WAR AND TRADE IN THE WEST INDIES

1739–1763

RICHARD PARES

BARNES & NOBLE, INC.   NEW YORK

PUBLISHERS   •   BOOKSELLERS   •   SINCE 1873

This edition published by Frank Cass & Co. Ltd.
10 Woburn Walk, London W. C. 1,
by arrangement with Oxford University Press

First published 1936
New impression 1963

Printed by Thomas Nelson (Printers) Ltd
London and Edinburgh

TO

THE VERY REVEREND

A. T. P. WILLIAMS

AND

C. G. STONE

TWO GREAT TEACHERS
OF HISTORY

PREFACE

THE reader will not find here a story told straightforward from beginning to end. No more, on the other hand, will he find an analysis carried out, subject by subject, without regard to sequence of time. In order to see a thing from all round, the historian has to combine different methods. Sometimes he has to describe a political, an economic, or a strategic system as a going concern, which can be viewed almost logically as a complex of ground and consequence; at other times he must relate the course of a campaign or a negotiation as a story complete in itself. In order to give a just idea of a great movement of history, such as a war or a succession of wars, he has to treat not only of diplomacy, but of law and party politics; not only of strategy, but of economics, the structure of society, and party politics again. He has therefore to vary the method. Some of these things, such as diplomacy, can hardly be rendered except by narrative; for other parts, such as law and economic history, narrative would be quite inappropriate. Movement therefore must alternate with standing still: sometimes the story goes forward, sometimes it comes to a stop at some point from which the surroundings can be surveyed at length.

This combination makes difficult reading. Where the difficulty is in the nature of the thing to be attempted, there is no need to apologize for it; only where the fault is of my clumsy contrivance, I have to ask the reader to excuse it. Perhaps he will get some help through the labyrinth if he constantly consults the tables of the principal events and dramatis personae which I have given in the Appendixes.

I have tried to describe two great colonial wars, in so far as they arose out of disputes in the West Indies and affected the way of living in the sugar colonies. I have tried to explain what the colonists expected from those wars, what part they took in fighting them, what demands they made upon the armed forces and the diplomacy of their mother countries. I have discussed at some length the economic effect of colonial wars upon plantation colonies in one of the great ages of imperialism. I have tried to show how much and how little patriotism meant to the colonists. Above all, I have tried to discover the policy of which those wars were the instruments, and to show how the relations of those great powers were determined by their ambitions in America, especially in the great diplomatic crises of 1739–41 and 1761–2, upon which I have spent what the reader may at first sight think a disproportionate time.

He may also be surprised at finding so large a book written about the West Indies. I answer, first that it is by no means all about the West Indies, and secondly that in the age of which I have written, nearly everybody still considered the West Indies to be the most important and valuable part of our empire. The scale of things has changed, and it is difficult now to conceive how those neglected and unprosperous islands, many of them hardly bigger than the Isle of Wight, could ever have loomed so large in the eyes of governments and peoples. Yet so it was; therefore to ignore the West Indies is to get a lop-sided and unhistorical view of the mercantilist empire of the eighteenth century.

Further, the reader may think it strange that a book about war should contain so few accounts of battles or even campaigns. Here again the answer is simple. There were very few battles or expeditions in colonial waters during the two wars which I have described. There was, on the other hand, a very interesting and important routine of blockade and trade defence, and it played a far more serious part in the war than battles or expeditions. Naval war in those days was a branch of business, not only for the colonists who claimed the protection of the navy, but for the strategists who planned the operations and most of all for the sailors who carried them out. However, I must acknowledge that even where there were conquests or engagements to describe, I have very seldom given a narrative of them. That is because I have been more interested in war as a social institution, as a system for satisfying certain ambitions or securing certain rights, than as a fine art. The reader who is interested in campaigns and encounters will do better to consult Admiral Richmond's excellent *History of the Navy in the War of 1739–48*, and Sir Julian Corbett's somewhat less valuable *England in the Seven Years' War*.

This book has other faults for which I offer an unqualified apology. It is impossible to give a satisfactory account of war or diplomacy between two nations, without consulting the records of both general staffs and both foreign offices. I have

tried to do this for England and France, but my courage failed
before the vast archives of Spain. Of the making of books there
must be somewhere an end. One day a more conscientious
historian will have to rewrite some of these chapters from the
records of Simancas and Seville. I can only plead, and it is a
bad excuse, that this book, imperfect though long, is a by-
product or excrescence from an original project of a history of
the British West Indies.

I have many debts of gratitude to pay. First of all, I owe my
thanks to the Warden and Fellows of my College, who have
enabled me to write this book, by electing me to a Research
Fellowship, and have more lately, with an excess of generosity,
helped me to bear the cost of publishing it. After them,
to the officials of the Public Record Office and the British
Museum for their patience. Next, to the librarians of many
historical societies and other learned institutions in the
United States. I should like especially to thank those of the
Library of Congress, the Historical Society of Pennsylvania,
the New York Public Library, the John Carter Brown Library,
and the Essex Institute at Salem; I name these not so much
because their kindness exceeded that of others, but because I
have made most frequent use of it. I am also very grateful to
several private owners of manuscripts; most of all to Lord
Chewton, who allowed me to use some papers of the first Earl
Waldegrave, and to Messrs. Wilkinson & Gaviller, who let me
spend several months in their office over the papers of their
firm. This unique series of merchants' letter-books is the
richest and best single source of information for the history of
business that I have ever seen, and I cannot enough thank the
owners for such generosity as I wish were commoner in the
business world. I must also thank Miss Jean Garlick for permission to use these papers, of which she hopes to publish a
selection shortly.

Last and most of all, I wish to thank two friends who have
helped me most generously with their advice. I cannot
express how much I have profited by the kindness, patience,
learning, and wisdom of Professor G. N. Clark and Professor
L. B. Namier. The only recompense I can offer them is, that
if they ever read this book again they will see how much it
owes to them.   R. P.

OXFORD, *June 1936*.

CONTENTS

ABBREVIATIONS

Add. MSS.	Additional Manuscripts, British Museum.
Adm.	Admiralty Records, Public Record Office.
A.E.	Archives du Ministère des Affaires Étrangères, Paris (Correspondance Politique).
A.E. Mém. et Doc.	Do. (Mémoires et Documents).
A. N.	Archives Nationales, Paris.
A.P.C. Col.	*Acts of the Privy Council, Colonial Series,* ed. Grant & Munro.
Arch. Gir.	Archives de la Gironde, Bordeaux.
C.J.	*Commons Journals.*
C.O.	Colonial Office Records, Public Record Office.
C.S.P. Col.	*Calendar of State Papers, Colonial.*
C.S.P. Dom.	*Calendar of State Papers, Domestic.*
G.D.	Gifts and Deposits, Public Record Office.
H.C.A.	High Court of Admiralty Records, Public Record Office.
H.M.C.	*Historical Manuscripts Commission.*
H.S.P.	Historical Society of Pennsylvania.
M.H.S.	Massachusetts Historical Society.
N.Y. Col. Doc.	*New York Colonial Documents.*
N.Y.H.S.	New York Historical Society.
N.Y.P.L.	New York Public Library.
Parl. Hist.	Cobbett's *Parliamentary History.*
R.I. Col. Rec.	*Rhode Island Colonial Records,* ed. J. R. Bartlett.
R.I.H.S.	Rhode Island Historical Society.
S.P.	State Papers, Public Record Office.
T.	Treasury Papers, *ibid.*
W. & G.	Letter-books of Messrs. Wilkinson & Gaviller, 14 Great Tower Street.
	These are described by Miss L. M. Penson in *The Colonial Agents of the British West Indies* (London, 1924), pp. 300–1; but since some volumes exist which Miss Penson does not appear to have seen, my numbering of the volumes is different.
Vol. I.	March 1739/40–Feb. 1741/2.
Vol. II.	Sept. 1743–Jan. 1745/6.
Vol. III.	Feb. 1745/6–Aug. 1748.
Vol. IV.	Aug. 1748–Aug. 1750.
Vol. V.	Aug. 1750–Aug. 1752.
Vol. VI.	Aug. 1752–May 1754.
Vol. VII.	May 1754–July 1756.
Vol. VIII.	July 1756–Nov. 1759.
Vol. IX.	Nov. 1759–June 1763.
Vol. X.	April 1765–Aug. 1768.
Vol. A.	Letters of Henry Lascelles, Nov. 1751–Sept. 1753.

I

THE ORIGINS OF THE WAR OF 1739

§ i. *The Beginnings of the Struggle for Spanish America*

SPAIN was the sick man of America at the end of the seventeenth century. Critics have sometimes been tempted to ascribe the decrepitude of the Spanish Empire to some moral or social blemish of the Spaniards themselves, or the revenge of God and Nature for the wholesale destruction of the aboriginal Indians. This is to do less than justice to the Spaniards both of Europe and America. The greatest fault of Spanish imperialism was attempting too much. Its claims vastly exceeded its performance. Her enemies never gave Spain a fair chance to show how she could have settled and organized the whole continent of America; but had they left her alone, she was too constantly preoccupied with European wars to give herself a fair chance.

There were hundreds of miles of coastline and millions of acres inland, where Spanish occupation was a mere pretence. Perhaps the most striking example is to be found by the side of the most important highway of Central America. The whole treasure of the South Seas was supposed to pass every year from Panama to Portobello; yet within a few miles of the road the Darien Indians were still unsubdued and even hostile to the Spanish power after two centuries of empire. The Lesser Antilles, the first seats of English and French colonization in the West Indies, were nothing more than a row of Spanish names upon the map, although the outward-bound galleons had to sail through them and take in wood and water there. The coast of North America between St. Augustine and the Bay of Fundy was not even complimented with a row of Spanish names.

This pre-emption of a continent defeated its own purpose in a violent manner. The other nations of Europe could do nothing lawful in America; they therefore did very much that was lawless. They did not merely want to jump the Spaniards' claim to land. Instead of building up colonies of their own, they fastened at first like parasites upon the Spanish Empire and bled it white. For peoples whose resources in men and especially in money were small, it was easier, no doubt, to fit

out a plundering expedition against the galleons than to find
the capital for beginning a plantation. There was also a political motive for attacking Spain in this way. Charles V and
Philip II used the treasure of the Indies to pay their troops in
Italy, and to pursue their ambition of dominating Europe.
Their enemies naturally believed that the best way to defend
Europe was to attack the West Indies. This doctrine was perhaps less true than it looked; but it suited large and active
classes of people, and it died hard. Above all, it was not land
but money that the English, French, and Dutch first came to
the West Indies to take. They might have pardoned Spain for
the fictitious pre-emption of a continent in which they had very
little interest; but they could not pardon her the real occupation, which almost amounted to a monopoly, of the mines of
gold and silver.

Whatever the reasons and justifications of this nearly universal obsession with gold and silver, for the Spaniards and
their rivals in America it was the prime motive of imperialism.
The rich plantations of tobacco, sugar, and indigo were only
a second best. Not until the Dutch had proved by their example
that a nation could live and prosper without any command of
the precious metals at first hand, did some economists come to
their senses on this subject. Even they preceded public opinion
by nearly a hundred years. The cramped and hard-living seaports of western Europe were haunted by dreams of gold to be
had for the taking. There soon grew up a legend that the
Spanish Empire was made of gold and silver. In the still
mysterious back-country between Brazil and British Guiana,
Sir Walter Ralegh believed that there lived a Golden Man.
This invincible belief in the abundance of precious metals must
have cost many a Spanish colonist his life or his limbs in the
days of the buccaneers, who tortured their prisoners in order to
make them reveal hoards which for the most part never existed.

Gradually it became clear that there were more ways than
one to get possession of the wealth of America. The crude
method of plunder could not succeed for ever. Though their
system of trade defence was always unwieldy, the Spaniards got
the habit of protecting the chief thoroughfares of their commerce, and the galleons were not often taken entire after the
reorganization of Pero Menendez. Yet the slipshod Spanish
Empire—more slipshod after every exhausting effort in Europe

and America—offered to the outsider opportunities of making money in other ways. Illicit trade with the colonists was very likely more profitable than privateering. For this illicit trade the Spanish Government itself was much to blame.

Before the reign of Philip II, Spain had possessed some industries which might have been developed. If she could have supplied her own colonies with manufactures, the competition of England, France, and Holland for the Spanish-American market would have been less necessary. This development, however, had been checked. The Spanish economists of the eighteenth century hardly recognized any other reason for this but excessive taxation. The foreign ambitions of Charles V and Philip II did indeed call for vast revenues, which were raised in such a way as to do the most possible harm to Spanish industry; but the economists did not take enough account of other things, such as the effect of American gold and silver upon the level of prices in Spain. Whatever the cause, Spain was only the channel through which the manufactures of the rest of Europe passed to her colonies. The Spanish Government made even this almost impossible by contracting the volume of trade.

The commerce of the Indies was confined to a few thousand tons of shipping which was meant to sail, from Seville or Cadiz, at regular intervals. One small fleet known as the 'galleons' was convoyed to Cartagena, and another known as the *flota* to Vera Cruz in Mexico. The supercargoes did their business at the fairs of Portobello and Jalapa; the two convoys then assembled at Havana with their cargoes of bullion, cochineal, and cocoa, and came home to Spain together. Single register-ships (so called from their registered cargoes) sailed to the smaller markets which could not be supplied from the fairs; there were also *azogues*, which carried out quicksilver for the silver-refineries of Mexico and brought home valuable cargoes. All this shipping together made up a very few thousand tons; the regulations of the fairs further hampered the trade, for the merchants of the colonies were forbidden to ship goods for their own account on the galleons and flotas, and the supercargoes from Spain were equally restrained from warehousing their goods in the colonies and selling them at leisure. Both the ships and goods in this trade were to be the property of Spanish subjects.

It was partly for the sake of the revenue that the trade of the
Indies was regimented. The Crown expected a great deal of
the duties, which it often increased in spite of its promises. The
attacks of foreign privateers also made some sort of convoy
necessary, and restricted the frequency of sailings. These limitations were less serious than they might have been, because most
of the exports were luxuries whose bulk was small in proportion
to their value, and the chief imports were gold and silver. That,
however, may be an effect rather than a palliation of the system.
The Spanish minister Campillo attributed it to the method of
laying the duties according to the measurement of the goods,
which made it most profitable to ship merchandise whose value
bore the highest possible proportion to the space taken up.[1]
Whether the Spanish Government shared the wish of the merchants that prices should be high in America, is not so obvious.
At any rate, whatever its motives, by damming up the trade
between America and Europe it created an excellent fishpond
for the foreign interlopers. As Campillo wrote: 'With such high
duties and such restrictive freights, and other notable hin-
drances, it may be said that we have shut the door of the Indies
upon the manufactures of Spain, and invited all the other
nations to supply those goods to the Spanish dominions, since
every port in fourteen thousand leagues of coast is open to them,
and those provinces must be supplied from somewhere.'[2] The
smugglers had all the advantage, for they escaped the crushing
duties; and the interruption of the galleons left the market for
longer and longer intervals without goods, which only the
smugglers could supply. This interruption is said to have begun
in the War of the Spanish Succession; the colonists then acquired a taste for smuggled goods which injured the success of
the galleons after the war.

Cause and effect moved in a vicious circle. The fewer galleons sailed and the seldomer, the greater were the interlopers'
opportunities and profits. Perhaps the wholesale merchants of
Lima and Mexico would as soon have dealt with the regular
fleets as with the smugglers; but they could not wait, and if
some of them began to supply themselves from the smugglers
the rest had to follow suit for fear of being undersold. The more

[1] Joseph Campillo y Cosio, *Nuevo Sistema de Gobierno Económico para la América*
(Madrid, 1789), p. 19. It is not quite certain that Campillo was really the author of
this book.   [2] Campillo y Cosio, op. cit., p. 20.

the markets were stocked with smuggled goods, the less inducement there was to ship on the galleons; they became smaller
and rarer, in spite of the repeated edicts which enjoined regularity. There was an interval of seven years in the 1730's, and
when the galleons sailed at last in 1737 the tonnage was less
than ever before. Yet when they appeared at Cartagena, they
found the market glutted; the merchants of Peru were so accustomed to buy smuggled goods, that they had neither inclination
to buy of the galleons nor money to pay for their purchases.[1]

A little more freedom of trade would have taken most of the
profit out of smuggling, for the excess of demand over supply
was largely artificial. The Creole nobles were luxurious, but
they were only a small part of the population; it does not
appear, from the relations of travellers, that the poor devils of
Indians can have had much purchasing-power. The interlopers
themselves often found that the trade was overdone, and even
when the French made their way into the fresh markets of the
Pacific, in the War of the Spanish Succession, they quickly
learnt that a very little competition among themselves lowered
their profits, although they were helped by some years' virtual
suspension of lawful traffic between Cadiz and America.[2]

The Spanish West Indies had for the trader as well as the
pirate all the charm of the remote and fabulous. The legend
of the great American market superseded the legend of the
Golden Man, or rather grew up by its side. There was some
conflict between these legends, or between the people who believed in them. It was not impossible to combine plundering
the Spaniards and trading with them; but it was not very easy.

---

[1] Geronimo de Uztaritz, tr. J. Kippax, *The Theory and Practice of Commerce and
Maritime Affairs* (London, 1751), i. 156, 209–13; Bernardo Ulloa, *Restablecimiento de
las Fábricas y Comercio Español* (Madrid, 1740), ii. 98–168. Ulloa was the father of
the traveller and sailor, Antonio Ulloa, who may have informed him of the state
of affairs in South America; but Antonio had not returned to Europe when his
father's book was published. See also Campillo y Cosio, op. cit., p. 159 *bis*.

[2] E. W. Dahlgren, *Les Relations commerciales et maritimes entre la France et les côtes
de l'Océan Pacifique*, i. 384–6. In 1715 the thirty French ships then in the South Seas
had so glutted the markets that the St. Malo merchants themselves suggested that
no more permissions to sail should be issued (Dahlgren, *L'Expédition de Martinet et
la fin du commerce français dans la Mer du Sud*, p. 30). (See also Frezier, *A Voyage to the
South-Sea*, English translation, 1717, p. 201.) The writer of an anonymous paper of
1715 (A.E. Mém. et Doc. France, 2008, f. 68) says that Brittany cloth, which used
to be 8 or 9 reals the varre, is now reduced to 2½ or 3. Fifteen ships, he says, would
do more good in the South Sea trade and bring home more money than forty do at
present.

At first sight it looks as if the combination was frequent, but
the truth is that trade disguised itself as plunder, or at least
pretended to use force, for the better justification of the Spanish
Governors who did not want to prevent it. Perhaps real violence
was sometimes used or threatened, in order to overcome the
scruples of the authorities; the inhabitants very seldom had any,
for they could not ask for a better opportunity to satisfy their
wants and to dispose of produce that had not paid duties or
silver that had not received the royal stamp. As the Governors
commonly excused themselves by the necessity of averting
violence, it is difficult to distinguish the instances where it was
really intended, from those in which the threat was at most a
piece of expiatory ritual.[1]

Sometimes trade and plunder were alternatives, for each of
which an expedition was equally ready. This happened especially in places where the disposition of the colonists to trade
was unknown; the English, Dutch, or French adventurer might
resolve to deal with the inhabitants if they would trade, and
plunder them if they would not. Perhaps the early voyages of
John Hawkins were made with this indefinite purpose.[2] A
hundred years later, when the South Seas were almost as little
known in England and France as the Caribbean had been in
Hawkins's time, some of the earliest schemes of French voyages
round Cape Horn showed the same uncertainty.[3]

Nevertheless, in spite of some exceptions, the antagonism
between piracy and trading was obvious and insurmountable.
It is seen very clearly in the politics of Jamaica; two factions
grew up there in the 1670's, the buccaneering party of Morgan
and the party led by Lynch, which preferred to promote the
trade with the Spaniards.[4] They represented two conflicting

[1] The Spanish Ambassador St. Gil complained of the piracies of the people of
Curaçao upon the coasts of his master's colonies; the States-General replied in their
resolution of Oct. 14, 1739, that what was described as piracy was only trade in
disguise. They went on to argue that just as smuggling can disguise itself as robbery, so on the other hand robbery can be committed on pretence of smuggling:
and they accused the Spanish colonists of tempting the people of Curaçao to come
and trade with them, in the deliberate intention of having them robbed by the
Guarda-Costas.

[2] Dr. Williamson has ascribed to Hawkins a more definite and elaborate design.
His argument is most ingenious: but possibly he has made more sense of Hawkins's
voyage than Hawkins could have made of it for himself when he set out (J. A. Williamson, *Sir John Hawkins* (Oxford, 1927), pp. 92 et seqq., 166 et seqq.).

[3] Dahlgren, *Les Relations commerciales et maritimes, &c.*, pp. 113–14.

[4] I use the term *buccaneering* because it is the commonest one in English, though

tendencies in the policy of the English Government, which hesitated at that time between bringing Spain to heel by means of the buccaneers, and trying to procure, with the consent of the Spanish Court if possible, a greater freedom of trade with the Spanish colonies. At one time Morgan's party had the upper hand, both at home and in Jamaica; but the Government tried afterwards to call off the buccaneers.[1] The tradition of plunder died hard, and the same conflict reappeared in the War of the Spanish Succession. Once more the Government supported the traders, whom it considered more profitable to the nation than the privateers.

French policy experienced the same hesitations and changes as our own. For France, however, and consequently for the rest of Europe, the Spanish question took a new turn at the end of the seventeenth century, and the stakes became higher than ever. It was a question of nothing less than the partition of the Spanish Empire or its appropriation by France alone. This was the dispute over the Spanish Succession, about which so many treaties were made and broken, so many battles were fought. The policy of Louis XIV was entirely changed. He had lately been the enemy, waiting to tear away provinces and conquer privileges by force; he now represented the heir, and became eager to keep the estate together and set it on its feet by a programme of reform and efficiency. Yet he was not disinterested. France meant to turn the tutelage of Spain to good account. Louis XIV pressed various schemes upon his grandson Philip V of Spain. Some were only reorganizations of the commerce between Cadiz and the colonies; France would only profit by them indirectly as the principal foreign trader to Cadiz. Others suggested a more active part for French efficiency: the galleons were to be convoyed by French ships, and the squadrons stationed in the colonies were to be put under French control. This would ostensibly have checked the illicit trade of the English and Dutch, but it would also have favoured that of the French. Other proposals again would have given an open monopoly of the colonial trade to a Franco-Spanish company— a leonine partnership in which the direction, the capital, and

M. Vignols was quite right to insist that we misapply the term to what ought to be called *filibustering*.

[1] An elaborate account of these politics is to be found in an unpublished thesis of Miss Margaret Hunter on the career of Sir Henry Morgan.

the profit would be predominantly French. Whatever benefits the French might derive from these reorganizations, they meant to keep to themselves. Michel-Jean Amelot, going Ambassador to Madrid in 1705, was instructed not to sign a treaty of commerce, as that would create public advantages which France might have to share after the peace with England and Holland. At the same time he was to discourage Frenchmen, so far as he could, from participating in the manufactures of Spain, as their development would interfere with the sale of French merchandise in the Spanish market.[1]

Besides trying to get special privileges from the Spanish Government, France took the law into her own hands. Since 1682 she had permitted and encouraged a smuggling trade from her colonies in America to those of Spain. She now connived at a bolder novelty—the voyages of French adventurers round Cape Horn to the markets of Chile and Peru. There is no need to describe the shiftings and cross-currents of French policy. Sometimes the interests of Nantes and St. Malo were sacrificed, or kept in the background, in order to please the Spanish Government or stifle the outcry against foreigners in Spain; but more often the merchants' influence and the needs of the treasury overcame the political scruples of Pontchartrain, and the trade was winked at or openly allowed. At any rate, eighty-eight ships left France for the South Seas during the War of the Spanish Succession; the affair made a great noise in Spain and among the enemies of France.[2]

The alteration in the policy of Louis XIV had required a reaction in that of his rivals. As long as France had been the enemy of Spain, England could pose as a friend. France now aimed at the control of Spain, though it was destined to be much slighter, in matters of commerce, than the enemies of both countries chose to think. There were three courses which England and Holland could take. They could persuade France to a partition of the Spanish Empire, in which they should reserve for themselves, or for some candidate of their own, the American colonies in which they were interested. Louis XIV consented to make such treaties, but broke them in 1700 by

[1] Dahlgren, *Les Relations commerciales et maritimes*, &c., pp. 330–1.
[2] This subject is discussed at great length by Dahlgren, op. cit., vol. i.

accepting for his grandson the whole inheritance of Carlos II. His enemies must then resist him by force, and oppose the Austrian King of Spain to the French King. This was their policy in Europe and America during the War of the Spanish Succession; they sent armies to Spain, and tried to provoke a sympathetic revolution in the Spanish colonies by playing upon the jealousy which the Creoles were supposed to feel against the French.[1] They could obtain for themselves, from their own candidate, such a special position as France would have liked to get from Philip V. In fact England secretly stipulated in the Treaty of Barcelona (1707) for very great privileges in trade, at the expense not only of the French but of her own allies the Dutch.

When it became clear that Philip V could not be turned out of Spain and Louis XIV could not be made to expel him, England decided to make the best of a bad business. She would accept the French King of Spain but nullify the effects of French influence upon the trade of Spanish America. It was no longer possible to insist upon the absolute exclusion of France from all direct or indirect trade with the Spanish colonies (the Dutch had been inclined to demand this in the peace negotiations of 1709). France could, however, be induced to forgo all special privileges in Spain. Intelligent negotiators like Mesnager had long seen that this would be a necessary condition of peace. At first a mere paper renunciation was not held to be enough guarantee against collusion between the French and Spanish Bourbons. French 'perfidy' was then as much an article of faith in England as English perfidy has ever been in France. England and Holland held out for a 'real security' for their commerce—we shall meet the phrase again. They meant by 'security' the possession of some towns in Spanish America. No doubt this would have injured the Spanish Empire. These towns would have been, at the least, advanced posts for illicit trade. England already had such posts in Jamaica and Barbados, Holland in Curaçao and St. Eustatius; but strongholds suitably placed on the mainland would have made smuggling easier still. In case of war they might be still more useful as starting-points for expeditions of conquest. France and Spain naturally resisted such a concession; and though Philip V unwillingly consented to make it, Mesnager was able to

[1] *C.S.P. Col. 1706–8*, nos. 33, 554, 735, 793.

divert the English from it by offering favours of another kind.[1]

Several Governments had long coveted the privilege of supplying the Spanish colonies with slaves. The Spaniards were forced to depend on foreigners, because they had no slave-trading settlements of their own. Spain had directed her efforts towards America and turned her back on tropical Africa. Portugal was the first great power on the West African coast, and in the years when the Portuguese Empire was incorporated in that of Spain, the Spanish Government commanded its own sources of supply. After the Portuguese had recovered their independence but lost their pre-eminence on the Slave Coasts, both the authorized and the illicit trade in negroes to the Spanish dominions were keenly competed for. Adventurers of several nations obtained *Assientos*, or contracts for furnishing the Spanish colonies with slaves; but it is doubtful if many of them made a profit. They were burdened with heavy duties and hampered by the high standards of quality which their contracts stipulated. Meanwhile, interlopers smuggled in cheap and inferior negroes, such as the colonists could afford not only to buy but to pay for. Yet the Assiento trade was an attractive prize, for it gave an opportunity of selling merchandise as well as negroes, and it was for this purpose that the nations competed to obtain it.[2]

One of the first effects of the accession of Philip V was the transference of the Assiento from the Portuguese to the French. England extorted from the Archduke Charles a promise of a contract which closely imitated the French Assiento. The Tory Ministry, which must have some advantages in trade to show for the fruit of its negotiation, now claimed the same concession from Philip V; and when Mesnager made difficulties over the 'real securities', Secretary St. John proposed to drop that demand if Spain would grant, by way of compensation, an Assiento for thirty years instead of ten. This was agreed to, and England was thus the only party to the war which obtained by it any special privilege in Spanish American trade beyond what was common to all nations. She afterwards got it increased in a very significant way. France had agreed in the provisional

---

[1] These subjects are treated in great detail by Legrelle, *La Diplomatie française et la Succession d'Espagne*, vol. iv (Ghent, 1892).

[2] G. Scelle, *La Traite négrière aux Indes de Castille* (Paris, 1906), ii. 107, 118.

negotiations of 1711 that England alone should have a reduction of 15 per cent. in the duties upon manufactures imported into Cadiz. It soon became obvious that England could not decently keep this privilege to herself at the peace treaty; she must at least impart it to her ally Holland. She therefore commuted it for another advantage which should be peculiar to herself—the right of sending a ship of 500 tons every year to the fair at Portobello.[1]

Everybody could see that the Assiento and the Annual Ship would lead to smuggling. Some clauses of the treaty were almost useless except as a pretext for it. The tonnage of the Annual Ship could be exceeded, and the hold filled up again and again by tenders which brought it 'refreshments'.[2] The Assientists might also send small vessels from time to time with 'necessaries' of various kinds for their factors and negroes in the Spanish ports. They had the right to hold land on the River Plate for the purpose of disembarking and refreshing their negroes; since Buenos Aires was in itself an unimportant market for slaves, this provision was meant to enable them to smuggle goods overland into Chile and Peru. Other privileges were copied from former Assientos, but these three were now invented for the first time, probably by Manuel Manasses Gilligan.

This adventurer had been deeply concerned, as a naturalized Dane, in smuggling to the Spanish colonies during the War of the Succession; his ship had been condemned as prize, and he had narrowly escaped prosecution for high treason by the Law Officers of Barbados. Carrying his case to London, he got the Vice-Admiralty sentence reversed, and returned to Barbados with strong support from the Government to organize a trade in slaves with the Spanish coasts. He turned up once more in 1712 as our chief commercial negotiator at the Court of Madrid, where the important finishing touches were being put to the Assiento treaty. This was the man who possibly conceived and at any rate procured the privilege of the Annual Ship; and if there were any doubt of the tendency of the treaty to encourage smuggling, it would be removed by the antecedents of its negotiator.[3]

[1] Scelle, op. cit., ii. 485–581.
[2] Juan and Ulloa, *Relación Histórica del Viage a la América Meridional* (Madrid, 1768), i. 142.
[3] *C.S.P. Col. 1702–3*, nos. 572, 661, 1065, &c.; *1704–5*, nos. 108, 203, &c.; *1706–8*, nos. 53, 777; *1708–9*, nos. 126 (i), 134, 180 (iv); Scelle, op. cit., ii. 528–9, 553–60.

As if this were not enough, the South Sea Company (to whom Queen Anne had assigned the Assiento) tried to obtain by a treaty in 1716 a further facility for clandestine introduction of goods into the Spanish colonies. It argued with some justification that one could not calculate exactly how much merchandise would be needed to buy a cargo of slaves on the coast of Africa, and that for this and other reasons the slave-ships might have to cross the Atlantic with some unsold goods. It therefore asked permission to bring these goods into the Spanish ports. It offered to warehouse them, but, Spanish officials being what they were, that was not a very real restriction on their sale. The King of Spain therefore refused to allow it except in Buenos Aires; he insisted that the Company's ships bound to the Caribbean ports should stop on their way in the English colonies and unload this superfluous merchandise.

Excepting these special advantages, the Treaties which England made with France and Spain at Utrecht professed to establish equality for all nations in the Spanish trade and to restore the state of affairs which had existed in the reign of Carlos II. Louis XIV promised in his treaty with England 'that he would not, for the interest of his subjects, hereafter endeavour to obtain, or accept of any other usage of navigation and trade to Spain and the Spanish Indies, than what was practised there in the reign of the late King Charles II of Spain, or than what should likewise be fully given and granted at the same time to other nations and people concerned in the trade'. England did not enter into the same undertaking with France. Philip V likewise promised 'that no licence, nor any permission at all, should at any time be given either to the French, or to any nation whatever, in any name or under any pretence, directly or indirectly, to sail to, traffic in, or introduce goods, merchandises, or any things whatsoever, into the dominions subject to the Crown of Spain in America'—except the Assiento for introducing negroes, which was at present granted to England, but might be transferred to another nation after the expiry of the contract. The King of Spain also promised that he would never alienate any part of his American dominions to France or any other nation; in return for this, Queen Anne guaranteed to him all the Spanish dominions in the West Indies as they had stood in the reign of Carlos II.

France consented to prohibit direct trade from her ports to

the South Seas. This prohibition was not always whole-
heartedly enforced and still less loyally observed. Dahlgren
gives the names of sixty-two French ships which departed for
the South Seas between 1713 and 1724.[1] It was not until Spain
sent out an expedition—officered by Frenchmen—that the
back of the trade was broken. The French Government had
perhaps some excuse for connivance, for nothing whatever was
done to stop the smuggling trade of the English and Dutch
colonies.[2]

Thus the settlement of Utrecht was supposed to have established an equilibrium or 'balance of power' in America. It
confirmed the doctrine that the much-agitated question of
Spanish colonial trade was best resolved by leaving the King
of Spain in possession of his empire. The trade was not thrown
open to foreigners in principle; certainly they might not sail
directly to Spanish America, and even the projects of reform
were dropped, by which the galleons and flotas were to be
abolished or the subjects of foreign nations to be allowed to
ship their goods in their own names. Everything had still to
pass under Spanish names—no great grievance, because the
Spanish merchants who lent them had the reputation of complete honesty. This trade was nominally equal for all nations,
but its security depended much on administrative connivance
and Court influence. France might, therefore, expect to have
the largest share of it, because a French king governed Spain.
It might be foreseen that France would become the champion
of the Cadiz trade while England would turn the patronage of
smuggling into an important article of national policy.

This did not happen at once in the complicated and chaotic
diplomacy which followed the Peace of Utrecht. Commonplace prophecies were falsified by the growth of an *entente*
between England and France; Spain was ruled by an Italian
queen, not a French king. But Europe began in the later 1730's
to recover from the age of adventurers, of unnecessary hostilities
and wild or improvised alliances, and to settle down once more
to colonial rivalries. Then the American equilibrium of Utrecht
was once more appealed to and called in question.

---

[1] Dahlgren, *Voyages français à destination de la Mer du Sud, 1695–1749* (Paris, 1907).
[2] *C.S.P. Col. 1714–15*, nos. 76 (i), 129 (ii).

§ ii. *The* Guarda-Costas, *the South Sea Company, and the Private Smugglers*

The treaties of Utrecht were hardly signed when complaints of Spanish 'depredations' began to come in from the West Indies. The first is dated from Bermuda, in January 1714; a Spanish coast-guard ship, or *Guarda-Costa*, had seized some English vessels for carrying goods reputed to be the produce of the Spanish colonies.[1] Examples were soon multiplied, and the volume of controversy and protest grew very quickly.[2] Lord Archibald Hamilton, Governor of Jamaica, was induced, chiefly, it seems, by his private advantage, to allow reprisals. This gave colour to the Spanish counter-complaints of English piracies; in the interest therefore of the friendship of the two nations (and because he was suspected of Jacobitism) he was recalled in 1716.[3] Even the critics of his policy of retaliation continued to complain of the Spanish captures, which soon began to poison the relations of England and Spain. It would be wearisome to follow this disagreeable subject through twenty years of agitations in the English press, strong resolutions passed or frustrated in the House of Commons, stiff diplomatic dispatches and references to commissaries. It can hardly be said that this petty plundering of colonial shipping was a principal cause of the two ruptures of diplomatic relations between England and Spain, in 1718 and 1727; but it produced in the West Indies a situation which subjected trade to some of the nuisances and expenses of war, and sometimes came near to causing more serious hostilities. English warships had to cruise in the Windward Passage for the protection of trade, and even to convoy the merchant fleets clear of the islands, just as in time of war.[4] The Spaniards went so far, on one or two occasions, as to descend upon shipping at anchor in the harbours of Jamaica, and often molested the coasting trade of the island.[5]

---

[1] *C.S.P. Col. 1712–14*, no. 544.

[2] See this list of 47 seizures given for the years 1713–21, in *The State of the Island of Jamaica, Chiefly in Relation to its Commerce* (London, 1725), p. 49.

[3] *C.S.P. Col. 1716–17*, nos. 158, 203; *1717–18*, no. 350.

[4] Commodore St. Lo to Secretary Burchett, June 24, 1728, Adm. 1/230; petition of the Kingston merchants to Rear-Admiral Stewart, May 28, 1730, Adm. 1/231; Commodore Dent to Burchett, Dec. 10, 1735, June 27, 1737, Adm. 1/1695; Commodore Brown to Burchett, May 8 and July 8, 1738, Adm. 1/232.

[5] St. Lo to Burchett, Aug. 25, 1728, Adm. 1/230. *C.S.P. Col. 1717–18*, no. 65 (i–iii); *1720–1*, no. 213.

Neither the naval commanders on the Jamaica station nor the Lords of the Admiralty could put up with this without trying to stop it; the former often solicited, and the latter sometimes gave, orders to supplement the defence of trade by active measures against the pirates. Such orders were given, for example, in 1723, 1728, 1730, and 1736. They hardly agreed with the more peaceful instructions which the Secretary of State sent to the colonial governors.[1]

On one occasion the English navy came near taking a step further. Some privateers of Porto Rico having seized the *Mary*, of Liverpool, in a particularly scandalous manner, the Admiralty instructed Rear-Admiral Stewart in 1730 to make reprisals on Spanish merchant shipping if he could not get her restored any other way. He tried in vain to get satisfaction from the Governor of Porto Rico, and was, therefore, preparing to execute this part of his orders, when he received a petition from the South Sea Company's agents, imploring him to do nothing of the kind. They pointed out that the Company's Annual Ship was then at Portobello for the fair, and would certainly be seized as soon as it was known that Stewart had laid violent hands on any Spanish traders. Besides this, the Governors of the Spanish colonies might all proceed to sequestrate the Company's property and embargo its trade wherever it had any. This would amount to an interruption of the Assiento and injure the English slave-traders. They added that the Spaniards would almost certainly issue similar orders against English shipping. Experience, they justly said, had taught them how hard it was to recover anything that the Spanish authorities had once seized. They therefore asked Stewart to confine himself to authorizing his ships to cruise against the Spanish *Guarda-Costas*. Stewart very prudently took the hint, and was approved by the Government; but he involved himself in one of those controversies with the merchants which hardly any Admiral on the Jamaica station succeeded in avoiding. It snowed petitions and counter-petitions, of which the purport matters very little. The adversaries of the Company declared that the situation of English shipping in those waters could not be worse than it was, for any orders that the Spanish governors might give in consequence of Stewart's action. But their chief motive was pro-

---

[1] For example, Newcastle's circular of Jan. 22, 1729/30, C.O. 324/36, pp. 171–192.

bably hatred of the South Sea Company, a feeling which was very prevalent among merchants at Jamaica.[1]

This time, then, the interest of the South Sea Company had saved the situation in the West Indies from developing into what would have amounted to a war. Meanwhile the depredations in general had been referred to English and Spanish commissaries appointed under the Treaty of Seville. These sat a long time, settled some cases, and left many others unsettled for want of such proofs and papers as would satisfy the Spaniards. But for a debate in the House of Commons, and an occasional article in the Opposition newspapers, the question dropped into oblivion.[2] The seizures still continued; according to figures given in the *Gentleman's Magazine*,[3] there were ten in 1731, one in 1732, six in 1733, one in 1734, nine in 1735, none at all in 1736; then, in 1737, there were eleven, and the whole controversy burst suddenly into flame.

Before considering the causes of this sharp renewal of the crisis, or the principles of the diplomatic argument which followed, it would be well to ask, who made these depredations, and on whom?

For more than a century before the Peace of Utrecht, the Spanish Empire had been victimized by marauders of three different nations, who had destroyed a great deal of its legitimate coasting trade. That trade must once have been considerable, because of the economic diversity of the Spanish lands in America; perhaps it was increased by the restrictions on transatlantic shipping which caused the colonies to become, except for luxuries and a few Spanish products, a self-sufficing system. When lawful trade is annihilated, it is not surprising if the seafaring population takes to piracy—an argument which the English used in their turn when they attributed the development of piracy among their own sailors to the Spanish depredations.[4] Robbers and adventurers create their own kind among the populations they attack. Therefore it is likely that the out-

---

[1] Pratter and Rigby to Stewart, March 4, 1730/1, Adm. 1/231; Stewart to Burchett, March 8, 1730/1; the merchants to Stewart, Sept. 24 and 27, 1731, ibid. The Admiralty's instruction is printed by R. G. Marsden, *Law and Custom of the Sea*, ii. 273.

[2] *C.J.*, Feb. 16 and 26, March 4 and 16, 1730/1, vol. xxi, pp. 631, 648-9, 660, 675.

[3] March 1738, vol. viii, p. 163.

[4] *The State of the Island of Jamaica, Chiefly in Relation to its Commerce* (London, 1725), p. 8; Charles Johnson, *A General History of the Pirates*, Introduction.

rages of the *Guarda-Costas* resulted partly from those of the buccaneers. Indeed, Governor Trelawny of Jamaica maintained
that their commissions were still, in 1751, based on an order
which the Queen Regent of Spain had issued in 1674, expressly
for the suppression of the buccaneers; he sent home a copy of
such a commission, to prove his point.[1]

If this was true, it goes some way to explain the violences
which the *Guarda-Costas* permitted themselves; and even if it was
not true, they could hardly be expected to abandon the habits
and livelihood of fifty or a hundred years, the first instant
after peace was concluded. The buccaneers themselves, after
all, were no more able than the *Guarda-Costas* to convert themselves into law-abiding citizens at the word of order from Rys-
wick or Utrecht. It is generally admitted that unemployment
among privateers caused the almost world-wide outbreaks of
piracy after King William's War and the War of the Spanish
Succession. Moreover, after the Peace of Utrecht the seamen
of England and Spain in America were asked to forget, not
merely the tradition of two long wars, but that of a century of
skirmishing and marauding. Indeed, the remarkable thing is,
not that they should have continued for a time the hostilities
and pillage to which they had been accustomed, but that they
should finally have been put down at all.

The English and French Governments contrived to suppress
their own pirates. It was perhaps the first time in the history
of the modern world that such a thing had happened, and is to
be attributed to the exceptional length of the peace and the
unusual whole-heartedness of the governments, who no longer
wished to foresee any possible use for buccaneers. The Spanish
Government was less able or less willing to restrain the *Guarda-
Costas*. Less able, for the revival of Spain was slow under Philip
V, and the effective control of colonial Governors was, if possible, even slighter in the Spanish Empire than in any other.
There may have been some truth in the charge which the
English made against these Governors—that they had sometimes an interest in the *Guarda-Costas* and shared their takings;
also that the *Guarda-Costas*, being unpaid and private individuals,
had to rely upon their prizes for their subsistence and profits,
and were forced to seize unjustly where they could not find

---

[1] Trelawny to Holdernesse, Dec. 1, 1751, C.O. 137/59. Marsden prints the
commission of a *Guarda-Costa*, op. cit. ii. 270.

anything to seize rightfully.[1] Certainly, as the Spanish Government afterwards admitted, there were some Governors who were not fit to be trusted with the power of issuing such commissions.[2]

Moreover, the Court of Spain had no desire to suppress the *Guarda-Costas* altogether, for it had work for them to do. Since the Treaty of Utrecht was meant to restore the old system of trade to Spanish America, interlopers must be put down, and a system of supervision was as necessary and legitimate as ever. In spite of the prohibition, the smuggling did not stop. England and Holland, whose illicit traders were old-established, continued to be the worst offenders.

Perhaps the South Sea Company was the greatest smuggler of all, carrying on an unlawful trade under cover of the lawful. The directors and agents soon got a bad reputation, but I do not know exactly why; for the declared profits of the Annual Ship were seldom large, and sometimes there were none at all. However, the declared profits of the Company might have very little to do with the private profits of the directors. The Company sometimes dismissed its agents for illicit trade; but that may have been as much a matter of self-defence as a proof of its sincerity to the Crown of Spain.[3]

The *Guarda-Costas* could do little against the Company, for it was able to penetrate, under lawful colours, inside the lines of the prohibitive system. They could do more against the private traders. Neither the Treaty of Utrecht nor the South Sea Company had succeeded in putting down this trade. The Assiento Treaty, which established a monopoly of the introduction of slaves, contained provisions for inducing the Assientists to defend it against the interlopers; they were to profit by the forfeitures of negroes introduced by such unauthorized traders. These clauses, and the obvious intention of the Company to supersede the private traders, caused very bad feeling between it and them, which developed into a political controversy; the Whig writers backed the private traders of Jamaica against the

---

[1] Trelawny to Holdernesse, Dec. 1, 1751, quoted above.

[2] Carvajal to Keene, Dec. 2, 1753, S.P. 94/144.

[3] Such resolutions are reported in the *Gentleman's Magazine*, i. 539, ii. 773, iii. 213; Add. MSS. 25504, f. 225. See D. Templeman, *The Secret History of the Late Directors of the South Sea Company* (London, 1735), a malicious but not very convincing piece of work. The same can be said of *The Particulars of the Enquiry into Mr. Benjamin Wooley's Conduct* (London, 1735).

Company, to which the Tories had handed over the Assiento as a monopoly.[1]

The private traders were said to have made a large profit to the nation, while the Company made nothing by the Assiento and little by the Annual Ship. The Company was thought to have convicted itself of losing by the Assiento, for it had obtained the Annual Ship from the King of Spain as a compensation for the unprofitableness of the contract for slaves.[2] Besides, it was argued that the Company, which was obliged to pay heavy duties to the King of Spain, could not make such a profit as the private traders, who took care to pay none, though they were liable to lose something by seizures and had often to purchase the connivance of the Spanish officers. The unprofitableness of the Company's commercial enterprises is shown by the fact that in 1734 the Spanish Ambassador persuaded it to ask the King for permission to commute its trading privileges.[3] It was also argued that the Company, having expensive establishments and large stocks in the Spanish colonies, had given hostages to the King of Spain which precluded the Government, or at least caused it to shrink, from taking proper measures to protect English shipping against depredations.[4] I have quoted an instance in which this happened; there were others in which it did not, and the Company had a long controversy with the King of Spain over the restitution of its effects which had been seized in 1718 and 1727 by way of reprisal for English hostilities.

The sugar-planters of Jamaica also disliked the Company. They thought it raised the price of slaves upon them by exporting so many to the Spaniards. Certainly the prices continued to rise in this period, but it would be wrong to attribute that to the Assiento contract. While the Assiento had been in Genoese and Portuguese hands, Jamaica had already supplied many of the slaves. Besides, the private traders were partly responsible for the rise, as the Jamaica Assembly recognized when it tried to burden with duties all re-export of slaves from the island.[5]

[1] *The British Merchant*, nos. 95, 98.

[2] *The Assiento Contract Considered* (London, 1714), pp. 6, 38; *Some Observations on the Assiento Trade* (London, 1728), *passim*.

[3] Petition of the Company to George II, July 4, 1734, Add. MSS. 25561, ff. 22-3, *Gentleman's Magazine*, ii. 824, v. 162, 273-4; Add. MSS. 25544, ff. 105-110; 25545, ff. 36, 41-2.

[4] Newcastle to Sandwich, April 11, 1747, Add. MSS. 32808, f. 62.

[5] *C.S.P. Col. 1716-17*, nos. 67 (i), 83, 85; *1717-18, passim*.

The colonists had another grievance against the Company which was perhaps better justified. They complained that it exported all the best slaves and left them only the refuse. The Company was in fact obliged by its contract to furnish negroes of a certain standard; this was a very great handicap, for the private traders continued to export the cheap inferior negroes and spoilt the market for the better and higher-priced article.[1] Three classes of negroes were said to be imported into Jamaica: the best sort, which the Company re-exported; the second, kept for the planters; and the worst, re-exported with very little profit by the private traders.

There were other arguments against the Company. It was alleged that the Annual Ship caused a net decrease of English manufactures exported, and therefore a net loss to the nation, however profitable it might be to the directors or even to the Company itself. The Cadiz merchants, uncertain what English goods the Company would export to America, were afraid of ordering so much of them as they would have done if they had had the trade to themselves and could have regulated the supply. The Annual Ships were also said to spoil the markets for such English merchandise as the Cadiz traders still sent to America; for as the smuggled goods came cheaper, they could be sold at a price which the supercargoes of the galleons could not afford to take. The decline of our trade to Cadiz was said to be greater than the whole turnover of the Company, to which it was attributed.[2] This was not fair to the Company. In fact our exports to Spain did not diminish; and if they had, the private traders of Jamaica would have been at least as much responsible for the decrease as the Company. In later days, when the Company was out of the question, this issue was joined.

The Company was also accused of shipping luxuries of foreign manufacture rather than English merchandise which was bulkier and less profitable; so that as much as two-fifths of its annual cargo consisted of re-exports. In fact, when the King of Spain took it into his head to confine the loading of the

---

[1] South Sea Company to James Pym, Dec. 12, 1723, in Miss Elizabeth Donnan's *Documents illustrative of the History of the Slave Trade to America* (Washington, 1931), ii. 307–8; Merewether to Burrell, Sept. 6, 1736, pp. 459–60.
[2] Malachy Postlethwayt's *Universal Dictionary of Commerce*, s.v. South Sea Company; *The British Trade to the Spanish West Indies considered*, Add. MSS. 32819, ff. 188–99; A.E. Mém. et Doc. Angleterre, 41, f. 191.

Annual Ship to English manufactures, the Company was extremely disconcerted.[1] Lastly, the enemies of the Company pointed out that it had never justified its title by a single voyage of trade or settlement to the South Seas. 'It was, for many years, like the dog in the manger, it neither traded itself nor would suffer those who would have done so in the like branch.'[2] This also was unjust. A Company founded in a war against Spain, to trade to her Pacific colonies without the consent of her Government, could neither expect nor be expected to combine such a trade with a monopoly conferred by that Government.

Although the private traders of Jamaica complained that the Company had destroyed them, they continued to exist. In fact they made their bargain with the Company. It soon discovered that there was little profit in the slave trade—at least with some of the smaller markets[3]—and licensed the traders to supply them in its stead, as the Treaty empowered it to do.[4] This cannot have been very advantageous to the traders, who had to pay the Company's profit as well as the King of Spain's duties. Probably most of them preferred to trade without a licence and take their chance of seizure.

The slave trade was only one article, and not the most important. English goods in general appear to have been smuggled briskly from Jamaica to all parts of the Caribbean.[5] No doubt the Company had an advantage in competition with the private traders; smuggling in port was probably safer than hovering on the coasts. The private traders, however, were not ruined by this handicap. They often received the protection

[1] *Gentleman's Magazine*, v. 273, 497; Add. MSS. 25545, ff. 42–3, 44–6.

[2] *The British Merchant*, no. 98, quoted by Postlethwayt, loc. cit.

[3] An article of the Treaty obliged the Assientists to supply the windward coasts of Caracas and Santa Marta with slaves at a maximum price of 300 pieces of eight.

[4] Some controversies in the Company about the licensing are reported in the *Gentleman's Magazine*, vi. 422; Add. MSS. 25545, ff. 35, 38, 39; 25506, f. 75, &c.

[5] Descriptions of this trade are not very common. The most celebrated is that of Captain Nathaniel Uring. The trader, accompanied by an interpreter who was usually something of a secret agent, appeared at some harbour just outside Cartagena or Portobello and sent in letters to the Spanish merchants. They came off to him in canoes and did business on board. The merchants of Panama came to Portobello disguised as poor peasants, with their money hidden in jars of meal, and returned through the woods with little packs of merchandise on their backs. (*The Voyages and Travels of Captain Nathaniel Uring* (reprint of 1928), p. 114. This description was abridged by Postlethwayt, s.v. Antilles, and lifted entire without acknowledgements by the author of *An Account of the European Settlements in America*.) See also Add. MSS. 32964, f. 65.

of the English men-of-war, who convoyed the interlopers upon their business, and were not always above taking a hand in the slave trade for themselves.[1] Indeed the navy had a special opportunity for it, since the Admiralty often sent out warships to the West Indies by way of the west coast of Africa, where the officers took in slaves on their own account. George II promised in 1732 that he would put an end to this improper behaviour, but it does not seem to have stopped.[2] The French Government was equally aggrieved, and entertained a controversy upon this subject with the English Ministry, about the time that the Anglo-Spanish crisis was at its height.[3]

§ iii. *The Depredations and their Redress*

These were the people with whom the *Guarda-Costas* had to deal. It would have been impossible to keep up a purely preventive system of defence against smuggling along the whole shore of the Caribbean Sea. The centres of population were too far apart for that. There were some·spots where smugglers were sure to be found at almost any time of the year; such as Baru, near Cartagena, and the Garote off Portobello. In general, however, the *Guarda-Costas* would have attempted the impossible if they had confined themselves to looking into all the places along the coasts where they might find interlopers. Moreover, they would have annoyed their fellow countrymen too much if they had intercepted the much-wanted European goods on the way to market. They did no such immediate and direct harm by confiscating the payment after it had been made. For these reasons, their method was punishment rather than prevention. They ranged at large, often at some distance from the coasts, and examined every English ship they met. If she was carrying anything which they chose to regard as Spanish produce, they concluded at once that she had been trading unlawfully, and carried her off for condemnation. Whether this procedure was conformable to the treaties, or founded upon a fair criterion of the English trader's guilt, was one of the points that most envenomed the diplomatic controversy, and proved hardest to settle.

---

[1] *C.S.P. Col. 1717–18*, nos. 566, 681 (iii).

[2] Add. MSS. 38373, ff. 130–1. A copy of Keene's and Patiño's declaration of 1732 is printed by Marsden, *Law and Custom*, ii. 281.

[3] P. Vaucher, in *Mélanges offerts à M. Bémont* (1913), pp. 611 et seqq.

If the *Guarda-Costas* had contented themselves with the repression of smuggling, no matter by what means, the War of 1739 might never have happened. They preyed, however, upon the lawful as well as the illicit commerce of the English colonies, especially upon that of Jamaica.

The prevailing trade-wind in the Antilles is easterly. The commonest course of ships bound from England to Jamaica was to get into the right latitude before they reached any of the West India islands, and then run down with the wind; this course took them near—but not very near—the southern coasts of Porto Rico and Spanish S. Domingo.[1] There they might possibly be snapped up by the Porto Rico privateers, and accused of hovering on the coast for illicit purposes. This, however, was not so great a risk as that which must be run on the way home. Ships from Kingston had two choices—they could go through the Windward Passage between Cuba and French St. Domingue, or take the 'Gulf Passage' round the west end of Cuba, past Havana, and through the Gulf of Florida. Either way they must pass very near some Spanish coast; for the Windward Passage is not very wide, and in order to avoid getting into the Bight of Leogane, between the two western prongs of St. Domingue, they had to keep on the Cuban side of the strait— besides, the land winds were said to be more useful there. Doing this, they must pass the privateering port of Santiago de Cuba. If they went through the Gulf, they had to coast along three-quarters of Cuba, keeping particularly close to the western point of it at Cape Antonio in order to avoid a contrary current which often runs from the Gulf of Mexico into the Caribbean.

It might seem that the Gulf course was the less natural, and that nobody would take it except for the excuse to smuggle near Havana. In fact, however, it was very often the most convenient if not the only possible one. The winds and currents on the south side of Jamaica were sometimes so strong that the homeward ships were a week or more rounding the eastern point of the island; after that, they had still to make against head winds through the Windward Passage, which lies nearer east than north from Jamaica. If they took the Gulf route, the winds favoured them until they had rounded the west end of Cuba, and then, although there were often calms off Havana, they

---

[1] In future the French colony in the western half of Hispaniola will be referred to as St. Domingue, the Spanish colony to the east of it as S. Domingo.

got another favourable wind and current to carry them eastward through the Florida Channel. This route was therefore proper and natural, but they might nevertheless meet a *Guarda-Costa* off Havana, who would very likely interrupt their navigation upon the pretext that they were about some illicit trade. It was in this course that several of the ships were taken in 1737, whose seizures renewed the agitation and disputes on this subject, and led to the war.

The trade of the other sugar colonies was not in so much danger, but even their ships went home through the islands for some distance, and might meet a Porto Rico privateer. Perhaps the shipping of North America ran more risk than any other, for it both came and went through the Windward Passage to Jamaica, or past Porto Rico to the other islands.

The *Guarda-Costas* judged these lawful traders by the same standards they used for the smugglers: that is, the places where they were found and the nature of their cargoes. By these tests the former were hardly more likely to be acquitted than the latter, because they often carried home the articles which the Spaniards chose to regard as proofs of illicit trade—cocoa, logwood, and money.

It was generally the lawful traders who complained loudest of these seizures; though a smuggler, who had a fair chance of concealing his real profession, might induce the Government to take up his case. At least one of these interlopers who had been selling slaves on the coast of Cuba posed as a lawful trader on his way from Jamaica to London through the Gulf of Florida.[1] Keene, our Minister at Madrid, admitted that the English Government sometimes intervened in favour of very dubious claims,[2] and Montijo, who had been Ambassador in London and was President of the Council of the Indies during the crisis, asserted that the English Government was often deceived by the clamour of disguised smugglers.[3]

Diplomatic representations were made, from time to time, to the Court of Madrid on such cases as seemed to deserve them. The Spanish Ministers generally answered that the Governors had not yet sent home copies of the legal proceedings: and however peremptory Keene might be in demanding immediate

---

[1] Geraldino to St. Gil, Jan. 20, 1739, S.P. 107/23.
[2] Keene to Newcastle (private and confidential), Dec. 13, 1737, S.P. 94/128.
[3] Keene to Newcastle, Nov. 18, 1737, S.P. 94/128.

justice, they would reply, with some reason, that they could not be expected to decide the case without hearing both sides.[1] In his heart Keene admitted this; the more so as the English complaints were only too often ill founded. When Newcastle sent him a great batch of petitions and protests in the autumn of 1737, Keene complained to a friend:

'Then my God what proofs! At most they can only be regarded as foundations for complaints, but not for decisions for restitution, must there not be an *audi et alteram partem*? Are the oaths of fellows that forswear themselves at every custom-house in every port they come to, to be taken without any further enquiry or examination, what should we say to a bawling Spaniard who had made a derelict of his ship at Jamaica, & afterwards swore blood and murder against the English before the Mayor of Bilbao? Should we give him his ship without knowing what the Govr of Jamaica has to say for his proceedings? Yet this is the case. I know not how Mr Sharpe could give such papers, I mean some of them, to the Council, I blush I am sure when I give them to this Court, yet it is in virtue of such performances that I am to get justice.'[2]

Sometimes the Spanish Ministers would point out that the English captain had not appealed, and must, therefore, be considered as acquiescing in the justice of the sentence; Keene had then to prove, if he could, that this was no fault of the captain's, who had been hindered by want of money or an abuse of the Governor's authority. But in fact the captains too often gave up all attempts to defend their vessels in the Spanish courts. They despaired of a favourable result, wanted to save the expense, and chose to rely on the good offices of the British Government, which would generally believe their story even if it was false, rather than on the justice of the Spanish courts, which would not believe it even if it was true.[3]

But supposing the captain had appealed—or supposing the English Government succeeded, as it sometimes did, in shoving in an appeal from above by its influence at Madrid—even then there were great difficulties. Keene reported that the Council of the Indies made it a rule never to allow new facts to be brought in evidence upon the appeal; anything therefore that was suppressed in the record of the inferior court would remain suppressed for ever. This was serious, because the Spanish

[1] Keene to Newcastle, Jan. 27, 1738, S.P. 94/130.
[2] Keene to Waldegrave, Dec. 13, 1737, Waldegrave MSS.
[3] Keene to Newcastle (private and confidential), Dec. 13, 1737, S.P. 94/128.

Governors were interested in obtaining a conviction by their share of the forfeitures. Profiting by the real reluctance of the English captains to defend their ships at law, or by their ignorance of what was going on, or at a last resort by their involuntary confinement, the Governors used to appoint a lawyer to make a sham defence for the Englishmen. (Indeed, there were other lawyers who were too much afraid of the Governor's wrath to undertake a real and wholehearted defence of their clients' interests.[1]) They cooked up a trial in which no evidence was admitted which would clear the ships or their cargoes.[2] Keene had no proof of this but the affidavits of the Englishmen concerned; and in any case the Spanish Ministers denied his major premiss, that the Council of the Indies refused to admit new evidence at appeals.[3] Indeed, when he put enough pressure on them, they procured reversals of sentences which seem to prove the truth of what they said.

The trouble did not stop there; indeed it only began. The Council of the Indies might order the ship and cargo to be restored, and give the claimants a *cedula*, or royal letter, for that purpose. The restitution could only be made at the place of condemnation; to which, therefore, the claimants had to make an expensive voyage. They often paid themselves very well for this; such a golden opportunity of going on lawful business to the Spanish ports did not happen every day, and the ship which carried out the injured claimant often took a valuable assortment of trade goods. The Spanish Ministers asserted that the claimants of the *Woolball* returned three times on such an errand to Campeachy, after they had been told, on their first visit, that the proper place to apply was Mexico.[4] When the claimant appeared, in good or bad faith, with the royal *cedula*, at the place of condemnation, he might find other compensations, but if his real object was the recovery of his property, he was often disappointed.

Sometimes the Governor would say the *cedula* had been obtained (as it often may have been) on false pretences, and

[1] Edward Manning to Drake and Long, Feb. 21, 1753, S.P. 94/145.
[2] Draft letter of Keene to La Quadra, sent by Newcastle to Keene, March 17/28, 1737/8, S.P. 94/132. For the interest of the Governors in the forfeitures, see Carvajal's note to Keene, Dec. 2, 1753, S.P. 94/144.
[3] La Quadra to Keene, May 26, 1738, S.P. 94/130.
[4] Ibid. The men-of-war were concerned in this, for they carried the claimants on these repeated journeys to Campeachy.

write home a protest, pending the answer to which nothing was done.[1]

The original ship and cargo had nearly always been sold; in view of the time it took to send the proceedings home, have them reconsidered by the Council of the Indies, and bring the *cedula* out, that was the best thing that could happen, especially if the cargo was at all perishable. The sale very seldom produced anything near what the English claimed as the first value of the cargo. A Spanish provincial capital was often a poor place where money was far from abounding; and while the cargoes of outward-bound ships might meet with a good sale because they consisted of goods which were badly wanted, those of the homeward-bound, which were more often taken, fetched much less than they would have done if they had reached their real destination. Besides, if the capture was unjust and the condemnation irregular—which may be assumed in the cases where the Spanish Court ordered restoration—the sale might well be collusive, at artificially low prices; and so no doubt it often was. For this reason many claimants refused to accept *cedulas* to colonial Governors, and preferred to resort once more to their own Government for a better and more immediate satisfaction.[2]

Even if the sales should be in every other respect satisfactory, there remained a further difficulty in recovering. The proceeds had been distributed, generally without any security to restore them in case the sentence should be reversed; for indeed the appeal was by no means always entered on the spot. They could not be recovered without prosecuting the captors or their securities individually. If the courts lent themselves to obstruct such prosecutions, the proceedings were interminable; and even if the courts expedited the business, the result was often useless, for the *Guarda-Costas* and their securities alike proved insolvent.[3] These shameful disappointments only admit of one extenuation —which is, that the conditions were nearly as bad in the English colonies; this the neutrals found to their cost in wartime.

The claimants insisted, with the support of their Government, that as the *Guarda-Costas* were, after all, doing the King

[1] La Quadra to Keene, Feb. 21, 1738, S.P. 94/130.
[2] Jenkins to King Charles II, Oct. 8, 1675, Wynne's *Life of Sir Leoline Jenkins*, ii. 779; Newcastle to Keene and Castres, May 8, 1739, S.P. 94/134.
[3] Ibid.; Wager to Keene, Sept. 30, 1730, *Private Correspondence of Sir Benjamin Keene* (ed. Lodge), p. 4.

of Spain's business though not in his pay, he ought to make himself responsible for restoring what they had unjustly taken. Philip V did in 1732 make a declaration which England believed, and Spain denied, to have this effect,[1] but it remained to all intents and purposes unexecuted. Even in the more propitious reign of Ferdinand VI, when England and Spain were trying hard to be on good terms, this promise, though better observed, had little effect. The King of Spain did not choose to pay at home; the treasures of the offending colony were drawn upon for the purpose. That colony would often have, or appear to have, no money in its chests; or else the fiscal of the exchequer on the spot would show his zeal for the royal revenue by the invention of chicaning difficulties.[2] For many reasons, therefore, the claimants and the English Government came to believe that the only acceptable form of restitution was payment out of the royal exchequer at Madrid; which, in a number of instances, they finally succeeded in getting. This was the origin of the famous sum of £95,000 which Spain was to pay to England according to the Convention of El Pardo; whose nonpayment was the proximate cause of the war.

This, then, was the situation in which the Anglo-Spanish crisis arose. The Spanish Government had hoped to stop the mouth of England with some lawful share of her colonial trade. She had not succeeded, and the smuggling continued, the authorized traders taking part in it with the others. She could only stop it by the *Guarda-Costas*, who got out of hand and molested the traffic of England with her own colonies. This was the foundation of the diplomatic dispute which must now be examined.[3]

[1] Marsden, *Law and Custom*, ii. 280; La Quadra to Keene, May 26, 1738, S.P. 94/130.

[2] Pedro de Estrada to Drake and Long, April 18, 1755, S.P. 94/148.

[3] This controversy has already been treated by Paul Vaucher, *Robert Walpole et la politique de Fleury* (Paris, 1924); A. Baudrillart, *Philippe V et la Cour de France*, vol. iv; H. W. Temperley, in *Transactions of the Royal Historical Society*, iii. iii. Professor Vaucher's account of the matter is especially to be recommended.

II

THE OUTBREAK OF THE WAR

§ i. *The legal argument; the Treaties of 1667 and 1670*

IN the autumn of 1737 the West India merchants complained to George II of the revival of Spanish depredations. The Duke of Newcastle, Secretary of State for the Southern Department, ordered Benjamin Keene to make strong protests at Madrid, and to ground his demand for restitution on the treaties existing between England and Spain.[1]

There were two treaties which might be held to apply to this matter—those of 1667 and 1670. The former seems to have been drawn up with a view to sparing the feelings of both Governments about the concessions which obviously must be made in America. The least that England could openly accept, Spain could not openly grant. The question of trade between the two countries was dealt with very gingerly. The subjects of each state might trade 'where they were accustomed to trade'— that meant, in the European but not in the American dominions of the contracting parties. The only article which expressly mentioned the Indies was the eighth; it put England on the same footing on which the Dutch stood by the Treaty of Münster. That is to say, Spain was not to interrupt the trade between England and her colonies, and vice versa. The English were only to enjoy this privilege on condition of undertaking, like the Dutch, to prevent their subjects from trading to the Spanish colonies.

The Treaty of 1667 was meant to serve also as a treaty of commerce, and for that reason included a number of provisions, in the mode of those times, for defining neutral rights. The manner of search was prescribed; nothing but the ship's papers were to be examined, and that without any show of force. A list of contraband was drawn up. It is reasonably certain that the Spanish Government did not mean these articles about search and contraband to apply to the English trade except in so far as the English might be neutrals when Spain was engaged in war. In fact it is doubtful if any article of the Treaty of 1667 applied to America, except the eighth. Seventy years after-

---

[1] Newcastle to Keene, Nov. 4, 1737, S.P. 94/129 (two letters, with numbers of papers enclosed).

wards, it was the 'right of search' which was the chief subject of discussion, and both sides frequently applied the term 'contraband' to the goods which English smugglers exported from the Spanish colonies contrary to the laws of Spain. This was an entirely unsuitable use of the term, but it sufficed to lead the Duke of Newcastle into a very silly mistake.

The Treaty of 1670 was known as the 'American Treaty' and there was no doubt of its applicability; but in at least one article it was drawn up with a face-saving vagueness which was perhaps necessary in order that it should be signed at all, but left a door open for future trouble. It confirmed the 1667 treaty in so far as it did not supersede it. It forbade English subjects to trade with the Spanish colonies (and vice versa), unless such trade was authorized by somebody with a proper warrant from the King of Spain for doing so; but it allowed certain help and refreshments to be given to the ships of either nation driven by storm or pursuit of enemies into the ports of the other nation's colonies. Nothing whatever was said of the legitimacy of the methods by which Spain repressed the English trade to her colonies. This omission was serious enough, but it was made worse by article 15, which tried to combine two incompatible pretensions by leaving them entirely vague. The first part of this article says that 'This present treaty shall in no way derogate from any pre-eminence, right or seigniory which either the one or the other allies have in the seas, straits, and fresh waters of America, and they shall have and retain the same in as full and ample a manner, as of right they ought to belong to them'. This is an allusion to the claim of Spain that all America, land and sea, belonged of right to her except in so far as she should allow privileges to other nations by way of exception; but at the same time there was nothing in the article to show that England admitted that claim. The latter part of the article makes the same compromise the other way round: 'it is always to be understood that the freedom of navigation ought by no manner of means to be interrupted, when there is nothing committed contrary to the true sense and meaning of these articles'. That is to say, Spain showed she knew that England claimed some unspecified right of navigation in some unspecified part of the American seas, without committing herself to recognizing its validity. Keene later said very justly of this treaty that 'it consists of reciprocal proposi-

tions made between an English and a Spanish Minister, correc-
tive of each other, without bringing the point to so precise a
conclusion as might effectually, and at all times, and in all
dispositions of the two Crowns towards one another, prevent
the evil it was intended to remove'.[1]

The immediate success of this treaty was the result of its other
clauses; Spain profited by the suppression of the buccaneers,
so far as England could suppress them, and recognized in
return the English occupation of Jamaica. It was a long time
before the rest of the treaty did any harm. The Government
of Carlos II was dependent on England for help against
France, particularly for the preservation of its sovereignty in
Flanders. As for the Indies trade, it was in such a chaos that
the smuggling from Jamaica was not much noticed or resented
at first. Philip V had no special motive of goodwill to England.
He no longer possessed Flanders; he was anxious, and increasingly able, to put the colonial system of Spain in order. Then
it was that the discussions arising out of the Treaty of 1670
showed how much trouble the judicious ambiguity of one
generation can bring upon the next.

The West India merchants who were heard before the Council in 1737 demanded that the behaviour of the *Guarda-Costas*
should be governed by the Treaty of 1667.[2] This would have
prevented them from making many real discoveries, because it
only allowed them to inspect the ship's papers, and gave them
no right to look into the contents of the cargo. It would not have
protected the smugglers altogether, for it appears from the
Jamaica shipping registers that many of them were foolish
enough to clear openly for the Spanish colonies, which must
presumably have been expressed in the papers they carried.
But it would have conferred even upon smugglers a further
advantage. If the *Guarda-Costas'* attitude to the question of
'contraband' were to be governed by the provisions of this
treaty, they would only confiscate the contraband goods themselves, leaving the ship and the rest of the cargo to go free;
whereas their actual practice was to confiscate everything, if
they found any one contraband article on board. In fact
several English claimants complained that their vessels and

[1] Keene to Holdernesse, June 30, 1753, S.P. 94/143.
[2] 'Short state of the several seizures, &c.' transmitted by Newcastle to Keene,
Nov. 4, 1737, S.P. 94/129.

cargoes had been entirely lost for the sake of one piece of log-wood or braziletto found in the hold—a story suspect by its repetition and improbable in itself, for what master of a ship would be such a fool as to carry about with him a single in-criminating article?[1]

The merchants' insistence on the Treaty of 1667 was pro-bably what misled Newcastle (who never really understood a legal or a commercial question in his life) to insist on it in his turn. Keene replied at once that the Treaty of 1667 had nothing to do with the West Indies; the clauses about contra-band and search were meant to enable Spain to stop certain kinds of trade with her enemies, while the object of the *Guarda-Costas* was to stop all kinds of trade with her subjects. The two things had nothing in common, and it would not be to our ad-vantage to confuse them, for while the Treaty of 1670 forbade the trade of British subjects with the Spanish West Indies, it did not establish any kind of search; whereas if we admitted the right to examine the papers according to the Treaty of 1667, we were allowing the Spaniards something which they could not claim by that of 1670. The latter treaty, if it justified any search at all, could only cover that which the *Guarda-Costas* exercised by Spanish laws within what were indisputably Spanish waters.[2]

This might be true, but Keene was too logical. There was no persuading the Court of Madrid to accept his reasoning against any kind of search; and we should certainly have been the gainers if we had induced Spain to accept, in lieu of anything worse, the almost harmless inspection provided for in 1667.[3] When we came to grips with the subject, we were forced to make larger concessions than this; and Keene himself later proposed a scheme somewhat like that of 1667, but that it gave the *Guarda-Costas* much greater rights in certain cases. Mean-while Newcastle's blunder—for a blunder it was—gave the Spanish Minister, La Quadra, an opportunity to elude for a time a real discussion of the subject, and to score a logical victory, by proving that the Treaty of 1667 was beside the point.[4] New-castle, forewarned by Keene's objections, was reluctant to own

---

[1] e.g. Capt. Way of the *Loyal Charles*, Capt. Vaughan of the *Sarah*.
[2] Keene to Newcastle (private and confidential), Dec. 13, 1737, S.P. 94/128.
[3] Stone's observations on Keene's letter of Dec. 13, 1737, S.P. 94/128.
[4] La Quadra to Keene, Feb. 21 and May 26, 1738, S.P. 94/130.

the mistake. Sir Robert Walpole and his brother were apparently anxious to do so, and to make a fresh start on the ground of the Treaty of 1670; but Newcastle, supported by Hardwicke, insisted at least on building a bridge from the old position to the new, in a passage of transitional nonsense.[1]

The original argument of the Spanish Government assumed that foreigners could have no lawful trade to the Spanish West Indies. Such trade was forbidden by the Treaty of Münster, whose provisions, in this respect, were applied to England by the Treaty of 1667. It was forbidden again in that of 1670; and in the settlement at Utrecht the powers of Europe had agreed that the trade of Spanish America should be restored to the footing of the reign of Carlos II, when foreigners did not ordinarily receive any general legal permission to engage in it. Admittedly the treaties did not prescribe how Spain was to put down unlawful trade—for the Spanish Ministers denied the relevance of the Treaty of 1667; but though that of 1670 had only condemned navigation and trading in Spanish ports, it was reasonably to be interpreted as including the *conatus proximus*, the sailing to and from Spanish ports on such unlawful business.[2] Even if there had been some omission in the treaties, it remained true that smuggling was forbidden. It was to be assumed that the smugglers were to be suppressed by the laws of Spain; and the only question was, what were the places to which Spanish jurisdiction extended?

The Spanish Ministers were quite clear in their own minds that it covered all the seas of the West Indies. The claim of Spain to be the rightful mistress of all America had never been explicitly abandoned, and La Quadra meant to revive and enforce it as far as he could. Keene described him and his colleagues as

'three or four mean stubborn people of little minds and limited understandings, but full of the romantic ideas they have found in old memorials and speculative authors who have treated of the immense grandeur of the Spanish monarchy, people who have vanity enough to think themselves reserved by Providence to rectify and reform the abuses of past ministers and ages'.[3]

[1] Horace Walpole to Trevor, March 7/18 and 14/25, 1737/8, *H.M.C. XIVth Report*, App. IX, pp. 13, 14; Newcastle to Keene, March 17, o.s. 1737/8, enclosing letter to be written by Keene to La Quadra, S.P. 94/132. Stone's observations quoted above.   [2] Keene to Newcastle, May 7, 1738, S.P. 94/130.
[3] Keene to Newcastle (most private), April 24, 1739, S.P. 94/133.

They could not deny that Spain had been forced to yield territorial and other rights in America to England, France, and Holland: for instance, she had undertaken to respect the principle of freedom of navigation in America, by the Treaty of 1670. But these privileges were only conveyed by grants from Spain; they were only exceptional derogations from her sovereignty in the Indies. Whatever she had not expressly yielded, was still hers by right; and even the concessions she had made, were to be judged in the light of her own laws.[1]

La Quadra kept this immense claim in the background as long as he could; no doubt he rightly feared that it would offend other nations besides those with which he was immediately in controversy. It had to come out sooner or later, for Spain could hardly give any other reason why she should exercise a right of stopping and searching foreign ships all over the West Indies without the express warrant of treaties for doing so. She had promised the English freedom of navigation in America, and meant to observe that promise; but they could not claim anything beyond the true sense of her promise, of which she was to be the judge. If the claim which they founded on that promise should come into conflict with her prior and indefeasible right to protect her colonial monopoly against smugglers, it must give way. Spain did not claim to interrupt the trade of English ships sailing between England and the colonies; this, she held, was the true sense of that 'liberty of navigation' which she had granted in 1670. There were recognized routes for such voyages, though they had never been defined in any treaty between the two nations. Traders who deviated from them without any necessity were held to have convicted themselves of meaning to traffic unlawfully in the Spanish dominions. This was presumably the point of the expression 'suspected latitudes', and of the exception which La Quadra made against vessels which 'voluntarily forsook their course'.[2] Spain was to judge what the latitudes were, in which English ships were justly open to suspicion; she was also to judge what was the 'course' from which they had deviated. The English Government resisted these definitions of guilt. It was thought neither safe nor honourable to let Spain mark out our sailing-routes for us in the open seas; and while the conception of 'suspected lati-

---

[1] Keene to Newcastle, May 7, 1738; La Quadra to Keene, May 26, 1738, S.P. 94/130.   [2] La Quadra to Keene, Feb. 21, 1738, S.P. 94/130.

tudes' made possible an agreement which would establish a right to pass by certain Spanish coasts, all English shipping in America was in danger from it, so long as no such agreement existed.

As to the way in which this fundamental right was to be exercised, Spain was more accommodating. The Government had lately upheld seizures of foreign ships in 'suspected latitudes', and ships which contained any goods which could only have come from the Spanish dominions. What those 'suspected latitudes' were, I do not know that it ever defined; but it ordered the restitution of one or two vessels, such as the *Woolball*, which were proved to have been seized elsewhere. No general rule was laid down as to the ships which, though taken where they ought not to have been searched, were afterwards found to contain 'contraband' goods. Were they to be condemned as having been guilty of illicit trade, or restored as unlawfully arrested? Here again the example of the *Woolball* seemed to show that they would be restored.[1] The question of ships in this case was one about which the English Ministers themselves were uncertain; even Newcastle doubted if he should be justified in claiming them.[2]

Early in the summer of 1738, Keene thought he saw indications that the Spanish Ministers would abandon their positions and take up another which would bring them much nearer to that of Walpole. They never gave it him in writing, but he believed he might say that they would adopt a new method of search and a new criterion of guilt. The *Guarda-Costas* should examine the papers of English ships, which were to express their ports of departure and destination. If their presence in the place where they were stopped was compatible with their pursuing, in good faith, the voyage described in their papers, they should be released without further examination; if not, they should be searched, as before, for 'contraband' goods, and condemned if they carried any.[3]

Keene was disappointed in the expectation that La Quadra would propose this; but he continued to believe that it was what Montijo, the President of the Council of the Indies, really desired, and that Montijo's opinion in such a matter was of more

[1] Report of the Fiscal of the Council of the Indies, forwarded by Keene to Newcastle, May 7, 1738, S.P. 94/130.   [2] *Parl. Hist.* x. 770.
[3] Keene to Newcastle, May 7, 1738, S.P. 94/130.

weight than La Quadra's.[1] The execution even of this project
would have needed a great deal of goodwill and adjustment.
It would still have left much to the discretion of the Spanish
Governors and *Guarda-Costas*. It would have left even more—
too much, in fact—to the honesty of English customs officials;
and it would probably have been incomplete without some
definition of the 'suspected latitudes'. Further, it must have
been supplemented by some strong action on the part of the
English Government against the smugglers and the commanders of warships who favoured and protected their trade.
But the project had this great advantage, that the lawful
traders would be subject to an inspection of papers only, so long
as they kept in their recognized courses; and so the original
demand of the West India merchants would have been satisfied.
At any rate it was something on which to build projects of
accommodating the dispute; and this is what Keene and his
masters proceeded to do.

Soon after this suggestion was made, the controversy took
another turn, and little more was heard of the Spanish attitude
to the question of search and free navigation until the meetings of the plenipotentiaries in the summer of 1739. By that time
the hope of averting war had been lost or thrown away, and the
exasperated stubbornness of the Spanish Ministers expressed
itself in an open revival of the old claim to universal sovereignty
in America. They explained the Treaty of 1670 in such a way
'that the navigation which the British nation can pretend to in the
American seas, is to be such as shall not diminish or lessen the pre-
eminences, rights, and dominions, which in those parts belong to
his Majesty. . . . Neither the pre-eminences, rights, and dominions
above mentioned, can remain whole and entire to his Majesty, as
long as the ships or privateers authorized by him, shall not be permitted to detain, examine, and search the vessels that navigate in the
American seas, and without such formalities as these, it can never
be verified whether in those seas anything be done or committed
against the genuine sense of the said article.'[2]

---

[1] Keene to Newcastle (most private), Aug. 2, 1738, S.P. 94/131. It does not
appear why the Spanish Ministers did not give Keene these proposals in writing,
which it seems they once meant to do. Lord Waldegrave, the English Ambassador
in Paris, suggested that it was 'from an opinion that they may get off upon easier
terms than they at first expected', which might or might not be due to hopes of
support from the Court of France. (Waldegrave to Keene, June 10, N.S., 1738,
Waldegrave MSS.).

[2] Keene and Castres to Newcastle, July 13, 1739, S.P. 94/133. The claim was

They condemned as a derogation from these principles the English claim to be exempted from search. This language would not have been used if Spain had still hoped for a settlement of the dispute; but it may, for all that, express the real thoughts and wishes of the Spanish Court.

The dispute between England and Spain was about a rule and an exception. Spain asserted that the Spanish sovereignty of the Indies was the rule and the English right of navigation was the exception; England retorted that the natural freedom of navigation was the rule, and the Spanish right to prevent smugglers was a derogation from it, which could only be lawful within the ordinary territorial limits of the Spanish dominions—for we allowed Spain no extraordinary sovereignty in America or anywhere else. The English Government never claimed or desired any right of smuggling in the Spanish Empire; even the Opposition, in their saner moods, acquiesced in the condemnation of real smugglers and were always careful to put the hardships of the lawful Jamaica traders in the forefront of the agitation. Where, however, the rule and the exception conflicted, they argued that the rule was to prevail. It was unfortunate, they said, that the King of Spain should find it so difficult to put down smuggling within his own territories. But he was not entitled, for that, to step outside his own sovereignty and exercise preventive measures in the open seas which were common to all; still less was he to molest our fair traders.[1] A right of search on the high seas could only come into being by virtue of treaties; nothing of the sort was known to the fundamental law of nations. If we started from the Spanish principle that smuggling must be prevented, and carried it to all its necessary conclusions, nothing would be left of the lawful trade of England with her colonies. When the Opposition orators were heated, they went farther, and even hinted a criticism of the Treaty of 1670, for giving up our right to trade to the Spanish dominions.[2]

This was not the opinion of responsible people. Still less was it the opinion of the Ministers, who may have known that smug-

---

repeated, even more imprudently, before an international public, in the King of Spain's *Raisons justificatives* (Rousset, *Recueil*, XIII. ii. 179).

[1] *Parl. Hist.* x. 683 (Pulteney), 748 (Carteret): *A Review of all that hath pass'd between the Courts of Great Britain and Spain* (London, 1739), pp. 36–8.

[2] *Parl. Hist.* x. 1222 (Bathurst): *A View of the Political Transactions of Great Britain since the Convention was approved of by Parliament* (London, 1739), pp. 25–8.

gling must continue with impunity if their demands were satisfied, but never were so silly as to say so. Indeed, both Walpole and Newcastle saw the necessity of giving Spain at least a promise to repress it by all means that were constitutionally in the Government's power.[1] Newcastle once went so far as to say that we were morally obliged to do so by the Treaty of 1670.[2] It is doubtful if such a prohibition would have been effective. The Ministers would hardly have dared to ask Parliament for an Act; the most they seem to have offered, in their projects of treaties, is a proclamation, and a promise to cashier any commanders of warships who should protect the traders or engage for themselves in the trade.[3] They made it perfectly clear, however, that they would never agree to any measure which would infringe the absolute liberty of the fair traders.[4]

Therefore they could not acquiesce in the Spanish doctrine about 'suspected latitudes' and voluntary alterations of course. They were not so unreasonable as to deny that there were some places where English traders could have no lawful business, if Spain would in her turn concede that there were some places in which English ships were not necessarily suspect of smuggling. There were several ways of settling this question. One was to establish a distance all round the Spanish coasts, outside which no search might be made. Something of the kind seems to have been nominally observed by the *Guarda-Costas* under an order of 1732;[5] but it was too rigid, and would have to be qualified by a declaration that it was not to be applied on the lawful routes of English trade. Another expedient was to except by name the Windward Passage and the Gulf of Florida from the places where English shipping was to be suspected and examined.[6] This scheme, which was approved by a well-informed French writer,[7] would have raised difficulties. It would have involved the abandonment of the whole island of Cuba to English smuggling, and would not really have protected the Spanish monopoly in the mainland, because Cuba would have been a door

---

[1] *Parl. Hist.* x. 1292, 1312.

[2] Newcastle to Hardwicke, 'Fryday noon', Add. MSS. 35406, f. 53.

[3] Article 3 of the first draft treaty, article 2 of the second.

[4] Newcastle to Keene and Castres, Nov. 13, 1738, S.P. 94/132.

[5] Report of the Fiscal of the Indies, quoted above, p. 35.

[6] Draft instructions to Keene and Castres, Nov. 13, 1738, S.P. 94/132.

[7] Silhouette to Amelot, Dec. 24, 1739, A.E. Angleterre, vol. 405, f. 360; March 12, 1740, vol. 407, f. 181; A.E. Mém. et Doc. Angleterre, vol. 9, f. 111; vol. 41, f. 200.

through which English goods would have reached the whole empire.

Yet another expedient was the proposal of Montijo.[1] The English Ministry did not dislike it, but could not accept it alone. For Newcastle, the chief point was *No Search on the High Seas*, because it made most noise. The investigation of the ship's papers, to see if she was really on her declared voyage, might be quite harmless to the innocent if it were properly conducted; still it was a search, and the Spaniards apparently proposed to practise it on the high seas. That would not satisfy the bellowing patriots in the House of Commons. Newcastle therefore combined all the schemes together, in order to make assurance treble sure: Montijo's scheme, the exception by name of the Windward Passage and the Gulf of Florida, and his own favourite project of establishing a reasonable distance round the Spanish coasts, within which English shipping should not go. Outside this distance, there was to be no search at all; within it, the papers only were to be searched for evidence as to the voyage, as Montijo had suggested.[2] Even if some discrepancy appeared between the declared and the actual voyage, that was not to suffice alone to condemn the ship and cargo. Legal proof of smuggling or intention to smuggle must be produced; and even so, only that part of the cargo which was brought for or from the Spanish dominions should be confiscated. The English plenipotentiaries did not criticize this; it does not signify what La Quadra would have said to it, because the great question of search and free navigation had hardly been discussed between the plenipotentiaries before the war broke out.

The English Ministers objected not only to the practice of search, but also to the Spanish doctrine of 'contraband'. That doctrine touched the national honour. Spain claimed, amongst other things, a right to interrupt the trade between one part of the British dominions and another. The *Guarda-Costas* not only searched, on the high seas, vessels that were actually coming away from the Spanish colonies; they extended their inquisitions to 'contraband' goods which had been safely landed at Jamaica and reshipped for England or North America. Once a Spanish product, always a Spanish product; there was a *vitium reale*, a taint in the thing itself, which rendered it liable

---

[1] *Vide supra*, p. 35.
[2] Draft instructions to Keene and Castres, Nov. 13, 1738, S.P. 94/132.

to confiscation, no matter where it was found, after how many voyages and changes of ownership.[1] There was no knowing how far this would go, as it was left entirely in the discretion of the Spaniards. If they seized Spanish coin in the Florida Passage to-day, they might seize it in the Channel to-morrow: if they seized cocoa on the ground that some of it was grown in the Spanish colonies, one day they might seize sugar for the same reason. Of course these fears were exaggerated, but Spain was nevertheless asserting a new and objectionable principle; she had in fact discovered, though not in the sphere of neutral rights, the doctrine of continuous voyage; and *mutatis mutandis*, some of the English arguments of 1739 became the Dutch arguments of 1759.[2]

The 'contraband' goods might have come into the possession of Englishmen in many lawful ways. Perhaps through the Assiento. It was all very well in 1670 to seize goods of Spanish origin as evidences of illicit trade; but since 1670 we had the Assiento Treaty and the Annual Ship.[3] The South Sea Company had its agents at Jamaica; most of its ships came straight home without touching there, but they did not all do so, and some of them may have disembarked goods in the island. Certainly this tap leaked; the Company no doubt exported more than it ought, and besides, there was a danger that all the Spanish products in Jamaica would be legitimated because some of them had entered into circulation through a lawful channel. Perhaps the Government might have adopted a suggestion of Keene's, that produce which really had been acquired by the Company should be protected by a certificate of its factors.[4] The certificates would undoubtedly have been sold to all and sundry, but the question would at least have received a nominal solution. Besides the lawful exports of the Company, there was some Spanish produce whose presence in the English colonies could be accounted for in another way. The Spanish Governors, on pretexts of scarcity of provisions, sometimes allowed their subjects to send ships to the English colonies to buy necessaries, and to export merchandise to pay for them. The impropriety of this practice, if there was any, lay at the door of the Spaniards

[1] *A State of the Rise and Progress of our Disputes with Spain* (London, 1739), pp. 5–6.
[2] *Parl. Hist.* x. 650.
[3] Keene to Newcastle, Feb. 3, 1738, S.P. 94/130.
[4] Keene to Newcastle (private and confidential), Dec. 13, 1737, S.P. 94/128.

themselves; and it was hard if the Spanish authorities should pursue with their vengeance the Englishmen at Jamaica who bought the goods so exported.

There was another reason why the criterion of 'contraband' goods could not be admitted. Some of them were said to be produced in the English as well as the Spanish colonies. Cocoa had once been grown in Jamaica, but the trees had died for want of expert care; yet a little was still grown here and there in the English dominions. This too was a very small tap which would let out a great deal.

More serious, because of its implications, was the question of dyewoods. Captain Kinslagh of the *Prince William* was convicted of illicit trade in 1737 on account of some braziletto wood in his cargo.[1] He said it was the growth of New Providence, in the Bahamas; but Spain had never admitted the English right to settle the Bahamas, and regarded them as Spanish possessions. Logwood created a yet more important difficulty. Some logwood grew, and still grows, in Jamaica; it was sometimes exploited commercially, especially by those who were clearing new plantations. Most, however, of what was imported into England came from the Spanish provinces of Honduras and Campeachy. The use of logwood in dyeing dark colours made it an article of great necessity to the woollen-manufacturers of Europe. It was a tree which grew in swampy ground near the creeks on both sides of Cape Catoche. The Spaniards of S. Francisco de Campeche cut and sold it in the seventeenth century. The English seem to have come to the trade from buccaneering: first they plundered the logwood ships, then they seized upon the piles of wood which lay ready cut near the creeks. Finally they settled down to cut it for themselves, especially after the serious attempts of the English Government to suppress buccaneering forced them to change their career. It was a life of hard work, up to the knees in swamp half the time, and heavy burdens to carry; but it was beguiled by drinking-bouts and native women, and recommended itself to those who had been accustomed to live outside the pale of law and order.[2]

Exactly when the logwood-raiding turned into logwood settlements cannot easily be ascertained. The Board of Trade

[1] Newcastle to Keene, Nov. 4, 1737, S.P. 94/129, with enclosures.
[2] William Dampier, *Voyages* (ed. 1699), vol. ii, part ii, *passim*.

afterwards made the most of the evidence that the process had taken place before 1667, or at any rate before 1670.[1] This point was held to be important, for the Treaty of 1670 recognized the *status quo* of the dominions of each party. Certainly the Spanish Government never meant to legitimate the logwood-cutting settlements; could it be held to have done so by mistake? They had no established government of any kind and were in no sense regular dominions of the Crown of England. Besides, it was doubtful if their sites could be regarded as having been left vacant by the Spaniards. Sir William Godolphin, Ambassador at Madrid, had been applied to for his advice in 1672; he answered that the province of Campeachy was as much occupied by the Spaniards as most of their other American possessions, and that the Spaniards 'may as justly pretend to make use of our rivers, mountains, and other commons, for not being inhabited or owned by individual proprietors, as we can to enjoy the benefit of these woods'.[2]

After this, the Spanish authorities continued to eject the logwood-cutters as best they could, and the English Government to protest from time to time. The English claim was further strengthened by the Anglo-Spanish Treaty of Commerce in 1713, which confirmed the Treaty of 1670 'without any prejudice however to any liberty or power which the subjects of Great Britain enjoyed before, either through right, sufferance or indulgence'. The Spaniards denied that there ever had been such indulgence and sufferance, and pointed to the number of times they had turned the logwood-cutters out, without any complaint made by the English Government. A demand of the Spanish Ambassador for the withdrawal of the English settlers from the Laguna de Terminos produced in 1717 a long and celebrated report on the subject by the Board of Trade.[3] Its reasoning is far from conclusive, though it was accepted as Gospel truth by most Englishmen.[4] Besides, whatever title it might establish for the logwood-cutters of Campeachy, it was open in 1739 to one insurmountable objection: since it had been written, the logwood-cutters had been finally ejected from Campeachy, and those who still pursued that calling lived at a

---

[1] *C.S.P. Col. 1717–18*, no. 104 (i).   [2] *H.M.C. Xth Report*, App. I, pp. 200–1.
[3] *C.S.P. Col. 1717–18*, no. 104 (i).
[4] Keene did not accept it (Keene to Under-Secretary Couraud, June 9, 1739, S.P. 94/133). See also Fuentes to Pitt, Sept. 9, 1760, G.D. 8/93; Bristol to Pitt (most secret), Nov. 6, 1760, S.P. 94/162.

much more recent settlement, hundreds of miles away, on the
bay of Honduras. It was not even, as Wager supposed, 'in
the same province of Yucatan', and the right to it could not be
defended on the same grounds.[1]

This was a dangerous subject to touch upon, because it
revived a controversy that had only been quieted in 1670 after
nearly a hundred years of war—the question of effective
occupation. Apart from the sophistry of claiming a right under
the Treaty of 1670, the only solid justification the English had
to offer for their logwood settlements was that they occupied
the country and the Spaniards did not. Spain had allowed the
doctrine of effective occupation to be applied once, when she
recognized Charles II's title to his American dominions in 1670;
but she had not assented to it in general. She still believed that
no settlement in America was lawful which she had not expressly licensed; therefore to claim the cargoes of logwood in
English ships as the produce of English dominions was to
advance from questioning her rights at sea to questioning her
rights on land. It was for this reason that Wall afterwards said
of those cases that the justification was worse than the offence.
When the depredations, the South Sea Company, and all other
sources of irritation had died away, logwood still remained to
play a considerable part among the causes of the Anglo-Spanish
war of 1762.

§ ii. *Newcastle and the Opposition; the Reprisals of 1738*

The argument between England and Spain was interrupted
almost as soon as it was begun. The question of search and free
navigation was complicated by disputes upon several other subjects; and even if the English Ministers had been able to keep
the Spanish Court to the main point, they were not masters in
their own house.

The two nations were drifting towards war in the spring of
1738. The agitation of the West India merchants made a great
noise. Moreover, a new element was introduced into the
situation. The English Opposition had seen a chance of making
party capital out of the dispute, and was pressing the Government for strong measures which would lead to war.

The Earl of Marchmont lamented, at the end of the Parlia-

[1] Wager's observations on the draft treaty, Nov. 8, 1738, Library of Congress,
Vernon-Wager MSS.

mentary session of 1737–8, that he had not succeeded in persuading the Opposition leaders to take up this question early
enough in the season; 'it was answered, that must arise from
the merchants themselves: and from them at last it did arise,
but too late'.[1] The Ministry therefore encountered little trouble
in Parliament until the session was some way advanced. Perhaps Pulteney and Wyndham wanted to be sure that there was
something in the agitation before they associated themselves
with it openly. They had already begun a spate of articles in
the press; and one of them had, intentionally or not, taken a
step which perhaps did more to bring on a war than anything
that any of them could say in public.

Newcastle heard in October 1737 that 'a certain Person'—
presumably somebody in Opposition—had talked of making a
particular attack on him for the conduct of the Government
about the Spanish depredations.[2] Certainly Newcastle must
have felt that the record of past achievements in this field was
not imposing. Complaints had been made, and had sometimes
been answered civilly. Commissaries had been appointed on
both sides to adjust these cases; but there remained a number
of English claims unsatisfied, and small appearance that the
abuses would cease in future. It was all very well for Hardwicke to reassure Newcastle that if the truth were known he
would be as well able to justify himself as anybody; he must
have been thrown into great agitation at this prospect of being
personally singled out for criticism.

Newcastle was above all a political coward. He was terrified
of public opinion—whatever that may have been in the
eighteenth century. Anything that could talk big and call itself
a tribune of the people could make him quiver with anxiety.
His fear of Pitt may be excused; for who was not afraid of that
great actor?—but he even stooped to be afraid of Alderman
Beckford, who was never more than Pitt's Sancho Panza. He
could not live without unqualified approbation, and one dis-
sentient voice was enough to disturb his peace of mind. Yet
with his colleagues, who had no popular influence to terrify him,
he was very far from compliant. In spite of the nervous agitation into which the least difficulty threw him, he had a bound-
less appetite for business; he loved the merit of arranging

---

[1] *Marchmont Papers* (London, 1831), ii. 100.
[2] Hardwicke to Newcastle, Oct. 12, 1737, Add. MSS. 32690, f. 394.

everything, and the praise of arranging it well. Though he seldom knew exactly what he wanted, he wanted it so strongly as to go almost any lengths to obtain it. It was not conscious treachery or desire for power that made him part with so many political allies and edge so many colleagues out of the nest; it was a firm conviction that his own policy, however nebulous, was right and necessary. Walpole, Carteret, Chesterfield, Bedford—it is an imposing list. Several of them were discarded for trying to do exactly what Newcastle himself did soon after their extrusion.

It was for this kind of reason that he was universally suspected of dishonesty. Admittedly he broke promises—that was because, in the fullness of his heart or as a line of least resistance, he had had the misfortune to promise the same thing to too many people. It is true that few men succeeded in remaining his friends and allies for long; but he was not, like Pitt, deliberately and artificially dishonest. His was the spontaneous dishonesty of weakness. He was a mercurial, always at the top or at the bottom of his spirits; he lived entirely in the present. He saw life neither steadily nor whole; but whatever he did see, struck him with an overwhelming force of conviction. While he believed a thing, he believed it strongly; and perhaps it was hardly his fault that he could not foresee the difficulties which would cause him to rebound so lightly from one doctrine or friendship to another. Besides, he was easily flurried and lost his head. He was then more determined than anybody that something must be done, and knew less than most what it ought to be. He would then recommend with equal earnestness almost all the possible expedients, and later events would enable him to proclaim with perfect sincerity that he had always been in favour of the course which finally seemed the most eligible. He never understood more than the politics of any subject, and was fascinated by the personal side even of politics. He has been charged with having no interest in life but jobbery; but that is not quite fair to him. True enough, his name is not associated with any great acts of legislation. He passed no Reform Acts, relieved no distress by wise laws; but domestic legislation was not then thought to be the chief business of Government. Ministers were generally preoccupied in the conduct of war and foreign affairs, and Newcastle was no exception. He lived for foreign politics, as the enormous correspondence testifies which he so futilely devoted to them. With long experience, he never formed anything like a general principle; the only two prepossessions in his mind which approached such a thing were a horror of Tories and a partiality for the House of Austria, in spite of everything that her intractable monarchs could do. He had picked these up in the heat of his youth and always looked upon them as the 'good old system'; but even from them he was brought to allow deviations, though with a wry face. Nothing but inexhaustible vitality could have enabled him to live forty years of so tormenting and haphazard a political career, and to prevail with such surprising and continued success against men of better capacity.

With such a light-weight, so sensitive to popular disapproval, in charge of the negotiations with Spain, the Opposition's policy became at least as important as that of the Government. Even before the Opposition had declared itself, Newcastle had already quarrelled with Walpole for his tameness to Spain; but the subject of that disagreement seems to have been something else.[1] It would be a trivial pedantry to ascribe all Newcastle's ill-judged zeal in the affair of the depredations to his apprehensions of the 'certain person', though Hardwicke's letter was followed remarkably soon by Newcastle's first sharp dispatch to Keene. Certainly he had other and more public motives, such as the petition of the West India merchants; but I think it remains true that his impatient bellicosity was very greatly due to his fear of criticism, not to say impeachment, and his desire to play a part worthy of a strong Foreign Minister.

The Ministry took a violent step towards war at the beginning of March 1738. The King offered to issue letters of reprisal for the English merchants to do themselves justice against Spain. This was a form of private war which had almost passed out of use. It was designed to satisfy the grievances of an individual against a foreign power, without incurring an open international conflict. If an English merchant was wronged, for example, by the King of Spain or his subjects, and could not get justice from the Spanish courts, he was entitled to apply for the interposition of his own sovereign. The King of England would then make a formal complaint to the Court of Spain, and demand a review of the sentence, or whatever form of satisfaction was most appropriate. If justice was still denied, the

---

[1] Hardwicke to Newcastle, June 16, 1737, Add. MSS. 32690, f. 299.

King of England might, after a due period, grant the injured parties letters of reprisal. This would entitle them to fit out a private vessel of war and take the property of Spanish subjects on the high seas, until they had recovered their loss, which they were generally obliged to prove beforehand in the English courts. It was a chaotic and dangerous way of doing business, though perhaps it was no worse than the modern trade embargo. It had been very common in former times, and the conditions of its use were often defined by treaty, as by those of 1630 and 1667 between England and Spain.[1]

Newcastle justified the letters of reprisal by the treaties;[2] but the practice had always been inconvenient and was becoming obsolete. Even though the sovereign who resorted to it usually took care to make his subjects prove their loss in his courts, he could not always make sure of the facts before he thus cut short the controversy and refused to hear the other party's version. He might claim to be as good a judge of the facts as any other; but if this claim was admitted and acted upon, there would be two courts of justice for every dispute where the parties were of different nations.[3] Besides, in those days reprisals could hardly fail to bring on a war, which they had once been designed to avoid. Diplomacy was assuming more and more of the responsibility for private international relations; the English Government in particular, which was more amenable than others to a sort of public opinion, would find it hard to distin-

---

[1] There was a case very much in point a few years after the second of these treaties was made; a certain Captain Cook was wronged at Havana, but got a sentence in his favour from the Court of Spain. He was to have it executed at Havana, which he looked upon as a hardship, for he believed that satisfaction would be delayed or eluded there. He seems to have petitioned Charles II for letters of reprisal, in order to save himself a fool's errand to the West Indies. Sir Leoline Jenkins advised the King that reprisals could not properly be granted without a denial of justice, which could not be presumed until Captain Cook had obeyed the Queen of Spain's *cedula*. (Wynne's *Life of Jenkins*, ii. 778.) Marsden prints many letters of reprisal in his *Law and Custom*. The earliest is dated in 1295 (i. 39).

[2] Newcastle to Geraldino, April 28, 1738, *Law and Custom*, ii. 284.

[3] The author of *Britain's Mistakes in the Commencement and Conduct of the Present War* (London, 1740) admits that Spain has the right to confiscate smugglers but denies that she is the sole judge of the facts: 'it is behaving like a little pettifogging Norfolk attorney, to allow the Court of Spain, or any Court in the World, to contest the fact with us'. This aphorism, which represents the opinion of the whole Opposition, illustrates the impracticability of the whole system of reprisals. How could peace be preserved if everybody acted upon this principle? The question asked itself again in the controversy between England and Prussia over the Silesia Loan.

guish for long between reprisals and war. Lastly, reprisals were probably impracticable in the eighteenth century. They had been common when the royal warships were few and small, but a privateer could no longer affront the navy of even a second-rate maritime power, unless he was sure that his own navy supported him. Privateering was therefore common enough in war, but too dangerous in peace.

Moreover, Newcastle's reprisals were not true reprisals at all, for they were offered not only to the merchants whose grievances were unredressed in Spain, but to all who chose to take them. This was war without a declaration and without a Royal Navy. There were precedents for it: the line which divided reprisals from privateering pure and simple had become obscure in the seventeenth century. Reprisals had been allowed without proof of loss in 1628. General letters of reprisal had been issued against Holland in 1664 and against France in 1689; they differed little from privateers' commissions.[1] Nevertheless, the letters of reprisal were much ridiculed in 1738.

The Government was trying to shirk its responsibility; perhaps this was due to a difference and a compromise within the Ministry, but more likely it is to be attributed to the cowardice of Newcastle and his faction, for his colleague and enemy Horace Walpole described it as 'that wild notion of leaving the people of England and the Queen of Spain to worry one another'.[2] The merchants would not let the Government leave them to fight their own battles like that; they required it to do the work for them with the King's ships of war, arguing no doubt, as Carteret did the next year, that 'Royal navies are kept by the merchants, and must protect the merchants'.[3] Nobody took out letters of reprisal; it would have been a great risk unless the Government was committed to war. The Opposition tried to stimulate applications by introducing a Bill, copied from the Prize Act of 1708, for giving the entire property of the prizes to the captors, and guaranteeing to adventurers, who should fit out expeditions of conquest against the Spanish territories, the perpetual possession of whatever they might take. Sir Robert Walpole resisted this malicious proposal, which

---

[1] Marsden, *Law and Custom*, i. 407; ii. 48, 123, 408.
[2] Walpole to Trevor, Oct. 24, o.s., 1738, *H.M.C. XIVth Report*, App. IX, p. 24. 'Horace Walpole' always means, in this chapter and the next two, the Ambassador to The Hague, and brother of Sir Robert Walpole, not the letter-writer and art-critic who was Sir Robert's son. [3] *Parl. Hist.* x. 1409.

would have destroyed his chance of settling the dispute with Spain. He pointed out that in 1708, when such an Act was first passed, we were already at war with France and Spain; we were now at peace with both, but should not long remain so if we took such a measure.[1] The Bill was defeated and the letters of reprisal remained unapplied for; the peace was for the moment saved.[2]

Newcastle must have been getting ready for war at the beginning of June 1738, for he had the English merchants in Spain warned to withdraw their effects from the country. A few days afterwards a sudden light broke; and though the negotiations which now began led to war in the end, their first appearance was very favourable to peace. At this time the Court of Spain must have sincerely desired a settlement or at least a delay. If it had been really warlike it would never have stomached the proclamation of reprisals, which La Quadra treated with surprising equanimity.

The Spanish Government yielded nothing on paper; but it was about this time that Montijo suggested a more tolerable

---

[1] *Parl. Hist.* x. 831–2.

[2] The Government repeated the letters of reprisal as a prelude to war in 1739, and that time the merchants, with greater confidence in its intentions, applied for them. The Seven Years War began in much the same way, but the institution of reprisals was still further distorted from its original form. The injury for which the reprisals were granted was in no sense a private wrong; it was the French aggression in North America. This was not quite without precedent, for the Law Officers, of whom Hardwicke was one, had reported in 1727 that in attacking Gibraltar the King of Spain had committed acts of war which would justify George II in committing any kind of reprisals or hostilities without a declaration (Marsden, *Law and Custom*, ii. 265). Yet there was another irregularity in the reprisals of 1755; they were only exercised by the Royal navy. (See the debates on this subject, *Parl. Hist.* xv. 544–615.) Choiseul tried to persuade Pitt in 1761 to allow compensation for the French ships taken in this way before the declaration of war; but Pitt would not agree to it. He argued that they were taken by way of reprisals for the encroachments in Canada. Choiseul replied reasonably enough, that if France had committed unlawful hostilities in time of peace, the right remedy for that was the war itself. Pitt stuck to his point that it was the aggression and not the war which gave the right to reprisals. Choiseul admitted this, but tried a new line of argument: it was not always easy to determine who was the aggressor, and the peace treaties protected private people from the bad consequences of this uncertainty by exempting enemy ships from seizures in port at the outbreak of a war. *A fortiori* ships should be allowed to pass free on the high seas. It would not do. Pitt insisted, and Choiseul gave up the point. (Instructions to Bussy, May 23, 1761, A.E. Angleterre, 443; Bussy to Choiseul, June 19, ibid.; French memorial of July 13, translated in Thackeray's *History of William Pitt*, ii. 550; English answer of July 25, ii. 559; French ultimatum of Aug. 5, ii. 568; Choiseul to Solar, May 1762, A.E. Angleterre, 446.)

method of exercising the right of search. This outline of a project does not seem to have satisfied the English Ministry. Keene and his friend Waldegrave were very disappointed; but the negotiations went on.[1] Geraldino, the Spanish Minister in London, had already got into conversations with an agent of Walpole about a plan for satisfying with a payment of money all just claims on account of depredations. It is not very clear why the Spanish Government allowed him to propose this. It seems to have thought that the English Ministers were more concerned to stop the mouths of the injured merchants than to settle the controversy for the future.[2] This was certainly not true of Walpole, who must have foreseen a clamour against the sale of our national rights for a sum of money.[3] However, the two objects were not really incompatible.

The draft convention which resulted from these conversations provided that Spain should pay the sum of £95,000 as a compensation for the depredations, and that the two Governments should appoint plenipotentiaries to discuss and settle within a few months the questions at issue in America. The terms of reference caused some difficulty. Walpole insisted on mentioning expressly the free navigation in the West Indies. La Quadra imagined that this would prejudice the question beforehand by establishing the existence of such a right; therefore he wanted some general phrase which should promise the settlement of all the pretensions between the two Crowns. This would have started interminable disputes, and would probably have brought up the Spanish claims to Gibraltar, the Newfoundland fishery, &c.[4] A form of words was found, which made it reasonably clear that only the respective pretensions of the two Crowns arising out of their treaties with each other were to be the subject of discussion.

These pretensions were of various kinds. England was most anxious to discuss the right of search, but it was not uppermost in the mind of Spain. Besides the controversy over the navigation, we had a question of boundaries to settle. Since 1670, when the two nations recognized the territorial *status quo*, the colony of Georgia had arisen on the undefined frontiers of

---

[1] Waldegrave to Keene, June 10 and 17, N.S., 1738, Waldegrave MSS. For Montijo's project, *vide supra*, pp. 35, 39.

[2] Stert to Horace Walpole, June 5, 1738, S.P. 94/131.

[3] Newcastle to Hardwicke, Aug. 25, 1738, Add. MSS. 35406, f. 39.

[4] Keene to Newcastle, Oct. 13, 1738, S.P. 94/131.

Carolina and Florida. It had caused a great deal of trouble; Newcastle and Geraldino had long been disputing whether, and in what sense, if the limits of these colonies were to be referred to commissioners, the English should evacuate Georgia during their sittings.[1] Newcastle did not know what the rights and wrongs of the question were; but he knew the politics of it—the Government could not afford to surrender Georgia.[2] The question was complicated by the annual grants of money which Parliament made for the support of the colony. The Treasury might be held to incur a responsibility towards the Spaniards.

Walpole seems to have been in two minds whether to give up Georgia to Spain—reports conflicted and varied from day to day on this head. His strongest desire was to have the affair kept out of politics, in order to avoid swelling the complaints and agitation, and to enable his own supporters among the colony's Trustees, of whom many were members of Parliament, to vote with the Government. The Trustees were equally anxious to escape from an unpleasant choice: if they allowed political capital to be made out of Georgia, they got no money from the Ministry, and if they did not, they offended the Opposition, which might come into power at any moment. With a little adroitness on both sides, this difficulty was overcome; the Trustees got their money and made little trouble.[3] Newcastle made Geraldino waive the demand for preliminary evacuation, but Spain got this matter included in the plenipotentiaries' terms of reference. The Convention was signed at last in January 1739, at the palace of El Pardo.

The English Ministers would not have been so eager to make a special reference to the liberty of navigation in this preliminary agreement, if they could have foreseen how it would be taken by the Opposition. When the Convention was published, everybody cried out that by consenting to discuss our rights we had sacrificed them. Great play was made with the word 'regulate' which was found in the text. If the plenipotentiaries 'regulated' the right of search, they must end by establishing it in some form or other; if they 'regulated' the

<hr>

[1] Keene to Newcastle, March 17, 1738, S.P. 94/130; Newcastle to Keene, April 12, 1738, S.P. 94/132; Geraldino to Newcastle, March 27, 1738, S.P. 100/59.

[2] Newcastle to Hardwicke, Sept. 25, 1738, Add. MSS. 35406, f. 49.

[3] *H.M.C. Egmont MSS.*, Diary, iii. 2–51, *passim; Colonial Records of Georgia*, ed. Candler, i. 336, 340–4.

freedom of navigation they could only diminish it.[1] Our Ministry should have asserted our rights without allowing any debate upon what, in the opinion of the Opposition, admitted of none.[2] The Government replied quite truly that no orders had been given for sacrificing anything of our lawful claims. In fact Newcastle's instructions were only too likely to embarrass the plenipotentiaries by their peremptory insistence on the abandonment of the right of search. He believed, or at least he said, that England really had the right to insist on her own interpretation of the freedom of navigation, by the terms of the Convention itself.[3] Horace Walpole pointed to the payment of compensation and argued that it implied a recognition that wrong had been done in the past, which amounted to a tacit undertaking not to repeat the offence in the future. This was unconvincing logic, for, as Pitt said, Spain only admitted in this way the existence of excesses in the past—nothing as to the legal rights of the case.[4] Moreover, this small mess of pottage for which we had sold our birthright, when would it be paid?

§ iii.   *The South Sea Company and the Convention of El Pardo*

The famous £95,000 was never paid at all; the negotiations broke down, and war became unavoidable. How did this come about? At first sight the explanation is to be found in the method by which the money was to be paid; but there were deeper causes, arising from the propaganda of a factious Opposition, the temper and ambitions of the commercial classes, and a fundamental incompatibility between the economic policies of England and Spain.

The figure of £95,000 resulted from a compromise. The English negotiator originally proposed a much larger sum, but the Spanish Government took advantage of some inconsistencies and indiscreet concessions to have it reduced. Perhaps the King of Spain would never have promised so much if he had thought he should have to pay it in cash; but somebody in London had suggested a method for making that unnecessary.

Since the beginning of its Assiento, the South Sea Company

---

[1] *Parl. Hist.* x. 1263 (Sanderson): *A Review of all that hath pass'd between the Courts of Great Britain and Spain* (London, 1739), p. 36.

[2] Cambis to Amelot, March 12, 1739, A.E. Angleterre, 404, f. 164.

[3] Newcastle to Keene and Castres, March 20, 1738/9, S.P. 94/134.

[4] *Parl. Hist.* x. 1253, 1282.

had had various financial relations with the King of Spain. It had lent him a sum at the outset. He had become a partner with a quarter interest in its trading operations; and as he did not choose to subscribe his share, the Company advanced it for him and charged him interest. A quarter of the profit on the Assiento trade and Annual Ships was due to him. Not much appeared to be payable on this head, for there seldom were any profits. The only Annual Ship whose accounts were examined on his behalf was proved to have made a very large profit. The Company would not let him inspect the accounts of any others, perhaps because it wished to defraud him of his share, by dressing up a gain as a loss.

The Company was also to pay him duties on the negroes it imported. Besides these, there were claims of an unforeseen nature. In 1726 the valuation of the dollar was altered, and a sum became due, or was at least claimed by the Spanish Court, on that account. Against this, the Company had some very large demands on the King of Spain. It argued that, as he was to have shared in the profits if there had been any, so he ought to bear his part of the loss. In the negro trade the declared loss amounted to £222,000 besides much larger deficits on the Annual Ship. It also charged him, rightly or wrongly, with a quarter of what it declared to be its running expenses; and on all these debts, which remained unpaid for many years, it demanded a very high rate of interest. In 1718 and 1727, when hostilities broke out between England and Spain, the effects of the Company in the Spanish dominions were seized by way of reprisals. Philip V had afterwards agreed to compensate the Company, but the accounts had never been settled to the entire satisfaction of both parties; still less had they been paid.[1] It had been agreed that if the reprisals were not paid for in any other way—and it was very unlikely that they would be—the King of Spain might allow the Company to recover the sum out of the negro duties which should be payable to him in future years. The Assiento had only been granted for thirty years from 1713—later altered to 1714—and was therefore likely to expire in 1744. The negro duties would not suffice to pay the Company's exaggerated demands within that time, especially as they had also been appropriated to the repayment of other debts due to it from the King of Spain.

[1] Add. MSS. 33032, ff. 256–7.

There was another dispute over the period of the contract's validity. The Assiento had been granted for thirty years; but there had been several interruptions in the exercise of the trade, and in particular there had only been seven Annual Ships, instead of twenty-four or twenty-five. The difficulties which had prevented the sailing of the rest had partly been chargeable to the Company itself; but that the directors overlooked. They started the doctrine that thirty years meant thirty trading years. They also claimed that as the negro duties would not have paid off their debt by 1744, the contract should be prolonged until the payment by this method should be complete. They refused to accept the settlement offered by the King of Spain except on these terms.[1] This enthusiasm for continuing the trade was surprising so soon after the Company had very nearly surrendered its trading privileges altogether.[2] Nor was it likely to be rewarded with success. Newcastle might think the claim 'plausible'; but the King of Spain did not wish to renew the contract. As for the huge demands of the Company, he meant to see the accounts produced in proper form. He particularly suspected the Company of grossly overrating its trading capital in order to increase the quarter share due from him, and concealing the real proceeds of the Annual Ships in order to charge him with a loss.[3]

All this while the negro duties, for which the Company was to be accountable every five years, were piling up. The directors were induced to admit that the Company had in its hands £68,000 which was due to the King of Spain in one way or another.[4] It was this sum which Geraldino proposed to have transferred to the English Government in order to pay part of the £95,000. The Ministry consented, but the Company at once made difficulties. The shareholders thought it unreasonable that they should pay what they owed to the King of Spain without receiving what he owed them. He ought at least to give good security for it by agreeing to extend the Assiento.[5] However, he refused to do any of this until the Company

---

[1] Add. MSS. 25561, ff. 75-6. [2] *Vide supra*, p. 19.

[3] Add. MSS. 32819, ff. 147-51. This is a document of 1749, but it is probably a repetition of earlier ones.

[4] Burrell to Newcastle, Aug. 9, 1738, Add. MSS. 35406, f. 43.

[5] South Sea Company, Minutes of the General Court, Add. MSS. 25545, f. 81; Newcastle to Keene, Aug. 21, 1738, S.P. 94/132; March 20, 1738/9, S.P. 94/134 (this last letter was not sent).

accepted his terms, and produced accounts in a regular form.[1]

He might still, according to the Convention, pay the £95,000 in cash; but he was so angry with the Company that, if he had to do so, he meant to suspend the Assiento altogether. At first he insisted on annexing this condition to the signature of the Convention itself. The English Ministry would not have that; but Keene could not prevent him from declaring this purpose at the same time as he signed the Convention. Keene took a great risk by accepting a Convention accompanied with such an encumbrance. Newcastle had warned him against doing so, but he argued that the Assiento was to all intents and purposes suspended already by the dispute between the Crown of Spain and the Company; he had always foreseen that he should never get the *cedulas* for the Annual Ships of 1738 and 1739 until that dispute was accommodated. Though the Government approved of his action, it was a long time before the public forgave the too Spanish 'Don Benjamin'.

This was sure to be a serious matter, for the Assiento affairs were no mere private dealings between the King of Spain and some English merchants; they were founded on a public treaty signed between King Philip and Queen Anne. All that the Ministry could do was to suppress the declaration as long as possible, and hope the Court of Spain would change its mind.

The last chance of this vanished in April 1739. Nearly a year before, the Government had sent out Rear-Admiral Haddock to reinforce the Mediterranean squadron. Keene, who knew the Spanish Court, had seen no harm in this, and had even thought a show of force would do good. It does not seem, however, to have done much to placate or impose upon the Queen of Spain.[2] When the likelihood of peace improved, the Government decided to reduce Haddock's squadron; but on March 21, 1739, Newcastle sent him counter-orders to keep all his ships with him. The English Ministers gave out to their friends that this was only a gesture to please the mob;[3] but when he heard it La Quadra looked very grave. He would not accept the vague and unsubstantial comfort which Newcastle ordered Keene to administer, and told Keene that he was no

[1] Keene to Newcastle, Sept. 8 and 29, S.P. 94/131.
[2] Keene to Newcastle, Feb. 23, 1738, S.P. 94/130; June 23, Aug. 29, S.P. 94/131.
[3] Cambis to Amelot, April 2, 1739, A.E. Angleterre, 404, f. 215.

longer sure of his ability to keep the peace between the two Crowns.[1] Soon afterwards the Spanish plenipotentiaries declared by order that as long as Haddock remained off the coasts of Spain they should grant no 'graces or facilities'[2]—in other words, that there was no hope of accommodating the disputes over Georgia and the right of search. In June the meaning of this threat was further particularized. Spain did not even carry out her design of paying the £95,000 and suspending the Assiento; she would not pay at all.

§ iv. *The Responsibility for the War*

Ministers are only responsible for the proximate causes of wars; they can seldom control anything more. What was the proximate cause of this war? Much has been made of Newcastle's counter-orders to Haddock. Certainly La Quadra's temper changed for the worse and the Spanish plenipotentiaries became more obstinate, soon after this measure was known in Spain. The English Ministers were wrong when they ascribed this change to the hope of support from France.[3] Spain was fortified by the marriage of Don Philip with Louis XV's daughter, but she had been refused the political alliance which she desired.[4] Yet supposing the counter-orders to Haddock had all the effect which Professor Temperley has ascribed to them, Philip V's declaration of January had already raised an obstruction to the good relations of England and Spain, which must have caused a war very soon unless Philip V himself had removed it.

One of the most remarkable things in the whole affair, which shows the majority of the English Ministers to have been really anxious for a settlement, is their readiness to accept the Convention in spite of La Quadra's declaration. Newcastle and Hardwicke may have expected and even hoped that the Spanish threat would be carried out, nor was there any love lost between the Government and the Company, which would be the chief loser in such a case; but that does not take away all the merit of an attitude which shows a real disposition to peace.

---

[1] Villarias (La Quadra) to Keene, April 20, 1739, S.P. 94/133; Keene to Newcastle (apart), April 24, ibid.

[2] Keene and Castres to Newcastle, May 18, 1739, S.P. 94/133.

[3] Hardwicke to Newcastle, April 26, 1739, Add. MSS. 32692, f. 52.

[4] A. Baudrillart, *Philippe V et la Cour de France*, iv. 525.

As for the dispute over the right of search itself, the proposals of England were not, for the most part, unreasonable. With good will, a real settlement could have been achieved along the lines of Newcastle's draft treaty. It would have been clogged, however, by other articles less acceptable. Newcastle instructed the plenipotentiaries on no account to give up the right to cut logwood;[1] this prohibition was certain to prejudice the main question of the right of navigation, because he insisted that logwood in the cargo was not to be a ground of condemning any English ship. Furthermore, the Spaniards would probably have attached a strong demand upon Georgia to any concession they might have made about the right of search.

There were then at least three questions—the Assiento, the logwood-cutters, and Georgia—on which no compromise was in sight when the war broke out. Newcastle wrote that Keene, after his return to England, had

'fortified Sir R. in his opinion, that Spain would have performed the Convention, had they not seen they must break afterwards in the future treaty; that Spain wished peace. Whoever doubted it, if they could have it on their own terms? and if we were to break on the future treaty, it is better to break now, for their non-performance of the Convention.'[2]

Disputes can always be compromised if they are yielded; no doubt the English could have had peace if they had been ready to give up every point. Walpole indeed was credited with the wish to do so, and certainly he was very disappointed when the war broke out in spite of all he had done. Yet he always proclaimed his dissent from the Spanish doctrine of search, and only differed from the Opposition in hoping to get the right renounced tacitly, instead of wishing to use force for its own sake.[3] It is not certain what he would have yielded in the last resort. His opinion about the logwood is not known; on Georgia, if the tittle-tattle picked up by Egmont is to be relied upon, he made up his mind to be firm. When Spain refused to pay the

[1] Silhouette, a competent observer, believed that the logwood question would be the hardest to settle. (Silhouette to Amelot, March 12, N.S., 1740, A.E. Angleterre, 407, f. 186.)

[2] Newcastle to Hardwicke, Sept. 20, 1739, Add. MSS. 35406, f. 137. Keene himself expressed very much the same opinion in a letter of August 17, N.S., to Lord Waldegrave (Waldegrave MSS.). He did not think any good would come of reopening the conferences, even if the money were paid.

[3] Parl. Hist. x. 662.

£95,000, even he admitted that it would have been even more embarrassing if she had paid it and suspended the Assiento Contract.[1]

Newcastle was for war nearly all the time. There was always too much of what Walpole called *invita Minerva* in his dispatches —a sharpness of tone which did not accord with the reasonable attitudes he was sometimes obliged to take. Yet he had his variations. He declined at first to draw up the Convention, and Horace Walpole (who was perhaps over-sensitive on this subject) afterwards accused him of trying to discredit it by a malicious phrase in the declaration of war.[2] Nevertheless he set his hand to the draft treaty, which made important concessions. In the same breath as he declared that he could not concede the right of search, he proposed almost accidentally an expedient which would have settled the controversy by doing so.[3] Yet he thought we had a title to cut logwood, and told Hardwicke that 'however the right may be, it will now be pretty difficult to give up Georgia'. He was often impatient to press our demands or unwilling to moderate them; by February or March 1739 he seems to have been convinced that even the supporters of the Ministry would hardly vote for a policy of peace, and that 'we must yield to the times, so far as is consistent at least with our own point'.[4] When the war became unavoidable, he expressed his eagerness and relief; he did not wait for La Quadra's open refusal to pay the £95,000, but acted at once upon his omission to do it.

Very few of their contemporaries accused the Ministers of wanting war; indeed their crime was rather that they did not want it, but brought it upon themselves by their too obvious desire to avoid it. Not only the Opposition but some French critics thought that the fault lay at the door of an inept diplomacy. It was the want of dignity and firmness, not the want of goodwill, which was held responsible for the final crisis. When George II first offered the general letters of reprisal in March 1738, Spain immediately appealed to France for help; yet some critics argued, like Admiral Warren, that if the Government had always been prompt to grant particular letters of reprisals to

[1] Hardwicke to Newcastle, June 2, 1739, Add. MSS. 32692, f. 64.
[2] Hardwicke to Newcastle, Aug. 17, 1738, Add. MSS. 32691, f. 301; Horace Walpole to Hardwicke, Oct. 14, 1739, vol. 35586, f. 202.
[3] Newcastle to Hardwicke, Sept. 25, 1738, Add. MSS. 35406, f. 50.
[4] Newcastle to Hardwicke, 'Saturday morning', Add. MSS. 35406, f. 111.

the sufferers from depredations, it need never have proceeded to the general measure, because Spain would have been intimidated into a real redress of grievances.[1] That was possibly true, but the Dutch of Curaçao did not succeed in stopping the seizures by this kind of retaliation. Keene can hardly be accused of cringing to La Quadra, or Newcastle to Geraldino. Keene in fact recommended a show of force, and the hint was taken. With what result? The decision to leave Haddock's ships at Gibraltar undoubtedly exasperated the Court of Spain. Perhaps this firmness came too late. Keene himself thought it ill timed.

'You will see', he wrote to Waldegrave, 'what a fine disposition this Court is in, on the news of our fleet's staying in the Mediterranean. I see the necessity of it with respect to our home affairs, but with regard to Spain I must own, that we shall only vex, not intimidate. We have gone too great lengths towards peace, to pretend we have still a mind to make war.'[2]

It is easy to criticize, but much harder to point out the exact temperament of patience with vigour which would have brought the insufferable Queen of Spain to submission without driving her to frenzy.

It is not enough to follow the progress of negotiations or pry into Ministers' minds—especially in this instance, because it was not the Government but the Opposition that made the war; and even they, being politicians, were only exploiting a much wider discontent. Perhaps the war was so necessary that the historian can absolve not only the Ministers but, what is much harder, the Opposition from blame. A country like England, which was beginning to be industrialized, and a colonial system like that of Spain could hardly coexist without conflict. Great profits, high prices, slow returns, and small consumption could not fail to result from the Spanish colonial monopoly, and these accorded very little with the pushing and expansive genius of English trade. Perhaps the English did not believe in free trade; they passed rigid laws against exporting wool, discouraged colonial manufactures, and restrained colonial commerce by Acts of Trade and Navigation. Nevertheless they could afford to see the mote in their neighbour's eye, for their own economic system was at least more progressive than that of

---

[1] *Parl. Hist.* xiv. 617 (Warren); A.E. Mém. et Doc. Angleterre, vol. 9, f. 105.

[2] Keene to Waldegrave, April 23, N.S., 1739, Waldegrave MSS.

Spain. The success of the English interlopers in Spanish America was accounted for by their readiness to take smaller profits than the regular traders—a thing they could well afford to do, since they did not pay the regular duties. Add to this the admirable situation of Jamaica as a smugglers' head-quarters, and the inaction of a Government which dared not suppress these unlawful exports and had no sufficient diplomatic motives for doing so; there was plenty of material for a conflict, provided each party adhered to its principles with only a little of that righteous obstinacy which inexperience of war inspires in statesmen and journalists.

Why had this agitation suddenly boiled up out of nowhere, over a practice which had continued for many years and affected smugglers rather than fair traders?[1] Did the merchants of England recklessly expose the whole volume of their foreign trade to remedy the misdoings of a few paltry privateers off the coasts of Cuba? There was some controversy over the nature of the propaganda for the Spanish war. Walpole maintained that the Opposition and the mob were entirely responsible for it; Argyll replied that it was a respectable middle-class movement supported by the merchants in general.[2] This dispute was carried into the City of London, always the home of faction and demagogy from the days of Pym to those of Alderman Wood. The supporters of the Ministry tried to turn the tables on the West India merchants who petitioned Parliament, by proving that they were not merchants and had nothing to do with the West Indies; but according to the Opposition newspapers this was only achieved by such means as describing a wholesale tobacco merchant as a tobacconist and a wholesale importer of spirits as a brandyman.[3] An Alderman who had voted for the Convention was overwhelmingly defeated at the election for Lord Mayor in 1739, despite his seniority, and the controversy raged for some years after the war broke out, until it turned itself into a constitutional struggle between the Aldermen and the Common Council.

If the merchants were really stirred by the legend of Jenkins'

[1] Silhouette asked himself this question, and answered, perhaps with too much faith in the importance of argument, that the agitation only rose to a great height when Carteret put the English case upon a strong foundation (Silhouette to Amelot, Dec. 24, N.S., 1739, A.E. Angleterre, 405, f. 360).

[2] Parl. Hist. x. 1142–3.

[3] Gentleman's Magazine, ix. 158.

Ear, why were they so?[1] Many of them would have profited by the suppression of the smugglers, and could only lose their trade by a war. Walpole tried to point this moral by stirring up the merchants who traded to Spain, to send in a counter-petition. He did not succeed; and he would have made very little impression if he had. Many years afterwards an anonymous writer remarked that 'this branch of trade by Old Spain to America, has ever been neglected by our ministers and ever will, as it lies among a set of people who can't be clamorous, vizt Roman Catholics and Jews'.[2] In general, our American trade was thought to be the most valuable trade we had; the statistics may not warrant the belief, but it was overwhelmingly strong. However that might be, the Opposition was quite right to argue that abandoning our American shipping to interruptions and insults was not the best way to procure security for our shipping in other quarters of the world.

However highly this branch of commerce might be rated, does it account for the behaviour of the merchants in general? Perhaps, as Professor Vaucher suggests, they were feeling the pinch of a trade depression, which heightened their desire for new markets.[3] The statistics of exports, for what they are worth, hardly seem to suggest this: the quantity was as great in the years 1735–8 as it had ever been. It is more difficult to be sure of the prices and profits, because the valuations which are given, for example, in Sir Charles Whitworth's tables, were founded on calculations which had not changed since 1722. Moreover, though the quantity had not diminished, it was increasing very little; it had been almost stationary for more than ten years. Complaints abounded that English commerce and industry were declining, or not advancing fast enough. Particularly they were not advancing so fast as the French. Economists and politicians were more obsessed than ever by the fear of French competition. France was thought to have re-

---

[1] Jenkins was a captain who declared that the *Guarda-Costas* had boarded his ship and cut off his ear; the Opposition took up his case very strongly. Perhaps if they had looked under his wig they would have found both his celebrated ears on his head; Alderman Beckford said so, and he might very well know. The War of 1739 is sometimes called the War of Jenkins' Ear.

[2] Add. MSS. 38373, f. 131.

[3] P. Vaucher, *Robert Walpole et la politique de Fleury*, pp. 296–302. Professor Vaucher apparently founds his opinion upon a graph in Mantoux's *Industrial Revolution in the Eighteenth Century* (English translation, 1928, p. 104). Mantoux's references do not really justify his graph, for they are to incomplete statistics.

covered faster than England from the wars of Louis XIV, and the pacific policy of Cardinal Fleury was known to be aimed at extending French commerce and manufactures. The competition of French merchandise in the Spanish market was thought particularly grievous. In a frenzy of apprehension and jealousy, the English pamphleteers excited their countrymen to strike a blow which would kill this bugbear stone-dead, and restore their own trade to an unshakable pre-eminence.

Some curious opinions were held as to the policy of waging war for the sake of trade. 'A rising trade may be ruined by a war; a sinking trade has a chance to revive by it.' That was the doctrine of *Common Sense*,[1] and more respectable writers endorsed it. Since the trade of our greatest rival had risen and ours had sunk, the moral hardly needed pointing. A silly and badly written pamphlet of 1745 expresses this doctrine of economic Chauvinism better than anything else. After a description of the various trades which we were in danger of losing to the French (of which the Spanish trade is one), the author comes to this conclusion:

'Since this, we say, is the real case between us, at present, however odd this position may sound in the ears of inconsiderate persons, we will venture to affirm, it is more the true interest of these Kingdoms in general, and even the merchants themselves (those who traded to Spain and the South-Seas excepted), that we should continue in a state of war with them (France and Spain), so that war is carried on only by sea, than in a state of peace. Nay, we will go yet further, and make no scruple to assert, whilst the Crowns of France, Spain and the two Sicilies continue united, as they are at present; our commerce, in general, will flourish more under a vigorous and well-managed naval war, than under any peace, which should allow an open intercourse with those two nations.'

He goes on to give his reasons, of which the most important is, that

'by such a war, we should not only distress our natural enemy to the last degree, but by ruining their commerce, and destroying their colonies, which they could hardly prevent, whilst we are so much their superiors by sea, we should in a great measure retrieve our own, and make them flourish again as formerly'.[2]

The measures he recommends for this purpose are mostly

---

[1] *Common Sense*, April 22, 1738.
[2] *The Present Ruinous Land-War proved to be a H——r War* (London, 1745), pp. 21–3.

destructive, such as a descent upon the French sugar-colonies for demolishing their plantations and carrying off their slaves.

Even those who passed for economists in those days made the same cynical calculations, prophesying that

'what trade they lose, we shall get, for by harassing their coasts, their merchantmen could not, without great risk, get out or in; the Turkey, East-India, fishing and sugar-trades would be rendered impracticable to them, and the bulk of them would fall into our hands again'.[1]

In fact the Yorkshire manufacturers preferred war to peace because they made a better living. The Archbishop of York told Newcastle in 1748 that the clothiers of Wakefield did not share the general joy for the peace, because their trade improved by war; Lord Kinnoull reported in 1759 that the trade of Yorkshire was so brisk that he feared the manufacturers would be disposed to carp at the peace. Contemporaries attributed this fact, perhaps wrongly, to the land campaigns of the French army, which withdrew men from the industries of France.[2] If this was true, war stimulated English trade as long as it lasted, but it could not last for ever.

Postlethwayt, a hack writer on commercial subjects, wished to discover so thorough a method of ruining our enemies that no national or political advantages would enable them to recover their ground at a peace. He wished

'so to distress the commerce and navigation of our ever restless enemy, as to disable them in future times from maintaining that lucrative competition with us in trade, they have too long done. . . . As the affairs of our trade and finances are at present circumstanced, a peace is far more dangerous than a war, for upon the continuance of a peace our trade must be ruined and undone, if that continues to be loaded with our tax-incumbrances, which we have seen . . . put it out of our power to support that commercial competition against France and others, that alone can save the nation.'[3]

Before Postlethwayt's eyes wars and taxes moved in a vicious circle; wars called for taxes and taxes necessitated more wars.

---

[1] (? W. Richardson), *An Essay on the Causes of the Decline of the Foreign Trade* (in Lord Overstone's *Select Collection* of tracts), p. 281.

[2] Archbishop Hutton to Newcastle, May 28, 1748, Add. MSS. 32715, f. 126; Kinnoull to Newcastle, July 28, 1759, vol. 32893, f. 331; *Parl. Hist.* xiii. 128 (Carteret), 316 (Bathurst); xiv. 582 (Egmont); Silhouette to Amelot, Nov. 26, 1739, A.E. Angleterre, 405, f. 287.

[3] *Great Britain's True System* (London, 1757), p. 270.

It remained for Dean Tucker, that most rational economist, to put his finger on the fallacy.[1]

The markets of Spanish America had long been eagerly competed for, and France was our strongest rival there. Many good patriots looked forward to the day when we should once again extend our trade in that part of the world, at the expense of the French, by a return to the policy of force which had been outlawed since 1713. This accounts for the curious fact that the probability of a war with France as well as Spain inspired enthusiasm rather than doubt or fear; from the language of some pamphleteers and orators, one might almost think it was France, not Spain, that was the real enemy from the beginning.

The eagerness of the merchants for new markets will appear better from the schemes which were freely put forward after the outbreak of war, for increasing our trade by conquests in America. In that moment of excitement and liberation, perhaps the veil was torn from ambitions which prudence had hitherto kept in the dark; perhaps the plans of campaign will show the real motives of the war.

---

[1] *The Case of Going to War for the Sake of Procuring, Enlarging or Securing of Trade* (London, 1763).

III

THE STRATEGY OF THE SPANISH WAR

§ i. *English Imperialism and the Liberation of Spanish America*

THE war with Spain was to be fought in the West Indies. The only person in England who seriously doubted or disputed it was the Prime Minister; and as he was an unwilling prisoner in the hands of his colleagues, poor Walpole's opinion was not to have much weight in the plan or conduct of the war. He was usually obliged to content himself with irritated acquiescence and protests which he was driven to withdraw, in order that something at least might be done, even on principles which he condemned.[1]

There were many reasons for this popular insistence on the American war. A wish, perhaps, to make the punishment fit the crime—Hardwicke more pompously called it 'vindictive justice'. It was in the West Indies that the *Guarda-Costas* had committed the offences which had provoked the war; in the West Indies, therefore, Spain should receive the punishment of her injurious obstinacy. There, too, Spain was most vulnerable. A long experience had shown that little was to be expected from attacks upon her coasts and seaports in Europe, and that, on the other hand, even her greatest strongholds in America could be reduced by quite small expeditions. Drake had taken St. Domingo city, the first capital of Spanish America. Pointis had taken Cartagena, and Henry Morgan, with a horde of buccaneers, had marched overland and sacked Panama. These exploits had been done in other days. The Spain of Philip V was not the Spain of Carlos II; but the English politicians and journalists do not seem to have understood that, and most of them believed that the Spanish Empire was still an effete, chaotic, defenceless affair that would collapse at a touch.

An American war with Spain was therefore just and easy; it was in fact the only kind of war that could be waged against her, the only kind that would bring her to her knees quickly. It may have been begun for the suppression of the right of

---

[1] There are descriptions of painful scenes in Council, in Hervey's minutes of April 28, May 6 and 22, 1740 (*Memoirs*, ed. Sedgwick, iii. 927–39), and in Newcastle's letter to Hardwicke, Oct. 1, 1740, Add. MSS. 35406, f. 237.

search; but no sooner had it broken out than the loud-mouthed patriots made up their minds that a mere confirmation of the rights which we had gone to war to defend, would not be enough. Artful Pulteney was even afraid that we might succeed too quickly and too easily in reducing Spain to submission; for that reason he disliked the Government's plan to send a powerful fleet against Ferrol. 'To ravage the coasts of Spain (supposing we could do it) seems to be with a desire only of forcing the Spaniards into a peace, before we have secured such advantages as we may reasonably hope for in another place.' That other place was of course the West Indies; and even there, he would rather conquer a colony which we could keep, than a strong place whose loss would merely disorganize the Spanish system of defences. 'Should it be to Carthagena first, even that action (great as it might be) would be a disappointment of our hopes; it might be a very sensible mischief to Spain, but what we immediately want is, advantage to ourselves.'[1] Carteret, intemperate drinker and still more intemperate talker, said to the Swedish Minister one night after dinner, 'What is the good of taking ships? We shall take from Spain some countries in America, and we shall keep them in spite of the whole world.'[2]

The Opposition leaders were suspected of saying this kind of thing in public in order to arouse extravagant hopes which they knew the Government could not satisfy. They were capable of such strategy, and had indeed employed it over the Convention. But if there is any truth in wine, Carteret meant what he said to Wasenberg, so far as he ever meant what he said at all; and besides, there is excellent reason for thinking him sincere in this. He was angling for a place—the chief place, for preference—in a 'National Government'. For some time he had been in some sort of collusion with Newcastle;[3] and now he disgusted his companions in Opposition by preaching the duty to avoid all factious obstruction which would disable the nation from carrying on the war efficiently.[4]

---

[1] Pulteney to Vernon, Aug. 17, 1740, *Original Letters to an Honest Sailor* (London, 1747), pp. 23–4.

[2] Wasenberg to Gyllenborg, Nov. 13, 1739, S.P. 107/34. See also Carteret's speeches in *Parl. Hist.* xi. 17, 723, 835, and Cambis's letter to Amelot, Nov. 26, 1739, A.E. Angleterre, 405, f. 274.

[3] Hardwicke to Newcastle, April 14, 1738, Add. MSS. 32691, f. 117. It is probable, but not certain, that the 'noble Lord' referred to in this letter is Carteret.

[4] Carteret to Marchmont, Aug. 15, 1739, *Marchmont Papers*, ii. 135–6.

While some of them ostentatiously rewarded the Government for doing their own will, others contrived to tie its hands and render peace impossible. At Wyndham's instigation, both Houses of Parliament addressed the King, asking him not to make peace until Spain would renounce the right of searching English ships in their voyages to and from the English dominions.[1] Pulteney revived, this time with success, the clause in the Act of 1708, which guaranteed to the fitters-out of expeditions the possession of whatever territories they might take from the enemy. In vain had Walpole protested that if any conquests were made, this proviso might make peace unattainable, and Bladen argued that it was contrary to the Treaty of Utrecht; in vain the South Sea Company trumped up its Charter of Queen Anne which gave it a monopoly of all Spanish America from the Orinoco to the Behring Strait.[2] Nobody now minded the Company; and one of the greatest grievances against it had always been, that it never made any effort to take advantage of its privileges. The clause passed, and aroused the greatest expectations.[3] It remained without sequel, a mere piece of bravado. Several projects of private expeditions, especially in the Pacific, were much talked of for a time; a silly scheme for the discovery of a non-existent passage to the South Seas was renewed, which had been rejected by the Admiralty some years before, and taken up in Russia of all places, until the war offered a new hope of its acceptance in England. It came to nothing, and the last heard of it is a strenuous effort of its promoter to foist it on the French.[4] I have found only two positive applications to the Government for commissions under this clause. Fotherby, Trahern, and Cole demanded one in June 1741; but there is no evidence to show where they designed their voyage or what became of it. The Royal African Com-

---

[1] *Parl. Hist.* xi. 213–45. Wyndham first wanted to make this renunciation a preliminary to any negotiation, but altered his proposal when Walpole denounced it for putting the cart before the horse (Silhouette to Amelot, Dec. 7, N.S., 1739, A.E. Angleterre, 405, f. 321). George II assented, but in the event the promise was neither performed by the King nor claimed by the Parliament.

[2] *C. J.*, Dec. 10, 1739, xxiii. 402; South Sea Company, Minutes of the Court of Directors, Dec. 7, 1739, Add. MSS. 25510, f. 59.

[3] *Parl. Hist.* xi. 603 (address of Speaker Onslow to the King, April 29, 1740), xii. 310 (Pulteney). Pulteney had tried to get this clause, with the whole of the Act of 1708, re-enacted in 1738; see Chap. II, p. 48.

[4] Bussy to Amelot, March 31, 1741, A.E. Angleterre, 411, f. 286; June 2, 1741, vol. 412, f. 126. There are further references to it in vol. 417, ff. 197, 216, and 304.

pany also asked for such a power, which was refused, because the proposed undertaking would contravene the Act against stock-jobbing.[1]

In all this, the Opposition leaders only obeyed the public voice. The press was full of pamphlets, leading articles, and anonymous letters, which all echoed, in one form or another, the cry of 'Take and Hold'. It was a sudden and noisy explosion of imperialism, a good example of the greedy turbulence which foreign observers attributed to the English nation.[2] Some writers tried to justify our ambitions of new markets and territories, by connecting them with our rights of free navigation. They revived the argument of Queen Anne's reign, when England had demanded the 'cautionary towns' in Spanish America. There could be no guarantee, they said, for our freedom from the right of search, unless we had in our hands securities for the good conduct of the *Guarda-Costas*. Hence the cry of 'Real Security', which had a great popularity as a complement, or justification, of 'Take and Hold'. When the news of Portobello had arrived to inflame the national cupidity afresh, the French *Chargé* wrote to his Court: 'The phrase "real security" has become a sort of national cry; it is on everybody's lips, from the Peer of the Realm to the cobbler; and everybody understands by it, taking and keeping some Spanish colony.'[3]

Very few people, outside the circle of those who were responsible for directing expeditions, doubted our ability to execute any fantastic scheme we pleased to conceive. Some, however—most of them supporters of the Ministry—doubted whether all things possible were things expedient. They had to reckon with foreign governments, who might dislike to see the 'equilibrium' of Utrecht upset by the substitution of England for Spain as the ruler of Central America. This fear of foreign jealousies had some slight influence on the choice of objectives.

The settlement of Utrecht, which left the Spanish dominions in America undivided in the hands of Spain, had once been considered equally fair to all the trading nations.[4] In spite of the precautions against a collusive French monopoly within

---

[1] C.O. 5/5, p. 169; *A.P.C. Col.* iii. 698, 723-4.

[2] See the chapter on this agitation in G. B. Hertz, *British Imperialism in the XVIIIth Century* (Manchester, 1908).

[3] De Vismes to Amelot, April 7, 1740, S.P. 107/41; see also Norris's diary, March 17, 1739/40, Add. MSS. 28132, f. 159.   [4] See Chap. I, p. 13.

the Spanish Empire, many Englishmen had come to believe, perhaps very unreasonably, that as long as Spanish America remained, on whatever terms, under the dominion of the House of Bourbon, France would have an unfair advantage. On the other hand, some of them recognized that impartial foreigners would dislike a conquest of those countries by the English even more than a virtual French domination under the Spanish flag. What remedy was there then? To acquiesce in Spanish rule was to hand over the richest part of the continent to French trade; to claim the Spanish colonies for ourselves was perhaps to incur the hostility of all Europe. There was only one course left—to promote an American Revolution within the Spanish Empire. This was much more likely to buy off diplomatic difficulties than the scheme of 'cautionary towns', for however strong might be the arguments for regarding such towns only in the light of securities, there can be no doubt that they would have been considered as something more. The plan had other advantages. Nobody could well conceive how we should hold down Spanish America by force. England could not spare the men; and though the conquered country itself might find the money, it would be a pity to seize Mexico or Peru for the pleasure of spending a great part of their revenue (as the King of Spain himself did) upon garrisons.[1]

The difficulties of this policy were underrated. Scraps of travellers' hearsay were collected and retailed, to prove the existence of discontent, especially in the Pacific colonies. There were three things, on one or other of which every projector of revolution relied. All the Spaniards of America, except the officials, were supposed to groan under misgovernment, arbitrary taxation, and the crippling system of trade monopoly. In particular, the English naturally flattered themselves that the French origin of the King of Spain rendered him unpopular. Of the Spaniards, the parties of Creoles and Chapetones[2] were supposed to dislike each other, and the Creoles, who were the

---

[1] Unsigned paper dated June 6, 1741, Library of Congress, Vernon-Wager MSS.
[2] Creoles were the Spaniards born in the colonies, Chapetones those who had emigrated there from Spain. The term Creole does *not* indicate any sort of racial mixture; on the contrary, a Creole was by strict definition a pure white Spaniard who was not born in Europe. The English extended this term to negroes, animals, and plants: a Creole negro was one born in the colonies as opposed to an African negro, one imported from Africa; Creole rice was a kind of rice supposed to be found growing wild in the colonies.

great majority, to be ready to discard their Spanish allegiance in order to satisfy this passion. Writers generally gave, as reasons for this state of affairs, the dislike of the colonist for the official (many of the Chapetones were officials), and the competition of the native colonial merchant with the more efficient trader who came out from Europe to get rich quick.[1]

Lastly, the English counted on the hatred of the Indians for the Spaniards in general. The Indians to the south of Chile were believed to be independent, very powerful, and always at war, or ready for a war, with the Spanish colonists.[2] Less was expected of the Indians of Peru and Mexico, but in the imperfectly subdued lands of Central America there were tribes which had the reputation of having never submitted to the Spanish rule. Such were the Darien and Samblas Indians of the Isthmus, the Moskito Indians of Nicaragua with their tributaries, and other Indians inland towards Guatemala, who were perhaps too liberally bestowed by amateur strategists and geographers upon the unoccupied spaces of the map. These Indians were all supposed to be impatiently awaiting their deliverance from Spain at the hands of the other powers of Europe. As an anonymous giver of unasked advice wrote of the Darien Indians, 'millions of miserable people would bless their Deliverers, and their hearts and their mines would be open to us'.[3]

The advantages which the people of the Spanish colonies would gain by accepting independence or an English government could be put before them in a proclamation. What was to be offered? Upon certain points there was universal agreement. The civil liberties, estates, and religion of the Spaniards must be safeguarded. As for religion, whatever dregs of anti-Popish sentiment remained in England, whatever penal laws in Ireland, publicists and politicians had at least seen the necessity of offering complete religious toleration to the inhabitants of conquered colonies. It was especially important in a country like Spanish America where priests counted for so much. In fact the author of one memorial suspected that clerical human nature was not very different in England and Mexico, and suggested that bare toleration was not enough; the priests should

---

[1] Frezier, *A Voyage to the South Sea*, English translation, 1717, p. 250.

[2] Ibid., p. 268; Shelvocke, *A Voyage Round the World* (reprint of 1928), pp. 63–4; Harris, *Navigantium atque Itinerantium Bibliotheca* (1764 ed.), i. 182.

[3] Add. MSS. 32694, f. 88. See also *C.S.P. Col. 1720–1*, nos. 47, 327.

be won over by promises of preferment.[1] The clearest orders were always given on this point of toleration, and were obeyed with naïve tact. Anson with ostentatious decency exempted only the two churches from the fire of Payta, and Knowles left the garrison chapel standing among the ruins of the demolished fortress of St. Louis.[2]

The liberties and properties of the colonists were to be not only preserved but enhanced in value. Political liberties they had none, but these were now to be offered by the generous hand of England. In what form, was the question.

Some writers thought that the Spanish Americans could ask nothing better than to share the rights of Englishmen.[3] They did not intend to promote an American Revolution but wished, if possible, to annex the Spanish colonies with the consent of their inhabitants. It was enough, they thought, to offer all the privileges of English subjects. This, however, would not have answered the purpose of diverting foreign jealousy; others therefore took the more imaginative course of suggesting that the colonies, if they could be induced to revolt, should set up governments of their own. What form of government, was a question on which little could be said with certainty. The Creoles were ambitious. There were nobles, descendants of well-beloved Viceroys. Some indeed were said to aspire to crowns. There was no counting on this, and the wisest course was to leave the colonists to make their own institutions, offering them a defensive alliance and an army and fleet sufficient for their protection. This was especially easy to promise in the Pacific colonies, for the Spanish fleets had hardly ever dared to pass Cape Horn, before Pizarro followed Anson in 1741; and the difficulty of transporting an effective army from Spain to Peru, or from one part of the Spanish dominions to another, over seas dominated by English squadrons, would have dismayed the Spanish Government.

If a considerable force of English ships and troops should succeed in reaching the shores of the Pacific, the invitation could as easily be coupled with a threat; for it would be plain that

[1] 'Project for attacking La Vera Cruz and Mexico, 1740, no. 1', Library of Congress, Vernon-Wager MSS.
[2] R. Walter, *A Voyage Round the World* (4th ed.), p. 277; Chastenoye to Maurepas, April, 8, 1748, A.N. Colonies C⁹ A 72.
[3] One projector even proposed the establishment of a Mayor and Aldermen at Portobello (J. Morris to Wager, May 1742, Vernon-Wager MSS.).

even if the colonists desired to continue their allegiance to the King of Spain, he could do nothing to help them. This perhaps would be the clinching argument; were they so blind as to reject a peaceable offer, the Creoles might yet be bombarded into liberty. If this fear would not avail with them, there was another menace in store. They were not the only people who could be appealed to, and if they did not take the chance of freeing themselves from the Spaniards their slaves, or at any rate their Indian enemies, might be tempted to rise against them. Even the Indians could offer a market for English manufactures which was worth gaining, and valuable returns too, especially if they had concealed many of their best mines from the Spaniards, as some English writers believed. Thus most of the schemes for liberation in Spanish America coupled vaguely as alternatives, or even as different parts of the same policy, incitement of the Creoles against the Government, and of the Indians, mestizos, and negroes against the Creoles.[1] As long as they were clearly conceived as alternatives, there was no harm in this; but they were obviously incompatible, and the muddled instructions to combine them, which the Government finally gave, could only have created confusion if they had been executed at all.

The future of trade with the revolted colonies was a more important and more difficult question, the suggestions more various. To the smugglers of Jamaica, or the English merchants in general, the independence of the Spanish colonies would be most valuable if we, and nobody else, should trade with the states we had set up. There might be objections to this from third parties, and from interested classes in Spanish America itself. The prospect that the grateful and dependent governments of the new world would barter with their protectors trade privileges for recognition and defence, might have alarmed the rest of the world as much in 1740 as it did in 1823; and the powers of Europe might have been driven to advocating a very different Monroe Doctrine before the birth of President Monroe. Some writers assumed that we could risk that; but at least one believed that though it might seem a 'romantic' thing to conquer and free the Spanish colonies in order that the whole world might be at liberty to trade with them, we should

[1] Wager to Vernon, Aug. 20 and Oct. 29, 1741, *Original Letters to an Honest Sailor*, pp. 51, 57.

be doing ourselves no harm by doing so. Our natural and acquired advantages, the situation of our colonies as bases for trade, and the cheapness of our manufactures, would give us a sufficient advantage against other nations in a commerce that was open to all. This anonymous projector of expeditions thus recognized that the policy of the Open Door is useful, or at least not injurious, to the nation which has most to send through the door.[1] Other writers assumed that we should make with the new states treaties of commerce which would be very much to our advantage; and this was the hope of the English Government.

Apparently the merchants of the Spanish colonies were also to be conciliated. Several anonymous advisers of the Government—especially those who thought of the Spanish colonies as put under some sort of English protectorate or dominion—recommended that we should keep up the galleons and *flotas*, and strictly prevent the unlicensed trade of Jamaica—a curious consequence, seeing how the war had been begun. These trading fleets would presumably sail from England and with English manufactures. So far, this is only another form of the claim for an exclusive trade; but it was plainly meant as a concession also to somebody in Spanish America. Presumably it would appeal to the great merchants, who bought regularly from the galleons and disliked the peddling, hand-to-mouth methods by which the interlopers supplied the small merchants and consumers without the help of a wholesale middleman. The galleon system must be reformed of its abuses; the irregularity, delays, vexations, and above all the high and arbitrary duties must be abolished. From this kind of improvement buyers and sellers would benefit alike (as the French thought, when they in the season of their power tried to make the Government of Philip V take up such reforms). It was important, however, that no change should be made in the system itself without the consent of the parties concerned in it, and England must promise to prevent illicit importations in the future. One writer made an interesting suggestion. The Spaniards forbade the growth of wine and oil in the colonies, in order to favour the agriculture of Spain. This prohibition could easily be removed by an English or free Anglophile Government. England would lose nothing, since she was not

[1] Paper of June 6, 1741, already quoted, Vernon-Wager MSS.

a grower of these articles; and the money that went to Europe to buy them, would stay at home, create new purchasing-power among the Indians, who would become growers of wine and oil, and so increase the demand for clothing of English manufacture. A retrenchment of the export of money which was sent to Spain for the purpose of buying official positions would have the same result.[1]

Nobody need take too seriously the schemes of anonymous memorialists; the eighteenth century abounded with them above all others. There are better witnesses to call. Edward Trelawny, Governor of Jamaica for fifteen years, did something in a small way to influence the policy of his superiors on Central American questions. He was not, like the author of the 'romantic' scheme, an advocate for complete national disinterestedness. Indeed, there was one place at least where he would like to see a new colony annexed to the British Crown; but he advocated the promotion of every kind of revolt against Spanish rule, especially among the Indians. By playing upon the discontent of the Creoles and Indians, he hoped to dismember the Spanish Empire:

'if we do not entirely destroy it in these parts, and lay a foundation for a most extensive and beneficial trade with the inhabitants in spite of France and Spain which will render his Majesty's reign as glorious as I wish it. It is a received notion I know that it is better that the Spaniards who are reckoned so indolent should have the possession of the West Indies, than any other Prince in Europe, and I believe it would be a right notion if they were not so greatly influenced by France, and so much of late inveterate to us; but be that how it will, surely it would be better for Europe in general that no European Prince whatsoever had the entire possession so as to exclude the others from trading with so great and rich a part of the world, but that it should be in the hands of the natives, who would naturally break into so many independent governments, no one of which could arrogate to itself the commerce of the whole. . . . I would not desire to exclude the Dutch (or even French when they behave well) from trading anywhere in the West Indies unless with our own settlements, so I think they would have no reason to complain, but would rather receive a benefit by this disposition while in alliance

---

[1] 'Project for attacking La Vera Cruz and Mexico, 1741, no. 1'; 'The same, no. 2'; undated paper entitled 'Proposal', all in the Vernon-Wager MSS. Some of these recommendations, especially the suggestion about the wine and oil, are extraordinarily like those of Don Bernardo Ulloa, *Restablecimiento de las Fábricas y Comercio Español*, ii. 237–60.

with us; tho' we should have, as we ought, I think, the greatest benefit by possessing the most advantageous places for commerce as Panama.'[1]

The Ministry itself was impressed by the arguments for encouraging Spanish-American separatism—in what degree, may be seen by the instructions of Cathcart, Anson, and Knowles. Cathcart was to command the main expedition to the West Indies in 1740; he had a powerful force, and he was to satisfy a strong expectation of conquest. The places against which he was to make his attempts were within easy reach of English colonies, therefore if they were taken they could probably be held. For all these reasons it was not to be expected that he should confer political independence upon the conquered peoples. The proclamation which he was to distribute, offered to all inhabitants of the Spanish colonies who should without committing any hostilities place themselves under His Majesty's protection:

'that they shall be received, protected, and maintained in their lands, houses, possessions and other properties . . . in the same manner as if they were His own natural subjects. They shall possess and enjoy the full and free exercise of their religion in the same manner and form which they do at present. They shall be freed from the increased imposts, alcavalas, duties, prohibitions and other oppressions, under which they at present suffer, from the nature and form of the government established in the Spanish Indies; and, in particular, the Indians shall be exempted from those royal tributes and services to which they have been subject. They shall have the privilege and right of trading directly to Great Britain and to all the British colonies in America, and finally, in all cases and in all respects they shall be attended to, assisted, favoured, and treated as the natural born subjects of Great Britain.'[2]

The policy of this proclamation (which was inexplicably divulged and made an embarrassing noise in the neutral press) was plainly not liberation but annexation by consent.

Anson's expedition to the Pacific was a more doubtful adventure. He had a much smaller force, and was going to a country about which hardly anybody in England knew anything certain. Therefore his instructions had to allow a great deal of latitude, and to be calculated on the assumption that his own

[1] Trelawny to Newcastle, Jan. 15, 1740/1, C.O. 137/57.
[2] C.O. 5/12, no. 71.

strength would hardly suffice for great conquests without some co-operation with the natives.

'As it has been represented unto Us,' they ran, 'that the number of native Indians on the coast of Chili, greatly exceeds that of the Spaniards, and that there is reason to believe, that the said Indians may not be averse to join with you against the Spaniards, in order to recover their freedom, you are to endeavour to cultivate a good understanding with such Indians, as shall be willing to join and assist you in any attempt, that you may think proper to make against the Spaniards, that are established there. . . . And whereas there is some reason to believe, from private intelligence, that the Spaniards in the Kingdom of Peru, and especially in that part of it, which is near Lima, have long had an inclination to revolt from the King of Spain, (on account of the great oppressions and tyrannies exercised by the Spanish Viceroys and Governors), in favour of some considerable person amongst themselves, you are, if you should find, that there is any foundation for these reports, by all possible means, to encourage, and assist such a design, in the best manner, you shall be able; and in case of any revolution, or revolt from the obedience of the King of Spain, either amongst the Spaniards, or the Indians, in these parts, and of any new government being erected by them, you are to insist on the most advantageous conditions for the commerce of our subjects, to be carried on with such government, so to be erected: for which purpose you shall make provisional agreements, subject to our future approbation and confirmation.'[1]

A proclamation was also drafted for Anson—apparently by Sir Charles Wager. It began by an ignorant invective against the French influence at the Court of Spain and the French trade to the Pacific colonies during Queen Anne's war (the first of which did not exist, and the second had by no means displeased the consumers in the colonies, however much it might impoverish the middlemen). Anson was then to declare that he had orders to support the Spanish colonists if they wished to set up a new form of government, and to treat them as enemies if they did not. He was to remind them that the King of Spain could do little to protect them against him; and to offer them a political alliance, the free exercise of their religion, a naval force for their defence (they were to pay a 'reasonable contribution' for its upkeep), a garrison, and lastly that

'We will supply you with all sorts of merchandise as you shall require from time to time without your being subject to impositions,

[1] S.P. 42/88.

fateagues and dangers in going to celebrate the Fairs of Panama, Portobello and Cartaxena.'[1]

Finally, the Government showed, by its instructions for Knowles's expedition to La Guayra in 1743, that it had not entirely renounced the hope of encouraging separatism. It thought it had a special reason to expect a response from the people of Caracas; the Guipuzcoa Company monopolized their trade, and its extortionate profits were believed to have excited great discontent. Knowles was therefore to inform himself of the disposition of the Creoles, and, if he found encouragement, to publish a declaration

'setting forth, that it is not the design of the English nation to make a conquest of their country, or to meddle with their property, religion, and liberty, but only to free them from the tyranny and oppression of the Guypuscoa Company, and to open a free and equal trade with them of their mutual commodities, without any exorbitant duties, charge, or imposition whatsoever'.

If this succeeded, he was to conclude a 'provisional agreement' —presumably, like that which Anson was ordered to make, of a commercial nature.[2] As Knowles's expedition was, like Anson's, a small one to an out-of-the-way destination, it was naturally prepared upon the same assumptions and with the same purpose.

§ ii. *The Sugar Interest and the Policy of Conquests*

This premature attempt at an American Revolution was not the main policy of the Ministers for their great expedition. There it was only conquests that would please. Over-estimating their chances of success, they imagined that almost everything was in their power; but the wide choice was only likely to embarrass a Government so constituted that it was certain to disagree wherever any choice was possible. The Ministers gibbered with indecision, and changed their minds over and over again, even before the Spanish fleets made a motion or the possibility of a French intervention set them a really difficult problem.[3]

There were three purposes for which new acquisitions of

---

[1] Add. MSS. 19030, f. 470. This proclamation is obviously founded on the 'Proposal' in the Vernon-Wager MSS., quoted on p. 74.

[2] Adm. 2/59, pp. 62–3.

[3] See Newcastle's letter to Wager, July 29, 1739, Vernon-Wager MSS.—a good example of his habit of suggesting everything and deciding nothing.

territory might be desired: trade, colonization, and protection. The last had very little importance; hardly any conquests of a purely strategic value were suggested. The nearest thing, per-haps, was the proposal to take Porto Rico because it could be used for intercepting the Spanish trade outward bound.[1] The people of Jamaica would also have been glad of the capture of Santiago de Cuba, as a place which commanded their home-ward trade through the Windward Passage.[2] Both these places were notorious nests of *Guarda-Costas*, which was an additional reason for at least destroying them.

Even these proposals had another side; and the main issue was between trade and colonization. Of course they were not incompatible. For example, the conquest of Cuba with Havana would eminently serve both purposes. Yet there was a real conflict or at least a distinction between those who wanted more lands for plantation and settlement, and those who wanted outposts for carrying on trade with the Spanish dominions—out-posts which they generally wished to strengthen and maintain with a colony of some kind.[3]

The ablest spokesman of the former class was William Wood, who held a post in the Customs Office; though connected with Jamaica, he does not appear to have been a sugar-planter, but had often represented before the Government the interests of the London and Bristol merchants trading to the West Indies. The arguments against a new sugar colony, and for a new smuggling settlement, are best put by Martin Bladen and James Knight. Both were connected with sugar-planting. Bladen received, for some reason, an annuity from the legislature of Nevis, and took an important part in promoting the interests of the West Indies.[4] He was a man of some influence, being a member of Parliament and of the Board of Trade; he was

[1] John Hart to Lord Townshend, May 8, 1729, copy in Add. MSS. 32694, ff. 37–8.

[2] Trelawny to Wager, Aug. 8, 1739, Vernon-Wager MSS.

[3] Some people hoped we should acquire some gold- and silver-mines in America. Others doubted whether such possessions would not have the same effect upon our national economy that they were thought to have had upon that of Spain. Gold-mines were believed to have destroyed the industry of Spain and converted its trade from an active into a passive one; none of the pamphleteers was economist enough to explain how (*French Influence upon English Counsels Demonstrated* (London, 1740), p. 13; *Britain's Mistakes in the Commencement and Conduct of the Present War* (London, 1740), supplement; see also Ulloa, op. cit., vol. i, introduction).

[4] See the Revenue Acts of Nevis, C.O. 185/4.

among the first and oftenest consulted by the Ministers and their committees, in the preparation of their plans for war, and he helped to draw up the instructions for Cathcart's expedition. Knight had been among the hotheads for reprisals against Spain in the time of Admiral Stewart, and was later one of the chief managers of the evidence against the 'depredations' at the bar of the House of Commons.[1]

Any new colonies of settlement or exploitation which we were likely to acquire in the West Indies would almost certainly become sugar colonies sooner or later. This would affect the prosperity of the sugar-planting interest, which had a certain influence in Parliament and with the Ministers. The attitude of this interest to the war is worth examining.

The English sugar colonies had suffered a depression since the Peace of Utrecht. In their early years they had prospered admirably, reduced the price of sugar to the English consumer, furnished the nation with an important article of re-export, and brought in large profits to the planters. The world's demand for their produce had been so great that the Government had to invent an elaborate system of precautions to stop it from being smuggled out of the Empire and finding its way straight to foreign markets. That prosperity was gone. The extension of sugar cultivation in the colonies of other powers had lowered the European price, and the English planters could not produce their sugar so cheaply as the French and Dutch.[2] Moreover, the increased consumption of sugar in Great Britain had begun to outstrip the somewhat slower increase of production in the British West Indies—not for want of land, for there was room in Jamaica alone for many more plantations.

For both these reasons the re-export trade had fallen off, and very few people seriously hoped to recover it. Few even of those who did, meant to achieve it by cutting costs of production—always excepting taxes, which they declared to be much higher in England than elsewhere. In the last ten years the West Indians had attended chiefly to maintaining a high price in the closed home market. For this purpose they had lately

[1] Report of proceedings in Parliament, March 1/12, 1738/9, A.E. Angleterre, 404, f. 161.
[2] It would take a long time to discuss the causes, and they are not necessary to this argument. I hope, therefore, that I may take it for granted here, and reserve it for a full examination in the book which I mean to write on the history of the English sugar colonies.

taken some very astute measures. In the first place, the Molasses Act of 1733 was meant to compel the North Americans to buy more rum and molasses from the English sugar colonies. Now rum and molasses are by-products of sugar, and by the methods used in the eighteenth century their quantity could be somewhat increased by making less sugar. If more rum and molasses were to be sold, without a corresponding extension of sugar cultivation, the quantity of sugar in the English market must be reduced, and probably the price must rise. This was said, and perhaps with some reason, to be one of the purposes of the Molasses Act.[1] It was much more certainly and avowedly the object of the Act of Parliament obtained by the West India interest in 1739, which permitted the direct export of sugar from the West Indies to certain markets in southern Europe.[2] There were some sugar-planters like Alderman Beckford who undoubtedly looked upon this liberty as a means, to be held in reserve, of browbeating the sugar-buyers at home into giving a high price. Had the Act not been encumbered by restrictions which made it almost useless, it might have been more used for this purpose.[3] Even without it, the downward tendency of

---

[1] *A True State of the Case between the British Northern Colonies and the Sugar Islands in America* (London, 1732), pp. 31–2; *The Consequences of the Bill now depending in favour of the Sugar Colonies* (n.d. ?1732). This imputation is denied without very much logic, by the author of *Proposals offered for the Sugar Planter's Redress, and for the Revival of the British Sugar Commerce* (London, 1733); but when the controversy had died down, an apparently knowledgeable contributor to the *Barbados Gazette* gave away the case by warning the planters against overseers who made more rum at the expense of making less sugar (*Caribbeana*, 1741, ii. 242–5). Yet it was possible, up to a point, to make more rum without reducing the output of sugar, by the method of distilling it weaker. This seems to have been done in Barbados after the Molasses Act (Paterson to Wood, July 5, 1751, Bodleian Library, North MSS. a 6, f. 174). The Boston *Weekly Rehearsal* of Sept. 18, 1732, reported from London, by way of Barbados, that the price of sugar was lower than ever; this was attributed to the failure of the Molasses Bill in that year, 'for we are assured the sugar merchants had housed vast quantities of sugars, which they expected would fetch a great price, upon the passing said bill'. That may be propaganda or uninformed comment.

[2] *The Sugar Trade with the Incumbrances thereon laid open by a Barbados Planter* (by John Ashley), MS. copy in C.O. 28/40; Ashley's second memorial, 1737, C.O. 28/25, Aa 62; William Perrin, *The Present State of the British and French Sugar Colonies, and our own Northern Colonies, Considered* (London, 1740), p. 17. Since Ashley was the chief agitator for the direct exportation, and Perrin one of the secretaries of the Planters' Club in London, their admissions are important.

[3] Beckford to Knight, June 18, 1743, Add. MSS. 12431, f. 125; *Parl. Hist.* xiv. 193–4 (Beckford). Henry Lascelles did not think very highly of the direct exportation, and reported with some pleasure that those who tried it did not find their account in it (Henry Lascelles to Thomas Applewhaite, Sept. 4, 1741, W. & G., vol. i; Lascelles and Maxwell to Samuel Husbands, Sept. 14, 1744, W. & G., vol. ii).

sugar prices in the English market was, for whatever reason, checked permanently in 1739.[1]

It would be impossible to keep up the price in the home market if the number of producers and the area of production were to be vastly increased. There was another thing to be considered. It was already becoming clear that the equilibrium of the northern and tropical colonies within the Empire was upset. As long as the West India islands could consume all the provisions and lumber of the Northern Colonies, the economic ambitions of the latter were more or less satisfied, and the internal balance of the Empire was maintained. After the Treaty of Utrecht, when the productive power of the Northern Colonies began to outgrow the consuming capacity of the English sugar islands, there were only two ways of preserving that balance—either to countenance the export of North American provisions to the foreign West Indies, or to acquire new West India territories.

The West Indian interest opposed both these remedies. It wished to confine the produce of North America to the markets of our own islands; thus it would assure itself of a cheap because over-abundant supply of fish, lumber, and provisions, and prevent its rivals in the French West Indies (who could not get enough provisions from their own northern colonies, and had to rely on the more expensive and infrequent supplies from France) from producing sugar to the same advantage, by raising

---

Lascelles disliked Ashley and was a sugar-factor; the promoters of the direct exportation had always reckoned with the hostility of the factors, who would lose their commissions on the sugars which went straight abroad.

[1] See the petition of the London sugar-refineries, March 20, 1753, which accuses the planters of artificially holding up the price by restricting production, because they gain more by a small crop than by a large one. The planters tried to repel the charge by pointing out the difficulty of getting the islands to co-operate for this purpose—as if the Planters' Club or the later West Indian Committee had never existed. They would have done better to deny the charge directly, for there is no evidence of a deliberate stint of sugar-production—the planters were far too greedy and individualist for that. Many of them had patented far more lands, especially in Jamaica, than they could possibly use; but we need not suppose this was calculated to keep down production. The refiners demanded some measures for extending cultivation in Jamaica, but according to Almon their real intention was to get permission to import foreign sugars (*C.J.* xxvi. 705; *Almon's Debates and Proceedings of the British House of Commons, 1751–60* (London, 1770), p. 55; Lascelles and Maxwell to Jonathan Blenman, March 14, 1753, W. & G. vi.; to Gedney Clarke, March 16). Lascelles and Maxwell were really afraid that Jamaica would produce too much for the English market (see their letter to John Frere, Sept. 4, 1756, W. & G. viii).

the price of their necessaries of life. This had been the ostensible, and to a great extent the real, purpose of the Molasses Act. It was designed, by levying very high duties on goods imported from the foreign sugar colonies, to make it impossible to export any provisions or lumber to them—for the French planters would not wish, and their own government would not allow them, to pay for foreign produce in cash.

The West India interest was now, at the outbreak of the war with Spain, trying to prevent the other solution of the difficulty, by discountenancing the acquisition of new West India territories, which might restore for a time the balance of the tropical and temperate colonies. If neither of these remedies could be used, the Northern Colonies must either manufacture much more for themselves than they had yet done, or send their corn to the markets of Europe, and compete with English agriculture. Wood pointed this out, speaking of the conquest of Cuba which was then being attempted by our forces.

'A very large additional employment will be given not only to the traders and manufacturers of this Kingdom but to the inhabitants of the British Northern Colonies, particularly to the inhabitants of New England, New York and Pensilvania, and prevent them from hurting their Mother-Country in many branches of traffic so soon as they will otherwise be able to do by a century at least.'[1]

He might well feel that he had scored a point here, for manufactures in the colonies were one of the greatest bugbears of English economists.

Some people in the Northern Colonies themselves shared his opinion. George Clarke, Lieutenant-Governor of New York, twice used this argument with the Assembly for giving a liberal encouragement to the volunteers who went on the West Indian expedition. 'By such acquisitions', he said, 'a door will be opened for a large consumption of provisions (the staple of this province) whereby the farmer, as well as the merchant, may be greatly enriched', and he later spoke of the possibility of obtaining such a territory in Cuba 'as may give large and numerous settlements to such a colony of people as may, in time, take off more of the provisions of these northern provinces than all the other islands in the West Indies'.[2]

West India conquests were expected to appeal to the North

[1] Wood to Newcastle, Sept. 10, 1741, Add. MSS. 32698, f. 26.
[2] Speeches of June 30, 1740, and Sept. 17, 1741, C.O. 5/1094.

Americans, not only as a market for provisions, but also as a field for emigration. The West India planters dreaded the very name of emigration from their own islands, for it was likely to deprive them of the few remnants of small planters and working-class white men who were believed to be their chief military security against the French and the negroes. Since losses by emigration could not be repaired, the planters were all the more anxious to prevent it. As James Knight puts it, the advantages attending the conquest of Havana

'will not compensate the damages our Sugar Islands will sustain thereby, as they will in such case be deserted and become an easy prey to the negroes, if not to the French and Spaniards, for if the midling and inferior sort of people remove, as undoubtedly they will even from Jamaica, the rich planters who are not many in number will not be able of themselves to maintain the possession'.[1]

It is curious that the great planters should have raised this complaint at a time when some of them were emigrating with their negroes to the Dutch settlements of Essequibo; but there was all the difference in the world between extending the area of sugar cultivation inside the Empire and participating in the profits of a sugar colony outside it.[2]

These considerations help to explain the traditional hostility of the English sugar-planters to colonial expansion in the tropics. They feared that sugar cultivation would be extended, the military population dispersed, and the prices of their necessaries of life raised by an increased demand. This attitude, which can be traced even in the late seventeenth century, is perfectly visible in the advice given to the Government by Knight and Bladen. Knight, for the reasons quoted above, recommended that Havana should be destroyed, rather than retained; Bladen, giving his arguments against attempting to conquer Porto Rico, said, 'We have more land already than we can people, more sugar and tobacco than we can dispose of to

[1] Knight to Newcastle, Dec. 3, 1739, Add. MSS. 22677, f. 32. Knight used every possible argument against the permanent acquisition of Havana. The French and Dutch would resent it; the situation was less central for 'interception' of Spanish trade and enterprises against Spanish colonies than that of Jamaica, which he assumed would be ruined by the competition of the new colony.

[2] Robinson to Townsend, Sept. 14, 1745, C.O. 28/47, ff. 47–8; *Storm van 's Grave-sande*, i. 204, 211–13 (Hakluyt Society, 1911). Governor Grenville spoke of the practice as uncommon a few years later (Grenville to Board of Trade, Oct. 20, 1752, C.O. 28/30).

advantage.'[1] Knight thought it necessary that in the settlement he proposed to make at Darien, the colonists should be
restrained from raising sugar, tobacco, ginger, and coffee, 'to
prevent giving any umbrage or discouragement to our other
Colonies in S. America'.[2]

Wood tried to answer such restrictive views.

'It is conceived', he said, 'Great Britain can never have too many
settlements in America, provided such settlements produce commodities vendible in Europe, and not interfering with the product
and manufactures of this Kingdom, and which must necessarily find
employment for our navigation and at the same time give Great
Britain an opportunity not only of supplying its own people cheaper,
but also of becoming rivals at all foreign markets to the French in all
West India commoditys, which is only to be brought about by selling
cheaper than the French, and this selling cheaper is only to be
effected by an increase of such commoditys in or from the British
plantations in America.'[3]

This aggressive policy involved cheap production and low
prices, which did not commend themselves to the conservative
British planters.

The sugar interest did not put a simple veto on all plans of
conquest in the West Indies. It used its influence in favour of
schemes which were not likely to result in the acquisition of a
new plantation colony. In fact it supported the various proposals of attacks upon places whose possession would make an
opening for British trade in the forbidden regions of Spanish
America.[4] This was natural, for Jamaica, the chief sugar island,
was also the head-quarters of the illicit trade.[5] Whatever com-

[1] Bladen to Harrington, June 12, 1739, Add. MSS. 32694, f. 21.

[2] Knight to ? Newcastle, Nov. 20, 1739, Add. MSS. 22677, f, 25. *Vide infra*, pp.
193–4, 199–200, for further applications of this policy.

[3] Wood to Newcastle, Sept. 10, 1741, Add. MSS. 32698, f. 26.

[4] See a letter of Bussy to Amelot, Dec. 26, 1740 (A.E. Angleterre, 409, f. 403),
in which he gives an account of the attempt of the Jamaica merchants to dissuade
Vernon from conquering Santiago de Cuba, where a rival sugar colony could be
established, by diverting his attention to Panama. The report has at least this
foundation, that both Bladen and Knight, the two strongest anti-expansionists
among the Government's advisers, tried hard to commit it to a settlement at
Panama. Governor Trelawny, in his dissenting minute of May 26, 1741, objected
to the expedition against Santiago de Cuba, and laid it down that 'no Possessions
but such as may be useful in commerce are for our benefit' (Council of War, May
26, 1741, S.P. 42/90, f. 174).

[5] The planters of Jamaica identified themselves with the smuggling merchants to
a remarkable degree. Their lawful navigation had been molested by the Spaniards
on account of the offences of the interlopers; but they bore it for the sake of the

petition the Jamaica smugglers had had to endure from the
South Sea Company and the London merchants trading
through Cadiz, was destroyed by the war which suspended the
operations of the two last; and the interest of the Jamaica
traders became, for the time being, the only national interest,
where trade with Spanish America was concerned.

§ iii. *The Plans of the English Government: Havana, Cartagena,*
Santiago, Panama

There are other things, besides the advice of interested
parties, to be taken into account in planning a naval expedition.
Ministers are called upon to determine, not only what is to be
desired, but what can be done; and in this light, the advice of
Admirals is at least as valuable as that of planters and merchants.

The first question to be resolved was the size of the expedition
and the importance of the object. Until the available strength
was determined, there was no saying whether success in a given
attempt was possible. Upon this subject there were two
opinions, or at least two tendencies of opinion. Newcastle and
his friends were for complying with the popular cry, which
demanded a great expedition in the West Indies with as many
ships and soldiers as possible. They waged the war as politicians; the success they most desired was in Parliament. Walpole on the other hand was much more interested in defending
the security of Great Britain and Ireland, and much more
afraid of attempts upon it. He was, therefore, on the side of
caution, and Newcastle on that of extravagance, in the allot-
ment of our strength to the West Indies; and whenever there was
a question of the forces to be sent there on any new emergency,
Newcastle was nearly always for more, Walpole for less.[1] Newcastle in fact was for the biggest possible expedition, and the
biggest possible success.

'All His Grace's politics', said Hervey, 'were founded on short
maxims of policy, gleaned in private conferences in the House of

illicit trade, and turned their resentment against the Spaniards, not against the
interlopers who were as much the cause of it. The resident merchants seem to have
been a much stronger and more influential class than those of other islands; in
fact, Jamaica was still almost as much a trading colony as a plantation.

[1] There were times when Walpole seemed to be converted, but he soon returned
to his attitude of reluctance (Newcastle to Hardwicke, June 19 and Aug. 15, 1741,
Add. MSS. 35407, ff. 31, 68).

Lords, during the Session, from Lord Carteret, who had over and over again told him, *Look to America, my Lord; Europe will take care of itself. Support Vernon, and you will want no support here.*[1]

Sir John Norris, Admiral of the Fleet, was often consulted by the Ministry at this time. He did not quite agree with Newcastle or Walpole. He wisely suggested that we ought above all to keep blockading squadrons off the chief Spanish ports.[2] This was only common sense; for whatever we were to do in the West Indies, could be much better done if there were no Spanish squadrons there to oppose it. It was not the same thing to let them get out and then send more ships after them to reinforce our own commanders. That was the way to waste time, give the enemy a start, and cause uncertainty and division of our own strength; moreover a moderate English squadron in the West Indies could venture and achieve more in the presence of a very small Spanish squadron than a large English fleet could do in the presence of a moderate Spanish one. Nobody seems to have seen the point of Norris's argument, except perhaps Lord Hervey, to whose opinion only Sir Robert Walpole would be likely to attend.[3] First of all Cadiz was watched and Ferrol not; two Spanish squadrons were allowed to join at the latter port, in such strength that the Admiralty could not spare enough ships to blockade them while the grand fleet was getting ready; and at last, just when the grand fleet was on the point of sailing to deal with it, a large force under Torres got out of Ferrol and went off to the West Indies.

There were three ways of carrying on the war: large expeditions directed to important objects; smaller expeditions directed to secondary objects; and no expeditions at all. Admiral Vernon, the commander in the West Indies since the autumn of 1739, disliked all combined expeditions of land and sea forces. He always discountenanced schemes for landings and colonies as expensive and unnecessary. Sea-power alone, he thought, would do all that could and need be done in the Caribbean; it would destroy the Spanish commerce, interrupt the return of the treasure to Spain, and protect the English smugglers with the Spanish colonies while hampering the trade of their rivals.[4]

---

[1] Hervey, note of Cabinet proceedings, May 22, 1740, *Memoirs*, iii. 940.
[2] Norris's diary, Nov. 26 and Dec. 14, 1739, Add. MSS. 28132, ff. 86, 99.
[3] Hervey, *Memoirs*, iii. 940; *Parl. Hist.* x. 1191, xi. 833.
[4] Vernon to Newcastle, Oct. 31, 1739, S.P. 42/85, f. 55.

Vernon in fact was for a purely naval war; perhaps for the reasons he gave, perhaps because such a war would be conducted by an Admiral alone (for he was one of the vainest of men and the most ambitious of glory).

Vernon's advice was little echoed or attended to; other admirals had their doubts, but none of them approached such a radical scepticism. Such arguments were, with Newcastle, beside the point. There must be an expedition, for political reasons, therefore an expedition must be practicable.[1] Besides, long before Vernon's advice came to hand, the Ministry had been thinking in terms of expeditions. The first plans to be made, after sending Vernon out to reinforce the West India station, were for small expeditions to Manila and the Pacific. Sir Charles Wager, the First Lord of the Admiralty, appears to have been interested in a small scheme for starting a revolt in Guatemala. This kind of thing might be good strategy or common sense, but it was not grand enough. Politics demanded something larger, and the Admirals had to produce it.[2] At the end of 1739 it was decided that the small expeditions would take away too much from the strength of the great ones. The squadron destined for Manila was therefore suppressed, and only Anson's expedition to Peru and Panama was left. For the same reason Wager's project against Guatemala was laid on the shelf, and he could not get the Ministry to recommend it to Vernon, even after the greater enterprise had come to grief at Cartagena.[3]

There was, then, to be a great expedition to the West Indies under Lord Cathcart; but what was to be its objective?[4] The obvious point for a great attack was Havana. It was reputed the strongest place in the Spanish West Indies; it was the rendezvous of the *flotas* and galleons, and commanded their homeward route. If we possessed it, we could intercept or delay the return of the treasure to Spain, and thereby put such pressure on the Court of Madrid that the war must be brought to a

---

[1] When Cathcart changed his mind about the practicability of Havana, Newcastle was furious and had him sharply silenced by the Lords Justices (Newcastle to Hardwicke, Aug. 28, 1740, Add. MSS. 35406, f. 229).

[2] Norris's diary, Oct. 16 and 23, Dec. 5, 1739, Add. MSS. 28132, ff. 52, 59, 87.

[3] Wager to Vernon, June 21, Aug. 20, Oct. 29, 1741, *Original Letters to an Honest Sailor*, pp. 45, 51, 57.

[4] See the full and excellent account of these discussions in Admiral Sir H. W. Richmond's *The Navy in the War of 1739–48* (Cambridge, 1920), vol. i, chap. ii.

sudden and striking end. This was a simple calculation, and it was probably a wrong one, for Spain was much better able than anybody expected, to bear the very considerable delay and diminution of the homeward treasure which we were able to effect without the conquest of Havana; in fact, Philip V had already given proof of this in the War of the Spanish Succession.[1] Be that as it might, Newcastle always preferred an attack on Havana to anything else that could be suggested.

The objections to it were two. Wager was persuaded by one Tassell, who had lately lived there as the South Sea Company's agent, that it was very strongly fortified and defended, and could not be taken by less than 10,000 soldiers.[2] This was more than could be spared, and the Ministry therefore decided in October to be content with something less ambitious. In November Newcastle brought up Havana again in a new form: why not make up the number of men with recruits from North America? Our Northern Colonies abounded with men who, properly used, were a great asset in any American war we might wage; for some people were already beginning to suspect, what proved true in the Canadian campaigns of the next war, that colonists made the best soldiers for colonial fighting. They could be attracted to the expedition by hopes of plunder and land. From soldiers they would turn settlers, and thus solve the problem how to people our new acquisitions without draining our older sugar colonies of men.[3] At first this proposal was thought to make no difference to the practicability of the scheme, but the Ministers later decided to raise troops in North America; indeed, Norris told Walpole that if they did not, the Opposition would make a cry of it. They even formed exaggerated expectations of the number of men that could be got from this source. Bladen had to explain 'that most or all the people in those parts had their employments to live and very few that wanted business',[4] and that 3,000 troops was the largest number that could be raised. In the event, the enthusiasm for

---

[1] The miserable end of Admiral Hosier at the Bastimientos in 1727 was a warning against merely trying to delay the sailing of the galleons (*The Grand Question, whether War or no War with Spain, Impartially Considered* (London, 1739), p. 18).

[2] Tassell to Wager, Oct. 24, 1739, Vernon-Wager MSS.; Tassell to Newcastle, Oct. 29, 1739, Add. MSS. 32694, f. 49; Wager's note on the same, f. 51; Norris's diary, Sept. 29 and Oct. 16, 1739, Add. MSS. 28132, ff. 47, 53–4.

[3] Norris's diary, Oct. 29, Nov. 22, Dec. 5 and 17, 1739, Add. MSS. 28132, ff. 68, 82, 87, 105.

[4] Norris's diary, Dec. 17 and 31, 1739, Add. MSS. 28132, ff. 105, 112.

the expedition was so great that the Government afterwards believed it could have raised more. 'There is a vast spirit by all accounts', Trelawny wrote, 'in those of the Northern Colonies who in their imagination have swallowed up all Cuba; 'tis true, they are undisciplined, but they will be supported by double the number of disciplined troops that Ld Cathcart brings.'[1]

The second objection to Havana was its situation. It was a long way to leeward of the chief English and French colonies; and the easterly trade wind was so strong in those seas that no naval commander liked getting to leeward if he thought he should have any occasion to come up to windward again. This would make little difference, if there were too few Spanish warships in the West Indies to take advantage of the Jamaica squadron's absence. As more ships went out from Spain to join those already in the Caribbean, and as the arrival of a French fleet in the West Indies became more and more likely, disquiet for the safety of Jamaica had more influence in determining the movements of our West India expedition. If there were French or Spanish fleets to windward of it when it started from Jamaica, a long leeward journey into the Gulf of Mexico would leave the island at their mercy. This made an impression not only on the Governor and people of Jamaica, but on Wager, who knew the facts because he had commanded a West India squadron in the War of the Spanish Succession. It strengthened his dislike of the Havana scheme, and his preference for the less serious undertaking—as it then seemed—of an attack on Cartagena.[2] Another thing to consider was, that Havana was difficult of access from December to March—the best part of the campaigning season—because of the strong north winds which made it hard for ships to ride off the coasts.

Vernon shared Wager's preference; he was already stationed at Jamaica and must have heard what the island politicians had to say. Perhaps he had another reason. The voyage of the last galleons which started before the war had been unusually slow;

[1] Trelawny to Wager, Aug. 29, 1740, Vernon-Wager MSS.; Newcastle to Vernon, Sept. 12, 1740, Add. MSS. 32695, f. 51. Wager thought that the Americans would be especially suitable for such an irregular campaign as the excursion into Guatemala. It appears, though not clearly, that this was because he thought them less likely than regular soldiers to alienate the Indians by violating their women (Wager to Vernon, June 21, 1741, *Original Letters to an Honest Sailor*, p. 46).

[2] Trelawny to Wager, Aug. 29, 1740, Vernon-Wager MSS.; Beckford to Knight, Oct. 11, 1740, Add. MSS. 12431, f. 116; Norris's diary, Oct. 29, 1739, Add. MSS. 28132, f. 68; Wager to Newcastle, June 3, 1740, C.O. 5/41.

though they had sailed in 1737, they were still in Cartagena harbour and had not yet held the fair at Portobello. However, they had done some business, according to the custom, in Cartagena, and had already received some money in return. They were, therefore, with this money and the remainder of their unsold cargoes, the richest prize that could be made in the West Indies. Whatever his faults of judgement, Vernon had a reputation for disinterestedness, but he would hardly have been human if these facts had no influence over his opinion. Besides, it was an important and honourable feat to catch the galleons, and it was an essential service to the trade of Jamaica. If their cargoes were destroyed, the smugglers would be left without competition; delaying the galleons in the harbour by a blockade until the goods rotted was very useful, but destroying them would be better still. It was to the smugglers' interest that some accident should happen to the galleons at Cartagena, before their cargoes came to market, rather than at Havana, when they were only carrying the returns, and had already spoilt the trade.[1] Vernon's preference for Cartagena can have had nothing to do with the presence of Torres and his ships of war in that harbour; for he had already conceived it before Torres came out to the West Indies at all, and he knew, before he finally sailed to attack Cartagena, that Torres had gone to Havana, where the French fleets might have joined him. In fact, if he had aimed at the destruction of the Spanish warships, he would presumably have made for Havana, not for Cartagena.

Newcastle put Havana back on the map by a characteristic compromise: the Government was to make no determination, but to leave it to the Council of War on the spot to say what was practicable. Having gained this point, he then tried, by a still more characteristic piece of dishonesty, to prejudge the decision of the Council of War, by causing it to be delayed until the expedition should arrive off Havana—from which place it was impossible to do anything except attack Havana or Vera Cruz. Wager detected and denounced this; it was given up, but the irrepressible Newcastle contrived to have the last word by sending Cathcart a private letter with his instructions, earnestly recommending him to try Havana if it was at all possible.[2] The

[1] Trelawny to Wager, Aug. 29, 1740, Vernon-Wager MSS.; Vernon to Newcastle, June 4, 1740, S.P. 43/93.
[2] Wager to Newcastle, June 3, 1740, C.O. 5/41; Newcastle to Cathcart, Aug. 14, 1740, Add. MSS. 32694, f. 472.

Opposition gave the same orders to Vernon; Pulteney told him that nothing but the conquest of Cuba would satisfy the appetite of the public.[1] Even after the first failure of 1741, Newcastle believed that a reinforcement of 3,000 men might enable Vernon to attack Havana or at least make another attempt on Cartagena.[2]

When the great expedition arrived in the West Indies and joined Admiral Vernon, the commanders made up their minds to attack Cartagena. This enterprise failed entirely.

There is no need here to describe the calamity or to distribute the blame between Vernon and Wentworth.[3] Admiral Richmond has done all that very well.[4] It may no doubt be true that Vernon was 'a silly, noisy Admiral', and that Wentworth lacked moral courage; but probably their faults and dissensions did not affect the result so much as has been thought. If it comes to that, there was equal discord behind the walls of Cartagena between the Viceroy Eslava and the General of the galleons.[5] Too much attention has been paid to the quarrel of Vernon and Wentworth. There are two reasons for this: in the first place, it has been too readily assumed that Cartagena was so weak that only some fault of our commanders could account for our bad success. In fact the place had been strongly fortified since Pointis took it in 1697, and it was a much harder nut to crack than the English supposed.[6] The second reason why the controversy was so envenomed (and why Wentworth always had the worst of it), was the unpopularity of the army. Old-fashioned Whigs and Tories had always railed against a 'standing army', and the Opposition could not forbear exploiting the cry. They affected to believe that the army existed, not to fight (for Walpole always avoided wars if he could), but to create comfortable places for the Minister's creatures. The soldiers were therefore under a cloud, and the fashionable rant was the wooden walls of old England, long before Wentworth's incompetence confirmed the legend. Lastly, it was sickness that put the finishing touch to failure at Cartagena, and that was no more Wentworth's fault than Vernon's. Vernon had been

[1] Pulteney to Vernon, Aug. 17, 1740, *Original Letters to an Honest Sailor*, pp. 23–4.
[2] Memorandum of June 22, 1741, Add. MSS. 32993, f. 154.
[3] Cathcart died on the voyage out, and was succeeded by Wentworth.
[4] Op. cit., vol. i, chap. vi.
[5] Larnage to Maurepas, March 21, 1741, A.N. Colonies C⁹ A 55.
[6] Larnage to Maurepas, Dec. 5, 1740, A.N. Colonies C⁹ A. 53.

in the West Indies before, and knew that the most important maxim of West India strategy was to begin operations at once, before the soldiers could fall victims to the climate and the rum.[1] It was to avoid delay and 'Captain Punch' that he had proposed at first to meet his reinforcement under Ogle and Cathcart at Cape Donna Maria instead of letting it come into harbour at Jamaica.[2] The miscarriage of a letter brought this scheme to nothing, and once in Port Royal, Ogle's fleet could not be got out in a hurry. Then Vernon spent time in looking for the French fleet instead of sailing straight to Cartagena; the decision was justifiable, but it gave the climate plenty of time to work upon the troops.[3] It is true, however, that if Wentworth had taken Cartagena at a rush, the soldiers would have had the satisfaction of dying of fever after victory, as they did at Havana in 1762, instead of dying frustrated outside the walls.

Vernon's and Wentworth's second choice after Cartagena was Santiago de Cuba. The south and east of Cuba were so little populated, and so far from Havana, that they might have made a permanent establishment there; it was no more than the French had done on the west end of Hispaniola. The people of Jamaica, especially those of the north side, would be glad to have the pirates of Santiago suppressed, so that their ships might pass safely through the Windward Passage. The planters would not be equally pleased to see a rival sugar colony growing up next door; but the planters were not always attended to, and if the east end of Cuba was not conquered and colonized by the English, it was because the commanders mismanaged the attempt, not because the sugar interest was holding the Government by the coat-tails. Newcastle expressly ordered Vernon to have it garrisoned and settled if he could take it.[4]

The North Americans were to have been glad of this conquest, for they were to have settled it. They were disappointed of their hopes; they should have remembered the two com-

[1] After the failure at Cartagena, Ogle was of the same opinion (Ogle to Knight, June 18, 1741, and Feb. 13, 1741/2, Add. MSS. 12431, ff. 112, 114).

[2] Cathcart to Vernon, June 22, 1740; Vernon to Cathcart, Dec. 26, 1741, S.P. 42/90, f. 12; Wager to Vernon, June 10, 1740, *Original Letters to an Honest Sailor*, p. 13.

[3] Already on Jan. 20 Wentworth reported that at least 1,400 of the soldiers were sick, of whom 500 seriously so (see his letter to Newcastle, C.O. 5/42).

[4] Newcastle to Vernon, Oct. 15 and 31, 1741, Add. MSS. 32698, ff. 138, 240. Knowles tried to capture Santiago in the spring of 1748. If he had taken it, he would have kept it, but only 'in hopes it may produce some good terms upon the conclusion of a peace' (Knowles to Newcastle, March 13, 1747/8, C.O. 137/58).

panies of Massachusetts volunteers, who arrived at Jamaica in
1703 to find no quarters or allowances, and to be enrolled, in
spite of their express wish and the entreaties of their Governor,
into the crews of Admiral Whetstone's ships.[1] The volunteers
of 1740 were not much better treated; Newcastle heard many
complaints that they had been drafted into the ships in exactly
the same way.[2] They might well be furious, for nobody disliked the service of the King's ships more, or went farther out of
the way to avoid the press-gang, than the North Americans.
They got no plunder, for there was none; no land, for none was
conquered, and if any had been, Wentworth strangely obstructed the proclamation which was to have offered it to them.
He alleged that most of them were unsuitable for colonization
and had not the necessary means; and if Vernon is to be
trusted (which perhaps he is not), the officers of the regular
army grumbled at having to fight battles in order to conquer
land for North Americans.[3] The unbounded expectations of
the use of North Americans in West Indian warfare were disappointed, and the idea of such a service was unpopular for
some years in the Northern Colonies;[4] yet volunteers were
found in 1762 for a very similar enterprise against Havana.

When both Cartagena and Santiago had resisted them, Vernon and Wentworth condescended to take some advice from
the people of Jamaica, and to reduce their pride to one of the
smaller but more practicable enterprises in which that island
was interested.

There was one expedition which was always more popular
in Jamaica than any other that could be proposed.[5] This was
an overland attack upon Panama, to be followed by a settlement upon the isthmus. Such a settlement was designed as an
advanced post for illicit trade into the Pacific, and for the
acquisition of gold-mines, or at least gold, in the neighbouring
province of Veragua.[6] In fact it was the first proposal which the

---

[1] *C.S.P. Col. 1702*, no. 1131; *1702–3*, nos. 30, 319, 322, 694, 764.
[2] Newcastle to Vernon, Aug. 28, 1741, Add. MSS. 32697, f. 482; Oct. 15, vol.
32698, f. 138.
[3] Wentworth to Newcastle, Dec. 20, 1741, C.O. 5/42; Vernon to Newcastle,
Nov. 11, 1741, *Original Papers relating to the Expedition to the Island of Cuba* (London,
1744).   [4] Vaudreuil to Maurepas, Feb. 22, 1748, A.N. Colonies C⁹ A. 74.
[5] Not only in Jamaica; Bussy reported that a large company was projected for
this purpose in London (Bussy to Amelot, June 2, N.S., 1741, A.E. Angleterre, 412, f.
112).
[6] Bladen to Harrington, June 12 and 18, 1739, Add. MSS. 32694, ff. 21, 25;

Government considered in this war. Bladen had urged it very strongly, and Lord Harrington favoured it; but Wager and Norris reported that it would need at least 2,000 soldiers and a large squadron. At first it was a project for attacking Panama from both sides of the isthmus, but then the Admirals made up their minds that no settlement could be made on the Pacific shore. The march overland from the Atlantic, which Wager and Norris thought more practicable, was soon forgotten for greater enterprises.[1]

The scheme had a long history, for the Isthmus of Panama was the short and narrow channel by which the produce of the Pacific colonies had passed to Spain for the last two centuries. The temptation to seize it was obvious to anybody with the slightest sense of strategy. There Drake had intercepted the treasure; Morgan's buccaneers had taken Panama in 1671. Near by were the mines of Veragua and St. Mary's, to which the privateers had made an expedition in 1702. The travellers Dampier and Wafer had reported favourably of the Indians, who had also shown friendship to the Scotch settlers at Darien in 1698.[2] The Governor of Jamaica had entered into relations with them in Queen Anne's reign. It was assumed that they still hated the Spaniards mortally, and would furnish valuable military help to an English army against Panama or the gold-mines; and finally, that they would be ready to sell some of their land for a small consideration, and for the sake of the colonists' protection against the Spaniards.[3]

It is very questionable how far these assumptions were justified. Vernon thought them out of date. In his opinion the

Knight to Newcastle, Nov. 20 and Dec. 3, ff. 9, 16; Trelawny to Wager, Aug. 29, 1740, Vernon-Wager MSS.; Trelawny to Newcastle, Jan. 15, 1740/1, May 27, 1741, C.O. 137/57; Beckford to Knight, Feb. 10, 1741/2, Add. MSS. 12431, f. 118.

[1] Norris's diary, Sept. 17 and 29, Oct. 16, 1739, Add. MSS. 28132, ff. 31, 47, 51.

[2] G. P. Insh, *The Company of Scotland* (London, 1932), pp. 129–35, 186–90. See Wafer's *New Voyage and Description of the Isthmus of America*, republished by the Hakluyt Society, 1934; also *C.S.P. Col. 1702–3*, no. 22.

[3] 'But as this tract of land is still in the possession of the aborigines who were never conquered by nor submitted to the Spaniards, . . . it will be necessary to have their consent and approbation, which I am persuaded may be easily obtained. . . . The Scotch met no difficulty in it. This will be acting agreeable to the law of nations, the principles of Christianity, and the constant maxims of the British nation, whose possessions are founded on reason and justice, and not chimerical grants, butchery of millions of innocent people, and other unjustifiable means.' (Knight to ? Newcastle, Nov. 20, 1739, Add. MSS. 22677, f. 27; see also Add. MSS. 32694, ff. 83–8.)

Darien project was unnecessary, for it would procure no advantages in trade that we did not possess already by our command of the sea. He thought it impossible too. Since the failure of the Scotch colony, the Spanish authorities had perceived the folly of estranging tribes placed in so important a situation, and had conciliated them.[1] This pacification of the Indians probably had something to do with the bad behaviour of the English 'marooners'—the dregs of the pirates, who abused the Indian women. Unscrupulous sailors enticed Indians on board ship, under pretence of trade, and then carried them off and sold them as slaves in Jamaica. This came to the ears of Wager, who remembered a project of a settlement at Darien from the days when he was Commodore at Jamaica. He was very upset, and wrote to Vernon and Trelawny to have these practices stopped and punished. The warning was not needed, for nobody set a higher value on Indian friendship than Trelawny, who had already persuaded the Jamaica Assembly to make a law against the enslavement of Indians.[2] He was the warmest partisan of the Darien scheme, but he had to admit that the Indians had made their peace with the Spaniards; however, this only made him insist with the more vehemence on the necessity of taking Panama in order to encourage them to join our side again.[3] But taking Panama in order to make an impression upon the Indians was a very different calculation from taking it with their help.

No doubt the Panama scheme was conceived with a vague and free imagination, helped out by confusions between the Indian tribes and anachronisms as to their attitude; but something had been done on the Isthmus more than once before, and Vernon might at least have given it a fair trial. Most of the witnesses agree that he did not. It was important to arrive quickly and safely at Portobello, and, before making any open appearance there, to have landed a force behind the town and seized the pass which led to Panama. Instead, he beat farther to windward than he need, so that the rainy season had time to set in and the soldiers to fall sick. He then sailed into the harbour 'with all the pageantry of a Spithead expedition',

[1] Vernon to Newcastle, Jan. 23, 1739/40, S.P. 42/85, f. 122.
[2] Wager to Vernon, June 10 and July 9, 1740, *Original Letters to an Honest Sailor*, pp. 13, 16; *Journals of the Assembly of Jamaica* (Kingston, 1797), iii. 563; Act of May 8, 1741, C.O. 139/15.
[3] Trelawny to Wager, Sept. 12, 1740, Vernon-Wager MSS.; Tassell to Walpole, Sept. 11, 1739, Add. MSS. 32694, f. 41.

sent the Governor a pompous message, and gave him time to remove all the valuables from the town, to occupy the pass, and to send the news to Panama.[1] The scheme was ruined. Wentworth, who never cared much for it, declined to proceed any farther, saying that his force was reduced too low by sickness; and Vernon can have hardly felt all the surprise he affected, when Governor Trelawny, the chief promoter of the expedition, insisted in a huff on going home to Jamaica to do other business.[2]

There was little more that Vernon could do; soon afterwards, he retired to England, with 'his laurels handsomely tipped with gold'. He spent the rest of his life quarrelling with the Admiralty, publishing pamphlets, presiding at meetings of the Order of the Anti-Gallicans, and making ranting speeches in the House of Commons. The great offensive against the West Indies had come to an end for a time, and Ogle was left with orders 'to protect the trade of the King's subjects in those parts, to hinder the return of the Spanish Treasure to Europe, and to prevent the Spaniards from opening or carrying on any trade at Cartagena, or Portobello'.[3] In the very fag-end of the war Knowles revived some semblance of activity by his destruction of Port Louis and his attempt on Santiago, and conceived a further scheme of attacking Vera Cruz; until then, the annals of the Jamaica station are free from expeditions. There was an attempt upon La Guayra and Porto Cabello, two ports of Venezuela, under Knowles in 1743. This expedition was sent out from England and strengthened with ships of the Leeward Islands station; for Venezuela is so far to windward as to be quite out of the way of the Jamaica squadron. For that reason

---

[1] Council of War, Jan. 20 and 22, 1741/2, C.O. 5/42; Trelawny to Newcastle, Jan. 31, C.O. 137/57; Beckford to Knight, April 30, 1742, Add. MSS. 12431, f. 124; J. Morris to Wager, May 1742, Vernon-Wager MSS.; Col. Burrard's diary, March 30, 1742, Add. MSS. 34097, f. 67. Vernon's best excuse was that he tried to kill two birds with one stone, and that he delayed so long off Cartagena because he hoped to intercept succours coming out from Spain (see the minute of the Council of War, March 4, 1741/2, S.P. 42/92, f. 77). Trelawny had wanted Vernon to undertake this expedition in 1741, but Vernon refused, and Wager approved his refusal because the rainy season had been coming on. For that matter, Wager appears to have vindicated Vernon in 1742, for the same reason and because if 500 men had been landed behind Portobello there would not have been enough to land before it (Wager to Vernon, Aug. 18, 1741, and Aug. 1742, *Original Letters to an Honest Sailor*, pp. 49, 62).

[2] Vernon to Newcastle, Feb. 11 and 25, March 5 and 15, 1741/2, March 31 and April 27, 1742, with enclosures, S.P. 42/92, ff. 1–149 *passim*.

[3] Newcastle to Ogle, Aug. 5, 1742, Add. MSS. 32699, f. 360.

its valuable trade was hard to intercept, and the best way of attacking it was to seize the terminal points and deprive the shipping of any refuge on the coast.[1] Knowles made a mess of it, and the attempt produced no benefit whatever.

§ iv. *Trelawny's Interference on the Moskito Shore*

After so many pompous failures, there is some satisfaction in dealing with an effort which, however small, met with any success at all. This was the interesting attempt of Trelawny to extend English influence and trade among the Spaniards of Central America, and to consolidate the logwood-cutting colony in Honduras.

Trelawny believed in the possibility of breaking up the Spanish Empire from within, by encouraging the Creoles and Indians to revolt. Like many other Governors of Jamaica, he took a special interest in the tribe of Moskito Indians. They dwelt on the east coast of Nicaragua, which was then known to the English as the 'Moskito shore'. They had long had friendly relations with the English; indeed, in a later controversy with Spain, we claimed that they had made us a cession of their territory in the reign of Charles I, which, if it really took place and was valid, would have given us a title to it under the American Treaty of 1670. Needless to say, Spain disputed both the fact and the lawfulness of this surrender. Be that as it might, the Indians' friendship to the English nation had continued intermittently.

Nearly all the witnesses, from Dampier downwards, described them as a very small tribe; some writers attributed to them no more than five hundred fighting men. The younger Hodgson, writing in 1757, said they had once numbered ten or eleven thousand people, but were much reduced after 1730 by the small-pox, which they caught in a successful expedition against the Spaniards; in his day they were eight thousand souls, with fifteen hundred fighting men. He distinguished among them

---

[1] 'A Proposal for the taking of La Guaira and Porto Cavallo', Vernon-Wager MSS.; paper of Daniel Campbell, July 22, 1741, ibid. The Spaniards, according to Admiral Richmond, had two months' notice of this attempt. Lord Hardwicke believed that Knowles himself had been talking about it before he left London (Hardwicke to Newcastle, May 27, 1743, Add. MSS. 32700, f. 148), but the French Minister, who usually got wind of projects almost before they were out of the authors' mouths, only learnt about this one after some months, and described the secret as perfectly kept (Bussy to Amelot, March 15, N.S., 1743, A.E. Angleterre, 416, f. 352).

three separate bodies of people. There were the pure Moskito Indians in the south, under a 'Governor'; in the centre, round Black River, they were ruled by a 'King', and consisted chiefly of Samboes, descended from the conquest of Indian wives by two shipwrecked cargoes of negroes;[1] in the north there was a mixture of Indians and Samboes under a 'General'. The King, Governor, and General were more or less coequal, but the English of Jamaica had accorded a pre-eminence to the first, on account of his title; he thus belonged to the class of native rulers who owe their state to the convenience or the defective imagination of the English authorities. The chiefs had little power, and the real decisions were taken by assemblies of elders—such worthies of fame in war and weight in council as 'Admiral Dilly', 'Colonel Morgan', and the like. They entertained a lasting hatred of the Spaniards, which Uring accounted for by supposing that they had been expelled by the Spanish authorities from the land of their fathers, a good land, into the disagreeable swamps in which they lived when the English knew them.[2] There is no telling whether that was the truth, or a prejudice instilled into them by the English and then repeated as their own opinion; but certainly one of the ways of attracting them to an alliance was to promise them the land of their forefathers. Their manner of life seems to have been a not extraordinary mixture of laziness with violent activity in fishing and hunting, punctuated by almost interminable drinking-bouts which usually ended in a 'general rape'. They had always been valued by the privateers as expert if temperamental fishermen, and gallant fighters so long as they were encouraged by proper example.[3]

To them Trelawny sent in 1740 a 'romantic' character or 'Don Quixote' named Robert Hodgson. He really seems to have been a fit man for the post; he felt some sympathy for the Indians, but tried to restrain the vices which he could not strongly condemn because he considered them to be chiefly due to contact with the English. He believed (what was probably

---

[1] This was not an uncommon accident, the Black Caribs of St. Vincent had a like origin.   [2] Uring, *Voyages and Travels* (1928 reprint), p. 159.

[3] The best connected accounts of this tribe are to be found in Dampier, *A New Voyage Round the World* (1699), i. 7–11; Uring, pp. 156–9; Hodgson to Trelawny, April 8, 1740, quoted above, and *The First Account of the State of that Part of America called the Mosquito Shore in the year 1757*, by Robert Hodgson (the son, I think), C.O. 123/1.

wrong) that the Moskitomen were descended of the race of Montezuma, and therefore looked for a deliverer from the 'grey-eyed people'; Hodgson had the modesty to doubt whether he could play the part.[1]

The Moskitomen were valuable allies. They lived mostly by desultory hunting, fishing, and turtling, and left the care of their plantain-walks to their wives; a high proportion of their men was, therefore, always available for expeditions against the Spaniards. A useful by-product of this military activity was their need for arms; Hodgson saw a good opening for trade here, and lamented that before he and Trelawny could make any use of it, the privateers would probably have supplied the want.

On the other hand they had their limitations. They were ungovernable, and needed disciplined troops to keep them in order; and they were a diplomatic liability. They had difficulty in accepting Hodgson's opinion, that the King of England was the best judge of the proper time for peace or war with the Spaniards; this gave little trouble during the war, but it was to cost Hodgson some anxiety and effort after the peace. They used their Spanish prisoners cruelly, which Trelawny instructed Hodgson to prevent so far as he could; for though it might be very convenient to browbeat the Spaniards into trading with us by threatening to set the Moskito Indians on them if they refused, the barbarity of these uncontrollable allies was a nuisance when it was not exercised according to plan. It could not, in any case, commend itself to a man like Trelawny, who hoped to work for an Anglophile Creole Revolution within the Spanish Empire. The behaviour of the Moskitomen to the other Indians was even more embarrassing. They had two dependent tribes called Piacos and Puttocks, but they were at perpetual enmity with certain other Indians, generally called 'wild', or Bravo Indians. Whenever they went warfaring, they insisted on treating their prisoners with great cruelty or enslaving them. In fact, they made a business of slave-raiding; it was deposed in 1762, before the Council of Jamaica, that they had reduced a small tribe of their neighbours from 300 people to 47 by this practice.[2] This gave a handle to all the critics of Trelawny's

---

[1] Hodgson to Trelawny, April 8, 1740, Vernon-Wager MSS.; Trelawny to Wager, July 26, ibid.

[2] Deposition of Richard Jones, in Council Minutes, Nov. 17, 1762, C.O. 140/42.

schemes; for how could we develop good relations with the Indians in general, as Trelawny wished to do, when our chief Indian allies did us more harm than good with the other tribes? Hodgson tried to prevent it, but he was not very successful. As he could not stop the enslavement of enemy Indians, he bought their freedom and sent them to Jamaica, whence Trelawny tactfully returned them to their homes.[1]

On his first appearance in 1740, Hodgson procured a new cession of the country from King Edward,[2] distributed some presents, immediately exhausted his supplies of rum in ceremonial visits, and persuaded the tribe to make an expedition against the Spaniards. Wager had been particularly interested in the scheme of a certain Captain Lea, who reported that the people of Guatemala and Nicaragua were ripe for revolt if they could receive some help against their Government; he supposed that the Moskito Indians could usefully take part in such an expedition.[3] Hodgson wanted the Indians to go to leeward, perhaps against Truxillo, but had been forestalled by an English privateer captain who had enlisted their reluctant support for a campaign to the southward, to some gold-mines at Veragua. It probably made little difference where they went, for though they surprised some places and destroyed some small Spanish forces, their ungovernableness in the hour of victory prevented them from profiting by it. The same useless success attended Hodgson in a second expedition which he made in 1742 with 700 Indians whom he had raised too late to take part in the attempt on Panama.[4] Beyond this the Moskitomen had no other military value in this war, except that in 1747, when the Spaniards were getting ready an expedition to destroy the English settlements in that part of the world, the Moskito war boats cruised actively against them and molested their preparations. Still, the tribe was a thorn in the side of the Spaniards which they could not draw out so long as the English were at Black

[1] Hodgson to Trelawny, April 8, 1740; Trelawny to Wager, July 26 and Aug. 29, 1740, Vernon-Wager MSS.; *Journals of the Assembly of Jamaica*, iii. 563, April 24, 1741; comments of Gerrard on Trelawny's letter to Stone, October 1742, C.O. 137/57.

[2] Declaration of Edward King of the Mosquito Indians, March 16, 1739/40, C.O. 123/1.

[3] Wager to Vernon, June 21 and Aug. 20, 1741, *Original Letters to an Honest Sailor*, pp. 46, 51.

[4] Trelawny to Wager, Aug. 29 and Sept. 12, 1740, Vernon-Wager MSS.; Trelawny to Newcastle, July 20, 1743, C.O. 137/57.

River, for it could only be attacked to any purpose by sea, which the English warships and the small craft of the few settlers prevented or rendered much more difficult.[1]

Trelawny had another interest in that part of the world—the promotion of an illicit trade with the Spaniards. He believed their country could be penetrated up rivers and Indian paths which their authorities could not watch, and that in return for English manufactures we could extract great quantities of Spanish produce, especially the fine Guatemala indigo, the best of its kind in the world. There was hardly any cultivation of indigo in the British colonies, that of Jamaica having languished into unimportance and that of Carolina being barely started; this was therefore a tropical product that would be the more welcome because it did not compete with any of our own, and furnished a dye which was useful to the English textile industries. Besides this, a way might be found to the Pacific sooner or later, and thus a South Sea trade established by an alternative to the Panama route.[2]

There were also some English settlers on the Moskito shore, living dispersed up and down the coast by fives and tens.[3] Some of them were mere misfits who chose to vegetate among the swamps surrounded by half-caste families. Others were traders of exceptionally low morals; so Hodgson said, but as he and Trelawny intended to combine a little private trade with politics he may have been prejudiced against them by their competition. Others again were rich 'masters of barcadiers' from the logwood settlements who thought their property safer behind the shoals and bars at Black River than at Belize.[4]

The most important of these was William Pitt, or Pitts, a man of great fortune and influence among the settlers, to whom the first establishment of the English at Black River was generally

[1] Spanish paper of Jan. 19, 1746, Add. MSS. 17566, ff. 170–7.
[2] Trelawny to Stone, Oct. 1742, C.O. 137/57; to Newcastle, Dec. 10, 1743, with paper enclosed, ibid.; 'Account of what has been done at Black River', ibid.; Vernon to Newcastle, Dec. 30, 1742, S.P. 42/92, f. 318; letter to Vernon, enclosed in his letter to Newcastle, Feb. 4, 1743/4, f. 328. See also a letter of William Lea, late South Sea Company's factor in Guatemala, March 3, 1740/1, Add. MSS. 32698, f. 145. This letter and Lea himself were sent out to Vernon at the end of 1741.
[3] In 1753 there were 106 whites and 240 coloured British subjects (C.O. 137/25, X 136). The character of the settlement is pretty clearly shown by the fact that the white men vastly outnumbered the white women, while the coloured women outnumbered the coloured men.
[4] A *barcadier* is the West Indian term for a wharf of any sort.

ascribed. He seems to have been the chief capitalist of the colony and to have bought a great part of its produce. He and some others continued to live on the Shore for safety while their partners cut logwood in the Bay of Honduras.[1] Whenever there was real danger from the Spaniards, the entire population removed from Honduras to Black River. Some said that this happened every year during the rainy season, but another witness denied that, for he said there was no time of the year when the cutters were not profitably employed on the spot; in the dry season they cut the logwood, and in the wet season, when the floods made cutting impossible, they floated it down the creeks to the shipping. However that might be—and the Board of Trade did not believe that this witness gave a fair account of the matter—there was some connexion between Belize and Black River.[2]

The 'Baymen', or logwood-cutters, had quite left their first and greatest head-quarters at Campeachy, and were now established round Belize in the Bay of Honduras. There were said to be about 500 of them. They were reputed to be more industrious and regular people than the squatters of Black River; they lived in comparative peace under a government of their own setting up, and some writers celebrated the probity and punctuality of their dealings. But their way of life troubled the imperial authorities, because, although they were mainly English subjects, they sold most of their wood—some said as much as three-quarters—to the Dutch. A great deal of the shipping which took off their produce was from New England; but that too carried it directly to Holland. This was an anomaly of long standing, but none the better for that. Since their settlement could hardly be called a British colony—in spite of the claims made on their behalf against the Court of Spain—this trade with foreigners could not technically be a breach of the Acts of Navigation; but could not this difficulty be overcome by giving them an established government and making them a regular colony?[3] Once or twice they had demanded such a

[1] Cusack to Vernon, Sept. 25, 1742, C.O. 137/57; Gerrard's comments, Feb. 23, 1742/3, ibid.; Cunningham to Trelawny, Dec. 1743, ibid.

[2] Gerrard's comments, Feb. 23, 1742/3, ibid.

[3] Cunningham to Trelawny, Dec. 1743; undated paper on Honduras, Vernon-Wager MSS.; Trelawny to Vernon, July 27, 1741, S.P. 42/90, f. 318; Vernon to Newcastle, Nov. 3, 1741, f. 389; Hodgson to Board of Trade, April 3, 1744, C.O. 323/11, N. 65. The same proposal had been made in Queen Anne's war (*C.S.P. Col. 1704–5*, 164, ii).

government for themselves, provided it were accompanied by a proper defence, such as the building of forts or stationing a ship of war in their river. The Dutch, they said, had offered them protection, if they would contract to sell them all their logwood; but they had declined it, preferring if possible to live under the dominion of His Majesty.[1] Now, plainly, was the time for a measure of this kind. Belize could not very well be annexed in time of peace, for fear of offending Spain; but since we were already at war, this was an opportunity to do it openly and then maintain it at a peace.[2]

This, however, was not Trelawny's scheme or Vernon's. They were more impressed by the possibilities of the little island of Ruatan, or Rattan as they called it, not very deep in the Gulf of Honduras.[3] It had one of the best harbours that were to be found in that part of Central America—though the champions of Belize said theirs was good enough—and a port so far to leeward might sometimes be useful to the men-of-war of the Jamaica station. As an island, it would be a suitable refuge for Baymen, Moskitomen, and settlers from Black River; but this merit was really less than it looked, since the Spaniards were unlikely to attack except by sea, and would find it harder to advance up a creek than to land on an island. Rattan was to be a sort of general head-quarters, or base-camp, for all the Englishmen and English shipping on both sides of Cape Gracias à Dios, a starting-point for illicit trade with Spaniards, and perhaps a post from which men-of-war or customs authorities could enforce the laws of Navigation and drive the Dutch out of the logwood trade.[4]

Some critics complained that Rattan was out of the way; that the logwood ships never came near it, so that it could be no protection to them; that the Baymen never had time or occasion to go so far afield; that Belize offered the same opportunities for

[1] Gerrard's paper of Feb. 23, 1743; Inhabitants of the Bay to Trelawny, April 28, 1743, C.O. 323/11, N. 67; Inhabitants to Parke Pepper, May 22, 1746, ibid., N. 84; Inhabitants to Caulfield, June 8, 1745, C.O. 137/57.

[2] Petitions of Parke Pepper, July 24 and 27, 1747, C.O. 323/11, N. 84 and 85.

[3] Hodgson afterwards claimed the merit of suggesting the settlement of Rattan (Hodgson to Knowles, Dec. 19, 1752, C.O. 137/60).

[4] Trelawny to Vernon, July 27, 1741, S.P. 42/90, f. 318; Vernon to Newcastle, Nov. 3, 1741, f. 389; Trelawny to Stone, Oct. 1742; Hodgson, 'Reasons for settling Rattan'; Trelawny to Newcastle, Dec. 10, 1743, C.O. 137/57; *Original Papers relating to the Expedition to Panama* (London, 1744), pp. 12, 131, 140.

illicit trade with the Spaniards as Rattan or Black River, and that to consolidate the settlement there would cost the Government nothing, while Rattan would—and did—cost a great deal.[1] There was probably truth in all this; for in spite of fortifications and a garrison of American soldiers, a ship of war generally stationed there, the influence of one of the chief logwood magnates, the liberal grants of land which Trelawny allowed him to make, the elaborate proclamation offering a free port, lands free from quit-rents for twenty years, a year's subsistence for every immigrant and his slaves—in spite of all this, the colony did not prosper.[2] After an auspicious beginning, the illicit trade with the Spanish dominions was not developed. The soil of the island was bad. Few inhabitants were attracted to it. Perhaps, as Trelawny said, they were afraid the Government would restore it at a peace; this was no uncommon reason for the shyness of settlers in new colonies. Trelawny lost most of his interest in it; his greater anxiety for the safety of Jamaica caused him to neglect that of Rattan.[3] It served some of the purposes for which it was intended, for in 1747, when almost all the Baymen were driven out of their settlements by fear of the Spaniards, they came to Rattan; but as they were afraid to venture back into the Bay from thence, they might just as well have been anywhere else.[4] When Rattan was restored to Spain according to the treaty of 1748, nobody seems to have much regretted it except Hodgson and the orators of the Opposition who wanted an opportunity of declaiming against the peace. The Spaniards themselves, when they tried to settle the island, found it impossible to attract inhabitants. The two more important settlements of Belize and the Moskito shore were saved by the want of formal annexation from the necessity of formal restitution.[5]

§ v. *Anson in the Pacific*

There was only one performance in America, during this war, that added anything remarkable to the history of the

---

[1] Gerrard's paper of Feb. 23, 1743, C.O. 137/57.

[2] Armstrong to Wentworth, Oct. 16, 1742, C.O. 137/57; Order in Council, Feb. 2, 1743/4, C.O. 323/11, N. 58; *A.P.C. Col.* iii. 761–9.

[3] Trelawny to Board of Trade, Dec. 19, 1743; C.O. 137/24 W. 64; Jamaica Council Minutes, July 20, 1747, C.O. 140/32.

[4] Trelawny to Newcastle, Aug. 9, 1747, C.O. 137/57.

[5] The English Government had some shadow of authority over Rattan in the nineteenth century; it was not formally ceded to the Republic of Honduras until 1860 (*Archives of British Honduras*, ed. Burdon, iii. 52–231, *passim*).

navy; that was Anson's campaign in the Pacific.[1] Anson received a general commission to do what he could where he could, and to take and fortify, if possible, some port or island as a permanent base for refitting the English squadrons. Only one definite enterprise could be recommended to him which would have any bearing upon the general course of the war; he was to try to communicate overland with Vernon, when he arrived off the Isthmus of Panama, and to concert a joint attack upon Panama city. This was no doubt a fruit of Bladen's original suggestion, out of which the plan of Anson's expedition grew: it had been represented that a settlement at Darien could not expect to maintain itself unless we held some posts on both sides of the isthmus—at Darien and Choco, or St. Mary's, or Panama itself.[2] For this purpose a strong naval force would be very useful. When, however, Anson at last approached Panama, he learnt that Vernon had already failed, so that no attempt at joint operations was ever made.

Anson's was not the first English force to penetrate the South Seas. Besides Sir John Narborough, who performed very little more than a voyage of exploration, there was a long list of privateering expeditions: Drake, Cavendish, the buccaneers who entered the Pacific over the Isthmus of Panama; Dampier, Woodes Rogers, and Shelvocke. Anson had, therefore, the light of some experience, some general principles were laid down; and his squadron, though a larger and more respectable force than its predecessors, only confirms their truth by its history.

The voyage out was a long one, the preparations must be exceptional and could hardly be concealed; Anson's voyage, like those of Dampier and Woodes Rogers before him, was no secret. In fact, the news was half round the world before he started. The delay was the fault of the Government, which was preoccupied by larger undertakings and unstable in its resolutions. It was indeed so long, that Anson had to get round Cape Horn in the very worst season of the year (from which his historian Walter deduces all his misfortunes and disappointments, especially the separation and shattering of his fleet and the enfeeblement of his crews by scurvy). The Viceroy of Lima

---

[1] See above, p. 76, for the connexion of this voyage with the proposed liberation of Spanish America.

[2] Tassell to Walpole, Sept. 11, 1739, Add. MSS. 32694, ff. 41–5; Anson's instructions, S.P. 42/88; Wager to Vernon, Aug. 6, 1740, *Original Letters to an Honest Sailor*, p. 19.

had not only heard of his coming but had waited for him until he concluded the news could not be true, and accordingly revoked his precautions. If any secrecy could have been observed in England, it would have been broken on the way; for a squadron on so immense a voyage must call at some place for refreshments before attempting Cape Horn, and the custom was to take them in at St. Catherine's island off Brazil. From this place, by the perfidy of the Portuguese Governors or the ordinary trading intercourse of the River Plate, the news could not fail to reach Buenos Aires, whence it would be carried overland to Lima. Walter may have imagined that he was the first to point out this danger; but Shelvocke, in his advice to commanders intending for the South Seas, had earnestly recommended them to avoid the coasts of Brazil, for this very reason.[1] Walter, however, made a suggestion which had an important sequel; he asked whether we could not use the Falkland Islands as a stepping-stone to the Pacific?[2] This suggestion he presumably had from Anson himself, under whose influence the Board of Admiralty projected in 1750 a voyage to explore them, which was countermanded out of delicacy for the Court of Spain. The scheme survived Anson, was executed after the Peace of Paris, and produced the very acute Anglo-Spanish crisis of 1770.

Once in the Pacific, various questions arose. Where to go for wood and water? Where to cruise for the trade? What to do with the prizes? They nearly always answered themselves in the same way. For refreshment after the passage of Cape Horn, the two favourite places were Chiloe and Juan Fernandez Island; later in the cruise, in the latitude of Panama, it was Gorgona or the Galapagos islands. As the English adventurers repeated themselves, the Spaniards, who were ready to provide against the obvious though quite unprepared for the unexpected, got the habit of watching the likely places. A small squadron was sent at once to Juan Fernandez, on the news of Anson's approach, and had only just given him up and left it when he arrived. The island was much valued by the English for the wild goats who had multiplied there. The Spaniards, therefore, resolved to exterminate them by importing a race of dogs, who, if they did not succeed in killing them, nevertheless

[1] Shelvocke, *A Voyage Round the World* (reprint of 1928), p. 230.
[2] Walter, *A Voyage Round the World* (4th ed.), pp. 128–9.

deprived the English of them by rendering the survivors so agile that nobody could take them. In other known resorts of privateers the Spaniards took precautions to the same effect.

All the trade of the Pacific coast proceeded in an almost straight line north and south. The adventurers, therefore, need only stand in the track and take. They must not let anything that saw them escape them, or the alarm was raised. A general embargo would then be declared, and the game would be up. When their presence was known, as it must soon be, they might as well be hanged for a sheep as for a lamb, and attempt to seize one of the towns in which some treasure might happen to lie. The greatest possible dispatch and surprise were necessary, or whatever was valuable, including the Governor, would be removed into the mountains, even a ransom would be denied, and bands of horsemen would appear on the heights behind the town, ready to fight. Anson could hardly have acted with more secrecy and speed than he did at the taking of Payta, yet he got little enough for his pains.

Suppose a great number of prizes or a rich plunder taken, it was often valueless. If it was money or provisions, very well. Never were portability and durability, those commonplace virtues of the precious metals, more highly appreciated than by captors in the South Seas; for they seldom had very much room in their own ships for what they took, and had an immense voyage over the Pacific before them, for which they must stow all the water and provisions they could carry. They might indeed man some of their prizes; but that could not go very far, for their crews could not suffice for many, even if they had all come round Cape Horn in perfect health, which was very unlikely. One captain at least (Clipperton) had suffered for weakening his forces by dividing them among too many prize ships. Therefore, unless the prizes contained provisions or goods of great value and small bulk, they were nearly useless. The captors might ransom them, or sell them to the Spaniards on the coast; but though this might be very well for privateers, it was beneath the dignity of a gentlemanly commander like Anson. Moreover the Spaniards often beguiled the captors in such bargains with a view to overcoming them by a surprise attack, or bullied them over the price, knowing they could not take the stuff away and could make nothing of it if they did not sell.

These expeditions to the Pacific always ended with an

attempt upon the Manila galleon off the coast of California. This was reported to carry the richest single cargo in the world, and was, therefore, a magnet to privateers. It conveyed the silver from Acapulco in Mexico to Manila, and returned laden with East India and China goods. The route and time of its arrival and departure were fairly regular, and as it came from such a distance, the returning galleon from Manila could hardly be forewarned against any definite danger. It was impossible, however, for the authorities at Acapulco not to know of it; and if there was any rumour of enemies on the coast, the sailing of the outward galleon from Mexico was commonly put off, as Anson found to his cost. The outward galleon carrying only money could disengage her lowest tier of guns; the returning galleon could not, for she was nearly always overloaded with bulkier goods. For all these reasons, it was generally the ship from Manila that was taken, not the galleon with the Mexican silver. Anson missed the first, and the second was not allowed to start while he was in the waters of Mexico. His originality, and the source of his great fortune, consisted in returning from Canton, where he went to refit, and taking the galleon which had sailed at last from Mexico, as it approached the Philippines.

After the attempt on the galleon, there was a long and dangerous voyage to be undertaken across the Pacific. The provisions and water were likely to give out, especially as the opportunities for procuring them on the Californian coast were not very good. The first islands in the route were Spanish; and to those that went farther, the jealous Dutch of Batavia gave cold comfort. Never was anybody in more danger of perishing than Anson, in this part of his voyage. From the East Indies the way was easy and frequented; but any cruise, however long, had to end in a new danger at the mouth of the Channel. Anson in fact found his way providentially through a French fleet which might very well have put an end to his career within sight of home, as the French South Sea ships *Louis-Érasme* and *Marquise d'Antin*, after rounding Cape Horn twice, were taken in fight off the Azores.[1]

---

[1] For the sources of these generalizations, see William Dampier, *A New Voyage Round the World* (1698); account of Dampier's 1703 voyage in Harris, *Navigantium atque Itinerantium Bibliotheca* (1764); Woodes Rogers, *A Cruizing Voyage Round the World* (1712); Frezier, *A Voyage to the South Sea* (English translation, 1717); accounts of Betagh's and Clipperton's voyages in Harris; G. Shelvocke, *A Voyage Round the*

§ vi. *The Interception of Spanish Trade*

So much for expeditions. They were not the whole war. Some people, like Vernon, thought it could very well be fought without them, and that Spain would be most effectively reduced to terms by the destruction of her trade and shipping. At first sight this doctrine was absurd, for Spain had not a large merchant marine, and England stood to lose a great deal more, absolutely if not relatively, by a war of trade destruction. That indeed was one of the chief arguments of Walpole and his supporters against entering into one; but the Opposition turned it into a reason for directing all our efforts to the conquest of the West Indies.[1]

But if the whole maritime commerce of Spain in Spanish ships was small, some parts of it were very rich and very necessary. These were the *flotas* and galleons, the *azogues* and Register-ships, the Manila Galleon and the Armadilla of the South Sea. It had been a commonplace since Queen Elizabeth's reign that the way to fight Spain was to intercept the galleons; and considering the many times it was attempted and the few times it succeeded, the legend may be said to have lived a hard life and died a hard death. Piet Hein had taken a treasure-fleet in Matanzas Bay in 1628; Blake had taken some of the galleons and burnt the *flota*; the allied expedition to Vigo in 1702 had surprised them after their arrival in Spain; and Wager and Littleton had caught and destroyed some of them in 1708 and 1711. These successes were just enough to keep up hope; the more so as the value of the prize was so great in

World (1726); R. Walter, *A Voyage Round the World* (1748). See also the chapter on Anson's Voyage in Sir Herbert Richmond's history.

[1] *Parl. Hist.* x. 1193 (Hervey), xii. 253 (Talbot); *Britain's Mistakes in the Commencement and Conduct of the Present War* (London, 1740), p. 46. I do not know of any reliable statistics which show how far this expectation was fulfilled. Those of the *Gentleman's Magazine*, which give a comparison of English and Spanish losses down to Jan. 1, 1742, are very vague. They give 332 English losses against 231 ships taken by the Spaniards; but the valuation, by which they make the two figures almost balance each other, is obviously arbitrary; besides, like almost all English statistics on this point, they include neutral ships on the profit side. It appears fairly certain that Spanish trade was, on the whole, a lean prey, in spite of one or two extraordinarily rich captures, and that our gains did not balance our losses before the last years of the French war (vol. xi, pp. 689–98). Two interesting pamphlets were written on this subject: *Hireling Artifice Detected* (London, 1742) is hostile to the Ministry, and therefore makes the most of the losses and the least of the gains; it is controverted by *The Profit and Loss of Great Britain and Spain . . . impartially Stated* (London, 1742).

proportion to that of any other Spanish shipping that could be attacked.[1]

The last galleons had gone in 1737, and were still in Cartagena. A *flota* was to have sailed in 1739, but when the war broke out the voyage was cancelled. At that moment it happened that some *azogues* were at sea in their return to Spain, and the eyes of all England—all Europe, indeed—were fixed upon them. Haddock lay in wait for them off Cadiz; Vernon was ordered to halt in his voyage to Jamaica and cruise for them; but all preparations were vain, for instead of making for Cadiz or Galicia, they appeared unexpectedly at Santander in the Bay of Biscay.

After this, one of Vernon's chief objects was to deal with the galleons already at Cartagena. The treasure was still on the way from Lima, and the great fair of Portobello had not yet been held. The first thing Vernon did, after he arrived on his station, was to take Portobello and pull down the fortifications; and to make sure of his purpose, he destroyed, a few months later, the castle of Chagre, where the overland route for bulky goods from Panama came down to the sea. By doing so, he adjourned the fair *sine die*, or caused it to be held with great inconvenience elsewhere, for the galleons could never have ventured into an undefended harbour. Indeed they would probably not have dared, even if Vernon had left Portobello untouched, so long as he remained in superior force at Jamaica; for Portobello was well known to be much less defensible than Cartagena (and this was one of the reasons why the galleons never stayed longer there than they could help). Perhaps, therefore, Vernon's action did not make so much difference as he expected; moreover Portobello was not the only place where the fair could be held. All the trade of Santa Fé and Quito was usually done at the 'little fair' of Cartagena. The route from Cartagena to the Pacific was not easy, because of the Andes beyond Quito, but it was just practicable, as the precautions show which the Spanish Government had lately taken, in the interest of the regular fair of Portobello, to prevent it from being used.[2] In

---

[1] The Danes, of all people, thought of seizing the *flota* without any declaration of war, in order to revenge themselves upon Spain for some injuries and unpaid debts. The Court of France was very angry with them for this silly notion (Rouillé to Ogier, July 21, 1755, A.E. Danemark, 129; Ogier to Rouillé, July 22 and Aug. 12, ibid.).

[2] Juan and Ulloa, *Relación Histórica del Viage á la América Meridional* (Madrid, 1768), i. 108–10.

fact the galleons, which could do nothing at Portobello after Vernon had dismantled the forts, did hold a sort of a fair at Monpox, near Cartagena.[1] However, the trade had been fatally disorganized. The cargoes had to be sold on long credit, the assortments had been broken up and could not be replaced from Europe. Thus the seizure of Portobello and the long detention at Cartagena made a fine harvest for the illicit trade of Jamaica and Curaçao.

There was nothing more that Vernon could do against the galleons, unless he could destroy them in port or take them in their voyage. The first of these he tried to do at Cartagena by the useless bombardment of 1740, which his enemies described as 'using guineas to break windows'; next year he tried to effect the purpose by conquering the town. Neither he nor his successors could prevent the homeward fleet from collecting at Havana and returning to Spain with Torres in 1744;[2] but that was the only time, in the nine years' war, that a regular treasure fleet returned to Spain from the West Indies.[3] Reggio was preparing for a second attempt in 1748 when he met Knowles between Vera Cruz and Havana, fought an indecisive battle, and escaped into Havana; he did not come home, therefore, till after the peace was declared.

The interruption of the Spanish trade in general continued throughout the war to be a very important part of the navy's business, especially in the West Indies. Some very rich prizes were taken. The effect of these losses and delays upon the Spanish Government was not so great as it was expected to be;

[1] Vernon to Eslava, Oct. 13, 1741, S.P. 42/90, f. 396; Eslava to Larnage, Sept. 13, 1741, A.N. Colonies C⁹ A. 55; Larnage to Maurepas, Oct. 13, ibid.

[2] Ogle seems to have made no attempt to intercept Torres, although he had kept back at Jamaica some almost unseaworthy ships in order to make himself equal to it. The reason for this may have been his natural lethargy, or the bewildering reports of his cruisers as to Torres's motions (but he seems to have got news before May 8 that Torres meant to sail home at the end of the month, which might have been almost time enough to try to find him, especially as he had a great part of his force together ready for an emergency). Or the real reason may have been that he was expecting a declaration of war against France and watching the motions of the French at St. Domingue. All he did was to send home an express to the Lords of the Admiralty, in order that they might, if they pleased, order the interception of the Spanish fleet in European waters; he had in fact already prepared them for the possibility of its departure (Ogle to Corbett, April 21 and May 8, 1744, Adm. 1/233).

[3] One Fournier complained in February 1747 that the owners of some French cargoes which had been sent out in 1730 and 1735 had not yet got their effects returned (A.E. Mém. et Doc. France, 2007, f. 124).

but they made a great difference to the regular lawful trade
of the Spanish Empire. Only one treasure-fleet came back to
Spain, and no galleons or *flotas* set out during the war. The
form of the trade was entirely altered; instead of fleets, single
'Register-ships' sailed by special permission. The system was
not entirely new, for it had long been used in the trade of minor
or distant markets, such as Buenos Aires, Havana, and Campeachy, which could not conveniently supply themselves from
the galleons and *flotas*. The 'register' was a list of the cargo,
outwards and inwards, upon which duties or *indultos* were
charged. All unregistered goods were subject to confiscation.
Needless to say, there was a great deal of them, for the temptation to avoid the duties was very strong. In this respect the
Register-ships did not differ from the galleons and *flotas*; what
was new in the War of 1739 was permitting them to sail to the
ports usually served by the galleons and *flotas*, and the greater
latitude allowed them in choosing the port of their return. The
Spanish Government drew the line, however, at Spanish ports;
a Register-ship which returned, for example, to France on the
pretext of necessity (but for the real reason that unregistered
goods and moneys could more conveniently be unloaded there),
got its owners, and especially those of the registered goods,
into infinite trouble.[1] Another novelty—though it had precedents—was granting some permissions for Register-ships to
foreigners, especially to Frenchmen.[2] Even Englishmen seem to
have received them. Indeed, if they could settle matters with
their own Court and their own privateers, they were more
eligible candidates for such a favour than anybody else could
be. That was not so easy. Messrs. Linwood and Clarmont petitioned the English Government for a pass for such a Register-
ship, but although they pleaded the advantageous market for
English manufactures, their proposal was rejected. However
they might belittle them, the advantages which the Court of
Spain was to receive by duties and the safe transport of its
treasure would have been very great. It would indeed have

---

[1] A.E. Mém. et Doc. Espagne, 80, ff. 105 et seqq.

[2] Many of the Register-ships were French, and other vessels were sent out from
France straight to the Spanish dominions, without any warrant from the Court of
Spain. La Rochelle had fourteen ships out on the coasts of Spain in 1743, and the
safety of these investments gave the Chamber of Commerce much anxiety; it tried
in vain to persuade Maurepas to take measures for protecting this trade (E. Garnault, *Le Commerce rochelais au XVIIIe siècle*, vol. iii (Paris, 1891), pp. 79–82).

been a complete stultification of the war to break our own blockade in this way, and even Newcastle hardly wavered.[1]

These reforms of the galleon system were not unlike those which the French had desired in the War of the Spanish Succession. Neither the French nor other licensees of Register-ships had cause to be wholly satisfied with the new regulations. The Spanish Minister Campillo revenged himself for the smuggling of the English in America, which he could no longer prevent, by throwing every possible difficulty in the way of the French smuggling in Spain, which he could still in some measure control. In fact, the critics of his policy complained that his increased precautions against abuses by Spaniards or neutrals played into the hands of the English.[2] Registers were only granted at a great price, jealously, and for small quantities of money. In order to detect the unregistered, seals were broken, private correspondence read, and decrees of confiscation founded upon the evidence so obtained. These terrors fell equally upon the innocent and the guilty; for as the goods had still to be shipped in the name of a Spaniard, and the same Spaniard acted this part for a great number of foreigners, anything unlawful done by any of their correspondents, with which he was found to be connected, forfeited the goods of all his clients.[3]

Besides these official vexations, the trade was disorganized by the unusual method into which it was now thrown. The buyers of America, accustomed to reckon with galleons of more or less regular period and calculable value, could never tell in advance how many Register-ships would be granted or for what ports; so for fear of being undersold, or in hopes of a better bargain from later comers, they bought from hand to mouth. The 'strong purses' were shut, and the prices, after exceptional fluctuations, fell below the usual level. At the same time the exports from Spain to the West Indies were smaller than they would have been for the same period in the normal régime of galleons and *flotas*. For as the great middlemen discontinued or reduced their operations, their customers might as well buy from the English and Dutch smugglers. The first Register-

---

[1] A.E. Mém. et Doc. Espagne, 80, f. 66; *A.P.C. Col.* iii. 770–2; Newcastle to Hardwicke, Oct. 6, 1743, Add. MSS. 35407, f. 281; Hardwicke to Newcastle, Oct. 7, 1743, Add. MSS. 32701, f. 151.
[2] A.E. Mém. et Doc. Espagne, 82, ff. 44, 65–6.
[3] Ibid., vol. 80, ff. 105, 109; vol. 82, ff. 38 et seqq.

ships of the war made good profits because they came after a
long suspension of trade; but those which frequented the Terra-
Firma provinces round Cartagena were hardly able to sell
their cargoes at all; and to make the matter worse, the merchants of Peru ordered back their treasures from Panama in the
hope that Register-ships would come directly into the Pacific
to deal with them.[1] Besides, the Register-ships were often taken,
even though their tracks were more scattered and less predict-
able than those of the galleons and *flotas*. The author of a
mémoire in the French Foreign Office calculated that out of 118
Register-ships which sailed from Cadiz between May 20, 1740,
and June 27, 1745, 69 had been lost.[2]

These alterations had permanent results, for though the
Mexican *flotas* were restored after the peace, the Portobello
galleons never were. The economist Ulloa had discussed
whether the trade-fleets ought to be kept up after the war, and
decided for it. He believed that single Register-ships would
overstock the markets. However, he recommended certain
reforms, such as a larger tonnage, greater regularity of sailing,
and direct voyages to the Pacific colonies; also the establishment of permanent warehouses in the colonies to supplement
the annual fairs. The smugglers would have been discouraged
and the prices kept steady by these means. Most of Ulloa's
advice was disregarded, and the effect of the change was considerable. It diminished the profit of smuggling, especially at
the Isthmus of Panama, for the Pacific colonies were better
supplied by the ships which came round Cape Horn. The
French Intendant at St. Domingue complained in 1755 that the
Spanish trade was almost dead, except in provisions, and everything as cheap in the Spanish colonies as in the French. He
wished for the galleons again; what better testimony to the
Register-ships could there be?[3]

§ vii. *The Protection of Trade with the Spanish Enemy*

At the same time that the English navy interrupted the lawful trade between Spain and her colonies, the Government

---

[1] A.E. Mém. et Doc. Espagne, 82, ff. 45 et seqq.; vol. 81, ff. 175, 180.
[2] A.E. Mém. et Doc. France, 2007, ff. 105 et seqq.
[3] Ulloa, op. cit., ii. 99–128; Laporte-Lalanne to Machault, April 11, 1755, A.N.
Col. C⁹ A. 97. See the very similar remarks of Trelawny, in his 'State' of Jamaica,
1752, C.O. 137/25, X 101.

ordered it to defend the English smugglers. This was nothing new. The interlopers had been countenanced and protected in the War of the Spanish Succession, and the pretence that the Spanish colonies favoured or might be induced to favour the English candidate for the crown, was so thin that nobody can have thought of it as the real reason for this intercourse. The allies had made a self-denying ordinance against trade with the enemy; the Dutch were the first to break it, and the English in America could not long be restrained from following their example. The Governors of colonies were ordered to encourage the trade, except in provisions and contraband stores, and to restrain the privateers from interrupting it. The traders of Jamaica were convoyed to the Spanish coast and protected there, and the Board of Trade condescended to inform the London merchants whether English goods were wanted there according to its last advices. Finally, in 1707 Parliament passed an Act which forbade any molestation of the Spaniards in the important region of the isthmus, between Rio de la Hacha and Chagre. The Government approved of Gilligan's attempt to settle a slave-trade between Barbados and the Spanish colonies, and only drew the line at breaking the Navigation Acts by allowing Spanish ships to import goods into the English colonies.[1]

Vernon had been employed on the West India station in that war, and its precedents were not lost on him, as he showed by his first measures in 1739. 'I have a particular pleasure', he wrote to Newcastle, 'in the pleasing hopes of a revival of a trade so beneficial to his Majesty's subjects, that I have formerly seen flourishing here in great prosperity.'[2] One of his strongest reasons, though not the most ostensible, for demolishing the forts at Portobello and Chagre, was the help such a measure would give to the interlopers. They could only gain by the destruction of the strong places within which their enemies the *Guarda-Costas* were used to retreat. If those places should become open roads, at the command of any English ship of war, the trade of a *Guarda-Costa* would be a difficult one to follow. The neutral smugglers benefited from this liberation of their

[1] *C.S.P. Col. 1702–3*, nos. 472, 487 (i), 1059, 1208 (i), 1243; *1704–6*, nos. 50, 116 (i), 285 (iii), 739, 871, 894, 994 (i); *1706–8*, nos. 350, 503, 593, 1073, 1108, 1250, 1477; *1708–9*, nos. 100, 111, 210, 226 (i), 445, &c. See also *C.S.P. Col. 1719–20*, nos. 247, 341 (i), 575.
[2] Vernon to Newcastle, Jan. 18, 1739/40, S.P. 42/85, f. 108.

trade as much as the English. This unexpected result annoyed the jealous English pamphleteers. Still, the Dutch were some sort of allies to us though they took the halfpence and left us the kicks; and their smugglers helped to make the Galleon Fair not only impossible but pointless, and lessened the returns to Spain.[1] It is significant that Knowles obtained help from the Dutch smuggling island of Curaçao for an expedition which should serve Porto Cabello as Vernon had served Portobello. The Dutch even imitated Vernon's example unofficially on their own account; the Spanish Ambassador had to complain at The Hague that a small force of small craft from Curaçao had destroyed the fortifications at Tucacas.[2]

The same desire to encourage trade evidently explains Vernon's surprising moderation at Portobello, where he spared the town and all it contained in order to make a good impression on the Spaniards. He published a proclamation offering them protection, and invited them to a free trade with all His Majesty's subjects.[3]

The Secretary of State, the Admiralty, the Opposition, and the merchants all applauded his prudence. At the request of the traders to Jamaica, the Government drafted a circular letter which ordered the colonial Governors to protect and favour the trade with Spanish America. Queen Anne's ministry had actually given such orders, but in 1739 the letter was not sent after all.[4] However, the Act of Parliament against trading with Spain during the war applied only to Spain in Europe, which

[1] Vernon to Newcastle, April 21, 1740, S.P. 42/85, f. 195; Pulteney to Vernon, Aug. 17, 1740, *Original Letters to an Honest Sailor*, p. 25; *Hireling Artifice Detected*, p. 47; Ogle to Newcastle, Aug. 19, 1744, S.P. 42/89, f. 146.

[2] *Journal of the Expedition to La Guira and Porto Cavallos* (London, 1744), p. 29; St. Gil to the States-General, Dec. 28, 1741, S.P. 84/396, f. 9.

[3] Vernon to Burchett, May 26–31, 1740, Adm. 1/232. The value of Vernon's self-sacrifice is uncertain. His enemies made the least of it by hinting that there was nothing worth taking, but the Governor of Panama, who ought to know, remarked with astonishment in an intercepted letter that Vernon gave up 700,000 pieces of eight, of which his own share would have been an eighth (Martinez de la Vega to Philip V, Feb. 12, 1740, S.P. 43/90). Of course Vernon seized the King's treasure which he found in the fortress. A certain Colonel Burrard tried to account for Vernon's obstruction of the Panama expedition in 1742, by attributing it to partiality for the people of Portobello who had paid him well for it. This is ignorant and vindictive military tittle-tattle, and deserves no more credit than what Vernon's admirers said of Wentworth. Vernon was not that kind of knave (Add. MSS. 34097, f. 67; see also Silhouette to Amelot, March 28, 1740, A.E. Angleterre, 407, f. 231).

[4] C.O. 5/5; Cabinet Minute, Nov. 12, 1739, Add. MSS. 33004, f. 23.

was as plain a hint as could be given without words, that intercourse with the Spanish colonies would be allowed.[1] The Government ordered Vernon to do all he could to protect and convoy it. The Act for encouraging privateers contained a clause which safeguarded the right of His Majesty's subjects to carry it on. The Opposition leaders and pamphleteers expatiated with pleasure on the useful trade which Vernon had opened with the Spanish settlements. Wager was loud in denouncing an English privateer who violated, a few months later, this neutrality of Portobello.[2] Merchants congratulated each other on the new markets for negroes and manufactures, and the orders that came into London for supplying them.[3] Indeed, it would not be too much to say that in the eyes of some people, the increase of our trade with the Spanish colonies was in itself a sufficient justification and motive of the war with Spain.[4]

Only the Spaniards and their friends deplored the success of these measures; not merely because it spoilt the market for the Cadiz trade, in which they were interested, but also because they believed that England, fortified by this new source of income against the severest taxation, would be able to continue the war for ever. Besides, it would accustom the merchants of the Spanish colonies to dealing with the English smugglers, and the habit might prove to be a permanent one when the war was over. English writers preferred to state the matter another way: we suffered great injury by our exclusion from the markets of old Spain, and it was only right that we should recover our losses in those of the new.[5]

In this war, as in the last, convoys were granted to the traders, even to the prejudice of services more important tacti-

---

[1] Byng to Board of Trade, Sept. 20, 1740, C.O. 28/25, AA 98.

[2] Wager to Vernon, June 10 and July 9, 1740, *Original Letters to an Honest Sailor*, pp. 13 and 16. The people of Jamaica wanted Trelawny to put into the privateers' instructions a special clause forbidding them to molest anybody in Portobello, but Trelawny was not sure if he had the power to do it (Manning to Wager, March 25, 1740, C.O. 137/56, f. 331).

[3] Henry Lascelles and son to Richard Morecroft, March 28, 1740, W. & G. i; 'Paper procured by Mr. Stone's friend', July 3/14, 1740, S.P. 43/92.

[4] *Considerations on the War* (London, 1742), p. 34; *The Present Ruinous Land-War Proved to be a H——r War* (London, 1745), p. 24.

[5] Harris, *Navigantium atque Itinerantium Bibliotheca*, i. 254; Van Hoey to States-General, Sept. 20, 1740, copy in A.E. Hollande, 436, f. 266; Silhouette to Amelot, Nov. 26, 1739, A.E. Angleterre, 405, ff. 289–90; Larnage to Maurepas, Sept. 1, 1740, A.N. Col. C⁹ A. 52.

cally.[1] Vernon was by no means indiscriminate in allowing all kinds of goods to be exported to the enemy; he exacted from the merchants an undertaking to load no contraband on their ships.[2] This given, he was ready to have them convoyed to the Bastimientos near Cartagena or the South Keys of Cuba. At the Bastimientos or at Baru, the ship of war lay at anchor, while the traders went off, or sent their boats, to neighbouring bays. Her commander had an opportunity, which he sometimes exercised, of taking into custody any ship which he suspected of carrying contraband. He seems to have accorded an equal protection to privateers and traders so long as they did not molest each other. Sometimes they even played into each others' hands, for the privateer would bring in prisoners whom the traders or the men-of-war could send with a flag of truce to the neighbouring Spanish towns, and create thereby a further opportunity for communication and trade. In the absence of a man-of-war, the traders were apparently protected by a fascine battery on shore. They sometimes made expeditions of their own against the Spanish forces gathering for the purpose of interrupting their business.[3] At the South Keys the warship had to stand a long way off the land; the traders or their boats went inshore every day to trade, and came out under her guns every evening. Sometimes she would send her boats with them, heavily manned and armed, to protect their trade. Whether this was a precaution against the Spanish officials or the mules who were an important item in this commerce, does not very clearly appear. The men-of-war would sometimes hunt out the galleys or xebecs which guarded this coast against illicit trade, and burn them or drive them into the swamps so far that the bushes hid them.[4]

[1] Ogle excused himself for making no attack on the French colonies at the outbreak of war in 1744, by the dispersion of his fleet in convoys (Ogle to Corbett, June 3, 1744, Adm. 1/233).

[2] Vernon to Newcastle, Jan. 18–31, 1739/40, S.P. 42/85, f. 107; Orders to Maynard, Oct. 1, 1740, ibid., f. 358.

[3] There is an account of an expedition of this kind, fitted out in September 1742 by two English vessels, four Dutch, and two French, against some Spanish *piraguas* preparing to surprise them (Deposition of the second mate of the *Fortune*, de Kaudran, H.C.A. 42/28).

[4] Captains' Logs, H.M.S. *Montague*, Adm. 51/615; *Sea Horse*, Adm. 51/903; *Fowey*, Adm. 51/340; *Enterprize*, 51/319; *Biddeford*, Adm. 51/110. A comparison of the trade of Jamaica and Barbados shows the importance of the convoys. The trade of Jamaica with the Spanish colonies increased during the war; that of Barbados declined, so that the slave-dealers had to look out for new markets. The difference

The convoys saved the traders great expenses in the manning and arming of their ships. The commanders-in-chief on the station charged a fee for these services—five per cent. was said to be the rule. It was contrary to orders and tradition to demand convoy-money; but the payment was masked under a more respectable charge for freight of the bullion which the men-of-war would, for greater safety, bring home to Jamaica for the traders. The Lords of the Admiralty thought this allowable, though five per cent. seemed, as they said, an extraordinarily high rate of freight. It was not complained of in this war until the great quarrel between the merchant Edward Manning and Admiral Davers in 1745, in which it appears that Manning was angry with Davers because he would only grant a general convoy, not a private one for Manning's sloops alone.[1]

The Spaniards were not the only enemies against whom the traders had to be protected. The old Jamaica antagonism between traders and privateers reappears in this war. Some of the privateers declared, what was probably true in law, that they had the right to take His Majesty's subjects found in trade with His Majesty's enemies. One John Ford put this detestable doctrine in practice by shadowing, and attempting to seize, a Jamaica ship trading at the South Keys. Christopher Edzery, or Edsbury, revived a still more injurious custom from the last war. He appeared off the South Keys, where he had been known as a trader, and sent in to the merchants the list of an imaginary cargo; when they came out to deal with him, he seized them and the money they had brought with them. The trading interest of Jamaica exclaimed with virtuous horror to Vernon, who sent a special convoy under Captain Boscawen, to protect the trade against such spoil-sports, and to restore the shaken confidence of the Spaniards on the south side of Cuba.[2]

can only be explained by the lack of convoy from Barbados (Robinson to Newcastle, Nov. 27, 1742, C.O. 28/46).

[1] Deposition of Manning, Nov. 10, 1745, Adm. 1/233; Counter-address of merchants to Davers, Nov. 23, 1745, ibid.; Lords of the Admiralty to Newcastle, Sept. 29, 1746, S.P. 42/31, f. 245. Commodore Kerr had given great offence by demanding money for convoying the traders of Jamaica in 1707 (*H.M.C., H. of L. MSS., N.S.*, vii. 99–111; *Lords Journals*, xviii. 449–50. According to an anonymous memorial of 1724, a percentage of the value of cargoes was usually paid to the men-of-war captains for this purpose (C.O. 388/28 R 155).

[2] Petition of the Merchants to Trelawny, ? Sept. 1740, S.P. 42/85, f. 355; Affidavit of Richard Lee, f. 356; Boscawen to Vernon, Nov. 27, 1740, f. 420; Vernon to Newcastle, Jan. 5, 1740/1, S.P. 42/90, f. 4. Perhaps the excesses of the English

This official protection from our own privateers was only enjoyed by the ships in the Spanish trade; on the contrary, in the trade with the French West Indies it was sometimes the privateers who protected the contrabandists against the men-of-war.[1]

The trade was so well protected during the war, that it probably increased. This is not quite certain, because the shipping registers of Jamaica hardly exist for the 1730's; but the vessels returning from the Spanish West Indies were more, absolutely and in relation to the total shipping of Jamaica, during the years 1743-6 than in any period for which deductions can be drawn after the peace.[2] Too much, however, must not be built upon these figures. In the first place, the smuggling trade of Jamaica was only one way of sending goods to the Spanish colonies during the peace; in war it was almost the only one, and might reasonably be expected to carry more goods. Besides, many of the ships returned to Jamaica in ballast or with unsold goods during the war. Ballast might be the sign of a good voyage, for when vessels brought home the returns in money (which is never declared in these statistics), they had to come in ballast. Returned goods, however, can only signify some kind of failure; but the statistics do not reveal the quantities, still less the cause, whether obstruction of the trade by Spanish officials or merely overstocked markets. Nevertheless, it was generally agreed that the trade of Jamaica to the Spanish colonies flourished best in war, and there were many complaints of dull markets in Jamaica after the peace, which were attributed to the cessation of trade with the Spanish colonies.[3]

The same statistics show a decline after 1743. In that year

privateers were the reason why the dispatch of vessels from Jamaica to Portobello was countermanded at the end of 1740, 'it being looked upon as too hazardous' (Henry Lascelles to Murray Crymble and George Peete, Jan. 27, 1740/1, W. & G. i). For a description of similar practices in the War of the Spanish Succession see *Parl. Hist.* x. 840 (Bladen), and *C.S.P. Col. 1704-6*, nos. 739, 871.

[1] For a further discussion of this subject, see Chapter IX.

[2] C.O. 142/15. I have to take the years 1743-6, for which the figures are nearly perfect; if those of 1740-2 had existed in full, they would probably have strengthened the impression, for the trade seems to have been better in the beginning than the middle of the war.

[3] *Gentleman's Magazine*, xix. 410; Trelawny's 'State of the Island of Jamaica, 1752', C.O. 137/25, X 101; petition of the Council and Assembly to George II, Nov. 20, 1752, ibid., X 115; William Lloyd to Henry Lloyd, April 29, 1749, *N.Y.H.S. Collections*, 1926, pp. 421-2. There is a good account of the trade in Add. MSS. 38373, ff. 130-1, a document of about 1763.

84 ships returned to Jamaica from the Spanish colonies, in 1744 there were 44, in 1745 there were 38, and 47 in 1746. Complaints of loss and dullness of trade had already been made in 1742;[1] they may have been caused by the number of Register-ships granted by the Court of Spain, or by the admittance into Spain of English goods in Dutch bottoms.

However, there were great schemes on hand. Some ships with quicksilver and Papal Bulls bound for Vera Cruz had been carried into Jamaica. If ever there was a cargo which the Spaniards would wish to ransom, it was quicksilver and Papal Bulls; without the former, the silver of Mexico could not be refined, and the latter were among the commonest necessaries of life all over Spanish America. A treaty was set on foot between Edward Manning and the Viceroy of Mexico, through the mediation of the French Governor's secretary at St. Domingue.[2] It came to nothing because the Viceroy would not admit English ships into Vera Cruz, and the Navigation Acts and Anglo-French Treaty of 1686 forbade not only Spanish but French ships from coming to Jamaica.[3]

Later in 1744, one Pedro de Estrada appeared in Jamaica with a recommendation from Governor Tinker of the Bahamas, in order to buy and carry away the Spanish prize goods.[4] It often happened that the ransom or repurchase of prize cargoes served as a pretext or introduction to a more extensive trade between enemies. It was so in this instance. The Bulls and quicksilver seem to have been an unprofitable venture, but next year Estrada was back again with a licence to the Governor of Havana to propose a trade for '2,000 Negroes, flour, rice, pulse, hams, sheet-lead, tin, pictures, linseed-oil, window-glasses, sail-cloth, several sorts of merchandise, and other effects as household furniture, diamonds set, looking-glasses and other small things'.[5] Some of these articles, such as sail-cloth and cordage, both Trelawny and Davers thought improper to be exported; but for the rest, they were willing to let the scheme go forward.

[1] *Gentleman's Magazine*, xii. 218, 601.
[2] Edward Manning had been an agent of the South Sea Company, and had some of its effects in his hands at the outbreak of war—most of which he succeeded in detaining for ever. At first an enemy, then an ally and perhaps a partner, of Governor Trelawny, he was later a leader of the mercantile or Kingston party in the Assembly, of which he became Speaker.
[3] Larnage to Maurepas, March 11, 1744, A.N. Col. C⁹ A 64.
[4] Trelawny to Newcastle, Aug. 16, 1744, C.O. 137/57.
[5] Paper enclosed by Trelawny to Newcastle, Nov. 15, 1745, C.O. 137/57.

Trelawny seems to have doubted whether he did right to allow it, but in view of what had been practised throughout the war, his nervousness is hardly comprehensible unless he was interested in Manning's scheme or it was one of unusual size. Though there might be a distinction between a loose, un-authorized smuggling and a formal contract with a Viceroy, this was not the first instance of the latter kind. Trelawny con-soled himself with the authority of Governor Tinker, and with the reflection that if we had not accepted this trade it would have fallen into the hands of the Dutch. The Council of Jamaica supported him; it expressed the opinion that the trade to the Spanish colonies was a beneficial one, especially because it promoted the exportation of prize goods. It desired that this trade might be put under some definite regulation in order that the merchants engaged in it might be emancipated from the caprices of the naval commanders-in-chief.[1]

Estrada was the cause of one of those elaborate and noisy quarrels into which Governors and Admirals often got them-selves in the West Indies. Davers seems to have repented of his consent, and to have set up his friends in the Assembly to make difficulties. They denounced Estrada as a spy, and accused him of causing the Jamaica shipping to be captured by report-ing its movements to the Spaniards. No doubt he saw what he could; nobody who went about that kind of errand in the West Indies omitted doing so. He was embarrassed by his connexion with the Havana Company; it had introduced into the Carib-bean the xebecs which preyed with such unexampled success upon the illicit traders in the South Keys. This was not the only way in which he injured the South Keys traders. They would probably be superseded (though some denied it) by an authorized trade to Havana; nobody will smuggle through the back door when the front door is open to him. Perhaps this is why the body of small merchants were on Davers's side against Manning in this dispute as in that of the convoys. The other aspects of the quarrel are unimportant. Very likely, as Estrada said, the clamour was raised by those merchants who had not succeeded in coming to terms with him, against the pernicious projects of those who had. Other sources of bitterness became mixed with the controversy; nothing definite can be extracted

---

[1] Trelawny to Newcastle, Nov. 15, 1745, C.O. 137/57; Jamaica Council Minutes, Nov. 11, 1745, C.O. 140/31.

from it, but I have the impression that on this issue, as on others, Davers supported the small traders against Trelawny who was in sympathy—his enemies said in partnership—with the big business firm of Manning and Ord.[1]

This venture seems to have come to no good in spite of the countenance with which it was started. Messrs. Lascelles and Maxwell, who did not think very well of the Havana Company or its credit, later advised a correspondent to have nothing to do with it.

'We know, that people of Jamaica have had contracts with the same Company, to supply it with Negroes and a proportion of flour, that Messrs. Manning and Ord have introduced many negroes into the Havannah, where we are informed, a huge balance is due to them, and although Manning has often gone there since the peace, he has not been able to recover payment.'[2]

They referred later to another misadventure.

'We remember an instance of the Governor of the Havannah executing a passport for the introduction of Negroes who died soon after, and some people from that island under the sanction thereof, sent down a cargo of slaves in the last war to the Havannah, where they were actually seized and condemned under pretence of an illicit trade. The owners of the cargo it's true appealed from the sentence to the Court of Spain, and after many years' trouble and a vast expence, obtained a reversal of the sentence, and an order for restitution from the Treasury, at the Havannah of the money arising from the sale of the cargo. There was some restitution made of money, but it fell short one third of the original cost and cargo of the charges. We have heard of other instances of the kind, and we think that no people of common prudence would ever be drawn into such a precarious trade however alluring the prospect may be made to them of great gain.'[3]

Although the English Government protected and encouraged the trade with the Spanish colonies, it forbade all intercourse with Spain in Europe. Philip V decreed the exclusion of English manufactures from all the Spanish dominions, no matter by

[1] Trelawny to Newcastle, Nov. 15, 1745, C.O. 137/57; Council Minutes of Jamaica, Nov. 11 and Dec. 2, 1745, May 14, 1746, C.O. 140/31; *Journals of the Assembly of Jamaica*, iv. 21–37.
[2] Lascelles and Maxwell to Dominick Lynch, Jan. 10, 1753, W. & G. vi.
[3] Same to Thomas Stevenson and Sons, May 6, 1758, W. & G. viii; see also Manning to Drake and Long, Feb. 21, 1753, S.P. 94/145; Estrada to Drake and Long, April 18, 1755, S.P. 94/148.

whom imported, and the English Parliament retaliated by an Act which contained some remarkable omissions; it only applied to Europe and only restrained imports. Even this limited prohibition was not universally held to be wise. Some pamphleteers defended it as a necessary reprisal for that of Spain, and argued that it would hurt Spain more than ourselves; most of our imports from Spain were luxuries, or they could be replaced from other countries, and if there was any article like dyestuffs which we must have from Spain, it should be excepted from the prohibition.[1] The commerce between Englishmen and Spaniards in Europe was thought to be equally advantageous to both; indeed, some maintained that we were Spain's best customer, and took off most of her wine, oil, and fruit. The smuggling trade which was carried on in America was advantageous to us alone. Therefore we should do Spain as much injury as possible by cutting off the former, and developing the latter in spite of her.[2] The author of the *Essay on the Causes of the Decline of the Foreign Trade* withered these calculations with a breath of reason. He showed that by prohibiting the use of Spanish goods we were only giving other nations an unnecessary monopoly against ourselves. For example, the price of Gallipoli oil had almost doubled since the prohibition.[3] If Spain had taken the lead in this absurd policy, she only hurt herself and there was no reason for us to follow her. Why tax ourselves unnecessarily in order to hurt the Spaniards, just at the time when we needed all our resources for carrying on the war?[4]

In spite of these arguments the Act stood, though it was not entirely in force. Both imports and exports to Spain sank to less than a fifth of their ordinary volume, but they did not cease altogether.[5] Moreover the King of Spain succeeded better in blocking our exports than the Parliament of England in restraining our imports. In 1740 and 1745 the latter exceeded the former—the only times that this happened for half a century. This appears to disprove the assumption that our trade was more necessary to Spain than hers was to us. It is not certain

---

[1] There was a special Act of Parliament in 1708 for allowing cochineal to be imported from Spain (*H.M.C., H. of L. MSS., N.S.*, viii. 557, 562, 592).

[2] *The Advantages and Disadvantages which will attend the Prohibition of the Merchandizes of Spain, impartially examin'd* (London, 1740).

[3] See the petitions in *C.J.*, Feb. 2, 8, and 9, 1742/3, xxiv. 401, 410, 413.

[4] In Lord Overstone's *Select Tracts*, pp. 263-5.

[5] See Sir Charles Whitworth's tables, *State of the Trade of Great Britain* (1776).

how much ought to be allowed for exports through neutrals. The Dutch and the French were the most likely to do this business for us. In fact our exports to France were considerably higher than usual between the outbreak of the Spanish and French wars; those to Holland rose little before 1743. Although the Spanish Government at first forbade the importation of English manu-factures in any kind of ships, there are evidences that the neutrals, especially the French, broke this rule quite early in the war. The Dutch shipping entered at Cadiz did not increase at all between 1738 and 1742, but the French almost doubled.[1] In 1742 the Spanish Ambassador announced verbally at The Hague that his Court would admit English goods in Dutch bottoms.[2] From that time the Dutch may have carried more English goods to Spain. Before the end of the war the pro-hibition of English goods in Spain was described as a dead letter.[3] However, it caused enough inconvenience to make the trading interest of England very anxious to remove it. Horace Walpole, who had introduced the Bill of 1739 for prohibiting the trade with Spain, moved in 1747 for its repeal; and though the proposal was not passed into law, the House of Commons requested the King to take off the prohibition as soon as Ferdi-nand VI removed it on his side.[4] The King of Spain declined to remove it, perhaps believing that the English were now more desirous than his own subjects for a renewal of commercial relations, and that the suspension would put more pressure on

[1] A.E. Mém. et Doc. Espagne, 82, f. 46.
[2] Trevor to Carteret, May 1, 1742, S.P. 84/397, f. 38.
[3] A.E. Mém. et Doc. Espagne, 82, f. 16.
[4] Walpole to George II, Jan. 19, 1746/7, in Coxe's *Horatio Walpole* (1802), p. 317; *C.J.*, Feb. 24, 1746/7, xxv. 299. According to a note in the *Gentleman's Magazine* (xvii. 76), the reason for the repeal was the smuggling of Spanish wines. The chief objection to it was the breach of the Navigation Acts which it must involve, by letting neutral ships carry on a trade which England did not allow in time of peace. It was hardly to be expected that Spain would let English ships enter her ports in time of war, even for the purpose of carrying off Spanish produce. In fact we learn that she did not, from the intercepted letter of Squillace to Moreno, Feb. 20, 1762 (Adm. 1/4125, no. 57). Squillace announced that the King of Spain would grant the people of the Canaries the same favours as in 1741 and 1743, namely the right to admit provisions and other necessaries of English manufacture in the ship-ping and for the account of neutrals but not of English subjects. At the end of 1746 the Canary merchants of London tried to obtain from the English and Spanish Courts permission to carry on this trade in English ships, but I do not think they succeeded (Add. MSS. 32709, f. 215). The New Englanders continued, however, to import Teneriffe wines disguised in Madeira pipes (see the case of the *Orotavo* dis-cussed by Weeden in his *Economic and Social History of New England*, p. 604).

England than on Spain.[1] The trade was not reopened until the preliminary treaty had been signed.

There was nearly an important exception in the last year of the war. Although there had been no great conquests or campaigns on the West African coast, the French slave-trade had been almost completely destroyed.[2] Perhaps the Spaniards could have relied on the Dutch or Portuguese, but these must have been insufficient, for in 1747 the Ministers of Ferdinand VI allowed Don Joseph Ruiz de Noriega to come to England in order to make a contract with the merchants for furnishing, 3,000 slaves at Cartagena. The English Government seems to have permitted one George Fryer to deal with him. Fryer, having made his bargain, petitioned for English passports to cover his ships. The South Sea Company suddenly intervened, urging that to relieve the Spanish colonies' need of slaves was to relieve the Spanish Government's need of peace. It complained also that if the markets were overstocked with slaves during the war, the renewal of its Assiento at the peace would be valueless. Plainly the Company hoped to make enormous profits by supplying the Spanish dominions with an article of which they had been more or less starved for nine years. It is not very clear what happened. Newcastle seems to have been impressed by the Company's arguments, and to have refused the passports. Fryer appears, however, to have begun to carry out the contract so far as it lay in him to do so; and it was the Spanish officers at Cartagena who put an end to the business by ordering his negroes back to Jamaica. He failed to get satisfaction out of Noriega, who died insolvent, so he petitioned the King of Spain after the peace and got permission to introduce the 3,000 negroes in his own name.[3]

The war of 1739 was unmistakably a war for trade. Its effect was to protect and increase certain branches of illicit commerce with the Spanish dominions. It may only have done this at the expense of other branches; moreover it would perhaps be too much to say that this was the only object for which the war was

[1] Le Man to Huescar, Feb. 16, 1748, Add. MSS. 32811, f. 169.
[2] Gaston Martin, *L'Ère des négriers* (Paris, 1931), pp. 225–9. The figures given for Nantes, the chief slave-trading port of France, are probably representative.
[3] Memorial of Noriega, Add. MSS. 32809, f. 55; Tabuerniga to Newcastle, July 15, 1747, f. 53; South Sea Company to Newcastle, May 21, vol. 25561, f. 101; Fryer to Stone, March 24, 1747/8, vol. 32714, f. 373; Bedford to Keene, April 10, 1749, S.P. 94/135; Keene to Bedford, Oct. 13, 1749, S.P. 94/136.

begun. However, it was certainly one of the objects; and the neutrals, who saw the result quite clearly, could hardly be expected, in that age of imperialist competition, to sit quiet and see the English merchants, supported by the English navy, run away with the most envied prize of America.

IV

FRENCH INTERVENTION, 1739–41

§ i. *French and Dutch Interests in Spanish America*

UP to this point the relations of England and Spain have been treated, for the sake of convenience, as if they had been isolated from the interference of any third power. In fact, however, the diplomacy of other courts was very much concerned with those relations and with their consequences. England and Spain became the centre of a storm which threatened to cover all western Europe. The Dutch Republic struggled with ingenuity and success to preserve its neutrality, but only an accident saved France from entering the war in the winter of 1740–1. After a very narrow escape, the English and French Governments kept up the appearance of peace at sea for the next few years, and did not come to an open rupture until 1744.

Any dispute which affected the Spanish West India trade interested all the commercial nations of Europe, particularly the French and Dutch. The settlement which had been internationally guaranteed at Utrecht was the foundation of the balance of power in America, and no innovation could be made by force or agreement without arousing the diplomacy of France and the Dutch Republic to vigilance and action.

The English Government tried to persuade them that they were as much interested as itself in securing the free navigation in America. That was only a half-hearted and unsuccessful hint to France, but to the States-General of the United Netherlands the argument was insistently and plausibly repeated. The difference is easily explained. Exemption from the right of search was not the most important interest that France had in the question, but it concerned the Dutch more closely.

The interests of the Dutch were nearly the same as those of the English. Curaçao was to them what Jamaica was to us, a base for smuggling into the Spanish colonies. It was an older settlement than Jamaica, and had never existed for any other purpose. Some merchants of Holland traded through Cadiz as well—so did some merchants of England; but the Dutch Government, like the English, identified itself with the American smuggling rather than the regular trade. The Spaniards treated the shipping of Curaçao in the same way as that of Jamaica, and its grievances were the same. The *Guarda-Costas* took Dutch vessels not only between Curaçao and the Spanish coasts, but on the way home to Europe. Vandermeer, the representative of the States-General at Madrid, had the same complaints to make as Keene, and they made a practice of supporting each other.[1]

A dispute had arisen between Spain and the States-General at the same time as that of England and Spain which ended in the War of Jenkins' Ear. Keene intended that both these negotiations should run the same course to the same result, and that Spain should be forced to yield to the simultaneous pressure of the two nations, whose unanimous firmness might compel what neither could obtain alone. With that view he stiffened Vandermeer's memorials, and drew attention, in their joint interview with La Quadra, to the menaces which he had himself inserted. He hoped the States-General would enforce their requests and commit themselves to acting with England, by arming some ships of war. He was disappointed. La Quadra, though firm, was not outrageous, and the wrath of the Dutch petered out in indecision, as it so often did.[2]

Keene was displeased; a few months later he was furious, for he believed that the States-General were about to give away England's case as well as their own, by offering to forbid their subjects to trade with the Spanish West Indies. He wrote on this subject a letter which is a remarkable example of national selfishness.

'The Republic, by going such lengths barely for beginning a negotiation, would throw away and deprive itself of one of the best and most essential means of carrying on and concluding a negotiation, that may have been successfully begun; and 2dly, by this previous step they would forestall and undersell, what His Majesty may possibly think proper to offer, according to the course and exigency of our negotiation; it being certain, that as France has made some tacite agreement on this head, and that if the States should be now so hastily coming into it, the Court of Spain would attempt to draw us into the same measures, merely out of the force of example, and not by an equivalent allowed us for a new precaution we have never, as yet, formally taken in favour of the

[1] Newcastle to Keene, Sept. 26, 1737, S.P. 94/129.
[2] Keene to Newcastle, June 23 and 30, July 7, Aug. 18, Dec. 15, 1738, S.P. 94/131.

exclusive commerce of Spain, and in terror of such of the King's subjects as should intrude upon it, in contravention to the treaties. I do not pretend, My Lord, to insinuate, that such measures may be agreeable to our constitution, or the present temper of our people. For let me suppose they are not, or ever will be so, yet it seems highly important to His Majesty's service, that the Dutch should not be so generous, at our expence, since no art will be able to convince these people of the sincerity of our intentions, if we do not consent to the same methods of prohibiting illicit commerce, that the popular Government of Holland would so hastily and roundly agree to. But if on the other hand, it should both be thought feasible and necessary . . . in that case, it will be impossible for us to get as much, or indeed any advantage from such a concession on our parts, as if we had the sole management of it, both as to the substance, the time, and the manner of making and agreeing to it.'[1]

In other words, the Dutch were to stand out when we stood out, and climb down when we climbed down. When we both stood out, they were to have at least half the danger and reproach; when we both climbed down, they were to have less than half the merit. That was the usual English conception of Anglo-Dutch co-operation, and it is no wonder that the States-General were beginning to shrink from such a leonine partnership.

Their controversy with Spain drifted gently to and fro without much definite direction—all Dutch negotiations of the time had a natural tendency to do that; and when the war broke out between England and Spain, the States-General were by no means implicated in it. Possibly there was a good reason why the question was a less pressing one for them. The Governors of Curaçao seem to have granted reprisals against the Spaniards; some of the smuggling vessels of that island went heavily armed, and in their encounters with the *Guarda-Costas* they gave as good as they got.[2] Perhaps this made the dispute harder to settle in the end, for it was complicated by counter-complaints of counter-depredations; but it was a reason why the States-General should be in no hurry to take the initiative of settling it, for their subjects could in some degree defend themselves.

[1] Keene to Newcastle, March 16, 1739, S.P. 94/133. The question is dealt with in an interesting letter from Trevor to Keene, of which there is a copy in the Waldegrave MSS. (April 9, N.S., 1739). Trevor thought the Dutch quite undetermined whether to throw in their lot with us or to make a better bargain for themselves; and if the latter, whether by *complaisant* or vigorous measures.

[2] See the Resolution of the States-General, Oct. 14, 1739, translated in S.P. 84/382, ff. 50–8; Trevor to Harrington, Nov. 6, 1739, ff. 76–7.

The situation of France was very different. There were, indeed, French colonies whose lawful navigation was exposed to the same dangers as the English. In particular, the French half of Hispaniola was very much in the same position as Jamaica. All its outward trade was forced to pass near the coasts of Spanish S. Domingo, and the shipping of the southern and western quarters might also find it convenient to go home round Cuba and through the Gulf of Florida.[1] Some Frenchmen admitted the existence of this difficulty, and their Government openly, though perfunctorily, recognized it, in order to claim the merit of impartiality by insisting that France was no advocate of the right of search.[2] The argument was even turned ingeniously against the English: France, it was said, being herself interested in the freedom of navigation, had a right to prevent the English smugglers from provoking the *Guarda-Costas* to an excessive severity; it was not fair that all trading and colonial powers should suffer for the abuses of one.[3]

The French colonies had also their smugglers to the Spanish West Indies. In the routine instructions to Governors and Intendants, the Minister of the Marine said that this trade was thought advantageous upon the whole, though it was liable to abuses. If it was properly carried on, it provided a market for rum and molasses, the by-products of sugar, which could not be used in France because they would compete with the brandy of the country; it might also be a means to dispose of some French manufactures. The return cargoes consisted of mules, which were indispensable to the production of sugar, and money, which alleviated the apparently incurable shortage of currency in the colonies. It was true that the colonists used the licences for this trade in very improper ways, by carrying sugar to the English and Dutch colonies and smuggling home slaves, but that could be prevented with care, and the trade was in itself worthy of encouragement.[4]

In spite, however, of this official benevolence, the trade did

[1] Most of the instances of this are in the French wars with England; they seem to be accounted for by the presence of English warships off Cape Nicola, rather than wind or weather.

[2] Fénelon to Amelot, Sept. 15, 1739, A.E. Hollande, 433; Silhouette to Amelot, Dec. 24, 1739, A.E. Angleterre, 405, ff. 360 et seqq.; A.E. Mém. et Doc. Angleterre, 9, f. 104.

[3] Conversation of Fleury, reported by Van Hoey to States-General, Sept. 10, 1740, copy in A.E. Hollande, 436.

[4] Instructions to Ranché, Intendant of the Windward Islands, Jan. 22, 1744,

not flourish like that of Curaçao and Jamaica. It is difficult to see why. No French colony was so admirably situated for smuggling as Jamaica or even Curaçao; but St. Louis, on the south side of French St. Domingue, ought to have been well enough placed, and Martinique was not too far to windward. There was no lack of merchants with capital and ability; for the *commissionnaires* of Martinique were at least as active and powerful as those of any English island except Jamaica. Martinique had plenty of seamen and shipping, and what trade was done between the French and Spanish colonies, mostly centred there. In St. Domingue the men and capital were probably all employed in the immense task of developing the plantations.

Perhaps the comparative failure of the French in the smuggling trade is best accounted for by supposing that they were undersold by the Dutch and English; they seem to have preferred the Cadiz trade, which was all based on calculations for keeping up prices, to the freer competition of the speculative smugglers, who were often in danger of overdoing their markets or suffering by the arrivals of galleons and *flotas*. One or two French writers, drawing, as it would seem, a bow at a venture, suggested that the French traders demanded higher profits than the English, who would not only take less, but spared out of their gains enough to bribe the Spanish Governors more handsomely than their rivals.[1] This was probably the wrong way of putting the facts; it was not so much a love of excessive profit as the high overhead charges which hindered the French competitor. French shipping seems to have been less cheaply navigated than English, and if, as the French ambassador told Keene, it was heavier armed and manned in this trade, the difference in favour of the English must have been accentuated, especially as the English were sometimes saved by convoys from the counterbalancing risks of the *Guarda-Costas*. Perhaps the French traders and manufacturers at home had smaller resources than the English; but the returns through Cadiz were so slow that at least the same capital must have been necessary to procure the same profits as in the smuggling trade, and on a smaller volume of business.

Whatever the reasons, the French traders and the French

A.N. Colonies B. 78; to Conflans, Governor of St. Domingue, July 16, 1747, B 85; Machault to Vaudreuil and Laporte-Lalanne, Jan. 31, 1755, B 101.

[1] A.E. Mém. et Doc. France, 2009, 'Annotations', ff. 171 et seqq.; 'Mémoire sur l'Amérique', A.E. Mém. et Doc. France, 2008, f. 82.

Government identified themselves with the trade of the galleons and *flotas* rather than that of the American colonies; their interest in the controversy with Spain was therefore not the same as that of England and Holland. They were certainly not eager to yield to the Spanish right of search; but they considered the prevention of the English and Dutch smuggling to be more important, and as they thought the entire abolition of the right of search would make that impossible, they must either find a middle way or give up the smaller interest for the greater.[1] The French ambassador at Madrid seldom complained of seizures in American waters—partly, as he said, because the French ships, like the Dutch, were better armed than ours and could look after themselves; partly because the French Government could easier afford to ignore complaints which would have made an intolerable noise in England.[2] His business consisted rather in getting grievances redressed in the Cadiz trade.

The two unchanging objects of French commercial diplomacy were to have the *indulto* fixed and to get permission to export coin from Spain. One of the things that most oppressed the shippers on the galleons and *flotas* was the arbitrary *indulto*, a duty which was levied at whatever rate the King of Spain chose to name. Like most Spanish taxes which were not tied down by law or treaty, it showed a certain alacrity in rising. The more it rose, the more it added to the already insupportable burden which the Cadiz trader had to bear, and offered, in effect, a premium to the smugglers in America.[3] The King of Spain could not afford to see this; even at the beginning of the war with England, when he could not conceal his need of a French alliance, he said he would rather go without it than give up the privilege of raising the *indulto* upon an emergency.[4] The other grievance—the prohibition of exporting bullion—was one which interested not only the nations engaged directly or

[1] As one anonymous memorialist puts it, 'we must take care not to sacrifice our own rights while sacrificing those of the English' (A.E. Mém. et Doc. Angleterre, 9, f. 104); see also Silhouette to Amelot, March 12 and 31, 1740, A.E. Angleterre, 407, ff. 187–8, 252.

[2] Keene to Newcastle, Dec. 13, 1737, S.P. 94/128; Vaulgrenant may have been speaking truth in his time, but during the war his successor Vauréal made several demands for restitution of ships seized in America.

[3] The Deputies of the French Conseil de Commerce said, in a *mémoire* which should be dated, I think, about 1744, that the duties amounted to about 70 per cent. of the value of the goods (A.E. Mém. et Doc. France, 2009, f. 91).

[4] Baudrillart, *Philippe V et la Cour de France*, iv. 538, 547.

indirectly in the Spanish American commerce, but all those that traded to Spain at all. It was the European counterpart to that system which treated all Spanish coin on board foreign ships as contraband. It had now subsisted so long that a thorough reformation could hardly be hoped for; and Keene would rather procure individual orders for exemption than attack the general principle.[1]

For these reasons, the English Government could not hope for more than a perfunctory support from France.

In November 1737 the French Prime Minister, Cardinal Fleury, excused himself, upon various pretexts, from joining his influence to those of England and the Dutch Republic in order to procure satisfaction for the violences of the *Guarda-Costas*. Maurepas affected to wish it, and Fleury himself regarded the depredations as a grievance; but he would only promise that Vaulgrenant should hold the same language as Keene and Vandermeer, though not in conjunction with them.[2]

Moreover, even if the interests of France had coincided with those of England, the profits of neutrality would have tempted her to keep out of the quarrel. In fact the French traders welcomed the war between England and Spain as an occasion to substitute their own manufactures for the English, to give the Spanish Americans a permanent taste for French goods, and to cultivate the art of imitating such English goods as were obviously indispensable.[3]

Keene had to reckon with a very determined and dangerous opposition from the French ambassador. For besides her commercial interests in the matter, which were opposite to those of England, France had political reasons for supporting Spain. She had endured a terrible war for the sake of the Bourbon succession, and she was not willing to lose the fruit of her blood and treasure. There were certainly times after the Peace of Utrecht when family quarrels seemed to stultify family ambitions, and others when Elisabeth Farnese's insatiable appetite for Italian duchies rendered Spain a diplomatic liability to France rather than an asset. There was no love lost between her and Cardinal Fleury; she taxed him with treachery and he less openly accused her of extravagance. But when it came to

---

[1] A.E. Mém. et Doc. Espagne, 80, ff. 111 et seqq., 'Observations' of 1749 or 1750.
[2] Waldegrave to Keene, Nov. 18 and 20, N.S., 1737, Waldegrave MSS.
[3] A.E. Mém. et Doc. France, 2007, ff. 105 et seqq.

the point, France could hardly be expected to stand by and see Spain the victim of a serious and successful attack by England, which might compel her to make undesirable concessions. There was also a slight and almost negligible danger that the Queen of Spain, disappointed in her expectation of help from France, would be glad to make peace with her open enemies at the expense of French commerce. This was hardly possible, and need not have been considered at all if she had not been notoriously vindictive and reckless when she was crossed, and rebounded already into one or two curious alliances.[1]

Lastly, there were influences which might drive Fleury into a war with England, quite apart from the merits or importance of the Spanish dispute. Maurepas, the Secretary for the Marine and Colonies, was a lifelong enemy of England; and as he was almost the only French Minister who was credited with a will of his own not entirely subservient to Fleury's, his animosity was the more to be feared.

§ ii. *English Opinion on the Prospect of French Intervention*

The question before Walpole and Newcastle was, therefore, whether France would support Spain outright or try to find a middle way between the English and Spanish pretensions, presumably a profitable one for herself and inclining to the advantage rather of Spain than of England.

Lord Waldegrave, our representative at the French Court, did not quite know what to make of Fleury's attitude. He knew from May 1738 that the Spanish ambassador, La Mina, was moving heaven and earth to bring about an alliance between the two Bourbon courts; but Fleury often protested that he was bound by no engagements to Spain and had given no assurances or encouragement to La Mina, whom he disliked exceedingly. Waldegrave was never quite sure whether he believed Fleury's word. He thought on the whole that France would maintain her neutrality as long as Fleury lived; but how long would that be? Fleury was a very old man, and subject to fainting-fits; nobody would have prophesied that he would keep his hold on life and power until the beginning of 1743. By August 1738 Waldegrave had convinced himself that 'France will be against us, especially if the Card[1] dies, and his life grows worse and

[1] Cambis to Amelot, Sept. 14, 1739, A.E. Angleterre, 405, f. 148; Silhouette to Amelot, Dec. 24, 1739, f. 366.

worse every hour'. For some months longer, in spite of La Mina's triumphant boasting, Waldegrave, Keene, and their masters continued to pray for the Cardinal's health. Waldegrave would not 'insinuate as if he thought we were likely to receive any advantage from the real friendship of this Court towards us', and 'should be sorry to try how far they might be pushed to the contrary', but hoped that so long as the Cardinal lived, we should see no experiments of that nature. But at the beginning of February 1739 there were rumours of a double marriage between the royal houses of France and Spain. Waldegrave had to acknowledge that 'things were going into their old channel', that is to say, that the Bourbon alliance was being revived, and that 'tho' the Card[l] dos not love the Queen of Spain better than heretofore, the name of Bourbon makes him overlook all private grudges'.[1]

The English Ministers soon made up their minds to expect no good from Fleury. Their suspicions were justified, but not exactly as they conceived them; for though negotiations for a treaty of alliance were carried on between Spain and France from the summer of 1738, and with some prospect of success, they do not seem to have had any direct influence on the course of the dispute with England. So far from it, that the Court of Spain seems to have taken all its decisive steps towards war at moments when the hope of concluding the alliance at once were dimmest, and to have shown the greatest disposition to accommodate matters with England when her negotiation with France seemed most forward. The Convention of January 1739, which might have led to a settlement of the controversy over the right of search, was made at a time when Fleury seemed likely to come to terms quickly; it was actually concealed from him in the hope that before it was known, the treaty of alliance between Spain and France might proceed to a conclusion. On the other hand, Villarias's serious words to Keene in April 1739, and his determination not to pay the £95,000, coincided with stoppages in the discussions between Spain and France.

There were reasons for these syncopations in the rhythm of Spanish diplomacy. Elisabeth Farnese was bargaining twice as hard with her friends as with her enemies. She hoped to

---

[1] Waldegrave to Keene, May 13, June 6, July 1, 14, 21, and 28, Aug. 11 and 28, Sept. 2 and 13, Oct. 27, Nov. 28, N.S., 1738; Feb. 3, June 22 and 27, N.S., 1739, Waldegrave MSS.

carry the day by a mere appeal to the sentimental cant of kinship which the rulers of the House of Bourbon employed when they wanted each other's help for nothing. She presumed, too, that when France saw Spain in difficulties, she must come to her help without being paid for it; with this view, she naturally hastened to get into the difficulties as soon as she could. Fleury seems to have acknowledged in his heart the force of this reasoning; he therefore tried to hold her back until he could make his market of her. He shrank from giving her *carte blanche*, knowing that her eyes were really set on Italy and that she could hardly obtain all she wanted without a general European war, which he was determined to avoid; and even against England she formed such designs as the recovery of Georgia, Gibraltar, and Minorca, for which he was unwilling to promise the help of France in all cases. Besides, he meant to be paid for the treaty of alliance by a treaty of commerce, and insisted on having them concluded to his satisfaction on the same day.[1] If there was to be a war between Spain and England, which would annul the commercial treaties between them, France would find an excellent occasion for transferring some of the English privileges to herself and obtaining other new ones without having to let Spain impart them to her rivals. Fleury did not mean to lose this opportunity; Spain, however, intended to have the alliance at once and postpone the commercial concessions to the Greek Kalends. Whenever she condescended to discuss them, she made so many difficulties as to justify her contention that the alliance could not wait for their settlement.[2]

The English Ministers could not see all this; with a commonplace judgement of his character, they soon gave Fleury credit for too much villainy and determination, and too little complication. After their eyes were opened to his dealings with Spain, they suspected him of having engineered the crisis, when he had really done little more than profit by it. They did not understand that he could hardly be said to desire an English war, or even a Spanish alliance, as an end in itself. Besides, they only knew the more alarming facts, without any of the reassuring difficulties. It happened that most of the letters

[1] Instructions to La Marck, French ambassador in Spain, Sept. 14, 1738, *Recueil des Instructions, Espagne*, iii. 201-3.
[2] This summary of the relations between Spain and France is drawn from the admirable account given by Mgr Baudrillart, op. cit. iv. 453-562.

which they intercepted were those of the over-confident La Mina, all hopes and no doubts.[1] Even Keene, who might have judged better, supposed that the double marriage treaty would give France a hold over Spain (whereas Elisabeth Farnese meant it to give Spain a hold over France), and that Fleury would use that hold to stiffen Spain's resistance to England. In fact Fleury did nothing of the kind for the next few months.[2]

The news of the double marriage reached England in time for the debates on the Convention, and may have been one of the things which determined Newcastle to leave Haddock's force on the Spanish coasts after all. A little while later, Newcastle got hold of some papers which purported to be drafts of the new treaty of alliance. He jumped to the conclusion that those treaties would very soon be signed, and that they explained the unusual obstinacy which La Quadra had lately shown, and his delay in paying the £95,000.[3]

England had therefore to make up her mind whether she would fight France as well as Spain, or yield to the combination. This choice had been discussed in public ever since the Spanish crisis had begun. Sir Robert Walpole and his supporters in the Cabinet had made no secret of their opinion that the strongest reason against precipitate measures with Spain was the unfavourable situation of England in European diplomacy. Some powers were likely to intervene against us, and none could certainly be expected to support us. This was a delicate and disagreeable argument for Walpole to urge, for the lack of allies was attributed to his own and his brother's policy. Their

---

[1] The most alarming of these intercepts were one of June 2, 1738, forwarded by Keene to Newcastle, Aug. 2, and one of Sept. 8, forwarded Oct. 13, S.P. 94/131. La Mina was the Spanish ambassador in Paris.

[2] Keene to Newcastle, April 24, 1739 (most private), S.P. 94/133. Fleury had other enemies at home who made criticisms equally ill informed. The Marquis d'Argenson taxed him with having got himself into Elisabeth Farnese's pocket by the Bourbon marriages, and attributed all the uppishness of Spain since their announcement, to assurance of French support. The Court of Spain may have felt such certainty, but not through any fault of Fleury. D'Argenson was a disciple of Chauvelin, Fleury's disgraced rival; he exaggerated the fatal results of the intimacy with Spain, in order to point the moral that Fleury ought not to have allowed her to be France's only ally; and the attitude towards Spain which he recommended was one which Fleury was trying hard to keep up (d'Argenson, *Journal et Mémoires*, ed. Rathery, 1859, ii. 294, 303–4).

[3] Newcastle to Keene (private and particular), May 8, 1739, S.P. 94/134; Hardwicke to Newcastle, April 26, 1739, Add. MSS. 32692, f. 53; Horace Walpole to Trevor, March 16, April 17, June 1, 1739, *H.M.C. XIVth Report*, App. IX, pp. 27, 28, 32.

neutrality in the War of the Polish Succession was especially criticized; it had offended our traditional friend, Austria, and earned no real gratitude from our traditional enemy, France. Walpole might urge that whatever our recent relations with Austria had been, we could hardly expect much support from her at present, for she was engaged by a disastrous war with the Turk; but that was small comfort, though it might be some justification, and did not affect the question whether France would take part in the war.[1]

The Government did not push its argument so far as to recommend submitting to Spain; it only pleaded for delay and caution. Since hardly any powers in Europe were prejudiced in our favour, we must be careful to conduct our case so as to convince the world that we only wanted to secure our lawful rights, not to make new conquests in Spanish America or force Spain to grant us a free trade to her colonies. If once the other trading nations should begin to fear for the equilibrium established by the peace of Utrecht, they would visit heavy displeasure on the first power to disturb it. These arguments were never better put than in a speech attributed to Newcastle.

'This, my Lords, has always been looked upon as a necessary step towards preventing any one nation in Europe from becoming too rich and too powerful for the rest; and the preserving the sole right of navigation and commerce to and from the Spanish settlements in America, to the Spaniards themselves, was not the effect so much of the Spanish policy, as of the jealousy which the powers of Europe entertained among themselves, lest any other should acquire too great a property in that valuable branch of commerce. They knew that while the treasures of the Indies were the property of the Spaniards, or at least while they centred in Spain, that sooner or later their subjects must have a proportionable share; because that monarchy is destitute of many of the advantages, which the other nations of Europe enjoy, from their manufactures and the industry of their inhabitants; and that, consequently, it was not in the power of the Spaniards, let them have never such an aspiring and politic prince at their head, to monopolize these treasures. Whereas, should too large a share of them come into the hands of any other nation in Europe, whose situation, power or trade, render them perhaps already formidable to their neighbours, they might be

---

[1] *Parl. Hist.* x. 693 (Walpole), 670 (Pulteney), 708 (Henry Pelham), 722 (Wyndham), 1254–5 (H. Walpole), 1268 (Sanderson); xi. 635 (Carteret), 645 (Newcastle), 1067 (Carteret), 1095 (Newcastle), 1270 (Pulteney).

employed to purposes inconsistent with the peace of Europe, and which might one day prove fatal to the balance of power, that ought to subsist amongst her several princes. In such a case there is no doubt but that a formidable alliance would be made against the power thus aspiring; and should the differences at last come to be made up by a treaty, it would be found that the most probable way to secure the general peace, is to suffer the Spaniards to remain in the same situation, as to their American settlements, they are now in.'[1]

The Opposition took two lines of argument which led to one conclusion. Some of them asserted that we could impose on France by bold action against Spain, and intimidate her into putting pressure upon Spain to yield. They also pointed out that France was concerned, like ourselves, to resist the right of search, and that she would have a strong inducement to keep quiet, from the profits which neutral traders would naturally make out of a war. In fact whatever we did, France would not interfere, therefore we ought to do what was right in our own eyes.[2] Her intervention was said to be a bugbear of Walpole's; he was compared to a spider, frightening his fellow spiders with the dreadful threat of an invasion of flies.[3] This was unjust at least to his sincerity; he really feared a French invasion, because he really feared a restoration of the Pretender. Most of his contemporaries thought one bogy as unreal as the other, and could not imagine that he believed in either; but it appears more likely that he earnestly believed in both.

Others treated French intervention as probable, but indifferent. Argyll announced that we could fight all the fleets of the world and should therefore dictate to all the trading countries; Pitt, with the oratory of theatrical jingoism, played upon the perennial hatred against the whole House of Bourbon. If France defended Spain against a cause so righteous as the liberty of navigation, then she declared that we could not have justice; and against such a denial of justice there was no remedy but war, let the success be what it might. If we abstained from pressing Spain out of deference to France, we allowed her to

[1] *Parl. Hist.* x. 772. The same arguments are in Walpole's second speech on the Convention, p. 1313. Perhaps I may here excuse my frequent references to the Parliamentary debates. The attributions of the speeches are not much to be relied upon, but whoever wrote or spoke them, they are for the most part far better argued than the average pamphlet or newspaper article.

[2] Ibid. 780 (Chesterfield), 849 (Pulteney); xi. 252 (Wyndham).

[3] 'Extrait d'une lettre de Londres', A.E. Angleterre, 409, f. 16.

prescribe our conduct and keep us in vassalage.[1] Nor did these orators profess to believe that a French war would add much to the difficulties of the Government; for the trade and therefore the taxes of France as well as Spain would be diminished by the interception of the treasure from Mexico and Peru. Wyndham appeared to think that the boldest way with France was the best; let her declare herself, even if it be against us, for we had nothing to gain from her false friendship and little to lose by her enmity. This is only one of many examples of the doctrine that neutrals are worse than open enemies.[2]

Of course this was extravagant rhetoric, but it helps to explain why those who had made up their minds to fight Spain were quite ready to fight France also. So successful was the campaign, and so much did the country believe that a war with France was unavoidable, that as soon as the first orders were gone out for hostilities against Spain, the provinces were filled with rumours that the Pretender had already landed with a French force.[3] Even the Government had come to believe what the Opposition declared. Whatever arguments Walpole and Newcastle may have used a year ago, they too were convinced by the Bourbon marriage and the discovery of the Franco-Spanish treaties, that if they were to enforce the nation's claim against Spain they must reckon with the very likely risk of French intervention. That risk they determined to take; for which reason it had very little deterrent effect upon them after the war was begun.[4]

§ iii. *Neutral Rights; the 'Azogues'*

The conduct of the war was almost certain to raise a more definite question. How could England put pressure upon Spain without injury to the real or supposed interests of France? The two easiest and most obvious ways of reducing Spain to submission were to conquer her colonies and intercept her treasure-fleets. But the colonies could not be conquered, or at any rate

---

[1] *Parl. Hist.* x. 848 (Pulteney), 985 (Wyndham), 1136 (Argyll), 1185 (Chesterfield), 1281 (Pitt); *French Counsels Destructive to Great Britain* (London, 1740); *French Influence upon English Counsels Demonstrated* (London, 1740).

[2] *Parl. Hist.* x. 986.

[3] De Vismes to Amelot, June 25, N.S., 1739, A.E. Angleterre, 404, f. 386.

[4] Newcastle to Waldegrave, June 8, O.S., 1739, S.P. 78/220, ff. 233–7. But the only thing that made Newcastle somewhat afraid of declaring war in October was the fear that France might prove to be formally engaged to defend Spain in such a case. (Stone to Waldegrave, Oct. 4, 1739, Add. MSS. 32801, f. 290.)

annexed, without upsetting the equilibrium of 1713, and the treasure-fleets could not be seized without involving the Government in disputes over neutral property. Very little of the cargoes on board the galleons and *flotas* belonged to Spaniards, and most of it was thought to be French property; the exact proportion cannot be known, but it was estimated as high as seven-ninths and as low as three-fifths. There was much debate in Parliament, before the war broke out, whether this time-honoured method of attack could prudently be employed. The difficulty was heightened by Pulteney's Bill of 1738 for giving the whole property of prizes to the captors. It would have prevented the Government from restoring at discretion neutral cargoes found in enemy ships.

The international law of the time, and our treaties with France in particular, unquestionably recognized the principle that neutral property in enemy ships was lawful prize. Besides, the trade of foreigners to the Spanish colonies was all carried on and registered in the name of Spaniards, so that even the cargoes, as well as the vessels, were technically Spanish. More-over, this trade might be said to be contrary to the Treaty of Utrecht, by which the King of Spain bound himself not to let foreigners trade directly or indirectly to his colonies. If France complained of the Jamaica smugglers, England might retort that the trade through Cadiz was no more lawful, and demand an inquiry into its abuses, which would show that the French had contravened the Treaty of Utrecht quite as much as the English.[1] Opposition orators made the most of this point; but, as Bladen replied, it might be very undiplomatic to insist on the law in a case of this kind. French merchants and Dutch insurers would complain, and our attitude, however righteous, would prejudice their governments against us.[2] The difficulty might take another form; the French fleet might be sent to escort the *flota* out from Cadiz, and bring back the galleons as well. Here again France might be in the wrong, for the right of neutral warships to convoy enemy trade was far from established. That would not be the point, since the matter was one of politics rather than law, and the question to be decided was

---

[1] *Parl. Hist.* x. 855 (Pulteney), 985–6 (Wyndham), 1193 (Hervey), 1213 (Bathurst), 1409 (Carteret); xi. 840 (Carteret).

[2] Ibid. x. 838 (Coster), 839 (Bladen); Bladen to Harrington, June 12, 1739, Add. MSS. 32694, f. 21.

not whether France would intervene justly, but whether she would intervene at all.

The debates of 1738 were academic, for Pulteney's Bill did not pass. Next year, as soon as the Government gave orders for reprisals, the issue became an immediate one. The *azogues* were at sea on their way home from Vera Cruz. They carried rich cargoes of silver, for the account of the French merchants and the King of Spain, and their seizure would be a small triumph which the hard-pressed Ministry of Walpole could not afford to lose. Without hesitation it took all possible measures to intercept them. Walpole declared publicly that he hoped to see them brought into the Thames, thus announcing that he did not intend to be frustrated in his warlike designs by the fear of France.

Fleury took the question of the *azogues* very seriously.[1] He expostulated strongly to Waldegrave, the English ambassador, upon the privileged or international character of the Spanish treasure-ships; all nations were interested in them, and the Court of Spain itself regarded their cargoes as a *depositum*, not subject to retaliation for national wrongs.[2] This was special pleading for a trade which had no higher title than that of collusion; Fleury would have done better to insist more on the argument that neutral property could not be seized without any declaration of war.[3] Waldegrave asked him how we could do ourselves justice upon Spain if we were not to attack the only kind of shipping whose loss would affect her seriously. If we must keep our hands off it, we must endure whatever injuries Spain pleased to put upon us. Walpole and Newcastle approved and adopted this argument, which had until lately been the undisputed property of the Opposition.

[1] The chief English spy in France—an unreliable twaddler to be sure, though he was a high official in the Foreign Office—even reported on August 8 that Fleury had sent word to the Court of Spain that the seizure of the *azogues* would be a *casus belli* between France and England (intelligence forwarded by Waldegrave to New-castle, Aug. 8, N.s., 1739, Add. MSS. 32801, f. 172). Amelot had in fact written to La Marck that Fleury would tell Waldegrave that such seizure would amount to a war (Baudrillart, op. cit., iv. 531), but one cannot gather anything of the kind from the much milder language reported by Waldegrave. Perhaps this is one of the cases in which his lazy confidence in Fleury's friendship led him to misunder-stand or misrepresent his words.

[2] Waldegrave to Newcastle, July 22, Aug. 15, 1739, S.P. 78/221, ff. 9, 80.

[3] He did use it a few weeks later. It was chiefly because the English Government recognized this difficulty that it converted the reprisals into a declared war in October 1739 (Horace Walpole to Trevor, Oct. 26, 1739, *H.M.C. XIVth Report*, App. IX, p. 35).

Walpole expressed no surprise at Fleury's language, and hoped to gain time by general promises of justice and favour to French subjects; but he would not allow the naval operations of the Government to be hindered by sacrifices to a precarious neutrality. Newcastle adopted a more definite suggestion which had lately been made by his colleague Harrington, and in Parliament by Carteret. Waldegrave was empowered to promise that the King should restore any proved French property that might be taken on the *azogues*, if the owners would pay him the *indulto* which they would have paid to the King of Spain, and if the French Government would undertake to remain entirely neutral (which Newcastle did not believe it would do). He was only to make this offer if he was sure that the *azogues* were the most important consideration in Fleury's eyes. Newcastle believed that they were not; but it appears from a letter of Amelot, the French Foreign Minister, to La Marck that this might have been an acceptable suggestion, and that France might on these terms have declined to take up arms on behalf of Philip V.[1] Waldegrave withheld the suggestion, contenting himself with vague and banal promises, and Fleury continued to ask him to promise that we should not take the *azogues* at all.[2] The danger of a serious dispute on this subject was soon afterwards removed by the unexpected appearance of the *azogues* in the port of Santander, where no English cruisers were waiting for them. The incident therefore ended ridiculously for England, but it shows the Government unwilling to give itself very much trouble to avoid a rupture with France.

The English Government believed at the beginning of 1740 that a French squadron would accompany the *flota* from Cadiz to America, and ordered Haddock to attack it, convoy and all, if he should find himself strong enough, or to send word to Vernon in order that he might do so in America.[3] However,

---

[1] Baudrillart, op. cit., iv. 531.

[2] Waldegrave to Newcastle, July 22 and Aug. 15, 1739; Newcastle to Waldegrave (most secret), July 27, S.P. 78/221, ff. 9, 49, 80; *Parl. Hist.* x. 1409 (Carteret); Newcastle to Hardwicke, Aug. 12, 1739, Add. MSS. 35406, f. 138.

[3] Norris's diary, Feb. 4, 1739/40, Add. MSS. 28132, f. 145. There must, however, have been some doubts of the propriety of intercepting the Spanish fleets under French convoy, for Wager made a note, on November 6, 1739, from which it appears that he or some of his colleagues thought it might be imprudent to attack the galleons if French warships should escort them out of Cartagena (Vernon-Wager MSS., Library of Congress. See also Waldegrave to Newcastle (most secret), Aug. 15, 1739, Waldegrave MSS.).

the neutrality of the treasure-fleets did not give any more trouble in this war, for the fleets themselves were almost completely paralysed by the danger of moving. Some French warships actually convoyed a sort of *flota* from Vera Cruz in 1745, but France was by that time as much a belligerent as Spain. In fact all the other disputes of international law, to which this war and the next gave rise, turned rather on enemy goods in neutral ships.

§ iv. *Proposals of Mediation, and Negotiations in Holland*

France and England still had to face the other and more important question—that of the equilibrium of Utrecht and the conquests in Spanish America. But for some time before it came to an issue, the possibilities of French mediation took up the foreground of the picture.

Fleury did not make much attempt at offering mediation by himself. He knew very well that he was suspected of partiality to Spain, and that his proposals would be received with caution.[1] However, he plucked up his courage to suggest in August 1739 an expedient which would have gained a little time for discussion. Spain should pay over the £95,000 into the hands of a third party, and Haddock should withdraw from the Mediterranean. This idea seems to have come to him from Count Lynden, a Dutch politician; he made a curious use of it. He sent word to The Hague that these terms could not possibly satisfy Spain, and that the English must withdraw not only Haddock but the reinforcements from Jamaica and Georgia as well; yet at the same time he entirely adopted the original suggestion behind the backs of the Dutch.[2] Newcastle, however, would not hear of this compromise; indeed it would only have served for a breathing-space, and offered no basis of final settlement.[3] If Fleury had now made up his mind to the Spanish alliance, a breathing-space was all he wanted, in order to make himself indispensable to Spain and to bargain for the services he should otherwise have to give perforce.

[1] Amelot to Fénelon, Aug. 3, 1739, A.E. Hollande, 433; Silhouette to Amelot, Nov. 26, 1739, A.E. Angleterre, 405, f. 287.
[2] Fénelon to Amelot, July 28, 1739, A.E. Hollande, 433; Amelot to Fénelon, Aug. 3, 1739, ibid.
[3] It had also the disadvantage that it gave the Dutch an excuse for doing nothing to help us or defend themselves. (Horace Walpole to Waldegrave, Sept. 8 and Oct. 1, 1739, Waldegrave MSS.)

Fleury never openly proposed a definite plan for accommodating the disputes of England and Spain; it is not certain what
terms he would have suggested.[1] He did not wish to mediate
alone; he would rather act jointly with the States-General, in
order to render his suggestions acceptable to the English Ministry, and to prevent it from leading the Dutch into something
more dangerous than mediation, namely a war with Spain.

Holland was the great battleground of English and French
diplomacy in these years. England might appeal to the memory
of William III and Marlborough, in whose days the Dutch
Republic had been unequivocally her ally and the enemy of
France; but those expensive glories could not be revived.
Lesser men now steered an uneasy course, not exactly mid-
way between the two great powers, but so as to incline on
the whole to England without incurring the anger of France.
The Stadhouder party, strongest in the smaller provinces, in the
country districts of the greater ones, and in the mob of the
towns, was still devoted to England. It received some of its
little influence—for the Stadhouderate was in abeyance—from
the marriage of the Prince of Orange with George II's eldest
daughter. There was another party, apparently much smaller,
which was definitely pro-French, because it feared a reinstate-
ment of the Stadhouder. This party was particularly afraid of
every kind of war, because it reasoned rightly that military
danger was the likeliest thing to restore the Stadhouder to his
powers. Most Dutchmen seem to have been moderate Republi-
cans, drifting between the two parties and hoping that Europe
would never fall into such troubles as would make it necessary
for them to choose one side or the other.

Fear played a great part in the determination of Dutch policy;
fear of an invasion by land from France, and of a suspension of Dutch navigation by England. These threats antago-
nized as much as they intimidated the interests to which they
were addressed. It was the landed classes and the provinces

---

[1] There are many memoranda on this subject in the archives of the French
Foreign Office: Silhouette to Amelot, Dec. 24, 1739, A.E. Angleterre, 405, ff. 360
et seqq.; March 12, 1740, vol. 407, ff. 180 et seqq.; 'Réflexions sur les differens de
l'Angleterre et l'Espagne', A.E. Mém. et Doc. Angleterre, 9, ff. 104 et seqq.;
'Plan de Negotiation', ff. 111 et seqq.; 'Observations sur la liberté de la Navigation', ff. 122 et seqq.; 'Mémoire sur la liberté de la navigation dans les mers des
Indes occidentales', A.E. Mém. et Doc. Espagne, 82, ff. 116 et seqq.; Mémoire
annexed to Mirepoix's Instructions, 1749, A.E. Mém. et Doc. Angleterre, 41, ff. 188
et seqq.

most exposed to a land war which were most anti-French, while the merchants were at least very jealous of England, though their hostility was somewhat mollified by their heavy investments in English funds. Besides, the shipping and trading interests were open to the highest bidder. England had little of her own to offer them, for the Navigation Acts excluded them from some important branches of her carrying trade. The most she could do was to help them to conquer some valuable privilege from France and Spain, as she had done in the War of the Spanish Succession. Spain was so intractably obstinate that nothing was to be expected of her, but France could prevent England from earning gratitude at her expense, and procure it for herself, by concessions to the long-standing ambitions of Dutch traders, especially in the fishery. She did so more than once when she found herself badly in need of Dutch favour; and it happened that, at the very moment when the war between England and Spain began, she was dangling before the noses of the States-General a nearly completed treaty of commerce. Fleury and his representative at The Hague proposed to make the fullest use of it, in order to keep them in a respectful suspense.[1]

Horace Walpole, the Prime Minister's brother, was titular Ambassador at The Hague and had obtained a considerable influence in Dutch politics. He had been on the point of retiring, but was now hurried off for a last visit, to procure a declaration of war against Spain, or at least a large increase of land and sea forces which might lead the States-General to that conclusion down the path of embarrassing inquiries and yet more disagreeable explanations. It became the English policy, in the later years of the struggle with France, to encourage the Dutch to increase their army but not their navy, because the former was calculated to annoy France and could be used against her, while the latter was even more likely to be directed against England. At present, however, this distinction was not perceived, and as the Dutch could only attack Spain by sea, England regarded an increase of their fleet as a favourable symptom. In fact, Horace Walpole was a little put out by the project of increasing the land forces at this moment, because though excellent in itself it would clog and retard the more important proposal of new warships.[2]

[1] Fénelon to Amelot, July 2, 1739, A.E. Hollande, 433.
[2] Horace Walpole to Harrington, Aug. 18, 1739, S.P. 84/381, f. 68.

He took with him a somewhat threadbare outfit of ready-made arguments. He pointed out the parallel between the interests of the two nations, and their grievances against Spain. Nothing but force, he said, could make Spain listen to reason; the Dutch would find it out when they had exhausted in vain all the recourses of diplomacy.[1] He used some documents from the controversy of Keene and La Quadra, which illustrated Spain's extravagant claims to sovereignty in the American seas. He received a little help here from the imprudent Marquis of St. Gil, the Spanish Ambassador, who would not be restrained by his French colleague from publishing a justification which asserted those claims. Yet though Walpole's arguments made a certain impression, and the augmentation which he set in motion was afterwards resolved upon, he had to return home, leaving Robert Trevor in charge of the negotiation, without bringing about any decisive step which would commit the States-General to war.[2]

The identity of interests upon which he insisted was not so great as English Ministers liked to believe. It was a piece of cant, a survival from the past, rather than a reality. The trade of Curaçao and Jamaica was the same, but they took somewhat different measures to defend themselves. Some people, moreover, believed that Curaçao depended on the monopoly which it existed to break.[3] Besides, so far as the Dutch and English interlopers carried on the same trade, their very identity was a cause of competition. This applies to the commerce of both nations in general. Moreover, when one great trading and maritime power goes to war, its chief rival is overpoweringly tempted by the profits of neutrality, however obviously common their cause. The English knew this very well, and did not conceal the irritation with which they saw the 'damt Dutch' run away with the carrying trade; no doubt this was one more reason why they strained so hard to drag their dear friends into their war.[4]

---

[1] Horace Walpole to Harrington, Sept. 15, 1739, S.P. 84/381, ff. 135–40; Hendrick Hop to Cornelis Hop, April 5, 1740, S.P. 107/41.

[2] Horace Walpole's paper to the Pensionary, Sept. 16, 1739, N.S., ibid.; St. Gil's 'Raisons justificatives', in Rousset's Recueil, vol. xiii, part ii, pp. 179–90; Walpole's reply, pp. 191–234; Amelot to Fénelon, Sept. 3, 1739, A.E. Hollande, 433; Fénelon to Amelot, Aug. 29, Sept. 8 and 22, 1739, ibid.; Newcastle to Hardwicke, Oct. 7, 1739, Add. MSS. 35406, f. 160.

[3] Fagel to Hop, Nov. 17, 1739, S.P. 107/34; Hendrick Hop to Cornelis Hop, April 5, May 3 and 9, 1740; Cornelis Hop to Hendrick Hop, April 12 and 27, S.P. 107/41–3.

[4] Hop to Fagel, Oct. 30, 1739, S.P. 107/32. Under-Secretary Couraud thought

The Dutch had yet another reason for neutrality. Unlike the English, they did not live upon an island; they had very nearly been subdued by a French invasion within the last hundred years. There was a chain of barrier fortresses between them and the French armies, but its efficacy was doubted, with only too good reason as the French marshals were soon to show. England could cheerfully face a Spanish war which might turn into a French war; Holland could not. For England, but not for Holland, it would still be a naval war.[1]

The Dutch could have only one strong motive for taking part in the war between England and Spain. If England should fight and win, before they had settled their own dispute with Spain, they might be in a disagreeable situation. England could extort some important concessions, which she would be under no obligation of gratitude to impart to the Dutch. Spain, defeated and humbled, would have every inducement to satisfy her anger at the expense of a less powerful and less respectable claimant for redress.[2] No doubt it was this possibility which caused the Dutch to regard with such attention the opening moves in the naval campaign. If the English squadrons had taken the *azogues*, the States-General would have been encouraged to enter the war; but the failure made them think twice of it.[3]

This at least was the opinion of the Marquis de Fénelon, the clever, perhaps too clever, diplomat who represented France at The Hague. It was his business to bring Horace Walpole's efforts to nothing. What exactly was the point of those efforts? Here Fénelon probably made a mistake through too much subtlety. He recognized in time that Walpole meant to induce the States-General to declare war, but his first thought, which he did not entirely abandon, was that the object of the farewell

it was unfair to exempt foreign ships from the embargo in our ports, 'for the moment they knew our own ships were embargoed, many of them flocked hither to carry the goods which our own people should have been the bearers of, who consequently lost the freight' (Couraud to Waldegrave, July 27, 1739, Waldegrave MSS.).

[1] Horace Walpole often encountered this argument (see his letters to Harrington, July 7 and 17, 1739, S.P. 84/380, ff. 119-21, 162-3; Aug. 18, N.S., S.P. 84/381, ff. 67-8).

[2] Hop to Fagel, July 14, 1739, S.P. 107/29; *Vrai patriote hollandois*, Aug. 1740. Horace Walpole hinted at this (see his letter to Harrington, July 3, 1739, S.P. 84/380, f. 107).

[3] Fénelon to Amelot, Sept. 1, 1739, A.E. Hollande, 433.

visit was a more recondite one. He saw that although the war was nominally begun because Spain had not paid the sum appointed by the Convention, the English immediately started to justify it as a crusade against the right of search. Of course this was necessary in Holland, because the Dutch were no parties to the Convention and were interested in the right of search. But Fénelon, putting the cart before the horse, supposed that the real aim of the English Ministry was to divert attention from the discredited Convention which had conceded the reference of questions of search and navigation to plenipotentiaries —a concession which he thought the English Ministers wanted to take back. So long as the war was waged by England alone it was a war about the Convention, and if Spain were to offer to execute the Convention, England could not reasonably refuse. If the Dutch joined in it as well, it could not be a war for the execution of the Convention, and must be a war against the right of search; the Convention could be conveniently forgotten, and an offer to fulfil it would be no excuse for stopping the war.

Fénelon might well believe this because he thought, like other Frenchmen, that it was not Spain that had broken the Convention by refusing to pay the money, but England by refusing to continue the plenipotentiaries' sittings.[1] As that opinion was not shared by the English Ministers, they did not feel they had any reason to be ashamed of their conduct in this respect, and the motive postulated by Fénelon did not exist. In Horace Walpole's instructions of June 1739 there is no sign of the plan which Fénelon attributed to him. True, the English Ministers did not mean to go back, now that they had made up their minds to a war, and they would have been embarrassed by a belated execution of the Convention. No doubt that was why Horace Walpole sternly rebuffed Count Lynden's attempt to propose a temporary appeasement; he said the state of the controversy was not what it had been before the Convention was broken.[2] He had also to shift the discussion from the Convention to the common grievances of English and Dutch traders

---

[1] Fénelon to Amelot, July 23, Aug. 18, Sept. 15, 1739, A.E. Hollande, 433; Fénelon's error was evidently shared by Amelot, the French Foreign Secretary, who was angry with St. Gil for talking publicly about the right of search and free navigation, instead of putting England in the wrong by sticking to the Convention (Amelot to Fénelon, Sept. 3, 1739, A.E. Hollande, 433).

[2] Fénelon to Amelot, Aug. 11, 1739, A.E. Hollande, 433; Horace Walpole to Harrington, Sept. 15, N.S., S.P. 84/381, ff. 134–41.

against Spain; but that was because the breach of the Convention was no argument for war in Holland.[1] Fénelon's error
was not as important as it was ingenious, but perhaps it accounts
for the embarrassing proposal which was suggested by Lynden,
possibly under Fénelon's tuition, and put forward by Fleury
in August.[2]

Fénelon was soon engaged on a business no less complicated
and more material. Fleury and the States-General became
involved in an elaborate contest about mediation. The object
of each party was to make the other propose something definite
without doing so itself. There is always, in all bargains, an
advantage in making the other side speak first; the principle
is as well known to Levantine peddlers as to Cardinals and
Grand Pensionaries. In this instance there was a more solid and
particular reason. Each party pretended to be impartial; the
pretence was equally false on both sides, though there was a
great difference in their desire to see the dispute settled and
their intention of intervening in it themselves. The States-
General preferred the interests of England almost as much as
France preferred those of Spain, though they had less wish to
fight for their allies, and had, unlike France, a strong interest
of their own in the controversy.[3] They were not willing to
annoy England by proposing something unacceptable. Fleury
had even stronger reason against indisposing the Court of
Spain, from which he was still trying to extort a commercial

[1] Instructions to Horace Walpole, June 12, o.s., 1739, S.P. 84/380, ff. 87-9; Horace
Walpole to Harrington, July 17, N.S., ff. 162-3.   [2] V. supra, p. 145.
[3] French diplomats do not seem to have entirely understood the interest of the
Dutch; they seem to have thought they could appeal to them, as a nation using the
Cadiz trade, by dwelling on the excesses of the English smugglers. Some even had
a faint hope of drawing the States-General into a war against England (Silhouette
to Amelot, Dec. 24, 1739, A.E. Angleterre, 405, f. 368). It must have been a mis-
conception of this kind that led Fénelon to declaim to the Dutch Ministers against
Vernon's throwing open the trade to interlopers by destroying the forts at Portobello and Chagre. He should have understood that the Dutch were themselves an
interloping nation, and that Vernon's action had made a great harvest for the
traders of Curaçao (Fénelon to Amelot, Sept. 15, 1740, A.E. Hollande, 436). He
had a better card to play when he excited the jealousy of the Dutch against the size
of Cathcart's expedition and the vast schemes which it seemed to portend. Some
Dutchmen were afraid that if England made conquests on the mainland, she would
put a stop to the interloping trade of other nations in the provinces which came
under her control (Trevor to Harrington, June 6, 1741, S.P. 84/393, f. 10). Others,
such as Van Hoey, the celebrated ambassador in Paris, professed to believe that
England would want to annex the French and Dutch colonies as soon as she had
conquered the Spanish (Waldegrave to Trevor, April 11 and 22, 1740, Waldegrave
MSS.; Trevor to Waldegrave, April 14, ibid.).

treaty. As no regulation of the questions at issue could be proposed which would satisfy the combatants, and as the combatants would be much more angry with their friends than with their enemies for attempting it, the reluctance of Holland and France to commit themselves to anything definite needs no explaining.[1]

For the English party in Holland, mediation was to be avoided as long as there was any hope of drawing the States-General into a war, and only to be tolerated as a second-best when there was none.[2] Horace Walpole believed that the only way to deter Fleury from taking the part of Spain, was to make the Dutch show some vigour on our side.[3] But mediation had its uses, even to the English, in spite of their abrupt rejection of Fleury's and Lynden's proposals in August 1739. In the first place, it might be possible to tie Fleury up, by an endless negotiation, from actively taking the part of Spain, or proposing a mediation of his own on terms which England could not accept. Fleury was equally anxious to entangle the States-General; but he did not mean to be tied himself, and warned Fénelon against encouraging any assumptions of reciprocity which would keep the Dutch neutral only so long as France remained so.[4] It was partly for this reason that Fénelon was told to hint that France had her own grievances against England, which might justify her intervention quite apart from the merits of the Anglo-Spanish dispute. Perhaps it was also why Fleury insisted, when he sent the French fleets to the West Indies in 1740, that France had taken this abrupt and warlike measure on her own and Europe's account, and not as an ally or partner of Spain. The danger against which he thus tried to guard was a real one, for in fact Trevor made the most of the argument that the junction of France and Spain would justify a similar union between the States-General and England.[5]

[1] Fénelon to Amelot, Aug. 7 and 11, 1739, A.E. Hollande, 433; Amelot to Fénelon, Oct. 18 and Nov. 29, 1739, vol. 434; Resolution of the States-General, Oct. 29, 1740, translation, vol. 436; Amelot to Fénelon, Nov. 6, 1740, ibid.

[2] Horace Walpole to Harrington, Sept. 15, 1739, S.P. 84/381, ff. 134–41. Trevor, instructed by Harrington, resisted an effort of the French party to tack an offer of mediation on to the augmentation of the forces.

[3] Horace Walpole to Waldegrave, Aug. 27, 1739, Waldegrave MSS.

[4] This was the only condition on which England would allow the Dutch to be neutral (Harrington to Walpole, Oct. 2, 1739, S.P. 84/381, ff. 235–6); even that was more than Horace Walpole thought proper (Walpole to Harrington, Oct. 9, ff. 222–3).

[5] Amelot to Fénelon, Aug. 23, 1739, A.E. Hollande, 433; Nov. 12, 1739, vol.

The Dutch had, moreover, an interest of their own in the matter, and saw a very good opportunity of killing two birds with one stone. They had not yet settled their own dispute with Spain about the rights of navigation. If they could now procure from Spain, directly or through France, a satisfactory adjustment, it would serve as a model for a reconciliation between England and Spain, and a bridge over which the English Ministry could crawl to peace and safety without dishonour. Fénelon saw through this design, but seems to have made the mistake of thinking that it was much more welcome to the English than it really was.[1] If, on the other hand, the Dutch should not succeed in bringing England into a peaceful settlement of this kind, at least it would be something to have got their own grievances redressed, for they would never have a better opportunity than a time of war between Spain and England, when they could threaten to join England if they were not satisfied.

As it was France's object as well as Spain's, or even more than Spain's, to prevent them from taking part in the war, the Dutch could make France pull this chestnut out of the fire for them by her diplomatic influence at Madrid. Fleury actually lent himself to their scheme; for he did not need to be told how important it was that Spain should satisfy the Dutch. If he was destined to enter the war on behalf of Spain, he certainly had the right to demand that he should not have the Dutch as well as the English on his hands; that would be coming near to the general war which he dreaded. Horace Walpole and his successor Trevor insisted chiefly on the argument that only force could extort any satisfaction from Spain; Fleury would therefore play a trump card if he could prove that the Dutch had more to gain by peaceful discussions and the influence of France, than by adhering to England and her warlike measures.[2] He never ceased to preach to Spain the necessity of detaching the Dutch by a slight concession, but he had little enough

434; Sept. 9, 1740, vol. 436; Horace Walpole to Waldegrave, Sept. 8, 1739, Waldegrave MSS.; Trevor to Harrington, Sept. 24, 1740, S.P. 84/387, f. 42.

[1] Trevor to Harrington, Dec. 15, 1739, S.P. 84/382, ff. 162-4; Harrington to Trevor, Dec. 11, ff. 180-1; Fénelon to Amelot, Aug. 25, 1739, A.E. Hollande, 433; Amelot to Fénelon, Aug. 30, ibid.; Fénelon to Amelot, Oct. 8, 1739, vol. 434.

[2] Amelot to Fénelon, July 12 and Aug. 30, 1739, A.E. Hollande, 433; Fénelon to Amelot, Oct. 8, 1739, vol. 434; Sept. 23, 1740, vol. 437; Resolution of the States-General, Sept. 27 and Oct. 29, 1740, ibid.; Amelot to Fénelon, Oct. 9, ibid.; Trevor to Harrington, Sept. 24, 1740, S.P. 84/387, ff. 42-7.

success for his pains, and the States-General thought in the summer of 1740 that they might as easily get what they wanted by direct negotiations at Madrid.[1]

Whether intentionally or not, their Ambassador Vandermeer seems to have promised that they would remain neutral during the war if they received satisfaction. This at once elicited a fulsome declaration from St. Gil. He protested that the King of Spain accepted the neutrality with gratitude, that he had never meant to infringe the lawful navigation of Dutch subjects, and would be glad to enter into discussions for preventing the abuse of that freedom by contraband traders. Vandermeer's supposed promise of neutrality gave great scandal in England,[2] and the reward which St. Gil offered seemed too small when closely examined; for nothing that he had said proved any real departure from the Spanish doctrine of 'suspicious latitudes' and the straight course to and from the colonies, which England had been unwilling to accept. Besides, the whole concession appeared to be conditional on some satisfaction to Spain on the question of smuggling, which could hardly be congenial to the owners of Curaçao. The Dutch therefore, both on their own account and on England's, continued to ask for higher terms. They hinted that they could take no part in mediation until Spain had redressed their own grievances, and that they could not accept any guarantee of free navigation which was conditional on an arrangement about the smugglers. Let Spain give an unconditional guarantee, and discuss the smugglers afterwards.[3] France would not treat on such terms, which were obviously designed to favour the interloping at the expense of the Cadiz trade; and if she had been willing, she could not have made Spain accept them, nor did she wish to incur her displeasure by asking her to do so.

---

[1] La Marck had told the Dutch ambassador as early as June 1739 that he was to put in a word for the claims of the Dutch in order to detach them from England (Keene to Newcastle, June 22, 1739, S.P. 94/133; see also Baudrillart, op. cit. iv. 530).

[2] Bussy said the Ministers secretly welcomed it, but I can find little evidence of this in dispatches (Bussy to Amelot, June 23 and 27, 1740, A.E. Angleterre, 407, ff. 398, 401); the *Pro-Memoria* of St. Gil, June 20, 1740, and Trevor's account of it, Trevor to Harrington, June 24, 25, and 28, July 1, 1740, S.P. 84/385, ff. 155–61, 163, 167–8, 186–7, 191–3; Harrington to Trevor, June 18, f. 183.

[3] States-General, Resolutions of Sept. 27 and Oct. 29, 1740; Cornelis Hop to Hendrick Hop. Oct. 18, 1740, S.P. 107/46; Hendrick Hop to Cornelis Hop, Oct. 25, 1740, ibid.; Cornelis Hop to Hendrick Hop. Nov. 18, 1740, S.P. 107/47.

Thus the whole complicated discussion ended with a dead-lock. Fleury had no more need to continue it, for he actively interposed between England and Spain at this point. It was no longer very likely that the States-General would take equally strong measures on the other side. Very soon after-wards they forgot the whole matter in their preoccupation with the outbreak of a new European war. The Dutch, with their weak land frontier, were more sensitive to that than England, and at last became really anxious that she should name the terms on which she would make her peace with Spain, and end the maritime war in order to devote all her strength to the continental troubles.[1] But the conversion of England to conti-nental measures was neither so sudden nor so complete; and when it was made, it did not take the form of courting media-tion, whether French or Dutch.

§ v. *Fleury threatens to intervene*

During the course of these elaborate machinations, the rela-tions of England and France had come to a crisis. Fleury naturally wanted to intimidate the English Government and keep it in suspense. Until he had come to terms with Spain, he could hardly do anything else. For this reason he had made a great fuss over the search of some French ships by Admiral Haddock off Cadiz. In their hearts he and Amelot did not take this incident very seriously, saying it was only the ordinary usage of war.[2] But they complained to Waldegrave and sent back their Ambassador Cambis from his furlough to London with an almost violent memorial upon the subject.

'The delay of satisfaction', it concluded, 'for grievances so well founded and of such importance to the honour of his Crown, would give His Majesty so much the more concern, as it would be looked upon throughout all Europe as a mark of the little regard Your Majesty would appear to have to his just complaints, if you should any longer refuse to cause a stop to be put to them, and to redress them.'[3]

Cambis presumably did not soften the rigour of his com-munication, for he prided himself on his fiery manner of exe-cuting his office, which had caused George II to cut him dead

---

[1] Trevor to Harrington, June 6 and 27, 1741, S.P. 84/393, ff. 10, 65.
[2] Baudrillart, op. cit. iv. 352.
[3] Cambis to George II, Aug. 30, o.s., 1739, S.P. 100/7.

in the Drawing-room.[1] Indeed, he hardly seems to have been the man to smooth over differences between the two Courts. His secretary justified him after his death against the charge of being too pro-English: in his last illness his attendants had been obliged to divert the conversation from the grievances of Spain against England, as it was a subject on which he felt so vehemently that he might do himself harm by discussing it. 'He never varied for a moment from these sentiments, and I have never seen him desire anything with more passion than to see a war well kindled between France and England'[2]—a curious qualification for a French ambassador at the Court of St. James. He nearly made matters worse on this occasion by threatening to reject Newcastle's reply. It was certainly very inadequate and tried to intimidate France from pursuing these controversies any farther.[3] All this was ado about nothing. Fleury only meant to create a vague uneasiness.

'You will notice', Amelot had written to Cambis, 'that the *mémoire* is drawn up in such a way as to inspire fear of definite action on our part, without representing it as taken or ready to be taken. You must speak in exactly the same sense, so that neither the English Ministry, nor that of Spain (from what it may hear of the matter) may be free from the uncertainty in which we must at present, on account of the state of our affairs, appear to be.'[4]

So long as Fleury lived, disputes over neutral rights had very little effect on the relations of the two Courts. Maurepas was credited, now and later, with a desire to make the most of them in order to bring on a war with England; but he never had his way.[5] Bussy was sometimes ordered to make complaints, which the English Ministers neglected with impunity—at one time he said he had given in over sixty to which no sort of reply had been returned.[6] When France refused to expel the Pretender and declared war in the spring of 1744, one of the chief reasons given was the breach of treaties and the violation of the rights of neutrals.[7] This was only a justification which Amelot had

[1] Cambis to Fénelon, Sept. 22, 1739, S.P. 107/32.

[2] De Vismes to Amelot, March 3, N.S., 1740, A.E. Angleterre, 407, f. 152.

[3] Couraud to Waldegrave, Sept. 6, 1739, Add. MSS. 32801, f. 252; Newcastle to Hardwicke, Sept. 9, vol. 35406, f. 144; to Cambis, Sept. 7/18, A.E. Angleterre, 405, f. 162; Cambis to Amelot, Sept. 14 and 21, ff. 158, 173.

[4] Amelot to Cambis, Aug. 30, 1739, A.E. Angleterre, 405, f. 86.

[5] Waldegrave to Newcastle, Jan. 9, 1740, Add. MSS. 32801, f. 361; Jan. 15, vol. 32802, f. 3.   [6] Bussy, memorial of Dec. 4, 1742, S.P. 100/8.

[7] Thompson to Stone, June 26, 1743, S.P. 78/228, f. 222; to Newcastle, Feb. 25, 1744, S.P. 78/229, f. 188.

held patiently up his sleeve for four years; it was not a real motive. The diplomacy of France was governed by grander and subtler considerations than mercantile complaints. The security of her overseas trade was not a matter of life and death to her, as it was to the Dutch, and she did not condescend to the desperate nagging with which the States-General urged their similar complaints against England.

This little storm was therefore allowed to blow over like that of the *azogues*, and the two Governments lived for some months in apparent cordiality. Fleury pursued his bargain with Spain, without ever reaching a conclusion. The English Ministers followed with alarm what they could learn of these negotiations. Waldegrave had told them that it was not consideration for England, but inability to make his terms with Spain, that made Fleury so passive in the first months of the war. They always expected that the signature of the treaty of alliance would be followed by a declaration on the part of France, and were almost prepared—so at least Bussy reported—to make that of the treaty of commerce a *casus belli* on their own account.[1]

Another very difficult problem began to arise out of the conduct of the war. What would be the attitude of France to the great expedition going out under Lord Cathcart to the West Indies, and to the glorious and profitable conquests which it would doubtless make? It is hard to comprehend the uncertainty of the English Ministers on this subject. Before the war or even the reprisals were begun, Fleury had told Waldegrave that France could not stand by and see England annex any important part of the Spanish dominions in America.[2] He repeated it again and again, after the war was declared, and further pointed his moral by applauding Vernon's behaviour at Portobello and Chagre, where the conquered towns had not been annexed or garrisoned, but had been virtually thrown open to the trade of all nations.[3] He had also shown great

[1] Bussy to Amelot, Oct. 3, 1740, A.E. Angleterre, 409, f. 122.
[2] Sir R. Walpole to Newcastle, July 17, 1739, Add. MSS. 32692, f. 152; Horace Walpole to Trevor, Oct. 24, 1738, *H.M.C. XIVth Report*, App. IX, p. 24. I cannot find the letter from Waldegrave to which Walpole refers in his letter of July 17. By the dates it ought to be that of July 22, N.S., but none of the dispatches which Waldegrave wrote on that day quite fits the description. On June 26, N.S., Waldegrave had sent Newcastle a long description of Fleury's state of mind, from which he concluded that Fleury would probably take no part at present.
[3] Waldegrave to Newcastle (most private), Nov. 23, 1739, Jan. 4, 1740, S.P.

interest in the proclamation by which the English Government offered to guarantee to private adventurers the possession of whatever territories they should take from the Spaniards in America. This proclamation (which was founded on Pulteney's Act of Parliament for that purpose) was hardly compatible with an intention to preserve the equilibrium established by the Peace of Utrecht; but the chances of private conquests were small, and the Government was not restrained from restoring places which might be taken by its own armies.[1]

Even if Fleury had never uttered a word of his intention, Newcastle might very well have guessed it, for it was easily deduced from the doctrine of the American balance of power, which Fleury and most of his diplomats held and proclaimed.[2] What makes Newcastle's uncertainty yet more curious is that he had made up his mind, before the war broke out, that France meant to enter it sooner or later in support of Spain; until the spring of 1740 he believed, in spite of Waldegrave's denials, that she would intervene that year. He then allowed himself to be converted to the view that Fleury would not meddle with Cathcart's expedition; he was not only surprised, but comically aggrieved, when Fleury did so.[3]

There are three possible explanations of this puzzle. The first is that Fleury meant to have the credit of giving fair warning, and the advantage of not being believed. He was so old and feeble, that he could easily deceive by an affectation of senility. He could appear not to mean what he said, and to say what he had meant to leave unsaid. Waldegrave, good easy man, was very much under his influence, and would believe anything that

---

78/221, ff. 272, 353; March 12, April 3, vol. 222, ff. 157, 233; July 22, vol. 223, f. 207; Jan. 15, 1740, Add. MSS. 32802, f. 3; July 8, 1740, S.P. 43/91.

[1] Waldegrave to Newcastle, May 4, 1740, S.P. 78/222, f. 321. *V. supra*, p. 67.

[2] Fénelon was already saying in July 1740, a month before the French fleet sailed, that 'an invasion of the Spanish possessions in America by us, is as much a *casus foederis* for France, as one of England by the Spaniards would be for the Republic' (Trevor to Waldegrave, July 28, 1740, Waldegrave MSS.).

[3] Newcastle to Waldegrave (most secret), Aug. 3, 1739, S.P. 78/221; Jan. 22, Feb. 27, 1739/40, S.P. 78/222, ff. 78, 129. See also his private letter of Feb. 27, in which he says: 'I dare say all their bravadoes are only to intimidate us, and prevent our American expedition, but that shan't do, it shall go on, with all possible vigour and expedition. Tho' this is the most probable conjecture, the consequence is too great to depend upon it, and therefore we must look out, and act, as if their intentions were as bad as possible, and if the Cardinal should drop, nobody can tell how soon, they might make us a visit here, and therefore we must always have an eye to that' (Waldegrave MSS.).

Fleury could pass off as the involuntary confidence of a dotard. So great in fact was Fleury's skill in handling Waldegrave, that it is almost an injustice to him as an artist to suppose that the curious effect which he produced in this instance was unintended. But it will not do. Fleury was an artful and tortuous old man, but he was not a devil. He was not the man to go out of his way to engineer an unnecessary war. Still less would he do so, before he was sure of his alliance with Spain.

It must therefore be supposed that Fleury intended the hint to be taken, and that it was not his fault if it was neglected. The blame then rests on Waldegrave, for it was he who persuaded Newcastle that Fleury would stay quiet and continue to watch events. He reported Fleury's threats, but either explained them away as meaningless, or prophesied that they would never be carried out because Fleury was too much afraid of a general war. Poor Waldegrave was lethargic, for he was dying of dropsy; he was unduly sure of his ability to penetrate Fleury's intentions. He was for these reasons a bad ambassador, and Horace Walpole (who as his predecessor would be more likely than anybody else to criticize him) had already found reason to complain of him on these accounts.[1]

Newcastle himself was as much to blame as anybody. If he had not wanted to be convinced by Waldegrave, he would have stuck to his first opinion. When he wanted to carry a point, he did not scruple to play fast and loose with the facts. In April 1740, when he was trying to dissuade George II from one of his unpopular visits to Hanover, he argued that France was likely to interfere with our expeditions or even to invade us. He therefore concealed from the King the strong assurances of Waldegrave that Fleury would take no part that year.[2] A few weeks later he turned round, and used Waldegrave's wrong information in his controversy with Walpole over the disposition of the forces. He had always wanted to press forward with the preparations for Cathcart's expedition, regardless of any danger, and to send as many ships as could be spared to the West Indies. Sir Robert Walpole began to argue that because the French were likely to intervene, the fleet must be concentrated

---

[1] Horace Walpole to Trevor, March 16/27, 1739, *H.M.C. XIVth Report*, App. IX, p. 27.

[2] See the two interesting letters of Newcastle to Waldegrave, April 11 and 18, 1740, in the Waldegrave MSS.

for defence in the home waters; for he believed that the hostility of France would take the form of an invasion of Great Britain or Ireland. This was not a very easy argument to answer—indeed, nobody was more fearfully aware of its force than Newcastle, sixteen years later. The best way of dealing with it was to deny that Fleury would interfere at all. Some reassuring letters had lately come from Waldegrave, and Newcastle used them in the Cabinet. Ogle and his ten ships could not possibly be sent to the West Indies if France was likely to strike some unpredictable stroke in the next few months; but Newcastle was determined that Ogle should go, therefore he believed that France would do nothing.[1] For the time Walpole and his supporters triumphed. Ogle was kept at home; but Newcastle was now quite converted to his new opinion; he announced to Vernon, and to Waldegrave himself, that he no longer thought France would take any part in the war that year.[2]

Not everybody agreed with him. Wager wrote in August that France must enter the war sooner or later. George II had already predicted that she would send her squadrons to the West Indies, in order to avoid giving a *casus foederis* to the States-General, who were bound by treaty to defend us against an invasion of our European, but not of our American, dominions. Harrington, the Secretary of State who accompanied the King to Hanover, thought that, a few days before Cathcart's expedition was ready to go, Fleury would put an embarrassing question as to its destination, or announce that he could not allow it to sail at all.[3] Newcastle persisted in believing that

---

[1] Newcastle to Waldegrave, June 12, 1740, S.P. 78/221, f. 111. But at the same time that he argued in this way, he prepared a private instruction for Sir John Norris, who was to command the Channel fleet, empowering him to get between the French and Spanish fleets if they should try to join in Ferrol harbour, and prevent it by force (Norris's diary, June 22, 1740, Add. MSS. 28133, f. 15). Fleury was very much afraid at this time that the English fleets would commit a sudden attack on French warships. This appears not only from Amelot's letter to Bussy of July 21 (which may have been meant to be intercepted, as in fact it was), but also from Maurepas's instructions to the commanders of ships in the Channel (Maurepas to d'Antin, July 26, 1740, A.N. Marine B² 311, f. 25). See also the accounts of proceedings in Cabinet, May 6 and 22, 1740, Hervey, *Memoirs*, ed. Sedgwick, iii. 933-40.

[2] Newcastle to Waldegrave, June 12, 1740, S.P. 78/223, f. 111; Newcastle to Vernon, July 23, 1740, Add. MSS. 32694, f. 239.

[3] Wager to Vernon, Aug. 6, 1740, *Original Letters to an Honest Sailor*, p. 18; Harrington to Newcastle, June 6/17, July 11/22, 1740, S.P. 43/25; Newcastle to Harrington (private and particular), June 24, o.s., S.P. 43/90; July 4, S.P. 43/91; July 22, S.P. 43/92.

nothing of the sort would happen. He had lately had a letter from Waldegrave, saying that Fleury had spoken 'as strongly as he could, to satisfy me he actually meant to declare against us, if the case happened. But for all that', the Ambassador continued light-heartedly, 'I wish to God, we took something from the Spaniards that would make it worth our while to stand a chance of his resentment.' Newcastle sent this off with satisfaction to Harrington, adding that the Cabinet was 'humbly of opinion, that what was thus said by the Cardinal does not import a resolution to make any declaration or demand relating to my Lord Cathcart's expedition, previously to his going hence. But however that may be, their Lordships continue firmly of opinion, that no alteration in the measures determined to be taken by His Majesty, can anyways be made, or the measures delayed by it.'[1]

Soon afterwards, however, a rumour reached Newcastle: Fleury had told Waldegrave outright that France could not let us make any conquests in America. This indeed was exactly what Fleury had always said, but Waldegrave had not reported it so. Newcastle now wrote to him for further light, and received a reassuring reply. Waldegrave thought that whatever Fleury had let fall to him was said 'in order that, without his appearing to menace, we may see what he would have us think he would resent, as well as what would be agreeable to him by keeping him out of the cases, in which, perhaps, he may have promised to assist Spain'; and that 'the Cardinal never had the least notion that any thing he ever said to me on these subjects, could be looked upon as a declaration or demand upon any intention of His Majesty for pursuing the war against his enemies'.[2]

At first sight this does not quite explain why Newcastle was so outraged when Fleury sent off d'Antin's fleet to the West Indies; for if Waldegrave's explanation of Fleury's words was comforting, the words themselves were dangerous. Yet there is really no puzzle at all. Newcastle was only sure that Fleury would say nothing about Cathcart's expedition 'previously to his going hence'. He knew perfectly well, for even Waldegrave's good-natured blundering could not conceal it, that

---

[1] Waldegrave to Newcastle, July 8, 1740, S.P. 43/91; Newcastle to Harrington, July 4/15, 1740, Add. MSS. 32693, f. 443.
[2] Newcastle to Waldegrave, July 15, 1740, Add. MSS. 32802, f. 158; Waldegrave to Newcastle, Aug. 10, 1740, S.P. 78/223, f. 268.

Fleury would interfere when he heard of victories in Spanish America. But he was prepared, like Waldegrave, to take his chance of that. He imagined that when Fleury said he could not suffer us to make conquests in America, he meant literally that he should do nothing until we had made them. He never thought that Fleury might try to prevent us from making them at all. He tried to steal a march on Fleury, and was surprised and grieved when he found that Fleury had stolen one on him. He complained that he had been cheated, because he had not been allowed to—I will not say, cheat Fleury, but it was something very like it. For while Waldegrave had purposely eluded giving Fleury a promise that we would keep none of our conquests, Harrington had allowed Trevor to deny that acquisitions were the object of the war.[1]

There was also an equivocation on Fleury's part. If Waldegrave may be trusted—which is admittedly doubtful—Fleury had never told him in so many words that it was Cathcart's sailing to make the conquests, and not the conquests themselves, which was to be the signal for his intervention. Probably he did not even give him to understand it. Certainly Waldegrave did not understand it. Nobody can blame Fleury for not announcing his movements in advance; but why did he order Fénelon and Bussy to imply that he had made it clear Cathcart must not sail?[2] His ubiquitous reiterations that the English Ministers could not be surprised at the step he had taken, indicate that he knew he had in fact surprised them.

He had surprised them indeed. Maurepas had sent out four ships to the West Indies earlier in the summer, but that had only reassured the English Ministers, who presumed he would send no more, or would at the worst reinforce them by inoffensive ones and twos until he had collected a respectable force there.[3] They had known very well that preparations were making at Brest and Toulon, but hardly a rumour, let alone any authentic news, had escaped as to the real destination of the squadrons. It was one of the few naval movements of the eighteenth century which were kept a complete secret from the

---

[1] Harrington to Trevor, April 15, 1740, S.P. 84/384, f. 174.

[2] Bussy's declaration, Sept. 18, 1740, S.P. 100/7; Amelot to Bussy, Sept. 11 1740, A.E. Angleterre, 409, f. 64; Amelot to Fénelon, Sept. 9, 1740, A.E. Hollande 436.

[3] Bussy to Amelot, Sept. 21, 1740, A.E. Angleterre, 409, f. 88; Waldegrave to Newcastle, May 4, N.S., 1740, Add. MSS. 32802, f. 131.

enemy; and this is the more remarkable because the two countries were not at war.

I do not know when Fleury first took his resolution to send d'Antin to the West Indies. Maurepas and the Spanish party were urging him to do so in May;[1] but the first written evidence of his intention is in d'Antin's instructions of August 14, N.S.[2] Perhaps he was determined by a letter which Bussy, the French Minister in London, wrote him on July 30, N.S. Amelot had written to ask whether it was true that Cathcart's expedition was bound to the Canaries. Bussy replied positively that he was sure its real objective was Havana, as he had announced for some months past.[3] He added a copy of Cathcart's draft proclamation to the Spanish colonists, which might in itself have been decisive in the eyes of the French Government, if they had not already had one in May from Silhouette.[4] It may have been Bussy's report of the Government's fixed intention to attack the strongest point in all Spanish America, which determined Fleury to go to the rescue at once.[5] Or it may have been Bussy's singularly ill-judged remark in the same letter, that 'it seems to me, from all I can hear, that the Ministers here were expecting that we should have explained ourselves more openly about the limits which we wish them to put to the progress of the war, and the expedients which we think proper for restoring peace'. There was nothing which they were more anxious to avoid.

Whatever else may have prompted Fleury's action, it was not Spanish influence. The measure was in no way concerted with the Spanish Court, which was not informed of it until d'Antin was already on the point of sailing, and had no time to order its naval commanders to co-operate with him until he was gone.

[1] Waldegrave to Newcastle, May 4, N.S., 1740, S.P. 78/222, f. 321.

[2] Between March 1700 and September 1752, the English calendar was eleven days behind that of the rest of western Europe. August 14, New Style, was August 3, Old Style, in England.

[3] Amelot to Bussy, July 21, 1740, A.E. Angleterre, 407, f. 443; Bussy to Amelot, July 30, ibid., f. 465; Amelot to Bussy, Aug. 3 and 16, vol. 409, ff. 2, 23. Bussy was not quite right; most of the Ministers hoped Cathcart would attack Havana, but it was not absolutely prescribed to him, and the final decision was to be taken by a Council of War. See also Newcastle to Harrington (private and particular), June 24, O.S., 1740, S.P. 43/90.   [4] *V. supra*, p. 75.

[5] Although both Bussy and Cambis had reported that Cathcart's force would probably go to Havana, they had not announced it as certain; and Maurepas does not seem to have known its destination on June 30 (Maurepas to Larnage, June 30, 1740, A.N. Colonies B 78).

In fact, at the same time as Fleury rendered it this remarkable assistance, he suddenly suspended the negotiation of the treaties of commerce and alliance. This curious scruple is hard to understand. It was quixotic to take such an abrupt and decisive way of proving to the world the disinterestedness which he claimed in his public manifestoes. He can hardly have hoped to avoid a war, for d'Antin's orders were almost sure to provoke one. Fleury did not mean to be the first to declare it, but he had little doubt of England's doing so, and had a *mémoire* drawn up about the naval and diplomatic steps necessary to be taken in that case.[1] The abandonment of the Spanish treaty of commerce was too high a price to pay for putting England in the wrong, even assuming that Fleury could do so, which was more than doubtful after the instructions he had given to d'Antin. The two chief reasons which he gave—fear of offending the Dutch by provoking their commercial jealousy, and of being dragged by Spain into a general war—might have justified him if he had never entered into the commercial negotiations at all, but do not seem to explain his withdrawing from them at this point. Perhaps he felt that they could never come to any good end, and chose a moment for suspending them when the Court of Spain would have other grounds of gratitude to him.[2]

§ vi. *D'Antin's Expedition to the West Indies*

Laroche-Alart sailed from Toulon on August 26, N.S., and d'Antin from Brest on the 3rd of September. For some days the news was kept secret; but Fleury soon admitted, without embarrassment, that d'Antin at least was on his way to the West Indies. He did not mean, he said, to go to war with England, to attack or molest any of her ships, or to deprive her of any of her possessions; but he must prevent her from becoming too powerful in America, and above all from engrossing the whole trade of the Spanish West Indies. He had reason to believe that the immense preparations for Cathcart's expedition portended something more than the seizure and dismantling of fortresses as at Portobello and Chagre. Amelot wrote to Bussy in very much the same strain. Fénelon was ordered to make a declara-

---

[1] *Mémoire* of Aug. 20, 1740, A.E. Angleterre, 409, f. 30. Yet Fleury declared to Van Hoey that though he did not suppose the first reaction of the English public would be towards peace, he hoped they might come round to it (Van Hoey to States-General, Sept. 13, 1740, A.E. Hollande, 436).

[2] Baudrillart, op. cit. iv. 560–1.

tion to the States-General, which should serve as Fleury's manifesto to neutral powers; d'Antin was furnished with another,
which he should publish as soon as he had struck the first blow
in America. All these documents harped upon the pacific intentions of France, and her disappointed hope that England would
have pursued her controversy against Spain by peaceful arguments, or would at least have confined her ambitions in the
war to obtaining redress of her grievances and securing a free
navigation for her lawful trade. France was acting not only in
her own interests but in those of Europe, and without any
collusion with Spain; she would do no more than was necessary
to preserve the equilibrium set up by the Treaty of Utrecht,
and to defend the Spanish colonies against aggression.[1]

The world in general might infer from this pompous display
of innocence that d'Antin was only instructed to prevent the
attack which Vernon and Cathcart were to make against
Havana or Cartagena. This was what the English Government
believed. How far it was from the truth, will appear from
d'Antin's instructions.

Torres, with the Ferrol squadron of fourteen ships, had sailed
a few weeks before d'Antin, and there were six Spanish warships already in the West Indies. Against these, Vernon at
Jamaica had only ten of the line, but he was to be reinforced
by a fleet of whose size the French were not certain, which
might have sailed, or be setting out, or on the point of setting
out, when d'Antin took his departure. When d'Antin had sent
back the escort which had strengthened his squadron in the
Channel, and picked up three ships waiting for him at Martinique, he would have twelve or fourteen ships of the line, of
which he was to leave one at Martinique.[2] Eight more under
Laroche-Alart were to join him in the West Indies. At his first
setting out, he had no orders to co-operate with Torres, so that
he had to rely on a force of twenty ships, against Vernon's ten
at Jamaica, and an uncertain number—his instructions said six
—which would probably not yet have reinforced Vernon.

He was to stop at Martinique and take on board some regular

[1] Waldegrave to Newcastle, Sept. 11 and 16, 1740, S.P. 78/223, f. 385, 78/224,
f. 10; Fénelon to States-General, Sept. 14, 1740, copy in Add. MSS. 35406, f. 233,
with copy of declaration to be made by d'Antin; Note of Bussy's declaration,
Sept. 18, 1740, S.P. 100/7.
[2] He was given the option of sending home four or six ships when he was clear
of the Channel.

troops and volunteers whom the Governor was to raise. He was to seek and fight the English, in one way or another. If he reached the West Indies before the English reinforcement, he was to waylay it in the Windward Islands without even waiting for Laroche-Alart to join him. If he could not do this he was to attack Vernon, whose squadron was said to be in a very bad condition. If he should not be able to meet either Vernon or the reinforcement before they joined, he must naturally wait until Laroche-Alart came up, when he would again be equal or superior to the combined English fleet. He was then to attack and destroy it, or blockade it in Port Royal, and if it escaped he was to follow and fight it at sea. Having defeated it he was to concert an invasion of Jamaica with the Governor of St. Domingue, who would have troops and volunteers ready for the purpose. He need not conquer and annex the whole island, but should confine himself to destroying the principal towns and forts, and carrying off the greatest possible number of negroes from the plantations. If, however, he took possession of it, he was to do so in the name of the King of Spain. He might find, on his arrival, that Vernon, already reinforced, had gone to the siege of Havana. If so, he was to follow him and drive him away. If the English should have divided their forces, he might do the same, provided each detachment could be superior to the English squadron to which it was opposed; otherwise, he was to keep his fleet together and deal first with any English division which might be attacking the Spanish possessions. As soon as he had struck any definite blow, he was to publish the manifesto with which he had been provided, and to send word to the Marquis de Champigny, Governor of the Windward Islands, in order that he might forestall the English in taking possession of the neutral island of St. Lucia.[1]

Two months later the situation was much changed. The French Government had come to some understanding with that of Spain about co-operation between their fleets, and the reinforcement which Ogle was taking to Vernon had been considerably strengthened as a result of d'Antin's departure. Maurepas wrote to d'Antin at first that Ogle was still waiting to set out, and that the increased size of the English fleet need make no difference to the execution of his instructions. But on October 23, when Maurepas knew that Ogle was to have between

---

[1] Instructions to d'Antin, A.N. Marine B² 311, Brest, ff. 58 et seqq.

twenty-one and twenty-four ships, he saw that even the united fleet of d'Antin and Laroche-Alart would be too small to deal with them, and dispensed d'Antin from that part of his instructions which enjoined him to intercept the reinforcement on its way to Vernon. The rest of his orders could still be executed, especially as Torres had been told to join him if it should seem advisable. He was to take all possible measures for the security of the French and Spanish colonies—particularly, of course, the former—against any attack the English might make. Torres also had been allowed a considerable latitude of acting as he should think best after informing himself of the position and number of the English ships. He was to fight Vernon, if he could find him alone and unreinforced, or to get between him and Ogle; and he might join with d'Antin for an expedition against Jamaica.[1]

This was Fleury's disinterestedness and moderation; this is how he interpreted his promise to respect the lawful commerce of the English in America, and to abstain from annexing a foot of English soil. It was a long time before he was found out; the English Government believed that the French fleets would try to hinder its operations against the Spanish colonies, but it had not an inkling of these elaborate plans of aggression. It only intercepted one of Maurepas's later letters to d'Antin, in which the full extent of the French schemes was not clear.[2]

Newcastle was shocked by what he regarded as Fleury's duplicity, though he did not know the half of it. Yet though he was staggered, he was not for a moment intimidated.[3] The first step of the Government was naturally to increase Ogle's strength so that the force he was taking out should make Vernon more or less equal to the combined French and Spaniards. The exact adjustment of this matter required a great deal of argument. It was not certain at first whether the Toulon squadron had gone, like that of Brest, to the West Indies; then each of them sent back to France a detachment which had strengthened it in the dangerous waters off the coasts of Europe. Something

[1] Maurepas to d'Antin, Oct. 7 and 23, 1740, ibid., Brest, ff. 172, 208; Copy of Torres's instructions, f. 173.

[2] The letter of Oct. 7, 1740, C.O. 137/57. It appears from Newcastle's private letter to Vernon, Oct. 15, 1741 (Add. MSS. 32698, f. 157), that they had found out by that time what d'Antin had really been instructed to do.

[3] Newcastle to Harrington, Sept. 6, 1740, Add. MSS. 32695, f. 6; Newcastle to Waldegrave, Sept. 5 and 20, S.P. 78/224, ff. 6, 68.

also depended on the movements which Vernon was going to make after he received this reinforcement. Admiral Norris thought Vernon would have to make for Cartagena, because the season of Ogle's arrival would be the wrong one for attacking Havana; he believed that Vernon would almost certainly have to deal with the French, and must therefore be as strong as possible.[1]

Another difficulty arose from Walpole's reluctance to strip the British Islands of all their naval defence. He continued longer than most of his colleagues to believe that the Toulon squadron had not really gone to the West Indies, but would prove to be employed in an invasion of Great Britain or Ireland; and when that was disproved beyond reasonable doubt, he still held out against Newcastle's plan for sending almost the whole available force of the navy to the West Indies.[2] For at one moment it was Norris's Grand Fleet of thirty-three of the line which was to go.[3] This proved to be unnecessary when it became clear that not all the ships which had left Brest and Toulon had gone to the West Indies. Finally Ogle took with him twenty-five ships, which would give Vernon thirty-five of the line against thirty-nine (or forty-one) if all the French and Spanish ships in the West Indies should join together.

This was the first time that so great a proportion of the fighting strength of three nations had been concentrated in the West Indies.[4] The French had orders to fall upon the English if they could do so with advantage. The English Ministers did not know this, so they presumably thought they were taking a very daring step when they instructed Ogle and Vernon to attack

---

[1] Norris's diary, Oct. 21, 1740, Add. MSS. 28133, f. 66.

[2] Newcastle to Hardwicke, Oct. 1, 1740, Add. MSS. 35406, f. 237; Newcastle to Vernon, Sept. 12, Add. MSS. 32695, f. 47.

[3] Newcastle to Harrington, Sept. 9, o.s., 1740, S.P. 43/94; Stone to Cathcart, Sept. 9, Add. MSS. 32695, f. 30.

[4] On Feb. 4, 1740/1, Vernon commanded thirteen third-rates, seventeen fourth-rates, twenty-two frigates, fire-ships, &c. He had so many small and middle-sized ships that there were not enough left for convoy and cruising in the Channel; this is probably the reason why the Spanish privateers were more successful there between March and December 1741 than at any other time (*A Short Account of the late Application to Parliament, made by the Merchants of London upon the Neglect of their Trade* (London, 1742), p. 13). The Government was criticized for fitting out so many capital ships in Europe, which were not wanted so long as France remained neutral; but what else was it to do when so many third- and fourth-rates were in the West Indies? (Wager to Vernon, June 21, 1741, *Original Letters to an Honest Sailor*, p. 47; *Hireling Artifice Detected* (London, 1742), pp. 53, 56.)

the French. Though they anticipated that the French fleets in
the West Indies would only hamper us and defend the Spaniards,
they had no intention of submitting even to so much. 'For if
the French and Spaniards get the better of us in the West Indies,
which they do, if they hinder our expeditions, or the success of
them against the Spaniards, we must for ever after be at the
mercy of France.'[1] Vernon was therefore ordered not only to
proceed with his plans against the Spanish colonies, regardless
of any obstruction which the French might interpose, but to
attack the French themselves if he should have sufficient force
for the purpose. Even Ogle, with his lumbering convoy of
transports, was told that if he should meet d'Antin on the way
out and find himself in a condition to fight him, he need not
scruple to do so.[2]

Here then was a strange situation. Each Government had
sent out its fleet to the West Indies with orders to commit an
unprovoked aggression against an enemy who was expected to
remain on the defensive. Each Government must therefore
have spent the winter waiting to hear of an explosion in the
West Indies, for which it believed itself to be entirely responsible.[3] Each side reckoned on attacking, and reckoned without
being attacked. Maurepas at least seems to have thought it
possible that d'Antin would have to defend the French colonies,
when he saw the huge additions made to Ogle's squadron; he
had not provided for this in his original instructions to d'Antin,
but gave him orders for it in his later dispatches.[4] Wager, however, his counterpart in England, entertained no such doubts.
He wrote cheerfully to Vernon that he thought it no bad thing
if d'Antin and Laroche-Alart should arrive in the West Indies
a couple of months before Ogle; they would have time to fall
ill before the fresh English crews could come upon them.
Wager had been Commodore on the Jamaica station in Queen
Anne's reign, when France had sent squadrons to convoy the
Spanish galleons home. He was under the impression that this

[1] Newcastle to Harrington, Sept. 6, 1740, Add. MSS. 32695, f. 7.
[2] Orders to Ogle and Vernon, Sept. 25, 1740, Add. MSS. 32695, ff. 138, 147;
Newcastle to Vernon, Feb. 28, 1740/1, vol. 32696, f. 140. This suggestion seems
to have come first from Harrington, Sept. 14/25, 1740, S.P. 43/26.
[3] Norris told the Cabinet that 'if I did not believe, thair would be an engagement, I should not be of opinion to send any ships to west indias; considering the
grate stres that was layed on our week situation at home' (*Diary*, Oct. 21, 1740,
Add. MSS. 28133, f. 66).
[4] Letters of Oct. 7 and 23, already quoted.

was the chief purpose of d'Antin's expedition, and that it was meant to do very little more. As he believed that the treasure could not be ready for some months after d'Antin's arrival, he was quite content to let him stew for a while in St. Louis. Besides, he saw better than anybody else how hard it would be for d'Antin and Torres to victual and repair such huge squadrons in the tropical colonies.[1] Yet he could not have been so light-hearted had he known the terrible danger to which Ogle's delay would have exposed the inferior force of Vernon for two months, if d'Antin had done his duty. Nobody in the Ministry seems to have seen that but Lord Chancellor Hardwicke (who often noticed points of strategy which were not revealed to professional soldiers and sailors). The Jamaica interest in London also saw this point; it invariably scented a danger to that rich and defenceless island at least as soon as one existed. Neither Hardwicke nor the absentee planters could make any use of their forebodings; for if d'Antin was between Ogle and Vernon, with intention to cut them off in detail, there was nothing for it but to hope they would join without meeting him, and to order Vernon to keep his squadron safe in Port Royal harbour.[2]

The English Ministers were of half a mind to go farther, and declare war. Fleury fully expected they would do it, and deliberated accordingly upon his preparations for fastening a neutrality or mediation upon the States-General, fitting out privateers, and attacking the credit of the English funds (this was a stock article of French plans of campaign against England, but I have never seen any convincing details of the way it was to be done).[3] Newcastle ransacked a similar store of well-tried expedients. He thought of obliging the States-General to declare war against France, either by appealing to the defensive alliance of 1678, which did not apply to the defence of possessions outside Europe, or by making the most of the new French fortifications at Dunkirk; these were certainly a technical violation of the Treaty of Utrecht, and the Dutch might well be induced to resent them. He threw out suggestions of a grand

---

[1] Wager to Vernon, Oct. 11, 1740, and Feb. 24, 1740/1, *Original Letters to an Honest Sailor*, pp. 26, 32; May 3, 1741, Vernon-Wager MSS., Library of Congress.

[2] Hardwicke to Newcastle, Sept. 12, 1740, Add. MSS. 32695, f. 56; Knight to Sharpe, Oct. 2, f. 178; Newcastle to Vernon, Sept. 12, 1740, f. 47.

[3] *Mémoire* of Aug. 20, 1740, A.E. Angleterre, 409, f. 30; Amelot to Bussy, Oct. 16, 1740, f. 156; see also Bussy to Choiseul, July 17, 1761, vol. 444.

anti-Bourbon alliance, although the difficulty of engineering it had been one of the chief arguments against going to war with Spain in 1738. He even gave a moment's consideration to the curious project of maintaining a neutrality in Europe while the two nations attacked each other's possessions in America—a sort of recurrence to the seventeenth-century doctrine of 'no peace beyond the line'. The historian would have a hard task who attempted a serious account of every fantastic idea that flashed across Newcastle's mind and found its way into his memoranda. This one was peculiarly impracticable, as Newcastle himself admitted in the same breath that suggested it. There would have been no trusting to such a precarious neutrality, which might expose the British Isles to a sudden danger of invasion; moreover we should lose the use of one of our chief weapons against France, namely the destruction of her European trade.[1]

In the end the Ministers decided to do nothing, and wait on events. For a few days they thought war unavoidable, and drew up declarations against France, but after a little reflection they decided to give Bussy no answer until the King returned from Hanover; in the event they did not answer him in writing at all.[2] Newcastle merely complained by word of mouth that France was making war upon England without declaring it. The King's Speech at the opening of the session announced vaguely the intention to pursue the war against Spain, whatever obstacles should present themselves; but it made no open reference to the dispatch of d'Antin to the West Indies. The French representatives in London judged that the English Ministers would be content to make war without declaring it, reserving the right to come into the open if news of a clash should arrive from Vernon or if the Opposition should insist on it.[3]

---

[1] Newcastle to Harrington, Sept. 6, 1740, quoted above; 'Considerations', Oct. 7, 1740, Add. MSS. 35406, f. 266.

[2] Newcastle to Harrington (private), Sept. 19, 1740, S.P. 43/94. There are three drafts of an answer to Bussy in Add. MSS. 35406, ff. 243-7. They all denounce the conduct of France, but none of them declares war. The Duke of Richmond, who was in the confidence of some of the Ministers, told Lord Waldegrave that 'The French sending these squadrons to the West Indias is I think as plain a declaration of war as can be made, and you will hear that it is looked upon as such here' (Richmond to Waldegrave, Sept. 11, 1740, Waldegrave MSS.).

[3] Bussy to Amelot, Sept. 21, Oct. 3 and 13, Nov. 28, Dec. 5, 1740, A.E. Angleterre, 409, ff. 88, 122, 148, 263, 305.

The Opposition leaders announced to Bussy, of all ill-chosen confidants, that they might be obliged to roar loudly against the Ministry for suffering d'Antin to set out and Dunkirk to be rebuilt; they might even have to demand a war with France. They gracefully palliated this intention by explaining that they should do so out of no animosity against France, but only a desire to get rid of their own Prime Minister. They suggested that when he had been ruined, and they had conquered political power for themselves, they would be in a much better position than he had ever been, to make a peace on terms which would satisfy Fleury. This was not to be believed, for they numbered among themselves not only many of the loudest shouters against France, but some of her worst enemies.[1]

The winter passed, but no echo of the awaited explosion reached Europe from the West Indies. Both the elaborate trains of powder, which the two Governments had laid, had missed fire altogether.

It would be a depressing business to relate in detail the series of misfortunes which so easily overcame d'Antin's will to execute his instructions. At Martinique the soldiers were unready and the volunteers non-existent. Governor de Champigny had failed to collect the first or to inspire the second.[2] D'Antin found the same state of affairs at St. Louis, on the south coast of St. Domingue, which he reached on November 7, N.S. Here the reason was a more respectable one. The *Fée*, sent out with instructions to Governor de Larnage, had been seized by H.M.S. *Norwich*, on pretext of a difference of opinion about a salute, and carried into Jamaica. After she had been very improperly searched for her dispatches, which had been thrown overboard, she was released, but she met with an accident on her way to St. Domingue, and never arrived at all. Larnage therefore did not hear of the great expedition which he was to

---

[1] Bussy to Amelot, Nov. 28, 1740, A.E. Angleterre, 409, f. 263. When Bussy came back to England in 1761 he lamented that 'there were no longer any Opposition leaders to enlighten foreign Ministers as to the Government's difficulties' (Bussy to Choiseul, June 26, 1761, vol. 443). The Opposition of 1739 tried to depreciate Walpole by expressing an exaggerated admiration for Fleury's talents (Silhouette to Amelot, Nov. 26, 1739, vol. 405, f. 286; to Fleury, Dec. 31, f. 394). This compliment took a less courtly form in the popular caricatures of the time, in whose tasteless and overcrowded allegories Fleury always appeared as the successful villain—Fleury rocking the English lion to sleep, Fleury winning the European race astride a fox, Fleury receiving the crown of three continents.

[2] D'Antin to Maurepas, Oct. 1740, A.N. Marine B⁴ 50, f. 77.

organize against Jamaica, until d'Antin arrived and demanded the troops.[1]

D'Antin had been expressly ordered to keep his ships in harbour as little as possible, in order to avoid sickness among the crews. But he had only ten ships on his arrival; two more joined him on November 22. He would not risk his ten ships against Vernon's ten, especially as the latter was not so badly provided as he had been led to expect; and he was further intimidated by a short-lived rumour that Norris had arrived at Cape Donna Maria with the whole English fleet. This was only Vernon himself with some transports from North America; but those very transports diminished the already faint hope of a successful attack on Jamaica, because d'Antin had in various ways been disappointed of the land force that was to accompany him. D'Antin therefore stayed in St. Louis and waited for Laroche-Alart; as he expected him to arrive soon, it would perhaps have been a mistake to delay the junction of their forces by a very problematical expedition against Vernon. Laroche-Alart had an exceptionally bad passage, and did not come in until December 15. By that time d'Antin's crews were very sickly, and he was himself laid low by a fever which probably weakened his resolution.[2]

In the meantime a fresh cause for delay had arisen. Maurepas's dispatches of October 7 had arrived, and announced to d'Antin the project of co-operation between him and Torres. It was plainly d'Antin's duty to get into touch with Torres, and (less plainly) to stay where he was until he had done so. He sent off a messenger who was intercepted; another had to be sent after him, and Torres's reply did not come back until December 30. The difficulty of concerting action between commanders of two different nations now began to make itself felt. Their first duty was to defend two different sets of colonies, and their junction only optional. Torres had met a hurricane off Porto Rico; Ogle would have met it too if his Government had not decided, with a flash of common sense, not to send him off so as to arrive in the season.[3] Torres had put in to port, badly dismasted. Since then he had got to Cartagena and joined the

---

[1] D'Antin to Maurepas, Nov. 13, 1740, ibid., f. 79; Larnage to Maurepas, Nov. 9 and 13, 1740, A.N. Colonies C⁹ A 53.

[2] Larnage to Maurepas, Nov. 20 and 26, Dec. 5, 1740, ibid.; d'Antin to Maurepas, Dec. 22, 1740, A.N. Marine B⁴ 50, f. 81.

[3] Newcastle afterwards claimed that this decision had been taken, but I can find

galleons. D'Antin had suggested that they should unite forces, but Torres replied by making difficulties as to the place. He could not get so far to windward as Santa Marta, or even, perhaps, to St. Louis. He therefore proposed that d'Antin should pick him up off Cartagena, or at Cape Corientes, at the west end of Cuba, and they should then proceed to attack Jamaica or relieve Havana.[1]

D'Antin was now beginning to be affected by two motives which only too often deterred French commanders in the West Indies from bold enterprises. In the first place, he had not unlimited time for action. This was because his victuals were running short. He and Laroche-Alart had been provided with six months' rations, and told to execute the whole campaign on them if possible. Maurepas had sent after him enough for another month, and empowered him to procure further supplies in the colony if he could, and if it seemed important that he should stay longer. The Governor and Intendant were able to furnish him with a month's victuals, but it was doubtful how much farther they could go. The southern quarter of St. Domingue, where his fleet lay, was thinly settled and produced little; the communication with the other quarters was difficult. It would have been just as easy to bring provisions from the Windward Islands as from Cape François or Leogane; but they had been stricken by the hurricane a few months earlier, and most of their ground-crops had been destroyed. There remained the recourse of Jamaica, from whence, strange as it may seem, Larnage and Maillart had already drawn supplies of flour which they resold for the use of the galleons; but that was stopped at present by an embargo. It began therefore to look as if d'Antin must make sure of being home by the end of April. That would still have given him two months for his campaign in the West Indies. To Vernon this would have been an unquestionable argument for doing something at once; in d'Antin it seems to have inspired doubts whether he should be able to do anything at all, and reconciled him to the thought of doing nothing.

He had, besides, another reason against accepting Torres's

do trace of it; perhaps it was Newcastle's *ex post facto* justification of an unintended nelay (Newcastle to Vernon, Feb. 28, 1740/1, Add. MSS. 32696, f. 142). The hurricane season was generally reputed to end in the middle of October.

[1] Larnage to Torres, Dec. 6, 1740, A.N. Colonies C⁹ A 53; Larnage to Maurepas, Jan. 2, 1741, vol. 55; d'Antin to Maurepas, Jan. 5, 1741, A.N. Marine B⁴ 50.

offer. Since he had received Maurepas's dispatches of October,
he had been charged with the additional duty of protecting St.
Domingue against a possible invasion by a large English force.
If Torres could not be sure of coming up from Cartagena to
St. Louis, it could not be safe or justifiable for d'Antin to go
down from St. Louis to Cartagena. What if the English should
attack the colony behind his back? Could he be sure of returning to the rescue? Still greater was the danger of going down
to Cape Corientes and Havana. D'Antin consulted Larnage,
who presumably did not fail, as Governor of the colony, to put
forward this point of view, though he afterwards denied that he
had said anything to deter d'Antin from decisive action. For
these reasons d'Antin determined to stay where he was, holding
himself ready to succour Torres at Cartagena or Havana if he
needed it.

Torres accepted the offer; but in the meantime two events
took place which made it less likely than ever that d'Antin
would join him. Ogle joined Vernon at Jamaica; the arrival
of four more French ships under Roquefeuille was very little to
set off against this colossal English reinforcement. On their
way, some of Ogle's ships met some French men-of-war coming
round from Petit-Goave to St. Louis. They fell into an engagement, in which each side showed great gallantry and some
stupidity, and parted without being sure whether their action
had provoked a war between the two nations. All this put an
end to d'Antin's prospects of action. He deliberated with
Larnage and Laroche-Alart whether to procure another month's
victuals in the colony, and cruise against Vernon and Ogle or
blockade them in Port Royal. They decided against it. They
were not sure of persuading Torres to come up to windward
and join them in time, without whom they would be inferior to
Vernon's fleet. Moreover, they thought Ogle's fleet could not
leave port for a month, because it would be employed in watering its ships and refreshing its crews, so that there would be
little point in blockading a force which did not mean to come
out in the period for which they could afford to keep it shut up.
They little knew Vernon; and Maillart, the Intendant, seems
to have believed they could have found victuals for more than
a month, though Larnage denied it. If anything more had
been needed to keep d'Antin at St. Domingue, it was the fight
of the four ships with the English. The English captains did

not appear to have had orders to attack French warships and possessions (Ogle having presumably kept his instructions to himself, for use by the whole squadron if an opportunity occurred); but it was not certain such orders would not be given after the incident had taken place.

The only other service d'Antin could have performed was to protect the General of the galleons in holding the fair, and carry the treasure back to Europe. There seems to be no word of this in his original instructions, but Maurepas afterwards signified that he thought it very important. But even if d'Antin had tried to set about it from the first moment of his arrival, he could hardly have had time for it. The fair could only be set in motion by a long train of comings and goings. Messages had to be sent to Panama and thence to Lima, and the treasure had to come back along the same route. Some of the merchants had their money at Panama, but most of them had sent it back to Peru. There was also a difficulty which was held to be almost invincible: Portobello was destroyed, and the fair must therefore be held, if at all, at some place whose communications with Peru were even longer and worse. For all these reasons d'Antin had little hope of doing this part of his duty, or even leaving Roquefeuille behind to do it.[1]

He therefore returned ignominiously home. He was conscious of his failure, and wished he had given orders for hostilities against English ships as soon as he heard of the seizure of the *Fée*. It was Larnage who dissuaded him from it, by the very sensible argument that it would be doing too much or too little. Hostilities ought to be signalized by a decisive act or not at all. That was certainly the spirit of d'Antin's instructions, and Larnage rightly added that d'Antin would do the French colonies a great disservice if he provoked Vernon against them without destroying his power to hurt them, and then went home at the end of the season, leaving them exposed to Vernon's vengeance.[2] D'Antin had, in fact, done the Spaniards an ill turn

[1] Minute of Larnage and d'Antin, Feb. 2, 1741, A.N. Marine B⁴ 50, f. 223; Roquefeuille to Maurepas, Feb. 7, 1741, f. 277; Larnage to Maurepas, Jan. 10 and 12, Feb. 6 and 17, March 29, 1741, A.N. Colonies C⁹ A 55; Torres to Larnage, Jan. 22, 1741; De Lezo to Larnage, Jan. 23, 1741, ibid.; Maurepas to Maillart, Aug. 10, 1741, A.N. Colonies, B 72; Maurepas to d'Antin, Nov. 14 and 15, Dec. 30, 1740, A.N. Marine B² 311, Brest, ff. 245, 246, 313.

[2] Larnage to Maurepas, Dec. 7, 1740, A.N. Colonies C⁹ A 53; Feb. 6, Sept. 22, 1741, vol. 55.

of this kind. His expedition had attracted to the West Indies a much larger English force than had first been intended for them. Without doing anything to weaken or frustrate it, he sailed back to France at the end of six months and left Torres to face it. Torres might be to blame for the difficulty he made of joining the French squadron; but for all he knew, it was come to help him and not to be helped by him, and he had a legitimate grievance when he was forced to leave Cartagena defenceless on his departure to Havana. This injury was long and bitterly remembered at the Court of Spain.

D'Antin left Roquefeuille behind him for a few weeks with six ships, to offer in vain a junction with Torres off Cape Tiburon, which was not on his route to Havana. The main French squadron sailed sadly back to France, and d'Antin, received with obvious coldness by Maurepas, died at Brest a few days after his arrival.[1]

The French squib had petered out; would the English squib explode? Fate was somewhat unkind to Vernon as well as to d'Antin; but he met her with a manlier resistance. He had meant to meet Ogle off Cape Donna Maria (the south-west end of St. Domingue) instead of letting him come into Port Royal. Unfortunately, the letter he wrote to Cathcart for this purpose did not reach him, and Vernon, waiting at Jamaica for news that the reinforcement was ready to join him at the rendezvous, was surprised to see the whole fleet preparing to come into harbour. There was no help for it. The ships must have wood and water, and might as well take it in at Kingston. Meanwhile the Council of War could be held, to determine the first objective. The commanders took a brave and wise resolution. They had orders to attack the French fleet if they thought fit; and they saw the danger to which they would expose Jamaica if they went off to any other destination and left a large French force ready to strike from the windward. They decided that no expedition could safely be undertaken against the Spaniards until the French had been cleared away; it was therefore the French whom they went out to seek.[2]

It was time wasted, for d'Antin had already got round Cape

---

[1] Instructions to Roquefeuille, Nov. 12, 1740, A.N. Marine B⁴ 50, f. 91; Roquefeuille to Maurepas, Feb. 7, 1741, ibid., f. 277; Begon to Maurepas, April 20, 1741, ibid., f. 279; Maurepas to d'Antin, April 26, 1741, A.N. Marine B² 313, Brest, f. 123; to Roquefeuille, April 26, 1741, f. 127.

[2] Wentworth to Newcastle, Jan. 20, 1740/1, C.O. 5/42.

Tiburon, unnoticed by the English cruisers, and was now slipping away from Petit-Goave. The delay was aggravated by the wrong information of Vernon's scouts, who mistook some merchant ships for the French fleet, and kept him off the coast of St. Domingue for more than a week longer than he should have needed, to find that the bird was flown. All these accidents made him lose nearly six weeks of his time, and arrive at Cartagena nearer the beginning of the sickly season. He might also have found and destroyed Torres's ships in the harbour if he had come sooner. This was all the service that d'Antin had done to the Spaniards by his presence; but perhaps it was enough, for the expedition miscarried at Cartagena, and the English squib went out as foolishly as the French.[1]

There were moments in 1741 when the history of 1740 nearly repeated itself. The French representative in London was almost imploring his Government to make war upon England while so large a part of her naval force was away in the West Indies and the Mediterranean.[2] In the late summer Maurepas thought of sending out Roquefeuille to intercept the reinforcements which the English were sending to Vernon. He was not to go so far as the West Indies this time, but he was to interfere quite as effectively with the great West India expedition. This design was given up, but perhaps the English Ministry had some inkling of it, for Newcastle told Vernon in October that a squadron was reported to be destined from Toulon to the West Indies, and instructed him to serve it, if he met it, in the same way as he was to have served d'Antin.[3] The necessity for this did not arise, and the two nations kept the peace at sea till the spring of 1744.

[1] Vernon to Newcastle, Feb. 24, 1740/1, S.P. 42/90, f. 20; Council of War, minutes of Feb. 8, 16, and 23, ff. 25, 28, and 39.

[2] Silhouette to Amelot, July 10, 1741, A.E. Angleterre, 412, f. 191. The prospect of this made Wager very uncomfortable. (Wager to Vernon, Aug. 18, 1741, *Original Letters to an Honest Sailor*, p. 48.)

[3] Maurepas to Roquefeuille, July 19, Oct. 2, 1741, A.N. Marine B² 314, Brest, ff. 26, 121; Newcastle to Vernon, Oct. 15, 1741, Add. MSS. 32698, f. 157.

V

THE WARS AGAINST FRANCE IN THE WEST INDIES

§ i. *The Objects of West Indian Campaigns, 1739–59*

IN the West Indies the war with France was a very different kind of struggle from the war with Spain. The former was dictated by the rivalry between one set of sugar colonies and another, the latter by an impulse to acquire new establishments, or at least new trades, complementary to those which already existed within the Empire. The French war was what the Spanish war was not, a matter of life and death.

The English and French had already been at war many times in the West Indies. Only one small territory—the French half of St. Christopher's—had changed masters in those conflicts. Even for this meagre acquisition there was a special cause. The Whigs had not stipulated for it at the negotiations of Gertruydenburg in 1710, but the English planters pointed out to the Tory Government soon afterwards that the division of the island between the two nations was an opportunity for illicit trade and a source of insecurity which discouraged settlers and investors.[1] So French St. Kitts was kept at the Peace of Utrecht. Perhaps if England had conquered more in the West Indies that war, she would have kept more; yet that is by no means certain, for the instructions proposed by the Admiralty for the expedition of 1703 seem to indicate that if either Martinique or Guadeloupe had been taken, it was to have been depopulated of Frenchmen and the plantations destroyed, but not colonized by the English.[2] On that occasion Sir Hovenden Walker—certainly no favourable critic of colonists—alleged that the Creoles did not want to keep possession of Guadeloupe, because it would reduce the price of sugar;[3] this was not the last time such a charge was made. The Government afterwards intended some revenge for the French devastation of Nevis and St. Kitts; but there is no proof that it meant to annex any of the French sugar colonies. At the same time the Secretary of State told Governor Parke that he was on no account to

---

[1] *C.S.P. Col. 1710–11*, nos. 336, 520, 810 (i).
[2] *C.S.P. Col. 1702–3*, nos. 170, 192.   [3] Ibid., no. 737.

favour an attempt on Porto Rico, because it would lead to a further depopulation of the strategically important Leeward Islands.[1]

The spokesmen of the West India interest were not so foolish as to proclaim aloud their aversion to new sugar colonies, or to veto annexations; but there was a remarkable silence on this head in the plans of operations which they put forward. James Knight, for example, in the suggestions which he made to the Ministry, offered many reasons for destroying the French West Indies but none for their permanent conquest. He argued that the French of St. Domingue were dangerous competitors to Jamaica in peace and still more dangerous neighbours in war, when they could threaten the shipping bound for England in the Windward Passage, or run down suddenly before the wind and sack the east end of Jamaica. We ought to prevent this by weakening them; it would diminish the trade and navigation of France, enable the English sugar colonies to recover their foreign markets, and encourage them to improve their settlements and re-establish the cultivation of indigo.[2] Governor Trelawny suggested more bluntly that 'unless French Hispaniola is ruined during the war, they will, upon a peace, ruin our sugar colonies by the quantity they will make and the low price they afford to sell it at'.[3] Instances could be multiplied, in which the same point was implied or stated with more decent vagueness. The French Government knew it very well. In the Seven Years War the French Ministers of Marine, Machault and Moras, were sure that England would attack St. Domingue before any other French colony in the West Indies, because it most excited their envy and rivalry; Moras only had a slight doubt how much of his forces Pitt would think it worth while to apply to a purely destructive conquest.[4]

---

[1] *C.S.P. Col. 1706–8*, no. 591.

[2] Knight to Newcastle, Oct. 21, 1740, Add. MSS. 32695, f. 309; July 22, 1744, vol. 22677, ff. 53–7.

[3] Trelawny to Newcastle, March 12, 1747/8, C.O. 137/58. But Trelawny wrote with apparent enthusiasm, a few weeks later, that the planters of St. Domingue might be induced to submit by guaranteeing them a free enjoyment of their religion and property (Trelawny to Newcastle, April 5, 1748, ibid.).

[4] Office minute of Aug. 31, 1755, A.N. Colonies C⁹ A 97; Machault to Vaudreuil, May 20, 1756, B 103; Moras to Bart and Laporte-Lalanne, Oct. 7, 1757, B 105. They proved to be mistaken, for St. Domingue was almost the only important French colony which the English did not try to conquer in this war. That was because even Pitt was afraid of offending Spain by exciting her fears for Cuba and

These are the ambitions of the respectable tradesman who hopes to increase his custom by hiring the racketeer to destroy his neighbour's shop[1]. They were not peculiar to the English planters. The French colonists seem to have disliked the prospect of expansion quite as much, in spite of their greater progress in sugar cultivation and the more flourishing air of their establishments. Those of St. Domingue were very much alarmed by the rumours that Corsica was to be exchanged for the Spanish half of their island, because they were afraid of the effect of expansion on the price of sugar;[2] at Martinique, Governor de Champigny did not want to allow sugar cultivation in the Neutral Islands. Nor did the Government's projects or instructions for attempts against the English colonies usually aim at annexation. D'Antin, for example, was to blow up the fortifications of Jamaica, destroy the towns, and carry off as many negroes as possible, but not to keep the island—or if he did so, it was to be in the name of the King of Spain. There might be a special reason for this in Fleury's desire to uphold his tattered reputation for disinterestedness; but that could not account for Maurepas's instruction to Caylus to take Barbados, 'not so much, however, in order to keep it as to destroy it and take away all the negroes'.[3] The need of slaves often inspired French strategy in this way. Always under-supplied, especially in time of war, the planters were only too willing to help themselves at the expense of the English. In fact, they had often done it during Queen Anne's reign, when they had matters very much their own way in the West Indies. The expeditions to St. Kitts and Nevis in 1706, and to Montserrat in 1712, seem to have been made for little other reason: 3,200 slaves were taken from Nevis, and the inhabitants obliged to sign a capitulation—not to surrender the island, but to hand over 1,400 more who could

S. Domingo. When Spain threw off her neutrality, the French colonists and Government recognized that the danger of St. Domingue was increased. (Bart to Berryer, May 25, 1761, A.N. Colonies C⁹ A 108; Louis XV to Bory, Oct. 13, 1761, B 111.)

[1] 'By a well-managed descent upon their sugar islands, of which they are as tender as the apple of their eye, we should at once ruin them, and promote the welfare of our own for many years. This might be done by only destroying their *ingenios* or sugar-works, and carrying off their slaves.' (*The Present Ruinous Land-War proved to be a H——r War* (London, 1745), p. 24.)

[2] Larnage to Maurepas, Sept. 27, 1740, A.N. Colonies C⁹ A 52.

[3] Instructions to d'Antin, Aug. 14, 1740, A.N. Marine B² 311, f. 59; instructions to Caylus, Oct. 6, 1744, A.N. Colonies B 78.

not at present be delivered, because they had regained their liberty during the invasion and taken to the mountain.[1]

Both Governments showed themselves indifferent to the acquisition of sugar islands during the war of 1744; the French only projected expeditions which would destroy without acquiring, and the English left expeditions alone altogether, except for the attempt which Admiral Townsend was empowered to make against Porto Rico or St. Lucia in 1745. This enterprise does not really prove any great interest in the conquests proposed. Townsend's mission was to save the Leeward Islands from invasion by Caylus, and he was only recommended to attack the French and Spanish colonies if he should find—as he did—that no such invasion had taken place and he had therefore nothing, else to do. He did nothing, because he met with no support from the planters and little from the Governors in this undertaking. Neither Barbados nor the Leeward Islands would give any help to an expedition against St. Lucia; Governor Mathew talked of attacking Porto Rico, but would rather send Townsend to sweep the roads of Martinique and Guadeloupe, in order to distress the French sugar colonies and to destroy their privateers which did so much damage to the trade of Antigua.[2] So far as the English Ministry had any desire for conquests at the expense of France in America, it looked to Canada and Cape Breton. This was very natural, for there the colonists were as eager for new territory as those of the West Indies were indifferent to it; they not only made the expulsion of the French from Canada a popular object in England, but proved their zeal by the expedition against Louisbourg in which they took the greatest part. It was therefore the colonies of settlement, not the tropical colonies of exploitation, that chiefly inspired the fervour of annexationists in this war.

There was, however, one interesting action in the West Indies. Admiral Knowles and Governor Trelawny wound up the war in 1748 by taking St. Louis, the strongest fort in St. Domingue. They do not seem to have set very much store by it, for they meant to attack Santiago de Cuba first and St. Louis only second, and it was the winds that compelled them

---

[1] *C.S.P. Col. 1706–8*, no. 357, ii–vii; *1712–14*, no. 38.

[2] Orders to Townsend, June 18, 1745, Adm. 2/64, p. 285; Townsend to Corbett, Oct. 1, 1745, Adm. 1/305; Robinson to Townsend, Sept. 14, ibid.; Mathew to Townsend, Sept. 23, ibid.

to change the order. The motives of this enterprise are not very clear from the English records. Both Knowles and Trelawny spoke of battering down all the forts of St. Domingue and putting the inhabitants at His Majesty's mercy. It might be supposed that they conquered for the mere sake of conquering; but the French officers took a different view, and so did Knowles's enemies in Jamaica, whom he called the 'Scotch party'. They thought he meant to engross the trade of the southern quarter of St. Domingue.

This was very likely true. The English had always had their eye on this quarter. It was the nearest part of the colony to Jamaica, and the best field for an illicit trade because it was the most neglected by the French merchants, and being the latest to develop, had more need of labour than any other. The merchants of Jamaica had diligently smuggled negroes there for some years before the war. The captains of His Majesty's ships of war did not disdain to protect this traffic and to dip into it for themselves, and Knowles had given particular cause of complaint to the French Governor. It would not be surprising if one of his first schemes, when he came back to the station as Admiral, was to take steps for starting the trade again. His friend Trelawny had had his finger in several big dealings with the Spanish enemy during this war, and might not share the common prejudice that while it was all very well to trade with the Spaniards who were not rival producers of sugar, there was something wrong in trading with the French, who were. Their actions gave colour to this view. The capitulation which Knowles imposed upon St. Louis provided expressly that English warships should enter the harbour unmolested. It did not add that English merchant vessels might do the same, perhaps because Knowles and Trelawny meant to keep the trade to themselves. Knowles and his officers repeated several times to the inhabitants of the quarter, that they meant no harm but to the French King's ships and forts, and were ready to 'favour' the planters. They particularly insisted that they must not be disturbed or opposed in wooding and watering their ships; considering the abuses to which wooding and watering had given rise on that coast, it is not unreasonable to suspect that it was meant to cover some kind of trade in this instance. Lastly, how else did Knowles come to receive, endorse, and remit to Europe in this year a bill drawn by merchants of St. Louis? No ransom was payable according to the capitulation, therefore this bill must be accounted for by some commercial dealings.[1]

Naval officers may be shocked by a suggestion which reflects so much upon the honour of their service, but the records prove that this kind of practice was very far from uncommon at that time. The officers of the navy seem to have traded again with the French islands after the war. Commodore Holburne and Captain Falkingham of the Leeward Islands station were complained of; and the commanders of French frigates who were sent out there to suppress smuggling were instructed to circumvent the English men-of-war so far as they could politely do so, and even to use or threaten force if they thought it safe.[2]

Both Governments changed their attitude to West India conquests in the Seven Years War. Great expeditions were sent out on both sides. France designed four for the West Indies, whereas she had only sent one in the last war. No doubt one reason why she could afford to do so was the unimportance of Mediterranean operations after the capture of Minorca. The Toulon fleet was released for service elsewhere; it was to have sent squadrons to the West Indies in 1757 and 1759.[3] In 1758 and 1761 detach-

---

[1] Knowles to Newcastle, March 13, 1747/8, C.O. 137/58; Knowles to Anson, Nov. 6, 1748, Add. MSS. 15956, f. 163; Chastenoye to Maurepas, March 26 and April 8, A.N. Colonies C⁹ A 72; Rancé to Maurepas, April 9, vol. 73; Lascelles and Maxwell to Knowles, Aug. 6, W. & G. iii. Knowles's smuggling of slaves had been the subject of a diplomatic representation by Amelot to Waldegrave, June 2, 1739, S.P. 44/225, p. 3; Larnage and Maillart to Maurepas, July 2, 1739, A.N. Colonies C⁹ A 50. The capitulations of the town and fortress are in Adm. 1/234.

[2] Bompar to Grenville, May 21, 1751, C.O. 28/29, CC 128; minute of Nov. 1749, A.N. Marine B⁴ 62, f. 217; Puysieulx to Albemarle, May 23, o.s., 1750, S.P. 78/236, f. 72. Of course Holburne denied the charge (Holburne to Clevland, Sept. 28, 1750, Adm. 1/306).

[3] The squadron of La Clue, which Osborn intercepted at Cartagena in the winter of 1757–8, was on its way to St. Domingue. I cannot find any evidence for Sir Julian Corbett's statement that La Clue was to have gone on to Louisbourg. Both Machault and Moras believed St. Domingue to be particularly threatened with an English invasion; La Clue was certainly to stay there until August or September 1758, when St. Aignan was to join him. He was then to receive further orders, but whatever they could have been, they could hardly have been to go to Louisbourg at that time of the year (Moras to La Clue, Sept. 19, 1757, A.N. Marine B² 357; to St. Aignan, Sept. 19, ibid.). La Clue's fleet which Boscawen caught at Lagos in 1759 is supposed to have been sailing round to Brest in order to join Conflans for an invasion of England; but there is some evidence that it too was at one time designed by Berryer for the defence of the West Indies. Berryer told Beauharnois on July 26 that he must expect no help before the end of the year, because the Government needed all its strength for the invasion of England; but in another dispatch of July 29, he distinctly implied that La Clue was to go to Martinique (A.N. Colonies B 109). La Clue was under orders to go to Cadiz, for

ments were made from the Atlantic fleet itself—so highly did
the French Government value the preservation of Martinique.
Bompar and Blénac, their commanders, had orders to recover
any French islands that had been taken by the English, or to
retaliate by seizing some English colonies; and whereas d'Antin
had been ordered not to annex Jamaica at all in 1740, or to
do so in the name of the King of Spain, Blénac was to take it,
if he could, for the King of France.[1] This, however, does not
prove that the French Government was converted to a policy
of annexation, for whatever France had conquered after 1758
could only have served to redeem her losses.

The English subdued all the Windward Islands in this war,
and annexed the Neutral Islands too.[2] This is the more surprising, since the avowed object of the war was not the West
Indies but North America. Yet there was logic in Pitt's
strategy. He attempted no conquest in the West Indies until he
was sure of Cape Breton and the entrance to the St. Lawrence.
His friend Beckford, the West India millionaire, said he had
never been for any West India expedition until Cape Breton
was ours, but now pressed warmly for an attack on Martinique.
Such a demand for West India conquests by the leader of the
sugar interest may seem to give the lie to all I have said about
its dislike of expansion; but notice Beckford's arguments. He
did not propose to keep Martinique; we were to take it in order
to exchange it for Minorca, and so avoid paying for that lost
island by restoring Cape Breton a second time.[3] In fact the war
had entered the stage of collecting counters to be used as
currency in peace negotiations, in order to keep the conquests
which we really cherished. It may be asked, why then did Pitt
not wait a little longer, until he had conquered Canada, before
he diverted his strength to eccentric operations of this kind?

which he was making when Boscawen came up with him. Berryer told Aubeterre,
at Madrid, that La Clue was to go on to the West Indies (A.N. Marine B² 363).
Berryer might have changed his mind, or concealed it from Aubeterre; but after
La Clue's disaster, when there was no reason for pretence, he told Beauharnois
that the squadron had been designed for Martinique (Berryer to Beauharnois,
Nov. 9, 1759, A.N. Colonies B 109; *mémoire* of March 3, 1760, C⁸ B 10). This is
not surprising, for Berryer was very anxious for the safety of Martinique, and
believed the English would have attempted it the next season after the conquest
of Guadeloupe, instead of waiting till 1762.

[1] Private instruction to Bompar, Nov. 15, 1758, A.N. Marine B² 359; to Blénac,
Oct. 12, 1761, vol. 368.

[2] For the history of the Neutral Islands, *v. infra*, pp. 195–216.

[3] Beckford to Pitt, Aug. 26, 1758, G.D. 8/19.

Several answers suggest themselves. To attack the French colonies in two places at once would be to disorganize the defensive combinations by which Machault and Moras had kept up the war. If Pitt wanted Canada he had the key of it already, for we had taken Louisbourg. Moreover, Pitt did not yet think the annexation of all Canada a necessary condition of the peace; he only insisted on establishing a satisfactory military frontier, and the rest of the province was no more a *sine qua non* than Louisbourg with its fisheries, Goree with its command of the slave trade, or even Guadeloupe itself.[1] Therefore 1758, rather than 1759, was the year when the prize was in our power, and the war became a general contest of endurance in which all ways of damaging the enemy and reducing him to submission were equally good, no matter whether they resulted in conquests which we had a mind to keep permanently.

§ ii. *The Conquest of Guadeloupe*

Pitt's first success in the West Indies was the conquest of Guadeloupe by Commodore Moore and Generals Hopson and Barrington in the spring of 1759. It was an open question whether the island would be permanently annexed to the Crown at the peace, but there were some questions which must be decided at once. What was to become of the French planters? Were they to stay on the island, and what rights were they to enjoy? Many English colonists expected that if we were to keep Guadeloupe, we should clear the French inhabitants off it and settle Englishmen in their room. Nothing of the sort took place, because it was uncertain at first whether the conquest would be permanent or provisional, and still more because the English commanders signed a capitulation which was very favourable to the French; indeed it was far better than the islanders had any reason to expect, for their own Governors had tried to fire their patriotism by foretelling that the English would drive them off the island.[2]

Moore and Barrington even allowed the capitulants to be neutral between England and France. They were to have complete religious freedom, and security for church as well as lay

---

[1] Newcastle to Hardwicke, Oct. 31, 1759, Add. MSS. 32897, f. 520; *v. infra*, pp. 216–26.

[2] Nadau du Treil to Massiac, Dec. 25, 1758, A.N. Colonies C⁷ A 17; Beauharnois to Nadau, Feb. 8, 1759, C⁸ A 62. This was an allusion to the unhappy fate of the Acadians.

property. They were to enjoy their old laws, which were to be administered by their own officers. For the present, they were to pay no more duties than they had paid to the King of France; if the island was kept at the peace, they were to pay the same duties as the most favoured of the English Leeward Islands— that presumably means the $4\frac{1}{2}$ per cent. on exports. They were to have the same freedom of trade within the Empire as any of His Majesty's subjects, saving the Navigation Acts and the privileges of companies. They should not be obliged to furnish barracks for troops or *corvées* for fortifications; negroes should only be employed on that work with the consent of their masters, and their hire should be paid. This was a remarkable concession, for it put the Guadeloupe capitulants in a better position than any other slave-owners in the West Indies, whether English or French. Owners of property in Guadeloupe might leave it for Martinique or Dominica after they had paid their debts in full. Absentees, and those in the service of the King of France, might keep their estates in Guadeloupe and manage them by attorney. Planters might send their children to be educated in France and remit there for their support. Perhaps the most remarkable of all the articles was the eleventh, which promised that British subjects should not be allowed to acquire any lands in Guadeloupe before the peace was signed; only then, if Guadeloupe remained an English possession, might the planters sell their lands to Englishmen.[1]

The planters of Guadeloupe cannot have looked upon themselves as losers by these terms. On the contrary, their submission to English rule was followed by a sudden transition from misery to plenty. Few ships had come from France to Guadeloupe in time of peace, and none at all in war. Its trade was in the hands of the *commissionnaires*, or factors of St. Pierre, Martinique, who took their toll of the feckless planters and had many of them in their debt. In war-time, the coasting trade from one island to another was at least as much interrupted as the voyages across the Atlantic. Therefore Guadeloupe obtained victuals and plantation stores with even greater difficulty than Martinique, and had large stocks of perishable sugar decaying on the plantations for want of transport. The English conquest made a great difference to all this. At first indeed it was

[1] Capitulation of Guadeloupe, Adm. 1/307. The English and French texts of the eleventh article do not quite agree, but this appears to be the sense.

a difference for the worse, because the island had been reduced to submission slowly and a great deal of valuable property had been destroyed; also some slaves were seized as plunder before the capitulation, and sold off the island.[1] But the English and American merchants soon rushed in to supply Guadeloupe with everything for which it had starved, and thus the planters had the direct trade with Europe, of which they had been deprived so long.

The capitulation was not quite perfect. There seems to have been a difficulty about importing coffee into England, or else it was less advantageous than sending it to the rest of Europe; the planters accordingly smuggled it out to St. Eustatius, and smuggled in French wine, which they could not very well obtain from England or any of its dominions. The English Governors tried hard to suppress this trade; the colonists, on the other hand, sent a certain Deshayes to London to get the capitulation modified and the inconveniences remedied. Nevertheless, these were only small grievances to set off against the immense advantage of a free and safe export of sugars to one of the best closed markets in the world.[2]

Barbados soon complained that the price of victuals was raised by the vast shipments for Guadeloupe. North American traders hurried their ships for the first market, hoping to arrive while the famine prices for lumber and provisions continued and produce, especially molasses, could be picked up dirt-cheap. Hasten as they might, most of them were too late, for a normal equilibrium of prices was soon restored. The slave-merchants made the best harvest of all. Although the captors had carried off a number of negroes at the conquest, there were 7,500 more in February 1762 than there had been in 1759; at the peace, the Liverpool merchants alone claimed to have imported 12,437

[1] Dalrymple to Egremont, Feb. 16, 1762, C.O. 110/2. William Mathew Burt, the commissary for the sale of captured goods, complained that the plunder of negroes was very small because the capitulation was too favourable and the army co-operated with the planters in keeping as much as possible out of his hands. We cannot rely much on the evidence of an official cheated out of commissions and a planter of a neighbouring island who disliked the leniency shown to Guadeloupe (Burt to Pitt, May 2, 1759, and March 7, 1761, G.D. 8/24).

[2] *Mémoire* on Deshayes's business, June 1760, C.O. 152/29, CC 52; Crump to Pitt, Oct. 4, 1759, Kimball, *Correspondence of William Pitt with Colonial Governors*, ii. 176; Dalrymple to Pitt, July 15, 1761, ii. 450. Choiseul said in 1762 that the fall of Martinique would bring relief to the absentee sugar-proprietors, who would at last be able to get some of their crops remitted to Europe (Choiseul to Ossun, April 5, 1762, A.E. Espagne, 536; Paris news of April 12, 1762, S.P. 84/499).

slaves into Guadeloupe.[1] As if the unprompted alacrity of the English merchants were not enough, the planters instructed Deshayes to stimulate them to send out goods on credit. This was very necessary because the island had lately been devastated, and because otherwise the *commissionnaires* of Antigua would get the planters as much into their hands as those of Martinique had done.[2]

The planters were presumably delivered for a time from the need of settling their accounts with the *commissionnaires* of St. Pierre, but they fell quickly into debt with their new purveyors. The laws of the French colonies were notoriously insufficient to enforce the payment of debts (though perhaps they were not so very much worse than those of the English islands, and the horror with which they inspired Governor Dalrymple was partly due to his inexperience of the West Indies). The protection of most forms of property from distraint for debt made it easy for the planters to avoid paying anything at all, unless the decisions of the law were enforced by the military officers, who were the real rulers of the French islands. The French Governors had not always been inclined to use this sanction. Punctuality in the payment of debts was not one of the points of honour upon which the accepted code of behaviour most insisted.

Dalrymple set himself to protect the interests of the English merchant creditors, by measures which may have existed on paper under the French rule but had seldom been executed. He introduced a summary jurisdiction for debt, with the penalty of imprisonment. This was the more necessary, and the more unpopular, when it became obvious that the Government

[1] Barbados Assembly Minutes, Oct. 2, 1759, C.O. 31/29; Caleb Cowpland to Thomas Clifford, June 14, 1759, Clifford Correspondence, ii, no. 185, H.S.P.; Thomas Tipping to Clifford, July 7, no. 195; Thomas Wharton, jr., St. Kitts, to Thomas Wharton, Jan. 2, June 18, and July 28, 1759, Wharton Papers, Box II, H.S.P.; Dalrymple to Egremont, Feb. 16, 1762, C.O. 110/2; *Considerations on the Present Peace as far as it is relative to the Colonies*, pp. 11–13. Already on June 27 George Dodge reported to his owners that molasses was very scarce and dear at Fort Louis; vessels were arriving daily—there were already twenty in the island—and they were raising the price so fast by their demand that it would soon be as dear as in the English islands (Dodge to Timothy Orne and Co., June 27, 1759, Timothy Orne MSS., xi. 77, Essex Institute). The market continued to disappoint the captains of Orne's vessels (John Hodgson to Orne, Feb. 4, 1761, xi. 101). Molasses rose in a year from 6½ pieces of eight to 11 at Guadeloupe, and touched 14 in 1761; by 1763 it had fallen back to 11.

[2] *Mémoire* on Deshayes's business, quoted above.

was going to give Guadeloupe back at the peace; for unless exceptional measures were taken, during the remainder of the English occupation, to collect the debts or at least to have them ascertained beyond the possibility of evasion, there was little hope that any real payment would be made within the period allotted for withdrawing English effects.[1] The French, on the other hand, became more determined than ever to avoid paying. By the transference from France to England, they had escaped from the old creditors to the new, and had obtained access to good markets for their produce. They now proposed to make the same advantage from their restitution to France: to escape back again from the new creditors to the old, and to send their produce as soon as they could to the French market, which had been very short of sugar since the loss of Martinique and would offer high prices to the earliest comers. For both these reasons they tried in the last months of the English occupation to withhold their effects from their creditors, and Dalrymple did all he could to prevent them from doing so.[2]

No doubt his popularity suffered for it; but in the main, the English rule was mild and well received in Guadeloupe. One or two of the articles of the capitulation were broken. For instance, Dalrymple threatened in 1761 to sequestrate the estates of such capitulants as still served in the French army at Martinique; this he did in order to sow dissension there on the eve of the English invasion, but he did not carry out his threat after the siege was over.[3] His predecessor General Crump seems to have introduced justices of the peace, which were not provided for by the capitulation, but were a necessary substitute for the rule of the military officers. They were ineffective according to the former *commissaire-ordonnateur* Marin, who

[1] These provisions opened a door to abuses by which Guadeloupe molasses continued to claim the benefit of a lawful importation into the English colonies some time after the peace. Such goods purported to be the effects of English creditors withdrawn from the island within the prescribed period; but it would appear that the value of the 'creditors' certificates' was doubtful (Israel Lovitt to Timothy Orne and Co., June 8, 1764, Timothy Orne MSS. xii. 63, Essex Institute).

[2] Dalrymple to Pitt, Feb. 21, 1761, C.O. 110/1; Sept. 14, Nov. 16, 1761, C.O. 110/2 (printed by Kimball, ii. 467, 483); Dalrymple's proclamation about weights and measures, May 4, 1761, C.O. 110/1; Dalrymple to Egremont, Oct. 21, 1762, Feb. 26, May 8, June 11 and 26, 1763, C.O. 110/2; Dalrymple to the merchants of Guadeloupe, Jan. 15, 1763, ibid.

[3] Dalrymple to La Touche, Dec. 25, 1761, C.O. 110/2; to Egremont, April 9, 1762, ibid.; Egremont to Dalrymple, Aug. 7, 1762, ibid.

thought they allowed too much licence to the lower orders of the people. Other departures from tradition were more welcome to the politicians of the island. The *Conseil Supérieur*, which had led a repressed and meagre existence under the French Government, was allowed more influence and consideration by Crump and Dalrymple, and some kind of representative assembly was called together upon several occasions.[1] The political leaders of the island seem to have used this freedom saucily, but Dalrymple overlooked it, as he was convinced that they only wanted to make a merit in case the island should be restored to its former master, by showing themselves good Frenchmen at small risk and expense. The Governors appear to have exercised a kind of patronizing tact and common sense, and though they doubtless flattered themselves with too high an estimate of their own popularity, it is certain that they were not hated.[2]

In fact the French authorities at Martinique soon began to hint that their subjects envied a little too openly the prosperity to which Guadeloupe had been admitted by the conquest—cheap slaves and necessaries, good prices, rapidly increasing cultivation, new creditors with clean slates. Whether this consideration was in any sense a cause of the speedy surrender of Martinique in 1762, is a matter open to doubt. The planters were happier and brisker under Governor Le Vassor de la Touche than they had been for some time past, and their spirits had been revived by a plenty of provisions, arising from a great number of English prizes. La Touche does not seem to have suggested this reason for the haste with which the inhabitants capitulated without the consent of their leaders.[3]

---

[1] Crump to Pitt, Oct. 4, 1759, C.O. 110/1 (printed by Kimball, ii. 176); Dalrymple to Pitt, Feb. 21, 1761, ibid.; Dalrymple to Egremont, Feb. 16, 1762, Feb. 26, 1763, C.O. 110/2; Marin to Berryer, July 10, 1759, A.N. Colonies C⁸ A 62; Le Mercier de la Rivière, *mémoire* on the siege of Martinique, Aug. 5, 1762, C⁸ A 64. Martinique seems to have had a similar assembly under English rule; its original purpose was the raising of funds (see its petition to Rufane in C.O. 166/2); Rufane to Egremont, July 19 and Dec. 1, 1762, ibid.

[2] Dalrymple's letters on the questions of language, laws, and religion show a very fair degree of enlightenment and understanding, and form an interesting appendix to the better-known history of the beginnings of English rule in Canada. The harshest thing he did was to dock the negroes of their too frequent Church holidays.

[3] Beauharnois to Berryer, May 17 and Oct. 2, 1759, A.N. Colonies C⁸ A 62; Le Mercier de la Rivière's *mémoire* already quoted. Berryer took the view that if there was any discontent or disposition to envy the lot of Guadeloupe, it was due

In the meantime the Governors of Guadeloupe had at least as much trouble to endure from their fellow countrymen as from the French. The capitulation had not introduced English law; in fact it expressly excluded it. Governor Crump was therefore forced to treat all English merchants as camp-followers of the army, and to govern them by the Articles of War. The Board of Trade half-heartedly suggested the establishment of an English judicial system for English subjects, but its hint does not seem to have been taken. The merchants remained subject either to the French law, or in their dealings with each other to the jurisdiction of the Governor as Chancellor. Some of them gave vent to a few cant expressions about the liberties of Englishmen, but Dalrymple made short work of them. As there were no English courts, though he had pressed for their establishment, and no English laws in force except the Acts of Trade and the Articles of War, he told the merchants that if they did not wish to live under such a government they must leave in three weeks. They stayed. Dalrymple was a good friend to them, as he showed by the zeal with which he helped them to collect their debts before the English occupation should terminate.[1]

When the terms of the capitulation were known in London, some West India planters were very angry. Newcastle wrote to Hardwicke, with a shade of alarm,

'Lord Anson told me there were letters in Town from some American proprietors, who are not satisfied with the capitulation; as the island, upon their total submission, is left as it was with regard to the inhabitants and their effects, whereas they wished to have had it destroyed, their negroes taken, and the whole demolished. But it is always a good thing to have in hand.'

(This last sentence shows that Newcastle thought of Guadeloupe rather as an asset to bargain with than as a permanent acquisition.) Hardwicke made light of the planters' selfish objection.

---

to recent misgovernment; see his letter to Beauharnois, July 26, 1759, and to Beauharnois and La Rivière, Aug. 27, A.N. Colonies B 109; see also May, *Histoire économique de la Martinique* (Paris, 1930), p. 288.

[1] Crump to Pitt, Oct. 4, 1759, C.O. 110/1, printed by Kimball, ii. 176; Dalrymple to Pitt, Feb. 21, April 15, 1761, C.O. 110/1; Oct. 20, 1761, C.O. 110/2; to Egremont, Jan. 27, 1762, ibid.; Board of Trade to George II, Aug. 31, 1759, C.O. 153/18, pp. 155–64; John Harper to Thomas Clifford, Dec. 24, 1761, Clifford Correspondence, iii, no. 264, H.S.P.; Rufane to Egremont, July 19, 1762, C.O. 166/2.

They have but one point in view, which is how it may affect their particular interest; and they wish all colonies destroyed but that wherein they are particularly interested, in order to raise the market for their own commodities.'

Orators and journalists continued to deplore the capitulation, which had turned what might have been a great advantage into a positive injury.[1]

The terms made it certain that Guadeloupe would remain a wholly French island under the English flag, at any rate until the end of the war. English merchants might reap the advantages of its trade, but planters could not establish themselves there.[2] Everything moreover was offered to the French that might persuade them to stay, even after the peace. This was exactly the kind of acquisition that did the old sugar colonies as much harm and as little good as possible. There was no opportunity for English planters, and the London market was flooded with Guadeloupe sugars. There were other reasons for the great fall of sugar prices in 1760, but the conquest of Guadeloupe was certainly one of the most important.[3]

How differently some West Indians would have treated the French colonies, may be seen from the 'Reflections on the true Interest of Great Britain with respect to the Caribee Islands', written by a planter of Barbados and sent home in manuscript by Governor Pinfold.[4] This author assumes that we must keep Martinique, Guadeloupe, and all the Neutral Islands. The Neutral Islands will never be settled, and the older English colonies will never be safe, so long as Martinique remains in French hands. If necessary, all the Frenchmen must be evicted from Martinique; force will not be needed, if the Government will edge them out by over-taxation, by exacting the oath of allegiance, and by setting up a representative form of government to be enjoyed by Englishmen alone. The French planters may also be encouraged to leave Martinique by the offer of land on extraordinary terms in the other conquered islands, where the military governors may administer French laws. The production of sugar must be forbidden in the other islands, and only allowed to the English population in Martinique, on

---

[1] Newcastle to Hardwicke, June 14, 1759, Add. MSS. 32892, f. 59; Hardwicke to Newcastle, June 15, f. 88; see also the complaint of W. M. Burt, already referred to, March 7, 1761, G.D. 8/24.
[2] It seems that Englishmen could rent plantations of the French.
[3] *V. infra*, pp. 481–2.   [4] C.O. 28/50.

account of its strategic importance. Cocoa and coffee are no
so objectionable, as they are complementary to the crops which
are already grown within the Empire. A conquest in this style
would not hurt the older English colonies like that of Guade
loupe.

A great deal of this argument was very weak, though Rodney
agreed with the author on the strategic importance of Marti
nique and the difficulty of settling the Neutral Islands while i
remained in French hands. This pamphlet illustrates the readi
ness of some West Indians to consent to new acquisitions on
condition that they were not permitted to hurt the interests o
the older colonies.

Since the Government would not impose such harsh terms
upon the conquered islands, the planters could only make
the best of a bad business. They tried hard to persuade the
Treasury that the capitulation was not to be interpreted as
admitting the produce of Guadeloupe to the English market
on the same terms as their own. They argued that the island
could not be deemed an English colony until it was annexed
to the Crown by Act of Parliament, and that the importation
of its sugars would be a breach of the Acts of Trade; but they
were baulked by an opinion of the Law Officers and dared not
bring the question to a trial.[1] After this they could only declaim
and hope that future conquests would not be spoilt by such
disastrous capitulations. Some of them must have been dis
appointed with that of Martinique, which did not vary much
from the terms given to Guadeloupe.[2] It did not contain the
obnoxious clause against alienating lands to Englishmen—
perhaps that would have been beside the point, for nobody
expected the island to be kept at the peace. The privileges o
neutrality between England and France, and the confirmation
of the religious orders in their rights and properties, were imi
tated from the Guadeloupe model. The existing laws and taxes,
however, were only to continue until the King's pleasure should
be known. In this and in some smaller points, Monckton was
a harder bargainer than Barrington. Even so, his work did not
satisfy everybody. The Barbados planter who has already been
quoted, was particularly displeased with the clauses which

---

[1] Lascelles and Maxwell to Gedney Clarke, June 19, Aug. 3 and 31, 1759,
W. & G. viii.
[2] Adm. 1/307, and C.O. 166/2.

allowed religious freedom and ecclesiastical landholding; the speculators of the neighbouring English colonies appreciated the value of a dissolution of the monasteries as well as speculators always do, and besides, the deprivation of these privileges might have driven the French inhabitants off the island.[1]

It would have been impossible to avoid giving Martinique a capitulation; but the English commanders did not want to grant any terms at all to the weaker French communities on the Neutral Islands. Rollo made Dominica surrender at discretion, and Rodney meant to force St. Lucia and St. Vincent to do so too, though he was ready to allow the small French colony at Grenada the same terms as Martinique. He probably differentiated thus between his conquests because he knew that the Government would very likely keep the Neutral Islands after the war; he meant therefore to leave it a clean slate for whatever policy it should think fit to pursue on the subjects of colonization, landholding, and political rights.[2]

iii. *The Neutral Islands*

All the greater West India islands and most of the smaller had been occupied by Europeans in the seventeenth century. Only one group had been left open for future development and conquest. These Neutral Islands, as they were called, were some of the smaller members of the chain which lines the Caribbean Sea to windward. Their pretensions to neutrality were various. St. Vincent and Dominica were supposed to belong to their Carib inhabitants; but Governor Caylus reported that the French had bought nearly half the lands of Dominica from the savages—he seemed to think that this gave the King of France a claim to the whole island.[3] St. Vincent was the head-quarters of the Caribs; the original stock of Yellow Caribs numbered about 400, and the Black Caribs, descended from the union of shipwrecked negroes with Indian women, about 1,100. St. Lucia and Tobago were only neutral

---

[1] Postscript to the 'Reflections on the true Interest of Great Britain', C.O. 28/50.

[2] Rollo to Pitt, June 8, 1761, C.O. 110/1; Rodney, orders to Hervey, Feb. 24, 1762, G.D. 20/2, p. 137 (in spite of these orders some provisional terms were granted to St. Lucia); orders to Swanton, Feb. 17 and April 17, 1762, pp. 131, 203; Rodney seems to have had his eye on some land in St. Vincent, and applied to the Ministry for a grant of it (Egmont to Rodney, Aug. 19, 1763, G.D. 20/20).

[3] Caylus's *mémoire* on his government, ? 1749, A.N. Colonies C^8 A 58; instructions to Bompar, Aug. 25, 1750, B 91.

in the sense that their title, disputed between England and France, had never been clearly established one way or the other, and neither nation openly occupied them.

Whether they were neutral or merely without a recognized sovereign, all four islands were inhabited or frequented by English and French. The latter far outnumbered the former as settlers, but did less than half the trade. In fact there were seldom found more than a handful of British families, most of them Irish. The number of Frenchmen was often over-estimated; probably there were never more than 400 men fit to bear arms on St. Lucia, and rather less at St. Vincent and Dominica. There were only a few dozen French families and no English at Tobago, but the turtlers of both nations often went there and sometimes set up huts for the season.

Some of the French families on Dominica were said to have lived there from father to son since 1660.[1] How and why they went there, is no mystery. All the West India colonies were largely peopled at first by the restless, the unsuccessful, and the misfits. In their early days they had wars, rapes, and disorders enough to content them; but when the hand of discipline tightened its grip about 1660, and the cultivation of sugar introduced or revived the difference of rich and poor, there were still some colonists whose original hatred of government, and of a stratified social system, was strong enough to make them prefer a slovenly hole-and-corner existence elsewhere. Buccaneering, and the newer settlements of Jamaica and St. Domingue, had carried away many adventurers from the Windward Islands for one more round of riot and disorder. But even Jamaica and St. Domingue, even the buccaneers themselves finally turned respectable for the most part. Piracy was suppressed. Those ways of escape were closed, and there only remained such distant backwaters as the Moskito Shore, the French establishments at Darien, and the Neutral Islands. People were still going to those islands in 1740 to get away, as they said, from laws, taxes, and governments.

Not all were good-for-nothings; no doubt there was a great deal of sober enterprise. The population of Martinique was abundant and almost all the cultivable soil occupied; the system

---

[1] Bompar to Grenville, May 21, N.S., 1751, C.O. 28/29, CC 128. Bompar's statement may not be worth very much, for he was making the most of the arguments against expelling the inhabitants.

of inheritance promoted large families, whose younger members could find little place as independent producers in a heavily capitalized agriculture. So long as there was uncleared bush in Martinique, they struck out into it for themselves; but when they had filled it up, their successors had no recourse but to emigrate to Guadeloupe or the Neutral Islands. These had no authorities which the Government recognized in time of peace, but seem to have elected their own commandants. Intendant La Croix appointed notaries, who sometimes acted as judges.[1]

These small communities were scattered up and down the islands; how widely, may be judged from the report of Commandant de Longueville, who complained that it took a week for 150 men to assemble in St. Lucia upon an alarm.[2] There were a few fair-sized estates in Dominica, but even the largest were understocked with slaves.[3] The people raised provisions and the minor West India crops—cotton, coffee, cocoa; they cut dyewoods and hardwood timber.[4] This last article was important, for the sugar mills of the settled islands needed a great deal of it; the lumber of North America was unsuitable, and the Dutch settlements on the mainland were the only other places where supplies were to be had. The sugar-planters of each nation were therefore interested in the sovereignty of the disputed islands, and pressed their Governments to claim it as the only way to avoid depending on foreigners for this kind of timber.[5] They also valued highly the ground provisions which they imported from these islands. The French seem to have needed these more than the English. They were worse supplied

[1] Poinsable to Maurepas, Jan. 8 and Feb. 8, 1744, A.N. Colonies C⁸ A 56. May, in his *Histoire économique de la Martinique* (p. 101), gives another reason for the emigration to St. Lucia: the cocoa-trees of Martinique were destroyed in 1727 by a hurricane, and some of the ruined planters had to leave the island.

[2] Longueville to Maurepas, Jan. 12, 1745, A.N. Colonies C⁸ A 56.

[3] R.P. Camille de Rochemonteix, *Le Père Antoine Lavalette à la Martinique* (Paris, 1907), p. 71.

[4] They do not seem to have produced any sugar, perhaps because nobody would dare to invest so large a capital as a sugar-plantation required, without a valid title to the soil and an assurance of the political future of the islands. Father Lavalette, who bought and cultivated a large estate on Dominica after 1748, would not begin a sugar-work, though he made preparations for doing so when the title to the island should be cleared up (Rochemonteix, op. cit., p. 74).

[5] Barbados Committee of Correspondence to Agent Sharpe, Oct. 31, 1753, C.O. 28/42; petition of John Maynard, 1754, ibid.; Lascelles and Maxwell to Philip Gibbes, Jan. 10, 1750/1, W. & G. v.

from North America, and perhaps they took less care to cultivate negro provisions.[1]

The French sugar-planters had yet other interests in these islands. They depended in part upon the negroes which were smuggled by that channel. Always under-supplied by their own traders, they were glad to receive the surplus of the Barbados slave-market. Both Governments objected to this commerce; it contravened the Treaty of 1686, by which they had agreed to restrain all intercourse between their West India possessions. The French Ministers of Marine never tired of repeating fruitless edicts, regulations, and penalties. The English Government took less trouble. That energetic martinet Sir Thomas Robinson, Governor of Barbados, complained of this trade in 1742; he thought it had increased since the outbreak of the Spanish war, which had forced the slave-dealers of Barbados to look for new customers. He feared it would result in the smuggling of French luxuries into the English colonies.[2] Be that as it might, the trade did not rest in war or peace. It was carried on briskly between Barbados and St. Vincent in 1759, when Commodore Moore's efforts to detect it cost him his popularity.[3]

The military value of the Neutral Islands was even greater. Tobago was to windward of Barbados; in French hands it would be a very dangerous base for interrupting the trade from England and North America as it arrived in the West Indies. The harbour was believed to be good and free from hurricanes.[4] St. Vincent and Dominica were chiefly valuable to France because they assured the communication of Martinique with Grenada and Guadeloupe.[5] St. Lucia was the most necessary

---

[1] This is only an inference from the more frequent objurgations of the French Government upon this subject; the English Government interfered much less with things of this kind, so that an equally serious evil might be less noticed in its correspondence.

[2] Instructions to Caylus, Oct. 6, 1744, A.N. Colonies B 78; to Bompar and Hurson, July 6, 1751, B 93; Rouillé to Bompar and Hurson, Feb. 26, 1752, B 95; Robinson to Newcastle, Nov. 27, 1742, C.O. 28/46; instructions to Richard Derby, Dec. 29, 1741, Derby family MSS., x. 2, Essex Institute. The French Government had complained of this trade to Newcastle in 1728 (*Mémoire* of Broglie, 1728, C.O. 28/21, Y 20).

[3] Moore to Cleveland, Oct. 3 and Dec. 13, 1759, Feb. 8 and 26, 1760, Adm. 1/307.

[4] Caylus's *mémoire* of 1749, A.N. Colonies C⁸ A 58.

[5] Maurepas to Caylus, Nov. 23, 1745, A.N. Colonies B 81; Caylus to Maurepas, Dec. 24, 1746, C⁸ A 57; Beauharnois to Nadau, April 9, 1759, C⁸ A 62.

of all to the security of the French Windward Islands. The soil was not so good as that of the other three islands, but its military importance made the French Government take more interest in it. It was just to windward of Martinique, and had one of the finest small harbours in the West Indies. The English knew this, but their views were purely defensive. They did not want to own the island themselves, so much as to prevent the French from doing so. St. Lucia in French hands would be an advanced post for French privateers, would interrupt the trade from Barbados to the Leeward Islands, and disorganize the squadron on the station.

There was only one purpose for which the Governments and colonists did not want the Neutral Islands. They had little or no wish to conquer them and plant them as sugar colonies. On the other hand, so far as they still hoped to compete in the world market, they would hardly be better pleased to see their foreign rivals settle the Neutral Islands. Thus Governor Grenville of Barbados said of the French colony on Tobago, 'The vicinity of this island is such that in times of war it will cut off the trade here by hostilities, its fertility is such that in times of peace it will undo this island by its crops.'[1]

The opposition of the sugar interest to expansion is very well illustrated by the history of these four islands. Already in 1664 the people of Barbados had shown themselves somewhat averse to an expedition to St. Lucia. Later in the seventeenth century, two English companies were formed to colonize Tobago under the authority of the Duke of Courland, one of the claimants to its sovereignty; but the first, under Pointz, was frustrated by the opposition of the Barbados sugar-planters, and the Courland agent who made the second agreement had to allow a clause forbidding the cultivation of sugar in the new colony.[2] For a

[1] Grenville to Sharpe, Jan. 26, 1748/9, C.O. 28/29, CC 23. The author of *The Alarm Bell, or Considerations on the Present Dangerous State of the Sugar Colonies* (London, 1749) calculates the rate of increase of sugar cultivation in the French and English islands; one of the measures he proposes for redressing the disproportion is to insist that the Neutral Islands shall remain unoccupied.

[2] He is reported to have said: 'This is an important article, and I do not believe the island will ever be settled unless this prohibition is inserted in the treaty; for the Barbados merchants are so far from being willing to join the Company that they rather begin to put difficulties in the way. I know very well how and why the wretched Pointz was ruined in the time of Charles II. Although the King himself gave him underhand encouragement, so that he got several ships ready in the Thames to carry the colony out, he (the King) changed his mind as soon as the Governor of Barbados whispered in his ear that if he allowed the settlement

long time the routine instructions of the Governors of Barbados contained a clause forbidding them to grant lands in any of the Neutral Islands, which were supposed to be within their jurisdiction; but in 1721, when drawing up the instructions for Lord Belhaven, the Board of Trade decided to make a change. They proposed that he should be allowed to make grants of not more than 300 acres in Tobago. He was not to grant any land to planters who already had estates in the older colonies, and it was to be an express condition of every patent that no sugar was to be grown. The first of those provisos was evidently designed to preserve Barbados from being weakened by emigration; the second, whose tendency is even more obvious, was disallowed by the Privy Council.[1]

About the same time two attempts were made to settle St. Lucia and St. Vincent—by Marshal d'Estrées on behalf of France, and the Duke of Montagu on behalf of England. Neither of these enterprises succeeded. That of Montagu was directly frustrated by the hostile intervention of the Governor of Martinique.[2]

The result of these attempts upon the Neutral Islands was to bring the matter under the eye of diplomacy. After some argument, the English and French Governments agreed to evacuate the islands pending a determination of the title. The proposal seems to have come from France, but was almost equally congenial to England. Since neither Government wanted positively to colonize these islands and each aimed only at preventing the other from colonizing them, there was little reason why the islands should not remain unoccupied for ever. However, there was a great difference in the zeal of the two nations to make the evacuation a reality. So long as the islands were left alone they were virtually French, and capable of becoming openly so at the first opportunity. The French Government would certainly suffer from the continuance of the illicit trade, which it took very seriously;[3] but that was a slight thing com-

of Tobago, the English sugar plantations, and especially those of Barbados, which paid such great taxes every year, must be ruined' (J. C. P., *Tobago Insulae Caraibicae in America Sitae Fatum*, Groningen, 1727, pp. 105–6).

[1] *C.S.P. Col. 1720–1*, nos. 6 (i), 148, 659 (i), 666, 693 (i); *1722–3*, no. 36 (i).

[2] *C.S.P. Col. 1722–3*, nos. 10, 36 (i), 126, 266, 419, 483, 820, 821.

[3] No doubt this explains why it was the French Government which added to the draft order for evacuation the clause forbidding all trade and navigation at the islands except for ships' wood and water. The English Board of Trade did not want to have breaches of this prohibition punished by confiscation; it would go

pared with the possibility of acquiring St. Lucia, the inconvenience of injuring a vested interest, and the injustice of depriving
French subjects of an established means of livelihood.

It was therefore the English Governors who were always pressing for a real evacuation, and Governor de Champigny who
showed himself uncommonly fertile in pretexts for delay. The
proclamation for the removal of all inhabitants was published
at St. Lucia in 1735, and that was all. If the settlers ever withdrew, they came back in a week or two. The six months which
they were allowed for taking off their crops lengthened into five
years; and in 1740 Governor Byng was still pressing Champigny,
and Lord Waldegrave was still pressing Cardinal Fleury, to
evacuate the islands in good faith. Champigny later said that
he determined in 1740 not to comply with any order for removal
he might receive, but to preserve St. Lucia for France. He
seems to me to post-date this good resolution by at least five
years. As for Fleury, he was assuring Waldegrave, a month
before d'Antin sailed, that effective instructions should be sent
at once;[1] but a few days afterwards Maurepas told Champigny
that as soon as he heard of d'Antin's first blow in the West
Indies, he was to forestall the English in seizing St. Lucia.[2] No
blow was struck, so that the 'neutrality' of St. Lucia was allowed
to continue four years longer, until the war broke out at last.
Byng and the legislature of Barbados became so impatient
that they asked the Admiralty to have the French settlements
destroyed outright.[3]

The English made little attempt, all this time, to colonize
St. Lucia. The Duke of Montagu's title to it was one great
obstruction; nobody liked to have the fatigue and danger of a
settlement, only to find, if the English claim to the island should

no farther than invoking His Majesty's displeasure, which, as experience had
proved and was to prove again, was not enough to kill a fly in the West Indies
(Poyntz to Newcastle, March 4, N.S., 1730, copy in C.O. 28/21, Y 18; *Mémoire* of
Broglie, 1728, Y 20; Plenipotentiaries to Newcastle, Sept. 17, 1730, Y 25 (i);
Newcastle to Board of Trade, Y 43 (i); Board of Trade to Newcastle, Nov. 26,
1730, C.O. 29/15, f. 218).

[1] Byng to Newcastle, Feb. 23, 1739/40, C.O. 28/45, f. 430; Waldegrave to Newcastle, July 28, 1740, S.P. 78/223, f. 208; Champigny to Maurepas, June 7, 1745,
A.N. Colonies C8 A 56; Champigny to Byng, March 13 and May 2, N.S., 1740;
Byng to Champigny, March 27, O.S., all in Barbados Council Minutes of April 29,
1740, C.O. 31/21.

[2] Instructions to d'Antin, Aug. 14, 1740, A.N. Marine B2 311, Brest, f. 60.

[3] Barbados Assembly Minutes, Jan. 10, 1739/40, C.O. 31/22; Warren to Corbett,
Feb. 6, 1742/3, Adm. 1/2653.

be made good, that he was an unauthorized squatter without rights against the noble Proprietor. Montagu was several times asked for some general permission to grant and take up lands; but he never gave it until the first year of the war.[1]

The French Government had not the same designs on St. Vincent and Dominica. It considered that the French population in the Windward Islands was enough to fill and defend two or three colonies, but not five. Besides, the settlements on St. Vincent and Dominica offered opportunities and excuses for illicit trade. Maurepas therefore ordered Champigny to recover the Frenchmen from those two islands, and keep them in Martinique and Guadeloupe—especially the latter—to strengthen the militia. Later, when the war broke out, he told him to send them to St. Lucia instead. Champigny was either very lazy or very obstinate, and did nothing of the kind. The French Government wanted the islands reserved for the Caribs, according to a treaty of 1660. That was the most convenient way of blocking the English claim without insisting on an inconvenient acquisition; but the settlers continued to buy out the Caribs in Dominica, and to obtain a hold over those of both islands by the two most powerful agents of imperialism, rum and missionaries.

There was nothing that could be called a French colony in Tobago before Caylus's expedition of 1749. The Indians were supposed to be subject to the Governor of Barbados, but some injuries done them by English privateers disgusted them, so that they fell under French influence and accepted presents and a 'General' from the French Governor as they had formerly had them from the English; later, however, they returned to their earlier affection for England.[2]

As soon as the war broke out in 1744, Champigny made ready to throw some soldiers into St. Lucia. The chief difficulty arose from the superiority of the English at sea; their warships might have intercepted the little expedition, or bombarded the

[1] John Bennet to Montagu, Sept. 17, 1726, C.O. 28/19, X 20; Robinson to Newcastle, July 7, 1745, C.O. 28/46.

[2] Maurepas to Champigny, March 17, May 15, Oct. 30, 1744, A.N. Colonies B 78; Poinsable to Maurepas, Jan. 8 and Feb. 8, 1744, vol. C^8 A 56; Champigny to Maurepas, Aug. 8, 1744, ibid.; instructions to Caylus, Oct. 6, 1744, vol. B 78; Robinson to Newcastle, Nov. 27, 1742, C.O. 28/46; Tyrrell to Moore, Oct. 19, 1757, C.O. 28/31, EE 17; Barbados Council Minutes, March 6 and April 10, 1759, C.O. 31/30.

batteries before they were set up, or landed a force and cut off all communication between St. Lucia and Martinique. If they took any of these measures, the new colony could not survive. Champigny was inclined at first to wait for a naval reinforcement which Maurepas had promised him for this purpose; but later he decided to take the risk. He succeeded, so far as any English opposition was concerned; a detachment of 400 Martinique militia and 50 regulars was landed, the cannon were safely sent, and the batteries raised without any interference by Commodore Knowles.[1]

The inaction of the English forces was criticized, and is a little hard to understand. Everybody on both sides knew that the longer the defences of St. Lucia were allowed to grow, the harder they would be to destroy; and Knowles had several months in which to use his superior force. The omission is the more remarkable in Knowles, for he was enterprising to a fault, and very much interested in the conquest of St. Lucia. (Later in the war, he asked leave to come southwards from Cape Breton and attempt St. Lucia; and while he was in the Leeward Islands for a few days on his way to Jamaica, in January 1748, he proposed to Pocock an attack on one of the French islands.) We can discount the suspicion that, having married a Barbadian wife, he was infected with the dislike of expansion which prevailed in that island. According to his own account, he now thought of destroying the new batteries, but preferred to go up to Barbados and get an expeditionary force to possess St. Lucia. There he found that nobody would volunteer. The ostensible reason, which was given to Knowles, was the Duke of Montagu's patent; so long as it was unextinguished, adventurers were afraid to undertake a settlement.[2] No doubt there were other reasons in the planters' minds, as the events of the next year plainly showed.

In the autumn of 1745 Vice-Admiral Isaac Townsend appeared on the Leeward Islands station with a large force. He proposed an expedition against St. Lucia; Governor Robinson passed on the suggestion to a select meeting of Barbados

---

[1] Champigny to Maurepas, May 26, Aug. 6 and 8, Sept. 7, 1744, A.N. Colonies C⁸ A 56.

[2] Robinson to Newcastle, March 24, 1744/5, July 7, 1745, C.O. 28/46; Knowles to Corbett, Oct. 15, 1744, Adm. 1/2007; Lords of the Admiralty to Newcastle, Jan. 12, 1744/5, S.P. 42/28, p. 10; Knowles to Anson, April 30, 1747, Add. MSS. 15956, f. 136.

politicians. The deliberations were traversed by the violent faction which raged in the island on account of the Governor's refusal to call the Assembly, which meant to inquire into the peculations of his stepson-in-law; but even if the project had not been so unfortunate as to be patronized by Robinson, there were genuine reasons why it should have failed of acceptance. The Speaker and the Attorney-General, the two most artful leaders of the Opposition, played upon the strongest passions of the planters. It was impossible, they said, for Barbados to spare a man without great danger; indeed, the colony was itself in need of further support and an increased garrison of regular troops. Besides, it was not to the interest of Barbados that St. Lucia should be settled; rather it should be left neutral.[1]

That was almost the end of English ambitions in the Neutral Islands during this war, but it was not the end of the troubles of St. Lucia, which came rather from within.[2] The Martinique militia had departed for that island unwillingly; Champigny had meant to raise six hundred men, but could only get together four hundred.[3] The colonial militia were always reluctant to leave their plantations exposed; how much greater must be their distaste for an expedition to another island, in which their communications with their home might, indeed must, be cut off. Champigny was to encourage them by a promise of land in St. Lucia, but he did not want to do so. He argued that it would be better to wait until a regular scheme could be adopted, so as to avoid abuses; but his real motive was the fear of new sugar colonies which might thrive at the expense of the old. Champigny was a planter as well as a Governor, and he did not want to bring down the price of sugar. Longueville, the new Commandant of St. Lucia, built more upon his hopes of making a fortune in the new island than on any property he may have possessed in the old; he was for allowing and encouraging sugar plantation in St. Lucia. He insisted that the colony would never be set on its feet without it; that the settlers already in the island

[1] Robinson to Townsend, Sept. 14, 1745, Adm. 1/305; Robinson's answer to charges, no. 15, Feb. 27, 1745/6, C.O. 28/47; Lascelles and Maxwell to Thomas Applewhaite, Jan. 15, 1745/6, W. & G. ii: 'We are intirely of your opinion that you did right not to send any of your people to make conquests of the French islands, as it would diminish your strength on which you are to depend when it may happen to be your turn to be attacked.'

[2] The Admiralty recommended Legge to take St. Lucia if possible (Instructions, Nov. 7, 1746, Adm. 2/68, f. 395).

[3] Longueville to Maurepas, June 20, 1744, A.N. Colonies C8 A 56.

had willingly furnished their negroes for the public works in the expectation that they would be rewarded by liberty to grow sugar; finally, he said, Champigny ought to know that the more sugar was made, the more was consumed. The Government ordered Champigny and Intendant Ranché to grant lands to people with capital and negroes, but Champigny continued to obstruct. He brought himself to issue 150 licences for small settlers to line and strengthen the sea-shore; but these were not the stuff of which sugar-planters were made, and hardly anybody applied for the licences.[1] In fact, nothing had been done before the summer of 1745, when Champigny was superseded by Caylus. Even then there was little progress for some time. The Government's surveyors proceeded with their business very slowly, and it was nearly the end of the war before any lands were actually granted.[2]

Besides land, the settlers wanted negroes. Martinique had never had quite enough for her own plantations, and could spare few to St. Lucia, especially as the French slave-trade was almost completely paralysed by the war.[3] Nor had owners of negroes much inducement to send them to the new settlement, where the *corvées* for work on the fortifications were exceptionally heavy.[4] Besides, there was a serious doubt whether the Government would see fit or be able to keep St. Lucia at the peace; this was increased by the delay to set up any regular authorities. Longueville said of the inhabitants in 1746 that 'until they see a regular Government established, clergy in the parishes, a judge, grants of land and troops to preserve the whole, they will never be reassured, whatever one may say to them'. He frequently repeated that the colony would never make much progress while the actual and possible planters remained uncertain of its political future.[5]

For all these reasons the forced enthusiasm of Martinique for its daughter-colony very soon cooled away. The detachment of

---

[1] Longueville to Maurepas, June 20, 1744, Jan. 12, 1745, A.N. Colonies C⁸ A 56; Champigny to Maurepas, June 7, 1745, ibid.; Maurepas to Champigny and Ranché, Oct. 30, 1744, B 78.

[2] Ranché to Maurepas, Sept. 20, 1746, C⁸ A 57; Longueville to Maurepas, Nov. 9, 1746, ibid.

[3] Caylus to Maurepas, July 19, 1745, C⁸ A 56; Longueville to Maurepas, March 15, 1747, vol. 57.

[4] Twelve days' *corvée* in the year for each negro was a good deal for a colony that had not been used to regular taxes.

[5] Longueville to Maurepas, Feb. 3 and Nov. 9, 1746, C⁸ A 57.

militia could not be relieved, for the gallant planters hid in the
woods to escape enrolment. The first four hundred trickled
home, so that in January 1745 there were only a hundred left,
and when Caylus arrived there were no more than nineteen.[1]
The fifty or a hundred regulars were not enough to defend the
colony: Longueville asked for five hundred. Thus St. Lucia
was in immediate danger of conquest by the English, if only
they should show a little spirit—a fact which naturally discouraged any but adventurers from embarking their fortunes in it,
and may well have given the old-established squatters some
cause for anxiety.

These squatters could muster, if they chose, four hundred
armed men; but besides that it took them a long time to collect
in sufficient numbers, not all of them had enough goodwill
to appear at an alarm. As Longueville said in the next war,
at least a third of them would stay behind in an emergency to
mind their women and their slaves. Most of them were ready
at first to contribute their negroes to the *corvées* (though some
concealed or understated the number of their slaves), but they
were soon discouraged. Longueville had to deal with a concerted opposition to *corvées*; but he put it down by banishing the
ringleader off the island.[2] As for the land, the Government had
to deal with a somewhat awkward state of affairs. Many of these
squatters, who were expected to be the mainstay of the colony,
had arbitrarily taken up and now claimed far more land than
they were cultivating. Maurepas ordered Champigny to cancel
those titles and all sales based upon them, and to regrant such
lands as the squatters should require and deserve by the capital
and labour at their command.[3]

It is not surprising that the population of St. Lucia increased
little. Champigny and Caylus were ordered to transfer to it the
French of Dominica and St. Vincent; but it was no easy matter
to induce them to leave their habitations where they had been
prosperous and happy in a higgledy-piggledy way, especially
as they could not (at any rate before lands began to be granted
in St. Lucia) be assured of any better title in their new homes.
Both Champigny and Caylus therefore neglected this duty.

[1] Champigny to Maurepas, Nov. 17, 1744, A.N. Colonies C⁸ A 56; Longueville
to Maurepas, May 12, 1746, vol. 57.
[2] Longueville to Maurepas, Jan. 12, 1745, C⁸ A 56.
[3] Maurepas to Champigny and Ranché, Feb. 10, 1745, B 81.

Champigny simply did not try to perform it; Caylus excused himself from doing so, because Dominica at least assured the communications between Martinique and Guadeloupe. Maurepas approved of Caylus's departure from his orders. In fact the people of St. Vincent and Dominica were so far from emigrating to St. Lucia that there was some movement the other way. No doubt some of the squatters of St. Lucia were true frontiersmen, ready to retreat a step for every one that regular government and orderly society advanced. Their repugnance to authority might perhaps be increased by the severity of Longueville. Both Champigny and Caylus complained of it; Caylus, who hardly ought to have cast the first stone, accused Longueville of behaving as if he thought he was God the Father.[1]

Longueville's fears for St. Lucia were well justified. The French Government hardly tried to keep it at the Peace of Aix-la-Chapelle. It instructed St. Séverin to ask for it, and to argue that the English did not need it because they had more land than they cultivated in the West Indies, while it would suit France very well to possess it on account of its neighbourhood to Martinique. As Sandwich, the English plenipotentiary, belonged to the same family as the Duke of Montagu, St. Séverin was told to bribe him with an offer to compensate his relative for the extinction of his title. Sandwich, however, had no love for Montagu, and thought it very important not to sacrifice the Neutral Islands. He prophesied that if the matter was neglected, 'under the general description of renewal of former treaties, the French will remain in possession and the thing neglected until some time after the peace; and then we must come to the fatal result of either leaving them there, or beginning a fresh war to drive them out'. He therefore asked for orders to insist on the evacuation of the Neutral Islands. He received such orders, but could not execute them, and the islands were left to be covered by the ambiguous clause of the *status quo*.[2]

Sandwich could not have prophesied more truly the troubles which arose from this uncertainty; but even he can hardly have expected them to develop as quickly as they did.

[1] ? Ranché to Maurepas, July 18, 1744, S.P. 42/27, p. 455; instructions to Caylus, Oct. 6, 1744, A.N. Colonies B 78; Maurepas to Caylus, Nov. 23, 1745, B 81; Caylus to Maurepas, Dec. 24, 1746, C8 A 57.

[2] Instructions to St. Séverin, Feb. 29, 1748, *Recueil des Instructions aux Ambassadeurs de France, Hollande*, iii. 131; Sandwich to Bedford, Aug. 29, 1747, *Bedford Correspondence*, i. 243.

A few weeks after the peace was signed, Maurepas wrote to Caylus and Ranché that he presumed the English would demand the evacuation of St. Lucia by virtue of the Treaty. If they did so, the King would reply (and Caylus was to do the same if any demand was addressed to him) that St. Lucia was a French island long before Champigny placed any troops there; but if the English insisted, the King was ready to have St. Lucia evacuated by both nations, and St. Vincent and Dominica left to the Caribs. In fact, if the Governor of Barbados should already be empowered to do his part, Caylus was to co-operate by ordering the settlers to leave at thirty days' notice. Maurepas added for Caylus's benefit that the King had no intention of giving up St. Lucia, but hoped the English would recognize his right to it upon a fair examination.[1]

Before this letter was received or even written, Caylus had acted for himself. He had already projected some lucrative scheme in St. Lucia, in partnership with the notorious Father Lavalette, the *Procureur* and afterwards Superior of the Jesuits.[2] He was therefore very unwilling to carry out the orders for evacuation. He now planned a new colony on Tobago. The excuse was, to find an occupation for ex-privateers which would prevent them from becoming pirates, as they had done at the end of the last war. This was in itself prudent enough, though founded on what proved to be a false analogy, for the privateers did not take to freebooting this time. Very likely, however, Caylus had some concern of his own in the enterprise, for there never was a Governor, English or French, who devised so many methods of enriching himself—and that is saying a great deal. He had lately asked for the grant of a whole island, to let or sell the land for his own profit; a mere estate would not suffice him, as he had no negroes to work it. In November 1748 he wrote to Maurepas that his measures for a colony on Tobago were in good forwardness, and he hoped to be able to send a commandant and some troops; he had not granted any lands yet, but had licensed a squatter who was already upon the island to continue his cultivation.[3] Governor Grenville of Barbados got wind of this, and took the empty precaution of sending a war-

[1] Maurepas to Caylus and Ranché, Nov. 25, 1748, A.N. Colonies B 87; to Caylus, Nov. 25, ibid.

[2] Caylus to Maurepas, March 19, 1747, A.N. Colonies C⁸ A 57; Maurepas to Caylus, Sept. 14, 1747, B 85; see also Rochemonteix, op. cit., p. 70, note 2.

[3] Caylus to Maurepas, Nov. 11, 1748, A.N. Colonies C⁸ A 58.

ship to assert King George's right to the island and to warn foreigners off. This gave Caylus the excuse he wanted. It became necessary to uphold at once the affronted dignity of his master; he therefore sent some troops to build a fort, and some warships to protect them.[1] There followed an awkward interview between their commander and an English captain, in which each represented himself as having stood his ground and the other as having gone off and left the field clear. Luckily they were content with high words; no shots were fired, but Grenville wrote home indignantly, and within a short time diplomacy was once more busy on this subject.[2]

The matter fell in the province of Bedford, still an enthusiast for colonies, and he took it up warmly. He ordered Colonel Yorke to declare in Paris that the King would on no account give up his right to Tobago, but would even repel foreign usurpations by force, if need be. Puysieulx and Rouillé overlooked this vivacity, and the affair was soon accommodated by agreeing that the island should be evacuated by both sides, and the title to it determined by commissaries.[3]

This treatment was extended to the other three islands a little later in the same year, and in good time the English commissaries came to Paris to exchange enormous memoranda on this and several other subjects, and to bicker over the order of priority of business until they produced a perfect deadlock. There never was a set of negotiators who had less chance of negotiating anything; even the Anglo-Spanish plenipotentiaries of 1739 had more. On the French side (if we may judge by the letters of Maurepas and Rouillé to the Governors of Martinique), there was no intention of giving up anything in dispute. The French Foreign Office seems to have thought, and perhaps with very good reason, that its case was overwhelming and that the English commissaries could not fail to accept it.[4] The

[1] Grenville to Board of Trade, Oct. 27, Dec. 12, 1748, C.O. 28/29, CC 15, 18. Both English and French foreign offices seem to have assumed that Caylus's expedition to Tobago was provoked by Grenville's proclamation; but the dates of his letters convict him of having intended it before, and it was actually the rumour of his intention which induced Grenville to send the proclamation.

[2] Captain Wheeler, H.M.S. Boston, to Grenville, Jan. 5, 1748/9, ibid., CC 24.

[3] Bedford to Yorke, March 23, 1748/9, S.P. 78/232; Yorke to Bedford, April 9 and 16, 1749, ibid.; Bedford to Albemarle, Sept. 21, o.s., 1749, S.P. 78/233. Puysieulx was at this time French Foreign Secretary, and Rouillé succeeded Maurepas in the spring of 1749.

[4] Rouillé to Caylus, May 2, 1749, A.N. Colonies B 89; Louis XV to Caylus, Dec. 19, 1749, ibid.

English Board of Trade, relying upon a different set of facts, did not see the matter in the same light; but it was not very much interested in St. Lucia. The controverted boundary of Nova Scotia was what it had most at heart; and much of the commissaries' time was taken up in arguing whether (as we wished) Nova Scotia should be discussed before anything else or (as the French insisted) it should be considered concurrently and at alternate sittings with St. Lucia. Newcastle at first resisted any such connexion of the two subjects, but later yielded. In the equation of these two disputes there might have been some hope of a compromise: that we should yield St. Lucia if the French would give us satisfaction on Nova Scotia. Perhaps this was what Puysieulx and Rouillé meant by joining the two things together, and the same idea seems to have occurred to Shirley, one of the British commissaries, and later to Holdernesse, who succeeded Bedford as Secretary of State. Since, however, the Nova Scotia business proved quite as in-tractable as that of the Neutral Islands, there was little hope there.[1]

It would not be worth while to follow the fortunes of the commissaries, or of the direct negotiation between the two Courts, which followed their obvious failure. Meanwhile suc-cessive Governors of Martinique were playing a tedious comedy over the evacuation.

Caylus had paid no attention to Maurepas's warning of 1748. So far from advising the settlers to make ready to withdraw from St. Lucia, he still allowed them to extend their cultivation. He told Longueville that he hoped no evacuation would be necessary; for which reason the people of St. Lucia were—or professed to be—very surprised when they first heard the rumour of what was to befall them. Caylus seems also to have been organizing a regular French Government on St. Vincent in 1749, taking advantage of the good relations of the settlers with the Carib chiefs.[2] The first order for evacuating the four

---

[1] Instructions to English commissaries, July 30, 1750, S.P. 78/238, ff. 96–103; commissaries to Bedford, Aug. 22 and 28, 1750, ff. 128, 134; Shirley to Bedford, Sept. 5/16, 1750, S.P. 78/237, f. 35; Bedford to Albemarle, Oct. 4, 1750, f. 82; Newcastle to Albemarle, Aug. 31 and Oct. 1, 1750, ff. 7, 78; Halifax to Newcastle, July 20, 1750, Add. MSS. 32721, f. 406; Newcastle to Bedford, Sept. 23, 1750, vol. 32824, f. 135; Holdernesse to Newcastle, May 15, 1752, vol. 32836, f. 301.
[2] Caylus to Maurepas, Dec. 22, 1748, A.N. Colonies C⁸ A 58; Caylus, *mémoire* of 1749 (?), ibid.; Longueville to Rouillé, June 5, 1750, ibid.

islands must have reached Martinique in the spring of 1750. Grenville sent down Commodore Holburne with his duplicate of the French order, to supervise the evacuation in detail. Caylus chicaned, lied, and picked an irrelevant quarrel in order to delay the evacuation; finally he died, and the interim Governor died too a fortnight later. The next successor refused to take the responsibility of executing the King of France's order, because he said he had not the legal power to do so.[1]

Nothing therefore could be done before the arrival of the new Governor-General, Maximin de Bompar. He was ordered to have the islands evacuated, if it had not been done already, and if it had, to see that the English loyally complied with the order, for which purpose he might use force.[2] Two months later he was given an instruction of a very different tendency. The King of France had only consented to the evacuation on the condition that the title to the islands should be decided as soon as possible; but Rouillé had now made up his mind that the English did not mean business. He thought their object was to avoid acknowledging the French claim until a suitable opportunity occurred for seizing the island, which he imagined they might do by surprise, without declaring war. Therefore, though Bompar was to proceed with the evacuation, he was to prepare for the reoccupation of St. Lucia, and was in fact to forestall the English if he should seriously suspect them of any designs upon it.[3]

Probably Rouillé had no direct justification for his guess. The English commissaries had excited his suspicion by refusing at first to discuss St. Lucia at the same time as Tobago, and by insisting that St. Lucia could not possibly be considered until the evacuation was complete. The French Government had pointed out that the evacuation had not been made a condition of the appointment of commissaries, and argued that it was hard to expel the settlers so relentlessly when their right might so soon be acknowledged. This reasoning exposed France in her turn to the suspicion of bad faith; it looked as if she meant to delay the evacuation until a favourable verdict, at least as much as England meant to delay the verdict for the evacuation. As for Rouillé's conjecture that the English Government would

---

[1] Grenville to Board of Trade, March 13, 1749/50, April 2 and 30, 1750, C.O. 28/29, CC 52, 74, and 81; Albemarle to Bedford, Sept. 2, 1750, S.P. 78/236, f. 383; Rouillé to Caylus, May 23, 1750, A.N. Colonies B 91.
[2] Instructions to Bompar, Aug. 25, 1750, A.N. Colonies B 91; Rouillé to Bompar, Sept. 2, 1750, ibid. [3] Rouillé to Bompar, Oct. 29, 1750, ibid.

give orders in full peace for the seizure of St. Lucia, that too was probably groundless, in spite of a few vapouring threats which Newcastle flung out from time to time. Yet though the English Government did not mean to do such a thing at present, it might have meant it one day, as it showed a few years later by its precipitate conduct in North America.[1]

These instructions of Rouillé, however founded, were not of a kind to make Bompar very earnest or thorough in performing the evacuation. He made as many difficulties as he could, and in particular he tried, upon various pretexts, to confine the evacuation to St. Lucia. The proclamation, ordering all settlers to withdraw, was finally published in all the four islands; the troops and cannon were withdrawn, and the fortifications pulled down.[2]

As in 1735, this was only the first step, not the last. What if the settlers would not go? Bompar said that would be very bad behaviour, and he should have to write home for further orders. He would not drive them out by force, nor let anybody else do so. This was the point on which the controversy turned for the next five years. Bompar's humanity to the settlers might not be unreasonable; but the fact remained that nothing short of force would drive them away, and as he had been instructed to use force to keep the English out of the islands, he ought hardly to have complained of Holburne for claiming the same right against the French.

Grenville continued to pester Bompar with nagging letters, demanding the expulsion of the inhabitants and offering to join his forces to those of Bompar for the purpose. Lord Albemarle continued to urge the French Ministers to do something effective, and to tax them with never having intended the evacuation at all. Puysieulx and his successor St. Contest warmly denied this. Puysieulx argued that Bompar had done enough, because the Governments had only agreed upon a military evacuation like that of 1720; but as Commissary Mildmay pointed out, that of 1735 had been meant to be complete.[3] Rouillé took an indecisive and ambiguous line in his dispatches to Bompar. He

---

[1] Newcastle to Albemarle, Aug. 31, Oct. 1, o.s., 1750, S.P. 78/237, ff. 7, 79; Albemarle to Bedford, Nov. 14/25, 1750, f. 167; March 6/17, 1751, S.P. 78/240, ff. 237-8.

[2] Holburne to Corbett, Jan. 21, 1750/1, Adm. 1/306; Bompar to Rouillé, Jan. 9, 1751, A.N. Colonies C⁸ A 58.

[3] Grenville to Bompar, May 3, Sept. 2 and 30, Nov. 2, 1751; Bompar to Gren-

thought Bompar had done right to refuse to drive the settlers out, and to decline Grenville's offer of joint operations against them; and once or twice he ordered him afresh to take care that the English should not seize St. Lucia. At the same time, however, he declared that the King of France meant to fulfil his engagements in good faith, and that the islands must be evacuated. Bompar was to confiscate the property in the other French islands of those who would not go. He was even to give them the impression that he was about to use force; but he was not to use it. If there were any English among the inhabitants, Bompar would be in an unfortunate position. As he would not drive out the French by violence, he could hardly do so to the English; he must therefore confine himself to complaining of them to Grenville. If they came for the purpose of illicit trade, he could easily disgust them of it by applying the penalties very heavily; if they were planters, 'could he not find some French settlers who, without compromising him, might give the English to understand that they would not allow them to make establishments at a time when he was pressing all the King's subjects to abandon theirs'?[1]

By 1751 Puysieulx had gone so far as to argue that no more could be done until the commissaries gave their decision. Rouillé was still willing to suggest that both sides should bring the unrepentant settlers to heel by forbidding all trade with them—a proposal which would suit him remarkably well, as it would stop up the channels of the illicit trade which he took such pains to prevent.[2] A year later he too had reached the same position as Puysieulx.

Meanwhile the English were losing patience. They did not break out into any violent projects, but they ceased to consider the evacuation as binding on themselves. Sir Thomas Robinson, the new Secretary of State, hinted to Albemarle that this would be the consequence of the French delays; but it had

ville, May 21, Sept. 17, Oct. 17, Nov. 17, 1751, C.O. 28/29, CC 127–8, 130–2, and 28/30, DD 2, 3, 5; Bedford to Albemarle, April 11, 1751, S.P. 78/240, ff. 313–19; Albemarle to Bedford, April 29 and May 5, 1751, ff. 330, 345.

[1] Rouillé to Bompar, May 19, 1751 (two letters), Nov. 9, 1751, A.N. Colonies B 93; Feb. 16 and 18, 1752, B 95.

[2] Yorke to Newcastle, 'Separate', July 16/27, 1751, S.P. 78/241; Bompar and Hurson thought that Rouillé went too far in this respect, and that his strictness would destroy the harmless trade in provisions, timber, &c., between Martinique and the Neutral Islands (Rouillé to Bompar and Hurson, Feb. 26, 1752, A.N. Colonies B 95; Instructions to Bompar and Hurson, July 6, 1751, B 93).

already resulted before he wrote. The people of Barbados had wanted for some time to cut hardwood timber once more in the Neutral Islands. At first they respected Grenville's proclamation against resorting to the Neutral Islands, but in 1753 a brigantine went to Tobago with a large crew to cut fustic. Grenville sent a warship to dissuade them, but in vain. On the brigantine's return, he tried to prevent her cargo from being entered at the Custom House, but Attorney-General Blenman, always ready to put a spoke in the wheels of government, told him he had no right to do it. This, as Grenville pointed out, showed how hard it was to enforce a royal proclamation in the colonies without an Act of Parliament. The owner, Maynard, and the master, Cranston, were prosecuted for high misdemeanours. When Bompar complained that English warships prevented Frenchmen from loading timber at the Neutral Islands while they allowed Englishmen to do so, the President of Barbados pointed with pride to this prosecution. But a prosecution without a conviction or penalty is nothing to boast of; and a few months later the President was obliged to have it discontinued, because no Barbadian jury would have convicted on a criminal charge of this kind. The public opinion of the island felt deeply the injustice of a prohibition which it considered to be one-sided. The legislature instructed its agent in London to represent the hardship of making the English observe the neutrality of the islands when the French did not, and to ask that until the French should act in good faith, the Barbadians might have leave to continue their valuable trade of cutting hardwood timber, which they must else buy at enhanced rates from the Dutch or the French themselves.[1]

On both sides, therefore, the evacuation was a complete sham. In the autumn of 1755 Bompar suddenly seized St. Lucia again. His pretext was the capture of the *Alcide* and the *Lys*, which had virtually started the war in North American waters; but obviously he had been on the alert for a long time. Machault approved his action warmly; it was the signal for the beginning of the war in the West Indies.[2]

---

[1] Robinson to Albemarle, Oct. 3, 1754, Add. MSS. 32851, f. 14; Grenville to Board of Trade, April 21, 1753, C.O. 28/30, DD 26; Bompar to Weekes, Jan. 28, 1754, ibid., DD 43; Weekes to Holdernesse, April 9, 1754, C.O. 152/46; Memorial of John Maynard, C.O. 28/42; Barbados Committee of Correspondence to Sharpe, Oct. 31, 1753, ibid.

[2] Bompar to Weekes, Sept. 15, 1755, C.O. 28/42. Machault had ordered

The history of the Neutral Islands in this war very much resembles that of the last. Longueville returned with some regular soldiers to St. Lucia, and hastily put together some fortifications which already had a tumble-down air within a few months. Once more he required more *corvées* than the inhabitants could or would support, especially as it was harder than ever to feed the negroes. In 1759 he had to suspend all further building. The inhabitants were no more and no fewer than they had been in 1744. The obstacles to the settlement of the island were the same as before—the danger of conquest, the oppressive negro *corvées*, the uncertain future of the colony. These drawbacks seem to have frightened prospective settlers even more than in the last war, for they were pointed out by that recent experience. Communications do not seem to have been improved, for Longueville still complained of the difficulty of getting his militia together in case of an attack. If he collected them beforehand, the victuals would run out, and if he did not, he would be overpowered before they could assemble.[1] In St. Vincent and Dominica, the Governors of Martinique continued their diplomacy among the Caribs. Le Vassor de la Touche instructed the chiefs of St. Vincent that the promises of the English were deceitful and their real purpose to enslave the natives. He obtained from them valueless promises of help in case Martinique should be invaded. Commodore Moore repeated Knowles's attempt to oblige the inhabitants of Dominica to a neutrality. Unlike Knowles he succeeded, but the neutrality seems only to have lasted until his back was turned, and then the French willingly returned to their natural allegiance.[2]

At the end of the war these islands were all conquered by the English. The conquest could not have been secure, even if it was possible, before Guadeloupe and Martinique had fallen into our hands. A force from North America descended upon Dominica in June 1761, and obliged the inhabitants to surrender at discretion; Rodney had no difficulty in reducing St. Lucia

Bompar on Feb. 17, 1755, to seize St. Lucia on the first information of a rupture between the two nations (A.N. Colonies B 101).

[1] Bompar to Machault, Aug. 1, 1756, A.N. Marine B⁴ 73; Longueville to Machault, July 14, 1756, A.N. Colonies C⁸ A 61; to Moras, Oct. 11, 1757, ibid.; to Berryer, Aug. 5, 1759, and Feb. 22, 1760, C⁸ A 62.

[2] Beauharnois to Nadau du Treil, April 9, 1759, C⁸ A 62; Croissier de la Berthodière to Beauharnois, April 22, 1759, ibid.

and St. Vincent to submission after the fall of Martinique. Tobago needed no conquest, for it was already to all intents and purposes in our power.

§ iv. *The Terms of Peace in the West Indies, 1761–2*

By these successes we won more than enough counters to set off against our losses and those of our allies. Indeed the game was so much too easy and successful that it began to embarrass the Ministers. They could not afford to throw all their gains away, and must keep something besides the original objects of the war. What was it to be?

This question was thrashed out in the celebrated controversy of Canada against Guadeloupe. Grant and Alvord have given such excellent summaries of the argument that very little need be said of it here.[1] The chief reason for keeping Canada was the necessity of preventing for ever such another dispute in North America as had caused the present war, and securing the frontier of settlement against the French and their Indian allies. The advocates of Guadeloupe answered that the annexation of Canada was too much or too little for the purpose. Too much, because a smaller adjustment of the boundaries would create a sufficient 'barrier'; too little, because if we wanted to prevent the French from making any more trouble for us in North America, we must expel them from Louisiana too. (Some Ministers thought of doing so, and the public expected that Amherst would be sent on that service in 1761 or 1762.) Besides, if French Canada could destroy the peace of mind of our Northern colonists, French Martinique was just as fatal to that of our sugar-planters. The cost of defence must also be considered. If the French were to be evicted from Canada, where should we find colonists to fill it? If the French were to remain, what sort of subjects would they be? We should have to keep an immense army in Canada, whereas the West Indies could easily be defended by a naval force. (This last argument might seem satisfactory at that time, because nobody guessed that England's enemies would ever again be a match for her at sea; it would not have appeared so convincing, if anybody had foreseen the misfortunes which the West Indies suffered in the

[1] W. L. Grant, in *American Historical Review*, xvii. 735–43; C. W. Alvord, *The Mississippi Valley in British Politics* (Cleveland, 1917), i. 49–74.

next war for want of the naval superiority which was so glibly postulated.)

The shadow of the American Revolution had begun to appear dimly. It was a capital argument against driving the French out of Canada and increasing our own holdings on the continent. We should thereby destroy the bugbear that kept the colonists loyal, and prepare for the growth of a Dominion so vast, so populous, and so powerful that it could not long continue subject to England. The West Indies, on the other hand, would always be weak; they must depend on the imperial Government for naval defence against foreign enemies and for the internal force which kept the slaves in awe. In reply to this, the advocates of North America could only hope that the colonies would pay for their own defence, and argue that the territory could be cut up into a number of new governments too weak in themselves and too independent of each other to resist the authority of England.

The balance between the northern and tropical colonies had to be considered. Here the argument was clearly in favour of keeping Guadeloupe. One side declared that we could not have too many West India possessions because they alone gave value to our northern colonies; the other replied that we could not have too many colonists in North America because they enabled our sugar-planters to subsist by selling them the necessaries of life. But in fact, though they did not admit it, the sugar-planters already had quite as much northern produce as they could consume; the exporters of North America were even forced to sell their goods in the French islands as well as our own. The immediate value of the trade of Canada was small—the fishery excepted, which was not in question. That of Guadeloupe was much greater, and would at once produce a revenue which would help the Government to pay at least the interest on the cost of the war. Both Pitt and Bute thought that the negotiators of a victorious nation should keep this in mind.[1]

It was argued that Canada, like the New England colonies, would be independent of Great Britain for many of the necessaries of life. Guadeloupe could never be so. This, however, was only true up to a certain point. As a market for English manufactures, the northern colonies were already far more

[1] Bute to Bedford, July 12, 1761, *Bedford Correspondence*, iii. 32; *Parl. Hist.* xv. 1265.

important than the West Indies. Colonies of settlement whose people, however poor, were nearly all free and white, naturally consumed more than islands full of slaves who bought few manufactures for themselves and had not much more bought for them by their masters. It was true that the northern colonies might one day manufacture for themselves, which the West Indies could never do; but this fear was beginning to be super-annuated, and economic writers were beginning to think that an Industrial Revolution was not very likely to happen in America soon. As for victuals, lumber, and other country pro-duce, the West Indies bought very little of these goods from England, so long as the northern colonies existed to supply them. It was only in the American Revolution that England became once more an exporter of agricultural produce to her own sugar islands; therefore manufactures were the only kind of necessaries for which the West Indies depended on England.

Of course the slave-traders were for keeping Guadeloupe; but that only inflamed the irritation of the English planters, who had long thought themselves under-supplied with slaves of the right sort. The traders had committed the unpardon-able sin of pouring negroes into Guadeloupe before they knew whether it would be kept or restored at the peace. Thus they did all they could to set a dangerous rival of the English sugar colonies upon its feet. If they were to devote themselves in future to supplying that and other new conquests with negroes, they would presumably neglect the older settlements, and the prices would continue to rise unless the extension of our trade and territories in Africa should keep pace with our acquisitions in America. The planters' advocates argued that expansion in the West Indies was injurious without expansion in Africa which furnished the prime motors of tropical industry. This set the Ministers a new problem, because we had conquered Goree and Senegal in the Seven Years War, and did not know whether to keep both.

Lastly the argument turned on the question where the profits of agriculture in the different colonies would 'centre'. Profits were small in North America, and were spent or invested upon the spot, though a few merchants in the colonies laid out their money in the English funds, and many more speculated in English lotteries. Very few of the continental Americans had any *animus revertendi*; but most West Indians of tolerable fortune or expectations were sustained in what they considered as a sort of exile by the hope of going 'home' to England—a fact which accounted for the surprisingly provisional character of their domestic arrangements. Not only did they return, but they brought some of their wealth with them, and English industry had the benefit of their often profuse expenditure, and of such capital investments as they were prudent enough to make. However they might be represented by the pamphleteers, these investments were probably rare, since the planters were for the most part borrowers rather than lenders, and at best subsisted upon remittances from the plantations they so cheerfully left behind them. It is therefore doubtful if they contributed much to the accumulation of capital—which must be the thing chiefly meant by the 'centring of profits'. Yet the accepted theory was that they did contribute to it, so this argument, for what it was worth, told in favour of West Indian acquisitions.

Although the weight of the argument was probably on the side of keeping the West Indian islands, yet it was Canada, not Guadeloupe, that was kept. As long as the choice was between those two conquests, there was hardly any doubt. Although it might not be the strongest, the most popular point in the whole controversy was the necessity of driving the French out of Canada in order to cut off the root of all future wars. The statesmen and the mob alike believed this to be the real object of the struggle and the most necessary.

It is sometimes suggested that the West Indian planters used their influence to the same end. Nobody advised the Ministers to keep Canada more strongly than Rose Fuller and William Beckford, the two most important West India absentees in English politics.[1] Rose Fuller was not an entirely typical sugar-planter in his views, but Beckford was class-conscious and proud of it. Yet it is doubtful if the West India interest as a whole resisted the annexation of new sugar colonies as it had

---

[1] Fuller to Newcastle, June 28, 1760, Add. MSS. 32907, f. 423; Beckford to Pitt, Aug. 26, 1758, G.D. 8/19. See Hardwicke's letter to Newcastle, April 2, 1762 (Add. MSS. 32934, f. 310): 'As to the retention of conquests, Mr Pitt made North America entirely his object. Some of his enemies objected to him that he did this out of partiality to his friend Beckford, and out of condescension to the particular interests of our sugar colonies; but in that I suppose they did him wrong.' See also the very interesting manuscript note of Israel Mauduit, quoted by W. L. Grant, in the *American Historical Review*, xvii. 742.

done in 1740.[1] In fact it had gradually been converted to certain conquests, though not to all.

What brought this about? The fortunes of the sugar-planters were somewhat better than they had been in the late thirties, although the effect of Guadeloupe produce upon the London market had not been pleasant. Prices had taken a turn for the better, and perhaps the planters could better afford to meet new rivals, or hoped to make a profit for themselves in the virgin soil of the conquered islands.[2] Professor Namier suggests, on the strength of a letter of Lord Morton, that there was a division between 'saturated' planters and 'planters on the make'.[3] I am not sure that this is quite right. Certainly a number of people from the older islands started sugar plantations on a large scale in the new. The Bourryaus, Youngs, Olivers, and Morrises of the Leeward Islands, the Blenmans, Husbands, and Clarkes of Barbados are to be found among the earliest proprietors in Grenada and Tobago.[4] But what was the precise difference between a saturated and an unsaturated planter? Had the latter more capital to invest than the former? Many of the new plantations were largely financed by borrowed capital. Were they readier to expose themselves to the dangerous climate of an uncleared island? Many new proprietors of the conquered islands were absentees.[5] Still, though it may not be easy to point out the distinction, there were two ways of thinking upon this subject among the planters.[6]

I think it was another consideration that converted the West India interest to annexation. Although no invader set foot on any English sugar colony during these wars, all were exposed

---

[1] This was not Bedford's opinion. In 1762 he prophesied that the sugar-planters would no more desire we should keep Martinique 'than they did in relation to Guadeloupe' (Bedford to Bute, July 9, 1761, *Bedford Correspondence*, iii. 25). However, Bedford never scrupled to exaggerate when he wanted to prove a point.

[2] See the very able letters of Paterson to William Wood, July 5, 1751, and Dec. 18, 1758, Bodleian Library, North MSS. a 6, ff. 174–83. Paterson, like Wood himself, was an expansionist and an officer of the Customs. He reported that the value of estates in Barbados had risen very high in recent years, as a result of the high valuation of sugar there.

[3] *England in the Age of the American Revolution*, i (London, 1930), p. 322.

[4] Daniel Paterson, *A Topographical Description of the Island of Grenada* (London, 1780).

[5] Lascelles, Clarke, and Daling to Samuel Husbands, May 2, 1763, and Feb. 10, 1766, W. & G., vols. ix and x; Lascelles and Daling to Richard Green, Sept. 19, 1767, vol. x; to Timothy Blenman, Aug. 4 and Oct. 7, 1768, vols. x and xi.

[6] So there were among the French; *vide supra*, p. 204.

to some very serious alarms; and above all, their trade was much molested by the privateers of Martinique and Guadeloupe. It is doubtful if the losses were greater in proportion to the shipping of the colonies than they had been in Queen Anne's reign; they may even have been less. But after discounting for the factious exaggeration of the complaints against Commodores Lee, Frankland, and Moore, it appears that, at two or three periods of these wars, Barbados and the Leeward Islands were brought near to scarcity by the interruption of their trade. These losses had an effect upon the colonists' attitude to the war. It can be seen in the increasing readiness of the legislatures to assist the expeditions against the French colonies. In 1745, Barbados had positively refused to have anything to do with the conquest of St. Lucia, and Governor Mathew had not been able to stir up any enthusiasm in the Leeward Islands for an attempt upon Porto Rico. In 1759 and 1762 there was no such obstruction.

Certainly there were misunderstandings which led to a good deal of controversy. The people of Barbados were deeply offended because General Hopson did not eagerly welcome some untrained volunteers under a political colonel in 1759. He did not think it worth while to transport them to the field of action; in consequence they had to be disbanded, and when Barrington sent for reinforcements a few weeks later, only two militiamen offered themselves. This gave a colour to the view that Barbados was still hanging back in order to discourage conquests; but it was probably due to the unfortunate effect which the professional snobbery of the regular soldier nearly always had on the easily outraged dignity of the colonists.[1] In Antigua at the same time the Governor and Council were afraid that the defences of the island would be weakened by the enlistment of volunteers for Hopson's expedition. They declared their satisfaction when the company which went to Guadeloupe was seen to consist chiefly of strangers, presumably privateers. This was only the selfish timidity of the planters, who could not believe themselves safe unless a large force was concentrated at their own island, nor content themselves with knowing that it was next door. The volunteers went, and were accompanied

[1] Barbados Council Minutes, Jan. 4, Feb. 13, March 13, 1759, C.O. 31/30; Pinfold to Pitt, July 10, 1759, C.O. 152/46; *A Defence of the Conduct of Barbados, published in a Letter to General Barrington,* by John Gay Alleyne.

by a large detachment of the regular troops who were stationed at Antigua.[1]

The Assemblies of the islands were more ready to furnish Hopson with negroes as pioneers and general drudges. It is true that they did not all compel the planters to furnish slaves, though they took other steps which conduced more slowly to the same result; nor were they forcing great sacrifices upon the owners, for Hopson had power to promise that the Government would make good any losses or damages which might happen to the negroes during their service. In 1761–2 all these preparations were repeated more thoroughly. This time Barbados furnished six hundred white volunteers for the reduction of Martinique; some of the island Assemblies which had formerly left the recruitment of negroes to the freewill of the planters, now made it obligatory.

Taken in the whole, these are evidences of goodwill and of a real desire to see Martinique and Guadeloupe conquered. Stronger proof is afforded by the congratulatory addresses which were presented to the King on these occasions. George Thomas, who was a member of an Antigua planting family as well as Governor of the Leeward Islands, was willing in 1759 to see Guadeloupe and some of the Neutral Islands annexed. The legislatures of Montserrat and Antigua ordered their agents to second Commodore Moore's request for forces which would enable him to hold Guadeloupe; that of St. Christophers went farther, and empowered its agent to press for the annexation of that and all other French Windward Islands at the peace.[2] The Grand Jury of Barbados petitioned George III that Martinique might ever remain annexed to the Crown of Great Britain. The legislature of Antigua congratulated him on the entire reduction of the French Windward Islands—

'and more especially of Martinico and the rich and fertile island of Guadeloupe, islands of the utmost importance to the preservation of your Majesty's sugar colonies, and to the security of the extensive trade and navigation depending upon them, as they have received more injury and interruption from those two islands while in the hands of the enemy than from any other of the French dominions'.

After a characteristic hint that these newly conquered islands

[1] Antigua Council Minutes, March 1 and 21, 1759, C.O. 9/23.
[2] Antigua Council Minutes, Feb. 7, 1759, ibid.; St. Kitts Council Minutes, Feb. 20, 1759, C.O. 241/7.

ought to pay some compensation for the expense of the war, which would prevent them from competing on too equal a foot with the older colonies, the address concludes thus:

'Permit us to hope for a lasting extension of your southern in proportion to your majesty's northern colonies without which we fear that the enlargement of the latter may redound more to the benefit and advantage of the French than to the British sugar islands, whose future existence seems to depend in a great measure upon an effectual extinction of that superiority which the French have always maintained in these islands, until the glorious era of Your Majesty's most auspicious reign.'[1]

I believe the legislatures meant what they said; their language is not a mere disguise for the victory of the unsaturated over the saturated. The planters had at last convinced themselves that Martinique and Guadeloupe were too dangerous neighbours, and that rival producers within the Empire were less damaging than the Martinique privateers. In other words, just as the North American colonists had always demanded the expulsion of the French from Canada in order to secure themselves against future American wars, some elements in the West India interest were beginning to look on the acquisition of Martinique in the same light. This was not only a military precaution; it had its economic side, for many of the West India planters had borrowed great sums in England, and had already begun to insure their West India property. The rate of interest and premiums would depend in part on the public as well as the private security of their property.[2] A letter from Admiral Rodney to Lord Lyttelton puts the whole point very clearly.

'The planters are divided between avarice and fear, they think if Martinique is retained, they will be obliged to lower the price or their sugars. On the other hand, if it is given up, they fear the loss of their own plantations in case of another war, and that the French will overrun them before they can receive succours from Europe, which as I said before, they may easily do, and the example of this war has taught them a lesson, which I fancy they will never forget.'[3]

The Canada-Guadeloupe controversy does not seem to have had much influence on the decisions of the Ministry or its deal-

---

[1] Antigua Council Minutes, April 15, 1762, C.O. 9/26.
[2] 'Reflections on the true Interest of Great Britain with respect to the Caribbee Islands; . . . by a Planter of Barbados', C.O. 28/50.
[3] Rodney to Lyttelton, June 29, 1762, Phillimore's *Lyttelton*, ii. 634.

ings with France. In fact the discussion had not much practical importance, though it was long, noisy, and interesting for the sake of the principles which it involved. Pitt once asked in the House of Commons, which of these two colonies he should be hanged for giving back to France? He seems to have been undecided or indifferent in 1759, and again at the end of 1760, whether he ought to demand all Canada or part of it with Guadeloupe.[1] Yet when the negotiation began in earnest, he seems to have made up his mind without difficulty that Canada and the fisheries were indispensable. (Fortunately, though Choiseul hinted to Stanley that he was in the same dilemma, he seems to have been as clearly determined to keep the sugar colonies as Pitt was to acquire Canada.)[2] In fact, so long as the choice was only between Canada and Guadeloupe, it seems to have been an easy one to make, and nearly everybody who had anything to do with the conduct of affairs came to the same conclusion as Pitt.

Hardwicke and Newcastle can scarcely have thought the question a very important one, nor disagreed seriously with Pitt, for there is little proof that they debated it, though they received some probably unsolicited advice. Neither of them appears to have felt much doubt about it until the spring of 1762, when the capture of Martinique shook their convictions. When that event was known, with Rodney's exaggerated eulogy of Martinique as the key of the West Indies—when, moreover, it was plain that all the Windward Islands would fall into our hands within a few weeks—Hardwicke wanted to reconsider the question, for the first time as it would seem. It was no longer a choice between Canada and Guadeloupe, but between Canada and all the French West Indies except St. Domingue. Newcastle replied, 'I own, it startles me, who never was startled as to the sugar islands before.' The whole tone of this correspondence gives the impression that the question now raised was one which he and Hardwicke had hitherto regarded as closed,

---

[1] Newcastle to Hardwicke, Oct. 31, 1759, Add. MSS. 32897, f. 520; Dec. 3, 1760, vol. 32915, f. 270. As late as March 1761 Pitt told Hardwicke he was not sure if we should be able to keep all Canada (Hardwicke to Newcastle, March 17, 1761, vol. 32920, f. 271). However, there is no proof that this was because he was uncertain whether to prefer Guadeloupe. He had decided by April that Canada and the monopoly of the fishery were to be a *sine qua non* (Newcastle's memorandum of April 10, vol. 32921, f. 381).

[2] Stanley to Pitt, June 12, 1761, Thackeray, op. cit. i. 528; Choiseul to Ossun, April 5, 1762, A.E. Espagne, 536.

or not worth discussion. While Newcastle is usually the worst possible authority for the history of his own opinions, he seems to have spoken truth this time.[1]

At this moment, when the question asked itself seriously for the first time, Newcastle and Hardwicke were on the point of leaving the Ministry, and it was Bute who was left to make the decision. The conquest of Martinique compromised a negotiation which seemed to be leading to an agreement. Choiseul and Pitt had squabbled about the Neutral Islands in 1761, but Egremont was ready in March 1762 to propose a division which would probably have satisfied France—we were to take Dominica and Tobago while France was to have the other two.[2] According to the ideas of that time, the restoration of a conquest must be paid for. The conditions of peace had therefore to be altered after the capture of Martinique, for Bute and Egremont were the last people in the world to expose themselves to the charge of giving anything up to France. It was a little difficult to decide what we should make her pay for Martinique. We could not go back to Pitt's terms and claim the monopoly of the fishery; we could never have a peace that way. Some were for demanding Louisiana, others for Guadeloupe, others again for Senegal and Goree. Newcastle was against making any of these claims, because he believed they would prevent an agreement. Egremont proposed to force Choiseul to choose between Louisiana and Guadeloupe.[3]

Bute was in a dilemma. He probably believed, like Newcastle, that we should get no peace if we asked France to yield us a settled colony; yet he knew he must ask for something. He

---

[1] Hardwicke to Newcastle, April 2, 1762, Add. MSS. 32936, f. 310; Newcastle's reply, April 2, f. 312. Newcastle had received advice, for the most part uninvited, from Alderman Baker, from Chesterfield, and from Lord Morton, a friend of Hardwicke. I can find no expression of his own opinion, and little proof that he discussed the matter, beyond his letter to Hardwicke of Dec. 3, 1760, in which he gives Pitt's opinion, or lack of opinion, rather than his own. Professor Namier (op. cit., pp. 323–5) seems to me to have underrated the effect of the capture of Martinique upon Hardwicke and Newcastle; naturally it made a difference to the perspective in which they viewed the question.

[2] Bussy's instructions, May 23, 1761, A.E. Angleterre, 443; Bussy to Choiseul, June 11 and 26, ibid.; Choiseul to Bussy, July 15, ibid.; Stanley's minute of Sept. 2, 1761, Add. MSS. 32927, f. 340; Egremont's draft letter to Viry, March 21, 1762, vol. 32936, f. 4.

[3] Newcastle to Devonshire, April 23, 1762, Add. MSS. 32937, f. 324; Egremont's draft answer to Choiseul, April 25, 1762, f. 343; compare this with his letters to Viry of May 1, vol. 32938, f. 3, and A.E. Angleterre, 446.

hit upon a happy compromise; we should content ourselves with Grenada and all the Neutral Islands, and the whole continent of North America as far as the left bank of the Mississippi.[1] This was a very clever proposal; it combined the greatest possible gain for England with the smallest loss for France. It was a way of assuring still further the original object of the war —the security of our North American colonists. If it saddled us in the West Indies with a chain of islands all exposed to attack from the French strongholds, it gave us the best and most defensible frontier in North America. Pitt had never asked so much. The territories which Bute proposed to demand, both on the continent and in the islands, were open fields for English capital and enterprise. They contained few Frenchmen to make political trouble for the Government, or to compete with English producers in the home market. They made an imposing show on the map without costing France many subjects or much pride. The only condition which they did not satisfy was one which Bute had once held to be necessary; they were not likely to pay for the war by bringing in an immediate revenue. Pitt made the most of this defect in his speech on the preliminaries—a factious performance in which he revived the controversy of Canada and Guadeloupe, and attacked decisions in which he had been the first to acquiesce.[2]

The treaty of peace followed the lines which Bute had chalked out. There was a hitch over St. Lucia. Choiseul would not give it up because it was necessary to the security of Martinique. That, as Pitt said, was the best reason for us to insist upon it; and Pitt's imitators in the Ministry tried to do so.[3] Bute made his colleagues yield St. Lucia in order to buy concessions from Choiseul on the other points in dispute.[4] One of these was the Mississippi navigation; and in this sense it may be said that Bute, like Pitt, showed a steady inclination to sacrifice the West Indies to North America. Like Pitt, he conquered in the islands in order to annex on the continent.

[1] Hardwicke to Newcastle, May 1, 1762, Add. MSS. 32938, f. 11; Bute to Bedford, May 1, 1762, *Bedford Correspondence*, iii. 75; *v. infra*, pp. 597–601 for the complications between England, France, and Spain over this cession.

[2] *Parl. Hist.* xv. 1263 et seqq. Pitt is made to say that he had been for demanding Guadeloupe in 1761, but had been overruled. This seems to be a lie.

[3] Ibid.; Comte de Choiseul to Solar, May ?, 1762, A.E. Angleterre, 446.

[4] Cabinet minutes of June 21 and July 26, 1762, Add. MSS. 34713, ff. 106, 110; Bute to Bedford, Sept. 28, 1762, vol. 36797, f. 12.

VI

THE DIFFICULTIES OF WARFARE IN THE WEST INDIES

§ i. *The Militia and its Duties*

IN describing the warfare of the West Indies, it is not enough to deal with projects of conquest. These were exceptional, and were carried out for the most part by regular forces at the will of the English Government. The merchants and planters were more concerned for the safety of their own property and trade; so far as they made any efforts themselves or exercised any influence over the Government, they directed its attention and their own to the routine of defence. In fact, West India strategy was mainly defensive.

This pre-eminence of weakness over strength is excusable, in view of the past history of West Indian warfare and the extraordinary vulnerability of sugar colonies. The events of 1664–6 and those of Queen Anne's reign had proved beyond doubt the great damage which a small armed force could do in a very short time, given a momentary command of the sea. Nevis, once the 'Garden of the Caribbees', had been reduced to desolation in a few weeks; St. Kitts and Montserrat had suffered the same fate. In the two last, the French were able to destroy most of the property on the islands without obtaining command of the principal fortresses. It was so easy to carry away the negroes, to fire the canes and sugar-works, and to depart within a fortnight, having caused more loss and damage than could be done in the same time anywhere else in the Empire, outside London and the home counties.[1] Neither Nevis nor Montserrat quite recovered from the eclipse into which the disasters of 1706 and 1712 had thrown them. St. Kitts succeeded better, by the help of its extraordinary fertility.

These facts are enough to account for the moans of terror which the West India interest so freely uttered upon the slightest apprehension of a French naval superiority in the Caribbean, and the extraordinary credulity with which it magnified the size of every French force which went that way. It was not enough to know that the enemy had no army in the West Indies

---

[1] *C.S.P. Col. 1706–8*, nos. 168, 195 (i), 282, 338, 357; *1712–14*, 33 (ii), 38, 57.

which was capable of subduing a colony; the planters were equally afraid of a few ships which could only snatch a momentary opportunity of devastation. 'I think as you do', wrote Knight during the alarm of 1745, 'that the conquest of the island [Jamaica] is out of the question; but if you and I are ruined it is the same thing to us.'[1]

Had they habitually insured their estates, the planters might have been less nervous. Messrs. Lascelles and Maxwell gave an amusing account of the scenes which attended the sharpest of these alarms, when Caylus and Conflans arrived at Martinique with a fair-sized force in the spring of 1745.

'The private insurance offices were seen crowded with planters endeavouring to insure their plantations for 6 months, but some, that had policies to insure £10000 could not get above £800 underwrote at £10. 10 p^r Ct. premio. It's said by an insurance broker of our acquaintance, who had several of those policies to get done, that the insurers would have wrote much more than they did but for the dismal countenances of the planters, which made them afraid to write, & had they stayed at home their policies would have been filled.'[2]

As this is almost the only mention of that kind of insurance in their correspondence before 1763, the practice must still have been rare.

Why could not the West India colonies defend themselves without a superior naval force? The chief reason was the smallness of the white population. From the time when sugar culture and large estates worked by slaves had taken the place of the small plantations of tobacco and cotton, the number of white men fit to bear arms had been sinking. Governor Parke had attributed the weakness of the militia to *latifundia* as early as Queen Anne's reign. The militia of Antigua had been depleted by great planters buying out the estates of the small, and elbowing them off the island. This evil was complicated by the planters' love of rank and position, which caused the available force to be divided into a large number of small units with a great many officers and very few men. Parke reported that the company of his enemy Colonel Codrington contained only three officers and one man; the militia of one parish in St. Kitts consisted of six men, of whom four were servants of the

[1] Letter of Knight, Aug. 15, 1745, Add. MSS. 22677, f. 48.
[2] Lascelles and Maxwell to Michael Longbotham, June 18, 1745, W. & G. ii.

captain. Of course both these instances are exceptional.[1] Another great evil was absenteeism, which not only deprived the islands of some of their military population, but may have contributed to the dangerous indiscipline of the negroes by removing the only influence and supervision which kept them in check.[2]

The numbers do not seem to have declined very much after Queen Anne's reign; in fact they began to rise again, perhaps as a result of the laws which were passed for the purpose in some of the islands.[3] No legislature went so far as that of Jamaica in recognizing the principle that the real military salvation of the sugar colonies could only lie in increasing the white population. Some schemes for mass immigration—of Palatines in 1709, of Scots in 1740—came to nothing.[4] Act upon Act went on the statute-book. Large tracts of land were set aside, and large sums of money spent, but the result of this showy and expensive legislation was depressing. In fact the only laws which produced any positive effect were the so-called 'deficiency laws'; they imposed a fine upon the landed proprietors for not keeping up a certain proportion of white servants on their plantations. According to Governor Trelawny, this fine had a slight influence upon the demand for servants, but

---

[1] *C.S.P. Col. 1706–8*, no. 519; *1708–9*, no. 597 (i); *1710–11*, no. 391; *1711–12*, no. 392.

[2] Jamaica Council Minutes, Dec. 18, 1760, C.O. 140/42.

[3] In 1703 Governor Handasyd estimated the military strength of Jamaica at 3,500 men (*C.S.P. Col. 1702–3*, no. 764); in 1706, at 2,550 including free negroes (*C.S.P. Col. 1706–8*, no. 221); in 1752, Trelawny put it at 4,400 and Knowles at under 5,000 (Trelawny's 'State of Jamaica', 1752, C.O. 137/25, X 101; Knowles's 'State', 1755, C.O. 137/29, Y 106). The spokesmen of the West India interest in London naturally gave a much lower figure when they were applying to the Government for help. Governor Parke reported the militia of the Leeward Islands to be as follows: Antigua 700, Montserrat 600, Nevis 250, St. Kitts 450 (*C.S.P. Col. 1706–8*, no. 473). In 1742 there were 1,360 militia on Antigua, 500 on Montserrat, 280 on Nevis, and 800 on St. Kitts. The numbers given by Thomas in 1755 are not very different. I cannot account for the great increase in Antigua; that of St. Kitts is presumably due to the extension of cultivation in the former French half of the island, which was almost uninhabited at the time of the earlier statistics (see Mathew's 'State' of the Leeward Islands, Oct. 26, 1742, C.O. 152/24, Y 54; Thomas to Board of Trade, Aug. 25, 1755, C.O. 152/28, BB 65). At Barbados there were supposed in 1707 to be 3,062 foot and 1,050 horse (*C.S.P. Col. 1706–8*, no. 1225 (vii)); the whole militia, without officers, in 1762, was 3,827 men (Pinfold's Answers to Queries, June 1, 1762, C.O. 28/32, FF 25). Something under 10 per cent. should be added to these figures for officers.

[4] *Journal of the Lords Commissioners of Trade and Plantations, 1708/9 to 1714/15*, pp. 58, 63, 75, 79, 82, 83. For the Scotch scheme of 1740, see Add. MSS. 22677, ff. 40, 41; vol. 12431, ff. 116, 120.

it generally became a mere tax, and thus the laws which had been designed to serve a social purpose were too readily diverted to fiscal uses. In fact, a scheme for peopling the island was frustrated in 1743 by the Assembly, which was afraid 'of losing 'the deficiency law, which if it does not altogether answer the intention of peopling the island, yet it serves to raise a large sum of money'.[1]

The Board of Trade reviewed these policies in 1753, when it tried to explain to the House of Commons why the population and sugar-production of Jamaica were so small. The families introduced into the island certainly could not be numbered by more than a few hundreds, and the cost was very high in proportion to the other normal expenditure of a colony at that time. Knowles summed it up by saying that some 700 persons had cost the island about £30,000. Both he and the Board described most of the immigrants as perfectly unsuitable. Many of them were good for nothing, the others knew nothing of husbandry. They therefore tended to drift into the towns, or to leave the island, whose economic life was so organized that new-comers could find little livelihood, unless they were qualified by patronage or education to take their places as underlings or skilled workmen in the management of the great sugar estates.[2] If they succeeded at all, they succeeded too well, and added to the prevailing *latifundia* by becoming sugar-planters. The legislature began to despair, and to repeal its own acts. However, the military population of Jamaica does seem to have risen, according to the figures quoted above; but the increase is not to be attributed to the artificial encouragements offered by the Government, so much as to the spontaneous spread of cultivation on the north side of the island, which had been very imperfectly settled in Queen Anne's reign.

These difficulties were by no means peculiar to the English sugar colonies. The French Government waged the same unequal struggle against economic forces by trying to impose white servants upon the colonies which no longer had any use for them. Colbert had invented the plan of obliging the master of every ship bound from France to the islands to take out two such *engagés*. But the ship-owners did not want to carry them,

---

[1] Beckford to Knight, June 18, 1743, Add. MSS. 12431, f. 125.
[2] Board of Trade, Report to House of Commons, Feb. 22, 1753, C.O. 138/19, pp. 405-52; Knowles to Board of Trade, Dec. 31, 1754, C.O. 137/28, Y 43.

nor the colonists to receive them, and a considerable recruitment of population could only be effected by frequent renewal
of the edicts and official vigilance in carrying them out. A few
years later, the Government gave the captains the option of
taking out two muskets instead; this duty was performed as
seldom or as badly as the other. In France, as in England, it
soon became impossible to recruit genuine agricultural labourers
for the sugar plantations, and such *engagés* as could be found
were rejected by the colonists as useless scoundrels. From the
dregs of the towns they came, and to the dregs of the towns they
returned in the colonies.[1]

Although both Governments failed equally to foist population
upon the colonies, the French islands were never so weak in
men as the English. Their greater size accounts in part for
their more imposing numbers. St. Domingue, for example, had
6,000 militiamen in 1739 according to Larnage,[2] while nobody
ever claimed more than 5,000 for Jamaica, and that was probably too high. But St. Domingue was a much larger colony than
Jamaica—in fact, it was really three colonies rather than one,
for the communication between its quarters was difficult. Likewise Martinique was larger than any of its English neighbours,
and might be expected to have a larger militia. In 1746 it
numbered 3,095 infantry and 710 cavalry besides officers, but
Le Vassor de la Touche estimated in 1761 that 8,000 planters
could be called upon in an emergency; this is not the same thing
as the number of the militia, though it should have been.[3]
According to one of its conquerors, Guadeloupe was supposed to contain between 3,000 and 4,000 armed men, but not
more than 1,600 appeared in arms.[4] The privateers who made
Martinique their head-quarters added something to its available force. Caylus thought there were 2,500 of them, but
Le Vassor de la Touche found only 1,200 in November 1761.

[1] Louis-Philippe May, *Histoire économique de la Martinique* (Paris, 1930), pp.
36–9.
[2] Larnage to Maurepas, Dec. 28, 1739, A.N. Colonies C⁹ A 50. Pierre de Vais-
sière quotes some figures of 1753—4,639 white men bearing arms, 1,853 white
boys, 1,332 mulattos and negroes—total, 7,824 (*Saint Domingue*, Paris 1909,
p. 116).
[3] Caylus to Maurepas, Dec. 23, 1746, A.N. Colonies C⁸ A 57; Le Vassor de la
Touche to Berryer, Nov. 20, 1761, vol. 63.
[4] W. M. Burt to Pitt, May 2, 1759, G.D. 8/24. In 1739 there had been 1,292
men and 1,497 boys bearing arms (Satineau, *Histoire de la Guadeloupe sous l'Ancien
Régime*, p. 384).

Le Mercier de la Rivière explained this apparent decrease; many of the privateers left Martinique when they were sure it would be invaded, for fear of being taken prisoners and sent to England.[1] It is impossible to say how many of these privateers were natives of Martinique and how many only used it as a base in time of war. It probably had a greater seafaring population of its own than any other West India island, because it had a greater local trade; the interruption of that navigation by the English blockade must have driven the crews to privateering even if they had no other inclination for it.

The disparity between the French and English populations in the West Indies was not vast; but the English planters exaggerated it and were obsessed by it. It became one of their strongest excuses for demanding that we should always keep a naval superiority in the West Indies. If Martinique was swarming with armed men ready to dash out and invade Antigua or St. Kitts at any minute, it was more important than ever to deny them the opportunity. The English estimated the military population of Martinique at ten or twelve thousand, all ready for an expedition at a moment's notice. How far this was from the truth, can be seen from the history of the meagre and reluctant reinforcement which Champigny scraped up for St. Lucia.[2] Yet there was something to be said for the legend. Though it was not true that the French sugar-planters as a whole greatly outnumbered the English, they really did so in the corner of the West Indies where they were likeliest to attack—namely the Leeward Islands. Martinique or Guadeloupe had many more men than Antigua or St. Kitts, let alone Montserrat or Nevis. If precedent and geography were any guides, it was those islands that were in most danger. They lay to leeward of Martinique; the easiest course of invasion was from windward to leeward, and that is why Barbados was never invaded at all and Antigua, which is set back a little from the others, only once, while St. Kitts, Nevis, and Montserrat were lost or ruined again and again.

The best hope of the Leeward Islands was help or a counter-

---

[1] Le Mercier de la Rivière, *mémoire* on the siege of Martinique, Aug. 5, 1762, A.N. Colonies C[8] A 64. Commodore Douglas also noticed the departure of the privateers. The reason which La Rivière assigns for it is plausible, for Douglas and Dalrymple had lately quarrelled with La Touche over the exchange of prisoners and begun sending them back to England.

[2] *V. supra*, pp. 204–6.

attack from Barbados, which was comparatively safe and well manned. Lieutenant-Governor Fleming suggested more than once that Barbados should at least pretend to be about creating some diversion. The Barbadians had willingly put themselves on shipboard and gone down to relieve Nevis and St. Kitts in 1666 and 1667; but the Leeward Islands were then lately peopled from Barbados, and every Barbadian planter might well have a friend or relation in the threatened colonies. In later years Barbados was too much preoccupied with its own defence to spend its military strength on behalf of other islands. It sent nothing more than good wishes to Nevis in 1706.[1] When there was question of a regular attack on Martinique, backed by regular troops and a decisive naval superiority, that was another matter; the island then felt itself safe in sparing a few hundred volunteers.[2] But it could not engage in anything more hazardous; for instance, one of the genuine reasons for the refusal to co-operate in the scheme against St. Lucia in 1745 was the feeling that Barbados would expose itself to danger by parting with any of its militia for an expedition without regular troops. How much the more would the colonists decline to succour the Leeward Islands over a sea commanded by the enemy?—for without such command, the French were very unlikely to attempt any invasion.

The selfishness of the Barbados planters was not exceptional, for the French militiamen were just as reluctant to leave their own islands in defence of others. There was a striking example of this in 1759, at the siege of Guadeloupe. The English attack was first aimed against Martinique, and the militia was embodied to resist it, with surprising success. When Hopson and Moore decided to go off to attack Guadeloupe, Beauharnois, who had disbanded his forces, could not send more than sixty-six volunteers to the rescue. The insufficiency of this effort is no doubt explained partly by Beauharnois's own inertia and by the danger of the passage across an uncommanded sea; this, however, was by no means so great as it was represented, especially after the arrival of a French squadron under Bompar had obliged Moore to concentrate his fleet and to leave the windward side of Guadeloupe unguarded. No doubt the

---

[1] *C.S.P. Col. 1706–8*, no. 383 (ii), 496; Fleming to Stone, Oct. 12, 1745, C.O. 152/44; intercepted letter of Fleming to Pinfold, June 29, 1757, A.N. Colonies C⁸ A 61.　　　　　　　　　　　　　　[2] *V. supra*, p. 222.

strongest reason was the unwillingness of the militia to leave
Martinique on any account.[1]

Only within the Leeward Islands government did one sugar
colony send real support to another in time of danger. In
Queen Anne's reign the Governors once or twice succoured
from Antigua the islands which were attacked by the French,
but already the forces they took with them consisted chiefly of
regular soldiers. At the beginning of the Spanish war in 1739,
Governor Mathew tried to induce all the colonies under his
government to pass laws for paying volunteers from the other
islands, in case of invasion. One or two of the legislatures complied, but their laws were never put to any use. Mathew himself appeared in the spring of 1745 at St. Kitts, as the point
chiefly threatened by Caylus; but he seems to have brought
only regulars with him.[2] In the same way Governor Shirley
came down from Antigua in 1782, and threw himself into St.
Kitts with some part of the garrison. These expeditions were
not impossible, even when the command of the sea was lost; for
the enemy would naturally attack the main fortresses and
towns, which were all on the leeward sides of the islands, so
they might leave the coasts clear for the landing of a relief force
to windward.

If the whole militia of the colonies had been large and easy
to move from one island to another in the face of danger, its
quality was still very low. Some of the islands had no militia
laws at all, or such bad ones that no sort of discipline could be
enforced. The people of Nevis were credited with the opinion
that 'Discipline is the first step to tyranny'. Monthly meetings
were appointed for exercise in most of the islands;[3] but the fines
for absence were so slight that anybody of moderate fortune
could quite cheaply buy himself out of the militia altogether.[4]

[1] Beauharnois to Berryer, Jan. 27, 1759, Feb. 15, 1760, A.N. Colonies C8 A 62.
When Beauharnois and Bompar at last screwed up their courage to try to raise the
siege, they do not seem to have taken any militia or volunteers with them.

[2] Antigua Council Minutes, Mathew's speech, July 31, 1739, C.O. 9/13; St.
Kitts Council Minutes, Jan. 19, 1740/1, C.O. 241/4.

[3] At Antigua, for instance, by the supplementary militia law of July 12, 1756
(C.O. 8/12). The lordly spirit of this militia is indicated by the clause forbidding
any private to have his arms carried for him to alarms by negroes. See Mathew's
'State' of the Leeward Islands, C.O. 152/24 Y 54.

[4] Lieut.-Governor Moore complained very loudly against the militia law of
Jamaica (Moore to Board of Trade, Nov. 7, 1760, C.O. 137/32 BB 9). It appears
from his speech to the Assembly on Sept. 18, 1760, that his chief objection to it was
the smallness of the fines for non-attendance.

Besides, there were numerous exemptions for so-called gunners, and the officers do not seem to have been strictly called to account for their appearances. Some islands dispensed whole-sale from their service assemblymen, councillors, judges, and other classes too.[1] Trelawny complained to the Jamaica legislature of the number of these exemptions, which obliged a few people to do duty for the whole. Robinson went a step farther at Barbados; he collected the fines appointed for absence from an alarm. He said this was the first time it had been done since the militia law was passed in 1697; he raised £5,700 at one stroke by this unexpected strictness, but it is not surprising that he was one of the most unpopular Governors the island ever had.[2] In the French colonies too the *noblesse* seem to have dispensed themselves and their negroes from regular service.[3]

It was therefore on the poorer whites that militia duty fell as a heavy burden, and the colonial politicians represented any sort of arduous or continued service as an especial hardship on the poor. Governor Mathew was so conscious of their discontent that he thought proper to deal with it in a speech to the Assembly of Antigua.

'I am told it has strangely prevailed among the poorer sort, that if in this cause or of any war, they are called upon, 'tis to defend the rich and wealthy only and at the expence of their lives, and therefore such a duty does not belong to them. But we ought all of us to cure them of this refractory error by letting them know, that the Articles of War, established by law, will certainly bring them to an ignominious punishment, or death, for avoiding an uncertain honourable one in the service of their country.'[4]

The militiamen were for the most part wretchedly trained. Some of the diatribes against their inefficiency may be discounted, for several Governors were professional soldiers from Europe accustomed to a superior, perhaps an unnecessary exactness in drill. Yet it does appear that the colonial forces were almost wholly unwarlike. At the beginning of the Seven Years

---

[1] For example, the Nevis Act of 1737 exempted the Councillors, the Chief Justice, and the Admiralty judge. That of 1741 added the Treasurer to this list. Both these Acts exempted the Assemblymen from the ordinary drill (C.O. 185/4).

[2] Nevis Assembly Minutes, April 11, 1748, C.O. 186/3; Trelawny's speech of March 18, 1739/40, *Journals of the Assembly of Jamaica*, iii. 505; Robinson to Newcastle, April 23, 1745, C.O. 28/46.

[3] Le Mercier de la Rivière's *mémoire* on the siege of Martinique, quoted above.

[4] Antigua Council Minutes, July 31, 1739, C.O. 9/13. See the complaint of the Grand Jury of Barbados, *C.S.P. Col. 1706–8*, no. 697 (ii).

War, martial law was proclaimed and continued for some weeks in Jamaica for the sole purpose of drilling the militia, which presumably needed it. Indeed, the training could hardly have been any better than it was, for the officers were all amateurs appointed for political reasons, because they were men of property or friends of the Governor. Faction ran so high at Barbados in Queen Anne's reign that the Governors ruined the discipline of the militia by repeatedly turning out and replacing the officers. Nothing quite so bad happened in the next war, but in the conflict between the true blue Protestants and the pro-Catholics of Montserrat, the Protestant Assembly demanded the deprivation of most of the chief militia officers.[1]

The French islands were little better off in these respects. Larnage lamented that the planters of St. Domingue were not the warriors they had been in the last century. Luxury and soft living had undone them; they were so used to lolling in chaises and coaches that they hardly knew the use of their legs.[2] Bory repeated the same complaints in 1762. The planters had altogether ceased to do guard duty, for which they hired mercenaries, so that they never got any military exercise except in great emergencies, for which they had to turn out quite unprepared. Bory could see no remedy for this state of affairs, but to embody the mulattos as a permanent professional militia; but Choiseul refused to sanction this reform.[3]

The military value of the population had fallen off everywhere in the West Indies for the same reasons, and thus the cultivation of sugar had lowered the quality and numbers of the militia at the same time. Martinique had a better reputation than most islands, but did not deserve it, if Le Mercier de la Rivière is to be believed. 'If the militia of France only left its labours once or twice in a year to stand in a sort of line and return home after being counted, without ever going through any exercises or learning how to handle its arms, the militiaman would always remain a boorish peasant.' But at least he would be fitted for military service by hard living, whereas the sugar-planter, equally untrained, was not even in the bodily

---

[1] *C.S.P. Col. 1708–9*, no. 179; Montserrat Assembly Minutes, *passim*, 1745, C.O. 177/4.

[2] Larnage to Maurepas, Dec. 28, 1739, A.N. Colonies C⁹ A 50; Oct. 31, 1744, vol. 64.

[3] Guichen to Berryer, July 24, 1761, A.N. Colonies C⁹ A 110; Bory to Choiseul, June 12 and 22, July 17, 1762, vol. 111; Choiseul to Bory, July 31, ibid.

condition to undergo a war. La Rivière certainly experienced one of the worst periods of inefficiency at Martinique under Beauharnois's Governorship. He admitted that Le Vassor de la Touche had put a little discipline into the forces, and that they behaved pretty well in the battle of January 27, 1762; but they had not the experience necessary to an orderly retreat, and their rout before the English counter-attack was the chief cause of the conquest of the island.[1]

So bad were the militia laws and so inefficient the militia that some Governors believed they could do nothing without martial law. Moore took off the martial law in 1760 at Jamaica when the back of the slaves' revolt was broken, but he found that he could not suppress the negroes entirely, because the militia shirked its duty, having nothing more to fear than a few paltry fines; so he had to proclaim martial law again at the request of the Assembly.[2] Martial law was sometimes represented as a hardship on the poor, but there were two opinions of that. Some welcomed and others detested it as a debtors' holiday. Factors made it an excuse for failing in their remittances.[3] Planters declined to pay their island or parish taxes. The lawyers on the contrary were exasperated, for martial law suspended the sessions of the courts and brought all legal business to a standstill. Gradually the legislatures departed from the principle of protecting debtors from suit during martial law; for instance the Jamaica Act of 1745 ordained that prosecutions for debt and collection of taxes should not be interrupted. This Act should have dispensed the Governor from the ridiculous necessity of deferring martial law till quarter-day was over; but it must have lapsed, for that was the situation in which Moore found himself in 1756.[4]

The militia laws obliged the colonists to appear in arms not only at the stated meetings for exercise, but upon every 'alarm'. This meant, every time that a certain number of three-mast or topsail ships were seen from the coast. The first person who

[1] *Mémoire* on the siege of Martinique, quoted above; Monckton to Egremont, Jan. 9, 1762, C.O. 166/2.
[2] Moore to Board of Trade, Nov. 7, 1760, C.O. 137/32, BB 9.
[3] Lascelles and Maxwell to Alexander Harvie, April 30, 1762, W. & G. ix.
[4] Montserrat Assembly Minutes, April 23, 1745, C.O. 177/3; *Journals of the Assembly of Jamaica*, iv. 668. The Barbados Acts of 1759 and 1761 for raising volunteers against Martinique permitted debtors for under £300 to be enlarged out of prison if they would serve against Martinique; to prison it seems they must return when it was all over.

sighted the ship was to fire a number of shots, and the signal was to be repeated through the island. There was no way of preventing the approach of our own fleets from causing false alarms. Sometimes the planters took the law into their own hands when they expected a convoy from England, and declined to turn out; but they might make a mistake here, as they did at Barbados when Bompar's squadron was sighted in 1759.[1] Penalties for deliberate false alarms were heavy, but the offence was hard to prove. The system was clumsy and harassing, especially when officious Governors like Robinson of Barbados multiplied the alarms by having them raised on the appearance of a smaller number of ships. Caylus found at Martinique that the inhabitants were pestered out of their lives by alarms, and tried to establish regular militia guards instead.[2]

This kind of guard duty was already exacted of the English militia, and very burdensome it was, especially to the smaller and more thinly populated islands. The legislature of Montserrat represented that a quarter of the militia would have to do guard duty every night if the regular troops were withdrawn; and although any West Indian body would exaggerate grossly in order to get favours from the Government, the statement is not incredible, for the militia of Montserrat only numbered 500. The object of this kind of service was not merely to give timely warning of an invasion—though both Antigua and Montserrat had been preserved from considerable French forces by the vigilance of the nightly guards in Queen Anne's reign—but also to prevent small incursions of privateers who came to pillage plantations on the coasts and to carry away negroes.

Such raids had been very common in earlier times, but about 1740 the authorities on both sides were beginning to dislike this form of warfare and wished to discourage it. Both Trelawny and Larnage would have been glad to enter into an arrangement for prohibiting it, but unfortunately that was impossible. Trelawny could barely have answered for the obedience of the Jamaica privateers, and had no claim whatever to bind or control those of the other colonies; therefore if Larnage had merely concluded an agreement with Jamaica, he would have tied the hands of the French subjects at St. Domingue, without affording

[1] Barbados Council Minutes, March 13, 1759, C.O. 31/30.
[2] Caylus's *Mémoire* on his government, A.N. Colonies C⁸ A 58. Something of the sort was done at Antigua; see the Act of Sept. 1, 1744, C.O. 8/9.

them any kind of security. At the end of the Seven Years War the question of prohibiting such descents was raised again. Admiral Holmes seems to have made a convention with Governor Bart of St. Domingue for discouraging them, by refusing to exchange any prisoners that might be taken from the raiders; but it cannot have had a permanent effect, for Governor de Bory was still asking for the same thing in November 1762. Le Vassor de la Touche fell into a quarrel with Commodore Douglas upon this subject. He said that he had not permitted the privateers of Martinique to pillage the sea-shore plantations of the English islands, but should very soon do so unless Douglas gave satisfaction for a descent which he had allowed one of his own warships to make.[1]

Jamaica in particular complained of these raids, for its coast-line was long and difficult for land or sea forces to guard. The legislature was very eager to have some small vessels of war allotted to this service, and the Lords of the Admiralty ordered Sir Chaloner Ogle and his successors in the command to provide for it. But the work does not seem to have been properly performed, for want of enough vessels of the right kind, until the time of Admiral Cotes in 1757–60. Cotes's successor Holmes was criticized for not looking after the coasts, but he threw the blame on the planters themselves, who either built no emplacements for defence at the landing-places most exposed, or, having built them, neglected to supply them with men and guns.[2]

---

[1] Larnage to Trelawny, Feb. 2, 1745, C.O. 137/57; Trelawny to Newcastle, Feb. 3, 1744/5, ibid.; Larnage to Maurepas, Jan. 29, 1745, A.N. Colonies C⁹ A 66; Maurepas to Larnage, Dec. 15, 1745, B 81; Maurepas to Caylus, Nov. 15, 1745, ibid.; Holmes to Bart, Aug. 8, 1761, Adm. 1/236; Jamaica Council Minutes, Nov. 3, 1762, C.O. 140/42; Le Vassor de la Touche to Berryer, Nov. 20, 1761, A.N. Colonies C⁸ A 63. The Governor of Cap François complained in 1747 to Governor Tinker of the Bahamas against the petty depredations of the New Providence privateers upon the coasts. Tinker replied that Vaudreuil was welcome to hang any of them if he could find them ashore without their commissions, and that he was sorry that he had not authority to chastise them himself. Soon afterwards Vaudreuil caught some of them, and determined to send them home to France instead of exchanging them for English prisoners in America—an inconvenience which was regarded by the colonists on both sides as a very heavy punishment (Vaudreuil and Samson to Maurepas, Feb. 24, 1748, A.N. Colonies C⁹ A 73. See the interesting directions for plundering Hispaniola, printed by J. F. Jameson, *Privateering and Piracy in the Colonial Period*, N.Y. 1923, p. 471).

[2] Bart and Laporte-Lalanne to Moras, Sept. 25, 1757, A.N. Colonies C⁹ A 100; *Journals of the Assembly of Jamaica*, iii. 557–8; Jamaica Council Minutes, May 18, 1743, C.O. 140/31; Council and Assembly to George II, May 8, 1747, C.O. 137/58; Holmes to Cleveland, March 18 and Oct. 27, 1761, Adm. 1/236; see the

Although the raids of privateers were so much complained of, they do not seem to have inflicted very great damage; there were very few demands for compensation. When a Bill was introduced into the legislature of St. Kitts for indemnifying sufferers by such pillage, there was only one case to be provided for—that of the Lieutenant-Governor, who was the real promoter of the law, and passed it by his casting vote. There were not more than half a dozen applications to the Assembly of Jamaica for compensation of this kind; it is impossible to say whether there were very few planters whose property had been damaged, or merely very few who had influence with the Assemblymen.

The inability of the militia to guard the coasts does not seem to have been a very serious trouble, though the burden was vexatious and was one of the principal reasons why the planters were so eager to have regular troops stationed in their islands. The difficulty of warding off a serious invasion with such small forces was a graver matter, and required some remedy. There were four principal ways in which the military strength of the sugar colonies could be supplemented—fortifications, armed negroes, regular troops, and above all a large naval force.

§ ii. *The Value of Fortifications*

The planters raised great sums for fortifying their islands. Unfortunately, the island legislatures not only paid for the work, but also directed it,[1] with such light as they could get, and were willing to take, from Governors who might or might not have had military experience. These Governors, especially if they had been professional soldiers, nearly always derided the work of their predecessors, and insisted upon altering it, only to have their own performances in their turn pronounced worthless and superseded by their successors.[2] Skilled workmen

French privateer's commission of 1746, printed by Marsden, *Law and Custom*, ii. 328.

[1] In Jamaica the fortifications in the out-ports were built and kept in repair at the charge not of the island but of the parishes concerned. It is therefore impossible to conjecture the whole expense, as very few of the parish records survive from this period.

[2] Knowles, for example, had an itch for fortifying, and ran down all the fortifications round Kingston except those which had been built under his own direction (Knowles's 'State of Jamaica', Dec. 13, 1755, C.O. 137/29 Y 106). Haldane, his successor, thought them still so weak that Fort Royal could not be defended half an hour without the help of the fleet, and asked for the services of a professional

were often lacking; when Peter Henry Bruce tried to put Fort Montagu in order at New Providence, he had to get masons from Philadelphia. Both in the English and French islands, there were many complaints of bad construction.[1] There were also popular prejudices and the interests of politicians to be considered. The planters would set an imaginary value upon some quite useless position, and insist on fortifying it to the neglect of everything else. Another cause of disturbance and delay was the danger that the legislatures might tack irrelevant clauses to the fortification bills, or raise the money in undesirable ways. In the Seven Years War the Assembly of St. Kitts tried to take advantage of the necessity of a powder duty in order to extend its constitutional privileges in financial matters. Governor Thomas had already rebuked this sort of trifling. 'Some of His Majesty's Colonys have been shifting off expences and disputing about little privileges, till the French have almost robbed them of the privilege of calling anything their own.'[2]

The result of all this was great confusion, inefficiency, and above all a prodigious waste, which would have been greater still if the Assemblies had not so much disliked raising taxes.[3] They would never do anything except in a great emergency. When the enemy was announced, they would proceed with energy on the works which they ought to have finished long ago. As soon as the danger passed over, they would leave everything standing as it was, and refuse to keep it up. The Assembly of Montserrat, for example, declined to open entrenchments in 1739, as the danger from a Spanish war was not great enough to be worth the expense: they would leave it until there were

engineer—though he attributed the fault largely to the badness of the guns (Board of Trade to George II, May 12, 1758, C.O. 138/20, p. 403; Haldane to Board of Trade, July 20, 1759, C.O. 137/30 Z 60). See also Laporte-Lalanne's letter to Moras, July 15, 1758, A.N. Colonies C⁹ A 101; Bart to Moras, Sept. 20, 1757, vol. 100; Remonstrance of the *Conseil Supérieur* of Port-au-Prince, July 19, 1759, vol. 103; Instructions to Clugny, April 4, 1760, B 111; Clugny to Berryer, Dec. 25, 1760, C⁹ A 107; Bory to Choiseul, June 22, 1762, C⁹ A 111.

[1] *Memoirs of Peter Henry Bruce* (London, 1782), pp. 386–7; Nevis Assembly Minutes, Feb. 4, 1747/8, C.O. 186/3; Berryer to Bart and Elias, June 23, 1759, A.N. Colonies B 109; Clugny to Berryer, Dec. 18, 1760, C⁹ A 107.

[2] St. Kitts Council Minutes, April 7, 1755, Dec. 6, 1756, C.O. 241/7.

[3] According to Trelawny, the legislature of Jamaica reasoned in 1749 'that it is better to run the risque of being destroy'd by the enemy, if not protected sufficiently by His Majesty's Ships and some soldiers from England, than absolutely and certainly to ruin themselves by an expence on their fortifications which they cannot bear' (Trelawny to the Board of Trade, June 8, 1749, C.O. 137/25).

signs of a French war. When the Governor warned them that a French war was in fact approaching, they set to with frenzied diligence. St. Kitts would do nothing to defend itself—not even pass a militia law—before the outbreak of the French war in 1744 (although its own agent, in company with the other representatives of the West India interest, had long been pressing the Admiralty to send out a large naval reinforcement on the assumption that a French war might break out at any moment). Then the legislature took all its measures in a desperate hurry. Beauharnois noticed the same thing at Martinique in 1758—everything had to be done at once.[1]

These fortifications were built by negro labour. The system was much the same in both French and English islands, but that the French *corvées* seem to have been apportioned and commandeered by the Governors, while compulsion could only be exercised in the English colonies under an Act of the local legislature. Probably much less was done in the English than in the French West Indies. The Governors of the latter were sometimes forced to suspend the *corvées* because they could not get victuals to feed the negroes, or the planters would not continue to furnish them; but the interruptions can hardly have been so frequent as those caused in the English islands by the sudden evaporation of the Assemblies' good intentions. This negro labour was generally unpaid on both sides; sometimes, however, the English legislatures ordered payment to be made, and Beauharnois could only persuade the planters of Martinique to furnish their *corvées* by paying hire for their slaves.[2]

The *corvées* were unpopular, especially if they happened to be demanded in crop-time, or for works distant from the owners' plantations. Vaudreuil of Cap François believed that the planters were more willing to furnish them in war than in peace, because the labour of their negroes could not then be so profitably employed on the plantations; but this argument has

---

[1] Montserrat Assembly Minutes, Dec. 8, 1739, C.O. 177/3; Nov. 28, 1743, C.O. 177/4; Mathew's 'State of the Leeward Islands', Oct. 16, 1742, C.O. 152/24, Y 54; Mathew to Newcastle, July 20, 1744, C.O. 152/44; Beauharnois and Givry to Moras, June 24, 1758, A.N. Colonies C⁸ A 64. For similar instances of eleventh-hour diligence see *C.S.P. Col. 1706–8*, nos. 281, 1251.

[2] Longueville to Berryer, Feb. 22, 1760, A.N. Colonies C⁸ A 62; Le Vassor de la Touche to Berryer, July 24, 1761, C⁸ A 63; Larnage to Maurepas, Oct. 30, 1744, C⁹ A 64.

the air of an *a priori* deduction. The colonists had some per-petual reasons for disliking the *corvées* which forced their slaves into the company of those from other estates, and gave oppor-tunities for mutual corruption of manners and even for plots. A money commutation was proposed several times, and the Government once or twice looked upon it with favour; but the planters objected to money taxes more than anything else, and were always monstrously behindhand with them, so the system of *corvées* had generally to be left as it was.[1]

An attempt at commutation in St. Domingue led to a con-stitutional quarrel between the Government and the *Conseils Supérieurs* of the island. The colonists appear to have consented to a tax upon negroes in 1713, by way of purchasing exemption from the *corvées*. The Government pocketed the tax, and frus-trated the exemption by distinguishing between ordinary and extraordinary *corvées*; the agreement only entitled the colonies to relief from the former, and the latter continued to be raised. The colonists acquiesced in this interpretation, and when the Government asked in 1750 for a special tax to put the fortifica-tions in order, the *Conseils Supérieurs* granted it for five years. At the end of that time the Seven Years War was breaking out, and the King ordered the tax to be prolonged. The *Conseils* made a difficulty of registering the order, raised a dispute over their constitutional privileges, criticized the way the money was spent, and asked what the Government had done with the revenues of the island since 1713. Finally the registration was pushed through, but the same trouble recurred when it had to be repeated in 1759. Berryer tried to bribe the colonists with a new Chamber of Commerce, but this registration provoked complaints like the earlier one.[2]

What was the use of fortifications without artillery? The colonists did not always stop to ask themselves this question before they planned their defences; in consequence there were sometimes emplacements without guns, just as there were at

---

[1] Maurepas to Caylus and Ranché, July 8, 1745, A.N. Colonies B 81; Caylus and Ranché to Maurepas, Jan. 30, 1746, C⁸ A 57; Le Vassor de la Touche to Berryer, July 24, 1761, C⁸ A 63; Vaudreuil to Maurepas, April 1747, C⁹ A 71; see the correspondence between Chastenoye and Vaudreuil on this subject, C⁹ A 67.

[2] Vaudreuil and Laporte-Lalanne to Machault, Dec. 1, 1755, A.N. Colonies C⁹ A 96; Remonstrance of the *Conseil Supérieur* of Port-au-Prince, July 19, 1759, C⁹ A 103; Berryer to Bart and Elias, July 28, B 109; Clugny to Berryer, Dec. 25, 1760, C⁹ A 107; Berryer to Clugny, May 31, 1761, B 111.

other times, for other reasons, guns without emplacements.[1] The islands expected the home Government to supply them at its own expense with ordnance stores, for which they petitioned extravagantly and often absurdly. The legislatures instructed their agents what to demand, very often without consulting the Governors; but even the Governors were sometimes at fault. Robinson of Barbados asked for heavier guns than the Ordnance had ever cast. No doubt he thought, as many people in the islands did, that the light cannon of the shore batteries were insufficient to reply to the fire of men-of-war; but he only betrayed his ignorance by asking for such artillery as had never existed. Another curious piece of waste and mismanagement happened in Montserrat about the same time. The legislature asked for a supply of 'buccaneer guns', a kind of muskets with exceptionally long muzzles, which carried farther than ordinary small-arms. The reason given for this demand does not seem a very good one—namely that whatever the real merits of buccaneer guns, the poorer classes, when armed with them, believed themselves to be invincible. As it was not their own money but the Home Government's that the Montserrat legislators proposed to spend, they could afford this psychological indulgence. The Board of Ordnance does not appear to have heard of buccaneer guns, so it sent a supply of rather similar weapons called wall-pieces, though it could not imagine what they could be wanted for, as Montserrat had no fortifications, and wall-pieces were too heavy to be discharged without walls to rest upon. Of course the wall-pieces were perfectly useless when they arrived, and the people hardly knew what to do with them.[2]

The Government drew a clear distinction between what it would supply gratis and what the colonists must buy with their own money. From 1735, it refused to provide without payment anything with which the colonists were bound by their own laws to supply themselves, such as small-arms or powder. After this the islands continued to apply for the stores which they could have gratis, and made no attempt to provide themselves with those for which they had to pay. This omission did not escape the Board of Ordnance, which very properly refused in

---

[1] Robinson to Newcastle, June 25, 1743, May 10, 1744, C.O. 28/46; Thomas to Board of Trade, April 26, 1758, C.O. 152/29, CC 32.

[2] Report of the Board of Ordnance, Feb. 25, 1745/6, *A.P.C. Col.* iii. 808; Montserrat Council Minutes, July 21, 1739, June 5, 1740, C.O. 177/3.

1740 to issue the one unless the colonists would buy the other. For example, it was utter waste to send out artillery to people who took no trouble to have any powder with which to fire it, so the Board began to insist that the powder duties should be put on a proper basis and really collected in kind, without which condition it would not send out the guns.[1] The legislatures and their agents thought this very hard, but of course it was the most reasonable precaution in the world.

The Board of Ordnance tried in vain to ensure that proper care should be taken of the stores after they were received. No power in the world could have procured that in the West Indies at that time. Many of the guns which had been so strenuously applied for, turned out to be unmounted at an emergency; they were lent to privateers, or embezzled, or allowed to decay.[2] The quality of the military stores shipped out to the colonies on public or private account was probably very low. Governor Haldane can hardly have been right when he said that most of the guns in the fortifications of Jamaica had been cast in the reign of Queen Elizabeth;[3] but very likely the Ordnance took the opportunity to send out to the colonies the oldest and worst of everything it had. The small-arms which the islands bought for themselves were no better. At Guadeloupe, not long before the siege, the commandant bought some muskets for the militia from Dutch merchants of St. Eustatius; but three-quarters of them burst at the first review. They had not been made to be fired, but only to be bartered in the African slave trade.[4]

There were three kinds of fortifications: batteries along the coasts, regular forts commanding the principal towns, and

---

[1] *A.P.C. Col.* iii. 557–60, 650; Nevis Assembly Minutes, March 26, 1741, C.O. 186/3; Montserrat Assembly Minutes, March 2, 1744/5, C.O. 177/4.

[2] Vaudreuil and Laporte-Lalanne to Machault, June 10, 1755, A.N. Colonies C⁹ A 96; Laporte-Lalanne to Machault, April 16, C⁹ A 97.

[3] Haldane to Board of Trade, July 20, 1759, C.O. 137/30.

[4] Nadau du Treil to Massiac, Dec. 25, 1758, A.N. Colonies C⁷ A 17. There was a curious dispute over the small-arms ordered by the legislature of Barbados in 1743. The business was done by Messrs. Lascelles and Maxwell; they had every qualification for it because one of their partners was a relation of the Surveyor-General of the Ordnance, who helped them to get the best of everything. One Wilson, a gunsmith in the Minories, heard of the order and bought up a number of old barrels in the hope that Lascelles and Maxwell would be obliged to deal with him. When they did not, he revenged himself by sending out a new musket to Barbados and pretending that he could have furnished arms of that quality for less than they had charged (Lascelles and Maxwell to Thomas Applewhaite, March 12, 1743/4, W. & G. ii).

places of refuge in the mountains. The first were beginning to be thought almost useless. They had been strong enough so long as the islands were unlikely to be attacked by more than a few ships; but they became powerless when the nations began to wage war in the West Indies on the same scale as in Europe. The conquests of Guadeloupe and Martinique proved this. Le Vassor de la Touche was blamed for letting the English land on Martinique in 1762; but how could he have prevented it when the batteries were so quickly silenced?[1] However, they still served small purposes well. They kept off small incursions of privateers, and prevented the enemy's cruisers from cutting merchant vessels out of roads. Sometimes the planters repulsed such attempts by musketry, but they disliked that kind of fighting, and threatened to give up trying to defend the shipping unless they were encouraged by the establishment of batteries.[2]

Nearly every island had some considerable fortress which it regarded as its main strength. Jamaica had Port Royal, which guarded Kingston Harbour and the open plains of St. Catherines. St. Kitts had the famous Brimstone Hill, which stood a great siege for several weeks in 1782. There was Monk's Hill at Antigua; Nevis and Montserrat had places of refuge up in the mountains, which they generally called 'Dosd'ânes' or 'Deodands'. Barbados had no such central stronghold, though Carlisle Bay was defended by several forts. Martinique had Fort Royal, besides entrenchments and refuges in the *mornes* or heights which commanded it. Guadeloupe had a fort at Basseterre and a refuge in the mountains. St. Domingue had strong places at Petit-Goave, Cap François, and St. Louis.

Many of these strongholds were on the coasts, for each colony must have one place where the merchant shipping could lie safe; the convoy system would be almost useless without such security at the end of the journey. The Governors often had a great deal of difficulty to persuade the merchant captains to stay in these fortified harbours, especially in the French islands where the chief places of commerce did not grow up round the chief fortresses. There was a perpetual rivalry between Fort Royal, the military and civil capital of Martinique, and St.

[1] Mathew's 'State' of the Leeward Islands, 1734, C.O. 152/20, V 46; Mathew to Dottin, Oct. 31, 1740, in Barbados Council Minutes of Nov. 25, C.O. 31/21; Rouillé de Raucourt to Berryer, June 30, 1759, A.N. Colonies C⁸ A 62; Le Mercier de la Rivière, *Mémoire* on the siege of Martinique, vol. 64.

[2] Guyonneau to ? Caylus, Aug. 29, 1745, A.N. Colonies C⁷ A 17.

Pierre where the trade collected. The Governors sometimes ordered all the merchant ships to lie at Fort Royal for their safety. The trading interest complained of the inconvenience, and argued that however insecure the open road of St. Pierre might be, and however easily ships could be cut out of it, at least it could not be blockaded, as Fort Royal harbour could. Similar conflicts arose in St. Domingue. The merchants preferred Aux Cayes and Léogane to the fortified harbours of St. Louis and Petit-Goave, because their ships could not lie far from the barcadiers where they were to take in sugar, without consuming the time and health of their crews in long boat journeys. Therefore Larnage and Chastenoye ordered the masters in vain to repair to the strong places. When the capital was removed from Petit-Goave to Port-au-Prince, the sailors and civilians disagreed as to the kind of harbour to be fortified: Périer de Salvert thought it useless to strengthen the merchant ports, because the King's ships of war were the real security of the trade, and it was their cruising bases that must be made safe. This argument, however, was only sound if the colony was constantly defended by a sufficient force; that condition was wanting in these wars. There were no such controversies in the English islands, though Vernon lamented that the ships would go to the outports of Jamaica instead of congregating in Kingston Harbour where he could more easily have protected them.[1]

Some of these fortresses were only indifferently strong. The great, the impregnable Fort Royal was so hard to defend in 1759 that Beauharnois was preparing to blow it up in a panic when a few hundred militia on Morne Tartenson repulsed the English attack, to their own and everybody's surprise, and drove the invaders from the island.[2] Basseterre Fort on Guadeloupe was tamely surrendered, and three years later Fort Royal had the same fate. On the other hand, the redoubt in the mountains of Guadeloupe was much better held; it is not certain whether it could have been taken at all if the inhabitants had

[1] Bompar to Machault, Oct. 20, 1755, A.N. Colonies C⁸ A 61; Givry to Machault, Oct. 28, ibid.; Letter from St. Pierre, May 12, 1756, Arch. Gir. C 4318, no. 58; Larnage to Maurepas, March 11, 1744, A.N. Colonies C⁹ A 64; Maillart to Maurepas, Feb. 22, 1747, vol. 70; Instructions to Bart, Dec. 15, 1756, B 103; Périer de Salvert to Machault, June 10, 1756, A.N. Marine B⁴ 73; Vernon to Newcastle, Oct. 31, 1739, S.P. 42/85, ff. 39–40.
[2] See the satirical rhymes and songs upon Beauharnois, quoted in Adrien Dessalles's *Histoire Générale des Antilles* (1847), v. 152–8.

not chosen to capitulate. Brimstone Hill and the Dosd'ane of Montserrat had held out in 1706 and 1712.[1] Port Royal at Jamaica was never put to the test; but Vernon and Lestock were reported to say that three 74-gun ships could take it, and that the real strength of Kingston Harbour consisted in the capital ships of the squadron, which could prevent an invasion by lying broadside across the narrows. Even there, they were commanded by several batteries which might be taken from the land side.[2] Perhaps nothing proved the weakness of forts against ships better than Knowles's capture of St. Louis; he got his cannon trained upon it and silenced it by a few hours' bombardment.[3] Moore's reduction of the Guadeloupe forts pointed the same moral.

Even if the fortresses had been perfect, their value in West Indian warfare was doubtful. The most that could be expected of them was to delay the enemy for a few weeks until his troops began to fall down sick; if they could do so much, the climate would do the rest. Some of them were already far too large for the forces which were to man them. This complaint was made of Brimstone Hill. In 1756 the people of Jamaica discovered that they had built works which needed three thousand men to defend them—a much larger number than could possibly be available if the rest of the island was to be defended at all; they therefore petitioned the King for another regiment.[4] Rochemore, the engineer sent out in 1760 to put the defences of Martinique in order, discovered that the entrenchments round Fort Royal were too long. The colonists had found fault for the same reason with Governor Parke's lines round St. Johns,

[1] Beauharnois's account of the siege of Martinique, Jan. 27, 1759, A.N. Colonies C⁸ A 62; there is another account of the siege, by an anonymous enemy of Beauharnois, ibid.; Le Mercier de la Rivière to Berryer, Jan. 10, 1760, ibid.; Gagnières to Berryer, Dec. 25, 1760, ibid. (but this is only hearsay). Barrington seems to imply that he could not have taken the Dosd'ane of Guadeloupe, for he said that if Beauharnois had come to the rescue a few hours earlier, the island need not have surrendered at all (Barrington to Pitt, May 9, 1759, C.O. 110/1). But Dubourg de Clainvilliers, one of those who made the capitulation, defended it as unavoidable, though he took care not to admit that to the English commanders (see his narrative enclosed in Beauharnois's letter to Berryer, July 12, 1759, A.N. Colonies C⁸ A 62).

[2] Knight, letter of Aug. 15, 1745, Add. MSS. 22677, f. 48. Vernon once said he would engage to take Port Royal with two 60-gun ships, but that must have been rhodomontade (Beckford to Knight, Oct. 11, 1740, Add. MSS. 12431, f. 116).

[3] Heron to Machault, Dec. 30, 1755, A.N. Colonies C⁹ A 97.

[4] Thomas to Board of Trade, Nov. 12, 1755, C.O. 152/28, BB 72; Legislature of Jamaica to George II, Oct. 14, 1756, C.O. 137/29.

Antigua.[1] A fortress too large to be strongly manned was worse than no fortress at all, for instead of being defended by the colonists against the enemy, it might come to be held by the enemy against the colonists. This was generally considered to be the disadvantage of such posts as St. Louis, on the south coast of St. Domingue, where the militia were very few and scattered.[2]

Still greater were the arguments against fortifying the outlying headlands of Cape Tiburon and Cape Nicola. These posts were immensely important, for they commanded not only the traffic through the Windward Passage, but the coastwise communications between the several quarters of St. Domingue. The French warships at that colony were paralysed by their inability to pass freely and safely round these two capes. The Chamber of Commerce of La Rochelle suggested in 1744 that the Government should try to fortify them; Maurepas had indeed long considered it, but found it impossible because of their desolate and exposed situation. Few settlers lived near Cape Tiburon, and most of them relinquished their habitations on the approach of a war which would subject them to great danger. Nobody at all could live near Cape Nicola, for the land was incultivable. There was therefore no hope of strengthening such fortifications in an emergency with neighbouring militia, and even if a garrison of regular troops was installed, it could easily be cut off from all help and subsistence. In spite of these difficulties, the French Government succeeded at last in setting up a fortress at the Mole of Cape Nicola, with the help of a free port. But that was after the Seven Years War was over, though the scheme was devised in the middle of it.[3]

The difficulty of holding fortifications was not entirely overcome by placing them in populous districts surrounded by large numbers of colonists. The militia could hardly be persuaded to enter them. When Knowles made his attack on Fort Louis in 1748, the militia of the neighbouring quarters was marched up; but many of the men deserted by the way, on one excuse or

[1] Rochemore to Berryer, March 13, 1761, A.N. Colonies C⁸ A 63; *C.S.P. Col. 1708-9*, no. 443 (ii).
[2] Larnage and Maillart to Maurepas, March 12, 1741, A.N. Colonies C⁹ A 54.
[3] Maurepas to Larnage and Maillart, March 10, 1739, A.N. Colonies B 68; Larnage to Maurepas, Dec. 2, 1739, C⁹ A 50; Larnage and Maillart to Maurepas, March 12, 1740, vol. 52; Aug. 31, 1744, vol. 64; Berryer to Bart and Clugny, April 4, 1760, B 111. *V. infra*, p. 301.

another, and those that arrived refused to enter the town, let alone the fortress.[1] According to Beauharnois, the attacks on Martinique and Guadeloupe proved that it was useless to expect the militia to shut themselves up in fortresses. In the fort of Basseterre, Guadeloupe, they threw down their arms and departed. Apparently many of them had got drunk on the garrison's rum; but they excused themselves by saying that some bombs had fallen into the cistern, and made the water undrinkable. The same kind of thing happened a few weeks later at Fort Louis, on Grande Terre. The militia would not go into the fortress, for the noise of the cannon. When the powder-magazine blew up and Beaulés decided to evacuate the place, he had to beat the militiamen in order to make them approach the fort and remove what they could save of the stores.[2] Scenes even more disgraceful took place at Fort Royal on Martinique in 1762. Seeing that the place was about to be invested, the commandant sent to La Touche for help. La Touche could send none, for the whole militia had abandoned him after the defeat of January 27; so the commandant had to shut himself up with what men he had. They were so determined to leave the fort, that some of them climbed over the walls before his eyes, in spite of his orders to fire upon them.[3]

This was not mere cowardice, though the experience of a cannonade in an enclosed place was doubtless very terrible to the planters, who were unused to it and preferred a sniping guerrilla warfare to regular fighting. There was a valid reason for this passionate aversion to entering the fortresses. The property which the militiamen left at home was very valuable and very precarious. To destroy and plunder it was the work of a very short time; negroes were a most portable form of wealth, because they had legs to carry them where the conquerors bade them go. Knowing the nervousness of the French planters for their estates, the English commanders in 1759, and still more in 1762, wisely adopted a harassing, plundering form

[1] Buttet to Maurepas, March 26, 1748, A.N. Colonies C⁹ A 74; Rancé to Maurepas, April 9, 1748, vol. 73; Larnage to Maurepas, Oct. 31, 1744, vol. 64.

[2] Hurault to Beauharnois, Feb. 28, 1759, A.N. Colonies C⁸ A 62; Beaulés to Beauharnois, Feb. 21, 1759, ibid.

[3] Letter of des Ligneris, Feb. 11, 1762, C⁸ A 64. The court martial decided that des Ligneris could not have prolonged the defence of Fort Royal, but he was retired at his own request because the Marshal de Sennecterre advised Choiseul that he had acted feebly.

of warfare. It made the militia anxious to remain as near as possible to their own plantations, or even to desert the distant encampments in order to protect their families and belongings. At Guadeloupe this plan was not fully carried out until after Hopson's death, though a great deal of ravage had been done in the Basseterre quarter before that. When Barrington began to dart up and down the windward coast, destroying the plantations here and there, the desertions from the French redoubt became more and more frequent. The planter could not bear to think what might be happening to his property behind his back.[1] The commanders of 1762 had the wisdom to make feints about the coast of Martinique before they delivered their main attack. A Frenchman who described the siege thought this a stroke of genius. It gave time for the first enthusiasm of the militia to fade away, as it infallibly must after a few days' entrenching and a few nights in the open. It also obliged Le Vassor de la Touche to disperse the forces which he had carefully collected at Fort Royal. He knew very well that these descents were only diversions, and continued at first to give orders for the further concentration of the militia; but the cries of the planters forced him against his better judgement to scatter his troops again. He had to make detachments to the out-quarters in order to check the ravages of English privateers, who were pillaging the plantations with impunity. Here again, as at Guadeloupe, the desertion of the militia after the first defeat, and their insistence on a capitulation, were greatly due to their fears for their property.[2]

It was not only the enemy who might play havoc with the planters' estates while they were defending the fortresses. At the siege of Guadeloupe the privateers whom the Governor pressed into the service burnt and pillaged so freely that they were thought to have done more injury to the colony than the

[1] See Dubourg de Clainvilliers's narrative, A.N. Colonies C⁹ A 62.
[2] Le Vassor de la Touche to Berryer, Nov. 20, 1761, A.N. Colonies C⁸ A 63; 'Journal of the Siege of Martinique', ibid.; La Touche to Choiseul, May 14, 1762, vol. 64; Le Mercier de la Rivière, *mémoire* on the siege, Aug. 5, ibid. Governor Dalrymple believed whole-heartedly that this form of warfare was the least troublesome and most effective; he thought it, in fact, the only way to reduce a small population in a mountainous island like Dominica, and also recommended it to be usen in Martinique (Dalrymple to Pitt, May 5, 1761, C.O. 110/1; see also the plan for attacking Martinique attributed to him, G.D. 8/98). He may have had some influence, through his friendship with Commodore Douglas, on the plan of action pursued at Martinique.

English. Le Vassor de la Touche had to guard against such outrages at Martinique by denouncing beforehand the penalty of death against any Frenchman who should loot the planters' property or set houses on fire without orders.[1]

  The only kind of fortification to which the colonists ever retired with anything like a good grace was the inland Dosd'ane, which was meant to hold their families, their negroes, and even their stock. In fact the people of Guadeloupe prepared for the siege in 1759, some weeks before it began, by turning into money as much of their effects as they could sell, and securing what was portable in the redoubt, or in other strong places in the mountains.[2] Le Mercier de la Rivière thought that the existence of this kind of refuges had a good effect upon the planters' morale; they would be unwilling to fight if they did not know that such a place of safety existed for their families and property.[3] But it is doubtful whether the presence of their relations, slaves, and movables really tended to improve their valour or endurance in the last resort.[4]

§ iii. *The Use of Negroes in War*

  The planters were not only afraid of the damage which friends or enemies might do to their belongings; they distrusted the loyalty of their own slaves. When French St. Kitts was taken in King William's war, many of the French negroes escaped from both conquerors and conquered, and ranged the mountains for nearly a year. At Iberville's assault on Nevis, a thousand slaves defended themselves for some time against both sides.[5] Jamaica had its tribes of Maroon negroes who waged war against the colony upon almost equal terms, and were not subdued for a hundred years.

  Opinions differed how far it was right to encourage the enemy's slaves to rise against their masters in the hour of invasion. In his scheme of 1740 for attacking Jamaica, Larnage reckoned with the probability that the English would arm their slaves.

  'But', he added, 'besides that soldiers of that kind are far from formidable, their effectiveness could be destroyed by proclaiming

---

[1] Le Vassor de la Touche to Berryer, Nov. 20, 1761, A.N. Colonies C⁸ A 63.
[2] Nadau du Treil to Berryer, Dec. 25, 1758, A.N. Colonies C⁷ A 17.
[3] Le Mercier de la Rivière to Berryer, Jan. 20, 1760, C⁸ A 62.
[4] *C.S.P. Col. 1706–8*, no. 281.   [5] Ibid., nos. 270, 357 (iv).

when we landed, that any slave found in arms should suffer the penalty of death, and on the contrary those who give up themselves and their arms should receive their liberty. I do not think that the laws of war and religion would permit us to offer a similar reward to slaves who should deliver the heads of their masters. The late M. de Fayet said he should do this if a war took place, but nobody liked it.'

About the same time, Larnage was under the impression that the Spaniards of Cuba had imported a number of muskets with which they meant to arm the negroes of Jamaica against their masters.

'I do not know', he wrote to Maurepas, 'if you regard this as a very Catholic way of destroying the English; and supposing that it succeeded, and that the negroes cut off the English altogether, surely an island occupied by more than a hundred thousand negroes would be a very disagreeable neighbour, because of our own slaves, for whom it would be a safe asylum from which we should never get them back.'

When a rebellion of the Jamaica negroes was reported, he observed that 'one ought not to wish for its success even against the enemy, for fear that the example might spread'.[1]

The English commanders against Guadeloupe do not seem to have agreed upon the encouragement to be offered to deserters. Hopson would only promise to respect the status of all free negroes and mulattos who should surrender within twelve days; Moore unsuccessfully tried to add a clause offering freedom to such slaves as should desert and do some signal piece of service against the French.[2]

It was a more contested question whether negroes could safely or usefully be armed in defence of their own masters. Even the optimists who thought it would be prudent in particular cases, hardly recommended it as a general principle. While each nation might think it could rely on its own slaves, it was not at all afraid that the enemy would derive any benefit from arming his. Larnage thought little was to be feared from the armed slaves of Jamaica. Knight returned the compliment.

'It is true', he said of the planters of St. Domingue, 'that they can arm some negroes, but these have very little affection to their

[1] Larnage to Maurepas, Aug. 24, 1740, A.N. Colonies C⁹ A 52; *mémoire* on attacking Jamaica, Oct. 17, 1740, vol. 53; Jan. 10, 1745, vol. 66.
[2] Proclamation of Hopson and Moore, Feb. 14, 1759, C.O. 110/1; draft proclamation by Moore, ibid.

masters, by reason of their severity and the hard labour they put them to, and therefore they can have no great dependance on them. The negroes in Jamaica have so terrible an idea of the French from some who were transported to Hispaniola, and sold there, and afterwards made their escape at a very great hazard of their lives upon the seas, that they think it the greatest punishment can be inflicted upon them to be transported and sold to the French.'[1]

In fact each side was reassured by the comfortable illusion that it treated its own negroes more humanely than the other.

Many colonists, however, extended this distrust to their own slaves, and with good reason. Jamaica had only just come to terms with the 'Maroons' of the north side before the war with Spain broke out, and had to suppress a dangerous revolt in the middle of the Seven Years War. Antigua had demanded a regular garrison in 1738, as a precaution against negro insurrections. The legislature of St. Kitts suspected a great plot among the slaves to desert in a body to the enemy in 1747, and professed a few years later to be afraid that unless the fortifications were garrisoned by regular troops, the negroes might rise and seize them. In view of this, it is not surprising that some colonists were not very willing to trust to their help in occasions of emergency.

When the legislature of Jamaica voted to raise 500 negroes for one of Vernon's expeditions, William Beckford thought it necessary to apologize for this decision to his correspondent Knight, who seems to have disapproved of the policy altogether. Only a third of these, Beckford hoped, would be 'shot negroes', the rest were merely to be 'pioneers' or general drudges of the camp; but he was afraid they might all be instructed in the use of arms before the expedition was over. A few months later he wrote again, acknowledging the folly of giving the negroes such an education, but still justifying the measure as a public proof of the excessive lengths to which the patriotism of Jamaica could go.[2] The slaves whom the islands raised for the expeditions against Guadeloupe, Martinique, and Havana were apparently meant for 'pioneers' only. The same kind of work was expected of slaves in cases of invasion. Governor Nadau, for instance, ordered each company of militia to furnish so many able negroes for distributing stores and the

---

[1] Knight to Newcastle, Oct. 21, 1740, Add. MSS. 32695, f. 309.
[2] Beckford to Knight, Aug. 19, 1741, Feb. 10, 1741/2, Add. MSS. 12431.

like; those of the religious houses were to be employed in such
non-combatant services as that of the hospitals. The English
colonies also appointed negroes to be furnished at alarms, and
to be equipped with bills, presumably for cutting away brush-
wood; they ordered others down to the rendezvous with carts,
for moving stores, victuals, and public records.

Even if the negroes were trustworthy, were they of any real
use as soldiers? Le Mercier de la Rivière thought them value-
lesss. He said they were so lazy and cowardly, that although
the promise of freedom if they behaved well inspired a few,
most of them were unwilling to bear arms, or only did so out
of vanity or the hope of escaping regular plantation work. To
make things worse, the *noblesse*, copied by some other planters,
assumed the privilege of refusing to let their slaves serve except
under their own eyes, with the result that the negroes were only
'a great number of superfluous domestics, victualled at the
expense of the King'.[1] Complaints were also made against the
insolence which the negroes showed when they found themselves indispensable. Nadau lamented that he should have to
arm some at Guadeloupe. 'Perceiving most of their masters in
great fear and poverty, and their own services in great demand,
they have assumed an impertinent and insubordinate air for
which we have to punish them.' When Bart ordered the planters
of St. Domingue to arm 5 per cent. of their slaves, the *Conseil
Supérieur* of Port-au-Prince protested: the armed negroes were
not only uppish, but sometimes refused to work with the other
slaves. The *Conseil* advised the Governor to follow the example
of Vaudreuil, who would not let anybody give arms to negroes,
or of Larnage, who had privately invited the planters to arm the
slaves of whom they were sure.[2]

In spite of all these dangers and inconveniences, the colonists
often armed their slaves for their defence. There were some
Governors who insisted upon it. Mathew and Thomas, of the
Leeward Islands, were never tired of recommending the legislatures of their government to pass laws for this purpose; some
of them disliked it, but generally had recourse to it when the
danger was great. St. Kitts, for example, which had for some

---

[1] *Mémoire* on the siege of Martinique, already quoted.
[2] Nadau du Treil to Berryer, Dec. 25, 1758, A.N. Colonies C⁷ A 17; Remonstrance of the *Conseil Supérieur* of Port-au-Prince, July 19, 1759, C⁹ A 103; Berryer
to Bart and Élias, June 23, B 109.

years paid no attention to Mathew's advice, suddenly complied with it in 1744. There was another great alarm there in 1757, in which Lieutenant-Governor Payne advised increasing the man-power of the colony with armed negroes.

'The negroes stood by their masters at Nevis in Queen Anne's war while our flag was flying, they are most of them (we see) good marks-men, they don't love the French, and tho' not brave in a close engagement they will be bold when out of danger, and in case of extremity we may arm three or four thousand of them who while their bodies are covered will do great execution. Your Honour knows whether there are arms for such a number but there are few planters that have not from five to fifteen spare arms.'[1]

The planters of St. Domingue, according to Larnage, would be glad of a further supply of arms to put into the hands of the negroes whom they could trust. At Guadeloupe precautions were taken against their infidelity, by embodying them in the same companies as the white militia and refusing to let them form separate units of their own.[2]

The free negroes and mulattos were thought to be far more reliable, and were almost universally included in the militia. They formed a sixth of that of St. Domingue. Both Larnage and Bory esteemed them the most valuable part of it, but Le Mercier de la Rivière thought those of Martinique useless, unless they had seen service with privateers.[3] Manumission seems to have been rarer in the English islands and the free coloured popula-tion smaller, but there were some coloured men in the militia. Governor Lyttelton was instructed to raise some free negroes in Jamaica for the expedition against Havana in 1762; but he had very little success. His enemies said he had not applied to the people who had influence with the free men of colour; but he ascribed his failure to their unwillingness to leave their com-fortable livelihood and their families in Jamaica, and above all to their fear that if they were taken prisoners they would be sold as slaves instead of being exchanged. Lyttelton tried to

---

[1] St. Kitts Council Minutes, Feb. 25, 1757, C.O. 241/7; Council of War, June 16, 1757, ibid.

[2] Guadeloupe, note of measures to be taken in case of an invasion, A.N. Colonies C⁷ A 17.

[3] Larnage to Maurepas, Dec. 28, 1739, A.N. Colonies C⁹ A 50; Le Mercier de la Rivière's *mémoire* on the siege of Martinique, C⁸ A 64. Bory thought the coloured men were the only ones on the island who could be relied upon to do militia duty (*v. supra*, p. 236).

eassure them, promising in a circular letter to the colonels of
militia that the Commander-in-Chief should insist on the
exchange of the free negroes along with the other prisoners of
war, and should detain a certain number of the enemy captives
until it was done. But this would not have sufficed, for the
Spanish authorities, who were past masters of evasion, would
certainly have declared with the deepest regret that the prisoners
had been sold and dispersed, and could by no means be traced.[1]

It is very much to the credit of the French capitulants and
the English commanders at Guadeloupe that the former should
have stipulated, and the latter consented, that the free negroes
and mulattos should be treated as prisoners of war, instead of
being reduced to slavery. There was a great temptation to
profit by the enslavement of such free negroes found in arms;
the conquerors of Guadeloupe did not yield to it, but those of
Martinique did so.[2]

§ iv. *The Regular Army in the West Indies*

Fortifications and the enlistment of negroes were not enough
to make the colonists think themselves safe. There was no other
measure they could take for themselves, except an artificial
increase of the white population which would have been incompatible with the social system. They had therefore to look to
the home Government for help.

They demanded both military and naval force. For some
time, regular troops had been stationed in the principal West
India islands, at any rate in time of war. Barbados, which had
been protected by a regiment in King William's War, does not
seem to have recovered this privilege during the next three—
perhaps because its less exposed position and greater white
population rendered such a force unnecessary. Jamaica and the
Leeward Islands had a regiment each in Queen Anne's reign;
they were withdrawn for a short time after the Peace of Utrecht,
but had been restored before the outbreak of war in 1739.

It sounds a very simple matter to station a regiment in a
colony; but in fact there was a number of difficulties. The
English Government had already laid it down as a principle
that the islands had no right to the protection of a regular mili-

---

[1] Lyttelton to Egremont, May 12, 1762, Jan. 11, 1763, C.O. 137/61; letter to
colonels of militia, May 5, 1762, ibid.; Capitulation of Guadeloupe, Adm. 1/307.
[2] Compare the terms granted to Guadeloupe and Martinique, Adm. 1/307.

tary force unless they would pay something for it. The cost of living was much greater in the West Indies than in England, and the Government thought it only fair that the colonists should make up the difference, without which the soldiers could not live on their pay; the more so because the high price of provisions was chiefly due to the planters' preoccupation with the more lucrative cultivation of sugar. The islands tried to avoid this obligation. Governor Handasyd had to complain in Queen Anne's reign of the 'penurious' way in which the Jamaica Assembly treated the soldiers. It allowed them no barracks or quarters, so that many of them had no roof over their heads; or else it would only pass the quartering act with unacceptable provisions tacked to it. On one occasion it declared that it would pay an allowance to the soldiers but not to the officers, as it did not want the latter; this was presumably a stroke at Handasyd, who was the colonel.[1] The Cabinet discussed in 1739 a demand of Trelawny for a reinforcement against a foreign invasion, and decided to ask first what Jamaica would do for the troops, since the regiment sent there some time ago had received no support from the legislature. Then or very soon afterwards, the island undertook to pay the soldiers a regular 'additional subsistence' on quite a handsome scale; but the appropriations for this purpose were annual and the Assembly soon tired of the burden, though it hesitated at first to carry out the threat of throwing it off. A little later, in its quarrel with Governor Knowles, it could not resist the temptation to put pressure upon him by holding up this supply.[2] The politicians of Antigua had expressed their dislike of Governors Parke and Douglas in the same way, during Queen Anne's reign; and the peculiar nature of the Leeward Islands Government caused further troubles, on which it is worth while to dwell for a moment, as they exhibit a perfect miniature of corporate selfishness.

Antigua had applied for a regiment in 1738, and offered to build barracks, with a contribution from the King, and to furnish an additional subsistence, on condition that there should never be less than 400 effectives on the island. When Dalzell's

---

[1] *C.S.P. Col. 1702–3*, no. 885; *1704–5*, nos. 557, 603 (i), 754.
[2] Cabinet Minute, Nov. 5, 1739, Add. MSS. 33004, f. 21; *Journals of the Assembly of Jamaica*, iii. 585, 669; Board of Trade to George II, Oct. 15, 1754, C.O. 138/20, pp. 61–2.

regiment went out upon these terms, its establishment was raised to 700, so Governor Mathew was able to spare some companies to St. Kitts, Nevis, and Montserrat. But the West Indies were the grave of English soldiers, and the planters would not have the regiments recruited among their own servants, so the numbers began to fall.[1] The people of Antigua were determined to have their 400 men, to secure them against another insurrection of their negroes, or else they would not pay for any. They considered that the Government had broken its bargain with them by preparing to send the regiment on Cathcart's expedition (but this was countermanded at the last moment) and then by actually putting it on board Knowles's ships for the attack on La Guayra. They were also angry with Mathew for dispersing part of the force among the other islands under his government. They therefore seem to have discontinued the additional subsistence.[2]

This reached the ears of Dalzell, who was of course in England (for the colonels of these regiments stationed in the colonies did not often condescend to share the exile of their men). He too was very angry with Mathew for taking a step which had caused his soldiers to lose a part of their pay; he demanded that Mathew should concentrate the troops again in order to entitle them to the additional subsistence.[3] Mathew was forced to make up the 400 men at Antigua by withdrawing the companies from Montserrat. The legislature of that island had done nothing for them—would not pay additional subsistence or even build barracks or guard-houses or hospitals, for want of which many lives had been lost. The politicians of Antigua were mollified by the return of these men, but not for very long. They soon demanded another sacrifice, and Mathew was very ready to give it, as the legislature of St. Kitts had annoyed him by refusing to follow his advice upon military matters. He

---

[1] Between 1739 and 1745 1,200 recruits were raised for Dalzell's regiment, of whom 960 were sent out; yet at the end of the period there were at most 492 effectives. If about 400 of the 960 can be accounted for by the raising of the establishment in 1739, that still leaves more than as many again who can only have died or disappeared in the West Indies, where in these years they only saw one short piece of active service, the expedition against La Guayra (Report of June 12, 1745, C.O. 152/44).

[2] A.P.C. Col. iii. 553–7; Antigua Council Minutes, Dec. 6, 1743, C.O. 9/15; Montserrat Council Minutes, Sept. 1, 1742, C.O. 177/3.

[3] Antigua Council Minutes, Nov. 24, 1743, C.O. 9/15; St. Kitts Council Minutes, Dec. 2, 1742, C.O. 241/5.

therefore withdrew all the troops from St. Kitts too, but restored them in 1744, when the Assembly, in the absence of his personal enemy the Lieutenant-Governor, dutifully voted an additional subsistence and came into all his other measures.[1]

Meanwhile an elaborate clamour had been rising from Montserrat. Elsewhere military arguments had not even been invoked in these transactions; but the Assembly of Montserrat glibly entered into considerations of strategy. It had already pointed out that without a powerful naval force the troops in one island were useless to another, because they could not be easily or safely transferred. Even if they could have been, the Assembly would rather have the soldiers on the spot, especially in a rocky island like Montserrat where it was easier to prevent a landing with twenty men than to drive the enemy away with a hundred. As for the danger of a negro insurrection, that was as great at Montserrat as at Antigua, and an island did not forfeit all claim to protection because it was poor. In fact, soldiers were more useful in Montserrat than in Antigua; the latter was well populated and protected by the constant presence of warships at English Harbour, therefore it was in no danger of small incursions, but only of an invasion. Montserrat, on the other hand, was nearer to the French islands and more accessible because farther to leeward than Antigua; the soldiers would do twice the service, because they would protect the island not only from great assaults but from small vexations.

The fact was, that the people of Montserrat wanted the troops to do nightly guard in order to save themselves the fatigue of keeping it up. (This was a common motive. In 1745 the Assembly of St. Kitts tried to deprive the soldiers of their additional subsistence for the period of the invasion scare, during which they had been stationed on Brimstone Hill, and had not been able to do nightly duty. This, it said, was their real business, in consideration of which the additional subsistence was granted.)

In 1744 the legislators of Montserrat adroitly changed their tune. Two years before, they had used the want of a naval superiority as an argument for cantoning out the troops among the islands where they might be needed. Now that we had a large force on the station they showed that neither Antigua nor any other island could be in danger of a great invasion, for if

[1] Mathew to Newcastle, July 20, 1744, C.O. 152/44.

any island was attacked, the soldiers could be hurried into it from the others; the moral was, that a company could safely be bestowed at Montserrat.[1]

This dialectical agility did not meet with its due reward. Antigua kept the troops, making the most of the strategical advantage of concentration, and professing that if any other island should be threatened, the soldiers should go to its rescue. How far this was true might very well be doubted; if the other islands had any hope at all, it was because the legislature of Antigua did not technically command the regiment. The Board of Ordnance had not relied on the altruism of the colonies in other matters of the same sort. When it recommended the dispatch of some field-pieces to the Leeward Islands, it urged strongly that they should be allocated among the islands before they left London, instead of being left to be distributed on the spot in case of emergency, 'it being hard to imagine should any one of them be attacked whilst unprovided therewith, that those who have them in possession will part with them readily, and seasonably for the relief of their neighbours, while they are hourly in expectation of the same fate'.[2]

Montserrat soon had its revenge. Antigua asked for a contribution to the cost of maintaining the prisoners of war, and alleged various reasons of equity why Montserrat should share this burden; the legislature of Montserrat replied, with what it conceived to be pathetic dignity, that the island could not possibly afford anything for this object, so long as it was put to the expense of hiring regular guards for want of a company of soldiers. Towards the end of the war the company was restored, the additional subsistence voted, and some barracks built; but Mathew must have taken the soldiers away again, for at the beginning of the Seven Years War Montserrat began the same round of argument and complaint.[3]

Jamaica was once tempted to exploit the necessities of its regiment in the same way, in order to procure a concentration of the troops at the point where it was desired. Some

---

[1] Montserrat Assembly Minutes, Oct. 6 and 16, 1740, May 26, 1744, C.O. 177/4; July 24, 1742, C.O. 177/3; Council Minutes, Sept. 1, 1742, ibid.; St. Kitts Assembly Minutes, June 26, 1745, C.O. 241/5.

[2] A.P.C. Col. iii. 560.

[3] Montserrat Assembly Minutes, June 6 and 16, Aug. 18, Sept. 1 and 26, 1744, March 18, 1744/5, C.O. 177/5; May 3, 1755, C.O. 177/8; Antigua Council Minutes, Sept. 29, 1755, C.O. 9/21.

companies were stationed for several years at Rattan and the
Moskito Shore. The legislature disliked this, and finally in 1753
it refused to provide any longer for the subsistence of the soldiers
then at the Moskito Shore, unless they were withdrawn to
Jamaica.[1]

The obligation to supplement the soldiers' pay was the only
thing which prevented the sugar colonies from calling upon the
Government for unlimited military support. In 1746 Antigua
proposed to petition for a whole regiment to itself, and St. Kitts
decided to follow its example. At the beginning of the Seven
Years War Antigua asked again for another regiment or for a
great augmentation of the existing one. After a struggle between
the Board of Trade and the colony over the rate at which the
additional subsistence was to be paid, the paper establishment
of the regiment was increased.[2] So was that of Jamaica; but
its Assembly, still unsatisfied, demanded and obtained another
regiment in 1758. Some companies of this second regiment
were left upon the coast of Africa, and the colonists insisted next
year that they should be transferred to Jamaica. The Government sent five more companies, and still Jamaica asked for
more. When the Secretary at War came to look in 1761 for
possible reductions in the American forces, the only crying
instances of superfluity he could find were at Antigua and
Jamaica, where the paper establishments and therefore the
officers had been augmented, but the privates had not increased, because of the difficulty of getting recruits to enlist for
West India services.[3]

These troops were not very actively useful. No doubt they
frightened the negroes into obedience, but there is little evidence
that they deterred the French from attacking the islands. It
was not the English soldiers that deterred Caylus and Conflans
from attempting St. Kitts in 1745.[4] These regulars served on
some of the West India expeditions, where they did not always
distinguish themselves. The companies were nearly always

[1] Jamaica Council Minutes, July 20, 1747, C.O. 140/32; Knowles to Holdernesse, Oct. 13, 1753, C.O. 137/60.
[2] *A.P.C. Col.* iv. 264–70; Antigua Council Minutes, Sept. 29, 1755, C.O. 9/21;
Board of Trade Report, Nov. 18, 1756, C.O. 153/18, pp. 84–91; *Journal of the Lords
Commissioners of Trade and Plantations, 1754–8*, p. 270.
[3] *A.P.C. Col.* iv. 367–70; Legislature of Jamaica to George II, Dec. 17, 1760,
C.O. 137/32, BB 19; Barrington to Newcastle, Oct. 2, 1760, Add. MSS. 32912,
ff. 287–8.
[4] Caylus to Maurepas, June 4, 1745, A.N. Colonies C⁸ A 56.

much under their full strength, because the poor fellows died faster than they were recruited. In Queen Anne's reign there had been great complaints of the equipment, clothing, and pay of the colonial soldiers, and of the absenteeism of the officers. They were repeated in a milder form once or twice during the next two wars, but were declared to be groundless.

The regular soldiers in the French colonies do not seem to have been worth much. Larnage complained that the recruits were mere children, and Buttet, who was indeed trying to exculpate himself for the scandalous surrender of St. Louis, said that they cried when ordered to remain under fire. Similar complaints were made at Martinique; and Longueville, commandant at St. Lucia, thought the officers lacked experience, since they came out to the colonies as young men and remained there all their lives without seeing any regular service or gaining a real knowledge of their profession.[1] St. Domingue was supposed to have 2,000 regular soldiers, French and Swiss, but the companies were reduced very low by fever and were seldom replenished.[2] The officers and men seem to have found it as difficult as the English to live on their pay, and had some strange ways of making ends meet. Vaudreuil wished there might be some workmen among the recruits whom Machault was to send out in 1756, because otherwise they would be

'useless to the colony and almost useless to His Majesty's service because most of them will starve to death in it. Workmen by their labour spread prosperity over the troop in which they are obliged to serve, and at the same time as they help their comrades to live, they prepare themselves to become useful colonists.'

This must surely mean that the soldiers were hired out as servants to the planters. The officers maintained themselves in a way which did equally little honour to their service. The Governor and Intendant urged Moras to increase their pay in 1757 because they could not live on it and no longer had the same supplementary resources as in peace. Then they could marry heiresses to plantations, or sponge upon the well-to-do

---

[1] Buttet to Maurepas, March 26, 1748, A.N. Colonies C⁹ A 74; Longueville to Berryer, Aug. 5, 1759, C⁸ A 62; Bory to Choiseul, June 13, 1762, C⁹ A 111.
[2] Instructions to Bart, Dec. 15, 1756, A.N. Colonies B 103; Moras to Bart and Laporte-Lalanne, July 1, 1757, B 105; Bart and Laporte-Lalanne to Moras, Sept. 20, 1757, C⁹ A 100; Jan. 5, 1758, vol. 101; to Massiac, Nov. 1, 1758, ibid.; Bart to Choiseul, March 13, 1762, vol. 111.

planters, but in war-time that was impossible unless they had relations in the colony.[1]

With all their fortresses, armed negroes, and regular troops, the sugar colonies still could not be considered safe. Their prime necessity was an adequate naval protection.

Governor Bart of St. Domingue illustrated the difficulties of defensive strategy in the West Indies very well when he wrote:

'We ought to rely on maintaining ourselves in sufficient force at the chief posts, so that the enemy cannot permanently establish himself there even if he obliges us to abandon them; by those means we ought always to be in a position to present ourselves on occasion in order to profit by the first reinforcement that arrives. In this condition he cannot reduce us, no matter what advantages he may have over us; in the nature of the ground and the help which our Spanish neighbours offer us, we have the means of keeping our hold on the country by harassing the enemy. But to preserve the country in this way is really to lose it, for nothing would really be preserved besides the King's troops and a show of possession; the enemy being master of the sea and the ports would really be master of the country. We can only recover it from him by a squadron capable of driving his ships away. . . . To insist on defending certain places in preference to others is to show the enemy where to make his attack, and to risk everything if he makes it in superior force, as he can. A wise retreat will protect the interior, but the trade and agriculture of the colony, which are its essence, will not be protected, and nothing but a fleet can really deliver them.'[2]

[1] Vaudreuil to Machault, May 30, 1756, A.N. Colonies C⁹ A 99; Bart and Laporte-Lalanne to Moras, Sept. 25, 1757, vol. 100.

[2] Bart to Choiseul, March 13, 1762, A.N. Colonies C⁹ A 111.

VII

NAVAL STRATEGY IN THE FRENCH WARS

§ i. *The English and French Systems of Colonial Defence*

IN these wars of the middle eighteenth century the English Government devoted more of its naval strength to the West Indies than it had ever consistently done before. It had kept a striking force at Jamaica during Queen Anne's reign in the hope of intercepting the galleons, or even of starting a movement in favour of the Archduke Charles among the Spanish colonists. From that time the Jamaica squadron had been a permanent institution. Elsewhere, however, the system of colonial defence had been primitive: a warship or two were attached to each colony for the protection of its coasts and trade. The men-of-war would convoy out the merchant vessels, remain for a time on guard, and convoy the merchants home again. Sometimes all these operations took place in a single year; but when nearly every important colony came to have more than one guardship allowed to it, the captains were able to relieve each other in rotation and stay for two or three seasons each. This system lasted until the establishment of the Leeward Islands station in 1743 and the North America station in 1745.

The size of the English squadrons in the West Indies varied so much from time to time that any given number must be arbitrary. The agents of the islands, seconded by influential merchants and absentee planters, were always on the alert to demand more ships of war, and to prevent the Admiralty from allowing the enemy even a momentary superiority in West Indian waters. Jamaica had asked for ten or twelve ships in the reign of Queen Anne, but had seldom obtained them. The island was so placed, some distance within the ring of the Greater Antilles, that it was an excellent base for a campaign against any of the Spanish dominions on the Caribbean sea, given a superior force to execute it. Without such a force the trade of Jamaica with England might be throttled, and perhaps the island itself invaded unexpectedly.[1] The few months in 1740, during which Torres was stronger than Vernon, made the agents very anxious, especially as they made it their business to

---

[1] Knight to Bedford, Aug. 5, 1745, Add. MSS. 22677, f. 58.

foresee the worst that might happen, and therefore suspected that Fleury meant to send out his squadrons to the West Indies.[1] Even they could hardly be dissatisfied with the enormous fleet which Ogle finally took out for Vernon's reinforcement. For the rest of the war, after Vernon returned home, the Jamaica squadron commonly had ten to fourteen men-of-war of various sizes, including five to seven line-of-battle ships.

That of the Leeward Islands varied much more. Here, too, the agents often applied for an increase between 1740 and 1744; but as long as the Government fixed its eyes on the Jamaica station and the glorious conquests to be achieved there, it attended little to the other West Indies. After all, they were in no danger from the Spaniards. The Lords of the Admiralty pointed out that if they had to comply with the wishes of Barbados and the Leeward Islands, they must leave more important services unprovided for. Newcastle made the same answer to critics in Parliament. We could not keep squadrons everywhere—indeed the English trade in the Channel suffered far more than Barbados by the concentration at Jamaica.[2] The agents, however, returned to the charge. They were afraid that France would suddenly declare war and attack our sugar colonies by surprise. The Admiralty and the Ministers always replied that they would be careful to anticipate such a movement by sending a proper force at the first sign of it. The agents thought at least twelve ships, of which six or eight of the line, would be needed in a French war; but in fact the squadron was very seldom so large. In January 1744/5 Knowles was supposed to have five of the line, five frigates, and three sloops; but this force was much weakened by accidents and removals just when Caylus took out six ships to Martinique.

Even the West India interest had never set up so loud a shriek of terror as it did upon this alarm. First the Admiralty tried to pacify the agents by promising that two large ships should be sent at once under Commodore Lee. The West Indians were not content; and as they knew where to clamour to the best purpose they took their request to Newcastle. He as good as ordered the Admiralty to reconsider its decision. The Board was at its wits' end. Not another ship could be spared

---

[1] 'Extract from the paper of observations', transmitted by William Wood to Newcastle, Sept. 12, 1739, Add. MSS. 32692, f. 290; v. supra, pp. 165–70.

[2] Admiralty Minutes, Oct. 31, 1740, Adm. 3/44; v. supra, p. 168, note 4.

from England, for the Young Pretender's invasion was at hand. The Admiralty could only offer to recall some of the foulest ships from the Mediterranean, refit them, and send them out to the West Indies. The Mediterranean was not a favourite service with that Board; perhaps Bedford, the First Lord, was already coming to prefer the American to the European war; so this concession to the West India interest was not a great sacrifice. Still the agents were not satisfied. Back they came to represent that if the ships were to come home from Cadiz, to refit and go out to the West Indies, Caylus would have had time to destroy all the English islands before they could arrive; so Vice-Admiral Isaac Townsend was forced to hustle out to the Leeward Islands, in the hurricane season, a force consisting largely of foul ships from the Mediterranean. Meanwhile the islanders had been in consternation. Even Knowles was apprehensive. He had eight ships, but only three of the line; he sent two to Barbados with instructions to come away if the island was attacked and rejoin him at Antigua, where he had moored four others across the mouths of English Harbour and Falmouth Harbour.[1]

Fortunately, though Caylus and Conflans had really been instructed to attempt some of the English islands, Conflans changed his mind and started difficulties, as the French commanders too often did.[2] He went home, and Townsend found upon his arrival that the command of the sea had passed by default to himself. He soon received orders to take off some of the ships to Louisbourg, and left Lee with no more than had been on the station before he brought out the reinforcement. The legislature of Antigua implored him not to go, or at least to leave several ships of the line behind, but he replied that he had only come out to counteract the French naval superiority; now that it no longer existed, there was no reason for his further stay, and if another French squadron should be sent out the Admiralty would take measures to deal with it.[3]

The next great alarm was in 1756. The squadrons on both

---

[1] Admiralty Minutes, Feb. 7 and 12, 1744/5, May 30, June 4 and 6, July 29, 1745, Adm. 3/49 to 51; Orders to Townsend, June 18, 1745, Adm. 2/64, p. 285; Knowles to Corbett, March 24, 1744/5, April 16, 1745, Adm. 1/2007.

[2] Caylus to Maurepas, June 4, 1745, A.N. Colonies C⁸ A 56.

[3] Legislature of Antigua to Townsend, Jan. 13, 1745/6, Adm. 1/305; Townsend's reply, Jan. 13, ibid.; Mathew to Townsend, Jan. 28, 1745/6; Townsend's reply, Jan. 28, ibid.

stations had been very much reduced during the peace, so that
Frankland, at the Leeward Islands, only had two of the line and
two frigates. One of the former was taken by a small French
squadron coming out to Martinique, and had it not been for the
lucky arrival of the *Bristol*, which he detained though she was
bound for Jamaica, Frankland must have shut himself up in
port as Knowles had done. Once more the West India interest
raised a cry of danger. Once more reinforcements were hurried
out, and the strength of that squadron was never allowed to fall
so low again.[1] At Jamaica in the same year the arrival of
Périer de Salvert with four of the line and two frigates caused
an alarm of the same kind. George Townshend, who commanded on the station, called in his capital ships and left only
his frigates cruising for intelligence. This was commonly done
at Jamaica when a superior French force appeared or was
expected at St. Domingue. Townshend repeated it during the
stay of Beauffremont in 1757, Cotes did it in 1759, and Forrest
in 1762. In moments of extreme danger the large ships were
even moored across the narrows of Kingston Harbour. The
panic was only increased by this measure, which Townshend
took quite unnecessarily in November 1756 and again with a
little more reason in the following spring. However, Jamaica
was never even threatened until the last year of the war, and
the squadron was sufficient for all the ordinary purposes of
attacking and protecting trade.[2] The Admiralty decided in
May 1757 to keep eight of the line and eleven smaller vessels
regularly stationed at Jamaica, eight of the line and eight
smaller at the Leeward Islands; but it could not always fulfil
this resolution.[3]

The existence of regular English squadrons in the West
Indies, and the lack of them on the French side, affected the
character of the war in those seas. The English and French
systems were produced by different conditions; each of them
had its advantages and disadvantages.

[1] Frankland to Cleveland, March 24, April 9, June 11, 1756, Adm. 1/306;
Thomas to Frankland, April 5, 1756, ibid.; Admiralty Minutes, May 27, 1756,
Adm. 3/64.
    [2] Townshend to Cleveland, May 23, June 28, July 24, Nov. 17, 1756, March 24,
1757, Adm. 1/234; Moore to Board of Trade, Nov. 26, 1756, C.O. 137/29; April
27, May 21, 1757, C.O. 137/30, Z 3, 5; Admiralty Minutes, May 20, 1757, Adm.
3/65.
    [3] Admiralty Minutes, May 18, 1757, Adm. 3/65.

When the French Government wished to have a striking force, or even a body of ships sufficient to protect the trade of its colonies, it sent them out specially for that purpose from France. Particular emergencies might cause the dispatch of such squadrons at any season of the year, but the time most commonly appointed for their departure was the late autumn or early winter, in order to avoid the hurricane months in the West Indies, which were generally held to last from the end of July to about the middle of October. The ships would be gratuitously exposed to danger if they arrived before that season was out—as Torres's squadron knew to its cost in 1740. Moreover, it might be just possible to make the ships do double duty by sending them out at the right time. After service in Europe during the summer months they could go to the tropics in the winter, which was the best season for operations there and the worst for doing anything at home. This plan was hard to combine. The French naval ports seem to have been slow in fitting out large squadrons—especially in periods of English blockade, when stores were interrupted and delayed in their journey along the coast to the arsenals. Unless the preparations were made well beforehand in the summer the ships which were to have started in November did not get off till the middle of January. Thus Bompar was delayed two months in 1759, and came too late to prevent the attack on Guadeloupe. The same thing happened to Blénac in 1762, and he arrived in the West Indies after Martinique had fallen. Périer and Beauffremont were likewise late in 1756 and 1757. For this sort of reason the Minister Moras was forced to send a squadron from the Mediterranean to the West Indies in 1757; but that did not answer any better, for though the Toulon squadron had no duties to detain it into the late autumn, as those of the Atlantic ports had, yet the English blockade in the Mediterranean was extremely efficient, and the French reinforcement never reached the West Indies at all.[1]

The campaign of these ships was generally limited to six or seven months by the quantity of victuals they could carry with them. Very few could take more on board without endangering their ability to manœuvre and to fight; frigates could not always

[1] Moras to Massiac, Aug. 7, 1757, A.N. Marine B² 357; see also the complaint of Laporte-Lalanne to Moras (Jan. 7, 1758, A.N. Colonies C⁹ A 101) and the good resolutions of the Ministers (Machault to Vaudreuil, June 8, 1756, B 103; Moras to Bart and Laporte-Lalanne, July 1, 1757, B 105); *v. supra*, p. 184, note 3.

carry even so much.[1] The officers of the navy often frustrated
the Minister's intentions in this matter. They had the deplorable habit of carrying out *pacotilles*—small ventures of European
goods which they generally received on commission from the
merchants of France and sold in the colony, laying out the proceeds in indigo or white sugar. The practice not only diverted
the attention of the officers from their duties and annoyed the
regular traders, whom they undersold; it also overburdened the
ships. Some of the men-of-war who went in Conflans's squadron
of 1746 to St. Domingue were said to be so heavily laden coming
out of Fort Louis that they could not use their lowest batteries
of guns. But the worst consequence was, that the full quantity
of victuals could not always be embarked because the space was
already taken up by the *pacotilles*; this happened to Bompar's
squadron in 1759, and to the warship which carried Intendant
de Clugny out to St. Domingue in 1760.[2] These malpractices
reduced still further the time which the squadrons could spend
in the colonies.

These may seem at first sight to be very trivial difficulties, but
in fact they were not so. There were ways of adding to the provisions which the ships took with them, but none reliable.
Additional supplies might be convoyed out in storeships under
the escort of the men-of-war themselves. The English squadrons were very largely victualled in this way. Another method
was to send out some ships of war *en flûte*—that is to say, with
their lowest tiers of guns unworkable because the hold was
stuffed with provisions. These were safer than the storeships,
but the French navy could little afford the sacrifice of fighting
power, for it was already weaker than the English.[3] Sometimes

---

[1] Larnage to Maurepas, Oct. 28, 1744, A.N. Colonies C⁹ A 64.

[2] Maillart to Maurepas, April 25, 1747, C⁹ A 71; Louis XV to Bompar, Dec. 20,
1758, A.N. Marine B² 359; Bompar's *Mémoire justificatif*, B⁴ 91; Clugny to Berryer,
May 12, 1760, B⁴ 98.

[3] The Ministers of Marine sometimes countenanced a practice equally fatal to
the fighting qualities of the ships, that of loading on freight the most valuable and
portable kinds of West India produce. No doubt this produced a certain revenue
to the King, when he could prevent the officers from pocketing it for themselves.
Those of Kersaint's squadron did so in 1757; their contracts had to be cancelled
by a royal edict (Arch. Gir. C 4256, ff. 59, 61, Minutes of Feb. 9, April 6, 1758.
See also the chapter in Garnault's *Le Commerce rochelais au xviii⁺ siècle*, iv. 192–216).
It was also a convenience to the planters and officials who obtained in this way a
safe conveyance for remittances, for though the King's ships charged a higher
freight than the merchants the insurance was much lower. Yet this was too often
monopolized by a few favourites, or by the Governors, Intendants, and Commo-

the unused guns could be carried out in the hold and mounted when the victuals were disembarked. The *Vaillant* and *Amétiste* went out in this condition with Bompar, but the men could not be found for completing their armament at Martinique.[1]

Even if these methods were used, and the necessary provisions were brought out to the West Indies, they would not keep wholesome in the tropics for very long. Caumont, for example, who executed one of Machault's combined campaigns in Africa and America, had to be sent home before his victuals were out, because they rotted and made his crews fall ill.[2]

Why not find provisions in the colonies themselves? It was not so easy. The Intendants were often instructed to prolong the campaigns, if they could, by procuring supplements of victuals in the colonies. But the English blockade was so successful, and victuals so hard to be got in the French islands, that I cannot call to mind any instance of an additional supply for more than two months.[3]

These conditions obliged the French to limit their campaigns in the West Indies. There were other reasons beside. If the squadron commonly sailed from France about the New Year, the ordinary period of a campaign ran out in June or July when the hurricane season was coming on. Both the King's navy and the merchants were afraid of it, and anxious to be gone before it. Conflans, for instance, refused to attack St. Kitts in 1745

dores themselves, most of whom had plantations. Macnémara carried in his ship a great part of the produce of his own plantation, freight free, but Maurepas detected it and insisted on a proper payment (C 4254, f. 279, Minute of Feb. 16, 1747). Intendants Ranché and Maillart seem to have helped themselves in this way (see the scandalous letter of Lambert to his cousin, Nov. 15, 1758, A.N. Colonies C⁹ A 102). The Chamber of Commerce of Nantes asked Maurepas to allow the warships which conducted the convoys to bring back some indigo on freight; perhaps Nantes was peculiarly interested in indigo because of its neighbourhood to some of the most important textile manufactures of France (Arch. Gir. C 4254, f. 226, Minute of May 20, 1745). But the habit was a bad one, and gave rise to abuses; it enabled the *pacotille* trade to be carried on under a lawful colour, and supplied an excuse for the overburdening of the King's warships. Accordingly the Ministers sometimes countermanded their orders for this purpose. See M. Tramond's article in the *Revue de l'histoire des colonies françaises*, vol. xv, pp. 176–7, 517–21.

[1] Private instructions to Bompar, Nov. 15, 1758, A.N. Marine B² 359; Bompar to Berryer, May 2, 1759, B⁴ 91; Bompar's *Mémoire justificatif*, ibid.

[2] Beauharnois to Moras, ? Oct. 1757, A.N. Colonies C⁸ A 61; Beauharnois and Givry to Moras, Oct. 13, ibid.

[3] It was even more difficult to send out naval stores to the colonies. The trade from Canada to the islands could not be relied upon (Laporte-Lalanne to Machault, Aug. 11, 1756, A.N. Colonies C⁹ A 99; Moras to Laporte-Lalanne, April 28, 1757, B 105; Fleury to Massiac, Dec. 23, 1758, C⁹ A 102).

because he should have to stay into the hurricane season, which he antedated so much that his reason looks like an excuse.[1] The crews as well as the commanders disliked a long stay in the West Indies. Latouche-Tréville, whom d'Aubigny left behind in the islands in 1756, had to conceal their destiny from his men till d'Aubigny was gone. Ruis reported in 1748 that his men were dying of chagrin at the prospect of a long stay. It would be hard to say whether this was rather an effect or a cause of the system of short campaigns.[2]

The English hardly ever undertook anything so important as an invasion in the West Indies after April or May.[3] The French squadrons could therefore retire in the summer without exposing the islands to danger, so long as a new force was ready to come out at the beginning of the next season. When the French navy was reduced to great straits in the Seven Years War, Berryer had to trust to the known laws of the climate to defend Martinique during the summer, in default of the naval force which he could not spare.[4]

The French Ministers of Marine did not regularly send out a squadron every year, even for the campaigning season. During the war of 1744 Maurepas confined himself almost entirely to the protection of trade by convoys. Except the small forces which Caylus and L'Étanduère took out to the West Indies in 1745, there was nothing that deserved the name of an expedition; and in the intervals between the convoys the islands were left completely unguarded. It was not until the middle of 1747 that the Minister was induced, by the repeated complaints of Larnage, to station so much as two small cruisers to protect the trade of St. Domingue. In the Seven Years War, Machault and Moras meant to keep the colonies guarded by a constant relief of squadrons; for which purpose they lengthened the stay of the

---

[1] Caylus to Maurepas, June 4, 1745, A.N. Colonies C⁸ A 56.

[2] Ruis to Maurepas, Oct. 1, 1748, A.N. Marine B⁴ 62, f. 129; Latouche-Tréville to Machault, Jan. 16, 1757, vol. B⁴ 77.

[3] The great exception is the conquest of Havana in 1762; but the Gulf of Mexico had a climate of its own, which dictated exceptions to the ordinary rules of West Indian strategy. Havana was not out of reach of hurricanes, but the north winds ruled out the best part of the campaigning season, from December to March. Therefore enterprises could not be undertaken there until near the beginning of the hurricane season. Besides, war was only declared against Spain in January, and the expedition could not have been got ready any faster. The invasion of Dominica in June 1761 is a much smaller exception, but this was a bagatelle, as Hardwicke said, and it needed no new force of ships from Europe.

[4] Berryer's *Mémoires* of March 3 and 6, 1760, A.N. Colonies C⁸ B 10.

ships in the islands—La Clue was to have remained at St. Domingue for as much as twelve months in 1757–8. But their system was soon disorganized; the intervals between the squadrons became longer, and the English force at Jamaica became so strong that even Kersaint was not able to keep the sea against it in 1757. Kersaint's was the last regular squadron in the West Indies during the Seven Years War. After Osborne had intercepted La Clue on his way out in the spring of 1758 the French Government gave up trying to keep the colonies perpetually defended. It tried to send out La Clue again in 1759, but Boscawen caught him at Lagos. The only large squadrons which succeeded in reaching the West Indies after 1757 were those of Bompar in 1759 and Blénac in 1762; both these were sent out to deal with special emergencies, and returned to Europe after they were over.[1]

Contrast with this the English system of stationing squadrons permanently in the West Indies. The victuals and naval stores necessary for their upkeep were abundantly provided, the most part from North America. The English navy was strong enough not only to throttle the trade which might have supplied these articles to the French squadrons, but to assure its own supplies. Naval stores were often convoyed from England or from Boston by ships belonging to the stations for which they were destined. There were occasions when the activity of the English commanders was hindered by shortage; for example, Cotes was once obliged to keep some of his ships in port, because he could only get enough bread to supply his crews from hand to mouth.[2] But this was an exception. In general the King's ships were subsisted without difficulty in the West Indies for as long a period as the Admiralty chose to keep them out. They were not obliged to go home to England to refit, for they had dockyards

---

[1] Larnage to Maurepas, June 30, 1744, A.N. Colonies C⁹ A 64 (Larnage appears to recant his opinion of the possibility of stationing ships permanently in the West Indies, Oct. 28, 1744, ibid.); Maurepas to Larnage, Dec. 15, 1745, B 81; to Chastenoye and Maillart, March 20, 1747, B 85; Caylus to Maurepas, June 6, 1745, C⁸ A 56; Minutes of the Chamber of Commerce of Guienne, Sept. 2, 1756, Arch. Gir. C 4256, f. 19; Chamber to Machault, Sept. 2 and 18, 1756, C 4263, ff. 249, 252; Machault to Vaudreuil, May 20, 1756, A.N. Colonies B 103; Moras to Bart and Laporte-Lalanne, July 1, Sept. 2, and Oct. 19, 1757, B 105; Bart and Laporte-Lalanne to Moras, Sept. 20 and Dec. 2, 1757, C⁹ A 100. The Ministers paid much more attention to St. Domingue than to the Windward Islands because they wrongly thought it more likely to be attacked.

[2] Cotes to Clevland, Aug. 7, 1757, Adm. 1/235.

in the islands, where almost any repairs could be done. On the Jamaica station there was Port Royal, with a much smaller base at Port Antonio on the north side; at the Leeward Islands, the chief arsenal was English Harbour on Antigua.

The equipment of these places left, no doubt, a great deal to be desired. Frankland complained that there was no proper staff at English Harbour, and that the common artificers were ignorant new negroes; there was not enough room for the stores, and the place was a festering unhealthy hole, especially in the hurricane season, when a great number of ships put in to refit at once and yellow fever ran through the crews. There were also too frequent opportunities of desertion during these stays in port; but of what dockyard could not that be said? Yet English Harbour had two still worse defects. It was very diffi-cult to get in or out of, and too small and shallow to hold the largest ships without lightening—if, moreover, they were light-ened at St. Johns they were incapable of turning up to wind-ward to English Harbour.[1] Therefore Frankland, Moore, and Douglas all sent their biggest ships away for refitting—either to Jamaica, or to Halifax, Nova Scotia.

The ships on these stations were relieved successively. Every year one or two convoys came out to the West Indies and one or two went home. The fresh ships which brought the trade out usually stayed to attach themselves to the squadron, while those which had been out longest or were in the worst condition escorted the homeward convoys to England. Ships of war some-times came out on other occasions, especially if reinforcements were needed to deal with a prospective or actual danger. Every two or three years a new Admiral or Commodore arrived, bringing with him a greater recruit of ships than usually came at other times.

The two West Indian stations had not much communication with each other. At moments of special emergency one Com-mander-in-Chief was authorized to call upon the other for such force as he could spare; but as these orders were only discretion-ary, they very seldom resulted in the detachment of large bodies

[1] Frankland to Clevland, Oct. 8, 1755, April 28, 1757, Nov. 19, 1757, Adm. 1/306; Moore to Clevland, Nov. 13, 1758, Adm. 1/307; Douglas to Clevland, June 4, 1760, ibid.; Rodney to Clevland, July 23, 1762, ibid. The legislature of Antigua was easily excited by criticism of English Harbour because it valued the protection of the warships which frequented the place (Antigua Council Minutes, June 27, 1755, Jan. 27, 1757, C.O. 9/21; Feb. 28, Dec. 14, 1758, C.O. 9/23).

of ships, for each was apt to believe himself short-handed already, or in almost as much danger as the other. A really considerable squadron only went once in these two wars from the Leeward Islands to Jamaica: Rodney sent down Douglas in 1762 on the news that Jamaica was thought in danger of an invasion. Apart from this, the pressing appeals for help which were sometimes carried from one station to another produced very small results.[1]

The Leeward Islands station had some advantages over that of Jamaica. It lay on the accustomed route from England to Jamaica, so that ships could be detained on their way out there and impressed into the service of the Leeward Islands; both Townshend and Holmes complained strongly of such detentions which withheld from them a part of their destined force.[2] Moreover, a squadron battered in an equal or unsuccessful sea-fight in the Leeward Islands might still save itself from disaster by taking refuge at Jamaica. This was not an advantage which the commanders on the Leeward Islands station were anxious to use. They were greatly influenced by the fear of finding their ships so much disabled after an engagement that they could not get back to their base and would have to drift down to leeward. This would mean abandoning the colonies under their care to the enemy—or, if he too was forced down, to the chance of the first arrival from Europe. Thus in 1759 Bompar would not fight Moore, lest he should have to abandon the Leeward Islands to him; Moore would not seek out Bompar for the very same reason.[3]

As the Jamaica station was to leeward of the Leeward Islands[4]

[1] Townshend to Clevland, March 24, 1757, Adm. 1/234.
[2] Townshend to Clevland, June 28, 1756, Adm. 1/234; Clevland to Holmes, July 22, 1760, Adm. 2/529, p. 120.
[3] Perhaps they were both right. Bompar had more to gain and less to lose than Moore, but his was a much smaller force. Moore could probably have afforded to fight Bompar without fear of being driven disabled before the wind at the end of the battle; but he had nothing to gain by it, for as long as he lay with his whole squadron between Bompar and Guadeloupe, the conquest of the island could proceed without disturbance, or at least if Bompar tried to interrupt it Moore could come down on him before he could get away (Moore to Clevland, July 25, 1759, Adm. 1/307; Bompar's *Mémoire justificatif*, A.N. Marine B⁴ 91).
[4] The name Leeward Islands is a misleading one; they were so called because they were to leeward of Barbados, but they formed part of a group which was called, as a whole, the Windward Islands; for example, the French islands of Martinique and Guadeloupe were known as the *Isles du Vent*, or Windward Islands, to distinguish them from St. Domingue.

it could receive reinforcements much faster than it could send them. This might have made no difference; for a long time taken to send a message, added to a short time for returning with reinforcements, amounts to as much as a short time for the message and a long time for the reinforcements. However, a danger to Jamaica was likely to be known at the Leeward Islands before it happened, for the French ships were almost sure to pass through, and to be seen or heard of, on their way from Europe to St. Domingue. Therefore the rescuers could start before any message arrived; Jamaica could not in the same way anticipate a danger to the Leeward Islands. Rodney therefore considered Jamaica to be perfectly safe as long as there was a sufficient force at the Leeward Islands. He still maintained the same opinion in the War of the American Revolution, and justified his detention of some ships which had been designed for Sir Peter Parker at Jamaica. Parker wrote indignantly to the Secretary of the Admiralty, denying the truth of Rodney's proposition. He argued that Jamaica could be attacked before the Leeward Islands knew it, though he did not very clearly explain how.[1]

The West India stations had also a traditional connexion with the Northern Colonies. In North America fighting was only possible in summer, because the ice froze up many of the great ports and rivers;[2] in the West Indies the summer was the only time when it was impossible, because of the fiery breezes and the hurricane season, which was also the sickly season in many places where there were no hurricanes.[3] There was an obvious advantage in combining the two stations in order to obtain a full year's service from the ships. The Admiralty had made a rule in Queen Anne's reign, that many of the North America guardships should pass the winter in the West Indies, cruising or convoying the Salt Tortuga fleet. This arrangement

---

[1] Rodney to Clevland, Dec. 11, 1762, Adm. 1/307; Parker to Stephens, Dec. 30, 1780, Adm. 1/242.

[2] There was even a doubt whether any ice-free port could be found in which the ships of war could pass the winter. Halifax, Nova Scotia (which was not founded until after 1748), satisfied this condition; but while the ships could lie there they could do no more. They could not be campaigning; and the importance of Halifax consisted only in this, that it enabled the English navy to be about in the mouth of the St. Lawrence early in the year, and helped to establish a perpetual blockade of Canada.

[3] The Gulf of Mexico was an exception, as I have already remarked (v. supra, p. 272, note 3).

also furnished occasional convoys between the Northern Colonies and the islands.[1]

Commodore Warren suggested in 1742 an elaborate scheme for sending nearly all the ships from North America to the West Indies, to cruise upon the Spanish main in the winter season. The Lords of the Admiralty did not approve Warren's plan in all its details, but they did combine the North America and Leeward Islands stations for a couple of years: Warren commanded in the tropics during the winter, and repaired to his proper duties at the Northern Colonies in the summer, leaving Knowles behind him to take charge of the islands.[2] In the winter of 1742/3 the presence of Warren's ships at the Leeward Islands also enabled Knowles to take off some of the ships of that station for the expedition to La Guayra. This amicable arrangement of Cox and Box ended in a violent quarrel at the beginning of 1745. There were only two ships of more than fifty guns on the Leeward Islands station; one of them was lost, and Warren insisted on taking away the other to the northward for the expedition against Louisbourg. Knowles egged on some of the island legislatures to protest, and to point out that a large force might appear from France; in any case the removal of the *Superbe* would make his favourite project against St. Lucia impossible. The prophecy of a French squadron was fulfilled, and the alarm over Caylus in 1745 made the deprivation of a capital ship a serious matter. Warren was already gone, having refused to listen to any arguments. He had married a wife from New York, and knew what Louisbourg meant to the people of the Northern Colonies. The Lords of the Admiralty vindicated him entirely.[3] A few years later Knowles, then commanding at Jamaica, suggested that he could find good employment for the North America ships in the winter months. In order to prove

[1] *C.S.P. Col. 1702*, nos. 603, 650; *1702–3*, nos. 77 (i), 950, 1150, 1208 (i), 1369, 1388, 1389 (ii). These convoys protected a trade which was very important to the New England fishery, because it was one of the chief supplies of salt. The salt-fleet generally collected at Barbados about April, and one of the station ships escorted it to Salt Tortuga where the salt was raked, and thence to a certain safe latitude to the northward. The liberty of raking this salt was granted by Spain in the Treaty of Utrecht; but according to French observers it afforded an opportunity of covering unlawful trade with the Spanish dominions, and ought to be suppressed.
[2] Warren to Corbett, March 19, 1741/2, Adm. 1/2653; Orders to Warren, Aug. 1742, Adm. 2/58, p. 439.
[3] Warren to Corbett, March 10, 1744/5, Adm. 1/2654; Antigua Council Minutes, March 10, 1744/5, C.O. 9/17; Lords of the Admiralty to Lords Justices, May 27, 1745, S.P. 42/28, ff. 251–3.

his disinterestedness he made such an offer as was rare in those days: he would sacrifice his share of the prizes which those ships might take while they were under his direction.[1]

Nevertheless, the two services were becoming more and more difficult to combine. The squadrons could not be out cruising for twelve months in the year; they must be cleaned and refitted, and although those operations did not need a whole summer or winter they could not be omitted altogether. If the ships were constantly passed to and fro between one active service and another there was a danger that their repairs would be scamped. Then there was the time consumed in the journeys between the stations. Sir William Gooch, Lieutenant-Governor of Virginia, denounced the whole system of combination for these two reasons—the ships did not return by the opening of the cruising season, and they were usually out of repair.[2] These considerations became much more important in the Seven Years War, when North America became for a time the centre of the most important operations, and everything depended on having a squadron outside Louisbourg and Quebec as early in the year as could be. Pitt seems to have believed at one time that a fleet could take Martinique on its way to or from Canada; but when Newcastle suggested it in 1760 he pooh-poohed it as impossible. Although Moore conquered Guadeloupe at the beginning of 1759 and Saunders took Quebec only at the end, Moore had not dispatched his business in time to send any help to Saunders. Some ships and troops came south in the summer of 1761 for the attempt on Dominica; but this was no true instance of the dovetailing of the two services, but rather a permanent transference of force from the theatre of war where the struggle was won, to that where it was still to be fought.[3]

Some instances of this combination are to be found in French strategy. The French commanders did not like to undertake it on their own initiative. Both Caylus and L'Étanduère thought of going from their commands in the West Indies to save Louis-

[1] Knowles to Corbett, March 13, 1747/8, Adm. 1/234.
[2] Dottin to the Lords of the Admiralty, July 16, 1741, Adm. 1/3817; Gooch to same, Dec. 1, 1744, ibid. In the same way, about that time, the notables of Barbados objected to Hawke's voyages to New England in the summer months. The Lords of the Admiralty promised that such removals should not happen again (Minutes, Oct. 31, 1740, Adm. 3/44).
[3] Newcastle to Hardwicke, Oct. 11 and 18, 1760, Add. MSS. 32913, ff. 51, 186; Hardwicke to Newcastle, Oct. 19, ff. 209–10.

bourg from Warren in 1745, but neither of them went; they would indeed have arrived too late, but Maurepas would have approved their action.[1] In the next year Conflans was ordered from St. Domingue, whither he had taken out the convoy, to join d'Enville off North America.

At the beginning of the Seven Years War Machault invented an ingenious scheme of co-ordination in Africa, the West Indies, and North America. Beauffremont was to go out at the beginning of 1757 to St. Domingue, which the Minister quite wrongly believed to be in danger. If the security of that island, which was to be his first object, was not threatened before April, he was to go on to Louisbourg, having been joined by d'Aubigny from Martinique. Meanwhile Kersaint and Caumont were to have destroyed English commerce and prestige in two different parts of the West African coast; they were to join, if possible, before they crossed the Atlantic, and proceed to Martinique. Caumont was to stay there, taking the place of d'Aubigny, while Kersaint was to move on to St. Domingue and fill that of Beauffremont. Most of this scheme succeeded to perfection. D'Aubigny did not, in the end, go to Martinique; but without him Louisbourg was relieved, by Beauffremont's squadron among others. Jamaica was terrified by the prospect of an invasion, and Townshend shut himself up for some weeks, during which the French commerce was very little disturbed. Kersaint and Caumont took a number of prizes, drove the English trade down the African coast, and arrived safe at their stations in the West Indies.[2] Possibly Moras designed something of the same kind for the next year, for he ordered St. Aignan to go down from Martinique at the end of the season and join La Clue at St. Domingue, as d'Aubigny was to have joined Beauffremont. But it does not appear that La Clue was meant to go on to Louisbourg.[3]

§ ii. *The respective Advantages of the two Systems*

When the working of the English and French systems is examined, the advantage seems at first to be entirely on the side

---

[1] Larnage to Maurepas, Aug. 5, 1745, A.N. Colonies C⁹ A 66; Maurepas to Caylus, Nov. 15, 1745, B 81.
[2] Instructions to Kersaint and Caumont, Nov. 5, 1756, A.N. Marine B⁴ 73; Caumont to Moras, June 1, 1757, B⁴ 77; Kersaint to Moras, May 5, June 7, ibid.; Jan. 15, 1758, B⁴ 81; Louis XV to Beauffremont, Dec. 21, 1756, B² 353; Machault to Beauffremont, Dec. 21, 1756, ibid.   [3] *V. supra*, p. 184, note 3.

of the English. The misfortunes which pursued the French squadrons were largely to be attributed to the shortness of their stay. If their passage out was more than ordinarily long, they found, like d'Antin, that they had consumed a great part of the victuals for the campaign before they reached the West Indies. They were forced to execute their instructions at once or not at all, and could not wait on circumstances.[1] At their first arrival in the tropics the crews often fell sick, so that several squadrons—for instance, L'Étanduère's and Conflans's in 1745 —were almost paralysed. As soon as the epidemics began to subside, the victuals were running out and it was time to go home. The whole campaign, therefore, was consumed in coming and going, and in sickness, and it is no wonder that the ordinary French squadrons in the West Indies took hardly one offensive measure, even against the English trade, in the whole of these two wars.[2]

In some of these respects the English were better off. At least their crews were seasoned, though at the cost of a number of men who died in the early months of their campaigns and were not always replaced. They could afford to wait their time; therefore, when a superior French force appeared they could retire into port until it went home, and then emerge to carry on their normal business of attacking and defending trade.

It might also be expected that the permanent English squadrons could reduce the French warships to starvation by blockading them until their victuals ran out. This very nearly happened several times. Mitchell shut up Macnémara in Cap François for three or four months in 1746, just as he was on the point of sailing home. Kersaint was blockaded for such a long time in 1757 that he had to take a desperate resolution. If he stayed any longer in Cap François he would be unable to get home for want of provisions, and his crews, with those of the merchant ships which wished to accompany him, would increase the scarcity in the colony. He must leave; but he dared not take the merchants with him, because the English warships were attended by swarms of privateers, who would raid his fleet under their protection. He therefore determined to go out and

---

[1] For the effect of this circumstance on d'Antin's campaign, v. supra, pp. 174-5.

[2] Daubenton to Maurepas, Nov. 7, 1746, A.N. Marine B⁴ 59, f. 187; Du Chaffault to Maurepas, May 5, 1748, vol. 62, f. 103; Larnage to Maurepas, Oct. 28, 1744, A.N. Colonies C⁹ A 64; Aug. 5, 1745; vol. 66; Laporte-Lalanne to Machault, April 30 and June 5, 1756, vol. 99.

offer battle to the blockaders. If he fought and won he would put back and take the trade under his convoy; if the battle was declined, or ended without a victory, he must proceed to France and leave the trade to take its chance. His plan succeeded, through the irresponsible zeal of Captain Forrest, who gave battle with an inferior force, was partly disabled, and had to raise the blockade. Kersaint returned to Cap François, made a few hasty repairs, and got away before Admiral Cotes could replace Forrest.[1]

The French did not always contrive to break out of port like this. Macarty tried to do so in 1761 and lost nearly all his ships. Kerusoret tried to lure the blockaders away by a feint and leave the coast clear for the merchants to escape; but he failed. Yet in general the English were unable to keep up a permanent blockade. This was because the squadrons had too many duties for their size; they had many cruising-grounds to fill, besides occasional convoys, and could not afford to keep their main blockading forces constantly relieved. The Admiral at Jamaica would send up his great ships with six weeks' or two months' provisions to lie before Cap François, on the news that a French convoy was intended home. They would stay outside the port as long as they could, but sooner or later they must go back unrelieved, and the French, after much anxiety and scarcity, could slip out.

The English system suffered from certain other difficulties. The men might be healthier than the French, but the ships were generally in worse condition. The French ships came out fresh from the arsenals, but on the English side the equipment for keeping ships in repair was inadequate at Antigua and far from perfect at Jamaica, though better than anything in the French colonies. Consequently the French ships often outsailed the English in West Indian waters, and the latter were sometimes so crazy after two or three years' service that the Commanders-in-Chief dared not send them home in winter.[2]

[1] Larnage to Maurepas, June 13, 1746, A.N. Colonies C⁹ A 68; Kersaint to Moras, Nov. 11, 1757, A.N. Marine B⁴ 77; Jan. 15, 1758, B⁴ 81. Sir Julian Corbett (*England in the Seven Years' War*, i. 365–7), represents Forrest's behaviour as uncommonly gallant. Kersaint gives a very different impression, and makes out that Forrest turned tail; but his accounts of his actions always glisten with self-satisfaction. He does not seem to have recognized that he had destroyed Forrest's rigging even more completely than Forrest had destroyed his, so that we need not accept his explanation of the English retreat. See also Tramond, op. cit., p. 526.

[2] Maillart to Maurepas, Jan. 29, 1746, A.N. Colonies C⁹ A 69; Dubois de la

However, the English squadrons could afford better than the French to risk an engagement of doubtful issue. Shattered ships could return to the arsenals of Jamaica and Antigua, where all but the greatest repairs could be done. The French had no such conveniences. This is one of the reasons given by Beauharnois for Bompar's failure to relieve Guadeloupe in 1759; but Bompar himself did not state his difficulties in quite the same way.

The hurricanes raised another serious problem which the insufficiency of the colonial dockyards complicated. If the English squadrons were always out in the West Indies they could hardly expect to escape these visitations. In fact the Jamaica squadron was paralysed by the storm of 1744, and Frankland's little force at the Leeward Islands by that of 1756. The French were not so much exposed to this risk because they did not usually spend the summer in the West Indies.[1]

The English had ways of avoiding it, especially on the Leeward Islands station, where the great ships were ordinarily sent for the hurricane months to the southward, to the Spanish main, or at least as far as Tobago. There they were supposed to be safe. In times of war with Spain this diversion might be a very profitable one to the commanders, for it afforded a chance of rich prizes. The people of Antigua objected to it. They had been at some expense to fortify English Harbour as a refuge for the squadron in the bad season, and they expected their reward from the presence of the warships at their island, which would help to defend them against invasion.[2] They claimed that the squadron, or at least the ships of the line, ought to spend the whole hurricane season in English Harbour and take the opportunity of refitting there. They made it an article of complaint against Lee, that he had sent most of his force to the southward for his private advantage—that is to say, the Commodore's

Motte seems to have outsailed Lee and perhaps Dent too (Dubois to Maurepas, April 8 and July 8, 1747, A.N. Marine B⁴ 61, ff. 282, 292).

[1] In fact there were two or three French ships at St. Domingue in 1744, but they were not damaged; those of d'Aubigny escaped the hurricane of 1756 by a month.

[2] It was doubtful whether English Harbour was impregnable or hurricane-proof, and it had other inconveniences. Champigny thought he could take it and destroy the ships with very little help. That may have been mere talk; Maurepas spoke of it as impossible. At any rate the Antiguans, like all the islanders, valued a man-of-war in times of alarm if only for the use that could be made of its cannon and crews on shore, and the impression it made on the slaves (Champigny to Maurepas, Oct. 5, 1744, A.N. Colonies C⁸ A 56; Frankland to Clevland, July 20, 1757, Adm. 1/306; Antigua Council Minutes, Jan. 19 and 27, 1757, C.O. 9/21).

eighth share of prizes. Lee was undoubtedly impelled by this hope of gain, for he referred to it in his orders to his captains; but he was acting under instructions. This arrangement was sometimes followed when there was no Spanish war, therefore no hope of prizes; and the only Commander-in-Chief who really can be accused of cupidity is Rodney, who sent away Swanton to the main in April 1762, long before the hurricanes could possibly begin. We must not judge the English navy by Rodney, for he sacrificed strategy to prizes throughout his whole career. Nor should too much attention be paid to the interested complaints of the legislature of Antigua, which criticized every disposition which took the men-of-war away from English Harbour; just as they complained of Lee for sending his ships away from the station, they denounced Frankland for keeping his on a cruise within it so that they were unfortunately struck by the storm of 1756.[1]

These drawbacks went some way to reduce the advantage of stationed forces over squadrons sent out for short periods from Europe. In the light of strategy the merits of the two systems were perhaps more disputable still. The French navy was annually concentrated and redistributed. At the beginning of every campaign France obliged England to do some painful and hazardous guesswork as to the destination of her fleets. Everybody in authority made it his business to suspect that the whole French force, or a formidable detachment of it, was aimed at the region under his charge. Each Governor and Admiral in the West Indies thought himself the most likely to be attacked, and the Ministers at home were afraid of an invasion. So well did the French statesmen know the disturbing effect of this uncertainty, that several of those whom Berryer consulted in 1760 proposed the creation of a fair-sized squadron at Brest, not to do anything—for it was far too weak—but to keep the English guessing and oblige them to detain a large part of their force at home.[2]

England kept France guessing too, but that was more natural because she could dispose of a larger navy. The benefit of her superiority was to some extent diminished by the rigidity of the

[1] Legislature of Antigua, Petition to George II, ? Aug. 1746, Adm. 1/305; Lee's reply of Aug. 26, 1746, ibid.; Lee's justification of Nov. 17, 1747, ibid.; Lee, orders to H.M.S. *Sutherland*, July 20, 1746, ibid.; orders to Lee, March 15, 1744/5, Adm. 2/63, p. 339.

[2] *Mémoire* of Belleisle, March 26, 1760, A.N. Colonies C^8 B 10.

station system. There was always a certain number of the
English force already, to all intents and purposes, accounted
for; of the French force there was very little. It was not only
because the Duke of Newcastle had 'minced the navy of England
into cruisers and convoys'—though that was bad enough—that
the Government sometimes found it so hard to collect a striking
force in the European seas. It was partly because the station
system imposed a permanent dispersion. In the summer of 1745
the Mediterranean service had to give way to a reinforcement
of the West India stations; and that was only after the Channel
fleet had been stripped of every ship it could afford.[1]

On that occasion the Lords of the Admiralty asked the
planters and merchants whether they did not think the ships
which they demanded would be better employed in keeping
command of the Channel? They answered no, for they took
an extremely pedestrian view of strategy, as people always will
who are afraid for their property.[2] Just as the islands quarrelled
with each other for soldiers and warships, the West Indians as
a body could not think themselves or their plantations safe
unless they were defended by forces upon the spot. Other forms
of protection they could not understand. They alone were
unmoved by the invasion scares in England and Ireland; they
expected the Government to call the enemy's bluff in Europe
that it might have the pleasure of convoying their trade and
surrounding their islands with warships.[3]

Yet it ought to have been obvious that the real defence of the
West Indies was in the Channel and the Straits of Gibraltar.[4]
A Government which could not keep up a proper system of
blockade in Europe was naturally forced to send fleets scurrying
across the seas to relieve the colonies. When Caylus got out in
1745 somebody had to be sent after him; when d'Enville got
past Martin the next summer and sailed away to North
America, he too ought to have been followed, and it was only
storms and scurvy that saved Louisbourg from recapture. On
the other hand it was the better organization of the Channel

---

[1] Lords of the Admiralty to Lords Justices, June 4, 1745, S.P. 42/28, f. 355.

[2] Admiralty Minutes, May 30, 1745, Adm. 3/50.

[3] See the letter of Messrs. Lascelles and Maxwell to Nicholas Wilcox, Jan. 15,
1745/6, W. & G. ii.

[4] I say the real *defence*; the West Indies could not be conquered in the Channel
except in so far as the blockade of colonial trade in the Channel weakened the
colonies and might perhaps make them the readier to surrender.

squadron under Anson that prevented the relief of the French colonies in 1747. Fortunately for the West Indies it was chiefly to North America that the French squadrons so freely made their escape in 1755-7; the same forces might have done irreparable damage in the sugar colonies. When the blockade was once more established, most of the French squadrons which were destined for the islands were intercepted, or so delayed that they came too late to be of any use. La Clue was twice frustrated in his attempts to get out of the Mediterranean; in 1762 Blénac's departure was so long delayed by the interception of stores and victuals on their way to Brest that he sailed two months late, and d'Aubigny, who was to have joined him, never got out of Rochefort at all. Several small reinforcements had to be countermanded for want of ability to break the blockade. Others were driven into the ports of Galicia on their way to or from the colonies, and shut up there for three or four months on end. It is obvious that the command of the Channel and the Straits, and a right use of them, had a very great influence on the course of events in the West Indies.

Unfortunately the command of the Channel could never be infallible. Blockading fleets might be driven from before the enemy's ports while his men-of-war slipped out. It was partly as an insurance against this imperfection that the colonists valued the station system. But this insurance would only have been effective, if our strength at the threatened points had been great enough to resist a French striking force as soon as it arrived. That it was not; no Government could pretend to make it so. Therefore there were several occasions when, in spite of their elaborate and permanent system of naval defence, our West India islands were chiefly indebted for their safety to the timidity of French commanders, or the disinclination of the French Government for aggressive designs in that quarter of the world.

The Admiralty might try to cover up the danger of these emergencies by hurrying out reinforcements as soon as it heard of the necessity. That was by no means an infallible remedy. French ships might get out unseen from an unexpected quarter, as Caylus did in 1745. It was long before the Admiralty knew where he was gone, and if he had tried to take St. Kitts, the English reinforcement under Townsend would have been much too late to stop him. In the same way d'Antin could have done a great deal of mischief in 1740 before Ogle could have joined Vernon. If Blénac had no chance of doing anything against Jamaica in 1762, it was partly because the English at Jamaica, instead of having to wait for help from England, were able to obtain it much sooner from the Leeward Islands. But it was lucky for them that Rodney had with him the very large squadron which had just been employed in the conquest of Martinique.

Permanent detachments for colonial defence could not, therefore, prevent an invasion of the islands had the French really designed one. The purpose of the system was defeated if the Government, after sending abroad such a high proportion of its fleet, had still to beat the French with their own weapons as well, by hurrying out ships to the colonies whenever the French did so. Still less could the station system dispense the English Government from sending out larger forces for its own expeditions of conquest. This, however, is no disparagement of the station system. It would have been insane to keep a striking force in such a climate when there was no intention to strike. Nevertheless the effect was unfortunate, for the necessity of fresh ships and fresh troops exposed the English enterprises over again to the danger of frustration by tropical disease, from which they were half emancipated by the station system and the seasoning of crews in the West Indies. It was a pity, but it could not be helped; and the English commanders no less than the French were forced to observe the rule laid down by Beckford: 'Whatever is attempted in that climate must be done *uno impetu*; a general must fight his men off directly, and not give them time to die by drink and disease; which has been the case in all our southern expeditions.'[1]

The station system had therefore most of the defects of a compromise. The permanent detachments usually withdrew a considerable number of ships which would else have been available for other services; but they were not large enough to withstand any force that might be sent against them, or to undertake any offensive movement against the enemy colonies without reinforcement from home. Hence the alarms which the West India interest raised in 1745, 1756, and 1757; hence also the great expeditions which had to be sent out from England against the French islands in 1759 and 1762.

But though it could not deal with the major emergencies of

[1] Beckford to Pitt, Sept. 11, 1758, *Chatham Correspondence*, i. 353.

the war, the system was very useful in the ordinary routine of defending and interrupting trade. The English squadrons had, at least for some months in every year, a local command of the sea. It might be disturbed by the intrusion of a disproportionate force from France, but that did not happen often. The French Ministers of Marine never spared large squadrons to the colonies, except for some special purpose, so that the English often preserved this superiority, or at least an equality, for a year or two together.

Their commanders could not always make the most of this advantage. The dispersion of their forces among a number of different errands prevented them from collecting a striking force for an important enterprise, or for an encounter with a body of enemy ships. Even Vernon complained of this, and he had far more ships at his command than any of his successors. For the same reason, at the outbreak of war against France in 1744 Ogle could do no more than 'show himself' on the south side of St. Domingue and worry the trade.[1] If the station commanders could have brought their whole forces into action with the French convoys the result could never have been doubtful; but the detachments which actually met those convoys were seldom decisively superior to them. Admiral Richmond seems to think this happened because the English commanders credited the enemy with a more serious strategic purpose than he really had; but I do not follow his reasoning. If Davers, Knowles, and Lee thought that a 'true military use' was to be made of the French and Spanish ships in the West Indies, it was their business to concentrate their forces more than they did; but the trouble was, that they could not or did not concentrate them enough, because of the multitude of their other services, and that they could not keep them out all the time, having squadrons too small to be worked in shifts. As to the 'true military use' of these ships, if Admiral Richmond considers that there was no justification for sending out ships to the colonies except for offensive operations, he may be right; but were not the English worse offenders than the French in the War of 1744? We kept more ships in the colonies and did just as little with them until the last months of the war.[2] Nevertheless, although they did not

---

[1] Vernon to Newcastle, Nov. 3, 1741, S.P. 42/90, f. 388; Ogle to Corbett, June 3, 1744, Adm. 1/233.

[2] H. W. Richmond, op. cit ii. 198. Caylus at least was enjoined to make a 'true

always succeed in catching the enemy's convoys, the stationed squadrons interrupted the trade of the enemy and protected our own more efficiently than they performed any other services.

§ iii. *The Attack and Defence of Trade*

The ordinary functions of the station squadrons were three: to attack the enemy's trade, to cruise for the defence of our own, and to give convoy. They were also to intercept and destroy any forces of the enemy which might come out to his colonies in the neighbourhood. In so far as the French sent their merchant shipping under the escort of such forces, this last function was bound up with the first.

What was the trade whose protection and destruction were so great a part of the navy's business in colonial waters? Most important of all were the ships from Europe, which brought out necessaries for the plantations and returned with loadings of sugar, coffee, indigo, cocoa, cotton, and other West India produce. The French islands relied far more than the English on provisions imported from the mother country. On the English side the trade from Cork was almost indispensable, as it furnished salt beef, butter, and candles; but with this exception, the arrival or interception of the ships from Europe had a greater effect on the plenty or scarcity of victuals in the French than in the English colonies.

For the English squadrons the worst complication in the whole problem of trade defence was caused by the North American shipping, which supplied so many articles of common consumption—especially flour and bread. The reason of the difficulty was the chaotic nature of the trade. A large number of small competitors, whose greatest object was to arrive alone at the most advantageous market, could not be induced to sail in regular convoys; they swarmed about the seas, scuttling imprudently from island to island in pursuit of the last halfpenny of profit.[1] A few of these might wish to take a cargo of

military use' of his forces. He was instructed that the best way to destroy English commerce and protect the French colonies was to beat the English squadron; this he was to do, if he could, before he ever anchored at Martinique, by seeking out the several detachments in their known cruising-grounds and overpowering them one by one.

[1] A merchant of Portsmouth, New Hampshire, wrote to his correspondent at Philadelphia for insurance on a ship 'from Portsmouth to Jamaica, with liberty

salt at Turks Island or Salt Tortuga, but they bore no great proportion to those who sailed straight home with their cargoes of rum and molasses. There was some intercourse of the same kind between Canada and the French West Indies; but that trade was never fully developed, and was annihilated during the wars.

Lastly there were the ships which arrived with slaves from the west coast of Africa. They were not many, but they were exceptionally valuable. They did not return to Africa, but loaded produce and went back to England or France.

Besides these important branches of commerce which brought necessaries to the West Indies from outside, there was some intercourse on a smaller scale between the islands and about their coasts. Perhaps this coasting trade was greater and more important in the French West Indies than in the English, especially in the Windward Islands. In order to explain this, it is necessary to know something about the organization of the English and French sugar trade.

In the English colonies most of the trade with the mother country was carried on at the risk of the planter. He ordered supplies from his factors in London, and sent home sugar on his own account. There were merchants in the islands who imported and exported for themselves, buying the planter's sugars and selling him goods on the spot; but I think—though there are no figures to prove it—that they were the exception rather than the rule. In the French islands the system appears to have been quite different. The merchants of France sent out cargoes at their own risk, for sale by their captains or other supercargoes in the islands; and most of the sugars which returned home were their property as the proceeds of their outward loadings. This was not universally true, and it was less so at St. Domingue than at the Windward Islands; but I think it was the rule, not the exception.

to touch at Guadeloupe, Nevis, Montserrat and St. Christophers'. If this kind of voyage, which was very frequent, set a problem for the insurers, it set a yet harder one to the officers of the navy charged with protecting the trade (J. Sherburne to John Reynell, June 6 and July 6, 1760, Coates-Reynell Papers, Box XI, H.S.P.). Many of these captains were limited to stay no more than a certain time in any one island unless they found a market or a freight to their liking (Davey and Carson, Philadelphia, to John Jordin, Antigua, Dec. 13, 1745, Letter-book of Messrs. Davey and Carson, Library of Congress). Or they were yet more commonly limited as to the prices they might accept or pay; this drove them from one island to another.

The ships which arrived at the French Windward Islands had their choice of three markets—Martinique, Guadeloupe, and Grenada—of which the first was the largest but not overwhelmingly so. They seem to have got into the habit of going to Martinique and dealing with merchants there who undertook to do one of two things. Either they acted as factors for the planters of the smaller islands and the windward districts of Martinique, finding freight for their produce or buying goods for them on commission; or they dealt in both European commodities and West India produce on their own account. That the first of these functions was their original one is shown by their name of *commissionnaires*; but the second was beginning to be the more important. In either the one capacity or the other, they had got control of the trade, so that few ships came from France to any port in the Windward Islands but St. Pierre; especially in time of war, when captains were more than ever glad to sit down and sell in any port they could make. This centralization required a coasting trade for collecting produce and distributing plantation necessaries. Intendant Maillart lamented the want of such a coasting trade at St. Domingue; but he only meant that it was not an independent form of enterprise.[1] There was plenty of coastwise navigation at St. Domingue, for the ships' boats had to carry their loadings long distances to and from the planters' barcadiers; and when the English blockaders cut off this intercourse, especially on the north side of the island, the planters' complaints were loud enough to prove its importance in the scheme of things.

The trade of Jamaica seems to have been gradually decentralized, and the volume of coastwise shipping accordingly decreased. This process was a comparatively new thing. Vernon complained in 1739 that since Queen Anne's reign the trade of the island was dispersed all over the outports instead of being carried on from Kingston and Port Royal. The planters of a district agreed to load a ship, which sailed directly for the nearest small port to their estates. Such a trade did not require any communication with Kingston; the coasting vessels and their crews began to disappear, because they were no longer needed.[2] Vernon attributed this development partly to the

[1] Maillart to Maurepas, Feb. 22, 1747, A.N. Colonies, C⁹ A 70.
[2] Vernon to Newcastle, Oct. 31, 1739, S.P. 42/85, ff. 39–40; Jamaica Council Minutes, May 27, 1742, C.O. 140/30.

traders' desire to escape the press-gangs which were so active in the neighbourhood of the men-of-war at Port Royal. In order to diminish the force of this motive, he ordered the captains who convoyed the trade round the island to press men from the trading vessels in the outports.[1] No doubt he was wrong to assign so trifling a cause to an important economic development; it was rather due to the settlement of the north side of Jamaica. Perhaps he also exaggerated the development itself, for there was still a fair number of vessels coasting round the island. Most of the other English sugar colonies were so small that they could be served by a single port. In these islands the sugar-droguers—as the coasting craft were called— were almost as much needed between the plantations and the shipping as at Martinique and Guadeloupe. But they were not needed between the islands, because none of them depended commercially upon any other.

The dispositions of the warships for protecting the trade were governed by the movements of the merchant shipping, and the way in which it arrived in the West Indies. The art of finding the longitude had not yet been discovered, or was at least very imperfect. The islands were not very large, and with a strong wind a ship might pass through them in the night without knowing it. As the trade wind was always more or less easterly, it would be very hard to repair this mistake once made by beating back. It was also difficult, and in time of war dangerous, to pass up and down the chain of islands to north or south, if you should happen to strike it at the wrong point. There was only one way of avoiding these inconveniences—to fall in with the exact latitude of the destination as far to the eastward as possible, and allow the trade wind to carry you down to it. In that way you could hardly miss your island; the worst that could happen was finding yourself uncomfortably near to its coast in the night or at daybreak.

The trade of Barbados, not only from Europe but from North America, made the latitude of the island. This trade was more important than the size of Barbados would have warranted, because many North American vessels used to arrive there first as the windwardmost and the best starting-point in their quest for markets down the range of the islands. Shipping bound for the Leeward Islands and Jamaica generally made the

[1] Vernon to Brown, Feb. 22, 1739/40, S.P. 42/85.

latitude of Deseada or of the eastern point of Antigua; only the North American trade for St. Kitts and St. Eustatius approached from the north instead of the east. In consequence the most frequented tracks to the English sugar colonies lay for some hundred miles to the east of Barbados, Antigua, and Deseada. In the same way the French shipping made the latitude of the northern or southern point of Martinique. Thus privateers or warships in quest of outcoming trade had only to place themselves on a certain latitude.[1] They could be pretty certain of meeting with prizes, unless the enemy's merchant captains followed the example of certain naval commanders, and gingerly approached their destinations from unusual angles, in order to escape the blockaders who lay in the accustomed stations.[2]

For the same reason, the frigates appointed to protect the trade knew roughly where to cruise for that purpose. Exactly how broad or how long was the belt of sea which had to be guarded, is a matter on which different opinions were expressed. Commodore Warren complained that the English traders made the islands at such a number of different places that he could not possibly preserve them all from the enemy. He thought that if only they would be more exact in choosing their latitudes, they could be more efficiently protected. Captain Middleton on the other hand attributed the many losses of our shipping to the opposite cause—it all made the same latitudes, and therefore the French privateers had only to stand in the path and take. The length of the tract was also a matter of doubt. Middleton criticized the commanders-in-chief of his day because they did not send their cruisers nearly far enough to the eastward to protect the trade from the enemy's most enterprising privateers. Probably that was because, however far the cruisers went, the privateers found that they could still push out a little farther with some chance of catching merchant shipping which had got into the latitude a long way off. Middleton's own earliest estimate for Barbados was ten to twelve leagues, his

[1] Middleton to Pringle, Oct. 21 and Dec. 4, 1759, *Letters of Lord Barham* (Navy Record Society, 1906), i. 1, 9; Middleton to Douglas, 1760, p. 27. Charles Johnson gives a similar description in the introduction to his *General History of the Pirates*, and explains how the pirates took advantage of this practice of finding the latitude some way east of the islands.

[2] De Kearney to Machault, Dec. 7, 1755, A.N. Marine B⁴ 68; Le Vassor de la Touche to Moras, May 15, 1757, B⁴ 77; Du Guay Lambert to Berryer, Feb. 17, 1761, B⁴ 103.

latest for the Leeward Islands was a hundred or a hundred and fifty.[1]

Whatever the exact definition of the danger-zone, it was obviously too large to be patrolled by the cruisers at the disposal of the English Commodores. One reason for this was the reluctance of the Admiralty to place enough small vessels on the station, and the strictness with which it scrutinized purchases of prize vessels in the colonies. There was hardly a commander-in-chief, whether on the Jamaica or Leeward Islands station, who did not constantly bewail the lack of small sloops and brigantines. Line-of-battle ships were almost useless for every-day cruising on these stations. The prevailing winds and currents were too strong and too constant, and the islands were set too close together, with too many little creeks and holes, and in some places too much shoal water to windward. The privateers escaped into refuges where their pursuers could not approach them. Even frigates were too unwieldy unless they sailed exceptionally well. Frankland and Moore complained, of course with some exaggeration, that their frigates chased French privateers four or five at a time, and never caught one. Périer de Salvert found the same difficulty at St. Domingue. Nothing would do but sloops, or, as Middleton would have it, brigantines; and of those, there were never enough. Moreover, the privateers were constantly changing their stations; if a Commodore broke up a nest of them in one place or made one of their cruising-grounds too hot to hold them, they cheerfully shifted to another. Thus when Moore cleaned up the latitude of Antigua in 1757, they swarmed in the seas to windward of Barbados.

The exchange of prisoners was another reason for the failure to deal with the enemy privateers. Few colonial privateers were large or heavily armed; their ships and equipment could be cheaply replaced. It was therefore the number of available men, not that of the ships, which limited the amount of privateering. The English navy could take the ships—Moore, for example, took fifty-seven, Douglas took forty; but as long as the crews were sent back to Martinique, they could reappear on different vessels and start their trade again.[2]

---

[1] Warren to Corbett, Feb. 7 and 9–25, 1744/5, Adm. 1/2654; Middleton's letters, quoted above.

[2] Moore to Clevland, Dec. 20, 1759, Adm. 1/307; Douglas to Clevland, June 4,

If the trade could not be sufficiently defended by sending ships of war to range up and down the tracts where it was in most danger, other methods had to be taken to extinguish the enemy's privateers. Of course the most perfect would be to conquer the islands to which they returned with their prizes. The English colonists came to desire this at last. When it was achieved in the Windward Islands in 1762, it had not all the effect that was expected. A great body of privateers got away from Martinique before the siege began, and cruised to leeward of St. Christophers. They continued their depredations, using the Danish island of St. Thomas as a base, and drew upon the Governor a severe animadversion from Rodney on the subject of the rights and duties of neutrality.[1] In fact, when the French flag no longer flew in the Leeward Islands, the French privateers were a greater nuisance than ever. Rodney and Monckton had only themselves to thank for this; they had refused to put a clause into the capitulation of Martinique, for allowing the privateers to return from the neutral islands on condition they made no more attacks on British property.[2]

Short of the complete conquest of their bases, other measures might be taken to suppress the French privateers. Governor Mathew asked Townsend in 1745 to 'sweep the roads' where they congregated, burning and bombarding their ships. This was not very effective, and brought the capital ships under the fire of the shore batteries for a purpose which was not important enough to justify the risk. Warships often seem to have got the worst of it in contests with those batteries, when they tried to cut out the shipping from the harbours. At least they wasted ammunition and incurred losses which were disproportionate to the object.[3] Moore judged rightly in 1759 that the bombard-

1760, ibid.; Middleton to Pringle, Dec. 4, 1759, *Letters of Lord Barham*, p. 12. For a further treatment of this subject, *v. infra*, pp. 446–50.

[1] Rodney, orders to Captain Keith, May 21, 1762, G.D. 20/2, p. 229; Rodney to Cleveland, July 23, 1762, Adm. 1/307; see also the letter of the Governor of St. Thomas to Dalrymple, Oct. 26, 1762, C.O. 110/2.

[2] Rufane to Egremont, Dec. 1, 1762, C.O. 166/2; Rodney to Cleveland, July 23 and Nov. 3, 1762, Adm. 1/307; Capitulation of Martinique, ibid. Samuel Herrick writes to Timothy Orne & Co. on July 29, 1762, that he shall lodge some money in the hands of some merchants of Guadeloupe for a safe carriage by land to another part of the island, 'for the privateers are thick round this island, here is scarse a day but one or two are taken' (Essex Institute, Timothy Orne MSS., xii. 26).

[3] Townsend to Corbett, Nov. 8, 1745, Adm. 1/305.

ment of St. Pierre would not be worth the damage to his ships, which ought not to be hazarded unless the fate of an island was at stake.[1]

Perhaps the simplest and best way to check the enemy's privateers and rescue our own trade from them, was to station ships off the ports to which they were most likely to bring their prizes. The capital ships could be used for this purpose; in no other way could they be of much service for the protection of trade. Middleton criticized his commanders-in-chief severely for omitting to do this, and Douglas decided in 1760 that it was the only course to take.[2] But if this plan was brilliant and sound, it is hard to believe that it did not occur to anybody before. In fact it was not so easy as it looked. There were many ports to which the privateers could carry their prizes at a pinch. They might not be able to sell them so well as at the chief places of trade, but they would get something for them and save their own skins. If St. Pierre and Fort Royal were blocked up, there was La Trinité to windward; or if Martinique was out of the question altogether, there were still Guadeloupe (till 1759) and Grenada. The French laws, and no doubt the owners' instructions, enjoined the privateers to return to the ports from which they set out, but they did not prescribe it absolutely. Moreover St. Pierre, which was the greatest centre of privateering, was an open road and uncommonly hard to blockade. In the spring of 1748, when there was nothing stronger than a small corvette in the harbour and a large English force outside, the privateers were able to go out and return safely with their prizes, given a little help from the shore and boats.[3] However, though recapture outside the French ports was not an infallible protection of the trade, it was recommended by all sorts of people, and in fact a certain proportion of the prizes was retaken.

The conditions were quite different on the Jamaica station. Here, too, the winds dictated certain methods of approaching the islands. The trade from England, having passed through the Leeward Islands, generally sailed down the southern coasts of Porto Rico and S. Domingo, where it was in danger from

---

[1] Moore to Hopson, Jan. 19, 1759, C.O. 110/1.
[2] Antigua Assembly Minutes, Aug. 6, 1747, C.O. 9/20; Douglas to Clevland, June 4, 1760, Adm. 1/307.
[3] Caylus to Maurepas, May 15, 1748, A.N. Colonies C⁸ A 58.

French and Spanish privateers.[1] Cruisers were therefore put out in this region to preserve the stragglers out of convoys and the 'runner' ships which came by themselves. They also served to intercept the shipping of the southern quarter of St. Domingue. The small vessels bound from North America for Jamaica sometimes made the Leeward Islands or joined this track from the Mona Passage, but more often came by the Windward Passage between St. Domingue and Cuba. Here they came under the protection of several English cruisers, for the stations in which the English warships annoyed the trade of the French colony were almost equally well placed for defending the track of English trade. The short stage from the Windward Passage to the east end of Jamaica was not so well policed, but it was not dangerous, for there was generally a ship or two cruising between Jamaica and Cuba to interrupt the trade to Louisiana and Vera Cruz. Commodore Forrest tried in 1762 to organize a chain of cruisers which would meet the trade at the confines of the station and hand it on to each other until it arrived at Jamaica. This elaborate system was never put to the trial, for it was thrown out of gear by the outbreak of the Spanish war and the invasion scare of 1762.[2] Special provision had to be made for the recapture of English ships from Spanish privateers; a frigate or two off Santiago de Cuba, and another from time to time off Baracoa, did something to prevent the Spaniards from bringing their prizes into port.

The coasting trade needed a separate system of protection, which the islands provided in part for themselves. Sometimes they fitted out small vessels, for which the commanders-in-chief furnished men and officers; sometimes they hired privateers to make special cruises off the coasts. The nuisances were not wanting here which attended every effort made by the colonists for their own defence—graft, constitutional obstructions, and efforts to throw the burden upon other islands. A quarrel between the Governor and Council of Barbados nearly prevented the equipment of a sloop in 1756, for the Council refused to pass a Bill for the purpose, in order to spite His Excellency,

---

[1] Héron to Machault, Dec. 30, 1755, A.N. Colonies C⁹ A 97. But there was no necessity for this. The outward trade could easily run down a different latitude farther south and come up with the east end of Jamaica from the southward; Cotes's convoy did so in 1757, when a large French force was rumoured to be at St. Domingue (Cotes to Clevland, May 24, 1757, Adm. 1/235).

[2] Forrest to Clevland, Jan. 28, 1762, Adm. 1/1788.

so that the whole had to be done by private subscription among the merchants.[1] The legislature of Antigua would not have such a sloop at all, for the characteristic reason that it would be of some benefit to the trade of other colonies which made that latitude, and therefore Antigua should not bear the cost alone, especially as she had contributed to the security of all the other islands by her heavy expenditure on English Harbour.[2] Jamaica tried, and at last with success, to make the Crown undertake this service, so that in 1757 the country sloop was put out of commission. The expense had been heavy—about £13,000 a year—and had been increased, according to his political opponents, by the corrupt prodigality of Lieutenant-Governor Moore's nominees.[3]

The defence of trade was not the only task of the squadrons, nor the most congenial. The inevitable consequence of the prize and salvage system was that the cruising-grounds which yielded the greatest harvest of defenceless enemy trade were more profitable than those where there was nothing to be had but hard knocks from privateers, or a certain proportion of the value of English ships retaken. This difficulty would not have existed, if the enemy's merchant ships and our own could have been met with in the same places. They were so in most parts of the Jamaica station; but in the Leeward Islands, though the station was much smaller, the two regions were distinct. The right place for intercepting French trade was to windward of Martinique; that for favouring the entry of the English shipping was to windward of Antigua or Barbados. The difference was not great, but it was enough to cause difficulties on the station.[4]

Several commanders-in-chief fell into great disfavour with the colonists for preferring attack to defence in this respect. The islands sometimes felt, or at least complained of, a great scarcity of provisions. They attributed this to the loss of out-coming shipping, and that in turn to the improper cruises

[1] Pinfold to Halifax, May 31, 1757, Pinfold Letter-Book A, p. 42, Library of Congress.
[2] Antigua Council Minutes, Oct. 25, 1756, C.O. 9/21.
[3] Moore, speech to the legislature, Sept. 27, 1757, C.O. 137/30, Z 12; *Journals of the Assembly of Jamaica*, v. 49–51.
[4] Middleton suggested that the cruisers should be appointed to the different parts of the station in rotation, so that each captain, having his fair chance of prizes, should be less tempted to stray, contrary to his orders, from the bad cruising-grounds to the good (Middleton to Pringle, Oct. 21, 1759, quoted above).

ordered by the Commodores and their neglect of the tracts to windward of the English islands. During the commands of Lee and Townsend, in 1745–7, over 170 vessels bound to the Leeward Islands were said to have been taken. The legislature of Antigua cried famine—with very little reason, as it would appear, for a North American supercargo reported at the height of the clamour that in spite of the captures, the markets were bad, 'there being such quantitys of provisions of all sorts here that there must unavoidably a great part of it perish'.[1] Lee was undoubtedly to blame for continually omitting to place cruisers in the situations where they could best protect this trade; the Admiralty did not acquit him of that, though it thought him guilty of no worse than an error of judgement.

Not only Lee but his predecessor Knowles had sometimes made the same mistake. But they had their reasons, of which the planters did not take enough account. Neither of them had a very large force, and neither could disperse it abroad with a sole view to promoting the convenience of the colonists. Every few months there was a French convoy, with a small body of warships, expected to arrive or to sail. It was not only the advantage but also the duty of the Commodore to intercept it. He had therefore to collect a great part of his squadron for this service, and as he had not always enough capital ships and frigates to be able to keep their duties absolutely distinct, he was forced to stint his striking force to keep up his cruisers, or vice versa. Lee's offences were indeed much aggravated by a succession of ridiculous failures to catch these French convoys. He was absurdly accused of cowardice, and of receiving 5 per cent. of their value to let them pass. He was known in the islands as 'Commodore Bottle' or 'the Bacchanalian Commodore', and the Council and Assembly of Antigua formed a special body of agents to procure his removal from the command. The entire Barbados and Leeward Islands interest was enlisted, and told the Lords of the Admiralty 'that their whole trade would be sacrificed if Mr. Lee was continued in the command'. In the reign of the Pelhams the West India merchants seldom clamoured in vain. Lee was suspended and tried; nothing but inefficiency was proved against him, and that was not enough, in those days, to prevent the restoration and even

[1] Edward Dowers to John Reynell, Aug. 27, 1746, Coates-Reynell Papers, Box IV, H.S.P.

promotion of an officer protected by the First Lord's father-in-law.[1]

The most remarkable result of the controversy appears in the instructions to his successor Legge. The 'principal point of his care and attention' was to be the protection of the trade to and from the colonies; only 'in the next place' was he to annoy that of the enemy.[2] This shows how far the offensive activity of the West India squadrons was paralysed by the demands of the merchants. It is not surprising that the men-of-war were inhibited from attacking the French colonies, for they were hardly sufficient for it; but it is extraordinary that the defence of our own trade should be allowed to take precedence over a service which was by common consent so important as the blockade of the enemy colonies—a service which, according to the partisans of colonial warfare, constituted the chief and almost the only success of the War of 1744.

The merchants would have wished to have the whole war conducted on their principles, which would have left it to be won or lost on land, or resulted in a stalemate. That was the point of the Cruisers and Convoys Bill of 1742, and of the complaint which they made to the Admiralty in the spring of 1747 against the concentration of force in the Channel. They 'did believe while Mr. Anson was out with that great squadron a greater number of captures were made than in other months, and while such a great fleet was employed to the southward it could not be imagined they could any way protect the trade'.[3] Yet within six months of this protest, the Admiralty had achieved, by ignoring it, the two most brilliant naval

[1] Legislature of Antigua, Petition to George II, Adm. 1/305; Lee's answer, Aug. 26, 1746, ibid.; Lee to Corbett, May 26, July 20, 1746, Jan. 17, 1746/7; Lee's justification of Nov. 17, 1747, ibid.; Instructions to Lee, June 23, 1746, Adm. 2/67, pp. 357–8; Antigua Assembly Minutes, May 16, July 10 and 18, Aug. 13, 1746, April 16, 1747, C.O. 9/17; Barbados Gazette, Oct. 4, 1746, April 23, 1747; Admiralty Minutes, May 30, 1745, Adm. 3/50; June 19, July 8, 1746, Adm. 3/54; Aug. 6, Adm. 3/55, Nov. 14 and 19, 1746, Adm. 3/56; Feb. 3, 1747/8, Adm. 3/58; Henshaw to Medley, Jan. 6, 1746/7, H.M.C. Ducane MSS., p. 161. It appears from a letter of George Maxwell to Edward Lascelles that Lee was seriously reported to be killing himself, presumably with debauchery (W. & G. iii). Legge and Pocock, Lee's successors and both diligent officers, thought Lee had been the victim of an unjust persecution (Pocock to Anson, Oct. 14, 1747, Add. MSS. 15956, f. 308). So did Judge King of Antigua (see his letter to Corbett, Nov. 22, 1746, Adm. 1/3881).
[2] Instructions to Legge, Nov. 7, 1746, Adm. 2/68, p. 395. These instructions were repeated to Osborn in 1748.
[3] Admiralty Minutes, April 14, 1747, Adm. 3/57.

victories of the war: Anson had taken La Jonquière and his convoy for Canada, and Hawke had beaten L'Étanduère and driven the French trade out to the West Indies without a single ship to defend it. If the merchants' advice had been followed, there would have been no such thing as strategy; only a number of cruisers, rigidly cantoned—perhaps by Act of Parliament—upon the stations which were most frequented by the trade.[1]

The same attitude is shown in the complaints against Commodore Moore in 1759. He had to collect a large part of his force for the attempt on Martinique and Guadeloupe, and to concentrate it still further when Bompar appeared at Martinique. Of course he could not afford cruisers in all the usual places; the French privateers flourished, and an outcry soon went up against him in Barbados. Unfortunately Moore, like Lee, failed to achieve the object for which he had sacrificed the normal security of the trade. He did not prevent Bompar from carrying troops to Guadeloupe, though the failure was quite unimportant as Bompar's move was too late to make any difference to the result.[2] He too was therefore denounced for adding inefficiency to neglect; but as the merits of his case were very different from Lee's, so was his fate. Unlike Newcastle and Bedford, Pitt would not even appear to give up a deserving sailor to colonial faction.[3]

[1] Yet in the next war Anson incurred some criticism of an exactly opposite kind. Joseph Watkins, one of Newcastle's advisers in the City, complained in 1756 that 'our cruisers are treading on one another's heels in our Channel: the protection of the trade is a great object I will allow but the annoying of the enemy is no less so. ... I am afraid Ld A. listens too much to some persons who may mean well but who direct his attention only to the protection of our own trade, but we shall never bring our enemies to reason but by destroying theirs and by hindering them from recruiting their forces in America' (Sept. 8, 1756—Add. MSS. 32867, f. 264).

[2] Barbados Assembly Minutes, Oct. 2, 1759, C.O. 31/29.

[3] Both Lee and Moore accounted for their difficulties in a manner very little to the credit of the colonists. Lee ascribed his to the secret hostility of Governor Mathew, who was concerned in a Flag of Truce vessel (the *Valeur*, H.C.A. 42/48) which had been seized by a man-of-war and condemned for carrying on an illicit trade with the enemy. The facts alleged by Lee were certainly true, but there is no direct proof of any open hostility between him and Mathew; indeed, that old fox maintained an ostentatious neutrality. Still, colonial Governors have sacrificed the reputation of Admirals for less (see Lee's papers of Aug. 26, 1746, and Nov. 17, 1747, also his letter to Corbett, May 26, 1746, Adm. 1/305). Moore attributed his unpopularity in Barbados, where he was burnt in effigy, to his vigorous prosecution of some people who had been smuggling goods to and from Martinique by way of the Neutral Islands (Moore to Clevland, Dec. 13, 1759, Feb. 26, 1760, Adm. 1/307). This account is borne out by Governor Pinfold. Holmes accounted in the

The commanders on the Jamaica station had a far easier task than those at the Leeward Islands. St. Domingue had few privateers, and the shape of its coast gave a peculiar advantage to a strong English force. Cape Nicola and Cape Tiburon jut out into the Windward Passage a long way from the body of the island. Their extremities were hardly inhabited at this period, so that the English warships could rendezvous there, and even lengthen their cruises by replenishing their wood and water, without any effective hindrance.[1] The French trade had to round these dangerous corners in its passage from one quarter of the colony to another. The roads were so bad and the country so difficult that the needs of one quarter could not be supplied from another by overland traffic. In fact, St. Domingue was for strategic purposes not one colony but three, almost as much separated from each other as Martinique and Guadeloupe, but forced to content themselves with a system of naval defence that would only have sufficed for one, and a single set of convoys. So completely did the English interrupt the navigation from one quarter to another, that some mortars which had been sent out to St. Domingue in 1745 were not yet moved round to their final destination at St. Louis by the end of 1747, and I doubt if they reached it before the end of the war; Larnage never found an opportunity which he could trust. If anything could add to the difficulty of securing the trade of the colony, the geography of the central, or western, quarter did so. The ports were situated on a broad and deep gulf called the Bight of Léogane; but the large island of Gonaïve, lying in the middle of it, obliged the trade to go through one of two passages, which could be watched without great difficulty. Most of the trade of the colony, however, was centred at Cap François, on the north side; there were several channels in and out, which could only be watched by a considerable number of warships. News—often unreliable—of the English movements off Cape Nicola was furnished by a service of look-outs.[2] Here the con-

same way for the criticisms of his strategy and efficiency on the Jamaica station (Holmes to Pitt, Oct. 27, 1761, Adm. 1/236).

[1] Larnage to Maurepas, Aug. 3, 1744, A.N. Colonies C⁹ A 64; Shirley to Halifax, July 20, 1764, C.O. 23/16.

[2] In order to escape the look-outs, the English ships kept out of sight of land so far as possible. The look-outs seldom made the mistake of underestimating the English forces; Épinay, Macnémara, and Dubois de la Motte were all kept in port for weeks by their exaggerations.

voys usually arrived in war, and the difficulty of getting round
to the other quarters of the colony favoured a yet further concentration of trade.

The Jamaica squadron also performed from time to time the
service of blockading the French colony at the mouth of the
Mississippi, by cruising between Jamaica and Cuba, and in
the channel between the west end of Cuba and Cape Catoche.
New Orleans never was for any important purpose the back
door of Canada, but South Carolina and Georgia sometimes
thought themselves threatened by invasions of French and
Indians, and the squadron could do a little to relieve them of
this fear. It captured some troopships and storeships for Mississippi in the Seven Years War.[1]

In times of war with Spain the duties of the station were far
more various. Vernon had his cruisers dispersed among six
separate tracts in 1741: one to windward of Rio de la Hacha,
to intercept the trade from Spain to Cartagena and Portobello;
another between Cape Corrientes and the Grand Caymanas,
for the trade from Cartagena to Vera Cruz and Havana—the
middle stage of the galleons' voyage; one in the Old Bahama
Channel to catch the trade which might go to Havana down the
north side of Cuba (an unusual route, but sometimes used,
notably by Pocock and Albemarle for the invasion of Havana
in 1762); another to windward of Cap François to protect our
own shipping from the Northern Colonies; another to the south-
east of S. Domingo to protect the trade outward bound to
Jamaica; and one off Santiago de Cuba, for recaptures.[2]

This dispersion left the Admiral a very small striking force,
let alone anything for convoys. His successors never had so
many ships; moreover, a war with France as well as Spain
necessitated the establishment of several new cruising-grounds
and an additional force on some of the old. However, a striking
force was not ordinarily needed against the Spaniards; they sent
few squadrons to the West Indies after the first year, and once
their ships were in the Gulf of Mexico, all the English Admirals
except Knowles seem to have regarded them as out of reach.
The deliberations of the Cabinet in 1740 show why Havana and
Vera Cruz were considered to be outside the sphere of the

[1] Townshend to Clevland, Jan. 22, 1757, Adm. 1/234; Cotes to Clevland, June
18, Aug. 7, 1757, Adm. 1/235.
[2] Vernon to Newcastle, Nov. 3, 1741, S.P. 42/90, f. 388.

Jamaica squadron: an Admiral who took his force so far to leeward would leave Jamaica exposed to the French behind his
back. Knowles was, therefore, an exception who proved the
rule; he could afford to lie off Havana in 1748 because the war
with France was over.

§ iv. *Convoys*

The navy had yet another service to perform in colonial
waters—that of convoy. The convoy system was a necessary
evil. Some merchants probably valued it more for the sake of
the insurance than for the safe arrival of their ships. The underwriters returned a part of the premium for ships which took
convoy. The masters and owners were therefore tempted to
begin their voyages with convoys which they meant to desert,
when they were so near home as to make the risk worth running,
for the advantage of arriving first at the market. This practice
was further encouraged by the underwriters' habit of accepting
proof that sailing-instructions had been received from the commander of the escort, as evidence that the insured had sailed
with convoy; also by the difficulty of proving misconduct against
anybody in case of separation at sea. No doubt these considerations account for the indiscipline and obstinacy of the merchant
captains. The commanders of convoys would have liked to
punish them by taking away their sailing-instructions, but that
might be hard on the owners if they were not responsible for
the captains' misconduct.[1] The underwriters themselves found
another remedy. Originally they made a return of premium
for the bare fact of sailing with convoy, but they introduced a
salutary innovation in 1746: they would only return part of the
premium if the ship sailed with convoy and arrived safe—not
necessarily with the convoy. The merchants did not like this,
but they had to endure it. It does not seem to have succeeded
in making the masters more obedient for very long.[2]

The lot of a convoy commander was one of the unhappiest
in the world. He bore a great responsibility, for the owners of
a lost merchantman were sure to complain, and the press would
take up the cry if it could make any political capital out of

[1] Capt. Man to Clevland, July 25, 1761, Adm. 1/2113.

[2] This rule was first made in 1746 for the ships which came home with convoy
late in the year, and were liable to dispersion by storms; but the next year it was
applied to all ships (Lascelles and Maxwell to Edward Pare, Sept. 17, 1746; to
John Fairchild, March 25, 1747; to Thomas Stevenson, Jan. 27, 1747/8, W. &
G. ii).

attacking the Admiralty. (The merchants' losses raised a great
ferment in 1741/2, and the House of Commons appointed a
committee of inquiry; the result was the wretched Bill for
Convoys and Cruisers, which was rejected by the good sense or
the Ministerial majority of the House of Lords.)[1] The trading
captains were only too often to blame for the misfortunes which
befell them. The men-of-war repeatedly denounced their dis-
regard of signals and even of cannon-shot. No degree of insubordination was any offence at law; Knowles suggested that it
should be made one, but the Secretary of the Admiralty replied
that such a Bill must be asked for by the merchants themselves.[2]
Some ships came out or went home too heavily laden or unfit
for the voyage. While these slow sailers expected the convoy to
stay for them, the ships which could get on faster crowded
ahead, especially at night, until they were almost out of sight.
The men-of-war had to cruise for leagues in every direction to
round them up by day, only to find them as far apart as ever
the next morning.[3]

Indiscipline reached its height as the convoy approached its
destination. On the voyage home, the temptation of getting
to market a day or two before the others was too great to be
resisted. There was a different motive on the way out: the convoys took nearly all the islands in their way, in order to do as
much work with as few warships as possible. They made Barbados first and left the trade there, then went down the Leeward
Islands and sailed from Antigua or St. Kitts with the shipping
for Jamaica.[4] Some of the masters bound for the Leeward
Islands and Jamaica disliked the delay and the additional risk

[1] Wager's notes of Jan. 27, 1741/2, on the evidence before this committee, and
his defence of the Admiralty, are in the Vernon-Wager MSS.

[2] The Law Officers reported in 1711 that it was no offence against the common
law to refuse to keep in convoy (Marsden, Law and Custom, ii. 221). See Knowles's
letter to Corbett, Aug. 16, 1744, Adm. 1/2007; Corbett to Knowles, Dec. 25,
Adm. 2/486, p. 118.

[3] Kirke to Clevland, Sept. 19, 1758, S.P. 42/41, f. 225; Alexander Innes to
Clevland, July 6, 1761, Adm. 1/1985; Man to Clevland, July 25, 1761, Adm.
1/2113; Ourry to Clevland, July 13, 1762, Adm. 1/2246; O'Bryen to Clevland,
Sept. 8, 1762, ibid. The best printed account of a convoy commander's difficulties
is in the Private Sea Journals of Sir Thomas Pasley (ed. R. M. S. Pasley, 1931),
pp. 35-49. Pasley was in charge of one of the homeward convoys from Jamaica
in 1778. See also the account of 'Commodore' Walker's meeting with a West
India convoy in 1746 (Voyages and Cruises of Commodore Walker (ed. 1928), p. 98).

[4] The Leeward Islands and Jamaica merchants disliked this arrangement, but
could not get the Admiralty to change it.

of this circuitous voyage, so they deserted the convoy in the night when it got into the latitude of Antigua.[1] They did not only expose themselves to danger by their selfishness; if they were taken the information of their crews might enable the enemy to intercept the whole convoy.[2] This was believed to have caused the loss of some ships out of Captain Lisle's homeward convoy in 1746.

The French captains spoke quite as ill as the English of the condition of the merchant ships and the masters' behaviour. They were too ready to ascribe all these shortcomings to the insurance. Wager and Burrell were no doubt right when they argued in the House of Commons that the masters of well-insured ships would not consult their safety too timorously. But that was nothing to the charges made by d'Aubenton, an officer or purser in Conflans's squadron. The enemy privateers, he said, had picked up three ships out of the convoy, which Conflans could not prevent because

'the captains of the ships in question did everything that was necessary to get taken, and succeeded in it; we have no doubt they had consumed part of their cargoes in the various ports where we were forced to stay, and being insured, were delighted to have an occasion to be captured'.

Kersaint was even more sweeping:

'Half the merchant captains and factors at Cap François are worse scoundrels than the *Cartouchiens*. The latter insure goods which they have not shipped, and the former, having spent more than they possess in port or gambled it away, unload goods from their cargoes to pay their debts, and have no hope of getting out of their difficulties short of having themselves taken.'

Very likely this was rhodomontade, and the relations between the King's sea officers and the merchant sailors were if anything worse in the French service than in the English, so we must not look for impartial testimony; but the kinds of barratry which Kersaint describes are not unheard-of.[3]

---

[1] Frankland to Clevland, April 28, 1757, Adm. 1/306.
[2] *C.S.P. Col. 1704–5*, no. 1510; Printed Instructions for Convoys, 1756. Cotes complained that a merchant ship bound to Jamaica had gone ahead of the outward convoy from Antigua, which might have had very bad consequences if she had been taken, for the French were believed to have a large force on the south side of St. Domingue (Cotes to Clevland, May 24, 1757, Adm. 1/235).
[3] D'Aubenton to Maurepas, Nov. 7, 1746, A.N. Marine B⁴ 59, f. 187; Foligny

The French officers also accused the merchant captains of cowardice: many of them struck to small English privateers, hardly larger than boats, from which, according to Larnage, they could easily have defended themselves if they had had any spirit. The Minister of the Marine had the right to remove them from their command for such offences. No such authority existed in England, where the Government might think itself lucky if a merchant captain who misbehaved himself under convoy happened to possess a letter of marque, so that his securities could be sued in the Court of Admiralty; nor do I know if that prosecution succeeded.[1]

The merchants complained of the men-of-war in return. Those of France denounced the haughty carriage of the naval officers to the masters of trading ships, and in particular their habit of commandeering boats to fetch their supplies of wood and water.[2] In England the commanders of convoys were charged with inefficiency and neglect. Sometimes they were to blame for leaving the trade in order to chase prizes or to engage enemy forces gratuitously.[3] The Admiralty tried to discourage the commanders of escorts from taking prizes. Some got round the difficulty by agreeing with privateers to cruise on their joint account in the neighbourhood of the convoy, and none declined the opportunity of a prize if it came in his way without causing him to leave his charge.

The printed instructions for the conduct of convoys ordered the men-of-war to protect the merchants from strange ships by getting between them. Of course this was the ordinary strategy of trade protection; in this way Dubois succeeded in preserving his convoy from destruction off Martinique in 1746, and L'Étanduère did the same in 1747, though at the loss of most of his warships. Dubois was less successful on his return in 1747, when Commodore Fox met him with an overwhelming force.[4] When two convoys met, as Mitchell and Macnémara did in 1745, Mitchell and Conflans in 1746, the warships on each side

to Maurepas, Feb. 28, 1747, B⁴ 61, f. 253; Kersaint to Moras, Jan. 15, 1758, B⁴ 81.

[1] Larnage to Maurepas, April 27, 1745, A.N. Colonies C⁹ A 66; Maurepas to Larnage, Jan. 12, 1746, B 83; Case of the *Ellis*, Oct. 6, 1759, H.C.A. 3/284.

[2] Chamber of Commerce of Guienne to Maurepas, March 30, 1745, Arch. Gir. C 4312, f. 14.

[3] A French commander, too, might get into trouble for this—Caumont, for example, was rebuked in 1757 for leaving his convoy to take a frigate.

[4] Dubois de la Motte to Maurepas, July 8, 1747, A.N. Marine B⁴ 61, f. 292.

might leave the merchantmen in the background and engage, so long as there was no danger of defeat or disablement which would expose the trade to capture by the victorious enemy; when that seemed likely, the weaker force was justified in retiring, rejoining its convoy, and getting away if it could.

The convoy system ought to have been easy to organize in the West India trade, especially that of the English islands. They all produced the same crop, and ought all to have had it ready about the same time. There should have been no difficulty in judging when convoys ought to arrive with plantation necessaries, some of which were needed for making the crop, and when they would be able to start home with their loadings of sugar. But rains might delay the beginning of the crop, or interrupt it half-done, or make the roads to the sea impassable; winds might fail, in the islands which ground their canes chiefly by windmills. Other accidents of an extraordinary nature, such as hurricanes or martial law, might put everything back.

In particular, there was a dissension about the times of convoy on the Leeward Islands station, which poisoned the lives of several of the commanders-in-chief. Barbados was unique among the English sugar islands in that it half-refined some of its sugars by a process known as claying. The amount of clayed sugar which the statistics of imports show was small, but the real proportion was much higher, for the Barbadians cheated the Customs by a long-sanctioned abuse, describing their sugars as *muscovados* in order to pay a lower rate of duty. The claying took time, and the sugars of Barbados were ready two months later that those of the Leeward Islands. The trade of Barbados was habitually obliged, in spite of many protests in Queen Anne's reign, to take the same convoy as that of the Leeward Islands. It was exposed to some risk by running the gauntlet of the principal French islands, even under escort, but that could not be helped; there were not enough ships for separate convoys. The great difficulty was to adjust the times of the homeward voyages. If the last convoy sailed at the end of July, as Antigua desired, many of the Barbados sugars could get no convoy at all, or must wait until next year; if it was delayed into September, some of the Leeward Islands trade had to wait into the hurricane season, which exposed it not only to danger, but to a heavier insurance, as the underwriters always charged an additional premium on ships which were not warranted to sail before

July 15/26.[1] Besides, so late a convoy would meet storms off the Banks of Newfoundland, or in the Channel, which made it quite impossible to keep the fleet together. No Commodore ever succeeded in satisfying both Barbados and Antigua so long as the allowance of only two convoys subsisted. In fact, for this reason among others, no Commodore could hope to please both islands. Legge, Osborn, and Frankland were hated in Antigua but popular in Barbados; Moore was burnt in effigy at Barbados but received the thanks of the legislature of Antigua. Only the very inept, like Lee, could be denounced by both at the same time. The Leeward Islands nearly always carried the day—perhaps because, as Lascelles and Maxwell suggested, they had a majority among the merchants who met in London to resolve upon applications to the Admiralty for convoys. At the end of the Seven Years War our superiority was so much assured in those seas that a third convoy could be granted for the trade of Barbados.[2]

But for this the planters disagreed little over the times of convoys. They wanted one to go out in October, another in February or March at the latest; one to come home with the first-fruits of the crop in April or May and a second later in the summer. These times were hardly ever kept: in Queen Anne's reign the trade sometimes had to wait three, four, or even five months for the outward convoy, at a great expense in wages, victuals, and demurrage. The delays were not quite so bad in the middle of the century, but they were still great. The merchants procrastinated as well as the Admiralty. They were often unready at the appointed day and applied for postponement; but the Admiralty was most to blame for deferring to appoint convoys. The lateness of the convoys home resulted from that of the voyages out, for some planters could not begin crop till they had received the cask or tools which they had ordered from England. However, the merchants of the islands aggravated it by applying for further postponements, chiefly

[1] The date was July 15 before the reform of the calendar in 1752, and July 26 after it.

[2] *C.S.P. Col. 1702–3*, no. 926; *1704–5*, nos. 197, 592; Resolution of the Council of Antigua, Aug. 22, 1747, C.O. 9/18; Legge to Corbett, Aug. 5, Adm. 1/305; Osborn to Corbett, June 21, 1748, Adm. 1/306; Barbados Council Minutes, July 28, 1747, C.O. 31/25; Lascelles and Maxwell to Nicholas Wilcox, Nov. 20, 1747, W. & G. iii; to George Walker, Aug. 6, 1757, vol. viii; to Thomas Stevenson, Oct. 13, 1757, ibid.; Frankland to Clevland, April 28 and June 16, 1757, Adm. 1/306; Rodney to Clevland, Nov. 3, 1762, Adm. 1/307.

because they were afraid that the convoy would reach England before their advices for insurance of goods upon it.[1]

Sailing with convoy was not compulsory in the English colonial trade during these wars; it had been so at some times during Queen Anne's reign. A last vestige of the compulsory convoys survived into the middle of the century. The Irish provision-ships were strongly suspected of getting themselves taken collusively in order to arrive at the enemy's colonies, where the markets were much better than in our own; the Lords of the Admiralty therefore put an embargo on their sailing, and refused to release them from it unless they would give bond to take convoy.[2] But for this the merchantmen were free to sail without convoy, and a certain number of masters did so, especially in such trades as that of the sugar islands, where the 'runners' who got safe home before the convoy earned increased profits for their freighters. From the correspondence of Messrs. Lascelles and Maxwell it appears that almost all the ships in the Barbados trade took convoy out, for there was little advantage to be made by arriving early in the West Indies; most of them returned with convoy, but many came home alone or by threes and fours, unaccompanied by men-of-war.[3] But Barbados was an exceptional island because much of its produce was shipped too late for convoy and had to come home without.

The merchantmen who wished to sail home from the islands without waiting for a regular convoy might apply for an escort to take them clear of the islands. Some warships were almost perpetually employed in this way among the English colonies. The French squadrons gave the same kind of help when they could spare the time, and when the Minister allowed the trade to return without a convoy for the entire voyage. In this way the shipping was protected through one of the dangerous zones, but had to run a more serious risk in the Channel. Both the English and French merchants were for ever entreating their

---

[1] C.S.P. Col. 1704–5, no. 562; 1706–8, no. 926; Knight to ? Sharpe, Aug. 10, 1745, Add. MSS. 22677, f. 61; Admiralty Minutes, April 14, 1747, Adm. 3/57; Clevland to Drake and Long, March 31, 1756, Adm. 2/704, p. 72; Lascelles and Maxwell to John Frere, Feb. 5, 1757, W. & G. viii.

[2] Admiralty Minutes, Feb. 27, 1745/6, Adm. 3/53; Lords of the Admiralty to Newcastle, Feb. 28, 1745/6, S.P. 42/30, f. 185; Sept. 18, 1746, S.P. 42/31, f. 194.

[3] Lascelles and Maxwell to Edward Jordan, Feb. 24, 1744/5, W. & G. ii. They mention another ship which was delayed a long time at Portsmouth by the desertion of her crew, who refused to continue in her when they found she was to sail without convoy (to Miles James, Jan. 14, 1745/6, ibid.).

Governments to keep some cruisers in the Soundings, in order
to protect the entry of these vessels at the seasons when they
were most expected.[1] Maurepas and Machault attended to
these demands as best they could.[2] The English navy was better
able than the French to meet the demand for protection in the
Channel because it disposed of a greater force. However, even
the English squadrons could not hold the sea at all seasons of
the year, and a scheme for enabling them to do so by setting
up a dockyard at Kinsale was pronounced to be impracticable.[3]

Single ships could also come 'north-about', that is to say,
round the northern coasts of Ireland and Scotland; but the
storms were more dangerous than the enemy's privateers in
the winter season, and in the summer the privateers themselves
countered this change of route by swarming along the northern
capes. They were far from their bases and could not hope to
bring back their prizes to France, so they carried them into
the Norwegian ports and sold them there, with or without the
formality of condemnation; this practice caused a bitter and
intractable controversy between the English and Danish
Courts.[4]

Convoy clear of the islands did not even halve the risk for the
shipping bound home to Europe; however, it was all the North
Americans needed. Their own coasts were very little vexed by
French or Spanish privateers, and the only dangerous place
seems to have been, in Vernon's time, about the latitude of 30°,
south of Bermuda, where Spanish privateers picked up prizes.
The English navy could not deal with them, and Vernon could
only suggest that the North American shipping should be

[1] *C.S.P. Col. 1702–3*, no. 1298; *1704–5*, no. 1262; *1706–8*, no. 461; *1708–9*, nos.
80, 214; Henry Lascelles and son to Governor Byng, March 18, 1739/40, W. & G. i;
Lascelles and Maxwell to Edward Jordan, Feb. 24, 1744/5, vol. ii; Admiralty
Minutes, Oct. 9, 1739, Adm. 3/43; Oct. 31, 1740, Adm. 3/44; Sept. 16, 1743, Adm.
3/47; Nov. 27, 1746, Adm. 3/56; Lords of Admiralty to Newcastle, May 22, 1740,
S.P. 42/23, f. 121; Wager's notes of House of Commons Committee, Jan. 27,
1741/2, Vernon-Wager MSS.

[2] Chamber of Commerce of Guienne to Maurepas, April 25, 1744, Arch. Gir.
C 4262, f. 284; Minutes, July 30, 1744, C 4254, f. 202; May 12 and June 10, 1746,
ff. 257, 261; May 31 and July 6, 1747, ff. 289 and 293; Chamber to Machault,
June 19, 1756, C 4263, f. 233; Minutes, Sept. 2, 1756, C 4256, f. 19; June 8, 1757,
f. 39.

[3] Admiralty Minutes, April 14, 1747, Adm. 3/57.

[4] Lascelles and Maxwell to Conrade Adams, Sept. 10, 1744, W. & G. ii. The
Admiralty tried to protect this route in the Seven Years War by establishing
cruisers on the north coast of Ireland (Bedford to Lords of Admiralty, April 10,
1759, Adm. 1/4123, no. 31).

obliged to go in convoys.[1] But it must be obvious, from what has already been said about the character of this trade, that it could not have borne such a regimentation. In fact convoys between North America and the West Indies became rarer. In Queen Anne's reign, when the guardships of the Northern Colonies came down in the winter to cruise among the islands, such merchants as wished to take the benefit of convoy had one or two opportunities of doing so; but these interchanges became less common in the war of 1744, and almost ceased after the establishment of the North America station in 1745.

§ v. *Maurepas's Convoy System of 1745*

The English system of colonial convoys was not much tested in these wars. It was a useful protection against privateers, but the general superiority of the navy relieved the convoys from serious danger of attack by warships at the landfalls of Europe or the West Indies. The real value and limitations of such a system are better seen from the history of Maurepas's attempt to organize the protection of the French West India trade in the War of 1744.

At first he had so many special services to employ his ships that he could not take proper care of the colonies or their trade. He had a squadron cruising off the capes of Spain in the early months of 1744, but had to withdraw it later; he promised Champigny a naval force for the Windward Islands, but could not send it. He contrived to dispatch Épinay to St. Domingue towards the end of the year, but gave him no positive orders to convoy the trade home. In consequence Épinay, who started from Cap François with a fleet of merchants, gave himself no great trouble to keep it together, and would not wait for the slowest sailers.[2] The news of this 'abandonment' scandalized the merchants; it reached France most inopportunely, when Maurepas had just finished working out a methodical scheme of convoys and presented it to the Chambers of Commerce.

The merchants had petitioned for regular convoys, but unhappily the Marine could not afford them; its funds were earmarked for paying old debts, and without some contribution from the trade it could do nothing. Maurepas suggested

---

[1] Vernon to Corbett, Oct. 31, 1741, Adm. 1/232. See also *C.S.P. Col. 1702-3*, nos. 906, 950; *1704-5*, nos. 155, 156, 1510.
[2] Épinay to Maurepas, Feb. 29, 1745, A.N. Marine B⁴ 57, f. 316.

an 'indult' of 5 per cent. on outward and return cargoes, but he would not take upon himself to collect such a tax unless the Chambers of Commerce would impose it of their own free will. The money should be accounted for to them, and if the indult produced more than enough, part of it should be remitted or the convoys should be strengthened. In return for this tax, the Marine would furnish every year four convoys, each consisting of two ships for Martinique and two for St. Domingue.[1]

This proposal was addressed to the Chambers of Commerce of the three great Atlantic ports—Nantes, La Rochelle, and Bordeaux.[2] The merchants of Bordeaux refused at first to have anything to do with it. Épinay's misconduct was fresh in their minds, and they were afraid the tax would become permanent even in time of peace. Their attitude was summed up in the phrase 'The burden is fixed but the success uncertain'. But Maurepas's emissaries promised that the indult should end with the war and that the commanders should have the strictest orders not to neglect their convoys. The merchants reconsidered their refusal, and promised an indult of 8 per cent. on returns only.[3] They did not state the reason of this variation from Maurepas's original suggestion. Perhaps they hoped to get as much as possible out of the ships of other places which returned with convoy to Bordeaux, Nantes, and La Rochelle. (These would probably be many, as no convoy would offer for the Mediterranean or the Channel Ports, and the law which obliged all ships to return from the colonies to the port of their setting out had been suspended at the beginning of the war.) Perhaps the merchants may have reflected that the indult would be a tax on West India goods which the seller might not be able to force the buyer to pay. They owned most of the outward cargoes, but by no means all the returns, for some planters sent

---

[1] Chamber of Commerce of Guienne, Minutes, Sept. 3, 1744, Feb. 4, 1745, Arch. Gir. C 4254, ff. 205, 213. Macnémara had given the same kind of offence as Épinay at St. Domingue in the first month of the war, but Maurepas exonerated him because he had no orders to give convoy (É. Garnault, *Histoire du commerce rochelais au xviiie siècle*, vol. iii (Paris, 1891), p. 112).

[2] I have only followed the history of this affair in the archives of the Bordeaux Chamber. Collateral material is doubtless to be found at Nantes and La Rochelle; but the attitude of those Chambers is for the most part sufficiently revealed in the letters which they wrote to Bordeaux, and the copies of some of their communications to the Minister—for the three Chambers generally consulted together before any of them approached the Government or replied to its proposals.

[3] Chamber to Maurepas, Feb. 13, 1745, Arch. Gir. C 4263, f. 12.

home produce on their own accounts, and some ships went out empty to load on freight; therefore to impose the whole tax on the returns might be to force the planters to bear part of it. This is crude economic reasoning, and leaves several possibilities out of account; but the study of taxation had not got very far in that day.

Maurepas's scheme was further embodied in the next few weeks. He promised to make the convoy commanders understand that the King's estimation of their services should depend on the opinion of the merchants; this pleased the Chambers, for the trade had had occasion to complain of the hauteur of the officers of the navy. The Chambers might even recommend captains for the command; they used this privilege once, and Conflans was appointed at their request to take out the trade in the spring of 1746.

Certain differences of opinion arose: Maurepas had suggested that the merchant vessels should be responsible for getting to the rendezvous, but the Chambers pointed out that this imposed upon them an excessive risk, especially at St. Domingue, where the danger was at least as great between the outports and Cap François as between Cap François and France. Maurepas therefore ordered the commanders to pick up and distribute the trade from port to port in the colonies.[1] It was a more serious question whether ships should be allowed to sail without convoy. La Rochelle advocated it, in the name of freedom of trade, but Bordeaux opposed it. Finally it was agreed that they should only do so when they unavoidably arrived late at the rendezvous, and even so, they should pay the indult. These cases were in practice often referred to the Chambers for their determination. The indult was to be charged upon the ships of Marseilles and the other Mediterranean ports which returned with the convoys to Nantes, La Rochelle, and Bordeaux; but Maurepas later induced the Chambers to abate half because these ships could have no convoy from the Mediterranean to the colonies, and must therefore incur high risks and insurance. The indult was also charged upon all ships belonging to the other Atlantic ports, no matter where they returned to France. Bayonne later tried to get an exemption, but Bordeaux resisted it because

---

[1] Maurepas to Chamber, March 4, 1745, Arch. Gir. C. 4312, no. 79; Minutes, March 4 and 18, C 4254, ff. 217, 219; Chamber to Maurepas, March 30, C 4263, f. 14.

Bayonne had really no colonial trade of its own, and, if the request were granted, every merchant who wanted to sail without convoy would send out his ship from Bayonne for form's sake.[1]

All these regulations threw the colonial trade into the hands of the three great Atlantic ports, and thus accentuated the tendency to concentration which was already produced by the war. Since it had become so difficult to trade between the Mediterranean and the West Indies, some merchants asked permission to transport sugars from Bordeaux to Marseilles by way of the Languedoc Canal; they were rebuffed at first by the pedantry of the Farmers-General, and then by the selfishness of the Bordeaux sugar-refiners, who wished to take advantage of the exceptional glut of sugars in their own market.

The Chambers attached one or two other requests to their acceptance of Maurepas's project. Bordeaux asked him to help the merchants to recruit their crews by ordering the Commissaries of the Marine not to raise men too strictly for the King's ships at the times when the convoys were about sailing. Maurepas agreed to this, but it was not an easy promise to keep, for the French seafaring population was too small to suffice the Royal and the merchant fleets at once, and both needed replenishing at the departure of a convoy. A year or two later, in fact, Maurepas was compelled to announce that he should not be able to grant a convoy for some little time because of the lack of men. The Chambers further asked Maurepas to use his power in order to prevent the seamen from demanding exorbitant wages while the shipping was waiting for convoy. Some form of administrative compulsion was to be exerted for this purpose. Maurepas also promised help of another kind to expedite the return of the convoys. The planters who bought goods of the merchant captains or supercargoes too often eluded or deferred the payment of their debts; postponement was always a grievance, but doubly so when the ships had only a short time to stay and must hurry home with the convoy. He therefore made an edict at this time to compel the debtors to greater promptitude.[2]

[1] Minutes, March 18 and 20, May 20, Oct. 16, 1745, June 30, 1746, Arch. Gir. C 4254, ff. 219, 220, 226, 240, 264; Chamber to Maurepas, Feb. 4, 1747, C 4263, f. 46.

[2] Minutes, April 29, 1745, Arch. Gir. C 4254, f. 223; Maurepas to Larnage, June 11, 1745, A.N. Colonies B 81; *v. infra*, p. 341.

The warships which went out with convoys were to remain some two or three months at the colonies to which they were destined; they were to cruise there for the protection of trade, and the King's share of any prizes they might take was devoted to the indult fund. At the end of their time they were to convoy the trade home to Brest or Aix Roads, from which auxiliary escorts would distribute it to the ports.

Admiral Richmond has criticized Maurepas's plan on the ground that it tied up too great a proportion of the French navy in the business of convoying the colonial trade.[1] If it had worked as it was designed, sixteen ships would have been devoted to it each year—a number no larger than was ordinarily to be found on the English West India stations and convoying trade there. But if what Maurepas wrote to the Chambers was true, want of funds might have prevented him from using these ships at all but for the convoys and the indult. It is certain that in the Seven Years War a great part of the French navy was only armed *en flûte*, which Maurepas was to some extent able to avoid. Besides, his system was never fully worked, so that he hardly employed so much as half the intended number of ships in the colonies and convoys; and the proportion of the French navy appropriated for colonial services was probably not so high as that of the English, while the absolute number was much lower. Even if it had been equal, the only important difference between them was that the French hardly ever had even a small striking force in the colonies. I doubt whether that was much disadvantage, for the reasons given earlier in this chapter. The French convoys probably saved the trade from some losses in the West Indies, though Admiral Richmond is quite right in saying that 'in home waters the security of the trade fleets depended to a great extent on evasion'. Even so, the annihilation of French trade between 1744 and 1748 does not seem to have been so complete as it was in the Seven Years War.

This was the system; on paper it was precise and impressive, but it was soon enough disorganized and came to pieces in the face of the superior numbers of the English fleet.

The convoys were never regular; there were delays from the very first. Bordeaux resented them more than the other ports, as it was the chief place for exporting to the colonies wines which leaked and flour which mouldered while the ships waited for

---

[1] *The Navy in the War of 1739–48*, ii. 193.

convoy. Yet even Bordeaux consented to some postponements, for the arrival of a convoy in the islands was sure to reduce the price of European goods, sometimes by as much as a half, and to increase the demand for produce. If another fleet should reach the market before the prices had recovered a satisfactory equilibrium, the merchant would find himself in danger of a losing voyage.[1] The merchants of France were full of philanthropic zeal to prevent the poor colonist from starving, but they did not mean to leave him much to spare. The delay was nearly always aggravated in the colonies themselves by the blockade which the English squadrons kept up when they heard or suspected that a French convoy was about to leave; it is true that the English were not strong enough to hinder them permanently from sailing, but they could retard them.

As the convoys got behind the time-table, the voyages became much longer, and therefore more expensive to the shipowner. The outward cargoes suffered from the long delays in Aix Road, and sometimes arrived rotten; the crews consumed in France and the colonies almost as much victuals as they had brought out, and the relief to the colonists was therefore small. The infrequency of sailings reduced the volume of trade which could be done by the limited number of ships and sailors that could be procured. Instead of four convoys a year, there were in fact never more than two. Perhaps this was no very great grievance; the English Government had never yet professed to find more than two convoys each way in a year. But as the convoys became fewer they became larger, and grew to such a size that the appointed number of warships could not possibly control them or ensure their safety. Conflans left Aix Road in April 1746 with 230 ships—a number almost twice as great as that of the largest English convoy of which I can find mention. Fromentières in the autumn of 1747 had 252. It is true that Conflans had four warships instead of two—indeed he had six as far as Martinique—and that Fromentières was to have been escorted clear of the capes by L'Étanduère; but the protection was not strong enough.

Larnage and Maillart suggested to Maurepas in 1746 that two strong convoys a year would be better than three weak ones; a

---

[1] Chamber, Minutes, May 26, Nov. 5, Dec. 30, 1745, Arch. Gir. C 4254, ff. 228, 241, 245; Chamber to Maurepas, May 25, 1745, May 17, 1746, C 4263, ff. 19, 36; to Nantes Chamber, May 14, 1746, f. 35.

respectable force was needed in waters where the English kept such large squadrons. Maurepas admitted that for a short time the risk would be lessened, but the English would soon find out when the convoys sailed, and oppose to them a still larger force. To increase the size of the convoys would be putting too many eggs in one basket; if one were taken, the colonists would starve immediately and for a long time.

This was the more likely because the merchants of France usually determined the size, nature, and destination of their cargoes by the advices they received of the sale of the last. If any goods had sold badly, they sent no more such next year; if all sales had been bad at St. Domingue, they transferred their enterprise to Martinique for the next voyage. This system was unnecessary in time of war, at least so far as the more perishable goods were concerned, for the arrivals of convoys in the islands were so few and far between that plenty had time to convert itself into scarcity between one convoy and the next. The merchants were none the less guided by it, and the consequences, harmless enough when the trade was a more or less continuous trickle, were injurious to the colonies when it came in great waves.[1]

It was, therefore, more and smaller convoys that were wanted. This lesson was in fact dictated to Maurepas by the Chambers of Commerce. After the news of a misfortune to the first outward convoy in 1745, the Bordeaux Chamber declared that the number of ships in each fleet was far too large, and asked for a small convoy every month. This scheme could not for a moment be entertained, for it would have required a prodigious number of warships; but the Minister entirely agreed with the principle. Unfortunately he could not follow it in practice, and, for all he might say, the convoys continued to grow huger and rarer.[2]

No more could he keep his promise to refrain from diverting the warships to other services. He ordered Conflans in 1746 to go on to Louisbourg from Cap François when he had seen the

---

[1] Samson to Maurepas, Dec. 14, 1745, A.N. Colonies C⁹ A 67; March 29, 1746, vol. 69; Maurepas to Samson, March 28, 1746, B 83; instructions to Capt. Thomas Morong, March 16, 1747/8, Timothy Orne MSS. i. 83, Essex Institute.

[2] Larnage and Maillart to Maurepas, Feb. 24, 1746, A.N. Colonies C⁹ A 68; Maurepas to Larnage and Maillart, Oct. 26, 1746, B 83; Chamber of Commerce of Guienne, Minutes, Feb. 10, May 12, June 8, 1746, Arch. Gir. C 4254, ff. 251, 257, 260; Chamber to Maurepas, Jan. 8, May 17, 1746; to Barrail, Aug. 10, 1746, C 4263, ff. 31, 36, 40.

merchantmen in there, leaving them without any escort home. It is true that Dubois and Foligny were hurried out after Conflans to repair this neglect, but that did not save the homeward trade from a very long wait, at a great expense of victuals and wages, besides the damage by the decay of the hulls in tropical water.

The cruises of the warships during their stay at the islands were almost useless. Caylus complained that the commanders would do nothing. The commanders of convoys at St. Domingue were handicapped by the sickness of their crews, lack of victuals, and the damages which two or three of them received in their slight engagements with the English blockaders. The service of distributing the convoys to the smaller ports and islands, and bringing the homeward trade to the rendezvous, was even worse performed. Caylus argued that the ships which came out with these convoys could only protect the trade between Martinique and France, and that the coasting trade needed a force permanently stationed in the colonies. No attempt seems to have been made, during the whole war, to establish any kind of communication between Martinique and Guadeloupe; Du Guay went once to Grenada, but only to carry some military stores there. In consequence, the English took nearly all the coasting craft of the Windward Islands; out of fifteen which ordinarily plied between Martinique and Grenada only one was left at the end of the first year of war.

At St. Domingue the task was attempted, but without very much success. The convoys usually arrived on the north side. The commanders would only sail round Cape Nicola to the western quarter, taking with them any trade which was destined there, and returning with the homeward ships to Cap François, whence the whole convoy would set out for France. (Dubois nearly went home without even this; indeed, he would have done so if he had not been reinforced.[1]) No convoy commander went right round the colony to St. Louis; the most that any of them would do was to prompt the ships of the southern quarter

---

[1] An incident in Dubois de la Motte's campaign shows the importance of local protection of trade in the colonies to the convoy system. Chastenoye and Maillart complained that as he could not or would not come round from Cap François, the shipping of the western quarter could not safely send out boats to get in their cargoes from the plantations; so that when he at last arrived there to pick up the homeward-bound vessels, many of them had to sail half-loaded or stay behind (see their letter to Maurepas, April 18, 1747, A.N. Colonies C⁹ A 71).

to sail out, and then cruise off Cape Tiburon for a day or two in the hope of meeting them. Sometimes this succeeded, but more often some of the trade was captured before it could get. into touch with the convoy. Only twice in this war did any armed force reach St. Louis. Both these visits were due to the accidents of the campaign, and neither of them gave the merchant shipping of the southern quarter an opportunity to get safely home to France.[1]

The imperfection of this service aggravated the tendency to concentration at the great places of trade, which alone were properly served with convoy. Many merchant captains had discretionary instructions to sell their cargoes in any port they could safely make. They durst not go farther than Cap François, even when they were offered convoys for the rest of the journey. In the same way, some of those who had such latitude were content to arrive safe at Martinique, and would not even risk the further passage to St. Domingue.[2] This concentration naturally played into the hands of the local merchants, who bought up both European goods and island produce as a speculation; it threw the planters still farther into their power. Such a slipshod way of seeing the trade to its destination would never have answered in the English colonies, where most of the outward cargoes were already the property of individual planters, and only the smaller part destined for sale in the open markets.[3]

[1] Épinay to Maurepas, Feb. 1, 1745, A.N. Marine B⁴ 57, f. 314; Dubois de la Motte to Maurepas, Jan. 7, April 8 and 10, 1747, B⁴ 61, ff. 278, 280, 288; Minute of a council of war, April 9, 1747, f. 282; Larnage to Maurepas, Oct. 28, 1744, A.N. Colonies C⁹ A 64; Aug. 5, 1745, vol. 66; Jan. 2, 1746, vol. 68; Chastenoye and Maillart to Maurepas, April 18, 1747, vol. 71; Tramond, op. cit., p. 339.

[2] In 1745 the crew of the *Providence* refused to go beyond Martinique unless the captain would ensure their private ventures; but this was a slave-trader, and the temptation to stop at the first port was always very strong in such vessels because of the dangers of mortality and rebellion (Petition of Vasselin, and letter of White to Segretain, *Postillon*, Segretain, H.C.A. 32/143).

[3] Yet the English colonies did suffer something in this way; the legislature of Jamaica complained that the enemy privateers molested the coasting trade and raised the rate of insurance between Kingston and the outports to 10 or 15 per cent.—about half the premium for a voyage without convoy between Jamaica and London. As a result 'great quantities of sugars and other commodities lie wasting at the aforesaid ports for want of small vessels to transport them, to the great impoverishment of many planters and settlers in these parts, and who for want of a free, and less dangerous intercourse, between them and the ports from whence in time of war they can only ship their increase for England, not only continue under the greatest difficulties but must soon become incapable to sustain and carry on their settlements; the expence of their contingencies for supporting them, increasing in proportion to the dangers and difficulties they find in sending their

The worst fault of Maurepas's convoy system was the danger of attack by the English squadrons. The Board of Admiralty devoted much thought and effort to the business of catching the French convoys; Sandwich, in particular, thought it so important a service that he was ready to delay for its sake the creation of an efficient western squadron in the Channel.[1] The navy made some attempt to intercept almost every French West India convoy at the beginning and end of each stage of its voyage. The St. Domingue convoys were most exposed to these encounters, for the Leeward Islands squadron might waylay them on their way out—thus Lee had an engagement with Dubois in 1746; or the Jamaica squadron might try to catch them between the ports of St. Domingue—thus Mitchell fought Macnémara and Conflans, and Dent attacked Dubois de la Motte.

Yet though the French trade had to run the gauntlet of so many squadrons, its losses in colonial waters were not very great. The commanders on the English stations could never afford to keep a sufficient and perpetual body of capital ships in any one place; therefore the outward-bound convoys seldom met an English force much stronger than that which accompanied them, and often slipped into port without any encounter at all. As for the return voyage, the blockaders outside the French colonial ports could not be relieved regularly enough to prevent a convoy from sailing home sooner or later.

There was another reason for the rarity of serious accidents: some of the French commanders behaved with the greatest possible skill and courage. Du Guay saved three-quarters of his convoy from Townsend, who ought to have succeeded in taking the whole. Conflans's tactics and vigour were very much superior to Mitchell's in 1746. Dubois de la Motte's defence of his convoy from Lee appears to have been a masterpiece, and he showed great resolution in repelling Dent, for he had singularly little help from his consort. In fact there were only two

produce to market' (Legislature of Jamaica to George II, May 8, 1747, C.O. 137/58). Jamaica seems to have complained already that the homeward convoys which sailed from Port Royal did not pick up the trade from the outports; the Admiralty resolved on April 16, 1747, to give orders for this purpose (Adm. 3/57). Vernon had provided for this service, but perhaps it had lapsed. These difficulties made shipowners and captains very reluctant to take freight for the Jamaica outports in war-time (Lascelles and Maxwell to Nicholas Newton, May 19, 1744, W. & G. ii; to Alexander Crawford, Sept. 8, ibid.).

[1] Sandwich to Bedford, April 24, 1746, *Bedford Correspondence*, i. 71; to Anson, July 20, Add. MSS. 15957, f. 6; Admiralty Minutes, July 12, 1746, Adm. 3/54.

occasions in the war when a considerable part of a French convoy was taken in the West Indies. One was when Townsend
captured some twenty odd ships from Du Guay's fleet just outside Martinique; but Townsend had a much stronger squadron
than was usual in the Leeward Islands because he had been
sent out to deal with Caylus. The other was in December 1747,
when Pocock once more picked up about a quarter of the outward convoy in the same place where Townsend had done so;
but then the French shipping was entirely unprotected, having
been stripped of its escort by Hawke in the Channel.[1]

In order to provide against the possibility of failure, the commanders in the West Indies were ordered to send home by an
express any information of the prospective sailing of a French
convoy, so that the Admiralty might take measures to intercept
it in the Channel. Sometimes the same kind of message was
sent out to the West Indies; in this way Hawke warned Pocock
and Dent that the convoy was coming out defenceless after his
victory over L'Étanduère.[2]

This system of vigilance began to meet its reward in 1747.
Already the French commanders had to dodge to and fro in
order to avoid the English forces that lay in wait for them on the
beaten tracks. An example of this painful agility is furnished
by Foligny, who escorted the trade home from Martinique in
the winter of 1746-7. First he sent out a Flag of Truce for news,
and heard that Lee was waiting for him in the Mona Passage,
where Du Guay Lambert had passed with his convoy the year
before (this information was wrong or rather misleading, and
he nearly ran into Lee's arms in consequence of it). He decided
to go out by the little-used channel between Sombrero and
Anegada. His rearguard had a busy time with privateers,
especially in the night, but he got safely clear of the islands,
with 99 out of 103 ships still accompanying him. When he
approached the Azores he began to wonder which side of them
he ought to go. The weather would be better to the southward,
for it was February—the worst time of the year for approaching
the coasts of Europe, yet all the better for that because the
English fleets might be unable to keep the sea. But he was

---

[1] V. infra, p. 324.

[2] Orders to Legge and Knowles, Aug. 15, 1747, Adm. 2/70, p. 277. But
the commanders in the West Indies had not waited for these orders; Davers,
for example, had sent home an express with the news of Macnémara's departure.

4274 Y

afraid that the English, having so often missed the French convoys, would come to the Azores to make sure of them, so he
steered clear to the north and ran into a terrible storm which
entirely scattered his convoy. Poor Foligny, too clever by half,
arrived at Brest unaccompanied by one vessel out of the hundred and three.[1]

The year 1747 was disastrous for the French West India
trade. Most of Foligny's convoy arrived more or less battered;
but in June, Dubois de la Motte, the hero of two encounters in
the West Indies, fell in with a squadron of eight ships under
Commodore Fox. He beat off the enemy until nightfall, but
then his only hope lay in tacking under the cover of darkness,
and hoping that the merchants would have the common sense
to do the same—he dared not order it by signal, for fear of letting Fox know his intention. Sixty tacked with him in the night,
forty held on their course; the forty were taken and the sixty saved.

Maurepas's system was breaking down, as he and everybody
else could see. The English fleets in the Channel were too
strong and too many; they could too easily inform themselves
of the prospective departure of the trade. They had opposed
system to system, and the stronger resources were beginning to
tell. Maurepas held consultations and took advice; he was
beginning to think he must try some other plan. Some were for
strengthening the convoys and increasing their frequency; but
they demanded for these purposes far more ships than the
King's navy could provide or the indult could support. There
had always been a school which believed that the trade could
be protected better by strong squadrons at the European and
West Indian landfalls—the system which Machault adopted for
a short time in 1756. The Chambers of Commerce wished to
pile these two systems on top of each other: more and stronger
convoys, with large squadrons to escort them clear of the
Channel, and to go out and meet them on their return. In
particular, the merchants had implored Maurepas to send out
the whole available fleet into the Channel to meet Dubois. This
advice was too late to save Dubois, but Maurepas determined
to try if he could not at least protect the outward convoy by
such a reinforcement.[2]

---

[1] Foligny to Maurepas, Feb. 28 and March ?, 1747, A.N. Marine B⁴ 61, ff. 253,
259.
[2] Chamber of Commerce of Guienne, Minutes, June 28 and July 6, 1747, Arch.

L'Étanduère was appointed to command a special squadron of eight ships in the Channel. He was to go to Corunna, find out what English forces were in the neighbourhood, and send word to Fromentières in Aix Road when it was safe to come out with the convoy; he was then to meet it and escort it clear of the Channel. But at Corunna he was to detach two of his ships to Martinique, and as his whole squadron had to be reduced, for want of men, from eight to six, that left him a very paltry force indeed. He represented to Maurepas that the plan was unworkable. There was no need to go to Corunna, to know that the English forces were still at sea; if he waited there long he was certain to meet one of the English squadrons soon, whereas if he only passed by he might hope to avoid them all. Besides, a wind which was good to send a message from Corunna would prevent the convoy from sailing, and when it turned the information might no longer be up to date. It would be much better to wait until October, when there would be fewer English ships out, and then to sail from Aix with the convoy and the two ships which were to have been detached to Martinique. He would have a respectable force of eight ships in the Channel, of which four would accompany the convoy all the way. He did not believe the enemy would try to attack the shipping which waited in Aix Road, for the attempt was too difficult; and as for the danger that the convoy would swell in the meantime to an unmanageable size, that could be prevented by forbidding any further departures.

All his suggestions were accepted but the last. Maurepas had foreseen his objections. No doubt L'Étanduère's plan might be safer, but it would lose the advantage of puzzling the English and making them guess what his squadron was going to do. If he went directly to Aix, they would be in no doubt and would devote all their endeavours to catching him. However, as L'Étanduère was dissatisfied with his instructions, he might put his own scheme into execution. At the end of September further doubts crossed the Minister's mind. The winds were

Gir. C 4254, ff. 292, 293; Chamber to Maurepas, Jan. 8, 1746, C 4263, f. 31. 'Réflexions sur les moyens de sauver le débris du commerce maritime de France', A.E. Mém. et Doc. France, 2007, ff. 159 et seqq., probably written about August 1747, recommends a greater regularization of the convoy system, but assumes that almost the whole French navy is to be employed in the protection of trade, and does not touch the problem how to avoid superior English squadrons in the Channel.

still contrary, and Hawke was said to have got notice of the convoy and to have sent a message to Warren to come out of port and join him. Should L'Étanduère wait until Warren, who would not be fit to keep the sea long, should have had to return to port? In the meantime the colonies would starve. Should L'Étanduère take out all eight warships to clear the sea and order the trade to sail in unprotected detachments behind him? Finally, Maurepas determined to take the risk and stick to L'Étanduère's scheme. The enemy might know the convoy was sailing, but he would not expect it to have so strong a force as eight ships, so he would probably scatter his forces over a wide tract, and L'Étanduère might meet nothing worse than small detachments whose opposition he could break down.[1]

These cogitations illustrate the perplexity to which the English superiority at sea had reduced the French Minister of Marine. They were all in vain. Hawke was cruising off Cape Ortegal with fourteen ships; L'Étanduère ran straight into his arms, and lost nearly all his squadron in battle. The convoy got away, but Hawke sent an express to the Leeward Islands and Jamaica with the news. Most fortunately Pocock was cruising off Martinique when Hawke's messenger arrived; the next day the convoy began to drop in, and the men-of-war were able to take twenty-seven of them, while the privateers accounted for about ten more. Even so, two-thirds of the French vessels reached Martinique safe. At St. Domingue they had better fortune still. Dent's captains were engaged in one of those tiresome courts martial which so badly interrupted the service when they were held on colonial stations, because nearly all the captains were requisitioned for the court and the commander-in-chief would not trust the ships to the lieutenants. As soon as Dent received the news, he broke up the hearing and beat up towards St. Domingue; but the whole convoy was already safe in port.[2]

The result of L'Étanduère's disaster might have been very much worse; but it ruined Maurepas's system of convoys. He was forced to suspend it until April 1, and to allow the merchants to sail freely during the winter season, which was the

[1] L'Étanduère to Maurepas, Sept. 1, 1747, A.N. Marine B⁴ 61, f. 181; Maurepas to Camilly, June 17, 1747, B² 331, f. 257; to L'Étanduère, Sept. 8 and 25, Oct. 3, 1747, ff. 98, 124, 131.
[2] Pocock to Clevland, Jan. 12, 1747/8, Adm. 1/2289; Dent to Clevland, Dec. 10, 1747, Jan. 12, 1747/8, Adm. 1/1697.

most favourable to unprotected trade because few English warships or privateers could keep the sea. He wanted the colonial authorities to detain till next September the merchantmen who could not sail home in time to arrive in the Channel before the English fleets were ready and about. In the meantime he tried to send out light vessels to bring home the trade from the colonies, but one of them was taken on her way to St. Domingue and the other, though she arrived at Martinique, was so weak that Caylus dared not even order her round from St. Pierre to Fort Royal. Much of the French shipping was taken in the West Indies or in Europe, and as for sending another convoy out, Maurepas does not seem to have considered doing so before the autumn; so that in spite of the fat fleets which had arrived, the last months of the war were a time of great privation in all the French islands.[1]

The Ministers of Marine did not try to re-establish the convoys at the beginning of the next war. How they proposed to assure the subsistence of the colonies is another story, and opens a new scene.

[1] Chamber of Commerce of Guienne, Minutes, Dec. 28, 1747, Jan. 25 and Feb. 1, 1748, Arch. Gir. C 4255, ff. 13, 15, 16; Caylus and Ranché to Maurepas, March 15, July 28, 1748, A.N. Colonies C⁸ A 58; Maurepas to Caylus, May 7 and June 18, 1748, B 87; Chastenoye to Maurepas, Jan. 3 and Feb. 15, 1748, C⁹ A 72. Some of these ships were insured with convoy warranted, and therefore could not take advantage of the season to sail by themselves (Vaudreuil and Samson to Maurepas, Feb. 1, 1748, C⁹ A 74).

VIII

THE FRENCH COLONIES AND THE NEUTRAL TRADERS

§ 1. *The Effects of War upon the French Sugar Colonies*

THE relation of colonies to the mother country was even more keenly discussed in the French Empire than in the English. The reason for this is not hard to conceive. The monopoly of colonial trade bore lightly upon the English colonists—at least upon the sugar-planters. The market to which their produce was confined was much better than those from which it was diverted; the manufactures of the mother country were becoming the most efficient in the world, except in certain kinds of textiles, some of which were admitted to the colonies upon very advantageous terms. The French colonies on the other hand made greater sacrifices to imperial self-sufficiency. Their produce was cheap and much desired in the open markets of Holland and Germany; the foreign smuggler offered them a method of conveying it directly to those countries, upon conditions beneficial to them and to himself. They needed slaves, which their own slave-traders could not or did not supply abundantly, and provisions, which could be most cheaply obtained from North America, where the French establishments were too difficult of access, and too little developed to supply the entire demand. The colonist and the merchant were therefore enemies in the French Empire as they never were in the English—especially as the English factor was often no more than an agent of the planter, while the French merchant habitually bought and sold for his own account, and therefore was involved every day with the planter in a warfare of prices. The French merchant justly suspected his customers of trying to escape from the necessity of dealing with him, and the French colonist retorted that the merchants wanted to tie him to a system which did not sufficiently provide for his interests.[1]

War aggravated this conflict in many ways. France had not a great merchant marine at this time; it was not so much ships as men that were wanting. The French system of *classes* gave the navy an option upon the available seamen, which it had

---

[1] See Gaston Martin, *L'Ère des négriers*, pp. 368–82.

to exercise, in time of war, with disastrous effects upon commerce. One of the reasons oftenest given in public and private correspondence for the virtual cessation of French colonial trade in 1757 was the difficulty of collecting crews.[1] No doubt this was very much increased by the great number of French ships and crews impounded by the English during the period of reprisals before the war began, and the long delay in returning or exchanging them. Privateering, even if successful, could add little to the tonnage of the French merchant navy, and worse than nothing to the man-power; it diverted from the trade a great proportion of the ships and an even greater proportion of the men, for privateers were far more heavily armed than the ordinary merchantmen. Neutral sailors might have been enlisted, but the shipowners did not trust them, as they seldom gave themselves much trouble to defend a French ship.[2] For these reasons the French merchants could not much increase the quantity of their shipping in a sudden emergency, nor could they easily replace losses unless the enemy should show great facility in the exchange of prisoners, which he was very far from doing in the Seven Years War.[3] This limitation of the quantity of shipping had important results.

The trade of the French colonies, especially of St. Domingue, was really a barter of goods against goods, in which money seldom changed hands and was in fact very rare. European goods were paid for in produce, whether at agreed, controlled, or current prices. So much sugar bought so much flour or wine or linen. The planters tried to keep up the value of their crops by combination, and even by invoking the interference of the Government—though that was more commonly reserved for their dealings with the foreign traders.[4] The prices so fixed were

[1] Chamber to Machault, Oct. 9, 1756, C 4263, f. 262; to Moras, May 14 and June 7, 1757, ff. 277, 278; Messrs. Brunaud, Bordeaux, to Danié, Jan. 31, 1758, *Juffrow Alida*, Kock, H.C.A. 42/73. On the other hand, when the Government tried to favour the merchant shipping in war-time, the ships of war were confined to port for want of men (see the letter of Ruis to the Chamber of Commerce of La Rochelle, April 24, 1757, Garnault, op. cit. iv. 157–8).

[2] Chamber to Moras, Feb. 7, 1758, Arch. Gir. C 4264, f. 6.

[3] This only applies to Europe; *v. infra*, pp. 447–50.

[4] An unsigned 'Account of what was transacted since my arrival in August 1761' describes a combination of the planters round St. Louis to raise the prices of their produce above the rates they had agreed to pay. The rains having made the roads impossible for three months, the supercargoes were in a hurry to get their sugars and be gone. The current price of sugar having for once risen above the fixed rate, the planters who had agreed to deliver it at the latter insisted on the former

nearly always above the market rate. The merchants and supercargoes, however, knew a trick worth two of that: they calculated the price of what they had to sell, by the valuation of the produce which was to pay for it—unless their customers were people in authority who had the power to impose upon them.[1]

The effect of war upon this economy was at once to increase the prices of imports and lower those of island produce. No doubt the merchant, who had to shoulder the increased freights and insurance, was justified in selling dearer and buying cheaper, and he had the power to do it because few ships set out for the colonies and still fewer arrived. A pound of sugar or coffee could only buy a quarter, a sixth, or some said an eighth of the European goods which it bought before the war. An outward cargo which could purchase the loading of one ship before the war could now purchase the loading of four, six, or eight in the same commodities.[2] Even in peace-time there had been a discrepancy between the tonnages of shipping needed to carry the outward and return cargoes, but it became much worse now.[3] It was therefore much harder to ship the

(*Archibald Adrian*, Karrestedt, H.C.A. 42/54). Machault ordered Bart to suppress any attempt at fixing the prices of imported goods or produce (Instructions to Bart, Dec. 15, 1756, A.N. Colonies B 103), but Bart does not seem to have obeyed where the neutrals were concerned.

[1] The discrepancy between cash prices and prices for payment in goods was sometimes striking—it might amount to 100 per cent. It existed in the English islands as well as the French (Pimont, Aux Cayes, to Chauvel, Aug. 27, 1757, *Juffrow Maria*, Vandervelde, H.C.A. 42/74; Dugué, Roullier and Co., Léogane, to P. and S. Locquet, Dec. 4, 1757, *Vreede*, Boon, H.C.A. 42/102).

[2] If flour rose from the ordinary price—about 60 livres the barrel—to about 120 livres, and raw sugars fell from 15 to 10 livres the hundredweight, a hundredweight of sugar would buy a third of the flour it had bought before the war. These are conservative estimates, because flour was often at 150 livres in war-time, and once or twice at 300, while raw sugars sometimes fell to 6—the better kinds did not fall so much in proportion (see the fragmentary collection of prices current in Martinique, A.N. Colonies C⁸ B 20. Adrien Dessalles gives even more striking figures in his *Histoire générale des Antilles*, iv. 468-9; but his authority is not very good). Besides, the colonists maintained that the average price of raw sugars in peace was not 15 livres but over 25 (see the controversy on this point in the two *mémoires* quoted by M. Gaston Martin, op. cit., pp. 388-9). Maillart speaks of it as falling from 26 livres to 10 in 1744 (Maillart to Maurepas, Aug. 10, 1744, A.N. Colonies C⁹ A 65). By the end of 1745 it rose to 13; in December 1757 it was 6 livres in cash, 12 to 15 in payment. Coffee seems to have lost even more of its value than sugar; according to Beauharnois and La Rivière, three-quarters (see their letter to Berryer, Feb. 13, 1760, C⁸ A 62).

[3] Clieu estimated the needs of Guadeloupe at 4,000 tons of imports and twice as much to carry away the produce of the island; though he was writing in 1747

proceeds of a cargo back to France. The result was a run on money, and on the more portable commodities such as indigo and fine white sugars. Money was already in demand, for there were occasions when the merchants believed that it was the only article of export on which there was not a loss. Insurance was at 55 or 60 per cent.;[1] freights might amount to 30 or 40 per cent. of the net sales, and seamen's wages were twice or three times the ordinary rates;[2] in these circumstances the transport of sugars to France was not always sufficiently recompensed by the price, for the re-export market on which the French traders so much depended might be partly supplied by prize sugars from England.

At the same time that money was drained out of the colonies, the interruption of their trade with Spanish America cut them off from its principal source, and the merchants of Marseilles who used to send out small Spanish coin to buy sugars were deterred from doing so by the unprofitableness of the purchase.[3] There were many complaints of hoarding or scarcity of cash, and the economic life of the islands was seriously deranged by it. The burden of debts and taxes was considerably increased, and with it the arrears. No wonder Maillart and Le Mercier de la Rivière wanted to introduce paper money—that favourite expedient of colonial communities in war-time—and collected taxes in bills on the principal *commissionraires*; but the French Government would on no account tolerate paper money.[4]

he seems to have been thinking of peace-time conditions. The authorities at St. Domingue complained that the French shipping, especially that of Nantes, often came out to St. Domingue in ballast (Clieu to Maurepas, March 30, 1747, A.N. Colonies C⁷ A 15; Larnage and Maillart to Maurepas, Feb. 10, 1746, C⁹ A 68; Laporte-Lalanne to Moras, Sept. 15, 1757, C⁹ A 100).

[1] Fifty-five or sixty per cent. of what? If brown sugar was bought in the colonies at 10 livres and sold in France at 28, insurance of the cost price would not be a very heavy article, but that of the sale price would. According to the 'Réponse au prétendu mémoire pour les colonies', quoted by M. Gaston Martin (op. cit., p. 396), the insurance was usually calculated on the former. That tendencious and abusive document is hardly to be relied upon for facts, but it seems to be right here. The Bordeaux Chamber of Commerce, trying to prove that the merchant received no profit on sugars, only charges insurance on the cost price in America (Arch. Gir. C 4263, f. 234).

[2] Of course freight rates and seamen's wages are alternatives not to be added to each other; the latter affected the shipowners who carried their own cargoes, the former was paid by the exporter of goods in other people's ships.

[3] Larnage and Maillart to Maurepas, Aug. 10, 1744, A.N. Colonies C⁹ A 64.

[4] Ibid.; Maurepas to Larnage and Maillart, Nov. 30, 1744, A.N. Colonies B 78; Moras to Givry, June 10, 1757, B 105; Le Mercier de la Rivière to Berryer, Jan. 20, 1760, C⁸ A 62; Berryer to La Rivière, March 29, B 111.

After the holder of money, the indigo-grower was the most favoured or the least injured by the war. The value of his produce was great in proportion to its bulk, and it could best afford the high freights. The importers of cargoes sought after it in order to make their returns in their own ships, instead of leaving their funds in the colony; the King's warships willingly carried it home upon freight. The indigo-planter could afford, if anybody could, to insist on receiving cash for his crop, and as he was not often in debt, the money was locked up in his possession.[1] There was also a particular reason for the high price of indigo in some parts of St. Domingue during the Seven Years War. The Governor fixed the rates of other kinds of produce above the real value; the market for indigo was left free; it could be had at current prices, and was therefore most in demand.[2] This prosperity tended to destroy itself. Indigo was overvalued in the colonies, and therefore answered no better than any other kind of cargo.[3] Some merchants thought it better to sell it in St. Eustatius, where the illusion of its superior advantage still kept up the price, than to send it to Europe, where it was as much a drug as any other West India goods.[4] At any rate, indigo was a resource for St. Domingue alone, for very little was made elsewhere in the French Empire.

After indigo, good white sugar was most saleable, then cotton; last of all came coffee and brown sugar. Nobody who received brown sugar in return for his goods could hope to carry back to Europe half the value of a full outward cargo in time of war. For this reason, the supercargoes sometimes refused to take anything but money, indigo, or white sugar in payment, and the colonial authorities had to oblige neutrals by special regulation to receive brown sugar in preference to other articles.[5] No

---

[1] Maillart to Maurepas, March 1, 1746, A.N. Colonies C⁹ A 64; Lambert to Moras, June 15, 1757, C⁹ A 100; Laporte-Lalanne to Moras, Dec. 15, ibid.; Kavanagh and Belloc to Bouteiller, Aug. 8, 1757, *Maria Joanna*, Lindeboom, H.C.A. 42/80.

[2] Ibid.; Pimont to Chauvel, quoted above (*Juffrow Maria*).

[3] Thus Messrs. van Marselis advised their correspondent at Port au Prince to get a return loading of white sugar if possible, for if the cargo consisted in brown sugar, three-quarters of their effects must be shipped in indigo, which was no longer profitable (J. and T. van Marselis to Danié, Dec. 19, 1757, *Juffrow Alida*, Kock, H.C.A. 42/73).

[4] Texier Brothers, Aux Cayes, to St. Martin Brothers and Angely, Feb. 12, 1758, *Vrouw Clara Magdalena*, van Houten, H.C.A. 42/99.

[5] Lambert to Moras, June 15, 1757, A.N. Colonies C⁹ A 100; Laporte-Lalanne to Moras, Jan. 7, 1758, C⁹ A 101; Lasserre, Port au Prince, to Klock, Dedel, and

doubt this also accounts for the French merchants' neglect of the trade of St. Louis and the southern quarter of St. Domingue, where brown sugar was one of the chief products. Intendant Maillart described thousands of hogsheads rotting away in that district; and as he had a plantation there, no doubt he was speaking from his own experience. The unpopularity of raw sugar with the exporters might have stimulated the planters to refine it; but the stimulus came at the wrong time, for they were least of all likely to possess the capital or credit for expensive new buildings and equipment in war-time, when they could barely meet their current expenses and the security of their property was impaired by the chance of invasion. In fact, they soon began to leave off producing this useless article, because they could not repair their losses of negroes during the war, and because they might as well save themselves the trouble.[1]

Both for the French merchant and for the planter who wanted freight, the widening gulf between the prices of imports and exports created a demand for more shipping.

If there was any advantage to be made by the carriage of goods from the West Indies to France, those who had ship-room to dispose of used it for themselves; only when nothing but loss could attend such an operation, were they willing to let out their space upon freight. On the whole, the impression to be gained from their correspondence and instructions is that they generally preferred taking goods on their own account, unless the rates of freight were very high indeed. For example, Jean White of Nantes was extremely angry with Captain Segretain of the *Providence* for sending home seventy hogsheads of sugar on freight in 1745, instead of loading her entirely on account of the owners; the high prices of West India goods would have made her a saving voyage.[2] Correspondents in the West Indies sometimes found it necessary to apologize if special circum-

Co., Jan. 13, 1758, *Juffrow Susanna*, Cornelis, H.C.A. 42/72; J. and T. van Marselis, Amsterdam, to Danié, quoted above.

[1] Samson, Cap François, to Maurepas, Dec. 20, 1744, A.N. Colonies C⁹ A 65; Larnage and Maillart to Maurepas, Feb. 24, 1746, C⁹ A 68; Larnage to Maurepas, Aug. 2, 1746, C⁹ A 68; Maillart to Maurepas, Nov. 20, 1746, C⁹ A 69; Chastenoye to Maurepas, Feb. 10, 1748, C⁹ A 72; Vaudreuil and Laporte-Lalanne to Machault, Aug. 27, 1756, C⁹ A 99; Bart and Laporte-Lalanne to Moras, Sept. 20, 1757, C⁹ A 100; Laporte-Lalanne to Moras, Oct. 2, 1757, ibid.

[2] White to Segretain, July 20 and Nov. 17, 1745, *Postillon*, H.C.A. 32/143; Bouwer and son to Beauchamp, Feb. 10, 1758, *Resolutie*, Johannesz H.C.A. 42/91; Charet to Fougou, Nov. 12, 1757, *Vigilantie*, Paauw, H.C.A. 42/101.

stances had caused them to take goods on freight.[1] The planters often complained that those who wanted to send home produce on their own account were unable to find freight for it, because in time of war the shipowners preferred to buy goods and bring them home for themselves.[2] But there were exceptions, for of course the equilibrium between shippers and shipowners righted itself by an increase of the rate of freights. A certain elasticity was rendered possible by the choice between very bulky and very portable articles, so that the proceeds of an outward cargo would load anything from half to double the tonnage of the ship, according to the class of goods in which it was invested.

If the demand for shipping was not to be met by invoking the services of neutrals or even enemies, the difficulty could only be overcome in one of two ways: either the colonies must live on credit, or their imports must be reduced.

Credit was almost unobtainable. The merchant who sent out goods to the West Indies was not very well satisfied to leave a large part of his capital there until the peace, especially as it must consist in doubtful debts or in perishable goods. The goods which kept longest in tropical climates were exactly those which were easiest to carry away; the most liable to waste was that which was oftenest condemned to remain in the colony for months or years—namely brown sugar. Some methods were proposed, and perhaps used, for avoiding such waste. Those planters who had the good fortune to charter a ship, French or neutral, to take off their crops in the islands, might sometimes find that she would hold more than the goods they had ready for her. They therefore offered to borrow sugars from their neighbours who could not get freight, and repay the debt in kind out of their next year's crop. But while this arrangement might alleviate the difficulties of individuals, it had no effect upon the trade of the colony as a whole, and in most of the cases in which it was contemplated, white sugar, not brown, was in question. Besides, there appear to have been obstacles.[3]

---

[1] Texier Brothers, Aux Cayes, to St. Martin Brothers & Angely, Feb. 12, 1758, *Vrouw Clara Magdalena*, H.C.A. 42/99.

[2] Larnage and Maillart to Maurepas, Feb. 24, 1746, A.N. Colonies C⁹ A 68; Maillart to Maurepas, Feb. 10, 1747, C⁹ A 70.

[3] Michel, Luker and Wailsh, Nantes, to Shee and Michel, Leogane, Dec. 31, 1744, *Arnaldus and Johannes*, Kool, H.C.A. 42/23; Beudet and Boutin to Danié, Sept. 25, 1757, *Sta Maria*, Robyn, H.C.A. 42/80; Nolivos to Danié, March 7, 1758, *Resolutie*, Johannesz, H.C.A. 42/91.

Supercargoes were occasionally ordered to invest the proceeds of their sales in a good plantation, if they could not by any means send them home.[1] This form of involuntary investment seems to have been rare. More commonly, the European merchant had to resign himself to hiring a warehouse in the colony and leaving a part of his capital there until a peace or some lucky accident should furnish an opportunity of recovering it;[2] this probably accounts for the vast quantities of West India produce carried to France during the first years of peace.[3]

The merchant might leave his capital in the colonies in another form, that of debts owed by the planters. Indeed, he could hardly choose but do so, how great soever the diligence of his supercargoes, for the purchasers could not or would not pay in time. For some classes of goods, such as negroes, credit of eighteen months or two years for part of the sums due had become an established custom in both English and French islands. Whatever degree of delay might be tolerated as normal, happy was the factor who could depend upon receiving payment at the end of the agreed period. This inexactitude seems to have been almost universal in the tropical colonies. It was partly due to the laws which protected so many classes of

[1] Feuilherade, Instructions to Captain Dumas, July 28, 1757, *Les Six Frères*, Dumas, H.C.A. 32/243.

[2] Van Alphen and Dedel, Instructions to the supercargo, *Gertruy*, Lachonius, H.C.A. 42/68; Bouwer and son to Beauchamp, Feb. 10, 1758, *Resolutie*; Grou, Nantes, to Lory, Nov. 19, 1759, H.C.A. 32/257.

[3] Malvezin gives some striking figures for Bordeaux. The greatest importation of sugar before the war of 1744 was 33,724,000 pounds. In 1748 it had sunk to 16,339,000, but rose in the next two years to 37,397,000 and 42,700,000; in the two years after that, it was much lower. The spring upwards at the end of the next war is yet more remarkable. The importation had fallen to 3,417,000 in the last year of the war. In 1763, for some reason, it rose no farther than 9,910,000; perhaps the commerce of France could not immediately provide itself with shipping. But in 1764 it went up to 63,821,000, a figure which it did not approach again, in spite of the very rapid progress of the colonies, till 1768. The figures for indigo are more extraordinary still. This may at first sight be surprising, since indigo was the most in demand of the West India commodities and the easiest carried to Europe in war time. But there may be explanations. Indigo was one of the best articles to keep in the colony until a peace, because it was less liable to wastage than most; besides, a great deal of the indigo was sent home on the King's warships, and would therefore be landed at Brest, not at Bordeaux, so that Malvezin's figures do not represent all the indigo that came home on account of Bordeaux merchants in war time. Further, though indigo might be the favourite form of return cargo from the West Indies, it was just as liable to be captured on the way home as anything else, and this interception of the homeward ships is what in the first place accounts for the reduction of imports into Bordeaux (Th. Malvezin, *Histoire du commerce de Bordeaux*, iii. 303–4).

valuables as real property, and interposed difficulties in the way of their sale or distraint; partly to the prevalent scarcity of money which limited the number of possible buyers of goods distrained for debt, and the prices they were likely to give; and partly to the wars, which upset the never very carefully balanced budgets of the planters and made them really incapable of paying even for their current supplies. Many were the entreaties which the merchants of Europe addressed to their correspondents upon this head: to be careful, in crediting purchasers, to choose only those of clear estate and good reputation, and to be diligent in exacting payment at the appointed times. Good purchasers at moderate prices were to be preferred to people of uncertain credit who would offer more; but, as one factor of St. Domingue replied, a reduction of the price could neither secure the debt nor render it more likely to be paid at once, when nobody in the community had any money.[1] The excuses of the factors were no less various or frequent. The officials, and any others who could protect themselves from prosecution, were particularly remiss in the performance of their engagements. 'As you will see', wrote some merchants of Léogane to their correspondents in Amsterdam, 'these returns are, the greatest part, in the hands of people in office, whose will and conveniency must be waited, and whom we cannot sue at law.'[2] Even the ordinary planter was well enough protected, not only by the customs of the colony, but by special legislation arising out of the war. If he had not been so, many of the plantations must have changed hands and fallen into those of the merchants of France, who gave out that it was indifferent to the national interest whether the present owners remained in possession.[3]

When the carriage of produce to Europe was so unprofitable as to cause the merchants to prefer money, debtors and creditors began to quarrel in both Martinique and St. Domingue over the manner of paying old debts. The creditors wished to take advantage of the terms of the obligations, which stated in money the sums due, and to exact payment in cash. The debtors, who could not have raised the cash, argued that the traffic of the colonies was really an exchange of goods against

[1] Kavanagh and Belloc to Bouteiller and son, Aug. 8, 1757, *Maria Joanna*, Lindeboom, H.C.A. 42/80.

[2] Dugué, Roullier and Co., Léogane, to P. and S. Locquet, Amsterdam, Jan. 28, 1758, *Vreede*, Boon, H.C.A. 42/102.

[3] Larnage and Maillart to Maurepas, April 21, 1745, A.N. Colonies C⁹ A 66.

goods, and that the money in which the prices were rated was only money of account. The local courts usually favoured the debtors, and decided that except when a payment in cash was stipulated, the calculation in money had no importance and the debt was payable in goods. Maurepas approved of these decisions. The supercargoes could still insist upon payments of cash in the future, if they were strong enough to make the planters buy on those terms; what would happen then was not very clear to Maurepas, who contented himself with vaguely surmising that the creditors would not long find their account in it. In fact the merchants forced the planters to pay cash, and consequently the *Conseil Supérieur* of Port au Prince revived at the beginning of the Seven Years War an ordinance of 1720 which commanded payments to be made and received two-thirds in cash and one-third in goods.[1]

The debtors tried to advance another step, and to turn all the disadvantage of the situation upon the merchants. Since they could not find freight for their produce, they might as well get rid of it in payment of their old debts.[2] This need not have been a grievance to the creditor; the current price of sugars was chiefly determined by the difficulty of exporting it off the islands, so that if he was embarrassed by having to receive his due when he could not make much use of it, he ought to have been compensated by the low rate at which the produce was valued. Yet when there was no chance of exporting the article, any price at which it could be estimated must be too high. Accordingly, the agents of some French creditors refused the proffered payment. Besides, the debtors did not propose anything so equitable; they wished to have their goods valued for this purpose at an artificially high rate. The courts of Martinique supported them in the war of 1744. That of the southern quarter of St. Domingue would not order indigo to be received at its peace-time valuation, but compromised by letting it pass at the price current at Léogane; this was a concession, because the indigo of Léogane was better than that of St. Louis, and therefore worth more. The court of the western quarter decided that the debtors who had neglected to pay goods when it would

[1] Laporte-Lalanne to Machault, Jan. 20, 1756, A.N. Colonies C⁹ A 99.
[2] The owners of plantations, or the creditors in Europe, sometimes complained that their agents grasped too eagerly this opportunity of wiping off debts within the colony, to the neglect of remittances which were badly wanted at home (Beudet to Danié, Feb. 26, 1758, *Resolutie*, Johannesz, H.C.A. 42/91).

have been to the creditor's advantage to receive them, should be prohibited from unloading them upon him when it was not. Maurepas tentatively approved this decision.

A stalemate was thus established between creditor and debtor for the duration of the war. The former could not demand payment in money, unless he should in future stipulate it when he made his bargain; the latter could not insist on paying in goods unless the creditor should consent to receive them. Of course he would consent, if the goods were of an acceptable kind, but there was a deadlock where they were not. The only remedy was patience—to secure the debt, charge interest, and wait for the day when there would once more be enough shipping to export brown sugar and coffee at a reasonable freight. This deadlock was the most equitable settlement of the difficulty. If the debtors had insisted on paying in war-time at a peace-time valuation, they would have halved the capital of their creditors; if the creditors had insisted on money, or money's worth at current prices, they would have doubled the burden of the debtors. Admittedly this virtual moratorium put a stop to the collection of old debts during the war, but that was no great hardship to the creditor, who could hardly have brought his effects to France if he had recovered them.[1] It only applied to old debts contracted before the war; the merchants had no interest in letting the planters fall behindhand with their current debts, and the Government supported their efforts to enforce greater punctuality.

I have discussed these difficulties in terms of planter and merchant, which are most appropriate to St. Domingue. In Martinique the situation was not essentially complicated by the intermediacy of the *commissionnaires*, or resident merchants.[2] In so far as they bought and sold on their own account, they might, by their command of money, render cash transactions somewhat commoner than at St. Domingue. On the other hand they made collection of debts a little harder. In St. Domingue the planter often owed directly to the supercargo or the French merchant. Most of the resident merchants of the island really were *commissionnaires* in the literal sense of the term, acting as factors or agents, without financial responsibility of their own though

---

[1] Larnage and Maillart to Maurepas, April 21, 1745, A.N. Colonies C⁹ A 66; Maurepas to Larnage and Maillart, Jan. 24, 1746, B 83; to Ranché, Nov. 11, 1744, B 78.　　　　[2] *V. supra*, p. 290.

they sometimes took debts to themselves in return for a special commission. The Martinique *commissionnaires*, on the other hand, had partly lost their original function and set up for themselves; they incurred the debt to the French merchant, and the planter incurred another to them. The French merchant's immediate security for his debt was therefore no more than the estate of the *commissionnaire*, which might consist only in credits on the planters. The difficulty of liquidation was exactly doubled, and perhaps this is why, as Intendant Hurson suggested, the merchants of France preferred the trade of St. Domingue to that of the Windward Islands.[1]

The exporters of goods to the colonies during the war were thus forced to give a sort of involuntary credit, which helped the planters to subsist. There was no other kind of credit upon which they could live. The financial relations of the planters and merchants seem to have been less developed in the French than in the English colonies—for instance, there were parts of St. Domingue where bills of exchange were practically unknown and could not be negotiated.[2] The reason of this was presumably the greater simplicity with which the trade was organized in the French colonies. There was little of that system of financial undertakings by which the English planter sent home his crop on his own account and drew bills upon his factor for what he supposed it would fetch. This system often developed, sometimes against the will of one or even both parties, into a state of affairs in which the overdrawn planter was entirely financed by capital from London. The same state of affairs sometimes existed in the French colonies, but I do not think it was common except among absentees, who were rarer in the French than in the English islands. Thus the English planter was already provided with a correspondent in Europe who was accustomed to being in advance for him, and could probably be driven a little farther in that direction, if the losses and disappointments of war required it. The French system had not the same elasticity, nor, perhaps, were the available capital resources so great.

Even if the French colonies had been much more familiar with the system of bills of exchange, the war would have dis-

---

[1] *Mémoire* of Hurson, July 26, 1759, A.N. Colonies C⁸ B 22.
[2] Rouvellette to de Windt, June 27, 1757, *Le Roy Indien*, Anderson, H.C.A. 42/92; see also Tramond, *Revue de l'histoire des colonies*, xv. 168.

organized it. The whole community was at straits for a method of remitting to the outside world. If the prices of West India produce had been very advantageous in the European market, those whose property had arrived safe would have disposed of a surplus on which they could have drawn bills, and the colonies could have supported themselves to some extent out of these funds. But it is far from certain that the trade yielded such a profit in time of war.

'You remember', wrote the Bordeaux Chamber of Commerce to its deputy in Paris, 'that in the last war several colonists agreed in Paris and the seaports to sell their raw sugars at six livres a hundred-weight in the colonies, and that those merchants who had their sugars brought home during the war made nothing by it; for you must also remember that several commission merchants in the sea-ports abandoned sugars for the payment of duties and expenses, or, which is the same thing, refused to receive the consignment of them.'[1]

The same Chamber estimated that the net sales of brown sugars after deduction of all costs and duties would be no more than 6 livres a hundredweight—not a very high price for a planter who had to pay more than double the ordinary rate for his stores and victuals. This calculation was not very far wide of the mark—a year after it was made, the gross sales of raw sugar were no higher than it stated them, and the rates of insurance and freight had increased considerably.[2] In the same sense, a

---

[1] Directors to Castaing, June 26, 1756, Arch. Gir. C 4263, f. 236. Most of the written information on this subject consists of fictitious and arbitrary calculations, designed to soften the hearts of tax-collectors—the very worst kind of evidence.

[2] Bordeaux to Nantes, June 26, 1756, Arch. Gir. C 4263, f. 234; Nantes to Bordeaux, July 21, 1756, C 4319, no. 7. Unfortunately I know of no series of prices current for sugar in France during these years. The nearest thing is the valuations for the payment of the duty of *domaine d'occident*, but the rates given are far too low, as will appear from a comparison with such prices current as I have been able to find elsewhere; for example, the valuations of 1757, given below, are much lower than the Bordeaux prices given in letters of June 1757—refined sugars 57 to 68 livres, *communes* 52 to 57, raw 33 (Guadeloupe) to 45 (Leogane); there is an even greater discrepancy in the first half of 1762, when raw sugars were quoted at 55 to 63 livres. These discrepancies can be accounted for partly by the fact that the *domaine* valuations deducted a fifth from the prices, presumably for payment of duties, and partly by the way in which the rates were fixed. There was a tug of war between the Farmers-General, who received the taxes, and the Chambers of Commerce, which argued that no tax was due where no profit was made, and failing the acceptance of that view, set themselves to underestimate wherever they could. However, I give the incomplete figures from the archives of the Bordeaux Chamber (Arch. Gir. C 4404), for what they are worth. They are partly confirmed by some figures furnished by a London merchant to George Chalmers in 1791

mémoire presented to Machault on behalf of the colonies stated that in the war of 1744 'effects shipped to France sometimes did not suffice to pay the excessive charges'; the reply of the Nantes merchants denied it, but not very convincingly.[1]

It appears at any rate that few merchants and still fewer planters were able to draw bills on France for considerable sums, because few could be certain of remitting goods to cover such bills, or dispose of credits already lodged in Europe. Those who had good bills to dispose of, knew how to exploit the planters' eagerness for them. They had only to 'try the merchants who are teased for remittances by their correspondents in France, and the planters who have wives and children in France to support'.[2] Those who gave bills as a commercial speculation and took upon themselves the risk of remitting produce, nearly always came to grief. The celebrated Father

(C.O. 318/1). He gives the prices of brown sugars at Bordeaux in 1758–60; in 1758 it varied between 20 and 30 livres, in 1759 between 22 and 32, and in 1760 between 24 and 33.

	Raw sugar per cwt.		White refined sugar per cwt.		Clayed sugar per cwt.		Indigo per lb.		Coffee per lb.	
	livres	sous	livres	sous	livres	sous	livres	sous	sous	deniers
1741 (1st half)	18	14	38	4	29	15	3	9	9	—
(2nd half)	17	4	37	15	28	—	3	3	8	—
1742 (first)	17	—	36	4	27	—	3	—	8	—
(second)	16	10	36	4	26	10	2	10	8	—
1743 (first)	17	5	35	11	27	10	2	11	8	—
(second)	19	5	39	12	30	5	2	10	8	6
1744 (first)	18	7	36	3	29	—	2	8	8	—
(second)	19	—	36	11	29	5	2	8	10	—
1745 (first)	19	10	38	17	29	7	2	8	10	—
(second)	20	10	39	—	30	3	2	10	10	6
1746	—	—	—	—	—	—	—	—	—	—
1747 (second)	22	—	39	—	32	10	2	10	13	—
1748 (second)	18	—	38	—	29	—	2	10	12	—
1749 (first)	19	—	38	9	29	10	2	17	13	—
1750 (first)	15	—	36	—	25	—	2	15	11	—
(second)	13	14	35	10	25	12	3	6	12	6
1751 (first)	13	18	37	8	25	12	3	16	12	6
(second)	14	10	40	—	26	—	4	—	12	—
1752 (first)	14	15	41	—	25	10	5	—	12	—
1753 (first)	14	10	41	—	24	—	4	5	12	—
1754 (first)	14	10	45	—	24	—	4	10	12	—
(second)	16	—	48	—	27	10	6	—	11	—
1755 (first)	22	—	48	—	32	—	8	—	11	—
1756 (first)	19	10	48	—	30	—	6	10	11	—
(second)	21	10	48	—	32	—	6	10	12	—
1757 (first)	21	10	48	—	32	—	7	—	12	—
(second)	22	—	48	—	32	—	6	10	11	—
1758	—	—	—	—	—	—	—	—	—	—
1759 (first)	24	—	52	—	35	—	5	5	10	—
1760 (second)	28	—	64	—	40	—	4	—	10	—
1761 (first)	25	—	64	—	36	—	3	10	9	—
1762 (first)	25	—	61	—	40	—	3	17	9	9
(second)	27	—	64	—	40	—	3	19	9	9
1763 (second)	25	—	56	—	35	—	4	—	10	—
1764 (first)	23	10	56	—	35	—	4	3	10	—

[1] Quoted by Gaston Martin, *L'Ère des négriers*, p. 396.
[2] Nolivos to Danié, March 7, 1758, *Resolutie*.

Lavalette furnished the occasion of the downfall of the French Jesuits by this kind of experiment. He drew bills on France and Holland, and hoped to secure them by sending home sugars, but a long run of losses reduced him and his Order to bankruptcy.[1]

In fact the French Government alone possessed enough credit in Europe to pay bills of exchange on a large scale. Maillart proposed in 1740 that it should turn an honest penny in case of a war, by offering bills to planters who were in a hurry to remit, at the high rate of 50 per cent. exchange, and covering them by remittances of sugar collected cheaply in payment of taxes. Maurepas discouraged this scheme, because he feared that the Caisse de la Marine could not stand such a burden.[2] When the colonists of Martinique could not dispose of their crops for want of shipping in the Seven Years War, they could not subsist without credit, so Le Mercier de la Rivière conceived the idea of supporting the colony on Government bills of exchange—for that is what his schemes amounted to, as Berryer indignantly pointed out. La Rivière was no luckier than Lavalette, with whom he seems to have had some sort of a partnership. The sugars which he remitted on the Government's account were just as liable to capture as those of the planters and merchants. Berryer was left to pay the bills at home. Unfortunately, this was the worst possible time to put an additional strain upon the finances of the King of France; an unauthorized extension of Government credit could least of all be tolerated at the height of a calamitous war. Berryer could not even pay the bills which La Rivière's predecessor had drawn on him for the first siege of Martinique. He stopped payment on all colonial bills in the autumn of 1759. The credit of Government paper was ruined, and La Rivière could not even negotiate the few bills which the Minister still allowed him to draw—let alone subsist the planters in this way. Fortunately the extremity of the crisis was past; Martinique was able once more to import and export pretty freely without such a stretch of credit.[3]

For all these reasons the unbalanced equilibrium between the

[1] Rochemonteix, *Le Père Antoine Lavalette à la Martinique*, chaps. 5 and 6.
[2] Maillart to Maurepas, Nov. 28, 1740, A.N. Colonies C⁹ A 53; Maurepas to Maillart, Feb. 25 and Aug. 10, 1741, B 72.
[3] La Rivière to Berryer, Nov. 16, 1759, and Jan. 20, 1760, C⁸ A 61; Beauharnois and La Rivière to Berryer, Feb. 13, 1760, ibid.; Berryer to La Rivière, Aug. 12, 1759, B 109; May 20, 1760, B 111.

prices of European goods and of island produce could not be righted by a voluntary extension of credit to tide the planters over the war. As long as they could buy on credit, their inability to return the whole proceeds of outward cargoes immediately was not of much importance. But so far from giving longer credit, the merchants of France were more anxious than ever to have their debts paid promptly. They persuaded Maurepas to give orders for this purpose. He issued an edict on the manner of arrest for debt. Hitherto, the person of a planter had been liable to seizure for a debt contracted to a supercargo, only so long as the ship remained in port; after her departure, gentler and less effective methods were to be employed. Maurepas extended the period for which arrest could be made. Though Caylus boasted of the promptitude of the people of Martinique to comply with the Minister's desire, it is impossible that they can all have done so; for the supercargoes could only have received and shipped these effects if they were paid in money, indigo, or white sugar.[1] The convoy system itself made it still more difficult to collect debts in a hurry; for so many cargoes arrived in the islands at once, that they could not all find a quick sale or a ready payment. Moreover, this punctuality which was enjoined upon the debtors produced a result which the merchants of France cannot have liked: the planters, fearing that for once they would get into trouble if they fell behindhand with their payments, bought no more than they could afford, and the price of European goods in the colonies became a little harder to keep up.[2]

There was only one other way in which the balance could be restored between the inward and outward cargoes: by reducing the size and value of the former. This was only too often done, in one of two forms. A ship which had sold her cargo for more sugar than she could hold, would return on the next voyage wholly or partly in ballast, so as to collect the effects of the original cargo and leave none behind her a second time. Or else the French merchant would send out on each voyage a cargo only just large enough to load his vessel back—another advantage was that a small cargo took a shorter time to sell and

[1] Maurepas to Larnage, June 11, 1745, A.N. Colonies B 81; Caylus to Maurepas, March 26, 1746, C⁸ A 56.

[2] Samson to Maurepas, Dec. 14, 1745, C⁹ A 67; Maillart to Maurepas, March 1, 1746, vol. 69.

the ship would the sooner be ready to return with convoy. There were frequent complaints of both these practices, especially of the former. Thus the quantity of victuals and manufactures which arrived at the French colonies in time of war depended, not directly on the tonnage of the shipping which frequented the trade, but on the value of the return cargoes which that tonnage could carry back to France. Therefore the number of vessels in the colonial navigation, often vaunted by the French merchants as a proof of their ability to carry on the trade by themselves, was no evidence of their intention to keep the colonies adequately supplied.[1]

This reduction of the imports from Europe may not have been quite so injurious to the colonists as it was represented to be. Their purchasing power had been severely reduced by the depreciation of their crops, and some of them were obliged to forgo the luxuries or even the common comforts of life which they had enjoyed in the time of peace. Some of them gave up imported flour and wine, and lived on country provisions like their negroes; indeed, if all had had the prudence to plant enough of these root crops, as the Government urged them to do, the problem of supplies would hardly have been so serious as it became. But the majority of white planters declined to change their diet before extreme necessity drove them to it. They suggested that it would injure their health, but perhaps racial snobbery was the real reason. They therefore planted only enough ground provisions for their negroes.[2]

The officials in the colonies sometimes expressed the fear that the planters would lose the habit of luxury altogether, and that the colonial trade would on that account become less valuable to the manufacturers and merchants of France. The colonists even alleged this as a reason for permitting the introduction of neutral ships during the war. The merchants of France, they said, would gain more by the continuance of the planters in their present standards of life than by insisting on a cramping monopoly of their trade in time of war.[3] They might have spared their surmises and their reasonings. The consumption

---

[1] Larnage and Maillart to Maurepas, Feb. 10, 1746, C⁹ A 68; Maillart to Maurepas, Feb. 15, 1748, C⁹ A 73; Ranché to Maurepas, Dec. 10, 1746, C⁸ A 57.

[2] Bart and Élias to Berryer, Feb. 11, 1760, A.N. Colonies C⁹ A 105; Peyrac to Berryer, March 22, 1760, vol. 106; Tramond, op. cit., p. 525.

[3] Clieu to Maurepas, Jan. 8, 1747, C⁷ A 15; Samson to Maurepas, Dec. 14, 1745, C⁹ A 67; Vaudreuil and Samson to Maurepas, Feb. 1, 1748, vol. 74.

of European goods in the colonies continued to increase after each war, though perhaps the momentary disuse of certain habits of life may account in part—but only in part—for the glut of which the merchants always complained for a year or two after the conclusion of each treaty of peace.

Thus the shortage of shipping helped to cause a decrease of production on the one hand and of imports on the other. There may have been other reasons for this decline of trade, but they were less easily controlled, while the need of ships could be relieved, as it seemed, by a stroke of the Minister's pen.

§ ii. *The Admission of Foreign Traders in the War of 1744*

For the first year of the war Maurepas could not organize any regular system of defence for the colonial trade. His inability to provide for this service does not seem to have distressed him so much as it ought; he admitted very freely that although the colonies themselves were presumably safe, the trade could not but suffer from the war. A year or two later he told Ranché that there was no question of maintaining the remarkable progress which the commerce of the Windward Islands had made in the last years of peace; the most that could be expected was to keep them supplied with victuals, and to furnish shipping to take off their crops.[1] Even this, however, he could not assure before the institution of the convoy system, for which he could spare neither ships nor money at first. He therefore resorted for a moment to a method which was quite contrary to the traditional policy of the French Government since Colbert's day; he issued three passports for neutral ships to trade to the French colonies.

France had yielded to the same necessity in the wars of Louis XIV, but always with reluctance. The great point of Colbert's colonial system was to drive the Dutch out of the trade between France and her colonies. Every relapse into dependence upon these officious carriers—themselves sometimes the enemies of the State—was an admission of defeat and entailed disagreeable consequences. Where the Dutch came, they stayed. Incredible efforts were required to dislodge them. They formed correspondences which enabled them to carry on the trade in secret when they could no longer do so with official

---

[1] Maurepas to Larnage, March 17, 1744, A.N. Colonies B 78; to Ranché, Aug. 11, 1746, B 83.

sanction; and in the brief periods for which their presence was permitted, they overstocked the markets so as to make them valueless to the regular French traders during the first year or two of peace.[1]

After the Treaty of Utrecht, the Government did its best to discourage the foreign interloper, regardless of the cries of the colonists, which even culminated in a revolt at Martinique.[2] The Dutch continued, however, to introduce dry goods and slaves from St. Eustatius and Curaçao. The English smuggler became an even greater nuisance—or blessing—to the colonies than the Dutch; for as the farmers and lumbermen of North America extended their production, they began to frequent the French markets in the West Indies in order to sell what the English islands could not consume. Besides, they took off the by-products of sugar, for which the French planters could not else have found a market. Upon certain emergencies such as fires and hurricanes, Maurepas permitted the introduction of foreign North America goods into some of the islands, but always found it attended with such intolerable abuses that he made up his mind not to repeat it. Other goods were imported besides those necessaries of life which were meant to be supplied by this method, and the finer West India products—sugars, indigo, and cotton—were exported instead of being reserved, as they should have been, for the mother country (the Government only meant to allow rum and molasses to be disposed of in this way). For these reasons, Maurepas and his successors refused to listen, in times of peace, to the most vehement demonstrations of the necessity of foreign mules and horses, or the most beneficent schemes for favouring the distilleries by forcing the New Englanders to take a certain proportion of rum with their molasses.[3] Besides the petty smuggler from North America, whose little sloops and schooners were hardly large enough to do great mischief unless they came in swarms, the English slave-traders haunted the least developed and worst guarded parts of the French colonies.

This trade, however salutary and indeed necessary to the

---

[1] May, *Histoire économique de la Martinique*, pp. 140–2.

[2] May, op. cit., pp. 143–6.

[3] Maurepas to Caylus, Dec. 10, 1746, A.N. Colonies B 83; Caylus to Rouillé, Oct. 6, 1749, C⁸ A 58; Rouillé to Conflans and Maillart, Dec. 4, 1749, B 89; to Caylus and Ranché, Jan. 28, 1750, B 91; Roma, *mémoire* on the illicit trade of Guadeloupe, Nov. 23, 1754, C⁷ A 17; A.E. Mém. et Doc. Espagne, 80, ff. 78–103.

development of the French plantations, aroused violent complaints from interested parties in France. The slavers of Nantes, the East India, linen, and milling interests, the fishermen of Cape Breton, the lumbermen of Canada, all had a word to say against the dilution of the colonial monopoly. Maurepas incessantly urged Larnage to enforce the penalties against smuggling, and Larnage replied again and again that they were so disproportionately heavy that he could never get anybody to bring forward evidence, nor induce any court to condemn.[1] The trade still went on. New England vessels put into French West India ports, in danger of foundering from fictitious leaks or quite disabled by imaginary cracks in their masts. The very merchant captains who cried loudest against the interlopers when they were at home in France, complaisantly certified the necessity of a number of illusory repairs, whose cost could only be defrayed by selling the cargo. Indeed, these captains themselves engaged in the illicit trade, sending their ships' boats to the Dutch islands for dry goods which they sold to the planters as part of their own cargoes. Even those branches of foreign trade which were genuinely patronized by the Government—such as the intercourse with the Spanish West Indies—were made the channels of all kinds of unintended imports and exports.[2]

It was the help of foreigners—neutrals and even enemies—that Maurepas and his successors were finally obliged to seek in time of war; but their conversion to such an unorthodox measure was tentative, compunctious, and hindered by the resistance of the merchants of France.

The three passports which Maurepas issued for neutral ships at the end of 1744 were not the first-fruits of a consistent policy; perhaps they were extorted from him by court favour or some other kind of special influence. Before he announced them to the Governors of the colonies, he had made up his mind that they were not to be repeated. The reason he gave for them was the difficulty of procuring Irish beef for export to the islands;

---

[1] Chamber of Commerce of Guienne, Minutes of Jan. 15, Feb. 5, March 5, 1739, July 14, 1740, Arch. Gir. C 4254, ff. 46, 47, 49, 74; Larnage and Maillart to Maurepas, July 2 and 4, Dec. 1, 1739, A.N. Colonies C⁹ A 50; Maurepas to Larnage and Maillart, April 19, 1740, B 70.

[2] Roze to Maurepas, June 11, 1745, A.N. Colonies C⁸ A 56; Poinsable to Maurepas, Jan. 8, 1744, ibid.; Ranché to Maurepas, June 8, 1745, ibid.; Roma, *mémoire* quoted above.

soon after they were issued, the trade between France and Ireland was reopened, and the case for admitting neutrals into the French colonies ceased to exist, in his opinion. He might grant a few more for the transport of ammunition, but in principle he should reserve the trade of the colonies for the shipping of France so long as it was able to carry the necessary supplies. The losses which the French traders had suffered in the first months of the war, before he had succeeded in providing for their protection, entitled them to the compensation of security against foreign rivals.[1]

To the colonists, Maurepas's logic must have appeared doubtful; if the French shipping had been diminished by captures, that was a cause, a proof, or an aggravation of its insufficiency to supply the needs of the islands, not an additional reason for insisting on the monopoly. However, Maurepas remained faithful to his principle that the sufferings of the French merchants must be rewarded by the increased profits and freights which the maintenance of that monopoly would presumably entail.

This attitude was of course entirely congenial to the merchants. As soon as the Chambers of Commerce got wind of the proposed issue of passports to neutrals, they concerted an agitation against it. Bordeaux demonstrated that French ship-owners could not hope to compete with Dutchmen whose expenses of insurance and seamen's wages were only half as heavy. Moreover, the neutrals once admitted into this trade would find ways of continuing it after the war, whatever efforts the Government might make to drive them out of it. (This indeed was only too true: Maurepas had to rebuke Caylus for allowing Dutch traders to return to the French colonies after the peace of 1748 on the pretext of recovering their debts—an excuse which they had used from time immemorial in order to maintain a position acquired by favour of a temporary emergency.)[2] La Rochelle added that the neutrals would ruin

---

[1] Maurepas to Champigny and Ranché, Nov. 30, 1744, A.N. Colonies B 78; to Larnage and Maillart, Dec. 9, 1744, ibid. See also the *mémoire* of 1745 in A.E. Mém. et Doc. France, 2007, ff. 133 et seqq., which recommends the admission of neutrals only as a temporary expedient until the navy can give the trade adequate protection.

[2] Maurepas to Caylus, March 6, 1749, A.N. Colonies B 87. For an example of the way in which the Dutch tried to keep the door permanently open, see the instruction of Messrs. L. André & Co. of Rotterdam to Messrs. Pasquier of Port au Prince, Dec. 24, 1757 (intercepted, in Adm. 1/235). If there were any goods of the outward cargo unsold when the ship set sail from the colony, Messrs.

both the manufactures of France and the re-export trade in French colonial produce; the Chamber appealed to the national honour and claimed that the shipping of France was quite able to furnish the colonies with all they wanted, if only the navy would protect it.[1]

Maurepas seems to have accepted the argument that the sufficiency of French shipping depended on proper naval protection, for soon after he had resolved upon the exclusion of neutrals he instituted his system of convoys. As he did not foresee the imperfections and breakdown of this system, he naturally hoped that it would resolve all difficulties and render foreign help unnecessary.[2] In principle he was right. The reason why England was not forced to suspend the Navigation Acts in these wars, as she had sometimes done in the past, was the efficient protection of her trade by her navy.[3] If Maurepas's system of convoys had succeeded, the French Empire would hardly have needed the neutrals.

He issued no more neutral passports after the first three. The Governors and Intendants presumed to doubt the wisdom of his abstention. They withdrew their first criticisms when they heard that he meant to provide for the protection of French trade; but at the end of the war, when the system of convoys had failed, they openly told him it was a pity that the French merchants had resisted the admission of neutrals. Those merchants would have saved themselves great losses (though nobody explained how they would have employed their capital, their ships, and what sailors the navy had left them). The cultivation of the West India colonies would have been maintained and extended, instead of declining for want of a market. The ordinary mortality of negroes would at least have been replaced (the French slave trade had been almost annihilated during the

Pasquier were to make a formal declaration that some of Messrs. André's effects could not be returned to them by their ship, 'which may procure us a permission for another such ship; if it does no good, at least it can do no harm'.

[1] Chamber of Commerce of Guienne, circular letter to other Chambers, Dec. 11, 1744, Arch. Gir. C 4263, f. 9; La Rochelle, *mémoire* of merchants to the Chamber of Commerce, Dec. 22, 1744, C 4312, no. 71.

[2] Maurepas to Ranché, Feb. 10 and June 13, 1745, A.N. Colonies B 81.

[3] In April 1747 the London merchants threatened to apply to Parliament for the suspension of the Acts, but this may have been mere rhetoric (Admiralty Minutes, April 14, 1747, Adm. 3/57). The Acts had been suspended, to all intents and purposes, in 1665 and 1672. In later wars only those clauses were relaxed which obliged English shipowners to employ a certain proportion of English seamen.

war by the risks in Africa and the West Indies, and by the fall of the price of negroes, whose value was in some degree determined by the price of the crops they were to make). The planters' standards of living would have been preserved—in fact, the economic machine of the French colonies would have remained in working order. Some planters might have gone farther; the high price of their produce might have enabled them to remit cash or Dutch bills to France in payment of their debts. The neutrals could thus have been used for correcting the rate of exchange, which was usually against the colonies. This plan of keeping the colonial trade in cold storage during the war was not only repugnant to most people's sense of mercantile patriotism, but also based on too sanguine a view of the planters' dispositions. History may afford some examples of colonial communities which cheerfully devoted the proceeds of an interloping trade to the payment of their lawful debts, but not one which gave up all connexion with the interloper upon the signature of a treaty of peace.[1]

It was only natural that the Governors and Intendants should feel the distresses of the colonists more strongly, and appreciate the merits of the mercantile system less than the Minister at Versailles. Most of them had acquired estates in the islands during their terms of office. Maillart had one near St. Louis, which perhaps accounts for his peculiar susceptibility to the woes of that quarter; Chastenoye had a plantation, and Vaudreuil and Laporte-Lalanne dealt largely in sugars. Champigny certainly had estates in Martinique, and his son possessed one in Guadeloupe. Caylus had interests in the Neutral Islands; Givry was accused of owning three large plantations, and pleaded guilty to one small one. Le Vassor de la Touche came of a planting family and inherited an estate in Martinique, so that his appointment as Governor was a solecism according to the strict tradition of the French Colonial Office. Besides these interests, which naturally moved the rulers of the colonies to sympathy with their subjects, other advantages accrued to them from the introduction of neutrals.

There were five kinds of foreign trade to the French colonies

[1] Larnage and Maillart to Maurepas, April 20, 1745, A.N. Colonies C⁹ A 66; Feb. 10, 1746, vol. 68; Chastenoye to Maurepas, Feb. 10, 1748, vol. 72; Maillart to Maurepas, Feb. 15, vol. 73; Caylus to Maurepas, Jan. 15, 1748, C⁸ A 58; Vaudreuil and Laporte-Lalanne to Machault, Oct. 20, 1756, C⁹ A 99; Bart and Laporte-Lalanne to Moras, Sept. 20, 1757, C⁹ A 100.

in time of war. At one end of the scale were the smugglers, who received no countenance from anybody and almost ceased to exist for the time being, because it became so easy to obtain a lawful entry. At the other end were the neutral ships which obtained passports from the King of France. Of these there were only three during the war of 1744. The merchants of Nantes who received them, passed them on to Francis Libault of Amsterdam. He sent out three ships to St. Domingue. Two of these were taken by the English and condemned as prize at New York, but were restored on appeal.[1] Besides these, there were the neutrals from Europe without permits, the neutrals from the Dutch and Danish islands in the West Indies, and the Flags of Truce, French and English.

Not many Dutch ships ventured during this war to come from Europe to the French colonies without first obtaining some authority to do so. Libault of Amsterdam, not content with the three passports which he obtained from Maurepas, sent out three more vessels which contrived to put into Martinique on the pretext of disability to continue their voyages, and got themselves compelled to sell their cargoes there. These vessels are the only ones of which I have found mention in the English Admiralty records,[2] but there were others which presumably escaped capture.

This trade was most repugnant to Maurepas's sense of propriety. He could tolerate the admission of small vessels from St. Eustatius and Curaçao, but the Dutch from Europe ought never to be allowed to trade until the resources of those islands had been exhausted. He reproached Maillart for merely turning away such a ship, instead of confiscating her for breaking the laws of France by entering a French colonial port without real necessity.[3] As he pointed out to Caylus and Ranché on a later incident of the same kind, the scarcity of victuals could be no excuse for such an omission, for the cargo would have

---

[1] *Arnaldus and Johannes*, Kool, H.C.A. 42/23; *Maria Elizabeth*, van der Kroon, H.C.A. 42/40.

[2] The *Endraght*, Edsert de Graaff, H.C.A. 32/108; the *Vryheid*, Vos, H.C.A. 42/50. There was also the *Amstel*, which probably got home safe. There may be more ships of this kind in the Prize Papers (H.C.A. 32), of which I have only looked at certain bundles, but I am sure there are none in the Prize Appeals Papers (H.C.A. 42), of which I have examined every bundle for these two wars.

[3] Maurepas to Maillart, Nov. 15, 1747, A.N. Colonies B 85; to Clieu and Marin, June 8, 1746, vol. 83; Maillart took the hint and confiscated the next vessel which appeared from Holland on a like errand.

been just as certainly brought to market by confiscation as by a free admission.[1] At the end of the war he had to deal with a complicated fraud from Martinique. A Dutch ship named the *Young Peter and Adrian* sailed from Rotterdam to Martinique, where she suffered a collusive confiscation for illicit trade. Most of her cargo was withheld from public sale—that is to say, it was presumably disposed of as if she had been an ordinary licensed trader—and the ship herself was 'bought' at an upset price by somebody concerned in her, who renamed her the *Société*, got her a cargo of produce, and dispatched her for Bordeaux. Her real destination seems to have been Holland. When she got clear of Martinique, she met an imaginary English privateer, threw her French papers overboard, and then, having escaped this bugbear, retired in equally fictitious terror to St. Eustatius, in order to provide herself with papers, namely the Dutch clearance she had always meant to take from St. Eustatius for Holland.[2]

Episodes of this kind were still rare in Maurepas's time. A more serious question was that of the trade from St. Eustatius and Curaçao.

These two Dutch islands had been thorns in the side of every power with West India possessions which it wanted to keep to itself. Curaçao had been expressly founded as a smuggling settlement, and St. Eustatius had never been anything else. As long as English sugar had a higher value in the world market than in England, it had been smuggled out by way of the Dutch and Danish colonies, which still performed that service for the French planters. Since they were no longer of much use in smuggling sugars out of the English colonies, they had now begun to smuggle them in. St. Eustatius was particularly important in peace or war, as the rendezvous of North American traders who wished to export their fish and lumber indirectly to the French Windward Islands and to receive French West India produce. Curaçao was more closely connected with the interloping trade to the Spanish colonies, but it had a short and easy navigation to the southern quarter of St. Domingue, to which it kept up a great trade in time of war. When the intercourse of St. Eustatius with its nearest French neighbours

[1] Maurepas to Caylus and Ranché, April 1, 1748, B 87.
[2] Maurepas to Caylus and Ranché, May 13, 1748, B 87; Caylus to Maurepas, July 29, 1748, C^8 A 58.

became too hazardous, as in 1758, the traders of that island turned their attention to St. Domingue, to which the voyage was pretty free from molestation, because, lying between the cruising-grounds of the two naval stations, it was not very closely super-vised from either.

The Danish island of St. Thomas had played a similar part in the War of the Spanish Succession, because the Danes, unlike the Dutch, enjoyed the advantages of neutrality at that time. Since then, they had settled St. Croix as well, but in these wars they were entirely eclipsed by the Dutch, whose command of capital and convenient situation, both in Europe and the West Indies, qualified them to be the greatest neutral carriers for the French Empire.

None of the French colonies could dispense in time of war with the help of these professional smugglers. Guadeloupe and Grenada lived by nothing else, for they had then no other communication with the world outside. In 1743 sixteen French ships came to Guadeloupe; in 1744 four; in 1745 one. St. Eustatius sent 168 vessels there in 1745, with a total tonnage twice as great as that of the French shipping in the very prospe-rous year 1743.[1] Clieu and Marin, the rulers of the colony, were so much impressed by its dependence on the Dutch, that they capitulated before their threat to discontinue the trade, and allowed them to declare and pay duties on only half their cargoes. As Maurepas and Caylus pointed out, the Dutch found their business far too lucrative to give it up for any consideration; Clieu himself was of this opinion later, for he spontaneously proposed to charge the neutral traders with three thousand livres for every permit.[2]

The complete abandonment of the trade by the French merchants, and its domination by the Dutch, affected each other in a vicious circle. Clieu justified the latter by the former, the merchants of France justified the former by the latter. Maurepas tried to keep the balance even by retailing Clieu's arguments to the merchants, and those of the merchants to Clieu. To the Chamber of Commerce of Bordeaux he wrote that he had given orders against the neutral traffic of which it complained, but he must point out that hardly any French

[1] Various figures in A.N. Colonies C⁷ A 15.
[2] Ranché to Maurepas, Feb. 25, 1746, C⁸ A 57; Maurepas to Clieu and Marin, June 8, 1746, B 83.

ships had gone to Guadeloupe or Grenada during the war, and if they would not supply those islands by themselves, they could not object to his letting the neutrals do so. He had already told Clieu that the King would not allow Guadeloupe to exist for the sole benefit of foreign traders; no doubt the French merchants were tired of sending ships to Guadeloupe, but that was because the trade of the island was entirely in the hands of the Dutch. He would try to induce them to frequent that trade again, but Clieu must make it worth their while by keeping the neutrals at a distance. The Chamber of Commerce, however, put its finger on the centre of this circle of argument when it said that the real reason why so few French ships went to Guadeloupe was the impossibility of getting there; there were no direct convoys, and the local trade with Martinique received no protection. The remedy therefore lay in Maurepas's own hands.[1]

Some quarters of St. Domingue were almost as much isolated and neglected by the trade as the lesser Windward Islands. Here too the pretext for the admission of neutrals was the scarcity of the necessaries of life. But the great bulk of the brown-sugar crops of those districts created a need for more shipping than would suffice to supply them with necessaries. Accordingly Larnage and Maillart argued that even if the convoy system was enough to assure the subsistence of the colony, yet more ships were wanted for taking off the produce which the merchants of France could not or would not carry to Europe. They proposed that the small craft of Curaçao should be admitted in ballast for the purpose of buying this crop. The Dutch would bring money into the colony to pay for the sugar, and need only be allowed to introduce cargoes of victuals when they were very scarce. The only objection could be, that they would raise the prices of brown sugar; Maillart wrote regretfully of a Dutch captain who, if he had been allowed to enter, would not only have taken goods on freight, which the French traders would hardly ever do, but would have bought brown sugars at 15 livres, for which the French would not offer more than 5 or 6. This might raise the price for the French buyer, who would not fail to complain to Maurepas, as he did in fact denounce the same state of affairs

---

[1] Maurepas to Clieu and Marin, June 8, 1746, B 83; Clieu to Maurepas, March 30, 1747, C⁷ A 15; Chamber of Commerce of Guienne, Minute of Sept. 7, 1747, Arch. Gir. C 4255, f. 7; Chamber to Maurepas, Sept. 9, 1747, C 4263, f. 57.

at Martinique. Maillart thought he could get over this difficulty by distinguishing between the rates at which Frenchmen
and foreigners might receive goods; for the former, the very low
prices of produce which had ruled after the departure of the
last fleet were to be preserved—in cold storage, as it were, for
there were few or no dealings. For the foreigner the price of
sugars was to be somewhat higher, and in order to prevent him
from raising the rate of his flour in proportion, that too was to
be fixed. Maillart began to put this scheme into execution, a
few months before the end of the war.[1]

Maurepas was not impressed by the arguments in favour of
admitting neutrals for the sole purpose of taking off the crops.
The only criterion of the necessity of neutral trade which he
recognized was the scarcity of provisions. Though he acknowledged that the St. Louis quarter would not be able to find a
market for its produce during the war, he did not wish, at
present, to enable it to do so by means of foreigners. In the same
spirit Caylus and Ranché rebuked Clieu and Marin for admitting small craft from St. Eustatius in ballast.[2] In fact, the
authorities determined to prevent the produce of the colonies
from leaking out to foreign markets without performing the
obligatory journey to France and passing through the hands of
French brokers. They were equally attentive to prevent another
of the commonest abuses of the neutral trade—the introduction of dry goods and negroes under cover of provisions.
The officials in the colonies had always been exhorted to take
great care of this point, whenever they had found it necessary in times of peace to have recourse to foreign supplies
of the necessities of life. They were to be no less vigilant
now. Ranché detected a case of this kind and punished
it with confiscation; Maurepas commended him and warned
him to be on his guard against a repetition of the offence,
for interested people would always try to deceive him in this
way.[3]

Where the shortage of provisions was the pretext for introducing neutrals, Maurepas made no objection to it at first. He

[1] Larnage and Maillart to Maurepas, Feb. 10, 1746, A.N. Colonies C⁹ A 68;
Larnage to Maurepas, Nov. 16, 1746, ibid.; Maillart to Maurepas, Feb. 10, 1747,
vol. 70; Feb. 15, 1748, vol. 74.
[2] Maurepas to Larnage, Nov. 19, 1746, B 83; Caylus and Ranché to Clieu and
Marin, Feb. 10, 1746, C⁸ A 56.
[3] Maurepas to Ranché, June 24, 1746, B 83.

warned the Governors and Intendants to confine it to cases of the utmost necessity, and above all not to let the neutrals spoil the market for the French convoys by lowering the prices of European goods and raising those of produce. The Governors and Intendants professed to be anxious to satisfy these conditions; according to their own accounts, they only allowed the colonists to live from hand to mouth, and suspended the dealings of neutrals as soon as the trade arrived from France. For a time, Maurepas made no criticism.[1] But in 1746 the merchants of France began to clamour against the licence which was allowed to neutral trade, especially at Martinique and Guadeloupe. They were very much excited by the rumour of an exceptional number of ships fitting out in Holland for St. Eustatius, and in Denmark for St. Thomas.

Maurepas warned Caylus and Ranché against the designs of the interlopers, and his advice appears to have produced a momentary effect, for in the spring of 1747 the merchants of Holland were very much alarmed to hear that a Dutch vessel had been refused admittance to Martinique because provisions were plentiful there. If this was true, wrote the English agent at Rotterdam, the Dutch would be deprived of one of the chief reasons for their neutrality, and the trade of St. Eustatius which had lately employed two hundred ships would be ruined. But Caylus could not or would not maintain this exclusion very long, the cries of the merchants redoubled, and Maurepas's note of warning soon became one of sharp reproach.[2] Caylus and Ranché tried to justify their own actions by necessity, and heaped accusations upon their subordinates. Guadeloupe had escaped altogether from their control, and was pouring millions of pounds of its best produce into St. Eustatius; members of the *Conseil Supérieur* absented themselves from sittings at which cases of illicit trade were to be judged; officers were guilty of smuggling, but nobody would bring forward any evidence against them.[3] The Chambers of Commerce found the same

[1] Maillart to Maurepas, Nov. 22, 1747, C⁹ A 70; Vaudreuil and Samson to Maurepas, Feb. 1, 1748, vol. 74; Maurepas to Ranché, June 3, 1745, B 81; to Caylus, June 8, 1746, B 83.

[2] Maurepas to Caylus and Ranché, Aug. 22 and Sept. 10, 1746, B 83; to Caylus, April 17 and May 19, 1747, B 85; La Rochelle intelligence, Feb. 6, n.s., 1747, S.P. 84/429, f. 71; Wolters to Chetwynd, Feb. 3/14, 1747, f. 65.

[3] Ranché to Maurepas, Dec. 10, 1746, A.N. Colonies C⁸ A 56; Caylus to Maurepas, Dec. 22, 1746, ibid.; Caylus and Ranché to Maurepas, July 1, 1747, ibid.

difficulty in procuring evidence against Caylus himself, or rather they hesitated to use the letters they had received on this subject, for fear of getting their correspondents into trouble with him. Bordeaux, however, complained to Maurepas in July 1747 that there were eighteen Dutch ships at Martinique according to last advices, selling goods so cheap and buying produce so dear that French merchants, with their high charges of freight and insurance, could not afford the competition.

Maurepas wrote to Caylus with real severity. At the same time he instructed Conflans, who was going out Governor to St. Domingue, to suppress all Dutch trade and to confiscate Dutch vessels which arrived in the colony upon any pretext.[1] Maillart, though he pursued a policy very like that of Caylus and Ranché, seems to have escaped a similar censure from Maurepas; but he had his enemies in the colony, particularly one Binau, who charged him with favouritism in the issue of permissions for neutrals and Flags of Truce. The accusation is quite plausible, for Intendants did much worse than that in the next war; but Maillart was defended by the acting Governor Chastenoye, and Binau's charge seems to have been prompted by a personal feud, of a kind which only too often arose between the civil and military officials.[2]

There is no telling whether Maurepas's indignation would have culminated in any effective action, for considerations of another order intervened, and affairs took a new turn. The tension between France and the States-General was developing into a state of virtual war. Orders for reprisals were issued on both sides, and the Governor of Curaçao began to seize French ships. Caylus laid his hands on the Dutch traders at Martinique, and rejected the argument that they were protected by his own permission to trade. Chastenoye with more hesitation followed in Caylus's footsteps. The cessation of intercourse with the Dutch was a very serious blow to the French colonies, for it deprived them of their chief source of supplies. The mercantile agility of the Dutch traders overcame this difficulty in some degree: they instantly metamorphosed themselves into Danes. Caylus and Chastenoye even had to continue granting passports openly to Dutchmen, not only for the last months of war,

[1] Chamber of Commerce of Guienne to Maurepas, July 18, 1747, Arch. Gir. C 4263, f. 61; Maurepas to Caylus and Ranché, July 26, 1747, A.N. Colonies B 85; Instructions to Conflans, July 16, 1747, ibid.
[2] Chastenoye to Maurepas, Feb. 10, 1748, C⁹ A 72.

but for the first of peace, until the new crop of wheat could be milled in France and sent out to the islands.[1]

The colonies had now to rely upon certain other resources. The privateers had always brought in a number of small victuallers from North America. Sometimes indeed their harvest had been rich in the Windward Islands, and sufficed to keep the colonists in plenty; but St. Domingue had hardly any privateers, and had to obtain the produce of North America in a more peaceful way, namely by the Flag of Truce trade.

The exchange of prisoners was the commonest pretext for this intercourse between enemies, though there were other excuses as well. The Flags of Truce from North America were especially welcome. They brought large quantities of flour, which was inferior to that of France, but a great deal better than manioc. Wine, the other great necessity of life in the French colonies, they very seldom supplied. The New England privateers took enough ships loaded with wine to have exported their prize cargoes, but the North Americans probably preferred to drink the French wine themselves, for it was a luxury not very easily obtained in the English dominions.

Larnage was shocked by the idea that enemies should trade with each other more freely in war than in peace, yet he allowed these cargoes to be sold whenever a scarcity required it, and the proceeds to be exported in rum and molasses. His successor Chastenoye admitted them quite freely to the ports which were already so well known that the enemy could learn nothing new about them; he reserved the less frequented ports for the neutrals. Vaudreuil of Cap François had a correspondence with Admiral Knowles, who wished to stop this intercourse altogether. The same reasons for which Knowles wished to suppress the trade rendered it politic for the French authorities to encourage it; Knowles was quite right, from his point of view, to be angry with the Flag of Truce traders, but though Vaudreuil might despise such unpatriotic scoundrels he thought

---

[1] Maurepas to Chastenoye and Maillart, Nov. 15, 1747, A.N. Colonies B 85; Chastenoye to Maurepas, March 10, 1748, C⁹ A 72; Faesch, Governor of Curaçao, to Caylus, April 15, 1748, C⁸ A 58; Caylus to Maurepas, May 31, 1748, ibid.; Case of the schooner *Pietre*, April 1748, Antigua Arsenal, Admiralty papers, bundle 1. It would appear that some merchants of Paris proposed at the very end of the war to borrow the names of Danish shipowners to a very considerable extent (Ogier to Rouillé, Nov. 18, 1755, A.E. Danemark, 130).

it his duty to take advantage of their disloyalty.[1] Maurepas had sanctioned the use of this resource in cases of extreme scarcity, but at the end of the war he ordered Conflans to put an end to the Flag of Truce trade, in which great quantities of valuable sugars and indigo leaked out of the colonies under cover of authorized exports of by-products.[2]

The Flag of Truce trade with the English West India colonies was less welcome even to Larnage and Maillart. The reasons which made any form of trade with North America valuable and justifiable could not be invoked here: dry goods were more likely to be imported than provisions, and the principal export was not rum and molasses which must else perish in the planter's hands, but the much prized indigo. Larnage asked the Governor of Jamaica to stop this illicit trade by making the English Flags of Truce come in ballast. He professed to restrain the French Flags of Truce in the same way; but owners would not send their sloops to Jamaica for nothing, and Larnage was sometimes, like the English Governors, forced to pay them for their trouble by allowing them to export indigo.[3]

Another kind of intercourse with the English might have arisen out of the practice of ransoming the ships and cargoes which were taken by privateers.[4] Ordinarily these ransoms were paid by bills of exchange upon the owners, but some masters of ships captured on the outward voyage wanted to export their ransom in West India produce. Maillart would have liked to allow it, especially as he was obsessed by his desire to get the brown-sugar crop shipped off by every possible method; but he dared not take the responsibility for such an innovation. He permitted one or two captains to go to Jamaica and buy back their ships and cargoes, though he pointed out to them that this was not a true ransom but a trade with the enemy. Caylus was mixed up in some such transactions, but Maurepas did not approve of them.[5]

[1] Larnage to Maurepas, Jan. 10 and Aug. 18, 1745, A.N. Colonies C⁹ A 66; Maillart to Maurepas, Jan. 5, 1748, vol. 73; Chastenoye to Maurepas, Feb. 10, 1748, vol. 72; Vaudreuil to Maurepas, Feb. 22, 1748, vol. 74. There seems to have been some Flag of Truce trade at Martinique, but no record of it appears to exist in the correspondence of Caylus and Ranché.

[2] Maurepas to Conflans, Jan. 31, 1748, B 87.

[3] Larnage to Maurepas, Aug. 18, 1745, C⁹ A 66; Feb. 19, 1746, vol. 68; Bart and Élias to Berryer, Feb. 11, 1760, vol. 105.

[4] For the dealings of this kind between Jamaica and Mexico, v. supra, p. 121.

[5] Maillart to Maurepas, Feb. 10, 1747, C⁹ A 70; Maurepas, to Maillart Nov. 15,

In spite of all these sources of supply, the islands complained of scarcity. They were often reduced to two or three weeks' provision of flour or wine, before the authorities consented to relieve them by sending permits to St. Eustatius or Curaçao. The bakers were sometimes forced to close their shops. The last few months of the war were those of the greatest distress. The famine in France was so great that very little flour could have been exported, even if there had been ships ready to carry it; in fact, some masters were forbidden to take any on board.[1] The trade of Curaçao and St. Eustatius was hampered, though not destroyed, by the strained relations of the French and Dutch Governments. Large English forces blockaded the colonial ports and interfered with the success of privateering. The Governors were at their wits' end and the planters were on the edge of mutiny. From the very beginning of the war, Larnage and Maillart had reported seditious agitations among the people of St. Domingue, who compared the naval protection of the French colonies very unfavourably with that of the English. These criticisms had been silenced by the institution of convoys, but revived when that system began to break down. Caylus and Ranché hinted at the possibility of similar discontents at Martinique.[2]

At the end of the war the eagerness of the planters to procure victuals broke out into insubordination. Chastenoye justified his admission of some Flags of Truce by this angry temper, and supported his argument by enclosing a letter from Champfleury, commandant at St. Marc. An English Flag of Truce arrived there at the end of January 1748. Champfleury had reason to believe that three principal innkeepers were preparing to buy up all the wine in the cargo, so that the rest of the town and the outlying quarters would get none; at the same time three merchants came to him with enormous orders for wine from their country customers, which they asked leave to execute. He instructed the captain of the Flag of Truce to deliver no wine without his permission, and sat down to think of a way to reconcile all interests, town and country, innkeepers and private consumers.

1747, B 85. Adrien Dessalles gives an obscure but highly coloured account of Caylus's commercial enterprises (*Histoire générale des Antilles*, iv. 519–21).

[1] Caylus to Maurepas, May 15, 1748, C⁸ A 58.

[2] Larnage to Maurepas, Oct. 28, 1744, C⁹ A 64; Maillart to Maurepas, Feb. 10, 1747, vol. 70; Caylus and Ranché to Maurepas, March 10, 1748, C⁸ A 58; Caylus to Maurepas, March 10, ibid.

'As I was trying to find means to please as many people as possible, the English captain came to my house, with a vast mob at his heels. He complained that as fast as he disembarked his flour, the mob seized it by force,—that two barrels were missing, and the mob was fighting over the flour upon the shore. I ordered him in the presence of forty people to deliver no more than two barrels to anybody. . . . In less than four hours, this captain, who had brought 240 or 250 barrels, had none left, and our bakers did not get a barrel. In spite of that, 150 persons more came to me asking for orders for flour; I did what I could to calm them, but they were very much annoyed. Some good people came to tell me that there was great talk in the town about the wine, and that the mob was saying it would have some, otherwise it would not allow any to be unloaded.'[1]

§ iii. *The Chambers of Commerce and the Neutral Passports, 1756*

As soon as the war was over, Maurepas and Rouillé set themselves to suppress the trade of foreigners afresh, and to prevent the licence, which their subordinates had allowed in the war, from having any permanent ill consequences. The colonists must have felt some annoyance when they found that the Government, which could not afford ships to protect them regularly in time of war, could so readily spare some in peace to put down some popular and necessary forms of colonial smuggling.[2]

Machault was the Minister in charge of the Marine and Colonies at the outbreak of the Seven Years War. He seems to have made up his mind not to repeat Maurepas's experiment of convoys. In his letters to the Governors and Intendants he admitted that the convoys had successfully protected the colonial trade—that most of the ships lost in the last war had sailed without convoy, or been separated from it before the moment of capture. Nevertheless, there was a prejudice against the system, and the King had other uses for his warships.[3] Machault intended, as Admiral Richmond would say, to make a 'true military use' of them, and indeed he did so: the years of his administration are not the least distinguished in the history of the French navy. He meant rather to take the alterna-

[1] Champfleury to Chastenoye, Feb. 1, 1748, C⁹ A 72; Chastenoye to Maurepas, Feb. 10, ibid.

[2] Maurepas to Ranché, June 18, 1748, B 87; to Caylus, March 6, 1749, B 89; Minute of Nov. 1749, A.N. Marine B⁴ 62.

[3] Machault to Bompar and Givry, June 19, 1756, A.N. Colonies B 103.

tive method of defending colonial trade—that of squadrons stationed at the landfalls of France and America, to protect the entry and departure of shipping.[1] It is doubtful whether this was really a more economical way of using the warships. Perhaps it combined the protection of trade with aggressive strategy better than the convoy system, but that is uncertain; the English squadrons in the Channel and the West Indies had not achieved those two objects with equal success in the last war, so long as they had to deal with forces of their own size.

Be that as it might, Machault's choice was made. In fact he and his successor could not continue to afford even that kind of protection which they had in mind. Kersaint's squadron at the end of 1757 was the last important one to spend any long time in the colonies, if we except those of Bompar and Blénac which were sent out to deal with special emergencies and returned to Europe soon after they were over. Nor was the French navy more successful in defending the coasts of France, and the all-important cruising-ground off the north-west capes of Spain; for want of which the French homeward trade often put into the Galician ports where it was almost permanently blockaded, and could only convey its cargoes to France by collusive transhipments into Dutch and Spanish bottoms.[2] So destitute of protection were the French coasts, that quite small English privateers, backed up by men-of-war in the neighbourhood, made a chain through which the trade could hardly escape. Even the mouths of the French rivers were not safe, and French privateers, returning with their prizes, often had the misfortune to lose them almost in sight of the coast. The Chambers of Commerce represented to Machault and Moras that a few frigates cruising and escorting the trade would force these privateers to fall back nearer to the men-of-war, and oblige even the latter to cruise in squadrons instead of doing so singly. The meshes of the net would so be widened, and more trade would slip through.[3] The Ministers were not often able to take this advice; Moras meant to send out Conflans with a

[1] Chamber of Commerce of Guienne, Minutes, Sept. 2, 1756, Arch. Gir. C 4256, f. 17; Chamber to Machault, Sept. 4 and 18, 1756, C 4263, ff. 249, 252.

[2] Chamber of Commerce of Guienne, Minutes, Aug. 5 and 25, 1756, Arch. Gir. C 4256, ff. 13, 17; Chamber to Macnémara, Aug. 7, C 4263, f. 243; to Machault, Aug. 21, ibid.

[3] La Rochelle Chamber to Moras, March 17, 1757, C 4320, no. 24; Minutes of April 14 and June 8, 1757, C 4256, ff. 35, 39.

large force to clear the Channel in the autumn of 1757, but he could not carry out his plan.

Since he did not mean to revive the convoys, Machault had to take into account the probability that the colonial trade would be entirely defenceless. The merchants still had the benefit of an occasional escort, whenever a squadron bound to or from the colonies was able to take charge of them; but as the commanders were no longer obliged to regard convoying as their principal business, they made little scruple of deserting the traders, like Caumont, in order to chase an enemy, or like Kersaint, because they had no longer the patience or the authority to insist on keeping the merchant fleet together. Moreover, if the royal navy was to put forth its full strength, and privateers were to be suitably encouraged, the merchants would be in straits to find crews, without whom they could not carry on their trade. Too many of their sailors had been seized by the English before the war had begun, and were not yet released. Besides, if the merchant crews were to navigate in future at the mercy of the enemy, they would only too probably become prisoners of war, and the navy could not count on their services again until they were exchanged. In the interest of the King's warships, which could not protect them, it was important that the seamen should not expose themselves to this risk.[1]

Machault therefore proposed to do what the colonial Governors had vainly urged upon Maurepas. He would put the French colonial trade in cold storage during the war, and rely on neutrals to supply the colonies and to carry their crops to market. He did not mean to prohibit the French merchants from trading to the colonies if they would, but he took his measures on the supposition that the enormous rates of insurance and the difficulty of getting seamen would prevent them from taking much part in that trade. In their opinion, these measures were such as to discourage them from taking any part at all.

The Chambers of Commerce learnt with displeasure in March 1756 that the Deputies of Commerce at Paris, nominally their own agents, had laid before Machault a complete scheme for throwing open the trade. The neutrals were to get permission

---

[1] We learn that this argument weighed with Machault, from the additional *mémoire* of Lamestrie and Jarreau, the special deputies of Bordeaux, May 15, 1756, Arch. Gir. C 4318, no. 55.

from the Minister, or rather from the Deputies themselves, and to pay a tonnage duty. This was to be distributed among the French ships which still used the trade, as an indemnity for their heavy expenses and for the damage which they would suffer by the neutral competition.[1] The Chambers at once struck up a violent agitation against this scheme. Some of them sent special deputies to Paris to combat it. Pamphlets were written on both sides of the question, and the affair made a great noise.

Spokesmen for the colonies argued that French shipowners were already, or soon would be, unable to carry on this trade. The risks would prove too great, the insurances too high. What right had they then to prevent the colonists from making use of the neutrals? The experience of the last war proved the extremities to which the islands were reduced by the high price of necessaries, the low value of crops, and the difficulty of getting freight or making remittances. The merchants were asking for a monopoly which, so far as they could use it at all, enabled them to extort high profits from the planters' distress.[2]

All this the Chambers of Commerce denied. They pointed to the number of ships now fitting out for the colonies, and to prove its sufficiency La Rochelle fixed the tonnage necessary to this trade at 50,000. This figure would have been generous in 1736 and perhaps equitable in 1746, but was certainly too small now.[3] Besides, there was no certainty that the ports of France would be able to furnish so much. There would have

---

[1] Chamber of Commerce of Guienne, Minutes, March 20, 1756, Arch. Gir. C 4255, f. 276. Most of the Deputies' letter is printed by E. Garnault, *Le Commerce rochelais au xviiie siècle*, iv. 76–8. Garnault has a whole chapter on this subject, pp. 75–117; he prints the *mémoire* of La Rochelle in full, with extracts from those of other Chambers.

[2] See the 'Mémoire pour les colonies de l'Amérique' presented to Machault and printed by Gaston Martin, in *L'Ère des négriers*, pp. 383–99.

[3] La Rochelle to Bordeaux, March 23, 1756, Arch. Gir. C 4318, no. 20. Beauharnois and Givry, who were no doubt as much inclined to exaggerate as the Chambers of Commerce to underestimate, claimed in 1758 that the Windward Islands alone needed 30,000 tons of shipping annually from Europe (to Moras, June 20, 1758, A.N. Colonies C⁸ A 61). Laporte-Lalanne wrote that the trade of St. Domingue had employed between 200 and 250 ships, upon an average, in the years of peace: in fact the number was 216, including 40 slave-traders, in 1754. If we suppose the burthen of a ship in the colonial trade to be about 200 tons, this would make 40,000 to 50,000 tons of shipping. Laporte-Lalanne adds, however, that some of them, especially those of Nantes, had always come out in ballast to load sugars home, so that the tonnage of the necessary provisions would be much less (Laporte-Lalanne to Moras, Sept. 15, 1757, A.N. Colonies C⁹ A 100; see also the figures he gave Machault on April 11, 1755, C⁹ A 97).

been no difficulty in times of peace. Bordeaux alone, according to its Chamber, annually employed 32,000 tons of shipping in the colonial trade;[1] but so much was not to be expected in war-time. In fact, not more than 22,000 tons appear to have left Bordeaux in the first year of the war, when the merchants were making every effort to prove the sufficiency of their shipping; and much of that was taken on the way out or home.

The Chambers denounced the reasons of the colonists as the clamours of self-interested individuals; one's own is always the public interest in a mercantilist controversy, all others are private. They accused the planters of trying to break through all the restraints and traditions of the colonial system, by obtaining a free trade with the foreigner upon the pretext of the war, and to escape from their debts by cutting off all relations with their correspondents in France.[2] The Chambers also tried to deal with the argument that the naval reserve of France must not be exposed in defenceless trading-vessels. They replied that if the seamen were not to be employed in this trade, they would take service in privateers, and surely a privateer ran even more risk of destruction or capture than a merchant ship?[3] This argument was both untrue and specious. Privateers may have been equally liable to those dangers, but they were not more so; besides, they played at least some part in the war by molesting the enemy's commerce.

Several distinct interests were enlisted together against the admission of neutrals. The manufacturers of France feared that the Dutch would substitute foreign goods for French in the colonial markets, perhaps in such quantities as would overstock them in the first years of peace, and with such success that the planters would lose the taste for French goods. The Lille and Lyons Chambers therefore took part in the agitation; but Lille made a significant reservation, by suggesting that if the scheme of neutral passports could not be prevented altogether, the Government should at least confine the neutrals to carrying goods of French growth and manufacture to the colonies.[4] This would have been small comfort to the French seaports. The interests of French agriculture were not so much concerned.

[1] Bordeaux to Dunkirk, Aug. 28, 1756, Arch. Gir. C 4263, f. 248.
[2] Bordeaux Chamber to Machault, Oct. 9, 1756, C 4263, f. 260; *mémoire* of La Rochelle, printed by Garnault, op. cit. iv. 91.
[3] Additional *mémoire* of Lamestrie and Jarreau, quoted above.
[4] Lille to Bordeaux, April 2, 1756, C 4318, no. 29.

French wine had no rivals for the preference of Frenchmen. Few countries in western Europe exported flour in great quantities to compete with that of France; the only other sources of supply were in the dominions of the enemy. The French colonies had long relied upon Ireland for beef, and the only change which the introduction of neutrals would make was the substitution of Dutch for French carriers. For these reasons the neutral scheme could hardly have bad consequences for French agriculture, besides those which must in any case arise from the suspension of French commerce by captures. However, agriculture had no organized body to express its will, and its name was taken in vain by the Chambers of Commerce which freely prophesied its ruin. None of them did anything to help it, except that of Bayonne, which justified itself for distributing passports to neutrals by stipulating that their ships should carry provisions of French growth to the colonies.[1]

The shipowners, merchants, and brokers were the classes really affected by the scheme. The shipowners feared the destruction of their capital by the depreciation of vessels lying idle in port, and the loss of their current profits, which would probably be larger than those of any other interest concerned in the trade if the monopoly were maintained. They pointed to the heavy expenses of insurance—if indeed it could be made at all—and the high wages of seamen. It was impossible to compete on such terms with neutrals who navigated cheaper even in time of peace, and would not be subject to the same extraordinary charges.[2] (To some extent the Chambers destroyed their own argument here, by foretelling on the other hand that the English would not respect the neutral flags, and that neutral vessels would be no safer than French; it came to pass as they said, and insurance on Dutch ships was little lower in 1758 than on their own.)

The merchants had something more at stake. Nantes, Bordeaux, and La Rochelle lived largely by re-exporting West India produce, especially to Holland, Hamburg, and the Baltic. In fact they often spoke of the re-export market as their chief salvation—an encomium which it seems to have deserved, if we may judge from the figures to be collected from Malvezin's

[1] Bayonne to Bordeaux, Jan. 22, 1757, C 4320, no. 5.
[2] Minutes of March 20, 1756, C 4255, f. 276; Chamber to Machault, March 23, 1756, C 4263, f. 226.

Histoire du commerce de Bordeaux.[1] For these towns, the point of the colonial monopoly was their command of the world market through the re-export trade. Any arrangement which would enable the foreigner to obtain West India goods without applying to them, would ruin the whole colonial system. They would be reduced to supplying the consumption of their own country, which could not nearly absorb the stocks on hand. It was the colonists' business—so the Bordeaux Chamber told Machault—to see that the merchants of France made an 'honest profit' on the sales of West India produce, by discouraging interlopers and forcing the foreigner to apply to France. He would then have to pay a price for it which would reimburse the owners of ships and cargoes for the high wages, freights, and insurance, and procure them a livelihood as well. If the colonists broke the united front against the foreigner, by allowing him to obtain their produce directly without the intermediacy of the French merchants, the remittance of goods from the West Indies to France would never be profitable, as the prices, which depended upon the re-export, would not keep up. The crops and importations from the West Indies had been large in recent years, and the merchants seem to have had a large capital invested in West India goods which they had not yet succeeded in exporting, but were forced to keep in entrepôt. It was the annihilation of this capital, by the reduction of the value of these stocks, which most oppressed them; in fact, they could hardly see beyond it.[2] Very little of these goods would keep throughout a long

[1] I quote his statistics for the years 1749 to 1756, the period from which the Chambers would naturally draw their arguments (op. cit. iii. 302–3, 308–9):

	Coffee		Sugar		Indigo	
	Imported (thousands)	Re-exported (thousands)	Imported (thousands)	Re-exported (thousands)	Imported (thousands)	Re-exported (thousands)
1749	4,804	4,577	37,397	14,388	1,171	940
1750	4,139	3,733	42,700	29,201	819	574
1751	3,348	4,214	28,878	30,412	546	558
1752	3,799	4,818	29,069	29,839	436	446
1753	4,480	4,650	46,173	35,526	640	537
1754	6,815	6,275	40,586	34,173	567	327
1755	5,978	6,004	39,703	28,713	598	396
1756	4,262	4,370	19,218	22,277	214	316

No doubt the re-exports must have been overestimated for the sake of exemption from duty.

[2] Minutes of March 20, and letter to Machault, March 23, quoted above; Chamber to Machault, Oct. 9, 1756, C 4263, f. 260.

war; and even if they had been imperishable, the right of entrepôt could only be enjoyed for a limited time, after which the goods must actually be exported or pay the heavy duties on consumption. This period was usually extended in times of difficulty; it had been so in the last war, but the merchants could never rely on obtaining any privilege which it depended on the Farmers-General to obstruct, and in fact they seem to have had trouble over this matter in the years which followed.[1]

The Chambers of Commerce won the day in 1756. Machault wavered; indeed, some thought he had never regarded himself as committed to the details of the Deputies' scheme. Laporte, the powerful first *commis* of the colonial department, used his influence on the merchants' side, and supported himself with quotations from his brother, Laporte-Lalanne, Intendant of St. Domingue, who is said to have asserted that the colonies did not need the neutral passports.[2] Machault interviewed the special deputies of Bordeaux, and told them that he only wanted to ensure a proper supply of necessaries to the colonies, and an outlet for their goods. He wished the trade of France might be able to perform these services by itself, but he thought the neutral passports would be a valuable supplement. He only meant, by proposing the scheme, to procure additional facilities for the merchants of France to carry on their own business (a phrase of which Bordeaux made excessive use in the sequel). Therefore he would send the passports to the Chambers of Commerce, to be distributed on what conditions they thought fit to impose. For himself, he would make none, except that the neutrals should carry provisions to the colonies and pay the duties of the *domaine d'occident*. (In fact, he never expressed any opinion about the regulations which the Chambers later submitted to him.) The Chambers were to inform him of the

[1] Minutes of April 22, 1745, C 4254, f. 221; Feb. 1, 1748, C 4255, f. 17; Chamber to Contrôleur Général, Dec. 23, 1756, C 4263, f. 267; Trudaine to Tourny, March 16, 1757, C 4320, no. 22; Nantes to Moras, June 28, 1757, no. 43.

[2] La Rochelle to Bordeaux, March 23, 1756, C 4318, no. 20; Lamestrie and Jarreau to Chamber, April 10, 1756, no. 37; Beudet to Danié, Feb. 26, 1758, *Resolutie*, Johannesz, H.C.A. 42/91. I have not found in the public archives any evidence that Laporte-Lalanne said anything of the kind. Beudet presumably refers to his private letters to his brother, which are not preserved in the Archives Nationales. All his dispatches to the Ministers recommend the admission of neutrals, though not in very pressing terms (Vaudreuil and Laporte-Lalanne to Machault, Oct. 20, 1756, A.N. Colonies C⁹ A 99; Laporte-Lalanne to Moras, Sept. 15 and Oct. 2, 1757, C⁹ A 100).

number of French and neutral ships which left their ports, and if he did not consider it large enough, he should take other measures.[1]

Machault did not know how this compromise would turn out. The Chambers were not entirely satisfied with it, but were glad it was no worse. They had in their own hands the power of expediting or obstructing the neutral trade.

Everything depended on the regulations which they imposed. The Bordeaux Chamber at once took the lead in favour of severity, and its influence had weight because the conversations of its deputies with Machault enabled it to pose as an authority on his intentions—which, as it delicately hinted, were 'susceptible of extension'. La Rochelle followed this example closely; Rouen even surpassed it. They preached the necessity of co-operation between the Chambers, and apparently induced some of them to promise to take no step without common consultation. Nantes wavered; Marseilles soon began to distribute passports, quite abandoning all thought of keeping up its own trade to the colonies, for the difficulty of getting safe through the Straits was indeed an exceptional hindrance. Machault had sent some passports to towns which had very little American trade of their own, and had no interest in them except their market value, which was no doubt considerable. Bayonne, always a centre of collusive international accommodations from its neighbourhood to the Spanish frontier, soon showed a tendency to make what it could of them. Dunkirk on the other hand, which was to the Dutch trade what Bayonne was to the Spanish, exhibited an inexplicable altruism: relying on the sufficiency of the ports properly concerned in the American trade, it decided to make no use of the passports.[2]

The chief interest of the affair lies in the obstinate struggle of Bordeaux and La Rochelle to avoid issuing the passports, or to subject them to such conditions as would prevent bona fide neutrals from applying for them. They insisted first of all that

---

[1] Minutes of June 16, 1756, Arch. Gir. C 4256, f. 7; Machault to Bompar and Givry, June 19, 1756, A.N. Colonies B 103. Some neutrals objected very strongly to paying the duties of *domaine d'occident*, but were obliged to do so (Laporte-Lalanne to Moras, Sept. 15, 1757, C⁹ A 100).

[2] Rouen to Bordeaux, June 28, 1756; Bayonne to Bordeaux, Aug. 28, Dec. 14; Marseilles to Bordeaux, Sept. 6 and 29; Dunkirk to Bordeaux, Sept. 29, C 4319, nos. 10, 22, 25, 39, 41, 60. The regulations of the La Rochelle Chamber are printed by Garnault, op. cit. iv. 105–7.

the neutrals must load and unload in French ports. They must load there, because, as La Rochelle observed, their outward cargoes would not otherwise consist of French manufactures. Goods could not easily be carried from France to Holland, nor could the loading be supervised there to see that foreign goods were not put on board. If the Chambers did not insist on this restriction, they could hardly justify their loud denunciations of the danger to French manufactures.[1] It was equally necessary, as Bordeaux argued, to demand effectual guarantees that the neutral ships should bring back their cargoes of West India produce to France. Otherwise they would reduce the volume of business in French ports, lower the price there by diminishing the foreign demand, and 'deprive us entirely of the compensation which we may expect from the real need in which the foreigner stands of these goods, for which he is unavoidably tributary to us'. The monopoly could not be too jealously guarded; the Chambers should on no account content themselves with a mere promise to return to a French port if possible, nor should they make allowances for circumstances which might render it impracticable. Indeed, all questions of guilt, responsibility, or intention were beside the point; it was essential that the produce of the colonies, carried for whatever reason or with whatever justification to foreign ports, should pay such duties as would annihilate the profit of such a short-circuit.

For this purpose Bordeaux insisted on security to pay the duties upon consumption known as the *cinq grosses fermes*, and would accept no substitute.[2] The Chamber even argued that Machault must have meant this condition to be imposed, in spite of the obvious proof of the contrary. Machault had indeed used language which might mean that he hoped the real benefit of the neutral passports would accrue to French traders, and he had made no open objection to the Bordeaux regulations; but neither had he criticized the proposals of the other Chambers, some of which were of a directly opposite tendency. The

[1] Nantes to Bordeaux, June 16 and July 21, 1756, C 4318, no. 70, 4319, no. 5; La Rochelle to Bordeaux, June 20, 1756, C 4318, no. 72.

[2] Bordeaux to Nantes, June 26, 1756; to Nantes and La Rochelle, July 3; to La Rochelle, July 14; to Machault, July 24; to Nantes, July 26, Aug. 28; to Machault, Sept. 28, Oct. 9, C 4263, ff. 235-60 *passim*; Bordeaux Committee for Passports to St. Malo and Bayonne, Sept. 11, 1756; to Bayonne, Jan. 29, 1757, C 4418, ff. 3, 5; Minute of July 13, 1756, C 4256, f. 11; Bayonne to Bordeaux, Jan. 22, Feb. 11, 1757, C 4320, nos. 5, 12.

only condition he had made—the payment of the *domaine d'occident* duty—would have been entirely unnecessary if the neutral ships were bound to return to French ports where they could not choose but pay it.

Given these indispensable conditions, Bordeaux saw no reason for making any difference between Frenchmen and neutrals. Relying on Machault's phrase about increasing the facilities of the French trade, the Chamber publicly assumed that he meant the real users of these passports to be Frenchmen; and indeed, if they set out from French ports and returned to them, the neutrals might be made to act as simple carriers in the French trade without any interest in it besides their freight. Bordeaux therefore deprecated the imposition of discriminatory tonnage duties.

Bordeaux and La Rochelle blandly professed to believe that neutrals would be eager to engage in the French trade upon these terms. For some time, however, they had very few applicants for the favour. A man of La Rochelle who had some effects in St. Domingue for which he could not get freight, requested of his Chamber a passport for a neutral ship. The Chamber pitied the poor fellow, and all Americans in like case with him, but austerely resolved to sacrifice the private to the public interest.[1] The Bordeaux Chamber was pestered for a passport by the Swedish consul, but hardly any one else asked for them. This is no wonder, for Bordeaux, La Rochelle, and Rouen openly declared their intention to issue no passports so long as they considered that there was enough French shipping in this trade.[2] Nor did they take a generous view of the colonies' requirements. La Rochelle proposed to regulate the number of passports upon 'the real needs, not the abundance' of the planters. Nantes amplified this grim phrase, by suggesting that they should only be issued when the colonies were known to have 'less than average plenty', or to be nearer starvation than abundance. The number of interlopers—that is to say, of vessels from St. Eustatius and Curaçao without passports from the King—should be taken into account in estimating the supplies.[3] As the merchants usually believed all they heard

[1] La Rochelle to Bordeaux, Jan. 9, 1757, C 4320, no. 2. A similar application was rejected at Bordeaux.

[2] Minutes of Nov. 18 and 25, 1756, C 4256, ff. 25, 26.

[3] La Rochelle to Bordeaux, June 20, 1756, C 4318, no. 72; Nantes to Bordeaux, July 21, C 4319, no. 5. The Rouen Chamber had asserted at the beginning of the

about the number of interlopers, this did not promise well for the colonists.

In fact, to make a long matter short, Bordeaux, La Rochelle, and Rouen did not mean to issue any passports at all. They anxiously exchanged proofs—slenderer and slenderer, but still satisfactory to their fond eyes—of the sufficiency of French shipping. The prices of European goods were reported to be low in the islands—some said, lower than in time of peace.[1] That of West India produce was constantly falling in France. Perhaps this last fact was partly due to the licence accorded in the islands to the traders of St. Eustatius. But the chief cause was the ease with which foreigners could supply themselves with prize goods from the English—a circumstance which neither merchants nor colonists could control, and did as little good to the one as to the other.[2] The Bordeaux Chamber was not afraid to argue that the merchants had only fitted out their ships in spite of great discouragements on the understanding that, as long as they did so, the neutrals would not be permitted to compete with them.[3]

Thus when Nantes first broke the ring and gave a passport to one Orry, Bordeaux complained that its merchants were betrayed. Nantes lamely excused it by the pressure of Machault himself, with whom Orry was somehow connected. Nantes reaffirmed its intention to withhold the passports, but changed its mind again a few months later, alleging that the shipping of France had already shown itself unable to carry on the whole trade. Bordeaux furnished some proof to the contrary, and the resolution of Nantes was rescinded; but evidence or interest was at last too strong, and Nantes announced once more in January 1757 that the time had come to distribute some passports. Sugar was lying in the warehouses of the islands, and merchants with

---

controversy that all the French islands except Martinique could support themselves upon their own food crops (Garnault, op. cit. iv. 82).

[1] This was not corroborated by much evidence from the colonies, nor did those Chambers believe it which had no objection to issuing passports. Vaudreuil and Laporte-Lalanne reported in August 1756 that many kinds of goods were four times as dear as they usually were in peace (to Machault, Aug. 27, 1756, A.N. Colonies C⁹ A 99).

[2] The Chambers of Commerce which, like Bayonne, wished to distribute the passports, made the most of this point (Bayonne to Bordeaux, Feb. 11, 1757, C 4320, no. 12; Rouen to Bordeaux, March 31, no. 27).

[3] Bordeaux Committee for Passports to Bayonne and La Rochelle, Jan. 29, 1757, C 4418, ff. 5–6; Bordeaux Chamber to Moras, Feb. 26, C 4263, f. 270.

funds there could not get them home for want of freight. Martinique was distressed for necessaries by a hurricane; the navy gave the trade no protection, and seamen were very scarce.

The slave-traders of Nantes apparently found it impossible to carry on their business under the French flag, and were ready to use neutral ships—not that this would be much reason for issuing Machault's passports, which were not applicable to that purpose. They had particular reasons for keeping up this branch of trade at a slight sacrifice. A long suspension might permanently destroy their influence among the native chiefs; the English and Portuguese would get hold of the trade, and equip with cheap slave labour their own colonies which competed with those of France in the production of sugar.[1] Moras gave them some passports for this purpose, though he would rather they had used them to import victuals into the colonies.[2]

Rouen, Bordeaux, and La Rochelle would not yield yet. They asked Moras, the new Minister of the Marine, to prevent Nantes from taking these measures. Bordeaux continued to inform him that all would be well—that enough ships were fitting out for the colonial trade, and would certainly sail if only he could give them some protection at the landfalls and help them to sailors by procuring the release of those interned in England. If the obstinacy of Bordeaux was exceptional, so were its efforts to keep up the trade. Vaudreuil and Laporte-Lalanne reported in October 1756 that it was almost the only port which had not abandoned St. Domingue, and its ships had brought enough provisions to save the colony from absolute want. But in the summer of 1757 the trade of the colonies, both outward and homeward, was visited by heavy losses. The Bordeaux Chamber could hold out no longer; it shamefacedly announced to Moras in October that it intended to give out the passports.[3]

This conversion was too late. Moras had already determined to admit the neutrals, though he had not quite decided upon the method of doing so. He acknowledged the indirect usefulness

---

[1] Nantes to Bordeaux, Sept. 29, Oct. 20 and 30, 1756, C 4319, nos. 40, 42, 49, 52; Jan. 26, 1757, C 4320, no. 8; La Rochelle to Nantes, Nov. 4, 1756, printed by Garnault, op. cit. iv. 111–14.

[2] Moras to Bart and Laporte-Lalanne, Feb. 3, 1758, A.N. Colonies B 107.

[3] La Rochelle to Machault, Jan. 29, 1757, printed by Garnault, op. cit., pp. 115–16; Bordeaux to Moras, Feb. 26; to Rouen, April 23; to Moras, May 15, June 7, Oct. 15; to Tourny, July 9, C 4263, ff. 270, 278, 280; 4264, f. 1; Vaudreuil and Laporte-Lalanne to Machault, Oct. 20, 1756, A.N. Colonies C⁹ A 99.

of Machault's passports in stimulating the French merchants to further efforts; but the fact remained that the Chambers had issued very few, and some new arrangements must be taken. Moras seems to have granted some passports underhand in the summer. The secrecy of his arrangements was advantageous, as even the Chamber of Bordeaux recognized; for the notöriety of Machault's passport scheme and the unconcealed distribution by public bodies could not fail to excite the attention of the English, who would keep a good look-out for the holders of such permissions. But whatever was done in the dark at Versailles in those days was almost certain to be done corruptly and unfairly. In fact the only people to obtain Moras's passports were absentee proprietors of American plantations, who possessed court or ministerial influence, such as the Comte de Conflans, Vice-Admiral of France and a former Governor of St. Domingue; Carbon, a law officer of that colony; the Marquise de Ségur; and Nolivos, a nobleman who afterwards became Governor of Guadeloupe. It was reported—I do not know with what truth—that they paid something for these licences.[1] This should be remembered and set off against the complaints which were made against the colonial officials for selling permissions. At any rate this kind of passport was of very little use to anybody else in the colonies. The recipients were planters, not merchants, and were chiefly concerned to stock their own plantations and get home their own crops. They were not likely to export provisions or plantation necessaries for sale, as a merchant would have done; whereas had the merchants received the passports they would have helped the planters as well as themselves, by taking their produce in payment of their goods.[2]

Moras made up his mind to preserve this business in his own office. Instead of allowing the Chambers to deliver the passports, which they were at last ready to do, he caused applications to be made to nominees of his own. He arranged these requests in order of merit. Those which would both sail from French ports and return to them would receive most favour; next, those which would set out from France and return to a neutral port; third, those which set out from a neutral port and returned to

[1] Moras to Beauharnois and Givry, June 10, 1757, A.N. Colonies B 105; Lemasne to Poy, Nov. 29, 1757, Adm. 1/235; deposition of the master in the case of the *Hoop*, Keetel, H.C.A. 42/70; see Tramond, op. cit., p. 515.
[2] Bart and Laporte-Lalanne to Moras, Sept. 20, 1757, A.N. Colonies C⁹ A 100.

France; and lastly those which both started and finished their voyage in neutral ports. This classification shows that Moras valued the export of French goods to the colonies above the preservation of the re-export trade. He explained to Bart and Laporte-Lalanne that the admission of neutrals would be useless unless they carried provisions, and that it was very unlikely they would do so unless they set out from France (for indeed such articles were not to be had so easily in their own countries); he would, however, do all he could to supervise their loading in the neutral ports, and to insist upon this condition. The Bordeaux Chamber had entreated him to insist above all things on the return of the neutrals to French ports; but he soon found that neutrals did not offer on those terms, and resolved to take other order.[1]

From this time little more was heard of the subject. It was too late for any passports, open or secret, to be of much use. The colonists complained that the Chambers of Commerce and their allies at Versailles had obstructed the remedy until it was worse than the disease, for the English were now fully informed of the scheme and would not spare the Dutch traders. This argument was a little precious, for the English Ministry knew all about Machault's scheme through Holland as soon as it was conceived. It is true, however, that the English men-of-war and privateers did not make many seizures of Dutch ships on their way home from the French colonies until the autumn of 1757, just at the time when Moras was thinking of throwing open the trade to neutrals effectually; perhaps, therefore, a larger number of Dutchmen could have escaped seizure in the first year of the war, and the colonies could have been better preserved from want for so long. Moras himself seems to have held this opinion, and blamed Machault for his delays and compromises.[2]

The wholesale seizure of Dutch vessels in 1757 and 1758 discouraged the French merchants from trusting to neutral flags, under which they ran no less risk than under their own. The

---

[1] Minutes of Oct. 10 and 17, 1757, Arch. Gir. C 4256, ff. 47, 48; Chamber to Moras, Oct. 15 and Dec. 3, 1757, C 4264, ff. 1, 4; Moras, circular letter to Governors and Intendants, Nov. 25, 1757, A.N. Colonies B 105; Moras to Beauharnois and Givry, Feb. 18, 1758, B 107; to Bart and Laporte-Lalanne, Feb. 3, ibid.; Mathieu Brothers to Desportes, Nov. 7, 1757, Adm. 1/235.

[2] Moras to Bart and Laporte-Lalanne, Feb. 3, 1758, A.N. Colonies B 107; to Beauharnois and Givry, Feb. 18, ibid.; Beudet to Danié, Feb. 26, 1758, *Resolutie*, Johannesz, H.C.A. 42/91; Nolivos to Danié, March 7, ibid.; Mathieu Brothers, Nantes, to Desportes, Nov. 7, 1757, Adm. 1/235; Lemasne to Poy, Nov. 29, ibid.

English Court of Prize Appeals upheld the condemnation of neutrals trading directly to the French colonies; after its decision in the *America* there could no longer be any question of issuing French passports to foreigners. Perhaps this accounts for the slight revival of French shipping in the French colonial trade towards the end of the war.

The public history of the neutral passports does not quite end here. Bernis and Choiseul tried to persuade the Dutch merchants to continue carrying on the trade of the French colonies, even after the English seizures and condemnations had begun. Choiseul went farther, and was ready to bribe them by promising to throw the trade open to them for some years after the peace. His ambassador at The Hague remonstrated against this proposal and pointed out the injury to the trade of France. It was a great price for a French Minister to pay in a mercantilist age, and Choiseul knew it; but he was ready, as he said, to sacrifice trade to politics. Nothing came of it, however, because Choiseul allowed himself to be convinced that it was not even good diplomacy; besides, it did not take in Holland.[1]

Berryer always took the complaints of the colonists very seriously. He believed that they were suffering from a shortage of negroes, which must be relieved at once if the plantations were to be saved from ruin. Bart and Laporte-Lalanne had strongly recommended Moras to let neutral ships import negroes during the wars. They calculated the annual mortality of St. Domingue at 5 per cent., or 8,825 negroes a year, and pointed out that since the largest number ever introduced in any year of peace was 15,000, it would take many years to repair the damage done by the interruption of the trade during a long war.[2] In 1761 Berryer set about granting passports to neutrals for this purpose. Nantes, which had obtained such permissions from Moras in 1757, now denounced them vehemently. They were so worded as to allow the neutrals to carry on this commerce for some years after the peace, if it should be made before a certain date. Nantes was afraid of losing its monopoly to the foreigner for ever; in fact, the new Chamber of Commerce and Agriculture at Cap François had demanded so much. There

---

[1] Choiseul to d'Affry, Dec. 27, 1758, A.E. Hollande, 499; d'Affry to Choiseul, Jan. 4 and March 27, 1759, vol. 500.

[2] Bart and Laporte-Lalanne to Moras, Sept. 20, 1757, A.N. Colonies C⁹ A 100; Bart and Peyrac to Berryer, May 6, 1760, vol. 105.

were other objections to the scheme. Even if the foreign slave-trader were only admitted in war time, he would stock the markets so that the French merchants, who had laid up their ships during the war, would lose the advantage of the scarcity prices which usually reigned for the first few years after the peace. It would also suspend the liquidation of the debts which the colonies already owed to the French slave-traders; but that was a flimsy argument, for the result would be the same when the planters bought of the French traders themselves. A cheap and plentiful supply of slaves, such as the foreigners were likely to offer, would in the long run do more good than harm to the French creditor, by putting his debtor upon his feet and enabling him to pay.[1]

After a slight hesitation, Bordeaux joined frantically in the agitation. Berryer replied that he was astonished at such a fuss, and that nothing was decided. Nevertheless, Nantes was not happy until Choiseul had replaced him. Choiseul too considered for a moment the admission of neutrals after the war, fearing that the French slave-trade would not pick up strength quickly enough to satisfy the crying needs of the colonists; but the Chambers convinced him on this head, and the national monopoly of slaves was restored at the peace. In this sphere, therefore, the privations and expedients of the war did not lead to any infraction of the old colonial system.[2]

§ iv. The Foreign Traders in the Islands, 1756–62

In this war, as in the last, the introduction of neutrals was managed not only by the Minister but by his subordinates in the colonies as well. The Minister hoped that his own passports would make all others unnecessary. Machault warned the Governors and Intendants not to let in any foreign ships from Europe or America without his licence, unless extreme necessity required it. In fact his own system had been designed to pre-

[1] The arguments on both sides are rehearsed in an able letter of Clugny to Berryer, Aug. 5, 1761, A.N. Colonies C9 A 108.
[2] Bart and Laporte-Lalanne to Moras, Sept. 20, 1757, A.N. Colonies C9 A 100; Chamber of Commerce of Guienne, Minutes of June 11, Aug. 13, Sept. 18 and 26, 1761, Dec. 2 and 29, 1762, Arch. Gir. C 4256, ff. 143, 147, 149, 150, 183, and 188; Nantes to Berryer, June 6, 1761; Castaing to Chamber, July 28 and Sept. 15; Nantes to Bordeaux, Aug. 8 and Nov. 7, C 4324, nos. 12, 33, 37, 47, 53; Chamber to Berryer, Aug. 18, 1761; to Trudaine, Aug. 18, C 4264, ff. 73, 74; Garnault, op. cit., pp. 238–56.

vent the abuses which always attended the admission of neutrals by the colonial authorities. Moras was more willing to entrust the officials in the colonies with this business, but when he decided to issue permits of his own he once more forbade them to do so—not this time in the interests of the French merchants, but in that of the neutrals whom he should license. They would never apply for passports in Europe if they were afraid of the incalculable competition of other neutrals in the islands.[1]

These admonitions had little effect; nor did they deserve much more, for hardly any of the neutral ships arrived which the Ministers promised. The Chambers of Commerce obstructed the distribution of Machault's passports, and most of the neutrals who received them from Moras were taken or did not start at all.[2] Vaudreuil and Laporte-Lalanne began to grant permits for neutrals quite early in the war; but they do not seem to have issued an inordinate number, and few of them were used. Bart and Laporte-Lalanne issued some more—we do not know how many—in 1757, and these were taken up.[3]

Bompar and Givry delivered 261 permits for the Windward Islands in 1756. This liberal dose could hardly be justified by any momentary necessity; besides, Bompar distributed 138 more at the beginning of 1757, before the first were all used. Moras could see no reason for this, but Bompar may have known he was soon to be superseded, and therefore resolved to make hay while the sun shone.[4] Even though not all Bompar's licences were used, the neutrals were far more freely admitted to Martinique in the Seven Years War than in Caylus's time: 145 vessels entered from foreign ports in 1757 against 70 in 1747.[5]

Bompar and Givry proceeded upon a specious principle. They did not think it proper to throw open the trade without

[1] Machault to Bompar and Givry, June 19, 1756, A.N. Colonies B 103; instructions to Bart, Dec. 15, ibid.; Moras to Beauharnois and Givry, June 10 and Nov. 25, 1757, B. 105.

[2] Bompar and Givry to Machault, undated (end of 1756), C8 A 60; Beauharnois and Givry to Moras, June 20, 1758, C8 A 61; Laporte-Lalanne to Moras, Jan. 5, 1758, C9 A 101.

[3] Laporte-Lalanne to Machault, July 13, 1756, C9 A 99; Bart and Laporte-Lalanne to Moras, Sept. 20, 1757, C9 A 100; Tramond, op. cit., p. 515.

[4] Just as Governor Denny of Pennsylvania dealt out commissions for Flags of Truce with extraordinary profusion during the last weeks of his administration.

[5] A.N. Colonies C8 B 21. The figures for the latter years of the war are very imperfect, but it appears from what there are that the number fell off considerably in 1758 and 1759—perhaps because of the English seizures—and increased vastly in 1760.

restraint or formality; nor, on the other hand, did they accede to private applications, for fear of favouritism. They delivered some fifty licences to public officials—including twenty-four to themselves; only a dozen or so to foreigners, of which the Governor of St. Eustatius got six; and over two hundred to 'principal merchants'. These people, they said, were the greatest dealers in the trade with France, and had large remittances to make there. They could, therefore, have no interest in allowing the best produce of the islands to leak out to the neutral markets. This argument was plain nonsense, for when the *commissionnaires* could not remit to France for want of shipping they had not the least repugnance to disposing of their sugars elsewhere; it deserves no more consideration than Givry's sentimental plea that the recipients of passports were 'indebted fathers of families'.[1] No planter received any of these licences; the *Conseil Supérieur* of Martinique later complained of this discrimination.

Unfortunately the system was not so free from favouritism and abuse as it was supposed to be. There were loud complaints of the merchants' ring which surrounded Givry; he rationed out the permits to St. Eustatius in such a way as to keep up the price of imports. Instead of entering freely and selling on his own account, the neutral had to find among the resident merchants a surety for his general observance of the laws, and for the payment of 3,000 livres, which the authorities charged for the permits. These sureties were often the real owners or buyers of the cargoes, or they took a high commission on sales and returns as a reward for the favour of procuring the licence. Others resold the licences in St. Eustatius, where an office was said to be openly kept for this sort of business; so that the cargoes were charged with their profits as well as the 3,000 livres—all of which, according to the planters, was paid by the consumer.[2]

There was the same kind of graft in St. Domingue under Vaudreuil and Laporte-Lalanne. Vaudreuil seems to have

---

[1] List of permissions issued, Aug. 21, 1756, A.N. Colonies C⁷ A 17; Bompar and Givry to Machault, undated (end of 1756), C⁸ A 60; Moras to Givry, June 10, 1757, B 105.
[2] Lieutenans du Roy of Martinique to Beauharnois, Jan. 1, 1759, A.N. Colonies C⁸ B 10; Rouillé de Raucourt to Berryer, Jan. 30, C⁸ A 61; *Conseil Supérieur* of Martinique to Beauharnois, March 7, ibid.; Allot to Berryer, ibid.; La Martinière to Berryer, May 28, C⁸ B 10.

made his market of the neutrals. One Rouvellette wrote to the Governor of St. Eustatius, whose interests he looked after in St. Domingue, that while Vaudreuil was in office, 'he had the same doings as the present Intendant, which sacrifices all things to his own interest, he is jealous of all the profits foreign merchants can expect from this trade in the French colonies. When the permissions were given out, the Intendant took the half to distribute to his favourites, and the General the other half for the same use. . . . I promise you, dear sir, the transactings I have been a witness of in this place are shocking.'[1] In other words, Vaudreuil and Laporte-Lalanne would rather keep the trade and the profit in the hands of two rings of favoured merchants, than admit the neutrals freely. They justified this policy in the same way as Beauharnois and Givry; the *commissionnaires*, who were well established in trade, could be made responsible for abuses or breaches of the law.[2] In fact, however, the privileged merchants seem to have discouraged the neutrals by asking for too great a profit; that is probably the reason why the passports of Vaudreuil and Laporte-Lalanne were not all used.

Messrs. Kavanagh and Belloc of Port au Prince described in great detail the failure of one of Vaudreuil's schemes. They obtained from him a licence for four large ships from the Dutch islands; the Dutch shipowners were to put on board some cargo and ship the proceeds for Holland, but most of the freight was reserved for Vaudreuil and for Kavanagh and Belloc at a very low rate. They could not induce anybody in St. Eustatius to accept of these terms: 'The Dutch', they complained, 'who will share nothing, and who might have been admitted without permission, would not be concerned; besides, as the large Dutch vessels were confined by their orders to load in their colonies, the captains did not dare to undertake the proposal, though it would have been much better for them.' It does not seem to have occurred to them that they were asking

---

[1] Rouvellette to de Windt, June 27, 1757, *Le Roy Indien*, Anderson, H.C.A. 42/92.

[2] Vaudreuil and Laporte-Lalanne to Machault, Aug. 27, 1756, A.N. Colonies C⁹ A 99. This policy seems to have been abandoned for a time, but was renewed at Cap François in Sept. 1760 by an ordinance which required all foreign traders to entrust their affairs to French merchants and pay them 10 per cent. commissions. This requirement could easily be evaded by collusion (Lopez to Henriquez, Oct. 4, 1760, *Young Moses*, Lopez, H.C.A. 42/109).

too much. They had to content themselves with selling one licence outright; the other three were never used.[1] One Clérisse, a merchant of Cap François, seems to have got leave from the Commissaire-Ordonnateur of that place to introduce two Dutch ships. He sent a friend to Curaçao to dispose of the privilege, on the terms that he and his partners should have half the profits without subscribing anything to the capital. One of the partners was the Commissaire-Ordonnateur himself, who seems to have been responsible for this extravagant demand. In consequence of it, the Dutch would not bite.[2]

Bart, who succeeded Vaudreuil as Governor in 1757, was an honester or at least a more plausible man; but even in his time the trade was subjected to some extortions and vexations. Under the pretext of submitting the foreign traders to a convenient form of control, the colonial authorities obliged them to deal with certain merchants. At Cap François a certain Macarty enjoyed a monopoly of this kind; at Aux Cayes it was Messrs. Texier. The strangers were also expected to compliment the secretaries of the Governor and Intendant with presents of money; and when Peyrac succeeded to the Intendance in the spring of 1760, he obliged all foreign traders to pay, or at least give security for, the duties of the *domaine d'occident* which they would have had to pay if they had imported their cargoes into France. He justified himself by the example of the passports which Machault had issued in 1756; but he acted without warrant, and contrary to the intentions of Berryer. He also provoked an extremely tiresome constitutional squabble in the colony. He was heavily rebuked; his impositions, with the other vexations and abuses mentioned above, came to an end in 1761 with the arrival of Intendant de Clugny, a factious prig who was strongly under Berryer's influence.[3]

Vaudreuil and Laporte-Lalanne seem to have got their crops remitted to Europe by the neutral traders, or else to have become dealers in other people's sugars. Sometimes they only granted permission to enter on condition of carrying on freight so much sugar for their account. Messrs. Texier of Aux Cayes

[1] Kavanagh and Belloc to Bouteiller and son, Aug. 8, 1757, *Maria Joanna*, Lindeboom, H.C.A. 42/80.
[2] Memorandum of Clérisse, Dec. 1758, A.N. Colonies C⁹ A 102.
[3] Berryer to Bart and Clugny, May 10, 1760, A.N. Colonies B 111; Clugny to Berryer, April 20, 1761, C⁹ A 108. Volumes 105–8 abound with furious controversy about Peyrac's duties.

asked pardon of their correspondents for accepting a hundred hogsheads on freight for Laporte-Lalanne.

'The Intendant, who gave his assistance at the admission of your ship, has desired that he might ship in her 100 hhds. of sugar, and we could not refuse him, for two good reasons, the first is that we shall want him for the admission of your ships if you follow your intentions of sending others, and the second was the 300 barrels of flour which he had taken for the King, and which he would have paid us in brown sugar, a commodity that would have turned out an entire loss for the want of being able to ship it, instead of which he has drawn bills of exchange upon France . . . we shall be obliged to you Gentlemen if you will use him favourably with regard to that, and if you incline to send ships to this colony we advise you to sacrifice something to make sure of his protection for your commerce, . . . he is here all-powerful, and he does everything to oblige those that make their applications to him and that prevent[1] him, and even if you had permissions from the Court for your ships his protection is always wanted.'

Another merchant reported that he had to buy some of the Governor's sugars at a high price, and take some of the Intendant's at a low freight.[2]

The Dutch ships which came from Europe without a passport and put in to the French colonies upon pretext of distress, were peculiarly liable to these impositions. They committed a technical breach of the French laws, and were therefore at the mercy of the authorities. Some of them were actually confiscated at St. Domingue in 1756, but Moras afterwards complained that others had been allowed to trade.[3] They had some hope of escaping confiscation if they were 'addressed to those that are a little in favour'. What this meant, may be judged from the elaborate instructions from Messrs. Auger to the master of the *St. Fernando*. They seem to have been confident of their interest with the authorities, but appearances must be kept up. He was to pretend to put in at Cap François for wood and water on his way to Curaçao. 'You are by no means to inquire of anybody for us at your coming on shore, you are to say that you are

---

[1] Presumably a too literal translation of *prévenir*, to prepossess. Most of the foreign documents which I quote from the Prize Papers are translated by the interpreters of the Admiralty Courts—sometimes very badly.

[2] Texier Brothers to St. Martin Brothers and Angely, *Vrouw Clara Magdalena*, van Houten, H.C.A. 42/99; Auger Brothers to Jouaneaulx and Parelle, Feb. 23, 1758, *St. Fernando*, Hilkes, H.C.A. 42/67.

[3] Laporte-Lalanne to Machault, Feb. 10, 1757, A.N. Colonies C⁹ A 100; Moras to Bart and Laporte-Lalanne, May 11, 1757, B 105; Tramond, op. cit., pp. 513-14.

unacquainted with any person at the Cape, we shall watch you and after all these ceremonies are over we shall meet you, and do what is needful, don't let anybody know that you know us and always say that you are put in.'[1]

The merchants of the islands advised their correspondents to procure passports from the French Government. It would save them infinite trouble and delay—though Messrs. Texier did not think it an infallible protection against the Governors and Intendants. Messrs. Auril and Capdeville impressed this lesson on John de Witt of Amsterdam. The passport would be cheap at the price of 20,000 livres, for the commandants could not then 'make their own laws', and a great deal of time would be saved. Roullier of Leogane threw a clearer light on the way the authorities made their own laws. 'He must have a permission and not otherwise or else he would run the risque of being confiscated or it might cost largely for his introduction, besides those in power would load one half of the ship and would limit the freight at their pleasure and not on condition of 25 p̄ Ct as you make mention.'[2]

The pretext on which these informal permits were granted was shortage of provisions. Machault and Moras had laid it down that no neutrals were to be admitted unless they brought provisions; but even the vessels which bore their passports sometimes failed of complying with this condition, and imported little but dry goods.[3] It appears from a paper in the archives of St. Domingue for 1757, that somebody in authority proposed to admit neutrals on condition that they carried a quarter of their cargoes in provisions. This proportion was criticized as too low; victuals were scarce, and it was the interest of French trade and even the colonies themselves that dry goods should not become too cheap. If a great quantity of dry goods was imported, the price must fall very low sooner or later, for the planter, who had to pay more for the necessaries of life out of a smaller income, could only afford luxuries if they were very cheap indeed. When dry goods no longer yielded a profit, the neutrals would cease to come at all and the colony would run short of provisions again, or else the dry goods would be stored

---

[1] Auger Brothers to Hilkes, Sept. 11, 1757, *St. Fernando*.

[2] *Vrouw Maria*, Marloff, H.C.A. 32/252; Dugué, Roullier and Co. to Orry, May 31, 1757, *Joannes*, Malmstrom, H.C.A. 42/77.

[3] Laporte-Lalanne to Machault, July 13, 1756, A.N. Colonies C⁹ A 99; to Moras, Oct. 2 and Dec. 14, 1757, C⁹ A 100.

and spoil the market after the peace. The writer therefore suggested a much lower proportion of luxuries, and added that the Governors and Intendants had better be left to regulate it; they would thus have a hold over the neutrals and could oblige them to put a reasonable price upon their victuals.[1]

Vaudreuil seems to have been indifferent to the introduction of provisions in neutral vessels; his concern as a planter was to get the crops of the colony shipped off, and he granted licences at a time when, as he admitted, there was no immediate danger of famine. He even forbade the neutrals to import such provisions as the Bordeaux and La Rochelle traders were likely to bring out from France, in order to keep up the market for them.[2] Bart proceeded on the opposite principle, and would not ordinarily admit neutrals unless they carried wine or flour. He and Laporte-Lalanne had a peculiar reason for their objection to excessive imports of dry goods. In all the other colonies, the captains, whether neutral or French, usually sold their cargoes wholesale to the merchants, but in St. Domingue they had the option of retailing them directly to the planters. The resident merchants, whose interests Laporte-Lalanne seems to have favoured consistently, had bought large stocks of dry goods from the first Dutchmen who arrived, and he did not wish to have them undersold in the retail trade by the later comers. Bart also tried to reserve the indigo and white sugars for the French ships, and confine the neutrals to exporting brown sugars and coffee, which would otherwise perish in the warehouses for want of a buyer.[3]

These restrictions seem to have been observed up to a point. Messrs. Auger advised Captain Hilkes of the *St. Fernando* to buy flour, even at a very high rate, at Monte Cristi where he lay waiting for admission. It would legitimize his cargo, as it were. Countless other letters could be cited, which express the opinion that a ship was sure of admission if she had wine and flour in her cargo, and not otherwise. The people of Curaçao,

---

[1] 'Observations sur les passeports qu'on veut donner aux vaisseaux neutres pour nos colonies, sous la condition qu'ils n'y seront point introduits s'ils n'ont en commestible le quart de leur chargement', C⁹ A 100. See also the letter of D. Argoût to Berryer, Dec. 14, 1760, C⁹ A 107.

[2] Vaudreuil and Laporte-Lalanne to Machault, Aug. 27 and Oct. 20, 1756, C⁹ A 99.

[3] Laporte-Lalanne to Moras, Dec. 14, 1757, C⁹ A 100; Kavanagh and Belloc to Bouteiller, Aug. 8, 1757, *Maria Joanna*, H.C.A. 42/80.

silly with greed, violated this principle at St. Louis and brought punishment upon themselves. Instead of bartering provisions for brown sugar and coffee, which was all they might lawfully do in the southern quarter, they openly exchanged dry goods for white sugar and indigo, to the great indignation of the French supercargoes. Worse still, they actually exported flour from St. Domingue to Curaçao when it suited them. The French authorities were very angry, and forbade them the port unless they came laden with provisions.[1]

Aucane, the director of the *Domaine* at Martinique, complained that the St. Eustatius trade did harm by the introduction of East India goods and European textiles, which stole the market from French goods of the same kind. He had lately seized a sloop which had applied for a licence with an invoice of victuals; she proved to be full of dry goods, without a single barrel of provisions on board. He went on to lament that these neutral cargoes were distributed to the several quarters without inspection, so that he could not prevent the importation of prohibited goods, having no ships or guards at his disposal.[2] Indeed, the whole coastguard service of the Windward Islands was soon afterwards disbanded by Le Mercier de la Rivière. Berryer approved of this measure, for there could no longer be any question of repressing smugglers when all neutrals were to be admitted freely; but perhaps he forgot that even he had not given the neutrals *carte blanche* to introduce any kind of goods they pleased.[3] There was a great scandal over a convoy sent to St. Eustatius in 1758 to bring some badly needed victuals which the Dutch traders no longer dared to send without protection. When the vessels arrived, they proved to be full of dry

---

[1] Labat to Counil, April 12 and June 13, 1756, *Juste*, Counil, H.C.A. 32/204; Bouché to Hotessier, April 26, 1758, Adm. 1/235; Laporte-Lalanne to Moras, Jan. 7, 1758, A.N. Colonies C⁹ A 101 (I am not sure if the ship referred to was a neutral, but it seems so from the context); Pieter Kock Jansz, Curaçao, to Berewout, Jan. 27, 1758, *Caterina Maria Galley*, Gestloff, H.C.A. 32/176; Mesnier, Cap François, to Lebeuf, March 2, 1758, *St. Fernando*; Kavanagh and Belloc to Bouteiller, Aug. 8, 1757, *Maria Joanna*.

[2] Aucane to Ranché, March 14, 1758, *Stadt Rotterdam*, Peer, H.C.A. 42/96. Some factors appear however to have had difficulty in obtaining leave to export West India produce in vessels which had arrived in Martinique without any provisions for sale (Diant Brothers to Klock, Dedel & Co., Feb. 4, 1758, *Snip*, Schultz, H.C.A. 42/96).

[3] Berryer to Le Mercier de la Rivière, March 29, 1760, A.N. Colonies B 111. Berryer blamed La Rivière in the same letter for hiring out the *Domaine* vessels to an adventurer like Father Lavalette.

goods. Rumour accused the Intendant of responsibility for this shameful abuse; he could only boast that he had turned away neutral vessels with cargoes of dry goods in the past, and retort on his principal accusers, the commanders of the convoy, the irrelevant charge of demanding a fee of 10 per cent. for their services.[1]

Moras and his successor Berryer disapproved of their subordinates' conduct, but for exactly opposite reasons. Moras gave ear to the complaints of the Chambers of Commerce, who attributed to the 'smuggling' through St. Eustatius the unprofitableness of remittances, the decay of the re-export trade, and the low price of West India produce in France.[2] He still forbade the Governors and Intendants to admit neutrals except in the utmost necessity, and ordered them to justify it by giving an account of the victuals in store on every occasion when they permitted a neutral to enter. Beauharnois and Givry resented this well-deserved insult to their integrity, and asserted that such statistics would be valueless because the shopkeepers and planters would always hide their stocks from such an inquisition, in order to establish a case for importing more.[3]

The year 1758 was a bad one for the French Windward Islands. Commodore Moore established a blockade which, though not always effective, paralysed the trade of St. Eustatius and reduced the merchants to despair. No shipping dared move between the French and neutral colonies, unless protected by a man-of-war or fitted out with a heavy armament and expensive crew after the manner of privateers. Few neutrals, however exasperated against the English, would dare to carry on the trade in this way.[4] The French privateers were employed to bring victuals from St. Eustatius, and sometimes contributed to the subsistence of the islands by making prize of

---

[1] Conseil Supérieur of Martinique to Beauharnois, March 7, 1759, A.N. Colonies C⁸ A 61; *Mémoire* of Givry, Nov. 21, A.N. Marine B⁴ 91.

[2] Bordeaux to Nantes, Nov. 10, 1756, Arch. Gir. C 4263, f. 263; Chamber to Castaing, Dec. 18, 1756, f. 267; Dubos, Bordeaux, to Rose, June 7, 1757, H.C.A. 32/258; Brunaud Brothers to Denohic, June 6, ibid.

[3] Moras to Beauharnois and Givry, June 10, 1757, A.N. Colonies B 105; Beauharnois and Givry to Moras, June 20, 1758, C⁸ A 61.

[4] J. P. Allier, St. Eustatius, to E. Bouwer and sons, June 24, 1758, *Vrouw Gesina*, Nicolaas, H.C.A. 32/252; Allier to van Marselis, June 5, 1758, *Helena*, Flor, H.C.A. 42/71; Locuillart, St. Pierre, to Doumer, March 1758, ibid.; Berryer to Beauharnois and La Rivière, July 26, 1759, A.N. Colonies B 109. Some Dutch vessels actually showed fight; see Cotes's letter to Clevland, May 11, 1759, Adm. 1/235; Nadau to Massiac, Dec. 25, 1758, A.N. Colonies C⁷ A 17.

English vessels with provisions on board. At present, however, the resource of prizes was not a great one, though Martinique almost lived on the proceeds of privateering in the later years of the war.

The situation of the islands was really pitiable on the eve of the English attempt in 1759. On New Year's Day the Lieutenans du Roy protested to Beauharnois against the high prices fixed by the merchants' ring. No neutrals had arrived for two months, the negroes were dying of under-nourishment, the cattle had all been slaughtered to feed the children and invalids. The *Conseil Supérieur* hinted, after the danger from the English had passed over Martinique, that the starving planters and their negroes deserved some credit for preserving their allegiance and repelling the enemy. Beauharnois consented to hearten them by opening the ports to all neutrals, without any fee or special licence, for four months from the first of February—not that he would admit the fee of 3,000 livres to be the real cause of the discouragement of neutrals, which he attributed to the English blockade and the resale of permits at a profit. This freedom was prolonged for the rest of the war.[1]

It might have been expected that Berryer would object in the style of his predecessors to this abandonment of all traditional restraints. On the contrary, he commended it. He believed that the colonists had a real grievance, and that the neutral trade could easily be carried on but for the extortionate monopoly by which the Governors and Intendants had confined it. Unlike Maurepas, Machault, and Moras, who had all thought that neutrals were too freely admitted to the colonies, Berryer believed that they were not free enough. Just as Maurepas had assumed that the economic and financial difficulties of the colonies would vanish if the exports and imports were kept up by the convoy system, Berryer expected the same result from the uninterrupted flow of neutral trade. He made the mistake of thinking that the Governors and Intendants alone could make it flourish by disinterested and liberal conduct. They had great difficulty in explaining to him that the English blockade was the real reason why the neutrals did not come; and as he believed that the trade would be best left to itself, he never could think it necessary for Le Mercier de la Rivière to assume

---

[1] Rouillé de Raucourt to Berryer, March 16, 1759, A.N. Colonies C⁸ A 61; Beauharnois to Nadau, Jan. 8, ibid.

the duty of importing victuals for the colony at the Government's expense, and exporting sugars on its account. No doubt La Rivière was too anxious to try his hand as a practical economist, but he did not deserve all the niggling, exasperated *marginalia* upon his correspondence with which the Minister relieved his impotent indignation.[1]

Less and less was heard of the difficulty of victualling Martinique after 1759. Some decisions in the Court of Prize Appeals caused the spirit of privateering to slacken in England. Although they brought little direct relief to the trade between St. Eustatius and Martinique, they indirectly helped it to revive.[2] The Martinique privateers were far more successful in the latter years of the war than in the earlier. It is hard to see why this should have been so, for Commodores Moore and Douglas were no fools, and disposed of a considerable force. Perhaps the English traders, confident in the command of the sea and relieved from the embargoes which had hampered their operations at first, spread themselves too carelessly among the islands and exposed themselves to too many risks. Perhaps the number of French privateers was swelled by those whose other occupations were become unprofitable—a very common thing in the West Indies, where small planters and merchant sailors turned privateers when their estates or trade had been ruined by the war. At any rate, Martinique lived cheerfully upon prizes and the imports of the neutrals. Sometimes there was a positive plenty, and the French captains who arrived there in 1761, on the eve of the English conquest, found the markets so well supplied by prizes and neutrals as to be quite disadvantageous.[3]

[1] Berryer to Beauharnois and La Rivière, July 26, 1759, A.N. Colonies B 109; Le Mercier de la Rivière to Berryer, Nov. 16, C⁸ A 62; Beauharnois and La Rivière to Berryer, Feb. 13, 1760, ibid.; Berryer to Le Mercier de la Rivière, March 15, 1760, B 111; see also Berryer to Bart and Élias, July 26, 1759, B. 109; to Bart and Clugny, May 10, 1760, B 111.

[2] I hope to deal with these decisions in a book, shortly to be published, on the privateers and prizes, 1739-63.

[3] 'Letter from Martinique', April 15, 1761, S.P. 84/494; various intercepted letters, Nov.–Dec. 1760, apparently taken out of the *Union du Cap*, S.P. 42/42, ff. 293-6; Dumas to Van Heyningen and Heyliger, June 15, 1760, *Don Carlos*, Poeste, H.C.A. 42/63; Laforcaud and Dargenton to Penistone, *Mary*, Correer, H.C.A. 42/80; Le Vassor de la Touche to Berryer, June 11, 1761, A.N. Colonies C⁸ A 63; Le Mercier de la Rivière to Berryer, ibid. These last letters speak of the plenty as somewhat precarious, and dependent upon the high prices which La Rivière characteristically thought it the duty of the Government to keep up by large orders for the victualling of the island. At the capitulation of the island, the English commanders would not recognize these contracts, or promise immunity

The situation of St. Domingue was unpleasant, though not serious, for the first two years of the war. There was no real scarcity in 1756, but at the beginning of the next year the colony would have wanted flour but for the prizes. The planters were forbidden to feed their negroes on wheat bread, and most of them were soon afterwards obliged to live on yams and cassava like their slaves; but nobody starved. When, however, the English began to treat cargoes of provisions in neutral ships as contraband, and still more when Moore declared his blockade, Bart and Laporte-Lalanne were really afraid of a famine, especially in the northern quarter where the drought had destroyed the ground provisions. The price of necessaries fluctuated greatly from month to month, and differed between one place and another because the coasting trade was suspended. Sometimes a few neutrals would slip past the cruisers, at others the scarcity was worse than ever. From October 1757 to February 1758, wine and flour were very dear in Cap François; the one cost 500 livres the hogshead and the other 300 livres the barrel. Wine was only 300 at Léogane at the same time. In March some cargoes were imported to the northern quarter, and the prices fell to 300 and 120, but afterwards the scarcity set in again.

In the autumn of 1758, Bart and Laporte-Lalanne hoped that the Danes would take the place of the intimidated Dutch, but the English soon put an end to that resource by condemning all neutrals alike.[1] However, the neutral trade revived after the middle of 1759 at St. Domingue as in the Windward Islands; neutrals must have come in freely, and the prices do not seem to have risen again to those of the winter of 1757–8, though they were still above the average of peace. They varied a great deal between one quarter and another; for instance, in May 1760 wine was at 250 livres the hogshead at Cap François and

to the neutral vessels which arrived to fulfil them (see the capitulation, C.O. 166/2).

[1] Vaudreuil to Machault, March 1, 1757, A.N. Colonies C⁹ A 100; Bart and Laporte-Lalanne to Moras, Sept. 20 and 25, ibid.; Bart to Moras, Oct. 17, ibid.; Chastenoye to Moras, Oct. 19, ibid.; Lambert to Moras, Oct. 14, ibid.; Bart and Laporte-Lalanne to Moras, Jan. 5, 1758, C⁹ A 101; Laporte-Lalanne to Moras, Feb. 15, ibid.; to Massiac, Nov. 1, ibid.; Bart to Massiac, Oct. 1 and Nov. 27, ibid.; Lambert to Moras, Feb. 10, July 15, and Oct. 12, C⁹ A 102. The history of prices is to be traced in the papers of the Dutch ships and Flags of Truce in the Prize Appeals Papers, especially the *Archibald Adrian*, Harstedt, H.C.A. 42/54; the *St. Fernando*, Hilkes, H.C.A. 42/67; the *King William III*, Robinson, H.C.A. 42/79; the *Queen of Bohemia*, La Tora, H.C.A. 42/90, and the *Vrouw Clara Magdalena*, van Houten, H.C.A. 42/99; see also Tramond, op. cit., pp. 509–39.

500 at Léogane, while sugars fetched twice as much at Cap François as at Léogane. The southern quarter, the most neglected in peace by the traders of France, was the best served during the later years of this war by the neutrals and Flags of Truce. Flour never rose above 150 livres the barrel, and it was as low as 50 and even 30 livres in 1760 and 1761. Brown sugar fetched peace-time prices at several times in those years, though it fell at the end of 1761 when the demand of the New England Flags of Truce fell off. Conditions were good in the northern quarter at this time; it was the west that suffered most of all, because it was the most difficult of access.[1]

The English Flag of Truce traders came into play about the middle of 1758. The North Americans had frequented the French islands more than ever in the interval between the two wars. They were commoner at St. Domingue than at Martinique, for several reasons. St. Domingue was farther than the Windward Islands from any smugglers' head-quarters until the establishment of Monte Cristi in 1755; a direct intercourse was therefore more necessary. It was nearer to North America, and the risks from French and English warships were much less. These considerations were even more important in time of war, consequently there was very little Flag of Truce trade with Martinique and a great deal with St. Domingue.

Although the French Ministers had done their best to discountenance this trade in the intervals of peace, the necessities of the colonists and the interests of the local commandants frustrated their intentions. There was usually some pretext, such as a fire or a drought, which would justify the admission of these useful interlopers. Vaudreuil or his underlings were probably concerned in illicit dealings with them before the war, and he naturally had recourse to them after it began.[2] He had very little success at first: the embargoes in North America kept the neutral and even the English islands short of provisions, and the

[1] Bart and Élias to Berryer, Feb. 11, 1760, C⁹ A 105; Bart and Peyrac to Berryer, May 6 and Sept. 22, 1760, ibid.; Peyrac to Berryer, March 22 and Sept. 23, 1760, vol. 106; d'Argoût to Berryer, Dec. 14, 1760, April 27, June 2, and Sept. 25, 1761, vols. 107 and 109; Clugny to Berryer, April 20 and July 1, 1761, vol. 108.

[2] Rouillé to Conflans and Maillart, Dec. 4, 1749, A.N. Colonies B 89; Instructions to Dubois de la Motte, March 31, 1751, B 93; Fournier de la Chapelle to Chastenoye, April 19, 1754, C⁹ A 98; Vaudreuil and Laporte-Lalanne to Machault, Jan. 6, 1755, ibid.; Dumesnil to Machault, Feb. 22, ibid.; Fontenelle to Machault, Feb. 22, ibid.; Laporte-Lalanne to Machault, July 5, ibid.; Machault to Vaudreuil and Laporte-Lalanne, Jan. 31, B 101.

Flour Act seems to have intimidated some Governors for a time.[1] The commanders at Cap François sent a sloop to the Bahamas to make an arrangement with Governor Tinker, who had supplied them with victuals in the last war. There was plenty of prize flour at New Providence, but this time Tinker dared not let them have any, because he was afraid to break his instructions.[2]

This shyness soon wore off, and before the end of 1758 the North Americans were pouring their goods into the French ports. Bart reported at the end of the next year that they had brought the colony a supply for four or five months.[3] In 1760 it was said that the North Americans 'revive the spirits of the sugar-planters who had given up cultivating, and now begin it again with some rays of hope; they make enough sugar to buy themselves victuals, and what they sell for money enables them to pay their taxes'.[4]

Berryer made not the least objection to this trade. He criticized the excessive zeal of Beauharnois, who only admitted some Flags of Truce and confiscated others; in Berryer's opinion he ought to have let them all enter freely. Blénac was shocked to find the trade so prevalent at St. Domingue in 1762; it was repugnant to his sense of patriotism, and he asked Choiseul whether he ought not to stop it. Choiseul told him to do nothing of the kind.[5] The French commanders took measures which might have injured the very similar Monte Cristi trade; a French warship entered the bay in December 1758 and burnt a number of English vessels at anchor. This, however, was only a reprisal for the like treatment of some French vessels there in 1757; it was not inspired by any hostility to the business, which the authorities of the colony continued to tolerate so long as it lasted.[6]

[1] This was an Act of 1757, which forbade the export of provisions from the British Dominions to foreign parts; v. infra, pp. 437–45.

[2] Laporte-Lalanne to Moras, April 9, 1757, A.N. Colonies C⁹ A 100; Lambert to Moras, April 15, ibid.; Bart to Moras, April 18, ibid.

[3] Bart to Berryer, Dec. 15, 1759, A.N. Colonies C⁹ A 103.

[4] Bart and Peyrac to Berryer, July 12, 1760, C⁹ A 105.

[5] Berryer to Le Vassor de la Touche, May 20, 1761, A.N. Colonies B 111; Blénac to Choiseul, March 28, 1762, A.N. Marine B⁴ 104; Choiseul to Blénac, June 20, B² 370, f. 321.

[6] Bory to Berryer, March 14, 1759, A.N. Marine B⁴ 81; Berryer to Bart, April 21, 1759, Colonies B 109. For a description of the Monte Cristi trade, see pp. 456–67. The Flag of Truce trade was much more seriously interrupted by the Spanish privateers after the outbreak of war between England and Spain in 1762. The President of S. Domingo refused to restrain them, because it was axiomatic that

These expedients could not entirely remedy the shrinkage of trade in the islands. The statistics of neutral and Flag of Truce shipping are fragmentary: putting the average tonnage of a St. Eustatius bark or North America sloop at seventy tons—and that is a high estimate—and the average ship in the French trade at something over two hundred, it appears that the former did not fill the void left by the virtual disappearance, during the worst crises, of the latter. Only at places habitually neglected by the French trade, such as Guadeloupe and St. Louis, can the imports and exports have been increased or at least maintained during the war; and in fact some of these deserted outposts seem to have been half-starved in spite of the help which the Dutch might bring them. No ship had arrived in Cayenne from France for fourteen months in June 1758, and until the Dutch found out the way from Surinam the colonists were living on cassava bread and on the verge of having to drink water.[1]

§ v. *The Value of the Blockade*

The effect of the English blockade upon the French colonies has, I hope, been sufficiently described in the course of this chapter and the last. Its impact upon France is much harder to judge. The clamour and lamentation of the merchants is not very good evidence, for there was always too much cry in that quarter, and often very little wool. There was talk of idle shipping, bankruptcies among insurers, unemployment among manufacturers, but all in terms so general as to be insignificant. The figures of exports and imports tell more. Those given by M. Martin for the slave-trade of Nantes show that it was almost destroyed in the War of the Austrian Succession and quite annihilated in the Seven Years War. Malvezin's statistics for Bordeaux prove likewise that the latter war was much more disastrous than the former. The combined value of imports and exports to the French colonies, which had risen to its highest at 24 million livres in 1743, was reduced to 7 in 1748, although the war was finished half-way through that year. In the years 1753 to 1755 it rose well above 30 millions, but fell below 8 in 1758

trade between enemies was forbidden in time of war (Bory to Choiseul, Sept. 2, 1762, A.N. Colonies C⁹ A 111).

[1] Guimar, Cayenne, to Widow Prévost, June 12, 1758, *Young Peter*, Daaler, H.C.A. 42/105; Pruite to his brother, June 6, 1758, ibid.; de la Rivière to his father, June 10, 1758, ibid.

and 1759 and below 4 in 1760. The next year it rose to nearly 7, and in the last year of the war almost touched 15.

The re-export trade fell off to an even more pitiable degree. That of sugar, which was round about 300,000 hundredweight between 1750 and 1756, was below 8,000 from 1757 to 1761. The other re-exports were less seriously affected, but that of indigo fell to a quarter, and coffee to a tenth, of the average figure for the period between the two wars.[1] This trade was very dangerous, for it was often interrupted by English privateers even though it was carried in Dutch ships; it was also unnecessary, because the Dutch had made their own contacts with the French producer through St. Eustatius and Curaçao, and with the English seller of French prize goods. In fact, Dutchmen were offering French sugars and indigo to the merchants of France, instead of asking for them.

The prices of West India goods in France do not seem to have risen so high as might be expected from these striking reductions; but that is not really surprising if the French sugar-trade depended so much upon the re-export market, which was itself almost entirely cut off during the war. For the first years of the Seven Years War the large stocks on hand, which could not be disposed of abroad as usual, kept the price of colonial goods low in the French ports; but as those stocks were absorbed, and imperfectly replenished, it began to rise, although the merchants had nothing left but the despised home market. In the last years of the war it was really high, and stories were told— only, indeed, in a French *alamain*, the most worthless of all forms of news—of Parisian housewives using honey instead of sugar for preserves after the fall of Martinique.[2] Brown sugars are quoted at 55 to 63 livres the hundredweight in Bordeaux at the end of March 1762, and whites at 75 to 90; these prices are nearly 20 livres higher than those of June 1757. Perhaps it was this revival of prices that stimulated the French merchants to their new efforts of 1761 and 1762; and it may be added as a corollary, that possibly the low value of West India goods in France in 1757 had something to do with the collapse of the trade which was usually attributed to the heavy losses at sea.

---

[1] Malvezin, *Histoire du commerce de Bordeaux*, iii. 306–7.

[2] Dubos to Rose, June 7, 1757, H.C.A. 32/258; Crozilhac to Coudesc, April 16, 1757, ibid.; Brunaud to Denohic, June 6, 1757, ibid.; La Rochelle to Bordeaux, June 29, 1758, Arch. Gir. C 4321, no. 28; Mme de Frémicour to Lamole de Feuille, H.C.A. 32/257; Paris intelligence, April 1, 1762, Add. MSS. 32936, f. 247.

If the object of the blockade was to put the French colonies permanently out of action, it was a failure. After every war French production of West India goods rose steeply to new high levels. Within eight years of the Peace of Paris, the colonial commerce of Bordeaux, which had never before handled 40 million livres' worth of imports and exports, only just fell short of a hundred. This rate of progress quite surpassed the plodding climb of the English colonies, even with all the conquests of 1763.[1]

Whether the blockade contributed materially to England's victory is equally questionable. The success of such an effort depends on the importance of overseas trade in the economic life of a country, and, in those days, on the strength of Ministers' nerves. At first sight there appears to be some reason for thinking that the colonial blockade brought France to terms when nothing else could have done so. The colonies of France had never appeared more completely in our power than in the spring of 1748; her navy was diminished by the loss of two squadrons, and her trade was disorganized and defenceless. Louis XV sacrificed brilliant prospects on land in order to save his country from starvation and commercial crisis. But the famine, which was the chief cause of this distress and despair, was no work of ours; on the contrary, we actually relieved it even before the war came to an end. Still less had it anything to do with the colonial trade.[2]

The Seven Years War demonstrates to my mind the impotence of blockade and colonial conquests to break the will of France. The French colonial trade did not slowly decline until in 1762 it reached vanishing-point and so forced the Government to make peace. On the contrary, it collapsed quickly in the spring

---

[1] This advance was due chiefly to the exploitation of St. Domingue. Martinique, like the older English islands in its neighbourhood, was too fully settled to be capable of such striking increases, as the figures show which M. May reproduces in the appendixes of his *Histoire économique de la Martinique*.

[2] A different impression is given by a dispatch which d'Argenson sent to his ambassador at Madrid in January 1746. He was to tell the Catholic King that France could no longer undertake to insist on so large an establishment for Don Philip as she had promised in the Treaty of Fontainebleau. She had neglected her navy for her army, in order, as d'Argenson here suggested, to render the more effectual help to Spain in Italy. The loss of Louisbourg and 200 million livres' worth of prizes had caused a complete collapse in the trade and manufactures of the kingdom; so disastrous a policy could not go on (*Recueil des Instructions, Espagne*, iii. 259). This, however, was special pleading for a policy whose real merit in d'Argenson's eyes was the Sardinian alliance.

and summer of 1757, and in the last two years of the war it was reviving a little. The colonial merchants simply went out of business, and contented themselves with getting home their old debts if they could.[1] If France was ever to have been reduced to submission by the loss of this trade, it would have been in 1758 or 1759. Bernis did indeed fill the air with lamentations over the deplorable state of the French overseas commerce.

'No trade left, consequently no money or circulation. No navy, consequently no strength to resist England. The navy has no more sailors, and having no money, cannot hope to procure them. What must be the result of this state of affairs? The loss of all our colonies for ever; our land forces cannot protect our coasts. . . . Even if we save Louisbourg, what help can we send to our colonies without ships or money? . . . I tell you, my dear Count, that even if the King of Prussia were crushed, we should be ruined none the less. England carries on all the trade there is, and we shall never reduce her to reasonable conditions unless we can interrupt it.'[2]

Choiseul, to whom he wrote this letter, was made of other stuff. He proved, with the circumscribed help of the neutrals, how easily a nation can live without colonial trade, and even without colonies. Pursued by the imprecations of the seaports and manufacturing towns, he continued a losing war at sea and kept his hold of Germany the better to recover the colonies and trade of France. If she made peace in 1763 on terms not unworthy of her, it was because her Minister would not yield to a form of pressure which only touched the circumference of her economic life.

[1] Gradis to Marin, Oct. 18, 1759, quoted by Jean de Maupassant, *Abraham Gradis* (Bordeaux, 1917), p. 91.
[2] Bernis to Choiseul, Aug. 20, 1758, *Mémoires et Lettres du Cardinal de Bernis* (ed. Masson), ii. 259.

IX

TRADE WITH THE ENEMY

THE necessity and propriety of starving the French colonies into submission were assumed without much question by English Ministers and commanders. The exact purpose of this blockade was not very expressly defined; the authorities who directed it could hardly have said whether it was to conquer the French islands without striking a blow, or to weaken them so that they could not resist a blow to be struck, or to put their sugar plantations out of action for the advantage of our own, or simply to create a general pressure which would make them uncomfortable for the mere sake of doing so. War is war, and those who wage it are not always at the pains of defining clearly the kind of success at which they aim. In those days a blockade only required definition when neutrals called its legality in question; the English Government did not think itself obliged to justify it either to the enemy or to its own subjects.

The French West India colonies were marked out for such a blockade. They all depended for the conveniences and even the necessities of life upon overseas traffic, for the French Government was no more successful than the English in forcing them to grow their own supplies of food. An English critic of the blockade tried to argue that while there was some hope of reducing Martinique by it, there was none at all of starving St. Domingue, where more land was available for the cultivation of provision crops; but the French records do not seem to show that St. Domingue relied any less than the Windward Islands on imported provisions, or was any less distressed by their interception.[1]

The blockade cannot be fully understood if it is treated only as a military measure or a question of international law. It was both those things; but it also provoked, or rather intensified, a long-standing conflict of interests, which must be examined as shortly as possible from its beginning.

---

[1] 'Observations on the trade which is now carrying on by the English to Monto Christi a Spanish settlement in Hispaniola', Add. MSS. 36211, ff. 256 et seqq. This manuscript was presumably drawn up for the use of Charles Yorke, Solicitor-General, who had lately been briefed in some Monte Cristi cases before the Lords Commissioners of Prize Appeals.

§ i. *The Interests Affected by the Blockade*

North America and the West Indies were made for mutual trade and intercourse; each depended on the other from a very early date in the history of the colonies. This is equally true of the English, French, and Dutch Empires. The Dutch of New York exported horses, lumber, and provisions to Curaçao before the English conquest. In the eighteenth century there was a small but growing commerce between Louisbourg and the French sugar islands. It never became so important as the similar trade between the English colonies. The French settlements in North America were thinly populated and for the most part inaccessible; moreover the French West Indies relied more than the English on foodstuffs from Europe.

The connexion of New England with Barbados and the Leeward Islands was almost as old as the colonies themselves.[1] The sugar-planters needed flour, horses, fish, and lumber, some of which they could only obtain from England with difficulty and after much administrative formality, others could scarcely be had there at all. Most of these branches of export to the West Indies were resigned by England to North America without much reluctance, and the only important class of provisions which the sugar-planters still drew from Europe was the beef and butter of Ireland. If North America was thus indispensable to the West Indies, the West Indies were hardly less necessary to North America. They furnished sugar, rum, and molasses— the last two articles were more necessary, if anything, than the first. They also offered a market for the agricultural produce which was almost all that the Northern Colonies were at that time capable of producing. This is not the place to illustrate the many ways in which the West India trade interwove itself with the economic life of North America, and the convenience it afforded, especially to small traders and beginners, for making remittances to pay for manufactures imported from England. It is enough to say that the merchants of North America professed, and perhaps also believed, that they could not profitably carry on any branch of business without liberty to export their produce to the West Indies and bring back West India goods.

In the seventeenth century the agriculture of the Northern

[1] V. T. Harlow, *A History of Barbados, 1625–1685*, c. vi.

Colonies could do little more than supply the needs of the English sugar islands; but already the farmers of North America were beginning to look for wider markets in the West Indies. In the reign of Queen Anne there were frequent complaints of an unpatriotic trade with Curaçao and St. Thomas, two nests of cosmopolitan smugglers from which provisions were finding their way to the French islands. The Board of Trade suggested some ill-considered measures against this trade.[1]

The disproportion of North American production to West Indian consumption continued to grow; New England, New York, and Philadelphia traded more and more with the French islands. I have already dealt with the French attitude to this trade, and referred in an earlier chapter to the Molasses Act, which was designed to stop it by laying heavy duties on certain goods imported from the foreign West Indies.[2] Many of the arguments which attended the passage of that law, reappeared in the discussion of the 'pernicious and unwarrantable traffic' which the Northern Colonies carried on with the enemy in these wars. It was only a new form of the old controversy between North America and the West Indies, sharpened by the charges of treason, or at least want of patriotism, which the disputants bandied about. The expedients with which the West Indians obstructed the trade with the enemy sometimes bore a likeness to those which they demanded in peace for the permanent protection of their interests; the traders' devices for eluding the duties or the penalties of unlawful commerce with the French, were very much the same in peace and war.

The Molasses Act did not determine the controversy, for it was not executed. The price of West India goods in England and America began to rise about 1740, as the North American merchants had prophesied; but that did not satisfy the West Indians, nor could it be ascribed to a cessation of the traffic with the French West Indies. That traffic continued and increased; the sum of the duties paid under the Act was absurdly small.[3] The customs officers hardly tried to collect them; for example, when those of Salem began in 1758 to demand a tenth of the duties, the merchants exclaimed against

---

[1] *C.S.P. Col. 1702*, nos. 498, 743; *1702-3*, nos. 16, 950, 1014, 1072 (i), 1150 (ii); *1704-5*, nos. 669, 671, 677 (i), 846, 914; *1710-11*, nos. 47, 104.

[2] *V. supra*, pp. 79-82.

[3] T 70/1205. The duties on foreign West India goods—apart from prize goods—did not amount to £1,000 until 1749.

the innovation as unprecedentedly burdensome.[1] Compounding for these duties was very common, and the Act must have had a very bad effect on commercial morality and on the probity of the customs officers.[2] When the traders with the French were brought up in the Prize Courts during the wars, they very often defended themselves by arguing that the customs officers of North America made no objection to the entry of French West India goods, whether they came from neutral or even enemy ports.[3]

The officers in the West Indies were equally to blame for the state of affairs: through their connivance or neglect, the traders got false clearances from our own islands for cargoes which were loaded elsewhere. At Kingston, Jamaica, North American vessels were allowed to clear out with imaginary cargoes representing what they intended to take on board in the outports where there were no custom-houses; nothing easier than to load at St. Domingue instead of going to the outports at all.[4] False clearances must have been obtained in other West India ports without even this respectable excuse.[5]

Yet even if the officers had always been honest, they had very little power. Sometimes an accident might make this trade so obvious that it could not be passed over—as when one of Peter Faneuil's vessels fell into the hands of the public authorities after suffering piracy and shipwreck. Nothing more than intention to smuggle could be proved in these cases, so that the worst the customs officers could do, whether backed or resisted by public opinion, was to exact the Molasses Act duties.[6]

---

[1] Timothy Orne to George Dodge, July 18, 1758, April 30, 1759, Timothy Orne MSS. iii. 136, iv. 35, Essex Institute.

[2] Letter to the *Boston Evening Post*, Nov. 21, 1763; letter of 'Shearjashub Squeezum' to the *Boston Gazette*, Aug. 27, 1764, *Colden Papers* (*N.Y.H.S. Collections*, 1877), ii. 371.

[3] See, for example, the deposition of George Williams in the *Chester*, Angell, H.C.A. 42/59.

[4] Knowles to Board of Trade, Jan. 10, 1753, C.O. 137/25, X 122.

[5] The Governor of the Leeward Islands charged Dunbar, the Surveyor-General of the Customs, with various irregularities designed to favour the illicit traders, especially with refusal to make vessels coming or going to St. Eustatius enter and clear; he even accused him of partnership with the smuggling Governor of St. Eustatius. This last accusation, however, was very freely thrown about in the West Indies, and Mathew seems to have had a feud with Dunbar, so his invectives must be discounted (Mathew to Yeamans, May 29, 1741, C.O. 152/44; Yeamans to Stone, Aug. 4, ibid.).

[6] Report of the Solicitor-General of St. Kitts, Assembly Minutes, May 18, 1752 (St. Kitts Administrator's Office). For the history of Faneuil's ship, see his letters

The planters soon set to work to get the Act reinforced. They aimed at forbidding all intercourse with the foreign West Indies —this had been the original form of the Molasses Act, as it passed the Commons in 1731, and many planters regretted that Parliament had contented itself in the end with imposing severe duties. A Bill was introduced into the House of Commons for this purpose in 1739, but it fell short of a complete prohibition; the precautions against fraud were too elaborate and onerous, and the representatives of planters and merchants disagreed about it. For these reasons the Agents of some islands took it upon themselves to resist it. Their constituents did not blame them, though the legislatures of Barbados and St. Kitts were ready to accept a partial measure if the complete prohibition could not be obtained.[1] The sugar colonies, headed by Jamaica and Antigua, tried again in 1749–51, making capital of the unpatriotic character of the trade carried on by the Flags of Truce in time of war. They petitioned Parliament, but the Agents of Pennsylvania and New York struck back by taxing the planters with monopoly and *latifundia*, and for the next few years the planters had to defend themselves against a similar attack from the sugar-refiners. Their Agents still blustered, and summoned the chief representative of the Northern Colonies to prepare himself for a final trial of strength in 1752; but the threatened Bill was never introduced, and the West India interest busied itself with other expedients.[2]

On the eve of the Seven Years War a new circumstance disposed the West Indian and North American interests to a reconciliation; the Ministry was known to have its eye on the trade as a source of revenue, and both parties concurred to

to Benjamin Faneuil, Sept. 26, 1738; to Jacques Castera, Oct. 11; to Capt. John Browne, Dec. 4, 1738, Faneuil Letter-book, New England Historical and Genealogical Society.

[1] St. Kitts Council Minutes, Nov. 7, 1739, C.O. 241/4; Barbados Council Minutes, March 19, 1739/40, C.O. 31/21.

[2] Antigua legislature to John Sharpe, Nov. 30, 1750; Minutes of Dec. 14, 1752 (Antigua Assembly Minutes, St. John's Court-House); St. Kitts Council Minutes, Nov. 10, March 11, 1750/1, May 1, 1752 (St. Kitts Administrator's Office); Legislature of Jamaica to George II, Nov. 21, 1749, Nov. 20, 1752, C.O. 137/25 X 48, 115; *C.J.* xxvi. 107–8 (petition of West India merchants), 156 (petition of Bollan), 169 (petition of Partridge), 183–4 (petitions of Charles, and of various merchants); Partridge to Greene, July 24, 1751, April 10, 1752, West Indian Agents to Partridge, July 11, 1751, Kimball, *Correspondence of Colonial Governors of Rhode Island*, ii. 131–5; Lascelles and Maxwell to Gedney Clarke, April 19, 1751, W. & G. v.

resist this as the worst possible settlement of their differences.[1]
I do not know whether the Government's project was an
anticipation of the Sugar Act of 1764 or that of 1766—that is
to say, whether it tended only to lower the duties on foreign
West India goods so as to make them payable, or to charge
British West India produce with them as well. The scheme was
dropped for the time being, like that of the Stamp Act, to be
revived after the war with fatal and disconcerting effects.

The North Americans imported foreign sugars chiefly for
their own consumption, but they might tranship some of it
and send it to London as English produce. This was unfair to
the English planters, whose produce would have had to pay
the 'Plantation duties' of 1674 if carried to England by the same
roundabout way, whereas the French sugar actually paid nothing at all. They petitioned the Treasury for the exclusion
from England of all West India produce not imported straight
from the West Indies, or at least for a rule that sugars thus
indirectly imported were to be presumed foreign and pay duties
as such.[2] The Treasury took this last piece of advice in 1756,
to the great discontent of some North American merchants.
The West Indians sometimes urged that the Plantation duties
of 1674 should be abolished. The Government, however, would
not hear of this.[3]

The planters resorted to other methods for protecting themselves against foreign competition. Besides the smuggling of
foreign sugar and rum into the Northern Colonies, they had to
meet a danger nearer home, by stopping the leaks in their own
islands. Measures had already been taken for this purpose.
The introduction of foreign sugars into the West India colonies
damaged the planters, for it tended to lower the price in the
home market. It ruined them when there was a large crop,
and took away the benefit they might have gained by a short

---

[1] Letter of William Bollan, Agent for Massachusetts, 1754, M.H.S. MSS. 91 L;
Bollan to Willard, Aug. 12, 1754, ibid.

[2] Petition of planters and merchants, ? 1754, Add. MSS. 34729, f. 350; Lascelles
and Maxwell to Nicholas Wilcox, Aug. 28, 1754, W. & G. vii. See also C.S.P. Col.
1720–1, nos. 44, 197.

[3] Lascelles and Maxwell to Florentius Vassall, Nov. 9, 1752, March 10 and 16,
1753, W. & G. vi; Trelawny to Board of Trade, Aug. 15, 1752, C.O. 137/25 X 104.
Paterson, the surveyor-general of the customs in the West Indies, thought that the
abolition of these duties would not lower the price but only put money in the
planters' pockets (Paterson to Wood, July 5, 1751, Bodleian Library, North MSS.
a 6, f. 176).

one. In 1715, as soon as this trade had begun to flourish, the legislature of Barbados passed an Act to load it with prohibitive duties, and Antigua tried to forbid it altogether.[1] In spite of these laws, French sugars were still smuggled into our own sugar colonies, and imported into England paying duty as English produce—insomuch that some exasperated pamphleteers absurdly charged the planters, during the Molasses Act controversy, with wishing to prevent the North Americans from smuggling in order to have the monopoly of doing it themselves. (This accusation was echoed in 1760 by the writers who pointed out that the Admirals at Jamaica spared the Flag of Truce trade which was carried on from that island while they confiscated all the North Americans.)[2]

At the same time the advocates of the Northern Colonies developed a contradictory but more serious argument. They attributed the decline of the English re-export trade in sugar to these West Indian laws which kept French sugar out of the Empire and forced it into the European markets.[3] It would have been more to our interest to allow, even encourage, the French to smuggle their produce out of their colonies into ours, and then let our merchants import it all to England or carry it straight to Europe. We should gain the benefit of the freights (an important matter for North American shipping) and should make England the 'staple' of the sugar trade, so that the world price would be fixed in London.[4] Of course this ambitious scheme could not be realized. It was not to be expected that the French Government would allow such a breach of its colonial system. But the suggestion contained the germ of

---

[1] There is an illuminating account of the arguments for and against this measure, and the conflict of interests involved, in *C.S.P. Col. 1717–18*, no. 495 (i). When the Crown had disallowed the Act, the legislature of Antigua substituted a duty like that of Barbados (*C.S.P. Col. 1720–1*, no. 557). The Customs Commissioners in London thought it equally objectionable (ibid., nos. 623, 641).

[2] Holmes thought it necessary to answer this in his memorial of Dec. 1760 on the Flag of Truce trade, Adm. 1/236. He said it was not the men-of-war but the Admiralty judges who were to blame. See also the letter of James Duncan to Bowler and Champlin, Dec. 24, 1760, *Commerce of Rhode Island* (*M.H.S. Collections*), i. 86. Cotes seized and prosecuted some Jamaica traders whom he caught carrying provisions to Hispaniola; but the Vice-Admiralty judge was persuaded by the merchants to acquit them (Cotes to Clevland, Feb. 14, 1760, Adm. 1/235).

[3] This point is made in *A True State of the Case between the British Northern Colonies and the Sugar Islands in America* (London, 1732).

[4] Something like this argument appears in Colden's letter to Pitt, Dec. 27, 1760 (Kimball, *Correspondence of William Pitt*, ii. 380) and in the MS. 'Observations in the Monto Christi trade', Add. MSS. 36211, f. 256.

important arguments, for on the one hand it challenged, in the interests of the English consumer, the sugar-planters' monopoly of the home market, and on the other it recognized that a great proportion of the French West India produce found its way to foreign markets, and proposed to substitute England or North America for France as the intermediary of that trade—a thing which could much easier be done in a war than in a peace, owing to the English command of the sea. All these considerations were set forth again in the controversy over the Monte Cristi trade.

They had little effect upon the sugar-planters. The legislature of Barbados confessed itself shaken in its convictions, and ready to give up obstructing the imports of French sugar into the islands, if a moderate duty could be collected which would equalize the prices of English and French produce at London, and enable them both to be kept up.[1] The other Assemblies, however, were unconverted, and those which had not already forbidden or penalized the importation of French produce did so after 1739. Jamaica prohibited the export of sugar-machinery to the foreign West Indies, and laid a heavy duty on foreign West India merchandise. The means of enforcing this law had to be strengthened repeatedly. In 1741 two special customs officers were appointed for the purpose; in the next year they were increased to seven, and in 1745 they were given a salary, obliged to take an oath, and furnished with boats and negroes for the execution of their offices.[2] Finally, the importation of French and Spanish produce was entirely forbidden in 1746 for the duration of the war.

Between 1750 and 1756 the island legislatures passed a series of laws for supplementing the Molasses Act. Some amounted only to a declaration that whosoever imported French sugars into the English islands was an enemy to his country and unworthy to be a member of civil society. Others obliged the masters of ships loaded for England to prove the English origin of their cargoes by furnishing the customs officers with certificates from the producers.[3] Some colonies went farther still. The Board of Trade had sent out in 1752 a circular which

---

[1] Barbados Council Minutes, March 19, 1739/40, C.O. 31/21.

[2] C.O. 139/15.

[3] Antigua Assembly Minutes, Nov. 15, 1750 (Court House, St. Johns); St. Kitts Assembly Minutes, May 18 and June 11, 1752 (St. Kitts Administrator's Office); Montserrat Assembly Minutes, Feb. 22, 1755, C.O. 177/8.

ordered the West Indian Governors to prevent at the same time the emigration of English planters to foreign sugar colonies, and the introduction of foreign sugars into our own.[1] On the strength of this, Jamaica prohibited such imports outright in 1756, and afterwards went so far as to establish the penalty of death in certain cases. The Board of Trade had always questioned the wisdom of such an extreme policy.[2] Since the Molasses Act allowed foreign produce to be entered upon payment of heavy duties, it did not become the legislature of a colony to exclude it altogether. For this reason among others, the Board advised George III to disallow a re-enactment of this law in 1761. The Assembly of Jamaica furiously refused to accept any of the alterations which the Board had suggested, and solemnly indicted it for negligence and folly.[3]

The trade from Ireland to the foreign sugar colonies had never excited so much controversy. The French fleets and colonies depended almost entirely on Irish beef, and to a less degree on Irish butter. The attempts to establish a cattle-raising and grazing industry in the south of France were almost entirely unsuccessful before 1775; so were the efforts to replace Irish beef with Danish.[4] The only question was whether the provisions should be exported from Ireland in French, Dutch, or English ships. The customs authorities disliked the French traders, because they smuggled tea, brandy, and silks into Ireland; but this branch of exportation was presumably too necessary to Ireland to be hindered in time of peace by restricting the use of foreign shipping. Although the sugar-planters sometimes included Ireland in their general condemnation of all forms of trade with the French West Indies, they did not usually ask to have the export of Irish provisions suppressed in time of peace; the agitation for an embargo in 1740 was exceptional, because everybody believed that we should very soon be at war with France. However, the suggestion was sometimes made. For instance, in 1748 the English merchants trading to Hamburg put it forward in a memorial on the ways

---

[1] Circular of June 3, 1752, C.O. 138/19, pp. 360–1.

[2] *C.S.P. Col. 1717–18*, no. 611; *1719–20*, no. 201.

[3] Act of Feb. 7, 1756, C.O. 139/18; Wood to Pownall, June 20, 1761, C.O. 137/32, BB 26; Pownall to Moore, July 6, 1761, C.O. 138/22, pp. 176–7; Board of Trade to George III, Jan. 27, 1762, ibid., pp. 227–39; Lyttelton to Board of Trade, Oct. 13, 1762, C.O. 137/32, BB 65.

[4] L. Vignols, in *Revue Historique*, vol. 159, pp. 79–95.

of meeting French competition; they lamented the complete decay of the re-export of English sugar to that market, and proposed to consolidate the slight advantage regained in the war, by depriving the French islands permanently of Irish beef.[1]

This was the background of the disputes which arose in war-time over the propriety of trade with the enemy. North America and Ireland found it increasingly hard to abstain from inter-course with the French colonies, regardless of peace or war; their livelihood depended on it. For the West Indies on the other hand the path of patriotism should have been smooth in war-time; they were entitled to demand as a military necessity an abstention which it had always been to their economic interest to enforce. Some of their arguments against the Flag of Truce and Monte Cristi trades rested entirely upon the assumption that the blockade was only a move or an incident in the economic war of the English and French sugar colonies.[2]

§ ii. *The Expediency of Trade with the Enemy*

Was it right, politic, or lawful to trade with the enemy? No doubt there were some unthinking conservatives who answered no to all these questions at once; but it needs something subtler than outraged patriotism to define the real interests of a trading nation. All sorts of distinctions were to be observed.

The advocates and critics of trade with the enemy started from incompatible premises. One of the most important questions in dispute was the effect of prohibition. One party assumed without proof that the enemy could never be reduced to extremities by withholding any branch of trade from him. Pulteney (if he was the real author of the notorious *Considerations upon the Embargo of Provisions of Victual*) went so far as to ask:

'Whether any folly be more exploded, if fatal and general experi-ence can explode a folly, than the supposition, that any nation can exclude the rest of the world from any branch of commerce? Whether it can be supposed that Providence has been so severe upon any country, as to put it in the power of another to starve her inhabi-

---

[1] Memorandum of English Merchants Adventurers in Hamburg, Oct. 8, 1748, S.P. 75/91.

[2] For instance, Admiral Holmes's apologists dwell on the evil effect of the Flag of Truce trade, which renders sugar-cultivation possible in St. Domingue and raises the value of its plantations, at the same time that it drains Jamaica of cash and raises the prices of the necessaries of life (Unsigned paper of 1760, and Memorial of Dec. 1760, Adm. 1/236).

tants? Whether it is possible to conceive, that any nation abounding in wealth can fail to be supplied with necessaries for money?"[1]

On the other hand, the partisans of prohibition pointed to the existence of certain natural monopolies or acquired superiorities, which would enable us to inflict real privation on the enemy.

One of the best examples of natural monopoly was Irish beef. The French Government talked glibly, at the beginning of each war, about supplies of Jutland beef and Iceland mutton. Experiments were made, and some orders placed; indeed the French victuallers were forced in the Seven Years War to buy a great deal more Danish beef than they wanted, in order to smooth the path of French diplomacy in the Baltic. The meat was wretchedly prepared, and stank; if the fleets and colonies of France could not have obtained Irish victuals surreptitiously in spite of the war, they must have been very severely embarrassed.[2] So far, experience seemed to show that in some cases a nation could inflict real damage upon another by refusing to export certain goods or services.

A particularly interesting case was that of insurance. Here we seemed to have built up a superiority even over the Dutch, by the greater punctuality and science of our underwriters (Beckford denied this, but most of the writers on the subject, such as Magens and Beawes, contradicted him). Sir John Barnard and others argued that this pre-eminence was not great enough to be presumed upon; they prophesied that if we refused to insure the enemy's ships, the Dutch would do it, or the French could insure themselves, and we should have sacrificed our own gain for nothing. Willimot adduced on the same side an argument peculiar to insurance. Our advantage arose from our lower premiums, which we could afford to take because we did a greater volume of business. Subtract from that volume, and you are obliged to increase the premiums; business flies away from London to Amsterdam. Yet, as Walpole pointed out, the mere fact that all foreigners applied to us for insurance proved that we could inflict a real damage upon them by withholding it. The advantage they gained from it consisted in getting it done at cheaper rates than any other underwriters

---

[1] This pamphlet is reprinted by Cobbett in *Parl. Hist.* xi. 867–74.

[2] Chamber of Commerce of Guienne, minutes of Dec. 15 and 22, 1740, Arch. Gir. C 4254, ff. 82–3. See also M. Vignols's article quoted above.

would offer. We could deprive them of that advantage at least, and by doing so we might prevent them from competing with us in the neutral markets. Some spokesmen on the same side went farther. Cheap and reliable insurance was indispensable, especially to traders with small capital. Without it, they must give up their business.[1] A writer in the *Gentleman's Magazine* even predicted that France would otherwise pursue her continental schemes in security without troubling to protect her maritime trade, knowing that we should in any case insure it for her. That might be an exaggeration; yet there was some absurdity, as Magens suggested, in the spectacle of a vast navy and a horde of privateers diligently engaged in interrupting a commerce which their own fellow countrymen had protected, at a price, from total loss.[2]

'Throwing the trade into the hands of the Dutch' was one of the great national bugbears, not only of England but of France. Those who did not absolutely deny that we could lose a trade in any circumstances, were forced to acknowledge that we might be unable to recover at a peace the customers we had flung away for reasons of state during a war. Economic thinkers were obsessed by the idea of 'channels' of trade, which they claimed to have derived from Locke.[3] A customer soon forgets the merchant with whom he dealt in the past, in favour of the shop which supplies him at present. Once alienate him and accustom him to dealing with a rival, he is lost for ever. No doubt there was good psychology in this, but there was also

[1] There is here a parallel with certain arguments used in the Molasses Act controversy. That discussion turned partly on the question whether, if the export of provisions and lumber from North America to the French sugar islands were withheld, the French planters would be forced to go out of business, or be put to serious inconvenience. The North Americans maintained that the only effect would be to stimulate production in Canada and Louisiana, which could easily fill their own place after a few years. Here they were probably wrong, but they were never proved so by experience, because in fact they never ceased to trade with the French West Indies in peace or war.

[2] See the debates of Feb. 27, 1740/1, Dec. 18, 1747, and Feb. 25, 1752, *Parl. Hist.* xii. 7 et seqq., xiv. 108 et seqq., 1208 et seqq.; *Gentleman's Magazine*, xvi. 17; Nicholas Magens, *An Essay on Insurances*, 1755, i, pp. vi–ix, 42–5; Wyndham Beawes, *Lex Mercatoria Rediviva*, 1771 edition, p. 272.

[3] 'When trade is once lost, it will be too late by a mistimed care, easily to retrieve it again, for the currents of trade, like those of waters, make themselves channels, out of which they are afterwards as hard to be diverted as rivers that have worn themselves deep within their banks.' (Quoted by James Knight, Add. MSS. 22677, f. 65, from the *Considerations of the Lowering of Interest and Raising the Value of Money*, vol. v, p. 14 of the collected *Works* of 1823.)

some economic unreason. Alderman Janssen pointed out that we had obtained our position as the leading insurers of the world by doing business on better terms than anybody else; even if we should forfeit that advantage during the war in order to distress our enemy, we could recover it after the peace by the same methods which first gained it for us. Yet the theory of 'channels of trade' was very dear to most writers, and justified in their eyes almost any kind of dealings with the enemy. Pulteney held up for imitation the example of the Dutch, who are 'so careful to preserve the inlets of gain from obstruction, that they make no scruple of supplying their enemies with their commodities, and have been known to sell at night those bullets which were next day to be discharged against them'.[1]

Bound up with the argument of 'channels' was that of 'dependence'. If we could continue to supply a nation with a necessary article for a long enough time, that nation would become so dependent on us that it would not dare break with us for fear of the privation. This suggestion was made on some very inappropriate occasions. For example, the South Sea factors at Cartagena, who had contracted before the war to supply the galleons with flour, tried to induce Vernon to let them fulfil their bargain, by arguing that

'not only this city and province, but all this coast, would in a small course of years, have been entirely dependent upon the English; for we gave the flour at so low a rate, that all ranks of people began to make use of that, instead of maize or Indian corn. The husbandmen in Santa Fé, which is the only place in all this Kingdom that produces wheat, began to neglect their tillage, for they could not afford to sell the quintal of flour, for less than near double what we sold it for . . . so that in two or three years more, we may safely affirm, no other flour would have been consumed in this province, but what was introduced from our colonies, which . . . would have made the Spaniards so dependent upon us, that it would not have been easy for them to have freed themselves.'[2]

---

[1] Debate of Nov. 25, 1740, *Parl. Hist.* xi. 849. The author of *The Advantages and Disadvantages which will attend the Prohibition of the Merchandises of Spain impartially examined* (London, 1740) both advances and denies the argument of channels of trade. Extraordinary as Pulteney's statement about the Dutch may seem, it did not go much beyond the truth. François Libault, a merchant of Amsterdam, sent out a consignment of arms to St. Eustatius in 1745, observing to his correspondents that they would be 'a very good article, whether we enter the war ourselves, or only to sell to the enemy privateers' (Libault to P. and J. Heyliger, May 15, 1745, in the *Vryheid*, Vos, H.C.A. 42/50).

[2] Ord and Gray to Vernon, Nov. 20, N.S., 1739, S.P. 42/85, f. 117. Vernon

There was little point in this contention at the very outbreak of a war. The argument was sometimes used in more respectable contexts. Governor Dalrymple proposed supplying the French with North America produce through a free port on Dominica, in order that we might keep control of that trade and, if necessary, reduce the French islands, grown dependent upon it, to instant starvation by a sudden suspension.[1] In fact the argument of dependence was at the bottom of the proposals to make England the 'staple' of the sugar trade by encouraging imports from the French colonies, and of all other schemes of national monopoly. It was not a very satisfactory piece of reasoning. Besides the miscalculation which might be involved in all such assumptions of dependence, it required the Government to tolerate a trade during one war in order to make all future wars impossible; and such a plea would presumably be repeated by interested parties every time a war should happen, for the ideal moment of dependence could never be proved to have arrived.

Even if we deprived the enemy of a real advantage by withholding our goods and services from him, did we inflict upon him a damage equal to our own loss? This must turn on the size of the profits in any given branch of trade, and on the nature of the goods and services themselves. The *Considerations upon the Embargo of Provisions of Victual* pointed to the vast reduction of profits and rents which must ensue in Ireland from a suspension of the export of beef; this must in turn diminish the subject's capacity to pay taxes and therefore the national resources to carry on the war. The same arguments came up in the debates on insurance. Walpole assumed without question that a lesser evil must be suffered for the purpose of inflicting a greater; and other speakers on the same side set the expenses of a further prolongation of the war against the much smaller loss incurred in order to reduce the enemy to terms quickly.[2] Murray and Ryder, the Law Officers of the Crown, set out to exaggerate the profits of the business, in order to justify insuring enemy ships in war time. Magens took them to task in his

thought this reasoning odd; see his letter to Newcastle, Jan. 18–31, 1739/40, f. 105.

[1] Dalrymple to Bute, Feb. 27, 1763, *Correspondence of George III* (ed. Fortescue), i. 44–9.

[2] This argument is also used in the discussion on the propriety of exporting corn to France, *Gentleman's Magazine*, xviii. 20–1 (Jan. 1748).

Essay on Insurances, but his arguments seem to assume that the underwriters knew very little about the conduct of their affairs. Here again, however, insurance raised issues peculiar to itself. Advocates of prohibition contrasted the smaller loss of individuals with the greater gain of the nation. If we refrained from insuring the enemy's ships, then every prize taken would be a clear addition to the national wealth; if on the other hand all these prizes were insured, the national gain could only consist of the insurer's profits.

Some people justified by its profits the trade between North America and the French colonies in time of war. Judge Auchmuty of Boston, in his long and elaborate sentence on the *Victory*,[1] found it necessary to meet the argument that the Flag of Truce trade was lucrative and brought in a profit of 5,000 per cent. He did so indirectly, merely admitting that it 'enriched some particular favourites', but denying that it ever added or would add a farthing to His Majesty's revenues, because the importers of French West India goods always eluded paying the duties. This was true, although the Flag of Truce traders defended themselves in the Prize Courts by alleging that the public Treasury benefited from the customs dues which they paid on their importations.[2] It was also relevant, for one of the strongest arguments for allowing any trade with the enemy was the increase of the public revenue. Moreover, there was something reprehensible in the spectacle of the English navy creating, by its blockade, high profits for the English blockade-runners— the more so as that blockade was maintained at the expense of neutrals. Admiral Holmes adverted to this point in the memorial which he wrote or inspired against the Flag of Truce trade.[3] Even if the trade was as lucrative as it was represented to be, we were buying the advantage by the sacrifice of our national honour and consistency.

Besides, Holmes denied that any profits were made in the commerce, for it was so overdone that North American goods were sometimes sold below their first cost, and the scramble for sugars and molasses was so great as to raise the prices to a height which afforded the buyer no profit. This assertion is in some degree borne out by the private correspondence of traders.

---

[1] H.C.A. 42/48.
[2] See the master's depositions in the case of the *Three Brothers*, Gilbert, H.C.A. 42/97.   [3] Dec. 1760, Adm. 1/236.

North American captains and supercargoes were slow to admit that trade was good at any time or place, so it would be unsafe to make too much account of their jeremiads; but certain statements are so precise as to leave little room for discount.[1]

The trade which the North Americans carried on with the French through the Spanish free port of Monte Cristi was defended by the same arguments as that of the Flags of Truce. It disposed of some English manufactures at high prices to the French colonists, whose produce was bought very cheap in return. A great deal of this produce was carried directly or indirectly to the neutral markets of Europe, especially Hamburg and Leghorn.[2] Here the North Americans were claiming the right to usurp the French carrying trade during the war, and pocket the profits of it. All these profits, they said, 'centred' in England. Such commerce was at any rate less harmful to the English sugar-planters than the unlawful importation of French sugar into the markets which were reserved for them alone; it only interfered with the hypothetical profit they might have made by re-exporting their produce to the neutral countries which were deprived of French sugars by the blockade. The benefit which English industry received from this commerce was not to be measured only by the manufactures which were sold directly to the French planters—for indeed that was one of the least important parts of the trade, and strictly discouraged by the French Government. All those manufactures ought also to be comprehended which the Northern Colonies were able to buy out of the profits of this commerce; thus quite apart from any direct increase in the yield of taxes, a general prosperity

---

[1] For example, Captain Randall reports from Port au Prince to his owners in Rhode Island, 'As for dry goods, the place is glutted from York, Philadelphia and Jamaica. Every store full. I am in hopes to make the first cost, but numbers are obliged to sink 20 & 30 & 50 per cent. who has purchased effects before the sale of their goods' (John Carter Brown Library, Nicholas Brown MSS., Brigantine *Providence*, March 5, 1760). Many other informations of the same kind could be quoted, e.g. Thomas Rimington, Monte Cristi, to the owners of the *Windmill*, Rhode Island, March 15 and 23, 1760 (Champlin Papers, R.I.H.S.).

[2] The following are some of the vessels employed in this trade—*Baron von Bernstorff*, Lemwig, H.C.A. 42/57 (Amsterdam); *St. Croix*, Debroskey, H.C.A. 42/61 (Hamburg); *Sharp*, Maitland, H.C.A. 42/95 (Venice); *Quebeck*, Pew, H.C.A. 42/90 (Hamburg); *Gregg*, Nichols, H.C.A. 42/68 (Gibraltar and Venice); *General Wolfe*, Thompson, H.C.A. 42/68 (Ireland and Hamburg); *Charming Polly*, Horton, H.C.A. 42/59 (Leghorn). A detailed view of the trade between New England, Monte Cristi, and Gibraltar can be obtained from the Derby Family MSS., vol. xii, in the Essex Institute, Salem, Mass.

would diffuse itself through the Empire if this intercourse with the enemy were allowed.[1]

This argument was borrowed directly from the debates over the Molasses Act,[2] and could only be answered, in so far as it was answered at all, by another of the same kind.

'If such commerce should be decreed in courts of judicature lawful, then such traders even paying the duty can afford to undersell his Majesty's good subjects in his sugar colonies, and much more so when according to their usual practice they pay no duty, to the impoverishing those plantations, and diminishing his Majesty's revenue, furthermore . . . these illicit traders bring back into the northern colonys rum, sugar, molasses, indigo, cotton &c., for all which we ought to depend upon his Majesty's colonies and not upon the enemy.'[3]

Thus the calculations of national profit and loss were by no means easy to adjust out of hand, and finally became embroiled in sectional controversies. There were other considerations from which the statesmen might get some guidance as to the kinds of trade with the enemy to be allowed and condemned. The popular economic doctrines of the time afforded a rough and ready criterion by distinguishing the countries with which, as a whole, trade was 'beneficial' and 'unprofitable'. This criterion was itself determined by the supposed balance of payments, and by the character of the goods imported and exported. On this last point, strategy and international law also had some advice to offer.

It would not be too much to say that many people thought of trade itself as a kind of warfare. Some regarded each individual bargain as a battlefield, in which one party must lose and the other gain. In the debate upon prohibiting the insurance of enemy ships, Baltimore argued that as we made a profit

---

[1] Horatio Sharpe, Governor of Maryland, to William Sharpe, July 8, 1760, *Correspondence of Governor Sharpe*, ed. Maryland Historical Society, ii. 442; 'Observations in the Monto Christi trade', Add. MSS. 36211, f. 256.

[2] So were those with which Governors Hopkins and Colden answered Pitt's circular letter of August 1760 about the Flag of Truce trade. They laid stress on the vast excess of North American production over British West Indian consumption, and the impossibility of paying for English manufactures except by exporting the surplus to the foreign colonies (Hopkins to Pitt, Dec. 20, 1760; Colden to Pitt, Dec. 27, 1760, Kimball, *Correspondence of William Pitt with Colonial Governors*, ii. 373–82).

[3] This piece of political economy comes from Auchmuty's sentence upon the *Victory*; it is a good and somewhat rare example of the incorporation of current economic controversy into the judicial pronouncements of the Prize Courts.

by underwriting foreign ships (without which we should not be ready to do the business), we must inflict a proportionate loss upon the foreigners whom we insured, and this trade was therefore fit to be continued during the war. Others did not consider each transaction in detail, but looked rather at the totality of exchanges between any two nations. It is commonly thought that this national gain or loss was measured only by the ultimate payment of money from one country to another. That is an injustice to the mercantilists, who had other criteria of success or failure in this economic struggle; for example, a nation might be regarded as the winner which exported all its products as manufactured as possible and imported those of other countries as raw as possible. The exact form of the judgement does not matter; the point is that international trade was thought of as warfare. The duty of the Government was therefore quite clear when a war, in the political sense, broke out. It must do the enemies of the state as much harm as possible by protecting all those branches of trade with them in which we gained, and cutting off all those in which we lost; or if the thing was conceived in terms of whole nations, intercourse with our enemies was to be favoured or discouraged according as our trade with them was 'advantageous' or 'unprofitable'.

Hence the distinction between the treatment of French and Spanish trade. We believed ourselves to be gainers in our trade with Spain, losers in that with France. In the former, manufactures went out and cash came in, while in the other we bought manufactures or luxuries with money.[1] The Government discriminated accordingly. A war with France was usually an opportunity of stopping up all commerce with her; the Act of 1740 against trade with Spain was drawn up very carefully so as to avoid proscribing the exportation of English manufactures to the Spanish colonies—or to Spain in Europe, for that matter, if she would receive them. In fact, although the preamble recited the necessity of a general suspension of trade with Spain, nothing was prohibited but certain imports; the enlarge-

---

[1] The Customs statistics do not support the opinion that we lost in our trade with France. The declared exports always overbalanced the declared imports; but there was a great deal of smuggling to be taken into account. The same figures show a contrast between the effects of the prohibitions against trade with France and Spain. The imports from Spain sank to about a sixth of the ordinary quantity, but the imports from France were abolished altogether (see Whitworth's tables, *State of the Trade of Great Britain*).

ment of the market for English manufactures in the Spanish dominions was not only a necessary consequence, but perhaps one of the principal objects, of the war.[1]

Even the suppression of commerce with France was rendered less rigorous by the disposition to spare exports while discouraging imports. An Act of 1691 had actually threatened exporters of any goods to France with a *praemunire*, but that was an exception. That of 1705, modelled on an earlier one of 1689, merely forbade imports, reciting in the preamble that

'it hath been found by long experience, that the bringing in of French wines, vinegar, brandy, linen, silks, salt, paper and other the growth, product or manufacture of France, or of the territories or dominions of the French King, hath much exhausted the treasure of this nation, lessened the value of the native commodities and manufactures thereof, and greatly impoverished the English artificers and handicrafts.'

Parliament discovered by 1710 that the prohibition against importing French wines injured the revenue and the nation at large. It therefore allowed them to enter in neutral shipping on condition that the vessel which carried them should have paid for them by exporting a cargo of English manufactures.[2] The same tendency to encourage exports can be seen in the treatment of the tobacco trade. A great deal of the Virginia and Maryland crop was exported in times of peace to France, where the Farmers-General had a monopoly of buying and reselling it. Both the producers and the London tobacco-merchants in this trade would have been injured, if not ruined, by a complete suspension of their very specialized business; nor could the Farmers-General supply themselves from any other quarter. Accordingly the export of tobacco from England continued throughout the wars of 1744 and 1756 in ships licensed for that purpose. One of the few conditions which the English Government made, was that no French goods should be imported in return. France was not in a condition to resist or resent this proviso.[3]

Most people thought it proper to distinguish the kinds of

---

[1] This subject has been dealt with at greater length in Chapter III, pp. 114-27.
[2] 1 W. & M., c. 34; 3 & 4 W. & M., c. 13; 3 & 4 Anne, cc. 12, 13; 9 Anne, c. 8.
[3] *A.P.C. Col.* iii. 796-8; iv. 328-33. Marsden prints a specimen pass in *Law and Custom*, ii. 375. Seventy-eight passes were granted for tobacco-ships between Aug. 13, 1756, and Jan. 1, 1760, all in the name of George Fitzgerald (S.P. 42/140).

goods which ought to be exported to the enemy or imported from him. Obviously the sale of warlike stores to the enemy was out of the question. Nobody defended it; even Pulteney, with his rhodomontade about the Dutch, did not really justify it. The same thing may in one sense be said of the export of naval stores and provisions. Although many arguments were found for this trade, hardly one of them was grounded on its inherent harmlessness. It might be a necessary or a profitable trade, but nobody denied that it was advantageous to the enemy and helped him to carry on the war. A writer on behalf of the Monte Cristi trade argued that as St. Domingue could never be starved out, there was no harm in carrying victuals there; but this assertion, itself quite false, seems to be almost the only argument for this trade which recognized that there were military as well as economic necessities to be considered. The exporters were content for the most part to smuggle *sans phrase*, or to put forward their own interests as a sufficient excuse. For example, the merchants of Barbados and Jamaica would allege that perishable goods such as flour and fish must rot in their stores for want of a market; they neither specified the places to which they wished to export them, nor faced the argument that their commodities had better perish than be carried to the enemy.

Even the objectors to the export of provisions had other reasons for their policy besides their desire to reduce the enemy to famine. Most of the North American embargoes were designed to serve a double purpose—to distress the enemy and to render possible the accumulation at a reasonable price of victuals for a military expedition. This is clear from the letters of Governor Clinton, Lord Loudoun, and General Amherst, and the coincidence of the embargoes with such operations.[1] When Vernon appealed to all colonial Governors in the autumn of 1740 to stop the export of provisions to the Neutral Islands, he did so both because he wanted to paralyse the enemy's fleets and because he was afraid that if a free trade was allowed, the forces under his own command might suffer hunger.[2] The

---

[1] Loudoun to Sharpe, Aug. 20, 1756, *Correspondence of Governor Sharpe* (Maryland Hist. Soc.), i. 463. Amherst, for example, took off the embargo in 1762 when it had served the purpose of enabling him to commandeer enough shipping and collect enough provisions (Amherst to Ward, June 13, 1762, *R.I. Col. Rec.* vi. 323).

[2] Vernon to Ward, Nov. 13, 1740, Kimball, *Correspondence of Colonial Governors*

victualling contractors were always suspected of prompting such embargoes. Whenever large forces were raised, or arrived in the colonies, they created a market for provisions and rum, and caused the prices to rise, to the disadvantage of the contractors, who had undertaken to furnish the supplies at a fixed rate. It was their obvious interest to have the price artificially depressed by confining the goods to the home market. For this cause, the Opposition ascribed the Irish embargo of 1740 to the victualling contractors, and Commodore Legge observed some years later that 'an Irish embargo was an English job'. There are some traces of such interference. Augustus Boyd was certainly concerned in the victualling during the Seven Years War; he called the attention of the Ministry to the clandestine exportation of Irish beef to the enemy, and argued strongly for its repression. In the Spanish War he had done the same, but with a virtuous disclaimer of interested motives—for, he said, if orders from abroad could be executed, he would have the handling of them.[1]

The opposition to the export of provisions did not proceed only from those who were charged with the business of supplying our own forces. The consumers were equally concerned in it. James Knight hinted that he was not sorry to see Irish beef embargoed for military reasons, because otherwise the West India planter would have had to pay too high a price.[2] In the islands this motive becomes much clearer. Trelawny allowed the export from Jamaica of such provisions as were plentiful there. Barbados, with its large population of poor whites, had always attended more than most other islands to their subsistence, and the real object of embargoes apparently military in

---

of Rhode Island, i. 185; Vernon to Newcastle, May 26 and Oct. 7, 1740, S.P. 42/85, ff. 222, 333.

[1] Boyd to Gore, Dec. 5, 1741, Add. MSS. 32698, f. 393; Clevland to Robinson, Aug. 8, 1755, S.P. 42/37, f. 235; Lords of Admiralty to Pitt, Feb. 2, 1757, Adm. 2/371, p. 103. Mason and Simpson, victualling contractors for the forces in the West Indies, complained of the high price of Irish butter, which they were obliged to supply, and suggested that its exportation to foreign parts should therefore be prohibited (Petition to Newcastle, Feb. 24, 1745/6, S.P. 63/409).

[2] Knight to Sharpe, Oct. 17, 1740, Add. MSS. 32695, f. 280. One Macfarland of London wrote to Corbett, Oct. 7, 1745, that he had bought beef last year for exportation to the West Indies, at 20 shillings the barrel; this year it was 25 shillings, on account of the many orders for St. Eustatius or Martinique. His correspondents in Ireland wrote to him that 'if you merchants in London do not get an embargo laid on ships bound to the Dutch islands or fall upon some other method to prevent this trade, it will raise the price more and more, and be detrimental both to the colonies and to His Majesty's service' (S.P. 42/29, f. 284).

character, was plainly to assure a cheap and plentiful supply of the necessaries of life. For example, Gedney Clarke was allowed in August 1741 to export some fish only after he had assured the Council that he had a great quantity in stock and was expecting more, and promised not to raise the price. At the beginning of the Seven Years War, scarcity and high prices appear to have determined the attitude of the legislature once more; and the Act which it passed in 1757 against trade with the enemy contained a permanent system of regulation to prevent forestalling and engrossing. Pinfold informed Pitt in 1760 that no licence was granted for the export of provisions without 'strict previous examination of the quantity then in the island and of the current prices'.[1] In almost all the islands, the prohibitions were relaxed or enforced by administrative action according to the plenty or scarcity of victuals. In fact, so far as the planters imposed upon themselves or upon others the duty of patriotic abstention, their interest impelled them to it.

Money was another article whose export to the enemy was sometimes deemed unpatriotic. This is not surprising, for even in the course of normal trade, the outflow of precious metals was commonly regarded as a disaster, and its introduction as a public benefit. The planters had often complained that the North Americans, in their eagerness for cheap molasses, had refused to buy at the English sugar colonies, demanding the proceeds of their outward cargoes in cash, which they carried to the French islands where the price of West India goods was lower. Exactly this argument was brought forward during the Seven Years War against the Monte Cristi and Flag of Truce trades. Jamaica complained that it was being drained of its currency by these methods. This, said a pamphleteer inspired by Admiral Holmes, was how the North Americans disposed of the great quantities of money which the English Government spent among them for the upkeep of the troops. He ought at least to have admitted that the Government itself was partly to blame for the state of affairs: when the export of provisions was embargoed, there was no article which could be sent to the French colonies with so much profit as gold.[2]

[1] Barbados Council Minutes, Aug. 4 and 5, 1741, C.O. 31/21; April 14, 1756, Jan. 19, 1757, C.O. 31/28; Pinfold to Pitt, Nov. 15, 1760, C.O. 152/46.
[2] Philip Cuyler to Henry Cuyler, Dec. 3, 1759, Letter-book, N.Y.P.L. The French authorities commented upon the large sums of money imported into St.

Besides the arguments which did duty in times of peace, there were others which applied to the export of cash to an enemy. Money was the sinew of war; it was included in the contraband list of certain treaties—for example, that of 1661 between England and Sweden—though certain others, such as the Anglo-Dutch Treaty of 1674, expressly excepted it. Obviously, therefore, it was a public service to draw out the enemy's bullion by means of trade, and highly unpatriotic to part with our own. For this reason, again, certain writers distinguished the lawfulness of the trade with the Spanish and the French West Indies. Judge Auchmuty put this point somewhat obscurely in his judgement on the *Victory*.

'Indeed to send to an enemy things that tend to the gratification of their luxury and wantonness is said to be lawful, for such supplies contribute to render them weak and effeminate, and from this reason whatever debilitates the enemy may be deemed lawful, which leads me into the consideration of the case put concerning the open trade now allowed between Jamaica and the Main. That there is such a trade in practice I believe, but that the same is lawful is what I deny, unless the same is fully within the meaning of the last mentioned law as a trade that weakens the enemy. For if I'm rightly informed the British manufactures are carried from that island to the main and there sold for silver and gold and not trucked for other goods of no account to the enemy as molasses. The carrying [off?] the enemy's bullion which are the sinews of war is a case no wise similar to the present case. The trade in the first weakens, the trade in the latter succours the enemy.'[1]

This point was important, because the North Americans sometimes asked why they should be forbidden to deal with the French enemy when the people of Jamaica were encouraged to trade with the Spanish enemy.[2] Holmes's pamphleteer of 1760 brought forward arguments very like those of Auchmuty. He denied any analogy between the two trades, because in that which Vernon had allowed to be carried on to the Spanish Main, English manufactures, not provisions, were exchanged

Domingue by the New England Flag of Truce traders (Bart and Élias to Berryer, Feb. 11, 1760, A.N. Colonies C⁹ A 105).

[1] *Victory*, Bardine, H.C.A. 42/48. There was a passage of Seneca, which international lawyers were never tired of quoting on this topic, though they usually applied it to neutral trade; it is quoted, for example, by Grotius, *De Jure Belli et Pacis*, iii, c. i, § 5.

[2] Francis Bernard, *Select Letters on the Trade and Government of America* (London, 1774), pp. 21–2.

against gold and silver;[1] whereas in the trade with the French, cash and provisions were exported, in return for West India goods which competed with the produce of the English plantations. If they would buy their sugar and molasses from the English West Indies alone, the North Americans would keep their money within the Empire.

This last argument is drawn from the stock-in-trade of the West India controversialists, and shows yet again how closely, in the minds of the planters, war patriotism was connected with their own economic interests. Another proof is afforded by the attitude of Jamaica to the imports in this trade. The law of that island which prohibited the importation of French West India produce was only a continuation, or accentuation, of a peace-time policy, and appears to have been occasioned by the smuggling of sugar. Governor Trelawny had already forbidden the commanders of Flag of Truce vessels to import from the French islands anything contrary to the interests of Jamaica.[2] This language implies that there were some articles which could be brought in without damaging those interests. Trelawny was undoubtedly thinking of indigo, and perhaps also of cocoa. Jamaica had once produced those crops, but the industries had almost died out; therefore indigo and cocoa were welcome imports, the more so as the former was needed for the dyeing industry of England.[3] Trelawny had openly allowed some indigo to be imported in a French Flag of Truce in the War of 1744; this trade was carried on freely between Jamaica and St. Domingue.

Among the papers of the *Providence*, owned by Messrs. Brown of Rhode Island, there is a cryptic letter from John Burges, at Kingston, Jamaica, to Captain John Randall at Port au Prince. Randall had sent Burges to Jamaica 'for the good of the consarn', and Burges was obliged to report that 'I have not been able to do anything with the admerl (Cotes), for him to give

---

[1] This was not quite true; see p. 435, note 3.

[2] Trelawny to Murray, Nov. 23, 1745, in *Journals of the Assembly of Jamaica*, iv. 18.

[3] The author of the *Histoire et commerce des Antilles angloises* (1758, p. 86) says almost all the indigo which the English bought under the name of Jamaica indigo, was really of French or Spanish growth. In 1720 there had been a quarrel between Governor Lawes and Commodore Vernon over the seizure of some French indigo which the traders attempted to export from Jamaica to England. The Governor wished to protect the interests of the Jamaica indigo-growers, but the Customs Commissioners and Board of Trade repudiated him (*C.S.P. Col. 1720–1*, nos. 340, 471, 603, 608, 609).

me a protection would be directly opposet to what he has set out in, that is to take all shuger & molases laden vesells that comes out of any French port if posable'. For this reason Burges resigned his half of a prize snow bought at Port au Prince, to a merchant of Jamaica, who presumably would have some immunity which would help her to get safe out of St. Domingue as Burges could not have done. Burges added, 'I would advise you whatever quantety of indigo you purchace to send it in sum Jamaica flag of truce to this place, for if you should go out before thare is a better prospect you have teen to one against your getting clear, and all indigo that is taken in any vesel laden with suger or molases is as lyable as any other part of the cargo, as I have been informed'. From all this it appears that Cotes connived at the Jamaica Flags of Truce, so long as they only imported indigo—a licence which he did not extend to the North Americans.[1] In this instance the sugar islands, so diligent to protect their own crops against competition, were making free with the interest of another class of producers within the Empire: indigo of a sort was cultivated in South Carolina. An attempt was made in 1757 to legalize the introduction of French indigo during the war. One Hutchinson Mure applied to the Board of Trade for leave to export slaves to St. Domingue and import indigo thence. The Board considered the proposal, but rejected it at the instance of the Carolina merchants.[2]

When Admiral Holmes at last made up his mind to interfere with the Jamaica Flag of Truce trade as well as that of the Northern Colonies, he seized among others the *Greyhound*, John Fowles master. The claimant in the Vice-Admiralty court argued that 'by the purchase of the said cargo of indigo and cocoa with the manufactures of Great Britain he has as much as in him lay advanced the commerce of Great Britain and the territories thereunto belonging without prejudicing any of its

[1] Burges to Randall, Feb. 28, 1760, John Carter Brown Library, Nicholas Brown MSS., papers of the Brigantine *Providence*, voyage of 1760. See also the letter of Bart to Élias, Feb. 11, 1760, A.N. Colonies C⁹ A 105. On the other hand some owners advised their captains not to carry indigo, presumably because it would prove that the cargo was French produce; they must have hoped that so long as their ships carried nothing but sugar and molasses, they could successfully pretend, with the help of false clearances, that it came from the English colonies (Instructions to Captain J. Brown, Dec. 5, 1758, Derby Family MSS., vol. xxiii, Essex Institute). Cotes would have stopped even the Jamaica traders from carrying provisions to the enemy, if he could (Cotes to Clevland, Feb. 14, 1760, Adm. 1/235).

[2] *Journal of the Commissioners for Trade and Plantations, 1754–8*, p. 371.

colonies in America', and further, that 'indigo has always been admitted to an entry from the French colonies and that it is notorious it is not produced in the English or any foreign colony except the French colonies in quantities sufficient to supply our manufactures'. In fact, he made out that the duties on French indigo imported in a single year of the war amounted to nearly £2,000 (a statement which the Receiver-General of the island confirmed). He pointed to the existence of permanent laws allowing the introduction of foreign indigo free of duty, which could not be overridden by the King's declaration of war (a line of argument very like that by which the North Americans justified the Flag of Truce trade from the existence of the Molasses Act). Judge Long impudently approved in this case a process of reasoning which he never would have accepted from a North American with sugar in his hold. He acquitted vessel and cargo, but the Court of Prize Appeals reversed his sentence.[1]

§ iii. *The Lawfulness of Trade with the Enemy*

The lawfulness of trade with the enemy might be considered in two ways—as it affected the vessel and cargo employed in the trade, and as it constituted a punishable offence on the part of the trader himself. On the latter point, some very wild and vague ideas prevailed in the colonies, but the Law Officers at home took for the most part a more temperate view. The state of the law was in fact pretty clear, in spite of the too comprehensive language of the statute of 25 Edward III, which defined as high treason the giving of any kind of aid and comfort to the King's enemies. This law was held to be insufficient in the reign of William and Mary, for the exportation of arms and ammunition to the French was once more made high treason. That act expired with that war, but was in effect renewed for the duration of the next, by the 3 & 4 Anne, c. 14. At the same time another law was passed, to prohibit during the war all trade with France; trade with Spain was only forbidden in contraband goods. These laws were not renewed in the later wars; the prohibitions which were then enacted were only partial, and in no sense covered all trade with the enemy,

[1] *Greyhound*, Fowles, H.C.A. 42/69. See also the letter of the Jamaica Committee of Correspondence to its agent, Dec. 19, 1761, against the Monte Cristi trade; the committee assumed that the trade of Jamaica with St. Domingue had been legal and even laudable so long as only indigo was imported, and only became pernicious when sugar also was introduced (*Journals of the Assembly of Jamaica*, v. 320).

whether French or Spaniards. The importance of the statutes of William and Mary, and of Anne, consisted in the fact that it had been thought necessary to pass them at all. The apologists of the Flag of Truce trade argued, in the press and before the courts, that commerce with the enemy could have been no treason by any permanent laws, or these special enactments would not have been needed.[1] This reasoning could not get the ships and cargoes acquitted, but it was enough to protect the persons of the offenders from extreme penalties.

It was only a high misdemeanour to trade to the enemy contrary to a royal proclamation, so long as no stores of war were exported.[2] This was the opinion of Sir Edward Northey, Attorney-General, at the beginning of 1704, before the Act of the 3 & 4 Anne had renewed the prohibition. The Law Officers of Barbados had already expressed the same view in the case of Manuel Manasses Gilligan, who was apparently acquitted even of misdemeanour. However, Northey's opinion does not seem to have been accepted universally or at once.[3]

Heneage Legge, counsel to the Admiralty, advised in 1745 that smuggling with the enemy was high treason, but very little attention need be paid to his opinion.[4] More weight is due to that of the Law Officers Ryder and Murray. At the beginning

---

[1] For example, the Vice-Admiralty Judge of Philadelphia held this language (Hamilton to Pitt, Nov. 1, 1760, Kimball, *Correspondence of William Pitt*, ii. 352). So did Daniel Laroche, Judge surrogate in the Bahamas, in his sentence on the *Thomas and Waddell*, C.O. 23/7, E 20. A private lawyer, John Reade of Boston, to whom the case of Aeneas Mackay was referred by the Council, reported in the same sense in 1740 (Shirley to Newcastle, Oct. 25, 1740, C.O. 5/899). See the letter of the Customs Commissioners, Dec. 8, 1704, in which they reported (before the Acts of the 3 & 4 Anne were passed) that there was no law which forbade the importation of goods from France and Spain, so that they were bound to admit them to an entry. This compares strangely with the Secretary of the Admiralty's letter, in June of the same year, upon the same subject; he said that admitting such a vessel to an entry was nothing to do with the Admiralty, but if any of the men-of-war caught one, she would seize it pursuant to the Queen's declaration of war (*H.M.C., H. of L. MSS., N.S.* vi. 203).

[2] In what this misdemeanour consisted is not very clear; perhaps, as Reade reported of Mackay, 'in exposing himself and crew to be corrupted or insulted by the common enemy of his King and Country'. This is not impossible, for the King's power of restricting or prohibiting his subjects from foreign trade appears to have been founded partly on his duty to preserve them from such 'corruptions', especially in matters of religion (see the arguments of Holt and Sawyer in the case of *The East India Company* v. *Sandys*, Cobbett's *State Trials*, x. 376–80, 474–88).

[3] *C.S.P. Col. 1702–3*, no. 1121; *1704–5*, no. 203; *1711–12*, no. 423; *1712–14*, no. 51. The papers of Gilligan's case in the Vice-Admiralty court are to be found in H.C.A. 42/11 (*Charles the Second*).

[4] Opinion of Dec. 14, 1745, Adm. 1/3675.

of 1748 the Government wanted, for diplomatic reasons, to renew, in as severe a form as it legally could, the injunctions against trading with the French which were contained in the King's declaration of war. It consulted the Law Officers, who reported thus:

'We are humbly of opinion that the war which is now existing between His Majesty and the French King by which the French King and his subjects are enemies to His Majesty and his subjects, and His Majesty's declaration of war against them are in point of law a prohibition of all commerce and trade between His Majesty's subjects and the French, and that every exportation of corn, or other commodities by His Majesty's subjects to France without licence from His Majesty, knowingly and designedly, is a misdemeanour; for which they are punishable by indictment or information in the ordinary course of law; tho' we do not recollect, nor can at present find any case where any person has been in fact tried for such a misdemeanour. And we don't know what can be done by His Majesty more upon this subject to prevent such exportations than by issuing a proclamation directing the laws to be put in execution against such offenders.'

Such a proclamation was therefore made, in order to bring it to the notice of the King's subjects that trade with the French was a high misdemeanour, forbidden by the declaration of war and therefore punishable by law.[1]

Again in 1756 Murray advised on a case of trade with the enemy, that while the vessel and cargo might be condemned in the High Court of Admiralty, there was no hope of getting any kind of conviction against the master and crew. Such trade was a misdemeanour, greater or less according to the circumstances; but he could find no prosecutions for it at common law since the reign of Edward I. Misdemeanours were local as to trial, that is to say the case must be tried in the county where the offence had been committed; but none had been committed in any county, and nobody could be punished for the mere intention.[2] The hot-headed officials of Antigua were presumably ignorant of this opinion when they had a certain William Pickles tried for high treason and condemned to death on

[1] Report of Ryder and Murray, Feb. 18, 1747/8, S.P. 84/431: Proclamation of Feb. 19, in Jamaica Council Minutes, May 18, C.O. 140/32. Hardwicke seems to have agreed with the Law Officers that trade with the enemy was already fully prohibited by the declaration of war (Hardwicke to Sandwich, Feb. 21, o.s., 1747/8, Add. MSS. 35590, f. 15).

[2] Murray to ? Fox, Sept. 15, 1756, S.P. 42/138.

account of trade with the enemy. The sentence was passed by a 'commission for trying pirates', and seems to have been chiefly founded on the application of an Act of the 18 George II,

'inasmuch as by supplying his Majesty's enemies in this part of the world with provisions they are enabled to carry on the war to their advantage and to the prejudice of his Majesty's subjects trading to and residing in the sugar islands more effectually than they would be by the personal service of many of his Majesty's subjects on board their public or private ships of war, the cruisers of the enemy in these seas being more and oftener in want of provisions arms and ammunition than of men.'

The Court recommended Pickles to mercy and he was reprieved.[1]

Since it was almost impossible to punish a trader with the enemy as a criminal, he could only be deterred by the confiscation of his property. Even this method of proceeding against him was sometimes obstructed in the colonies by the sanctity with which English property was hedged about. Some colonial lawyers said that the King could not lawfully interfere with this trade by any proclamation or declaration of war. The claimants' proctors at Jamaica often suggested that the property of Englishmen could only be taken away, or their trade restrained, by a statute of Parliament. They also pointed out that the Molasses Act was regularly renewed every seven years, even in time of war; they argued that Parliament, by continuing the duties upon foreign West India produce, had tacitly admitted the legality of importing it, and thus recognized a right to trade with the French, which could not be taken away except by another statute.[2] This was very bad logic. If the Molasses Act had expressly referred to French produce, there would have been something in the argument; but even then, a royal declaration of war might well be held to modify or override such a statute. The Act, however, only specified foreign produce, and did not create a right to import the dutiable goods in all circumstances from any given places.

[1] Commissioners for trying piracy to Governor Thomas, Jan. 1759, C.O. 152/46. I cannot find in the Statutes at Large any Act of the 18 George II which appears to cover this case. The legislature of Massachusetts enacted in 1744 that exportation of provisions, naval stores, &c., to the French should be high treason for the future (C.O. 5/884, FF 29). Auchmuty thought it ought to be felony without benefit of clergy (*Gentleman's Magazine*, xv. 356).

[2] Popple to Board of Trade, Oct. 10, 1748, C.O. 37/16, M 158; Appellant's appeal case in the *Chester*, Angell, Add. MSS. 36212, f. 69.

Even when they did not thus explicitly challenge the royal authority, the claimants and their proctors generally insisted on the British property of the vessels and cargoes in question, and left it to be inferred that such property could not become prize. The captors attempted to turn this position by arguing that as the King's subjects could not lawfully have any transactions with the French during the war, no valid transference of ownership had ever been made from the French, in whom therefore the property still resided. On that account the cargoes at least would be lawful prize like any other French effects—how the vessels came to be included in the condemnation, the captors did not give themselves much trouble to explain. Since this somewhat metaphysical distinction was much used in the libels of the Advocate-General of Jamaica, it may fairly be presumed to have commended itself to the judges of that court. Judge Edward Webley dealt with the argument that not even an Englishman who traded with a public enemy could be deprived of his lawful property consistently with Magna Carta. He replied that property could not lawfully be acquired from an enemy during a war, therefore Magna Carta could not protect the goods in this trade.[1] Judge Morris of New York, on the other hand, adopted exactly the argument rejected by Webley. He said in the *Catherine*, 'I am clearly of opinion that the property of an English subject made out by clear and concluding proof is not subject to condemnation as prize to any private vessel of war tho' taken in any unlawful or forbidden commerce.' Had the property been clearly made out in the case of this vessel, he should have acquitted her and should have left the offender to be punished for his crime by fine, imprisonment, or otherwise by prosecution at the suit of the Crown as the law directed.[2] In fact, he acquitted a Jamaica Flag of Truce on this kind of grounds. The Philadelphia judge in the same war

---

[1] With the appeal case of the *Charming Elizabeth*, Fay, H.C.A. 42/59, there are some notes of Charles Yorke's argument on this point; but unfortunately they are almost unintelligible (Add. MSS. 36210, f. 289). See also the pronouncement of Judge Auchmuty of Massachusetts in the *Victory*, Bardine, H.C.A. 42/48.

[2] *Reports of Cases in the Vice-Admiralty of New York*, ed. C. M. Hough, p. 203. Morris added that such property 'may be forfeited when informed against by proper officers legally appointed to carry into execution the Acts of Trade'. But that was an illusory concession, for the Acts of Trade did not deal with the subject. Charles Yorke's argument on behalf of the claimant of the *Beaver* seems to follow these lines; but it was unsuccessful, for the Court of Prize Appeals condemned her (Add. MSS. 36212, f. 81).

acquitted traders with the enemy for the same reason, so that captors did not think it worth while to bring such cases before him.[1] The malice and partiality of these judges left the state as well as the captors without an effective remedy, for that which they indicated was least of all likely to be applied by a colonial jury. Their opinions cannot have commended themselves to the Lords Commissioners of Prize Appeals, who condemned all the Flag of Truce traders.

By its decisions this court appears to have established the principle that an Englishman who traded directly with the enemy during a war, without a special licence, forfeited his ship and cargo. There remained one possible exception to this rule. What was the status of an Englishman naturalized as a neutral? The question was an important one in the West Indies, for a great number of North Americans and people from the Leeward Islands inhabited such neutral colonies as St. Eustatius and St. Thomas, where naturalization was all too easily obtained.[2] This practice had already been common in earlier wars; and one of the many questions involved in the case of Manuel Manasses Gilligan was the right of English-born subjects to trade with the enemies of the state as neutrals. The Governor of Barbados then pointed out that if Gilligan's Danish naturalization was to entitle him to trade where he would, a great many people would follow his example; and it appears from later evidence that a great many did so. Northey advised that Gilligan's transference of his allegiance without the Queen's leave was invalid, and did not discharge him of his natural duty to her; but as he was really settled in St. Thomas, and had received no orders to return to Her Majesty's dominions, his trade with the enemy was not a capital offence, if it was any offence at all. The Queen, however, might call upon her subjects to return from the neutral islands, and might proceed against them criminally, if they refused to comply and continued to trade with the enemy.[3] Gilligan, it may be added, was afterwards an accredited representative of England at Madrid, and appears to have died an inhabitant of Barbados.[4]

---

[1] Lt.-Gov. Hamilton to Pitt, Nov. 1, 1760, Kimball, *Correspondence of William Pitt*, ii. 352.

[2] This was one of the chief grievances against St. Eustatius in the War of the American Revolution.

[3] *C.S.P. Col. 1702–3*, no. 1223; *1704–5*, no. 203; *1706–8*, no. 53.

[4] *V. supra*, p. 11.

The same question came up at the beginning of the war of 1739. One Aeneas Mackay divested himself of his allegiance after the outbreak of reprisals, and took the oath of a citizen of Amsterdam. Soon afterwards, he was captured in command of a vessel partly owned by Spaniards, which was condemned with its cargo by Judge Auchmuty at Boston. The authorities were perplexed what to do with Mackay himself; some were for sending him in chains to England, as guilty of high treason, but the Governor favoured him and even protected him against a trial for misdemeanour. Finally, he was bound over to appear in England before the Secretary of State. I cannot discover what Newcastle did with him; most likely nothing at all.[1]

The right to be naturalized a foreigner, and the privileges of Englishmen so naturalized, do not seem to have been conclusively defined in these wars;[2] but two decisions of the Prize Appeals Court somewhat softened the rigour of the prohibitions. In the case of the *Hoffnung* (September 1744), the Court seems to have admitted that an Englishman naturalized as the subject of a foreign power might trade with the enemies of England, if his naturalization had taken place before the war had begun; otherwise he fell under the rule that 'we are not to trade with our enemies—we are not to support them but to distress them by all manner of means'. In the case of the *Humility*, the right of an Englishman to trade with Spain as a naturalized Swede was likewise recognized, but for the special reason that he was in partnership with other Swedes, from whom his interest could not be distinguished.[3]

In the Seven Years War, several Englishmen naturalized at St. Croix were concerned in the Monte Cristi trade. Their

---

[1] Shirley to Newcastle, Oct. 25, 1740, C.O. 5/899.

[2] Judge King of Antigua had a controversy with the Governor of St. Eustatius on this subject. Heyliger reproached King for condemning Dutch property, but King replied that it was English; letters of burghership of St. Eustatius might entitle an Englishman to the benefit of Dutch laws but could not withdraw him from his English allegiance. (King to Heyliger, Nov. 12, 1745, Adm. 1/3881; to Corbett, Nov. 22, 1746, ibid.)

[3] Notebook in H.C.A. 30/875, ff. 10–11, 20. This is the book quoted by Marsden, *Law and Custom of the Sea*, ii. 436. There are some observations on the same cases in Stowell's note-book, copied by Rothery, in the High Court of Admiralty Registry (pp. 51, 102, 122, 138, 213, 216). This volume is the first described by Mr. E. S. Roscoe in his *Lord Stowell*, p. 104. It appears to be a collection of old opinions; the cases are seldom named and the authors never, but both may sometimes be identified. Most of them seem to come from Dr. Andrewe, an eminent civil lawyer of the 1740's.

vessels were seized, and carried to the English sugar colonies. The *St. Croix* was condemned at New Providence on grounds which necessarily imply that the judge considered her owners as Englishmen; but the Lords of Prize Appeals reversed the sentence, and it appears from a note of Charles Yorke, one of the advocates, that they applied to her the criteria by which they judged neutral ships.[1] Another vessel was condemned at Jamaica because her owner's naturalization was invalid, and the claimants deserted their appeal. However, a vessel in the same case which had been likewise condemned at Antigua, was restored on appeal in 1760.[2]

§ iv. *The Embargoes and the Flour Act*

It was not enough to forbid commerce with the enemy. The restriction could not be complete without a control of all exports from the King's dominions to neutral as well as enemy countries. This was particularly necessary in the West Indies, for the North Americans had long established a trade with the French through the Dutch and Danish islands. The legal right of the Government to prevent it was doubtful. To restrain trade with the enemy was one thing, but to interfere with English property which was not demonstrably designed for his ports was another.

Besides the uncertainty of the law, the Government had to deal with practical difficulties when it tried to limit or suppress the trade. The control could only be effective, let alone popular, if it was general. An embargo on Irish beef and butter were useless, so long as the North Americans contrived, for want of supervision, to carry the same articles to the French. Such partial vigilance could only divert trade and prosperity from one part of the Empire to another.[3] In the same way the North Americans resented the system of restraints which was designed to keep their trade within the Empire, when ships loaded with Irish victuals played themselves into the hands of the enemy or slipped their convoy and ran into Martinique on pretext of distress. The West Indians thought it hard they should be forbidden to re-export provisions while the Irish and North Americans could carry the same articles straight to the French

[1] *St. Croix*, Debroskey, H.C.A. 42/61; Endorsement of Charles Yorke, Add. MSS. 36213, f. 2.

[2] *Baron van Bernstorff*, Lemwig, H.C.A. 42/57; *Jane*, van den Bergh, H.C.A. 42/78.

[3] Albert Nesbitt to Chesterfield, Oct. 23, 1746, S.P. 63/409.

islands.¹ Finally, even if the Government established the necessary control in those parts of the Empire which produced
victuals and warlike stores, that was not enough when other
colonies, consumers rather than producers of those articles, were
free to re-export their surplus. The burden of patriotism was
already borne by the producers of provisions, while the consumers received a positive advantage from it; but if the West
Indians were to get Irish and North American exports restricted,
and then ship off from their own islands whatever they could
spare, they would have the privilege of stopping all the other
leaks in the system in order to enjoy a monopoly of turning on
the tap themselves. Thus both Ireland and North America
complained that it would be of no use for them to confine their
exports loyally to the English sugar colonies, unless proper
measures were taken to see that the goods remained there.²

Whatever limitation might be imposed must therefore be
general to Ireland, North America, and the West Indies. It
must also be general within each of those areas. This was not
easy to enforce. In Ireland the great port for victuallers was
Cork—insomuch that the Government sometimes thought it
could achieve its purpose by laying an embargo at Cork alone.
This was neither fair nor effective, for Dublin, Waterford, and
other towns took part in this trade. The Mayor of Cork protested against the discrimination, and the West India planters,
concerned for the entirety of the restriction, took the same side;
on the other hand, when the embargo was coupled with a permission to proceed to the English colonies under escort, Cork
had the advantage, for the convoys started there and the
shipping of the other ports often had some difficulty in picking
them up.³

Much more important than this resistance to discrimination
was the unpopularity in Ireland of the whole policy of embargo.

¹ Sir Charles Hardy, Governor of New York, reported that the North American
Assemblies would not prohibit the trade to the French colonies, so long as Ireland
carried it on with impunity (Hardy to Board of Trade, June 19, 1756, *N.Y. Col.
Doc.* vii. 117; see also Colden to Pitt, Dec. 27, 1760, *Colden Papers* (*N.Y.H.S.
Collections*, 1876), i. 49–53; Thomas to Pitt, Dec. 8, 1760, C.O. 152/46).
² Devonshire to Newcastle, Jan. 10, 1741/2, S.P. 63/405; Lt.-Gov. Clarke to
Newcastle, Feb. 28, 1740/1, *N.Y. Col. Doc.* vi. 180; Frankland to Cleveland, March
10, 1756, Adm. 1/306.
³ Mayor of Cork to Newcastle, Feb. 22, 1744/5, Add. MSS. 32704, f. 81; Sharpe
to Corbett, Feb. 18, 1744/5, S.P. 42/28, f. 62; Irish merchants to Corbett, Oct. 8,
1746, S.P. 42/31, f. 264.

Cattle-raising and dairying were the chief livelihood of southern and western Ireland; indeed, it was argued that the Government itself had driven the Irish into these branches of business by its restrictive commercial policy, which proscribed both the woollen industry and the importation of unfattened cattle into England. To destroy the export trade in beef and butter without the gravest necessity, was to impose upon Ireland too large a part of the burden of patriotic endeavour. The new season's beef and butter would depress the prices of the old (a strong argument in the eyes of the merchants with stocks on hand); the slaughtering must fall off, rents must come down, and in fact the whole country must be ruined. The Lords Lieutenant, Devonshire, Chesterfield, Hartington, and Bedford, all protested with various degrees of vehemence against this interference with Ireland's prosperity. Chesterfield induced the Admiralty to exempt certain goods, such as tallow and candles, from the prohibitions, and finally persuaded Newcastle to remove an embargo altogether in 1746, very much to the annoyance of that Board.[1]

The Government always tried to compensate Ireland for the loss of markets by ordering large quantities of beef and pork for the Royal Navy. Ireland naturally obtained some relief from the increased orders which the Government must in any event have placed in war-time; but she was deprived by the embargo of larger profits still, for all nations increase their naval and military establishments during a war, and all, friends and enemies alike, would have bought their rations of beef and pork from Ireland had she been free to sell. Besides, the Government never took off anything like all the season's killing. The Admiralty and War Office seldom ordered more than five or ten thousand barrels at a time, while the total production of beef alone was estimated at a hundred thousand barrels a year.

At the beginning of hostilities with France in 1755 Hartington heard that beef was on the point of being exported to France, so he ordered it to be unloaded and bought up for the Government. Some of this was of the old season's killing, and

---

[1] Nesbitt to Newcastle, March 7, 1744/5, S.P. 63/407; Nesbitt to Chesterfield, Oct. 23, 1746, S.P. 63/409; Mayor and Sheriffs of Cork, petition of March 8, 1744/5, S.P. 63/406; Lords of the Admiralty to Newcastle, Feb. 25, 1745/6, S.P. 42/30, f. 184; Chesterfield to Newcastle, Nov. 3, 1746, S.P. 63/409; Hartington to Lords of the Admiralty, Oct. 16, 1755, S.P. 42/38, f. 135; Hartington to Robinson, Oct. 31, 1755, S.P. 63/413; Bedford to Pitt, Sept. 2, 1758, G.D. 8/19.

the Victualling Commissioners could not recommend its purchase; but the Lords of the Admiralty decided to sacrifice the digestions of their crews to political expediency, and ordered the beef to be bought if it was found passable upon a survey. So far, so good; but the new season's beef would be upon the market in a few months, and the Government could not think of buying the whole of that. Hartington did not see how else he could restrain the merchants from exporting it where they would. To make the matter worse, half of what he had already reserved for the navy proved on survey to be cow beef, which the Victualling Commissioners would not take. He was providentially delivered from embarrassment by the great earthquake of Lisbon. The Government determined to send relief to the sufferers, and Hartington's two thousand barrels of cow beef were conscientiously shipped off, as no worse than 'the poorer sort of people amongst the Portuguese' would have bought in the ordinary course of trade.[1]

Earthquakes could not turn up in this way every year, but within a few months war was declared, and the Lord Lieutenant was invested with the proper power for restraining the trade by means of an embargo. Bedford had been the First Lord of the Admiralty who so much objected to the removal of the embargo in 1746; but now he protested, as Lord Lieutenant of Ireland, against the wanton or light-hearted use of embargoes. They seem to have been fewer than usual in Ireland during his reign, and the merchants of Cork did a lively trade with the French colonies in Dutch ships through St. Eustatius.

In the intervals when their vessels were released from the embargoes, the Irish shipowners often instructed their captains to get themselves taken by the enemy's privateers. One or two of them made elaborate arrangements for trading in this manner on a large scale. The ship was 'captured' by a privateer belonging to the real consignee of the cargo, who, having appropriated the provisions as prize, sold the vessel collusively back to its owner for a nominal sum, and got her loaded with West India produce. In order to stop this abuse, the Lords of

---

[1] Hartington to Robinson, Aug. 21 and Dec. 12, 1755, S.P. 63/413; Clevland to Amyand, Sept. 2, 1755, S.P. 42/38, f. 2; Amyand to Clevland, Sept. 4, 1755, Adm. 1/4120, no. 46; Horatio Townshend to Clevland, Oct. 14, 1755, S.P. 42/38, f. 109; Hartington to Lords of Admiralty, Oct. 16, 1755, f. 135; Lords of Admiralty to Robinson, Oct. 31, 1755, f. 129; Robinson to Hartington, Nov. 29, 1755, S.P. 63/413.

the Admiralty insisted that the Irish exporters should not only give the usual bond to land their goods in the King's dominions, which would of course be void in case of capture by the enemy, but also take convoy, and bind themselves not to depart from it during the voyage. This arrangement was burdensome to the merchants, for convoys were few and often caused expensive delays. The Admiralty sometimes dispensed individuals from it in particular cases, but insisted on the principle in both wars.[1]

Ireland might well resist the Government's attempts to confine her trade during war-time, when even England carried the necessaries of life to the enemy. Great scandal was caused at the end of 1747 by the export of large quantities of corn from England and Ireland to the famine-stricken ports of France. Vessels cleared out under neutral colours for the colonies or neutral ports, and promptly made the best of their way to Bordeaux.[2] Sandwich, our Minister at The Hague, was particularly embarrassed by this practice, for he was trying to drive the States-General into a war with France by inducing them to break off all commercial relations with her, and he could have wished for a better example to be shown in England. So long as the trade was a fraudulent one under foreign colours, the Government could have claimed plausibly that it was doing all that lay in its power to suppress such an abuse.[3] It could not gracefully palliate the resolution which the House of Commons passed in January 1747/8, to the effect that it would not be for the advantage of the country to prohibit the export of corn. The Duke of Newcastle tried to explain this away:

'Some officious, designing fools had given out, that, in order to prevent carrying corn to France, there must be a total prohibition of all exportation. The country gentlemen, and some *others* were so

[1] Bussy to Amelot, Oct. 27, N.S., 1740, A.E. Angleterre, 409, f. 183; *Gentleman's Magazine*, xii. 273; Holburne to Corbett, Dec. 25, 1744, Adm. 1/1884; Warren to Corbett, Feb. 7, 1744/5, Adm. 1/2654; Yeamans to Newcastle, May 31, 1745, with annexed letters to Bradshaw, C.O. 152/44; Admiralty Minutes, May 6, 1742, Adm. 3/46; Lords of the Admiralty to Newcastle, Feb. 28, 1745/6, S.P. 42/30, f. 185; Sept. 26, Nov. 20, 1746, S.P. 42/31, ff. 194, 323; Nesbitt to Chesterfield, Oct. 23, 1746, S.P. 63/409; Lords of the Admiralty to Fox, Sept. 15, 1756, Adm. 2/371, p. 71.
[2] Sandwich to Chesterfield, Nov. 21 and 28, Dec. 1, N.S., 1747, S.P. 84/427, ff. 79, 121, 126; extract from Van Deurse's letter, Nov. 10, 1747, f. 96; *Vrai patriote hollandois*, no. vi, Jan. 1, 1748, S.P. 84/433.
[3] Chesterfield to Sandwich, Dec. 8, O.S., 1747, S.P. 84/427, ff. 209-10; Hardwicke to Sandwich, Dec. 15, O.S., 1747, Add. MSS. 35589, f. 396.

alarmed at this, that without considering the consequences, or knowing what had passed in Holland, they came to a resolution against
prohibiting the exportation of corn; but this is only general, and
can't authorise the carrying it to France, which, as all commerce is,
is prohibited by the declaration of war.'[1]

That was all very well; but foreigners found it hard to understand how such a resolution came to be passed in defiance of
the wishes of the Ministry, which they credited with a degree
of control over the House which it possesses now but did not
exercise in the days of Henry Pelham. Besides, it is more than
likely that the country gentlemen and their advisers deliberately
meant to strike out of the Government's hands the weapons it
was preparing against the clandestine exports to France:[2] if so,
they were claiming a liberty to succour the enemy which they
allowed the Government to deny to the farmers of Ireland and
North America.

The embargo was far more difficult to enforce in North
America than in Ireland. Nothing short of extreme danger
could bring into line so many governments subject to popular
influence. The chief commercial colonies keenly rivalled each
other, and those which did not possess any first-class trading
town were for ever trying to emancipate themselves from the
domination of those which did.[3] No branch of trade was the
object of more mutual jealousy than that of the West Indies.
Pennsylvania tried again and again to monopolize the trade of
Maryland; the legislature of Maryland warded off the attack,
and attempted to build up an indigenous carrying trade to the
West Indies, by high duties on the exportation to Philadelphia
of articles which could compose a West India cargo. Connecti-

---

[1] Newcastle to Sandwich, Jan. 29, o.s., 1747/8, Add. MSS. 32811, f. 125.

[2] Sandwich had for some time been urging Chesterfield and Newcastle to stop
the trade by exacting security from the masters of vessels for the landing of their
cargoes of provisions in the ports to which they were nominally bound. This
measure, which he represented as necessary to the satisfaction of the Dutch, must
have been seriously considered, for, even after the House of Commons resolution,
Newcastle comforted Sandwich with the hope of it. Mischief-makers may have
known this, and determined to intimidate the Government beforehand, by a
resolution which would appeal to the self-interest of the landed gentlemen in the
House (Sandwich to Chesterfield, Dec. 1 and 23, N.S., 1747, S.P. 84/427, ff. 126,
276; Chesterfield to Sandwich, Dec. 8, o.s., 1747, ff. 209–10; Jan. 19, o.s., 1747/8,
S.P. 84/431; Newcastle to Sandwich, quoted above).

[3] Some details of this rivalry can be obtained from A. A. Giesecke's book on
American Commercial Legislation before 1789 (Philadelphia, 1910). The subject of
embargoes is discussed on pp. 80–6.

cut and New York fought in the same way. Moreover, the imports and even the exports in the West India trade were among the commonest sources of indirect taxation, whose rates varied from colony to colony. Just before these wars began the Lieutenant-Governor of New York deplored the lack of uniformity in the provincial customs duties; a colony which laid no tax on a particular article, allowed it to be smuggled overland into the territory of a neighbour which laid a high one.[1] It is easy to imagine the difficulties which a common policy of abstention would meet from the mutual suspicion of the colonial merchants and legislators.

Admiral Vernon tried to inspire such a policy in 1740, by a circular in which he asked the Governors of North America to prevent victuals from being exported to any place but the King's dominions. Some at least of the Governors complied, and the others were soon afterwards relieved of responsibility by the Flour Act of 1740, which forbade such exportation to foreign parts for the critical year 1741. Vernon was dissatisfied with these endeavours, for he informed Trelawny in January 1741/2 that flour was still exported to the foreign sugar islands from North America and even from Jamaica itself. Vernon does not seem to have taken the precaution of sending his circular to the authorities in the other West India islands; but Lieutenant-Governor Clarke of New York guessed the possibility of such an omission and forwarded copies of Vernon's letter to them. Trade, however, will always find the leaks in a system of restriction, and such a leak existed at Bermuda, where neither Vernon's nor Clarke's letter was received for a long time. Captains from New York found that having entered their cargoes in Bermuda they could re-export them without any conditions, and the Governor could not at first persuade the Council, which contained some eminent professional smugglers, to prevent the abuse. Finally, however, copies of the Act of Parliament arrived, and determined the question.[2] The system seems to have worked well for a short time. Judge King of Antigua called for its revival in 1746. He declared that there was no other way of stopping the export of provisions to the neutral colonies, and that it had obliged the people of St. Eustatius to

---

[1] Clarke to the Board of Trade, June 13, 1740, C.O. 5/1059.
[2] Clarke to Newcastle, Feb. 28, 1740/1, *N.Y. Col. Doc.* vi. 180; Alured Popple to William Popple, Dec. 21, 1741, C.O. 37/14, M 56.

sue to Antigua for leave to buy victuals for themselves at the beginning of the war.[1]

The Assembly of Pennsylvania told Governor Thomas that it would be useless to restrain the exportation of flour unless it was done by all the colonies alike.[2] Massachusetts and Rhode Island passed acts for confining the export of provisions to the British dominions, but they expired in 1742 and were not renewed; indeed, the active stage of West Indian warfare being finished, it would have been a futile piece of self-sacrifice to continue them. With the outbreak of the French war in 1744 a new wave of enthusiasm passed over the colonies, at the height of which Massachusetts and New York enacted new laws for depriving the enemy colonies of provisions and warlike stores; but the Massachusetts Act only continued in force eleven months —at the end of which time, none of the other colonies having followed the example, the General Court declined to renew it. Governor Shirley told the Board of Trade again and again that nothing could stop the trade but a general Act of Parliament restraining all the colonies. The Board tentatively agreed, but feared that it could not be done immediately.[3]

Nothing, in fact, was done for the rest of that war. Before the outbreak of the next, Shirley was already repeating his advice, and trying to bring about a general embargo throughout North America. Other Governors had the same policy at heart, and there was some chance of pursuing it as long as the Northern Colonies were interested in the reduction of Cape Breton. Both Massachusetts and New York passed laws in 1755 to restrain trade with the French colonies. Each of these laws was designed to last a very short time unless the neighbouring colonies would come into the scheme.[4] The attempt to procure a concert of

---

[1] Vernon to Ward, Nov. 13, 1740, Kimball, *Correspondence of Colonial Governors of Rhode Island*, i. 185; to Trelawny, Jan. 5, 1741/2, S.P. 42/92, f. 19; King to Corbett, May 21, 1746, Adm. 1/3881. Governor Mathew, however, said later that the Flour Act of 1740 was not obeyed (see his letter to the Board of Trade, Sept. 19, 1746, C.O. 152/25, Y 162).

[2] Assembly to Thomas, May 26, 1741, C.O. 5/1234.

[3] *Laws of the Colony of New York* (1894), iii. 569–71; Shirley to Board of Trade, June 16, 1744, C.O. 5/884, FF 27; Feb. 6, 1747/8, C.O. 5/886, GG 3; Board of Trade to Shirley, Feb. 21, 1744/5, C.O. 5/918, p. 141. Although the Flour Act had expired in 1741, the Board seems to have regarded the Order in Council of Feb. 19, 1740/1, made in pursuance of it, as remaining valid for the rest of the war. (Report of March 26, 1746, C.O. 153/16, p. 273).

[4] *Acts and Resolves of the Province of Massachusetts Bay*, iii. 814, 865; xv. 270. Shirley to Sharpe, Feb. 17, 1755; Delancy to Sharpe, Feb. 24, 1755, *Correspondence*

measures seems to have failed. Next year it was tried again. New York led the way once more, with an Act which was to continue in force for three months if New Jersey and Pennsylvania would pass similar laws, but was to end in three weeks if they would not. Pennsylvania passed such a law, likewise depending on the concurrence of her neighbours; New Jersey also came into the scheme, but it broke down because the King's Counties (the modern state of Delaware) would only keep up the prohibition for three weeks. Hardy tried to effect the same purpose by a concerted embargo; New Jersey agreed, but some others did not.[1] Meanwhile Pennsylvania complained that Maryland, likewise a bread colony, remained at liberty to export. The Governor of Maryland promised to do his best at the next session of the Assembly, 'tho' I apprehend they will not be very fond of it and will be apt to say that Virginia as well as Pennsylvania should set us an example'. Finally the knot was cut by the arrival of a letter from Lord Loudoun, Commander-in-Chief, requiring an embargo to be declared. A few months after it was laid, the Governor of Virginia relaxed it, Maryland followed suit, and the chain was broken again.[2] All this time, Massachusetts had kept up, by a succession of laws and proclamations, a very rigid system of prohibition; it was unlawful to export provisions even to the British West Indies, without a special order of the legislature. Unfortunately, Massachusetts was not one of the colonies which produced important quantities of food, so its abstention did not make much difference.[3]

Another proof of the futility of isolated action came from Rhode Island. The legislature had brought itself to pass, in good faith or bad, several laws against trade with the French and even against exporting provisions to foreign parts. The evasion of these laws by the Monte Cristi traders provoked a new and violent Act in June 1757; but in May of the next year

of Governor Sharpe (Maryland Historical Society), i. 169–70; Laws of the Colony of New York (1894), iii. 1050, 1121, 1139.

[1] Hardy to Board of Trade, May 10, June 19, Oct. 13, 1756, N.Y. Col. Doc. vii. 81, 117, 163; Laws of the Colony of New York, iv. 84, 96; Statutes at Large of Pennsylvania, 1682–1801, v. 223; New Jersey Archives, xvii. 23, 55–7.

[2] R. H. Morris to Sharpe, July 19, 1756; Loudoun to Sharpe, Aug. 20; Sharpe to Morris, Aug. 25; Dinwiddie to Sharpe, Sept. 8, Correspondence of Governor Sharpe, i. 458, 463, 472, 480; Loudoun to Pitt, June 17, 1757, C.O. 5/48.

[3] Acts and Resolves of the Province of Massachusetts Bay, iii. 806, 814, 865–6, 870, 880, 901, 949–50, 955–7, 998, 1028, 1069–70; xv. 270–1, 317, 383, 621, 657.

the General Assembly repealed it, finding that 'all the British subjects in North America, except those of this colony, are allowed to carry on trade and commerce with the subjects of His Catholic Majesty, at a place in the West Indies, under his jurisdiction, called Monti Christo . . . and no bad consequence can attend such a traffic'.[1]

The same mutual suspicions caused no less difficulty in the West Indies. Although the planters had a strong interest in assuring themselves of proper supplies of victuals, the merchants had influence enough to get leave to export whatever was left over when the island consumers were served. Perhaps they obtained this influence by threatening to reduce the importations for the future if their request was not granted. For example, Richard Morecroft obtained leave to send off some beef which was in danger of decaying on his hands, by pointing out that

'the quantity of old beef remaining upon the spot must necessarily prevent the importation of new, which your Petitioner is well assured from the advices he has received is to be expected. But while the old is permitted to remain, and thereby the proper vend for the new prevented, your petitioner will be obliged in justice to his employers as well as others, to send away the vessels consigned to him with new beef to some other and better market.'[2]

Other motives produced the same result in Jamaica, where the merchants addressed Trelawny in 1745 for leave to export flour, alleging that otherwise the factors would be

'under a necessity of advising their correspondents to stop shipping, which may be of bad consequence as it will put them on sending the provisions (which must be exported or perish) to Curaçao and other Dutch islands from whence the Spaniards have been constantly supplied and of course has enabled the Dutch to send great quantities of dry goods (a branch of trade well known to be of great consequence to this island). And . . . if an export be allowed, the merchants of New York and Philadelphia will be constantly supplying the markets in the hopes of a call from the Spanish market.'[3]

[1] R.I. Col. Rec. v. 423–5, 499, 516–17; vi. 11–12, 58, 147–8.
[2] Barbados Council Minutes, Dec. 1, 1741, C.O. 31/21. The same motive can be seen at work in Boston in 1713; corn was scarce, and the people was provoked to riot by Capt. Andrew Belcher's sending some to Curaçao. 'The Selectmen desired him not to send it; he told them, The hardest fend off! If they stop'd his vessel, he would hinder the coming in of three times as much' (Diary of Samuel Sewall, M.H.S. Collections, ii. 384).
[3] Jamaica Council Minutes, Aug. 26, 1745, C.O. 140/31. At the beginning of

Even if the merchants and factors of the islands had taken no measures to control the supplies as they threatened, the North American traders themselves would have done the same thing. The supercargoes, generally at liberty to sell at any market according to their judgements, and accustomed to try one port after another until they had suited themselves, would not knowingly approach an island from which no re-export was allowed. When the legislature of Antigua laid an embargo in October 1740, it ordered all pilots to swear 'not to inform any person whatsoever on board any vessels inward bound that such embargo is laid', so that the North Americans should be committed to selling at the island before they could discover the trap into which they had walked. The Assembly of Montserrat refused to pass a law for continuing in force the imperial Flour Act of 1740, 'because we think it will be prejudicial to the importation of that kind of commodity amongst us'.[1] St. Kitts and Antigua passed laws in 1745 for preventing the export of provisions, but were forced to repeal them the next year, because they found that in spite of the system of licensed exports which they grafted on their prohibition, the Northern Colonies left off supplying them, so that prices rose instead of falling. Governor Mathew excused this retreat by charging the people of North America with something like a definite conspiracy against these unwisely patriotic islands. 'The Northward Colonies took fire at what we did, and were resolv'd and actually did refuse supplying these islands (that had pass'd the law) with provisions. We then were in danger of famine, without a repeal of the law for preventing exporting provisions.' This palliation did not

the war, when the South Sea factors had asked leave to continue supplying the galleons with flour, Trelawny and the Council had refused it; but the factors put it about that they had agreed to connive at it in private. They were made to withdraw this accusation, but that proves little (Jamaica Council Minutes, Aug. 7 and 8, Oct. 2, Nov. 6, 1739, C.O. 140/30; Trelawny to Stone, Nov. 5, 1739, C.O. 137/56, f. 262). In fact large quantities of flour were sent from Jamaica to the Spanish ports. A certain James Christie made a contract with the Viceroy of Santa Fé to supply several cargoes to Portobello; he took the opportunity of importing other kinds of goods as well, and one of his vessels was seized by a *Guarda-Costa* and condemned. The merchants of Kingston complained to Admiral Ogle of this 'breach of public as well as private faith, and of the rights and privileges the English ought to enjoy on that coast', and Ogle, so far from leaving this double contrabandist to his fate, sent some ships to demand instant redress and to batter down the walls of Portobello if it was withheld (Petition of Kingston merchants to Ogle, April 2, 1744, S.P. 42/89, f. 150; Ogle to Newcastle, Aug. 19, 1744, f. 146; various papers annexed, ff. 149–91).

[1] Montserrat Council Minutes, Jan. 2, 1741/2, C.O. 177/3.

satisfy the Board of Trade, which advised George II to disallow the repealing Acts, both for certain technical reasons and because they conflicted with the policy of the imperial Government. The two islands were therefore legally tied to maintaining the restriction.[1]

No wonder Frankland found, at the beginning of the next war, that though the prohibition of exports had been suggested in Antigua, yet 'by some distresses which arose last war in consequence of a similar law, I fancy they will not enact another of that kind in haste again.'[2] The legislature consented, however, to pass such another Act in 1757; but in this war, as in the last, the mutual distrust of the four Leeward Islands was so great that none of them would commit itself until it was quite sure the other three would do so. St. Kitts only agreed after Governor Thomas had promised that he would withhold his assent to their Bill until he could ratify at the same time similar ones from the other three islands.[3] The Assembly of Antigua declared that only an Act of Parliament binding all the colonies could effectually stop abuses.

The Government was already moving towards such a policy. The Secretary of State sent out a circular to the Governors in March 1756, ordering them to get laws enacted for prohibiting the export of provisions to the French. Not all of them could do so. In October the Board of Trade recommended a general embargo, and at the end of the year it made up its mind to introduce a Bill into Parliament.[4] This became the Flour Act of 1757, which, unlike that of 1740, continued in force for the duration of the war.

[1] Mathew to Board of Trade, Sept. 19, 1746, C.O. 152/25, Y 162; Board of Trade, Representations to the King, March 26, Dec. 3, 1746, C.O. 153/16, pp. 273–5, 292–4. The sugar islands suffered in another way from the excessive though occasional zeal of the Northern colonies. Some of their laws—for example, the New York Act of 1744 and the Massachusetts Act of June 25, 1755—prohibited the export of provisions so rigidly as to interfere with the trade to the British West Indies. Particular exceptions were obtainable in Massachusetts by special order of the legislature; the New York and Pennsylvania Acts of 1756 provided that British colonies in need of provisions might apply to the Governors for permission to export a reasonable quantity.

[2] Frankland to Weekes, April 2, 1756, Adm. 1/306; see also Antigua Council Minutes, Nov. 17, 1756, C.O. 9/21.

[3] St. Kitts Council Minutes, Feb. 16, 1757, C.O. 241/7; see also Antigua Council Minutes, Nov. 20, 1740, C.O. 9/13; Assembly Minutes, Feb. 17, 1740/1, C.O. 9/14.

[4] Fox, circular to colonial Governors, March 13, 1756, N.T. Col. Doc. vii. 76; Board of Trade circular, Oct. 9, 1756, p. 162; Journal of Commissioners of Trade and Plantations, 1754–8, Oct. 1, 1756, Jan. 12, 1757, pp. 257, 285.

A long series of administrative measures culminated in this Act. The Government had frequently held the whole or parts of the King's dominions under embargoes; these were sometimes applied to all shipping, English and neutral—sometimes to all kinds of victuals, and sometimes only to certain classes whose export it particularly wished to prevent. These embargoes were imposed, withdrawn, and reimposed at the will of the Ministry. The Act of 1757 was meant to be more permanent than the embargoes, but it was not in every sense more complete. It applied to 'all kinds of victual', but it was to be in force only in the colonies. The export of corn and its products from England and Ireland was forbidden at the same time, but for one year only, and for a special reason—the scarcity which then prevailed.[1] Thus the English landed interest was to be free to send corn abroad as soon as the ease of the consumer would allow it; it was doing so in 1759. Further, the export of beef, pork, and butter from Ireland was not affected by the measure; that is why the Government continued to depend on embargoes for the control of this branch of trade. There was an exception in favour of the privileged rice-growers of Carolina, who had already been allowed a partial release from the restraints of the Acts of Trade.

The Act was to be enforced by demanding security that all victuals exported from any part of the King's dominions should be landed in some other part. Certificates were to be brought back from the place where the cargo was unloaded, and until they had been produced, the bonds were not to be cancelled. This system had a long history; it was in fact the most natural way of keeping within the Empire such articles as must be carried, in the ordinary course of trade, from one part of it to another. Nottingham had ordered the Governors to put it into force in 1703.[2] Vernon recommended the same thing to them in 1740, and when the colonial legislatures passed laws for the

---

[1] It is worth noticing that the temporary Act of 1740 owed its introduction in part to a similar scarcity. The first draft of that measure was so stringent as to prevent all intercourse between North America and our own West India colonies; it needed strenuous efforts both by the West Indians who depended on such trade for their subsistence, and by the North Americans who depended on it for their prosperity, to get this clause modified (Bussy to Amelot, Dec. 12 and 15, N.S., 1740, A.E. Angleterre, 409, ff. 353, 360. See also the petitions against the Bill, *C.J.*, Nov. 25 and 26, Dec. 1, 1740, xxiii. 538–9, 543–4).

[2] *C.S.P. Col. 1702–3*, no. 1194.

prevention of trade with the enemy, they often took this method of getting them executed.[1]

The system would only have worked well if the Customs Officers in the colonies had been many, upright, and efficient. Unfortunately they were few, and for the most part unworthy of their trust; all the efforts to regulate the export of provisions were thwarted by their negligence and by various abuses. Perhaps the commonest of all was the return of certificates for provisions which had never been landed in the English dominions. This practice was widespread and notorious.[2] A particular form of it existed between Barbados and the Leeward Islands. A vessel would clear from one of those governments for the other, sell her cargo at St. Vincent or Dominica on the way, and get a certificate at the end of her journey for provisions which were no longer on board. Pinfold offered to exchange with Thomas the lists of shipping entered and cleared, that the entries of one colony might be compared with the clearances of another.[3] Some ships took their cargoes to the English sugar islands, landed them and had the bonds cancelled, and then re-embarked them secretly.[4] False papers, or falsely obtained, were used likewise for covering the return cargo of French produce. Some masters went to Jamaica, cleared their vessels with imaginary cargoes of French prize sugars, and then loaded at St. Domingue; others cleared at Kingston with cargoes which were to have been put on board in the outports—a malpractice which was common enough in peace-time.[5]

Another sin of the officials was allowing the bonds to remain uncancelled after they ought to have sued for their forfeiture. Further abuses arose from the irregularity or incompleteness of the clearances themselves. Many vessels were cleared out from

[1] For example, Rhode Island in 1741 and 1755 (*R.I. Col. Rec.* v. 27, vi. 11).

[2] James Hamilton, Lt.-Gov. of Pennsylvania, to Pitt, Nov. 1, 1760, Kimball, *Correspondence of William Pitt*, ii. 354.

[3] Pinfold to Thomas, April 29, 1759, Pinfold Letter-Book, Library of Congress.

[4] Captain Edward Smith caught one of these—a Rhode Islander—red-handed at Antigua and got her condemned (Smith to Burchett, May 20, 1741, Adm. 1/2459; Mathew to Yeamans, May 29, C.O. 152/44).

[5] Holmes to Clevland, Oct. 27, 1761, Adm. 1/236. False papers seem to have been obtainable at Guadeloupe after the conquest (G. G. Beekman to Metcalfe Bowler, July 1, 1761, Letter-book, N.Y.H.S.). Governor Dalrymple attributed many of the abuses there to the participation of the revenue officers in trade (Dalrymple to Pitt, July 15, 1761, Kimball, *Correspondence of William Pitt*, ii. 450).

North America for the West Indies in general. Perhaps this vagueness was necessary to the supercargoes, who did not always know where they should sell their goods; but it did not help the customs officers to get the certificates returned. Other vessels were deliberately cleared for places where no Custom House existed, like the Moskito Shore, and then proceeded straight for the French colonies; no certificate could be expected from them. Others again cleared for ports where the officers were notoriously corrupt. The chain of imperial restriction was only as strong as its weakest link, and a few scoundrels at New London or Tortola could frustrate the whole system.[1] The former was especially frequented by illegal traders; exactly what kind of fraud was practised there, is not quite clear.[2] Lieutenant-Governor Colden noticed that vessels cleared from New York for New London with cargoes of onions, boards, and apples, which was like sending coals to Newcastle. Certainly these cargoes were not wanted at New London, and perhaps they never went there; Colden could only guess that the provisions were really landed and then reshipped without a new bond given.[3] Colden put all the blame on the New England

[1] The following entry is taken from the 'Journal of a Captive, 1745–8' in the Library of Congress: 'Feb. 4th 1747/8. Captn Austin went away in a small boat to Spanish Town another of the Virgin Isles to clear out his vessel, he finding it impracticable to clear out at Tortola as usual, for since Captn Purcell has been Governor he has sworn all his officers not to clear out any vessel but such as completely load here,—for formerly the North American vessels used to load at St. Thomas' or St. Cruz, two Danish islands, then stand over to Tortola and purchase a barrel of sugar and a little cotton, and by virtue of them clear out the whole cargo as the produce of the British islands, which now Captn Purcell's laudable conduct hath prevented those abuses.' Some practices of this kind had revived a few years later (John Gardner to Timothy Orne & Co., May 10, 1760, Timothy Orne MSS. xii. 6, Essex Institute). The same malpractice accounts for the cargoes of sugar entered in North America as from Turks Island, which produced nothing but salt.

[2] See an intercepted letter of James Thompson, Cap François, to Capt. Edward Dishington of the *Prosper*, April 6, 1762, Adm. 1/237; also the case of the *Black Joke*, Packwood, H.C.A. 42/57. Philip Cuyler of New York wrote to one Lechmere, a corrupt official in Connecticut, 'Inclosed you have a certificate for the landage of 300 barrels flour on board the schooner Dolphin John Hickey to your place which I request you'll be good enough to endorse and send it me per return of the bearer, the charge thereon be pleased to draw for and your bill shall be paid on receipt. I have also the brigantine Charming Sally Capt. Joseph Hunt cleared from Amboy to Kingston, Jamaica with 318 barrels flour, should be glad likewise youd send me a certif^t for the landing of it with a clearance for Jamaica as well for the former' (Aug. 19, 1760, Letter-book, N.Y.P.L.).

[3] Colden to Amherst, April 23, 1762, *Colden Papers* (*N.Y.H.S.* Collections, 1876), i. 195.

colonies and New Jersey, whose officers connived at a trade which, he implied, was not carried on directly between New York and the West Indies. This was an exaggeration, for the Prize Appeals records contain many cases of New York vessels which seem to have proceeded to the West Indies without touching anywhere in North America to adjust their papers on the way; perhaps Colden erred out of tenderness to a son in the New York Custom House.[1]

Sometimes a master would declare only a very small part of his cargo, and give bond to land it in His Majesty's dominions. He would sell all the undeclared goods among the French or Dutch, and then proceed with what little he had formally cleared to an English colony, where he would get the bond cancelled.[2] There were other abuses so ingenious and so mixed up with Custom House technicalities that to describe them would be to overload this topic with detail.[3]

It would be a thankless work to follow all the devices by which the merchants cheated the mediocre vigilance of the Custom House men, or corrupted their less than mediocre integrity. Even if the supervision had been as diligent as it was lax, the officers could do nothing without the courts; and, as Colden informed Pitt, it was difficult to prosecute with success for breaches of the Flour Act 'against the bent of the people, while they are under the prejudice to think that the sugar islands have gained a preference inconsistent with the true interest of the mother country'.[4] This difficulty is illustrated by the classic squabble in Massachusetts over the writs of assistance, which originated in the seizure of smuggled French molasses during the war. The obstructive strength of public

---

[1] Colden to Pitt, Oct. 27 and Nov. 11, 1760, *Colden Papers* (1876), i. 27–8, 36.

[2] 'This night expect to saill for Montsuratt in a sloop belonging their with what fish and mackl cleared out in order to cansall my bonds' (George Dodge, St. Eustatius, to the owners of the schooner *Beaver*, July 23, 1757, Timothy Orne MSS. x. 88, Essex Institute).

[3] See the report of J. T. Kempe, a law officer of New York, to Governor Monckton, Nov. 3, 1762, *Aspinwall Papers* (*M.H.S. Collections*), i. 469–72. The Collector of the Customs at Rhode Island allowed provisions to be exported to Surinam in spite of the Flour Act; I do not know if there was any complicated fraud or a plain breach of the Act. Some people distinguished Surinam from the other Dutch colonies because it had hardly any commercial intercourse with the French; but French privateers could victual there and thereby prolong their cruises (John Bowditch to Timothy Orne & Co., Nov. 7, 1757, Timothy Orne MSS. x. 82, Essex Institute).

[4] Colden to Pitt, Dec. 27, 1760, Kimball, *Correspondence of William Pitt*, ii. 382.

opinion is also proved by the curious complaint of George Spencer, an informer of New York who was maltreated in coffee-houses and packed off to prison by the device of buying up one of his debts from a creditor and suing him for it.[1]

Finally, the best supervision in the world could not have looked after so immense a coast-line, without a number of subordinate officers far greater than the imperial Government allowed. Many, perhaps most, of the traders with the enemy took on board the best part of their cargoes in remote bays without clearing at all, or after clearing a nominal loading of small value; and perhaps even more brought home their cargoes to such unauthorized outports and smuggled them on shore.[2]

The Flour Act had other defects which made it useless. In the first place, the export of provisions to foreign parts could only be proved after they had been landed; there was no punishing an English subject for an intention.[3] Secondly, the Act did not offer the captors enough incentive to make seizures under it. It only applied half the forfeitures to their use; they were entitled to the whole value if the vessel and cargo were condemned as lawful prize. The officers of the navy naturally showed what ingenuity they could in avoiding the half for the sake of the whole. For both these reasons, they made no attempt to stop English vessels on their way into the French ports, but concentrated their attention on catching them as they came out. There are conclusive proofs of this. The mate of the *Speedwell* deposed that she was stopped on her way into Port au Prince by H.M.S. *Viper*, which, having searched her cargo, let her go and watched her proceed into the harbour. The *Defiance*, Northam, was allowed to carry a cargo of fish into Monte Cristi in the same way. Both these ships were taken on their way home. Richard Mercer, a supercargo at Monte Cristi, gave other instances of the same kind, and advised his employers to send a ship to Monte Cristi with a cargo of flour, even if she went away in ballast. 'The men of war would take no notice of them, they don't care what they bring provided

---

[1] Spencer to Colden, Dec. 16, 1761, *Colden Papers* (*N.Y.H.S. Collections*, 1922), p. 93.

[2] See the owners' instructions in the *Betty*, Freeman, H.C.A. 42/56; *Fair Lady*, Lovett, H.C.A. 42/67.

[3] Less scruple was shown on this point where neutrals were concerned.

they have not loaded here with French produce. This they told me on board the Defyance.'[1]

A memorial inspired by Admiral Holmes puts one side of the case very clearly. Condemnations under the Flour Act will never be enough to stop the Flag of Truce trade, because they can never be procured. Only the exportation of provisions contravenes the Act; the return voyage does not incur the penalties, since a ship can only be condemned for an offence committed on the voyage in which she was taken. But it is almost impossible to take a vessel on her way to the French colonies.

'For whenever any of these vessels are met with by the King's ships, they are bound for Jamaica; their clearances are for Jamaica; and upon this assertion, and her clearances produced, she goes free from molestation. His Majesty's ships have given chase to them when they have attempted to make the Cape [Cap François]; the *Defiance* chased the schooner *Resolution*, Abraham Whipple master, belonging to Rhode Island, crowding all the sail she could make for Cape François, following and in company with a French privateer. When she saw that she could not escape she brought to, declared herself bound to Jamaica, was brought in by the *Defiance* but could not be condemned, because she had not actually entered the port. She was to distrust all colours; was not obliged to know the *Defiance* to be the King's ship; and might be, tho' ignorantly or foolishly, prosecuting her voyage; therefore she was returned by the opinion of counsel without being libelled. Many are the instances of vessels spoken with by his Majesty's ships at sea, when cruising off the enemy's coast, who were bound to Jamaica and with all the favourable circumstances of wind and weather never arrived there, but have gone into the enemy's ports, discharged their cargoes, taken in the enemy's produce and proceeded to sea, on their respective voyages. Wherefore, none of the North Americans can be taken on their voyage outwards, it is only in their return, when they are loaded with the enemy's produce, that they are liable to be seized and condemned by the King's ships; and then they cannot be condemned by the Act against exportation of flour, corn, &c., but as ships and produce of the enemy.'[2]

[1] *Speedwell*, Lake, H.C.A. 42/93; *Defiance*, Northam, H.C.A. 42/62; Richard Mercer to Greg and Cunningham, New York, Nov. 6, 1760, *Recovery*, Castle, H.C.A. 42/92 (the *Defiance* referred to in this letter was a man-of-war). See also, to the same effect, William Drope, Monte Cristi, to Hugh White, Oct. 11, 1760, *General Wolfe*, H.C.A. 42/68.

[2] Memorial no. 1, Dec. 1760, Adm. 1/236. The force of Holmes's complaints is possibly diminished by the fate of the *Fox* in the Jamaica Court in 1762. She was

No doubt the difficulties here described were real; but the officers of the navy had another reason for what they did and left undone. Edward Long, the new judge of the Jamaica Vice-Admiralty, attempted in 1760 to overcome their difficulties for them, and his efforts were most unwelcome. He allowed the Advocate-General to alter the libels of certain Flag of Truce prizes, and to claim condemnation under the Flour Act instead of demanding it as lawful prize; and then he condemned them half to the King and half to the captors, for the curious reason that

'if the bare design to export such commodities contrary to the intention and letter of the said statute be punishable with the (forfeiture of the) said vessel and cargo, how much more shall the carrying of that design into execution fall under the same penalty? . . . It did manifestly appear to his Honour that the homeward-bound cargo of sugar and molasses was the actual proceed and return of the said contraband provisions so unloaded and landed as aforesaid out of the said sloop in and upon the enemy's territory.'[1]

So far from accepting with pleasure this unexpected facility for executing the Flour Act, the captors resisted every step of the proceedings, appealed, and got the sentence reversed and the Advocate-General condemned in costs. Holmes asked the Lords of the Admiralty to dismiss Long, whose doctrine he denounced as 'a chimerical conversion of flour into indigo'. The ancient rule was restored, and the captors continued to enjoy the whole benefit of their prizes so long as they only took them on their return.[2] Whether Holmes was inspired by motives of private gain, or obliged by circumstances to act as he did, is an immaterial question. Whatever the cause, the blockade of

seized on her way to Port au Prince, and showed her clearance for Jamaica. The ships of war made a prize of her in spite of that. In the trial the mate produced the owner's orders to keep her close into the Bight of Léogane until she should meet with an English ship of war which would convoy her to Jamaica. Nevertheless Judge Long condemned her; but he may have done so because papers had been thrown overboard—a circumstance which was nearly always sufficient by itself to procure a condemnation. It is therefore impossible to ascertain how far this gives the lie to Holmes's assertion that confiscation of outward vessels was impossible. In any case the whole affair took place after his death (*Fox*, Tosh, H.C.A. 42/67).

[1] *Catherine*, Seabury, H.C.A. 42/60; see also the *Polly*, Easton, H.C.A. 42/88; *John and William*, H.C.A. 42/72; *Burrell's Reports*, ed. Marsden, p. 194.

[2] Holmes to Clevland, Aug. 22, 1760, March 18, 1761, Adm. 1/236; Clevland to Holmes, Nov. 17, 1760, Adm. 2/529, p. 512; Opinion of Advocate-General Hay and Solicitor-General Yorke, Nov. 1, 1760, Adm. 7/299, no. 23.

St. Domingue was robbed of all its direct military effectiveness by the dispensation which let provisions in and only stopped sugars coming out. A long series of seizures might ultimately destroy a trade either way; indeed the North Americans were almost entirely frightened out of the Flag of Truce trade by the condemnations at Jamaica, which were all upheld on appeal; but it is a curious blockade which deliberately omits doing the chief thing a blockade is instituted to do.

The failure of all its measures for the suppression of this trade was very soon apparent to the Government. At the end of 1757 the Board of Trade, which had hitherto taken the lead, gave orders for the collection of evidence upon the subject; but, for some unknown reason, the whole matter was dropped.[1] Perhaps Pitt may have been responsible for this change. Mr. Hubert Hall has pointed out the curious fact that Pitt took no action at all against the commerce with the enemy in the first three years of his Ministry.[2] The omission may have no significance, for many things were naturally forgotten in the confusion of public business. But these abuses must have been most repugnant to Pitt's ideal of patriotism—indeed, this appears from the strength of his language in the circular of August 23, 1760. Therefore it may be presumed that there was a reason for the delay; which may probably be found in his anxiety to avoid annoying the Americans while their help was necessary to the reduction of Canada. This object once achieved, he denounced the trade and called for its suppression. He chose his time wrongly; the colonists of North America had been ready enough to stop the trade with the enemy who threatened their own settlements, but did not see the point of this kind of patriotism when they were out of danger.

The colonial Governors returned what information they could, but held out little hope of stopping the trade. Some, like Fauquier of Virginia, declared with the pride of virtue that they had never granted a Flag of Truce in their lives; others, like Bernard of Massachusetts, simply lied, or evaded the question. Hamilton of Pennsylvania lamented his inability to put down this unwarrantable traffic, and asked exactly what kind of offence it was in law; Stephen Hopkins of Rhode Island defended the trade whole-heartedly, while Colden of New York

[1] *Journal of Commissioners of Trade and Plantations, 1754–8*, p. 337.
[2] *American Historical Review*, v. 668–9.

impersonally put forward the arguments that were used on its behalf, and threw the blame for abuses on the Custom Houses of every colony but his own.[1] The trade seems to have continued very much as it had been carried on before. Rodney discovered in 1761 evidences of a complete scheme for supplying Martinique with large quantities of flour from North America in ships with double papers. Amherst made a great fuss in the spring of 1762 over a similar revelation in New York; but nothing very startling or exceptional was exposed by the documents which he handed over to Colden. In May of that year somebody in New England wrote to Barbados, perhaps about the same affair, that French passports were sold in Boston and elsewhere for 200 dollars apiece.[2] In fact the trade continued throughout the war, in one form or another. It excited some indignation in England. The Agent for Rhode Island was afraid that some leading politicians would bring forward in Parliament further measures for stopping it; but he prophesied rightly that the Government would be content with the condemnation of vessels and cargoes in the Court of Prize Appeals.[3]

§ v. *The Flag of Truce Trade*

How was this trade carried on? There was direct intercourse with the enemy, and intercourse through neutral ports. The former was nearly all covered by Flags of Truce, for the French authorities themselves sometimes punished the English traders who dared to approach without any sort of official licence. French passports were sometimes sent to the English colonies, but only towards the end of the war, when the Flag of Truce trade was suppressed. As long as it was safe, it remained the commonest form of direct intercourse with the French islands.[4]

The volume of the trade is not easy to guess. In the Prize

[1] Pitt's circular is printed in Kimball, *Correspondence of William Pitt*, ii. 320. The Governors' answers are to be found in pp. 344–429, *passim*; see also *Colden Papers* (*N.Y.H.S. Collections*, 1876), i. 26.

[2] Rodney's Memorandum, Dec. 14, 1761, G.D. 20/2, p. 36; Amherst to Colden, April 15 and 16, 1762, *Colden Papers* (*N.Y.H.S. Collections*, 1922), pp. 136–9; Extract of a letter from New England to Gedney Clarke, May 3, 1762, Adm. 1/237.

[3] Sherwood to Hopkins, May 30, 1761, Kimball, *Correspondence of the Colonial Governors of Rhode Island*, ii. 320.

[4] Flag of Truce trade was by no means a new invention; Marsden produces what looks like an instance of it from 1485 (*Law and Custom*, i. 139). It existed and was subject to abuses in the War of the Spanish Succession (*H.M.C., H. of L. MSS., N.S.* vi. 112).

Appeals papers only 49 cases are recorded, of which 40 from Jamaica; but that is no guide, for the claimants must have given up a number of ships and cargoes for lost, and compounded or deserted their appeals, when they saw that the Court of Prize Appeals had set its face against the trade. The captors tried to induce the witnesses at Jamaica to admit that there were 300 ships employed annually in this trade, but none of them ever did so, and some expressly denied it. Cotes believed in February 1760 that there were then 85 in the ports of French St. Domingue; that is almost the only positive figure that was ever given.[1]

Where the exchange of prisoners was in the hands of the colonial Governors or legislatures, merchant vessels were always employed.[2] This might be free from abuse if certain conditions were observed. The most important was, that the owners of the vessels should be so well paid, either by the Government which sent the prisoners or by that which received them, as to be above the temptation to cover their costs by trading with the enemy. This necessary condition was very seldom realized. The colonial politicians strongly disliked expense. They sometimes agreed to it with a bad grace and for a short time, and were generally more willing to pay for sending the prisoners away than for maintaining them. This qualified compliance was more often found among the West Indian than the North American colonies—that is doubtless one of the reasons why the Flag of Truce trade was never scandalously large there, at any rate in the Windward Islands. The North American Governments almost always expected private shipowners to carry the prisoners at their own cost, and allowed them to repay themselves by the profits of trade.

The Flag of Truce traders often justified themselves, when they were brought up in the Vice-Admiralty Courts, by arguing that prisoners must be exchanged, that the Governments could not afford to subsist them or to pay for their transport, and that nobody could be expected to carry them for nothing.[3] All this

---

[1] Cotes to Clevland, Feb. 14, 1760, Adm. 1/235. Governor Bart said that 253 foreign vessels came to Cap François between July and Nov. 1760; but many of these—there is no knowing how many—must have been neutrals (Bart to Berryer, Sept. 14, 1761, A.N. Colonies C⁹ A 108).

[2] The control of prisoners was finally vested in the officers of the Navy by an Order in Council of March 25, 1761.

[3] The appellants' appeal case in the *General Amherst*, Add. MSS. 36213, f. 212;

was true, and might have been a valid defence, if the exchange had been loyally carried out for its own sake, instead of becoming a mere pretext for trade. In the first place, some of the claimants who urged these excuses had never carried any prisoners at all, or so few as to render the argument ridiculous. Reasons were sometimes given for this absurdity: the master had been in a hurry to get away before the rivers were frozen up, or to take advantage of a fair wind. Sometimes there were no prisoners to exchange, so that they had to be brought from the neighbouring colonies.[1] Governor Hopkins of Rhode Island refused to issue a Flag of Truce commission because the prisoners were purchased in Boston for the voyage. Clinton, of New York, was taxed with selling French and Spanish prisoners at several pistoles a head; and his refutation of the charge was far from convincing.[2] Frenchmen were sometimes hired to serve as prisoners for the voyage; they were brought back to North America for further use, and during their absence the ship's owners took care of their wives and families.[3]

The worst abuses were committed in Pennsylvania by Governor Denny. He issued blank Flag of Truce commissions, with lists of imaginary French names. At first he seems to have dealt them out in moderation, but towards the end of his career he scattered them freely over his own and the neighbouring colonies at twenty pounds sterling apiece. They were bought up and resold at advanced prices, and some were still in circulation several months after his departure. Eager inquiries were sent to Philadelphia from New York and New England.[4] In Rhode Island the Assembly granted Flags for some strange errands, quite unconnected with the return of prisoners, such as the pursuit of insolvent debtors.[5] A very common pretext for com-

William Popple, Governor of Bermuda, to Board of Trade, Oct. 10, 1747, C.O. 37/15, M 107.

[1] *Young Charles*, Carr, H.C.A. 42/109; *Venture*, Hymers, 42/100; *Three Brothers*, Gilbert, 42/97; *Polly and Fanny*, Tudor, 42/87; *Nancy*, Rooke, 42/84; *Greyhound*, Shoales, 42/68.

[2] *R.I. Col. Rec.* vi. 173; Representation of the Assembly of New York to Clinton, May 19, 1747, C.O. 5/1095.

[3] *Tryton*, Bowd, H.C.A. 42/97; *Sarah*, Borden, H.C.A. 42/94.

[4] Hamilton to Pitt, Nov. 1, 1760, Kimball, *Correspondence of William Pitt*, ii. 351-5; G. G. Beekman, New York, to Thomas Clifford, Philadelphia, Dec. 12, 1759, Clifford Correspondence, H.S.P., ii, no. 265; *Louisburgh*, Nuttle, H.C.A. 42/79; *Greyhound*, Shoales, H.C.A. 42/68.

[5] General Assembly of Rhode Island, Aug. 20, 1759, *R.I. Col. Rec.* vi. 218; *Windsor*, Clarke, H.C.A. 42/104.

mercial intercourse between enemies was the ransom or repurchase of necessary goods which had been taken as prize on their way to the West Indies. This led to the settlement of a regular correspondence between Jamaica and Havana in Trelawny's time; one or two attempts were then made at a similar trade with St. Domingue. In the next war the Governor of St. Domingue sent one Tanguy du Chastel to Jamaica to make a regular business of repurchasing French ships and goods. Caylus seems to have allowed Governor Mathew to ransom a cargo of wine in which he had been interested, and himself sent a merchant to Barbados for the like purpose.[1]

These irregularities could only be checked if the Imperial Government undertook the whole management and cost of the prisoners, which it would not do until 1761. Failing that, the only possible expedient was to insist on exchanging them in such large batches that the occasions for Flags of Truce would be extremely few. This is what the English Admirals always tried to do. Knowles in 1748 and Holmes in 1761 proposed to the French authorities to send not less than forty at a time. The French replied that it would be inhuman to keep the prisoners in the jails until the complement of forty should be made up, or to insist on sending them to Jamaica when they wanted to go elsewhere.[2] Some of the colonies ordained that the exchange should take place whenever a certain number of French prisoners had accumulated—fifteen in Rhode Island, twenty-five in Montserrat.[3] The importance of this arrangement is obvious. If it was not adopted, the prisoners were doled out to the merchants by ones and twos in order to create an excuse for as many Flags of Truce as possible. There are so many instances of this that it would be tedious to name them all. The most remarkable is to be found in Bermuda, where Governor William Popple seems to have made a point of supplying each vessel of the colony, no matter what her voyage, with a French prisoner to protect her against the questioning of French privateers. Presumably the whole shipping of Bermuda was covered by Flags

[1] Petition of Manning and others to Trelawny, Nov. 11, 1745, Jamaica Council Minutes, C.O. 140/31; Deposition of Tanguy du Chastel in the *Florence*, Breakill, H.C.A. 42/67; *Valeur*, Derny, H.C.A. 42/50; Barbados Council Minutes, March 24, 1745/6, and May 13, 1746, C.O. 31/23. *V. supra*, pp. 121, 357.

[2] Knowles to Newcastle, Nov. 20, 1747, Add. MSS. 32713, f. 473; Knowles to Vaudreuil, Jan. 23, 1748, A.N. Colonies C⁹ A 71; Vaudreuil to Knowles, Feb. 6, 1748, ibid.; Holmes to Bart, Aug. 8, 1761, Adm. 1/236.

[3] *R.I. Col. Rec.* v. 241; Montserrat Assembly Minutes, Nov. 19, 1757, C.O. 177/9.

of Truce, and hardly any vessel carried more than one prisoner. The Board of Trade rebuked Popple for this fault, but it became general to the colonies in the next war.[1] The advocates of the Flag of Truce trade defended it by arguing that it expedited the exchange of prisoners, who would otherwise be kept in prison until the batches of twenty or forty were made up; but Holmes retorted that the return of prisoners to their own ports was positively delayed by the commercial demand for them, as the Governors found it more profitable to deal them out one by one, than to send off as many as they had in one vessel. The suggestion is plausible, but very few instances of delay for this reason can be proved.[2]

Some colonies tried to regulate the Flags of Truce so as to prevent at least the export of provisions and naval stores. Trelawny ordered the Naval Officer at Jamaica to search the vessels in this trade at least as carefully as any others, and prevent them from carrying away any 'contraband'.[3] This gentleman chose to neglect the duty, and could do so with impunity because he was protected by his powerful relation, the great Lord Mansfield. Even Rhode Island, the home of all abuses, passed laws which would have been excellent if they had been obeyed or enforced. A committee was appointed to examine the Flag of Truce vessels on their departure, and to certify that they carried no warlike stores and no more provisions than would suffice to victual the crew and prisoners. Unfortunately the committeemen only too often certified without examining, or else they calculated the victuals at a generous allowance for more than the full crews, and for a number of prisoners vastly greater than was likely to be found on board. It is even possible that these certificates were bought and sold, like the Flags of Truce themselves.[4]

[1] Board of Trade to Popple, June 29, Dec. 21, 1748, C.O. 38/8, pp. 490-4, 505-6; Popple to Board of Trade, Oct. 10, 1748, C.O. 37/16, M 158.

[2] Holmes's memorial, no. 1, Dec. 1760, Adm. 1/236. The *Nancy*, Rooke (H.C.A. 42/84) and *Charming Elizabeth*, Fay (H.C.A. 42/59) are possibly examples. M. Tramond mentions another in the *Revue de l'histoire des colonies*, xv. 516.

[3] Trelawny to Murray, Nov. 6 and 23, 1745, in *Journals of the Assembly of Jamaica*, iv. 18.

[4] *R.I. Col. Rec.* vi. 93; Hopkins to Pitt, Dec. 20, 1760, Kimball, *Correspondence of William Pitt*, ii. 374-5; Philip Cuyler, New York, to William Tweedy, Rhode Island, Sept. 14, 1759, Letter-book of Philip Cuyler, N.Y.P.L. (This letter-book contains some very interesting light on the purchase of Flags of Truce, chiefly from Rhode Island and Philadelphia.) An instance of such overestimation is to be found in the *Sarah*, Borden, H.C.A. 42/94.

Many of the colonial Governors profited by the sale of Flags or dipped into the trade itself. The merchants in Trelawny's circle were undoubtedly concerned in the trade to both Spanish and French West Indies. Robinson of Barbados was suspected, perhaps unjustly, of remissness in its suppression, and he certainly granted Flags for curious errands, such as going to look for other Flags which had not returned. Mathew was interested in the *Valeur*.[1] Tinker, Governor of the Bahamas, was concerned in the *Bladen* Flag of Truce—indeed, she was named for his father-in-law. He was also said to have threatened to hang as a pirate the mate of a New York privateer who having caught another of his vessels, was foolish enough to bring her into New Providence.[2] Clinton of New York and Popple of Bermuda were accused of criminal compliances with the traders. In the Seven Years War, President Gambier of the Bahamas granted a Flag to a vessel owned by himself.[3] One of Governor Hopkins's sons commanded a Flag. No more need be said of Denny. Henry Moore, Lieutenant-Governor of Jamaica, and Thomas Cotes, Admiral on that station, were rumoured to have partaken in the trade.[4]

Not all the Admirals were so complaisant as the Governors. Knowles was a determined enemy of the Flag of Truce trade to the French islands, though he had partners who carried on a similar business with the Spaniards. Vaudreuil attributed his rigour to a feud with the North Americans, and indeed it was only against North American Flags that Knowles issued his severe orders. A French Governor is never a very good witness to the motives of an English Admiral, but Vaudreuil may have been near the mark, though he probably gave the wrong explanation of Knowles's animosity.[5] Holmes was a no less

[1] Barbados Council Minutes, March 24, 1745/6, May 13, 1746, C.O. 31/23; *Valeur*, Derny, H.C.A. 42/50; Lee to Corbett, May 26, 1746, Adm. 1/305.

[2] *Bladen*, H.C.A. 42/24; Case of George Ring, 1746, C.O. 23/5, D 40. See the letter of Bart to Moras, April 18, 1757, A.N. Colonies C⁹ A 100, which says that Tinker was afraid to break the Flour Act by trading with the French colonies as he had done in the last war.

[3] *King of Prussia*, Micklethwait, H.C.A. 42/79.

[4] Moore may have been concerned in the *Tassell*, Ross (H.C.A. 42/98). The obscure struggle between Moore and the Assembly of Jamaica over the expediency of returning prisoners to St. Domingue looks as if it may have been inspired by a jealousy over the profits of the trade (*Journals of the Assembly of Jamaica*, v. 207-10, 215). Cotes was slandered in a letter, of which the author withdrew the charge (Jamaica Council Minutes, Oct. 11, 1759, C.O. 140/38).

[5] Knowles, orders to Capt. Hughes, Feb. 10, 1747/8, Adm. 7/744; Vaudreuil

violent persecutor of Flags of Truce, and went a step farther than Knowles or Cotes, in that he finally took measures against the trade which was carried on from Jamaica itself.[1]

Though the privateers lived by their prizes, they spared their countrymen more than the men-of-war. They very seldom made real seizures of vessels belonging to their own colonies, and they sometimes did service to the traders by capturing them collusively.[2] Such collusive capture was a very serious offence at law, but instances of it abound in the High Court of Admiralty records. No doubt the profits fully compensated for the risk, especially as the counterfeit captor seldom forfeited his own ship, though he often lost his prize if a real captor lighted upon her. The practice was sometimes excused by the argument that it was only meant to protect the trade against the notorious Bahama privateers, and would never have been pleaded in bar of a real capture by a man-of-war. Certainly the collusive captors seldom made any attempt to vindicate their claims against the King's ships in the courts of law.[3]

The privateer would make arrangements for the farce to be played just outside the enemy port upon the return voyage. A gun would be fired, and a prize-master put on board. Sometimes he would be the sole member of the prize-crew—a circumstance which may be taken by itself to prove the falsity of the seizure. He would receive a copy of the 'captor's' commission, and instructions for an imaginary voyage to some privateering port. When another captor appeared, the prize-master was to step forward and claim that the vessel was already a

to Maurepas, Feb. 22, 1748, A.N. Colonies, C⁹ A 74. Vaudreuil thought Knowles resented the refusal of the North Americans to engage in an expedition to Florida. But the real reason was more probably the riots against the press-gang at Boston. Although Knowles treated the rumour of his partnership with Manning and Ord as the invention of scandalmongers, he was certainly connected with the firm at some time, for his correspondents in London wrote to him in 1754, 'We are extremely sorry for the vast loss you are apprehensive of suffering by Messrs. Manning & Ord' (Lascelles and Maxwell to Knowles, Feb. 12, 1754, W. & G. vi). V. supra, pp. 183-4.

[1] For Cotes's attitude to the trade, see pp. 417-18.

[2] Some North American privateers made prizes of North American Flags of Truce, but seldom those of their own colonies; for example, the *Hope* privateer of New York took seven Flags belonging to Philadelphia, Rhode Island, and the Bahamas (Philip Cuyler to Richards and Coddington, March 25, 1760, Letterbook, N.Y.P.L.).

[3] *Belle Savage*, Lindsay, H.C.A. 42/57; *Pompey*, Tucker, 42/89. The only cases in which they appear to have done so are the *Mary and Ann*, Chiapple, H.C.A. 42/82, and the *Young Jan*, Navaret, H.C.A. 42/109.

prize. Some of these feigned prize-masters were very little
suited to their parts, and the real captors generally saw through
the pretence.[1]

Sometimes the privateers accompanied their feigned prizes
for some distance, and gave them signals for keeping together.[2]
This amounted to convoying the trader, who paid a great deal
for the service except where the captor and the prize belonged
to the same owners.[3] Such convoy, with or without collusive
capture, was very common in all branches of the trade between
North America and the West Indies, for many of the vessels—
even those employed in the Flag of Truce and Monte Cristi
trades—were armed and commissioned as privateers.[4] The
traders could not rely entirely on the fidelity of their escorts,
who sometimes converted a farce into a seizure in good earnest.
This happened to the *Adventure*, a brigantine in the Monte Cristi
trade, and even to a neutral, the *Vrouw Ursula*.[5]

Prosecutions under the Act against collusive captures only
became frequent at the end of the Seven Years War. The forfeitures were to be divided equally between the King and the
informers, therefore the latter would rather libel the traders as
lawful prize, since they would receive the whole in case of

[1] See the very entertaining deposition of Peleg Rogers in the *Nancy*, Rooke,
H.C.A. 42/84.

[2] *General Amherst*, Hunt, H.C.A. 42/68; *Miriam and Ann*, Lake, H.C.A. 42/82.

[3] The best instance of this is the *Recovery*, Castle, H.C.A. 42/92, which was taken
by the *Harlequin* privateer. Both vessels belonged to Messrs. Greg and Cunningham
of New York. The *Catherine*, Henshaw (H.C.A. 42/59), is probably another case
of the same kind. Both she and her captor belonged to New York, and Francis
Koffler, commander of the captor, had formerly been master of the prize.

[4] For instance the *Thurloe*, Ireland, H.C.A. 42/97; the *Charming Polly*, Horton,
H.C.A. 42/59; the *General Johnson*, Little, H.C.A. 42/69; the *Ranger*, Crowninshield,
H.C.A. 42/92. The *Prussian Hero*, Campbell (H.C.A. 42/88), actually made prize
of some neutral vessels in her voyage to Monte Cristi. Other English privateers,
however, convoyed neutrals to and from the French colonies (Douglas to Cleveland,
Feb. 6, 1761, Adm. 1/307). There are many references to convoys in the intercepted correspondence of other prizes. Robert Purviance, a supercargo at Monte
Cristi, described a negotiation with a New York privateer, to whom 500 pieces
of eight were offered for convoying eight or ten vessels through the Bahamas. He
held out for 700, so that the traders decided to sail by themselves, though few or
none of them had guns. Purviance made the reflection that 'nothing will do here
if a man is not able to fight his way' (Purviance to Irwin, Sept. 2, 1760, *Stadt
Flansbourg*, H.C.A. 42/93). The author of an intercepted letter of Aug. 13, 1761
(S.P. 42/42, f. 440), says, ''Tis dangerous now convoying, that scheme is blown.'

[5] *Adventure*, Graisbery, H.C.A. 42/53; other cases are reported in a letter from
Joseph Gale to Hugh White & Co., Oct. 17, 1760, *General Wolfe*, Thompson,
H.C.A. 42/68. For the history of the *Vrouw Ursula*, see a letter of Nicholas Gouver-
neur to J. R. Faesch, July 22, 1758, *Resolutte*, Rieverts, H.C.A. 42/91.

condemnation;[1] but when the Court of Prize Appeals decided that Monte Cristi ships were not lawful prize, the captors naturally preferred the half to nothing.[2]

While the privateers usually abstained from molesting the illicit trade of their fellow countrymen, they freely interrupted that of other colonies. Sometimes this created what one Governor called 'the kind of civil war that has been waged by the privateers on these traders belonging to different provinces'.[3] Resentment ran high between North Americans and West Indians. The master of a condemned Flag of Truce vessel exclaimed against the severity of the Jamaica court: 'I know of no other way to get satisfaction, but to fit out a small vessel against the Jamaica men who have at least 40 sail of vessels running up and down to Hispaniola.'[4] These were only words; but there was nearly an open quarrel between Rhode Island and Antigua. The Antigua privateer *Hawk* seized two trading vessels on their way to Monte Cristi in the autumn of 1759, 'which', as William Grant wrote to his correspondent in Newport, 'I believe will be attended with very bad consequences in case they are condemned, as there is two or three more here and only waits to hear the fate of those already carried to port before they begin to make reprisals'. Next year a Rhode Island privateer made prize of an Antigua vessel belonging to one Hanson, who indignantly reminded the captor that 'he ought to consider how many of his countrymen were then in my power. . . . I owned three privateers that were cruising off Hispaniola, and I imagined the same liberty allowed me to steal vessels out of a road at anchor, as what Captain Michener had, there were many vessels then in the same port belonging to Rhode Island.'[5] It does not appear whether privateers ever rescued their fellow countrymen out of the hands of captors from other colonies; but possibly this is what Captain Randall

---

[1] In the case of the *Catherine*, Henshaw (H.C.A. 42/59), the captors refused to associate themselves with a libel for collusive capture, appealed against the sentence, and won their case.   [2] *Pompey*, Tucker, H.C.A. 42/89.

[3] Boone, New Jersey, to Pitt, Oct. 23, 1760, Kimball, *Correspondence of William Pitt*, ii. 344.

[4] Duncan to Bowler and Champlin, Dec. 24, 1760, *Commerce of Rhode Island* (*M.H.S. Collections*), i. 87.

[5] *Commerce of Rhode Island*, p. 79; *Good Hope*, or *God Haal*, Felan, H.C.A. 42/69. Hanson's privateers seem to have given convoy to North American as well as West Indian traders (Purviance to Irwin, Sept. 2, 1760, *Stadt Flansbourg*, H.C.A. 42/93; Philip Cuyler to Richards and Coddington, July 28, 1760, Letter-book, N.Y.P.L.).

of the *Providence* meant by telling his owners (after his seizure by a Bahama privateer) that 'if I meet with any Northern crusers shall beg my releaf if can be don'.[1]

The judges were as partial as the privateers to their own countrymen; it seldom happened that any of them condemned the Flags of Truce belonging to his own port. Three New York Flags were indeed condemned at New York;[2] but that seems to be exceptional. In general, North American judges acquitted these traders, and West Indian judges condemned them;[3] but Judge Bullock of Jamaica accumulated a great number of cases, which contrary to all expectation he acquitted wholesale in May 1760. Within a week he was removed from his office.[4] Samuel Gambier, whose doctrines were almost subversive on this topic, had a very short career as an Admiralty judge at New Providence.

It was the opinion of the Lords Commissioners for Prize Appeals that finally determined the fate of the Flag of Truce trade. That court uniformly condemned both vessels and cargoes. Its sentences in these cases are not recorded in full, but its policy was so clear and sweeping as to need very little interpretation. It can hardly be presumed to have taken into account the nature of the cargoes exported to the enemy, for the condemnations would not then have been so universal. More likely it regarded all direct intercourse with the enemy as unlawful. This probability is strengthened, as will be seen, by its attitude to the Monte Cristi ships. By the middle of 1760, the condemnations at Jamaica, backed by the decisions of the Prize Appeals Court, had virtually suppressed the Flag of Truce trade, and driven the North Americans into subtler forms of unpatriotic conduct.[5]

[1] Randall to owners of the *Providence*, May 18, 1760, Nicholas Brown MSS.
[2] Hough, *Reports of Cases in the Vice-Admiralty of New York*, p. 198.
[3] No doubt this was why the master of the *Keppell* offered money to the captors' prizemaster if he would allow the vessel to be carried to any port in North America (*Keppell*, Chambers, H.C.A. 42/79).
[4] Jamaica Council Minutes, May 17 to 25, 1760, C.O. 140/42.
[5] Philip Cuyler chartered a vessel for a Flag of Truce voyage at the beginning of 1760, but her owner repented of the bargain and Cuyler had to get another. The condemnations at Jamaica staggered Cuyler himself, and in May he thought it wise to put off his enterprise for a time. Bullock's acquittals did not much reassure him, for the captors insisted on having the cargoes lodged as security for appeal, so that they were as much lost to the owners, for the present, as if they had been condemned. A few days later, he got his courage back and decided to send a Flag of Truce to Cap François in the hurricane season, when the risk would

§ vi. *Indirect Trade with the Enemy: St. Eustatius and Monte Cristi*

If direct intercourse with the enemy was out of the question, indirect trade was by no means so. The warehouses of St. Eustatius were fuller than ever of North American goods, which were sent down in small cargoes to the French islands, usually at the risk of French or Dutch merchants, hardly ever of English subjects. Factors flocked to the place from Ireland and the Northern Colonies, and profited by the excessive ease of naturalization. Ships as well as goods were in demand, and a cargo sometimes sold to better advantage if the vessel which carried it was included in the bargain.[1] The English navy and privateers seem to have satisfied themselves with intercepting the trade between St. Eustatius and the French colonies, in which the North Americans do not appear to have engaged. They did not try to stop the English ships on their way to or from St. Eustatius; at least the Prize Appeals records show no trace of interference with such voyages.

St. Eustatius was an old-established free port whose commerce was merely swelled by the war; the same thing may be said of St. Thomas and St. Croix. A completely new trade of the same kind sprang up at the Spanish colony of Monte Cristi. This was a small settlement on the north coast of Hispaniola, not far from the boundary of the French and Spanish possessions. Some time not long before the war the authorities appear to have made it a free port in order to encourage the introduction of provisions—a proceeding which France imitated soon afterwards at Cape Nicola Mole. A Lieutenant-Governor was appointed, and a battery mounted; but Monte Cristi seems at all times to have been a one-horse place. A North American sailor wrote home in 1758: 'This place has been settled about six years. Their houses are built of cabbage-trees—they have a church, a gaol, six pieces of cannon for to guard the town, wherein there is about fifty houses, about one dozen chairs in the place to sit in, they ride on jackasses, for the most part, with

be less because fewer men-of-war would be about (Letter-book, Feb. to July 1760, N.Y.P.L.). About the same time, G. G. Beekman of New York expected to lose £7,000 by Flags of Truce; many merchants of North America must have agreed with him in his heartfelt cry of 'I say dam them all'.

[1] A great deal of information on the North American trade with St. Eustatius during these wars can be gathered from the Timothy Orne MSS. in the Essex Institute, Salem, and the Hancock MSS. in the Graduate School of Business Administration, Harvard University.

a saddle made of straw.' Nor did he think much better of the people: 'I am among a parcel of Romish savages, I may call 'em with safety. I assure you they are a compound of the greatest knavery in life, which I believe is the chief thing they study.'[1] The place was described in April 1760 as 'a poor settlement of about a hundred families'. Captain Hinxman, of H.M.S. *Port Royal*, who went into the harbour in March 1761, reported that the harbour was only two feet deep for two hundred yards from the shore, and that in the season of the north winds, to which the road was exposed, boats could not come within a quarter of a mile of the land for the great surf. On shore there was a guard-house, three 'suttling huts', and five sheds for coopers and carpenters; the town was two miles away.[2]

Such a place did not promise to be the seat of a lively commerce, but it served well enough for an accommodation address, and even for more. As the North Americans did not come there to trade with the Spaniards, it mattered little to them that there were no merchants, no wharves, and no sugar-plantations at Monte Cristi. For their own police and security, they did not rely on the Spanish forts and officers, but on the guns which some of them possessed, and the vigilance of their 'commodores'.[3] Only once did the trade suffer any interference from the French. Nor did the Spanish authorities molest it; the Lieutenant-Governor appears to have doubted its propriety at first, but he was soon converted or superseded, and the authorities began to make a handsome profit by their connivance.[4]

The trading vessels from North America lay in the open road, sometimes as many as 130 at a time.[5] There was no need for any communication with the shore, except for reporting and clearing the vessel, paying duties, and perhaps negotiating a counterfeit bargain with a Spanish intermediary. In fact, some witnesses deposed that the English supercargoes were forbidden

---

[1] Jonathan Clarke to Moses Brown, April 17, 1758, R.I.H.S., Moses Brown Papers, i. 24.

[2] Deposition of William Taggart, April 21, 1760, C.O. 23/7, E 3; Hinxman to Holmes, April 13, 1761, Adm. 1/236.

[3] Intercepted letter from Monte Cristi, April 13, 1761, S.P. 42/42, f. 440.

[4] See the letter of 'Dom Gaspar' to Chastenoye, Aug. 11, 1757, A.N. Colonies C⁹ A 105.

[5] This figure, reported by Cotes (Feb. 14, 1760), is almost the highest of those given. Shirley on March 29, 1760, put the number between 80 and 90; seamen reported various figures between 50 and 100. Hinxman only found 42 in March 1761. Moore sent home a list of 29 in Feb. 1759.

to land at all. Sometimes the ship's master would himself go down to the French settlements; but this was dangerous, because it might be a ground of condemnation in the English courts (the only reason I can assign for the sentence against the *Ranger* was the visit her captain paid at Fort Dauphin).[1] There were certain factors who resided at Monte Cristi to do business for correspondents in the Northern Colonies, and others at Fort Dauphin and Cap François.[2] No doubt these had some communication between them. A master arriving without recommendation could send down a message to the French settlements, if he did not choose to go himself, or apply to a Spanish *prête-nom*, preferably the Lieutenant-Governor or his secretary.

Some North Americans arrived in ballast and bought molasses with cash; those who had cargoes of goods unloaded them directly into small barks which carried them down to Fort Dauphin and Cap François or even farther.[3] At whose risk this part of the voyage was made, does not clearly appear; the depositions of witnesses conflict. Felice Russo, a boatman in the trade, denied that the Spanish *patrons* of barks ever had any interest in the cargoes. They were sometimes made to sign papers which made the sugar and molasses appear to be their property; this device would at the same time protect the goods from seizure between Fort Dauphin and Monte Cristi, and justify the English claimants when they declared in the Vice-Admiralty courts that the return cargo was lawfully bought of Spaniards. But according to Russo there was no truth in these papers; and another witness in the same case deposed that the merchants had to stop demanding them, because the *patrons* sometimes took advantage of them to behave as if they were the real owners of their loadings, and sell them to Englishmen for whom they had not been intended.[4] On the other hand, witnesses in other cases said they believed the Spaniards of

[1] Long to Moore, Dec. 31, 1760, C.O. 137/60; *Ranger*, Crowninshield, H.C.A. 42/92.

[2] The most prominent of the former class were Purviance and Mercer; of the latter, Waag and Carnegy.

[3] Sometimes, according to Holmes's memorial on the trade (Adm. 1/236) the Spanish craft ventured right round Cape Nicola into the Bight of Léogane or even to the south side of the island; but their chief trade was with Fort Dauphin and Cap François.

[4] Depositions of Felice Russo, Antonio Russo, Joseph Baliente, and Francis Mayole, *Sea Nymph*, Mitchell, H.C.A. 42/94; Hinxman to Holmes, April 13, 1761, Adm. 1/236.

Monte Cristi were sometimes concerned in the cargoes; and it is plain from many indications that the produce which was brought up to Monte Cristi was not always earmarked for a particular English vessel. Some North American supercargoes preferred buying their sugars at Monte Cristi to making arrangements at Fort Dauphin; one letter-writer described 'people almost fighting for sugars when it came up'.[1] Thus the trade between Monte Cristi and the French settlements took a number of forms: the interest and property might be English, French, or even Spanish. On the return voyage, the cargo would be put straight on board the English vessels, and was seldom or never landed on the shore. Witnesses sometimes tried to make the best of their belief that the goods came from 'towards' the shore, but in fact they neither need nor could come from it.

When the Monte Cristi traders were brought into the Vice-Admiralty courts, they always said they had dealt only with the Spaniards. They could hardly pretend that the Spanish merchants bought their goods for consumption in Monte Cristi, which was a desolate little hole, or in the rest of the Spanish colony, with which it had very little communication. Countless witnesses deposed that Monte Cristi by itself could hardly consume a single cargo of imports in a year. Nor could the sugar and molasses in the return cargoes be passed off as Spanish produce, for there were no sugar-works at Monte Cristi, until Lieutenant-Governor Cavrejas thought of setting one up for this purpose;[2] and that was merely a concession to the human weakness for acting the lies we mean to tell. There was no concealing the obvious truth that the French were the real recipients of the provisions and lumber that passed through Monte Cristi, and the real producers of the sugar which was exported in return. But the trade might still be lawful, so long as the supercargoes had no direct dealings with Frenchmen.

For this reason, some shipowners advised or ordered their agents to deal only with Spaniards. Thus the owners of the *Dolphin* of New York wrote to their captain, 'You are positively ordered and directed that while you are at Monte Cristo you

[1] Deposition of Augustin Jorba Calderon, *Sea Flower*, Gelston, H.C.A. 42/95; John Carnegy to James Baillie, Nov. 18, 1759, *Amherst*, Maddocks, H.C.A. 42/53; see also the deposition of the master in the *Sally*, Napier, H.C.A. 42/96.

[2] Holmes's memorial of Dec. 1760 on the Monte Cristi trade, Adm. 1/236; Mercer to Greg and Cunningham, Nov. 6, 1760, *Recovery*, Castle, H.C.A. 42/92; Long to Moore, Dec. 31, 1760, C.O. 137/60.

do not by any means deal trade or traffic with any subjects of the French King but solely with Spaniards, that the rascals who act as judges in some of the Admiralty courts in the West Indies may not have so much as a pretence to confiscate the vessel and cargo.'[1] Where such instructions as these could not be complied with, there were ways to cover up transactions with the French. The Lieutenant-Governor of Monte Cristi and his nephew made a living by certifying that the North American masters had dealt with none but Spaniards and residents of Monte Cristi. They did not even shrink from this perjury in cases where it afterwards appeared in evidence that the super-cargo had gone down to the French settlements and transacted all the business there.[2] These certificates soon lost all credit with the Admiralty courts of New Providence and Jamaica; Judge Bradford and Judge Long expressly refused to pay any regard to them at all.[3] The Jamaica court was also impressed by the consideration that the Spaniards, if they really had any concern in the matter at all, were only factors or agents for the French, and not traders on their own account. This view was no doubt supported by the abundant evidence of the poverty of the inhabitants of Monte Cristi, most of whom could not conceivably have done any business except as men of straw.

The Admirals at Jamaica were at first perplexed how to treat the Monte Cristi ships. Cotes and Holmes wrote to England repeatedly for advice, but received none. They regarded this trade as an unjustifiable extension or substitute of the Flag of Truce trade, which they had just succeeded in suppressing. It injured the interests of Jamaica in the same way, and ought to be put down in the same manner. Lieutenant-Governor Moore also sent to England a description of the trade; he thought it especially pernicious because some English vessels

[1] Livingston and Welch, instructions to Capt. Candy, Aug. 26, 1761, *Dolphin*, Candy, H.C.A. 42/63; Capt. Crowninshield of the *Ranger* was ordered to be sure to take bills of parcels for his sugars, with an oath of neutral property (H.C.A. 42/92).

[2] Shirley to Cavrejas, March 1760, C.O. 23/6, D 89. Good examples of Cavre-jas's certificates are to be found in the *Speedwell*, Davis, H.C.A. 42/96, and *Industry*, Putnam, H.C.A. 42/73.

[3] See Long's judgement of March 2, 1761, on the *Recovery*, Castle, H.C.A. 42/92. This was apparently a leading case in the Jamaica court, and the worthlessness of Cavrejas's certificates, as established by the evidence and papers, was there-after assumed by Long in all other cases. See also Long's letter to Moore, Dec. 31, 1760; Bradford's judgement in the *Ranger*, H.C.A. 42/92.

arrived at Monte Cristi in ballast, and bought their cargoes with cash which had been drained away for the purpose from the English sugar islands. The Board of Trade was indignant, and represented to the King that though the traffic with a neutral port might not be contrary to law, yet it was contrary to good policy to allow it when the neutral port was only interposed to cover a trade with the enemy. It suggested a royal proclamation against the trade. This would have been to prejudge a question which the Government most likely preferred to leave to the Court of Prize Appeals; therefore the representations of Moore, the Jamaica legislature, the Board of Trade, and the Admirals were all ignored until the eve of the Spanish war.[1] Meanwhile, pending the instructions which never came from England, the Jamaica squadron seized the vessels as they left Monte Cristi and brought them up before the Admiralty courts.

Monte Cristi was so near Cap François that though the two places could not be closely watched by the same ships at once, a small squadron could easily divide itself between the two services in normal times. Nevertheless, it was also very well situated for the traders; Cotes reported that they slipped away by night and were among the Caicos shoals next morning, where the men-of-war dared not follow them. Therefore they could not be efficiently intercepted without going into the harbour.

The temptation to cut the knot in this way must have been overwhelming, and one or two commanders yielded to it. The men-of-war and privateers made several captures within the harbour of Monte Cristi. The *Prussian Hero* was taken at anchor there by some Philadelphia privateers.[2] The *God Haal* was seized within a pistol-shot of the shore, and Cavrejas wrote a stiff letter to Governor Hopkins, to complain of this and other

[1] Cotes to Clevland, Feb. 28 and June 4, 1759, Feb. 14, 1760, Adm. 1/235; Holmes to Clevland, July 25, Nov. 11, Dec. 31, 1760, March 18, April 14, June 16, July 14, 1761, Adm. 1/236; Moore to Board of Trade, March 28, 1759, C.O. 137/30, Z 43; Board of Trade Representation to George II, Aug. 31, 1759, C.O. 138/20, pp. 447–50; Jamaica Committee of Correspondence to its Agent, Dec. 19, 1761, *Journals of the Assembly of Jamaica*, v. 320–1; Shirley to Board of Trade, March 29 and Aug. 1, 1760, C.O. 23/6, D 87 and 23/7, E 1.

[2] She nearly escaped condemnation by an extraordinary ruse. The captain waited until midnight when the captors' prize-crew were dancing drunk; then he threw all his contraband goods out of the port-hole. Having done so, he ordered some more cable to be paid out, so that the ship might change her position, and the captors, when they discovered the loss of the arms, should not know where to dive for them. Unfortunately some of the captors were just too sober for him, and finally recovered a number of muskets and cutlasses from the water (*Prussian*

outrages of Rhode Island privateers.[1] The men-of-war committed far more serious offences. Not only were they guilty of 'low conniving arts'—sending their boats at dusk into the harbour, to find out which ships were ready to sail; sometimes they openly violated Spanish neutrality.

Three trading vessels, the *Edward*, the *Superbe*, and the *Don Philip*, weighed anchor from Monte Cristi on September 24, 1760. They were hardly out of the bay before they saw three ships-of-war—which later proved to be the *Hussar*, Captain Carkett, the *Boreas*, and the sloop *Viper*. The traders turned back for the harbour, but the *Hussar* sent a boat after them under the ensign of a red handkerchief. As this boat came up quickly, the *Don Philip* fired a shot at her or towards her. The three traders reached the harbour in safety, but the men-of-war came in behind them, and after some vapouring threats to hang the captain of the *Don Philip* at the yard-arm, seized all three of them in the midst of the shipping that night. The next day Carkett had an interview with the Lieutenant-Governor. What passed there was afterwards disputed. Carkett said he had asked Cavrejas to detain the *Don Philip* for insulting the English flag, and Cavrejas, unable to do so for want of the necessary force, had permitted him to remove the offenders for himself, the more willingly because they had behaved badly in the harbour and had not paid the proper duties. Cavrejas afterwards gave out a different version, and denied that he had ever given Carkett positive leave to take the ships away. However that might be, Carkett bore them off to Jamaica, where Judge Long acquitted them on the sole ground that the seizure had been a violation of Spanish neutrality. The Court of Prize Appeals upheld the sentence.[2]

Hero, Campbell, H.C.A. 42/88). For a similar attempt, see the intercepted letter of April 13, 1761, S.P. 42/42, f. 440.

[1] Cavrejas to Hopkins, Aug. 7, 1760, *Good Hope*, or *God Haal*, Felan, H.C.A. 42/69. In 1759 a certain Silas Cooke petitioned the General Assembly of Rhode Island against the seizure by a Rhode Island privateer of a vessel belonging to Cavrejas's secretary. He observed sagely 'that there are many vessels with cargoes owned by the inhabitants of this colony now at the said Monti Christo, and in the power of the said Antonio Gomez Franco who is the King of Spain's secretary there, and will undoubtedly detain some or all of them, by way of reprisals for this act of violence done against the laws of nations'. I do not know that the Assembly took any definite action on this hint (*R.I. Col. Rec.* vi. 184, Feb. 26, 1759).

[2] *Edward*, Bishop, H.C.A. 42/64; *Don Philip*, Smith, H.C.A. 42/89; *Superbe*, Waters, H.C.A. 42/94. See also their appeal cases in Add. MSS. 36212, ff. 128–45, 170–88, with notes of Charles Yorke on the sentences, ff. 145, 177. The affair is

This outrage displeased the Spanish authorities; nor did Holmes's treatment of Spanish shipping give them any more satisfaction. For a time Holmes seems to have meant to keep his hands off the Spanish craft which plied between Monte Cristi and the French settlements;[1] but in September 1761, with or without his leave, Captain Mackenzie of H.M.S. *Defiance* seized twenty or thirty of these boats on their way into the harbour. He even came within pistol-shot of the shore, and refused to leave the place. The new Governor, Las Sobras, hastily mounted some guns and sent him a very rough letter, which caused him to release most of the vessels and crews; but the cargoes he took with him to Jamaica for condemnation.[2]

This filled the cup of Holmes's offences. He had already been in correspondence with Azlor, the President of Santo Domingo, over the right of Spain to protect this trade. Holmes had sent copies of Cavrejas's false certificates, and explained how the English traders abused them. He had also argued, on the strength of extracts from treaties, that English and Spanish subjects could have no lawful trade with each other in America. He even denied the King of Spain's right to set up such a free port without consulting his neighbours in America on a step so prejudicial to their interests. If such a port had been created in time of peace, France would have objected to it; its establishment during the war could only be regarded as an act of collusion with France. Thus Holmes tried, with his muddle-headed Admiralty logic, to apply the Rule of the War of 1756, which denied the legitimacy in war of those branches of colonial trade which the enemy would not have admitted in peace. Besides, this free port had no regulations, no officers, and no police; the first omission was important because only a positive regulation could have taken off the force of the time-honoured Spanish prohibitions, which must be considered as still subsisting. From this Holmes seems to have concluded that he had a right, by Spanish laws, to take the ships, whether English or Spanish, which used this trade.[3]

described in a letter of James Turner, Monte Cristi, to Andrew and Alexander Symmer, Maryland, Dec. 1, 1760 (*Recovery*, Castle, H.C.A. 42/92).

[1] Holmes to Clevland, Nov. 11, 1760, Adm. 1/236.

[2] Las Sobras to Azlor, Sept. 9, 1761; Las Sobras to Mackenzie, Sept. 8, 1761, *Sea Nymph*, Mitchell, H.C.A. 42/94.

[3] Holmes to Clevland, July 25, Dec. 31, 1760; Memorial on the Monte Cristi trade, Dec. 1760, Adm. 1/236.

Azlor expressed great displeasure with Cavrejas and deprived him of his post. The new Lieutenant-Governor had orders to prevent the English from frequenting Monte Cristi, and Azlor asked Holmes to co-operate in putting a stop to it. So far, so good. Holmes could ask nothing better than to be desired by a Spanish Governor to suppress the trade. Azlor, however, did not mean to tolerate violations of Spanish neutrality or seizures of Spanish ships. He dismissed most of Holmes's reasoning as irrelevant, which, indeed, it was. If he had wished to do so, he could easily have justified the establishment of a free port by the article in the Treaty of 1670 which reserved to the King of Spain the right to license English subjects to trade to his dominions on such terms as he saw fit.[1] However, Azlor confined himself to claiming the Spanish vessels which Holmes's squadron had taken, and insisting with asperity on the privileges of the Spanish flag.[2]

The news of Mackenzie's outrage reached England at a ticklish point in the Anglo-Spanish negotiations. The Court of Spain never made any complaint about the behaviour of the English officers at Monte Cristi, but the English Ministry resolved to forestall it. At the same time merchants of London who were concerned in the trade (especially in the transport of sugars from Monte Cristi to Venice, Leghorn, and Hamburg) denounced Holmes's conduct to the Government.[3] Lord Egremont ordered the Admiralty to send out a frigate to Holmes with a rebuke for his violations of Spanish neutrality, and prepared to prime our Ambassador at Madrid with an apology and an explanation. This was hard on Holmes, who had always asked for instructions and received none. It was also unnecessary, for Spain had not raised the question of Monte Cristi, and too late, for the Ambassador had already left Madrid and diplomatic relations were broken off between the two countries. This created a new situation, for, as the Admiralty foresaw, the Jamaica squadron might very well be blockading the English traders in Monte Cristi when the news of the war arrived, and thus might cause them all to fall into the hands of the Spaniards.[4]

---

[1] The ingenious claimant of the *Charming Polly* made this point in the Vice-Admiralty court of Gibraltar (H.C.A. 42/59).

[2] Azlor to Holmes, Sept. 27, 1761, *Sea Nymph*, Mitchell, H.C.A. 42/94. Holmes's letter to Azlor is missing, but can be guessed from the reply.

[3] Bourdieu and Lewis to Under-Secretary Wood, Dec. 16, 1761, S.P. 42/42, f. 514; this firm was concerned in the *Sharp*, Maitland (H.C.A. 42/95).

[4] Clevland to Wood, Dec. 17, 1761, S.P. 42/42, f. 499; Egremont to Lords of

In fact the Spanish authorities had turned against the traders some months earlier. Las Sobras, who had succeeded Cavrejas as Lieutenant-Governor, revoked the licences of the Spanish craft, and tried to force the English vessels out of the harbour. These measures had no effect. The trade had never received any protection from the Spaniards on shore; it stood in no need of their help, and had nothing to fear from their menaces. The supercargoes had usually done most of their business afloat, and they made their habitations in large storeships which sometimes lay as far as three miles from the shore. Thus when H.M.S. *Port Royal* came into the harbour to warn the traders of the war with Spain, most of them disregarded her. When the Spaniards began to fire, they moved down the coast to Fort Dauphin, where they apparently found protection from the French, with whom they had so long been connected. A few supercargoes were caught on shore at Monte Cristi and imprisoned, but the rest had no difficulty in winding up their affairs on French soil— a fact which proves how little part the Spaniards had ever played in the trade.[1]

Nearly all the Monte Cristi vessels were condemned in the courts of first instance, especially Jamaica, New Providence, and Gibraltar. The Court of Prize Appeals reversed most of these sentences. This is the more remarkable when it is compared with the sweeping condemnation of the Flag of Truce trade. The court appears to have distinguished between direct and indirect commerce with the enemy. The claimants of the *Pinguin*, appealing against her condemnation at Jamaica, could argue that

'The question has been repeatedly adjudged, that an English vessel taken in the return voyage from Monte Cristi to the Northern Colonies, with a cargo purchased wholly of Spaniards, and no proof of any correspondence with the French, is free, and not liable to condemnation; the captors have themselves proved the ship in question to be within this predicament, and the former determinations supersede the necessity of any reasoning upon the case.'

A lawyer who attended this trial described it to his correspondent in Massachusetts:

Admiralty, Dec. 22, 1761, Adm. 1/4124, no. 146; Admiralty Minutes, Dec. 25 and 26, 1761, Adm. 3/69.
[1] Forrest to Clevland, April 14, 1762, Adm. 1/1788; depositions in the cases of the *Walnut Grove*, Taylor, H.C.A. 42/104; *Keppell*, Chambers, H.C.A. 42/79; *Sea Nymph*, Mitchell, H.C.A. 42/94; *Sea Horse* (Hough, *Reports*, p. 206).

'Altho' the whole evidence taken in the court of Vice-Admiralty agreed that all the sugars came from Cape François in Spanish boats and had never been landed at Monte Christi, but was immediately put on board, and altho' the several depositions agreed that the supercargo was never ashore at Monte Christi; yet my Lord Mansfield would not permit the appellants' counsel to go into their defence, but immediately reversed the sentence given below and acquitted both these vessels, declaring the trade to be legal, he went so far as to declare that if the sugars had been bought of Frenchmen at Monte Christi, yet the trade would have been legal for a Frenchman residing at Monte Christi for the sake of trade, he said was to all commercial intents a Spaniard.'[1]

The reasoning of the court appears further from the cases of the *St. Croix*, *Young Abraham*, and *Stadt Flansbourg*. It affirmed the condemnation of the first two because 'the evidence was sufficient to prove an authorized and licensed trading', and acquitted the last because it was not.[2] It is not quite certain how far this criterion was applied to Englishmen, since all three vessels had some claim to be regarded as neutral property[3] (for the Dutch and Danes in the West Indies took the same advantage of Monte Cristi as the English, and introduced, in particular, large parcels of slaves into St. Domingue through that channel).[4]

The few condemnations which the court upheld, throw yet more light on its attitude. The *Africa* was condemned, probably because it was in evidence that she sent down a number of empty hogsheads to be filled with molasses, an act which implied a scheme prearranged with somebody in the French settlements. The *Kingston* was also condemned, either because the master had destroyed some papers, or because he sent his mate down to Fort Dauphin; the *Ranger*, probably because the master had

[1] Add. MSS. 36212, f. 8; John Gardiner, Inner Temple, to Richard Derby, March 19, 1762, Derby Family MSS. xii, Essex Institute.

[2] Endorsements of Charles Yorke, Add. MSS. 36213, ff. 2, 26.

[3] *St. Croix*, Debroskey, H.C.A. 42/61; *Stadt Flansbourg*, Christian, H.C.A. 42/93; *Young Abraham*, Hassell, H.C.A. 42/109.

[4] For this reason Holmes thought the Monte Cristi trade even worse than that of the Flags of Truce; the latter could only be carried on by the King's subjects, but the former 'gives an unbounded latitude to the whole world, and besides the innate baseness of it, will be taken soon into the entire possession of the Dutch, who can undersell his Majesty's subjects at the market, in all things except lumber, and they will be greatly preferred before them as carriers to the French' (Holmes to Clevland, Dec. 31, 1760, Adm. 1/236).

gone to Fort Dauphin 'for his health'.[1] If these surmises are right as to the causes of the rare condemnations, it becomes more obvious that evidence of direct intercourse with the enemy in his own settlements was the criterion of guilt.

Thus the Court of Prize Appeals recognized the legality of the Monte Cristi trade in most of its forms. In this it did no more than was expected of it. Underwriters had already insured the trade as one which would certainly be proved legal; customs officers not only in America but in Ireland and London had given clearances for Monte Cristi and had admitted to an entry the return cargoes from the port.[2]

The trade was revived after the war, but it never was so important again, partly because the French of St. Domingue set up a free port of their own. Possibly the free-port movement, which gained such strength in the West Indies after 1763, owed something to the example of Monte Cristi.

The persistence of the trade between North America and the French colonies taught many lessons. It strengthened the demand of the French planters for the free admission of some kinds of North American produce. It must have destroyed whatever public spirit the North American merchants still possessed, for it proved once more that the burdens of patriotism were imposed by England and the West Indies but borne by Ireland and North America, and that America might not always find it convenient to fight in England's wars. It may also have increased the tendency to law-breaking which is the most disastrous legacy of the British Empire to American business men. In the Flag of Truce trader and the privateer we have the boot-legger and the hijacker; sometimes they were at war with each other, sometimes they combined to cheat the police—the men-of-war—by a collusive capture. The men-of-war themselves, like other policemen in America, were not above connivance in some cases, or the third degree in others. The commerce made the Northern Colonies very unpopular not only in the West Indies but in the political circles of England. It accustomed the men-of-war to the suppression of illegal

---

[1] *Africa*, Saltonstall, H.C.A. 42/53; *Kingston*, Poaug, H.C.A. 42/79; *Ranger*, Crowninshield, H.C.A. 42/92.

[2] Anderson and Macniel, Gibraltar, to Richard Derby, Salem, Aug. 6 and 11, Oct. 1, Nov. 1, 1760, Feb. 11, 1761, Derby Family MSS. xii, Essex Institute. See the arguments in the *Charming Polly*, Horton, H.C.A. 42/59; Mercer to Greg and Cunningham, Nov. 6, 1760, *Recovery*, Castle, H.C.A. 42/92.

trade—a function they had never performed so thoroughly in the colonies before—and thus prepared the way for the disastrous efficiency of Grenville and Charles Townshend.[1]

[1] The Admiralty had ordered naval commanders in the Colonies to help the customs officers put down illicit trade as early as 1740 (Adm. 2/56, p. 197); and indeed the Navigation Acts empowered all Admirals and other naval officers to do so. But the navy's first experience of wholesale suppression of smuggling was gained in the attack on the Flag of Truce and Monte Cristi trades.

X

THE ENGLISH SUGAR ISLANDS IN WAR-TIME

IT is a difficult thing to calculate the cost of a war to a community. Reliable statistics of prices are wanting for almost all American trades in this period. The prices current printed in the newspapers seem to have been carelessly edited; they were often left unaltered for long periods and then brought up to date with a jerk. It is unlikely, however, that they are very far wrong. Better still, if we had enough of them, are the prices current which merchants often gave at the foot of their letters. Unfortunately it is almost impossible to compile a satisfactory series of them for any one market. There were so many islands in the West Indies and so many commercial ports in North America, that the great mass of available information is spread rather thin over them all. The records of actual sales are really the least reliable and precise kind of evidence. We know too little of a single transaction to be able to tell whether it was a representative one. 'Rum' in a North American day-book may mean Jamaica, West India, or New England rum; it may have been good or bad of its kind, sold at special rates of credit and payable at different valuations in money or other goods. The categories of the London sugar-market were yet more specialized. There was clayed sugar and muscovado, to say nothing of the bastards and pannels in which there were only a few dealings. The muscovados of each island had a special range of prices; and in the course of years, or even less for particular circumstances, they might exchange their reputations and values. The prices of each sort usually varied eight or ten shillings according to the quality; we can seldom discover whether a given parcel of sugars was good or bad of its kind. There are tables which show the prices of the King's sugars, but do not indicate the times of the year at which they were sold—an important consideration; moreover the transactions of each year are too few to enable us to strike an average confidently.

The details of an insurance policy must be scrutinized in the same way. An amateur speculator of small means might take a less premium than a man of substance; but would he be able to pay the loss, and if not, who would insure the insurer? The difference between the rates charged by public companies and private underwriters in London sometimes amounted to 5 per cent. of the sum insured.[1] A great deal depended on the place where the insurance was made. The London underwriters charged far more than those of Philadelphia or Boston for insuring voyages between two ports in America, because they could not satisfy themselves that the ships were seaworthy; they particularly disliked the complicated and uncertain itineraries of North American traders, because they had not enough information to judge the risk.[2] It is therefore important to distinguish between the rates given on these voyages in England and America. We must also be certain what was the sum to be paid in case of a loss; the Dutch underwriters only paid 96 per cent. of the sum insured, the English 98.[3] Above all it is often difficult and always necessary to know what was being insured against. The premium often depended on the likelihood of an immediate convoy; for example, at the end of the war of 1744 the London insurers usually underwrote a ship bound outward for Barbados at 15 guineas, to return 7 if she chanced to take convoy for the whole voyage; but when a convoy was appointed to go soon, the rate was 12 guineas, to return 4. The premium with convoy did not vary, but the premium without convoy depended on the likelihood that a convoy would be taken.[4]

The rates of wages in the North American ships are equally deceptive, for the payment in money was not the most important part of the sailor's earnings. Each man had the 'privilege' of shipping on his own account a certain quantity of goods without paying freight; and the pre-eminence of the captain over the other sailors was marked rather by his greater privilege than by higher wages. (Whether the officers and men found the capital for these adventures may well be doubted; probably the system accounts for the commonness of small loans upon bottomry.)

For all these reasons, whatever statistics I offer to the reader are put forward with very little dependence on their exactness, and should be received in the same spirit.

[1] Lascelles and Maxwell to Florentius Vassall, Feb. 4, 1743/4, MSS. of Messrs. Wilkinson & Gaviller, vol. ii; to Samuel McCall, Feb. 4, 1743/4, and May 10, 1744, ibid.; to Jacob Allin, May 31, 1746, vol. iii; to J. and A. Harvie, April 1, 1757, vol. viii.

[2] Lascelles and Maxwell to D. and A. Lynch, Nov. 30, 1743, W. & G. ii; to Samuel McCall, Feb. 4, 1743/4, ibid.

[3] Lascelles and Maxwell to Samuel McCall, May 1, 1747, W. & G. iii.

[4] Lascelles and Maxwell to Thomas Stevenson, Jan. 27, 1747/8, W. & G. iii.

§ i. *The Volume of Trade in War-time*

The wars affected the English colonies much less than the French. In spite of alarms and even dangers, the navy was able to preserve them from invasion, and their trade from catastrophic alterations. Some branches of it even prospered more than in peace; but the planters could not altogether escape loss and discomfort.

Less shipping reached their ports. There are not many figures to prove this, but if there were none, it could be inferred from several things—the captures at sea, the ships taken up for the service of the Government, and the prevalence of the Flag of Truce trade in North America.[1] The statistics of the tonnage duty at Barbados prove a considerable fall in the number and size of the vessels which traded there during the Seven Years War, but on the other hand a paper of figures in the collection of George Chalmers shows an increase for the same period in the shipping which left England for the West Indies.[2] The

[1] H. Lascelles and son to Francis March, Sept. 13, 1740, W. & G. i; John Reynell to Samuel Dicker, Oct. 29, 1740, Reynell Letter-book, H.S.P.; Thomas Clifford to J. and T. Tipping, Oct. 6 and Nov. 16, 1759, Clifford Correspondence, xxvii. 35, 41, H.S.P.

[2] I give the figures for the sake of comparison:

	(C.O. 28/32, FF 25)			(C.O. 318/1)	
	Barbados number of vessels		*Average Tonnage*	*English West India Trade*	
				Ships	*Tons*
		(1745–9)	21·010		
1751	511			263	37,955
1752	574	(1749–53)	34·491	309	44,599
1753	608			315	43,125
1754	650	(1753–6)	35·206	301	43,718
1755	604			255	34,394
1756	446			361	47,007
1757	292	(1756–9)	20·740	376	53,886
1758	230			397	59,704
1759	302			342	52,894
1760	247	(1759–60)	21·460	403	57,089
1761	⎫			332	53,594
1762	⎪			419	72,893
1763	⎬ No figures			451	74,479
1764	⎪			372	64,862
1765	⎭			373	62,573

The estimated tonnage at Barbados is no doubt far too low. No tax was more consistently evaded by under-declaration than a tonnage duty; but the amount of the fraud may be supposed constant. The average tonnage in the trade from

contradiction can be reconciled. In the first place, one paper shows the ships which left England, the other those which reached Barbados; there might well be some loss on the way. Secondly, Chalmers's figures cover all the West Indies, including the conquered colonies, which gave employment to many ships in the later years of the war; probably they also include store-ships in the Government service. Lastly, the trade from England kept up better than any other in war-time because it was the only one to be properly protected by convoys. As these ships usually went out half-empty and carried no lumber but hoops, no provisions but some beans and oats, they had little to do with the plenty or scarcity of plantation necessaries in the islands. That was affected by the losses of North American shipping, which were heavy.

One branch of the English trade, however, furnished an article which entered into the costs of production in the islands. This was the slave-trade. Here again there are contradictions in such figures as exist. The shipping which sailed from England to Africa fell in the war of 1739, but the number of negroes imported into Jamaica increased. Jamaica was only one market out of many, and perhaps it was the most frequented in the war with Spain because the slave-trade to the Spanish colonies was expected to be brisk, especially after Vernon's conquest at Portobello.[1] The re-export of negroes did not prove very great until the last years of the war, but the traders may have expected something better, and once their ships were at Jamaica they could go no farther but must sell, so that the planters benefited by their mistake.[2] On the other hand, the captains in this trade did not willingly go on to Jamaica if they could decently stop in the Windward Islands. Besides the additional risk of capture, there was the ordinary danger of disease, suicide, and revolt among the negroes, who were often more exasperated or dejected when they passed land without stopping, than when they were first put on board ship.[3] These two considerations probably

England seems to have gone up on the whole. A large ship was thought more profitable in war-time, a middling one in peace (Lascelles and Daling to Philip Gibbes, Sept. 12, 1765, W. & G. x; to Nathan Lucas, Nov. 14, 1768, vol. xi).

[1] H. Lascelles and son to Richard Morecroft, March 28, 1740, W. & G. i; Henry Laurens to John Knight, Dec. 21, 1756, Laurens Letter-book, ii. 359. (I am in debt to the kindness of Miss Elizabeth Donnan, who lent me her transcript of these letter-books.)

[2] *For table see opposite.*   [3] *For note 3 see opposite.*

cancelled each other out, and a third explanation of the figures is possible; the ships may well have carried more slaves to the ton in war than in peace. The charges and risks were high, but no higher for a large cargo than for a small one, and there was less than ordinary danger of arriving at an overstocked market; those are just the circumstances to cause overcrowding in such a trade.

Although the plenty of necessaries did not depend on the arrival of any other ships from Europe, they were still needed to carry off the crops. The production of the English sugar colonies does not seem to have been affected by the war. It was rather the weather which caused yearly fluctuations of the size of crops. The small islands were so fully cultivated that they could hardly yield more. Jamaica alone had room for new plantations, and seems to have increased its crop almost steadily

	Slaves imported to Jamaica	Re-exported	Slave ships leaving England	Tons
	(C.O. 137/25, X 41, and 137/28, Y 54)		(T 64/274)	
1735			67	6,250
1736			101	9,019
1737			104	9,959
1738			114	10,029
1739	3,008	115 last half	95	8,585
1740	5,621	495	62	4,244
1741	4,792	562	53	4,785
1742	4,938	792	60	5,465
1743	8,540	1,368	71	6,532
1744	8,755	1,331	52	4,201
1745	3,843	1,344	32	3,081
1746	4,703	1,502	60	5,820
1747	10,898	3,378	68	6,365
1748	10,483	2,426	92	9,906
1749 }			85	8,418
1750 }	15,296		85	7,906
1751 }			89	10,073
1752			104	11,361
1753	6,758	2,336 (Sept. 25, 1752, to	125	11,642
1754	8,843	Sept. 25, 1754)	112	10,794

There are some slightly different figures for 1730 to 1746 in T 70/1205, A 10. Those in T 64/274 show that the slave-trade of London declined more in the war than those of Bristol and Liverpool, especially the latter. Liverpool had a great advantage over other colonial ports in war-time, because the channels of its trade were much less frequented by French privateers (see the quotation from *Williamson's Liverpool Memorandum Book*, quoted by Gomer Williams, *Liverpool Privateers*, pp. 37–8).

[3] Henry Lascelles to Richard Morecroft, April 20 and Oct. 27, 1741, W. & G. i; Lascelles and Maxwell to Gedney Clarke, vol. iii; to Anthony Lynch, June 17, ibid.

through peace and war. Whitworth's figures show a slight drop in all the figures during the war of 1739. This was probably caused by a run of bad crops, the captures at sea, and perhaps the deliberate policy of restriction which some critics accused the planters of pursuing at this time. The price of sugar satisfied them after the Peace of Aix-la-Chapelle, and the imports of West India produce into Great Britain rose again. This rise continued throughout the Seven Years War and the years which followed it. To judge by other standards—rates of freight and insurance—the war of 1744 was no more dangerous to the sugar trade than the Seven Years War; since the latter did not prevent production from rising, it is not very likely that the former was the cause of the fall which happened at the same time.[1]

[1] These are the figures calculated from Whitworth's tables (*State of the Trade of Great Britain*, 1776). It should be remembered that they represent fluctuations of quantity, not of value, because the valuations of goods in the Custom House statistics were not altered in this period.

Average value of imports into Great Britain from

	1729–38 (peace)	1739–48 (war)	1749–55 (peace)	1756–63 (war)	1764–70 (peace)
	£	£	£	£	£
Antigua . . .	220,782	194,747	233,511	242,059	234,801
Barbados . . .	237,266	203,698	224,337	227,190	280,335
Montserrat . .	65,939	54,053	62,228	65,272	72,506
Nevis	66,352	45,470	49,645	57,808	66,949
St. Christophers . .	256,797	217,178	238,648	260,091	279,920
Jamaica . . .	550,877	542,648	760,290	968,385	1,185,979
West Indies generally .	8,259	4,165	..	..	..
Spanish West Indies .	38,985	6,563	..	..	35,981
TOTAL . . .	1,445,257	1,268,522	1,568,659	1,820,805	2,156,471

In these figures I have included 1748 and 1763 as years of war, because, though peace was signed half-way through the former and at the beginning of the latter, the canes were planted and the goods ordered from England in war-time. The figures from Jamaica, which show the largest increase, are somewhat equivocal. They certainly include the goods imported through the colony from the Spanish West Indies. (Those classified as 'Spanish West Indies' probably represent little before 1739 besides the Annual Ships of the South Sea Company.) There is no guessing the amount of the Spanish goods imported from Jamaica; presumably it was larger in the second period than the first, because this trade flourished more in the war of 1739 than in the peace before it. It was probably smaller in the last period than in the fourth, because there are evidences of a stop in the trade after the Peace of Paris. Probably we need not allow for a very serious error in the Jamaica figures, in order to discover the amount of the island's own produce. Far the most important article in the Spanish trade of Jamaica was bullion, which was not included in any of Whitworth's tables. The class 'West Indies generally',

The volume of the exports from Great Britain to the West Indies increased considerably in this time. This may appear surprising when that of the imports altered so little, but it is easily explained. The prices of West India produce improved permanently after the turning-point of the thirties, and the planters could afford to buy more though the size of their crops (which is all that the figures represent) remained nearly the same. Very likely they bought even more than they could afford; the inventories in the Jamaica Record Office show a steady increase of luxury, and the islands were running deeper and deeper into debt with the London factors. The wars appear to have stimulated exports to the West Indies, which fell back a little after each peace; probably this can be accounted for by the exports of naval and military stores in war-time.[1]

§ ii. *The Sugar Market in War-time*

The price of sugars was rising in England after the thirties. The production of the English colonies was not increasing so fast as the demand in the home market. People who had used brown sugar began to use white, and as there was some wastage in refining, more raw sugar was needed than before. The sugar-bakers had not the art of keeping their products good in cold weather, and were therefore obliged to refine in winter, even at a loss, in order to keep their sugar-houses warm. This spread the demand for raw sugar over the year, and perhaps increased

which disappears from 1750 to 1762, presents another difficulty: does it represent English or foreign West Indies, or both? Since the increase of exports in the third period is pretty evenly distributed among all the colonies, perhaps this indiscriminate category was so too. (See next note.)

[1] Average value of exports from Great Britain for

	1729–38	1739–48	1749–55	1756–63	1764–70
	£	£	£	£	£
Antigua . . .	31,026	44,586	75,243	124,302	124,181
Barbados . . .	64,346	91,793	167,592	183,997	181,749
Montserrat . . .	4,476	5,011	10,684	16,355	19,907
Nevis . . .	5,472	2,640	10,667	15,692	13,330
St. Christophers . .	23,220	27,333	70,110	110,806	109,108
Jamaica . . .	140,627	218,771	321,889	479,071	463,426
West Indies generally .	161,465	322,787	49,335	4,947	1,021
Spanish West Indies .	54,353	388	..	..	5,261
TOTAL . . .	484,985	713,309	705,520	935,170	917,983

For the interpretation of these figures, see the preceding note.

it altogether.[1] When the price was too high, especially in war-time, things went the other way; the middle classes used brown instead of white, and the poor ate molasses instead of brown sugar.[2] The changes of price were thereby attenuated, but they were still very considerable. The bare possibility of a war or a peace was enough to make them jump up and down. For example, they rose 3 shillings the hundredweight in two days when the French King declared war in 1744, and fell 10 shillings in a short time on the signature of the preliminary treaty at Aix-la-Chapelle; later in 1748 they came down again, so that the whole fall was over 15 shillings. They were more indifferent to the alarms of 1755, because the crops were so large as to keep the prices down in spite of everything; but the Spanish war of 1762 caused them to rise 6 shillings.[3]

These changes were considerable, for the average price of brown sugar in peace was not much more than 30 shillings the hundredweight. They were partly due to speculation. The price of brown sugar did not by any means keep pace with the charges and risks of production and importation; sometimes it rose above them, sometimes fell below. Other circumstances such as hurricanes or droughts affected it by reducing the crops. For instance, it seems to have touched the highest point of the war in the winter of 1745; the Jamaica crop was very much diminished in that year by a hurricane. The price rose again in the winter of 1747-8, and that time there had been a hurricane at St. Kitts. All this time the insurance premiums and the freights remained pretty steady. A more remarkable proof is furnished by the prices of 1759. The crops of all the islands except Jamaica were considerably smaller than usual. The insurance, for example from Jamaica to London, had fallen from 30 to 12 guineas since the beginning of 1758; yet the prices rose higher than they had done for decades. Barbados brown muscovado fetched 53 shillings, and white clayed sugar 84; a year later they were at 30 and 53 shillings respectively, and the insurance was a little higher.

The markets were affected in these years by the sale of prize

[1] Lascelles and Maxwell to Benjamin Charnock, Jan. 16, 1753, W. & G. v; to Jonathan Blenman, March 14, ibid.

[2] Lascelles and Maxwell to John Frere, May 20, 1747, W. & G. iii; to William Bryant, Nov. 20, 1747, ibid.

[3] See the correspondence of Lascelles and Maxwell, *passim*, for the years 1744, 1748, 1755-6, and 1762-3.

goods, and by two unusual circumstances—a re-exportation to Europe and the conquest of a French sugar colony. The English re-export trade in sugar had fallen off and lost its importance since about 1730. In those days the pamphleteers used to recommend a war with France by arguing that if we destroyed the French trade and settlements in the West Indies, we should recover our position in the world market for sugar.[1] The history of the wars does little to bear out this calculation. The few years of this period in which the re-exportation rose high are almost equally distributed between war and peace.[2] The most remarkable are 1743, 1756, and 1759. In the first of these we were at peace with France and the cause was the failure of crops in the foreign colonies. In the second, the capture of French sugars at sea may have played a part. The last is the nearest to an unequivocal proof that we could oblige Europe to buy our sugars by holding up those of the enemy, for everybody recognized that the scarcity abroad was caused by the detention of the French West India produce in neutral ships. This could only continue while the appeals remained unheard; the acquitted and condemned cargoes were alike exported abroad, and the shortage came to an end.[3]

The introduction of prize goods into a protected market created a serious difficulty for the legislatures. On the one hand they desired to encourage the captors by giving them the greatest possible liberty to dispose of their prizes; but collusive seizures and smuggling flourished under the cover of prizes, and the producers of similar goods within the Empire struggled hard to keep up such monopoly as the laws allowed them. There was also the interest of the consumer to be considered; even the planter was thankful for a cheap supply of prize European goods, while he disliked the competition of prize sugars with his own.

The privateering interest and the consumers had their own

[1] *An Essay on the Causes of the Decline of the Foreign Trade* (Overstone's *Select Collection*), p. 281; *The Present Ruinous Land War proved to be a H——r War* (London, 1745), p. 23.

[2] The re-export of brown sugar rose above 100,000 cwt. in 1743, 1748, 1749, 1750, 1755, and 1756; also, I think, in 1758 and 1759, but the figures in T 64/274 stop in 1757.

[3] *Considerations relating to a New Duty on Sugar* (2nd ed., 1746), p. 26; Lascelles and Maxwell to Conrade Adams, Sept. 16, 1743, W. & G. ii; to T. Stevenson and sons, Jan. 20, 1756, vol. vii; Aug. 23, 1756, vol. viii; to J. and A. Harvie, April 13, 1756, vol. vii; June 29 and Aug. 12, 1758, vol. viii; to John Frere, Oct. 29, 1758, and July 7, 1759, ibid.

way in the reign of Queen Anne. Foreign colonial produce imported into England as prize appears to have paid duty as if it were of English growth.[1] However, an Act of 1710 imposed upon it the usual foreign duty, by providing that it should enter the English market as if imported in the ordinary course of trade.[2] If it was brought into the colonies, it should pay such duty there as the local legislature should levy; at this time very few of the islands taxed the produce of their foreign competitors as they began to do after the Treaty of Utrecht. A year later the privateers received a favour at the expense of the planters; prize goods were put once more on the same foot as the produce of the English colonies, and permitted to pay duty as such. This seems to be no more than had been granted before 1710, but it was now confirmed by Act of Parliament.[3] Meanwhile the planter as consumer had benefited by these Acts; prize European goods might be brought into the colonies, first on payment of the duties on importation into England minus the drawbacks, and finally in effect duty free.[4]

These Acts had lapsed with the war, like most of the others which dealt with prizes. It therefore needed a new law to exempt certain prize goods from exclusion or very heavy duties.[5] That of 1741 appears to have favoured the captors. Prize colonial produce might once more be imported into the English market from the English colonies, and pay duty as if it were of their own growth, on production of a certificate of condemnation.[6] There does not seem to have been any need to re-export it. The captors, however, were not so well off as they might appear to be; before their prizes could reach the English market they had to find their way into that of the colonies, and to encounter several kinds of duties. First there were those of the Molasses Act, which taxed heavily all kinds of foreign West

---

[1] So the preamble of 10 Anne, c. 22, recites; see also *Tudor and Stuart Proclamations*, no. 4356.

[2] 9 Anne, c. 27. This clause is probably designed to get over the Navigation Acts, which forbade the importation of certain goods unless they came directly from their place of growth or usual shipment. Prize goods imported from the English colonies might else have been excluded. An act of the same kind was passed in 1741 to enable prize quicksilver to be imported (15 Geo. II, c. 19).

[3] 10 Anne, c. 22.

[4] 6 Anne, c. 37, 9 Anne, c. 27, and 10 Anne, c. 22; *C.S.P. Col. 1710–11* and *1712–14, passim* (the index should be consulted, s.v. 'Prize-goods').

[5] H. Lascelles and son to Turner and Cowley, Sept. 19 and Oct. 5, 1740, W. & G. i.

[6] 15 Geo. II, c. 31.

India produce imported into the English dominions. This was not a very severe obstruction, because the Act was not always complied with, nor the duties always paid. There was some difference, however, in this respect between the Northern Colonies and the Sugar Islands. The interest of the latter was to oblige the captors to pay these duties, and the importers of prize goods sometimes had to comply.[1] In New York the Commodore refused to pay them; the Vice-Admiralty judge gave a decision in his favour, on the ground that prize sugars should be accounted as English from the moment of their condemnation.[2] Yet there were some colonies in North America where these duties were exacted.[3]

The colonies also had imposts of their own, to which prize goods were subject like all others. Those of North America were only laid for revenue, but the legislatures of the sugar colonies had for some time protected their planters against foreign imports by very heavy taxes.[4] The English Act of 1710 which authorized the imposition of these duties on prize goods was presumably not in force, but there was so little doubt of their being payable that the appeals against them were never prosecuted.[5] The Assemblies of some islands often let the captors off the duties on such articles as prize wine and brandy; but that of Jamaica clung to the policy of making prize goods pay the ordinary duties, and even thought of a special tax on prizes. In the end, however, it relented so far as to let the captors re-export their prize goods without paying anything.[6]

Parliament was less tender to the privateering interest in the Seven Years War. It allowed prize goods to pass through England free of duty, but obliged the importers to pay most of the ordinary duties on whatever stayed to be consumed in the country. Thus prize sugars were subjected to the heavy protective taxes which were laid on foreign sugars. They could not

---

[1] Lascelles and Maxwell to Gedney Clarke, junior, Feb. 10 and May 7, 1757, Oct. 9, 1758, and Jan. 6, 1759, W. & G. viii.

[2] Hough, *Reports of Cases in the Vice-Admiralty of New York*, p. 23; Clinton to Newcastle, Oct. 9, 1744, *N.Y. Col. Doc.* vi. 260.

[3] Account of the duties paid, 1734–49, in T 70/1205.

[4] *V. supra*, pp. 399–402.

[5] Lascelles and Maxwell to John Fairchild, Oct. 30, 1747, W. & G. iii.

[6] Antigua Assembly Minutes, July 11 and 24, 1744, C.O. 9/16; see the Assembly Minutes of St. Kitts, 1744 and 1745, *passim*, C.O. 241/5; *Journals of the Assembly of Jamaica*, iv. 7, 8, 17; see also the Act of Oct. 15, 1756, C.O. 139/18, and the Board of Trade's comments on it, C.O. 138/22, pp. 207–27.

even escape it by paying the Molasses Act duties in the colonies, to which they were liable as well.[1] In this way prize sugars were kept out of the English market, unless the colonists started them into English casks and sent them home as English plantation produce; the island legislatures tried to guard against this abuse. Though, however, the planters kept the English market to themselves in this war, they could not for ever prevent the world price from finding its own level. The prize sugars which could not advantageously be sold for consumption in England were sent abroad, undersold English produce in the neutral markets, and thus interfered with the re-exportation of English sugars.[2] In the Seven Years War the legislature of Jamaica passed a strange Act which was presumably meant to prevent this; it obliged all prize goods, whether acquitted or condemned in the Jamaica court, to be exported first to England.[3]

On the other hand the West India islands sometimes received a cheap supply of European merchandise from a French or Spanish vessel captured on her way out. The prices of dry goods at Barbados were lowered in this way twice in the war of 1744, to the disadvantage of the merchants who imported from England. At the beginning of the hostilities against France in 1755, the Leeward Islands were stocked with negroes in the same way, and even the Jamaica market was probably affected, as the low prices at Barbados and Antigua drove more ships down there than usually went.[4]

Prize goods could not be entirely prevented from affecting the economy of the Empire, especially in North America where the Acts of Parliament were slightly observed. Merchants sometimes reported that the market for English produce or even for smuggled French produce was lowered by the sales of prizes (these complaints were commonest in 1756, before the Act of 30 George II was passed or in force).[5] Prize goods often affected

[1] 30 Geo. II, c. 18; Lascelles and Maxwell to Gedney Clarke, June 2, 1759, W. & G. viii.
[2] Lascelles and Maxwell to T. Stevenson and sons, Aug. 23, 1756, W. & G. viii; Waddell Cunningham to Halliday and Dunbar, Oct. 13, 1756, Letter-book of Messrs. Greg and Cunningham, p. 133, N.Y.H.S.
[3] See the Board of Trade's report, Jan. 27, 1762, C.O. 138/22, pp. 207–27.
[4] Lascelles and Maxwell to John Harvie, May 29, 1744, and March 16, 1744/5, W. & G. ii; to W. and H. Hasell, Aug. 6, 1748, vol. iii; to J. and A. Harvie, Jan. 31, 1756, vol. vii.
[5] There seems to have been a leakage in Philadelphia for some years after the Act was passed. The prize goods were landed without paying the duty, upon a

the rates of exchange between England and the colonies. The colonial merchants were no longer puzzled for a method of remitting home to pay their debts; they exported prize goods—whether to England or Europe is no matter—instead of drawing bills.[1]

The war affected the price of English sugars in other ways. The conquests of Guadeloupe and Martinique let into the market a flood of French sugars, especially whites half-refined on the plantations. This was one of the principal reasons for the fall of the price in 1760. Messrs. Lascelles and Maxwell complained that they could not sell a correspondent's inferior clayed sugar from Barbados at any price.

'The sugar-bakers could not be prevailed on to take them as they have been supplied with Guadeloupe claids at very low prices. . . . Had it not been for the unlucky acquisition of Guadeloupe, sugars must have been as high now, as at any time since the war, but from the large importations from thence, claids are in no request, and brown sugars quite unsaleable, and the small demand we have is only for fine muscovados.'

'Several cargoes of Guadeloupe sugars have lately been sold, and first whites, superior in colour to any that came from Barbadoes, have gone so low as 52/9 p̄ Cwt, and such last year sold once as high as 84/- p̄ Cwt, and muscovadoes have sold as low as 30/- p̄ Cwt and under, and once last year sold as high as 45/- p̄ Cwt.'

Guadeloupe sugars soon lost their reputation.

'Indeed we have applied to almost all the sugar bakers in town, and as they have formerly worked Guadeloupe sugars, at great loss, on account of their foulness, they do not chuse to work any more.'[2]

The island poured greater quantities of sugar, good or bad, every year upon the market, and when the news of the reduction of Martinique reached London in 1762, the sugar market fell three shillings.[3]

promise to re-export them, which was not performed. The Collector of the port received orders to stop this in 1760; the market for prize sugars was lowered by this reform (Thomas Clifford, Philadelphia, to Isaac Cox, July 26 and Dec. 9, 1760, Clifford Correspondence, xxvii. 99, 130, H.S.P.).

[1] Loudoun to Pitt, April 25, 1757, C.O. 5/48.

[2] Lascelles and Maxwell to Thomas Stevenson, June 28, 1760; to T. Stevenson and sons, July 18; to Thomas Stevenson, junior, Sept. 13, W. & G. ix.

[3] Lascelles and Maxwell to Thomas Stevenson, Aug. 6, 1762, W. & G. ix. The average importation from Guadeloupe in the years 1759–63 was £380,964; that of Martinique, 1762–3, was £316,293; that of Havana (partly sugars) in 1763 was £249,387. A comparison of these figures with those given on p. 474 will show what an impression the conquests must have made on the sugar-market.

The West India interest tried to protect itself against this competition by raising a doubt whether the produce of a colony so conquered could count as English. The Treasury wished to honour Barrington's capitulation by admitting Guadeloupe sugars at the same duties as English; but the planters and merchants questioned whether the island could be deemed an English dominion until it had been annexed to the Crown by Act of Parliament. The Treasury consulted the Law Officers, who supported it; so in spite of a contrary opinion of Hume Campbell, the Guadeloupe produce was entered as English.[1]

It is difficult to judge exactly the effect of these various circumstances and policies upon the sugar market. It must be taken as roughly summed up by the history of the prices themselves, and even that is hard to ascertain. If, however, we try to strike an average from what figures we possess, we may say that the price of Barbados muscovado sugar in the 1730's was about a guinea per hundredweight; during the Spanish war down to 1744 about 32 shillings; during the French war which followed, about 38 shillings. It fell back at the peace but advanced a great deal in the last years before the Seven Years War; we might strike an average for the whole period of peace at 34 shillings. It is hardest of all to name a figure for the Seven Years War itself, because the fluctuations were unusually violent; we have to take into account the high price of 52 shillings in August 1759 and the low one of 30 shillings in August 1760.[2] Perhaps 40 shillings would be a fair estimate. These figures show less variation than the Amsterdam prices, such as we have them. That is not surprising, for the English market differed from the free markets of the world in several ways. The prices fell less in peace because the market was protected and the production little more than enough to supply the demand; they rose less in war because the sugar convoys were protected by the most powerful navy in the world, which was able to intercept the produce of the French colonies on its way to neutral countries. It would, however, be a waste of time to theorize very subtly about these statistics, for none of them is much better than guesswork.[3]

[1] Lascelles and Maxwell to Gedney Clarke, June 19, Aug. 3 and 31, 1759, W. & G. viii.

[2] There is a further difficulty because the figures on which I most rely are deficient for the later years of the war.

[3] I give them here for purposes of comparison:

§ iii. *The Market for By-Products in War-time*

Since every sugar-plantation and refinery must make some molasses, the price of molasses and rum was almost as important to the planters as that of the sugar itself. Both these articles were the objects of keen speculation in North America, and the markets there and in the islands fluctuated widely in peace as well as war. Hurricanes, short crops, or sudden demands often raised the price very much in peace; but it kept up a higher average in war. For example, molasses only once got to two shillings a gallon in Philadelphia between 1728 and 1738, according to the prices current of the *American Weekly Mercury*; it never fell below that price between January 1742 and March 1743, and returned above it for another long spell after November 1744. The prices in the islands do not always seem to have kept pace with those of the North American ports; for instance, rum was exceptionally low at 1s. 8d. the gallon in Barbados in the spring of 1757 and 1758, while it was fetching high prices at Philadelphia and New York. In the year 1759, however, when prices broke records all over the world, there was more correspondence between the islands and the continent. Rum was at 4 shillings in Barbados in October (the average price was 2 shillings); at 3s. 6d. in Antigua most of the winter; nearly 6 shillings in New York and Philadelphia, where it seems to have been about 3 shillings upon an average in ordinary times.

Many circumstances entered into the determination of these prices. In the first place, they seem to have moved steadily upwards, war or peace, like those of sugars in the London market. The thirties were the turning-point for rum and molasses as well as sugar. It would be a mistake to ascribe all this to the Molasses Act which was not obeyed, or the direct exportation to Europe which was hardly ever used.[1] The

					London	Amsterdam
1730–8 .	.	.	.	.	22 shillings (1735–8)	3¾ florins
1739–43	.	.	.	.	32 ,,	6 ,,
1744–8 .	.	.	.	.	38 ,,	8 ,,
1749–55	.	.	.	.	34 ,,	5½ ,,
1756–62	.	.	.	.	40 ,,	8½ ,,

The Amsterdam figures are taken from the lists which a certain Mr. Collow, of Broad Street Buildings, supplied to Chalmers on Oct. 23, 1791 (C.O. 318/1). I do not know who was this Mr. Collow, or how he came by his information. See also J. J. Reesse, *De Suikerhandel van Amsterdam* (1908), vol. i, Appendix D.

[1] *V. supra*, pp. 79–82.

population of America was rising faster than that of Europe; molasses and rum were among the first necessities of life in that age and climate, so that the consumption must have risen greatly. The power of the planters to make more rum was as limited as their power to make more sugar; it could not go beyond a certain point without new colonies. More rum was being drunk in England, especially that of Jamaica. The prevalence of the punch-bowl favoured this trade; so did the wars with France, which diminished the imports of French brandy until after the Peace of Paris, when it seems to have come back into fashion.[1]

The planters were sometimes favoured by bad harvests of grain in England, which obliged Parliament to prohibit the distilling of corn spirits in order to keep down the price of bread. This was a gift to the West Indians, for the distillers had to use molasses or even brown sugar. It might as well happen in peace as in war; but since it took place for a long time in the Seven Years War, it is worth some attention.

The harvest of 1756 was very bad and the price of corn high. The ports most concerned in the West India trade, and certain towns represented by West India members, took the lead in petitioning for the prohibition of the corn distillery. The distillers and the barley-growers struggled against this measure, but Parliament agreed to it and continued it for more than three years.[2] The scarcity of corn ceased, and great quantities were exported in 1759, but Parliament did not face the necessity of repeal till 1760. Meanwhile the West Indians were making

[1] H. Lascelles and son to Nicholas Wilcox, May 21, 1740, W. & G. i; to Gedney Clarke, Oct. 27, 1741, ibid.; Lascelles and Maxwell to John Collins, Sept. 16, 1743, vol. ii; to Robert Belgrove, Jan. 15, 1745/6, ibid.; to Alexander Harvie, Oct. 5, 1765, vol. x.

[2] C.J. xxvii. 664 (petition of Lancaster), 694 (distillers' petition), 707 (Ipswich merchants' petition), 847 (petition of Bristol); xxviii. 6 (Liverpool petition), 9 (Leeds petition), 322 (Bristol petition), 327 (Liverpool petition). It is worth noticing the part played in this agitation by the chief West India ports—Liverpool, Bristol, and Lancaster. The manufacturing towns were complaining at the same time of the high price of food, but it was the colonial ports which insisted that the prohibition of the distillery was the proper remedy. Bath and Salisbury were on the same side; Pitt, the greatest defender of the West India interest, was M.P. for Bath and a Beckford sat for Salisbury. The chief petition in 1760 came from the City of London. for which William Beckford was a Member. The chief petitions on the other side were those of Suffolk (1756), Norwich, Berwick-upon-Tweed, South-West Essex, and Ross and Cromarty (1759), Uxbridge, Herts. and Essex, Surrey, Lewes, Croydon, Aldborough, Southwold, Cambridgeshire, Forfarshire, the East Riding, Sheppey, and others, in 1760.

good profits. Molasses rose from about 10 shillings to 37 shillings a hundredweight, and the sugar-bakers who turned it out as a by-product were encouraged to refine more raw sugars. The price of the latter rose 6 or 7 shillings on this account alone in the spring of 1757, when the prohibition was first made; and Messrs. Lascelles and Maxwell acknowledged a year later that 'the distillation has been a great aid in the consumption of sugars, which must otherwise have been miserably low at this time'.[1]

The West Indians charged the distillers with raising the price of bread; the distillers answered that it was strange the planters should feel such concern for the poor consumer of bread when they extorted so much from the poor consumer of sugar. The high price of bread did a real injury to the planters, for the more the poor spent on bread the less money they could afford for sugar; but the sugar interest did not make the most of this point in public, though it complained privately.[2] It accused the distillers of consuming corn which could have been exported from the country and affected the balance of trade in our favour. The distillers replied to all this that they only used the damaged corn. The planters denied it, and added an argument so far-fetched that nobody could have thought of it but a West Indian in defence of his pocket: they asserted that the flesh of hogs fattened upon distillers' refuse was unwholesome meat for the Royal Navy.

They supported their case by a pharisaical concern for the morals of the poor. The result of the prohibition was to raise the price not only of molasses but of spirits. Less was drunk, and the working class became soberer, to the great satisfaction of its employers. The City of London suggested further, in its petition to Parliament, that the soldiers and sailors became braver from the same cause. The distillers retorted that the question was not whether people should drink, but what they should drink; but the planters rejoined that if there were nothing but molasses spirits to be had, there would be less to drink altogether.[3] At last in 1760 a committee of the House of

---

[1] Lascelles and Maxwell to Thomas Stevenson, Feb. 5 and Dec. 3, 1757, Feb. 25, 1758, W. & G. viii; to J. Frere, Jan. 7, 1758, ibid.; to Henry Allin, Feb. 24, ibid.

[2] Lascelles and Maxwell to Gedney Clarke, Sept. 3, 1757, W. & G. viii.

[3] *C.J.* xxviii. 640 (Spitalfields petition), 718 (Lewes petition), 817 (City of London petition); *Gentleman's Magazine*, xxix. 630, xxx. 18, 22. The *Monitor*, quoted on p. 18 in favour of the prohibition, had been founded by Beckford and was probably still his property.

Commons went into the matter. It reported that the high price of liquors had indeed contributed to the health and sobriety of the people, and that the best way to keep it up was to lay a heavy duty upon all spirits. The discrimination against the corn distillery was to be removed.[1] The planters fought hard, and often divided the House. They seem to have been countenanced by Pitt, that unfailing champion of West India causes right or wrong. They tried to get the distillers confined to using malted corn, and offered to prohibit the use of sugar in molasses spirits at the same time; they also asked for a drawback on exported molasses spirits, equal to that on corn spirits. A few days later they only failed by three votes to get the Bill recommitted.[2] It became law in spite of them. The sugar-factors lamented in one breath the deterioration of the market and the repeal of 'that salutary and beneficial prohibition to which we attribute the reformation of the people with their increased industry and uncommon sobriety'. The price of molasses fell from 30 shillings to 13.[3] A few years later the corn distillers carried the war into the enemy's country: they exported to North America great quantities of spirits which lowered the market for West India rum.[4]

The more rum was sent to England, the less there was for North America. The other islands made a weak kind of rum which was used in the Northern Colonies; Jamaica could have made much more of that strength if its finer produce had not been so popular in England.[5]

The North American traders made up the deficiency from the French islands. They were the readier to do so because the French planter was glad enough to get rid of his raw molasses

---

[1] C.J. xxviii. 746, 788, 816, and 817.

[2] On the first of these occasions the tellers for the ayes were Nugent, member for Bristol, and Gibbons, a West Indian; on the last, Beckford and a Mr. Coventry whose connexions are unknown to me (C.J. xxviii. 822, 829). For Pitt's attitude see Watkins's letter to Newcastle, March 17, 1760, Add. MSS. 32903, f. 338. Not all West Indian Members of Parliament thought as planters on this occasion; Rose Fuller, for example, was against continuing the prohibition (see his letter to Newcastle, Nov. 19, 1759, vol. 32898, f. 372).

[3] Rowland and Richard Oliver to Abraham Redwood, March 18, 1760, The Commerce of Rhode Island (M.H.S. Collections), i. 81; Lascelles and Maxwell to T. Stevenson and sons, April 29, 1760, W. & G. viii.

[4] John Watts, New York, to Francis Clarke, Jan. 2, 1762, Letter-book of John Watts (N.Y.H.S. Collections, vol. 61), p. 6.

[5] Lascelles and Maxwell to Florentius Vassall, Nov. 21, 1751, W. & G. v; to Thomas Stevenson, Sept. 2, 1754, vii.

without insisting on selling it distilled into rum. There is no telling whether the trade to the French colonies was greater or less in war than in peace; since it was secret and for the most part unlawful, we cannot expect to find perfect statistics of it. To judge from the references to it in merchants' letters, it appears to have increased continually if not steadily. Perhaps this intercourse did not injure the English planters so much as they said. It was reported once or twice that no shipping was to be had for the West Indies, because the Monte Cristi trade employed so much, or that North American producers hoped for once to recover the first cost of their goods in the British West Indian market, because they were exporting so much to the French islands. Since, however, the same evidence shows that the price of flour always remained high in St. Kitts because so much was shipped off by night to St. Eustatius, it is impossible to be very sorry for the English planters. They should have put their own house in order before they complained of the Northern colonists.[1]

The North Americans had even more reason than the English consumers to be thankful for the conquests of the Seven Years War. They had never been able to buy as much rum and molasses as they wanted in the English sugar colonies, and lately they had made no attempt to do so. Their commerce with the French islands presumably kept down the price of the English produce as long as it lasted; but one important branch of it—the Flag of Truce trade—was killed by the navy and the courts in 1760, though a roundabout form of the same trade survived at the Spanish free port of Monte Cristi. The annexation of Guadeloupe and Martinique enabled them to do openly what they had long done against the law. They bought vast quantities of molasses at those two islands; indeed, most of what they lawfully imported from 1760 to 1763 seems to have come from thence.[2] No doubt they took advantage of the opportu-

[1] Thomas Clifford to J. and T. Tipping, Oct. 6 and Nov. 16, 1759, Clifford Correspondence, xxvii. 35, 41, H.S.P.; Thomas Wharton junior to Thomas Wharton, Dec. 26, 1757, and March 16, 1758, Wharton Papers, Box II, H.S.P. A fuller description of this trade has been given in Chapter IX.

[2] Most of the molasses imported as from the other New England colonies, and a great deal of that classified as coming from the 'West Indies', may be presumed to be foreign produce originally smuggled in without paying the Molasses Act duties, from St. Eustatius, Monte Cristi, or the French islands. Since the figures were probably compiled by the provincial, not the imperial, revenue officers, there was no need for concealing the imports from the 'West Indies'; and as for what purported

nity, and brought in more from these sources than they could have done before the conquests; this may have been one reason for the fall of the price from 1759 to 1762, though it was not the only one. The figures probably represent commerce which had always existed but only dared to come into the open when Guadeloupe and Martinique became English possessions; there are also indications that the clearances from Guadeloupe could be bought or forged for the produce of islands which were still French. Such documents would save the traders some risk and trouble, for it was easy to tell French cask or goods from English.[1]

to come from Connecticut and Rhode Island, the Collectors of those colonies had a reputation for giving false clearances to cover merchandise which was really imported from the foreign islands.

Hogsheads of molasses and rum imported into Massachusetts, 1760–1:

	1760		1761	
	Molasses	Rum	Molasses	Rum
From Guadeloupe . . .	3,604	36	3,361	31
From Jamaica . . .	1,211	90	636	141
From other English islands, by name	190	674	225	1,363
From 'West Indies' .	1,176	6	4,421	112
From other North American colonies	1,433	229	1,275	540
Total	7,614	1,035	9,918	2,187

(M.H.S., Lowell Papers, pp. 29, 33.)

Hogsheads of molasses and rum imported into Salem, 1762:

	Molasses		Rum	
	Hhds.	Tierces	Hhds.	Tierces
Guadeloupe	1,610	1,335	..	..
Martinique	1,615	912	..	60
Jamaica	197	..	10	..
English Islands altogether .	209	3	371	9

(M.H.S., MSS. 91 L, p. 41.)

These figures suggest that the North Americans bought their West India rum from the English colonies, and the molasses for their own distilling from the French—for indeed the English planters would not let them have it, preferring to sell it manufactured as rum. The same distinction is to be observed within the English sugar colonies; Jamaica was the only English colony to supply any molasses, but exported far less rum than the other islands. There was, however, a special reason for this: Jamaica rum was much better and dearer than that of the other islands, and was sent to England where it was the only kind good enough for the market.

[1] G. G. Beekman to Metcalfe Bowler, July 1, 1761, Letter-book, N.Y.H.S.

Thus the conquest of the French islands affected the market for sugar and its by-products. The planters found compensations in war-time for this breach of their monopoly. Even defensive warfare called for some increase of the colonial forces, and an active campaign for a great one. The soldiers and sailors received generous allowances of rum. The English planters supplied this demand in the West Indies, and took care to make their market of the Government. When Hosier's squadron arrived at Jamaica in 1726, the price of rum was said to have risen to three times the ordinary rate, and none to be had. The contractors for the victualling tried to protect themselves against a repetition of this extortion in 1740. They meant to use rum from Barbados and the Leeward Islands; it was cheaper though worse, and the liberty to import it into Jamaica would enable them to break the ring of planters and merchants which would certainly try to raise the price again. Jamaica had protected its own producers by a heavy duty on imported rum; the contractors knew that, and made the Duke of Newcastle recommend to the Governor to have this duty remitted on what was imported for the service of His Majesty's forces. Although Newcastle's suggestion was backed by an Order in Council, it might be ignored; in that case, the Government bound itself to indemnify the contractors for any duty that might be exacted. The agent of the contractors eventually found himself obliged— or so he said—to make use of this permission. He ordered down a hundred thousand gallons from Barbados, and asked the legislature of Jamaica to let him introduce it duty free. The legislature refused, so he advertised that he would buy Jamaica rum at three shillings the gallon. More was asked, so he resolved to import the Barbados rum after all and give bond for the duty.

The planters of Jamaica were patriotic, but they did not mean to sacrifice their profits to a victualling contractor. The Assembly addressed a long remonstrance to the King. It accused the contractors of importing French rum. (That was probably untrue; it cannot be disproved, but there are evidences that a great deal of rum was bought in Barbados for the forces at this time, and that the price went up there in consequence.)[1] The Assembly's concern for His Majesty's pocket and the welfare of his forces was quite touching: it pointed out 'how prejudicial these foreign rums are to the health of your Majesty's subjects,

[1] Henry Lascelles to Nicholas Wilcox, March 4, 1740/1, W. & G. i.

in comparison to the pure Jamaica rum, and as your Majesty allows the same price for those rums, as for the rum of this island, it is evident that your Majesty is hereby defrauded of above fifty per cent.' It complained that the loss of public revenue would be great if the duty were remitted, at the same time that the planters would be disabled from paying taxes by the reduction of the profits on their rum. A few months later, a committee went into the question and controverted the agent's history of the prices. It made him admit that he had bought rum earlier in the year at 2 shillings; it maintained that he could have had the whole year's supply at that price, and charged him with deliberately running short for the sake of an excuse to import the rum from Barbados. It denounced the large profits which the contractors had made upon this article in late years; it admitted that rum had risen from 1s. 8d. as far as 3 shillings, but asserted that it had fallen back to 2s. 3d. soon after. The contractors appealed to the Privy Council, and the Admiralty supported them. The Law Officers advised that the King had the right to import rum into Jamaica, as into England, duty free. The case seems to have been suspended for a long time, nor can a definite result be traced.[1] The Jamaica Assembly continued to protect the planters not only against rum but against wines imported for the navy. At least two of its members made a handsome profit out of this policy. William Beckford found it worth while to pay the Agent Victualler a secret rebate on a large contract for rum, and Speaker Price followed his example, though with some hesitation.[2]

The price of rum was raised all over the colonies by Cathcart's expedition in 1740. This had an unforeseen effect in Barbados, where some ships from Jersey, Ireland, and North America used to buy rum and draw bills of exchange for it. It

---

[1] Commissioners of the Victualling to Burchett, Jan. 23, 1739/40, S.P. 42/23, f. 22; Lords of the Admiralty to Lords Justices, Aug. 19, 1741, S.P. 42/24, f. 409; *Journals of the Assembly of Jamaica*, iii. 543, 545, 548, 572; *A.P.C. Col.* iii. 670–3, 713–17. The Admiralty was eager to break the ring at Jamaica (Minute of July 17, 1740, Adm. 3/44). It was finally so exasperated by the obstructions at Jamaica that it asked the Attorney-General to draw up a bill to permit the importation of provisions for the forces into the colonies without paying duty (Minute of April 21, 1742, Adm. 3/45).

[2] It must have been a very profitable contract indeed: the rate was 2s. 3d. or 2s. 4d. sterling a gallon, which amounted to about 3s. 4d. Jamaica currency (Jamaica Council Minutes, May 17, 1746, deposition of Richard Beckford, C.O. 137/57; May 22, deposition of Charles Price, ibid.).

now became too dear for them, so that they bought it no longer; there were consequently fewer bills to be negotiated at Barbados, and the rate of exchange upon London was depressed. The North Americans likewise found Barbados rum too dear, and took the payment for their cargoes in cash, which they spent in the Dutch or French colonies.[1] The decline of the distilling business in Boston was also attributed to the demand for rum in Jamaica, which encouraged the planters to distil their own molasses, and lessened the quantity which could be exported to New England. This complaint was possibly a little far-fetched. It is certain that the Boston distillery declined, but the cause of that was the rise of the industry elsewhere in North America; and in so far as the planters made more of their molasses into rum, they were partly encouraged to do so by the growing demand for it in England.[2]

The later West Indian expeditions, such as the conquests of Guadeloupe and Martinique, stimulated the demand for rum, which was often stored in expectation of them.[3] The campaigns in North America likewise had their effect upon the market. The soldiers were supplied largely with New England rum, but the price of West India rum usually kept pace with that of the home-distilled kinds, for there was not an unlimited amount of molasses to distil. The merchants of North America often wrote as if the demand for the forces was the thing which most determined the price of rum and even molasses.[4]

§ iv. *The Market for Provisions in War-time*

The planters' gain was mixed with some loss which arose from the same kind of causes. The King's forces in the colonies increased the demand for victuals as well as rum. For the finer kinds, such as only white people ate in the colonies, they must

[1] Robinson to Newcastle, Oct. 23, 1743, C.O. 28/46; Robinson's answers to queries, Feb. 20, 1746/7, C.O. 28/47.
[2] Report of a Committee, March 16, 1742/3, *Boston Town Records, 1742–57*, p. 12 (*Boston Records Commission, Report no. 14*). For other petitions on this subject, see *Report no. 12*, p. 120; *Report no. 14*, pp. 100, 221, 238, 280.
[3] Samuel Leacock to Thomas Clifford, May 10, 1760, Clifford Correspondence, iii, no. 55, H.S.P.; Richard Derby to Capt. John Bowditch, Jan. 1762, Derby Family MSS. xxvii, Essex Institute.
[4] For instance, Thomas Clifford to Jonas Maynard, Aug. 11, 1759, Clifford Correspondence, xxvii. 19; W. Cunningham to W. Woodbridge, July 4, 1756, Letter-Book of Messrs. Greg and Cunningham, N.Y.H.S.; G. G. Beekman to Rhode Island Committee of War, April 19, 1756, Letter-book, N.Y.H.S.; *Letter-Book of John Watts* (*N.Y.H.S. Collections*, vol. 61), pp. 3, 6.

have almost doubled it. The crew of a single third-rate ship of the line numbered more than the militia of Montserrat or Nevis; the arrival of a really large expedition like Cathcart's or Hopson's must have made a great impression on the market and raised the price considerably. The colonists of Jamaica complained in 1740 that the victualling contractors bought up all the provisions that arrived.[1] The victualling contractors themselves lamented that the price of bread and flour rose in Philadelphia and New York.

A paper sent from Jamaica in 1741 asserted that 5,000 barrels of flour could be had from New York and 5,000 from Pennsylvania without advancing the price, because a much larger quantity was sold to the Spaniards in time of peace. It is doubtful, however, whether the trade in flour with the Spanish colonies was effectively cut off. There are some interesting details about the victualling at this time in the letters of Henry Lascelles and son. Lascelles had the contract for supplying the forces on the Leeward Islands station. The year 1740 was an especially difficult year, for the harvest in England was very small, so that the victuallers could not keep down the price of North American produce by threatening to send out from England. Lascelles's correspondent at Philadelphia was disappointed of a proper supply of biscuit because a Mr. Allen, the agent for the Jamaica contractors, had engaged the town and country bakers of Pennsylvania and New York for all they could make for some months to come. The price of biscuit rose; the bills drawn on England to pay for these purchases altered the exchange in favour of the colonies, and so increased the price still more. Soon afterwards the Government took the Jamaica contract into its own hands, and appointed a different agent at New York, whose unskilfulness in handling the market was reported by an unsuccessful competitor to be the occasion of a further advance.[2] It is hard to see how the utmost delicacy of touch could have kept the prices down in such a year; but be that as it might, the price of provisions rose all over North

---

[1] 'Extract of a letter from Jamaica', Dec. 12, 1740, Add. MSS. 22677, ff. 42–5. This is really a pamphlet by James Knight, but he was in touch with many correspondents in Jamaica.

[2] Henry Lascelles and son to Edward Lascelles, May 10 and 17, Sept. 13, and Dec. 6, 1740, W. & G. i; to Robert Watts, New York, Nov. 21 and Dec. 11, 1740, June 5, 1741, ibid.; to Samuel McCall, Philadelphia, Feb. 6, 1740/1, ibid.; C.O. 5/41, no. 109.

America and the West Indies in 1741. Philadelphia flour still fetched 35 shillings in Antigua in August—a price unusually high when we were at peace with France. Yams had to be issued instead of flour to the men-of-war's crews in Barbados. There was very little bread in Jamaica besides what was in the hands of the Agent Victualler.[1]

It was many years before so great a force came out to the West Indies again, but the squadrons were always above their ordinary strength in war-time, and kept up a demand for the finer sorts of provisions; besides, many North American privateers cruised from the West India islands and replenished their supplies there. The merchant shipping from England, which generally bought its provisions for the homeward voyage in the islands, did not increase; it did not, however, diminish very much, and it probably stayed longer and consumed more in the islands because of the infrequency of convoys.[2] On the whole, therefore, it may safely be supposed that the regular demand for provisions was swelled during the war by the addition of a number of mouths to feed. Moreover, the troops in North America itself diverted from the West Indies a great supply of provisions which would else have gone there; it is hard to guess whether it would have reached the English or the French islands. The conquest of Guadeloupe and Martinique opened new markets for provisions and slaves. The French islands had long been starved of both, and were ready to take off great quantities. The English traders had supplied them with these articles in peace-time, but not so freely or largely as they could do after their annexation. Since there had never been much intercourse with these islands by Flags of Truce, and the commerce of St. Eustatius had been almost suppressed in 1758, the immediate effect of the reduction of Guadeloupe upon prices and trade must have been very great in 1759. It may account partly for the upward spring of both in that year.[3]

It is hard to judge how much the prices of plantation neces-

[1] Lascelles and Maxwell to Edward Lascelles, April 20, 1741, W. & G. i; to Robert Watts, June 5; to Samuel McCall, June 5, ibid.; Adrian Renaudet to John Reynell, July 4, 1740, Coates-Reynell Papers, Box II, H.S.P.

[2] Thomas Wharton, junior, St. Kitts, to Thomas Wharton, Feb. 12, 1759, Wharton Papers, Box II, H.S.P.; John Watkins to Thomas Clifford, March 9, 1757, Clifford Correspondence, i, no. 222, H.S.P.; Birkett and Booth to John Reynell, Feb. 12, 1752, Coates-Reynell Papers, Box VII, H.S.P.

[3] Thomas Wharton, junior, St. Kitts, to Thomas Wharton, July 24, 1759, Wharton Papers, Box II, H.S.P.

saries increased in the West Indies on account of the war. They varied suddenly and widely even in peace. The markets were small, and a few cargoes more or less made the difference between very high and very low prices: for instance, flour sold at 13s. 9d. upon an average in Antigua on January 5, 1752, was up to 32s. by June 27, down to 20s. 6d. on July 29, and to 15s. 6d. on January 13, 1753.[1] Unless, therefore, we could follow the market from week to week, two or three quotations might mislead us entirely about the average price for a particular year. Unfortunately there is no island for which I know of full statistics. Certain things can be said: extremes of price are worth notice so long as too much is not deduced from them.

Flour and bread seem to have been very high in Antigua in the autumn of 1741—flour at 35 shillings and ships' bread at 42s. 6d. This is to be accounted for by the embargoes, the drought, and the forces at Jamaica. The prices never rose so high, so far as I know, in the War of 1744; indeed, they were seldom more than 22 and 30 shillings respectively. They seem to have been continually low in the first years after the peace; the average seems to have been about 18 shillings for flour and 22 shillings for ships' bread. They were some 3 or 4 shillings higher in 1754 and 1755, and increased little after the war broke out. Suddenly they rose very high. Ships' bread was 52s. 6d. in March 1759 and 45 shillings in July 1760; flour bore a correspondingly high price. Then they sank quite low. The fluctuations at Barbados, which are even harder to trace, did not follow by any means the same course, but coincided on one or two of the most outstanding points. Here, too, the highest years seem to have been 1741 and from the end of 1758 to the spring of 1760; the lowest 1742–3 and 1748–51. There is no reason to expect an exact correspondence between the prices in different islands; less than ever in time of war, when some captains were glad to sell where they could, and afraid to run the risk of capture by wandering from island to island in search of a market.[2]

[1] The market prices at Antigua for part of the 1750's can be followed very closely in the Coates-Reynell Papers, H.S.P.

[2] Jonathan Cowpland was bound for Antigua in Dec. 1756 but was chased by a privateer into St. Kitts and durst not go farther, though he was sure the markets were better elsewhere; a month later John Harper, in the service of the same shipowner, was forced in exactly the same way to sit down at Antigua instead of St. Kitts. This is a good instance of the way the risks of war interfered with the freedom of the market (Cowpland to Clifford and Penington, Dec. 23, 1756,

§ v. *War Costs*

The West India pamphleteers sometimes tried to calculate the increase of their costs. Their estimates are to be suspected, because their object was to escape a tax on sugar, and very few people had less regard for truth, even among the hack writers of the eighteenth century. There is one, however, whose figures are correct in other respects and may perhaps be trusted here; he puts the advance in the price of necessaries at 35 per cent. and that of negroes at 50 per cent.[1]

The rise of insurance is easily traced; there was a standard rate for peace, and very often a standard rate for war as well at the London market.[2] Ships returning from Barbados were ordinarily insured at 2½ or 5 per cent. in peace according to the season of the year; from the 26th of July to the 26th of January the risks of hurricanes in the tropics and high seas in the Channel were at their greatest, and the underwriters naturally demanded a greater premium than for the other six months. The insurance home from Jamaica alternated in the same way between 5 and 8 per cent. The rates fluctuated rather more in war. The insurance for ships sailing from Barbados to London remained pretty steady about 7 per cent. in the Spanish war, while that of the ships from Jamaica sometimes got up above 12. That was natural, for Barbados was almost outside the theatre of war so long as France remained neutral, while Jamaica was the centre of it. As soon as the French war was declared, the insurance from Barbados went up to 25 guineas; it came down to 20 when the first alarm was over, but returned to 25 on the news of Caylus's expedition to the West Indies, and stayed there

Clifford Correspondence, i, no. 195, H.S.P.; Harper to Clifford, i, no. 208). The underwriters may have contributed to the same result by the terms of their policies: their custom was to insure a voyage to certain islands and return a part of the premium for each one the ship did not touch at.

[1] *Considerations Relating to a New Duty on Sugar* (2nd ed.), especially pp. 34, 41. A very much worse production of the same kind is *The State of the Sugar-Trade, showing the Dangerous Consequences that must attend any additional Duty thereon* (London, 1747). This author starts from the assumption that insurance, freights, and taxes mechanically advanced with the price of sugar in the London market. That was nonsense.

[2] Most of these figures are taken from the letters of Messrs. Lascelles and Maxwell. So far as possible, I give only those of their dealings with the public companies; they do not always distinguish, but they appear to have disliked dealing with private underwriters, and only did so as an exceptional thing when their correspondents pressed them very hard for low premiums.

for the rest of the war. The insurance from Jamaica seems to have been at 25 guineas. In the Seven Years War the variations were somewhat greater. For voyages from Barbados to London, the insurance went up to 20 guineas at the beginning of 1757 and to 25 at the end of the year, perhaps because of Kersaint's and Caumont's squadrons in the West Indies. It came down to 20 next year; for some time after, I have no figures, but in the middle of 1760 it was at 12 guineas. The fluctuations of the Jamaica rate can be followed more easily. It rose to 20 guineas in the autumn of 1755, when the war was still only probable; returned soon afterwards to 12, but rose again for a short time to 15 on the declaration. After a slight fall, it went up to 25 and even 30 guineas in 1757. The reason is obvious: Beauffremont's and Kersaint's squadrons at St. Domingue caused great alarm at Jamaica, which was soon reflected in the insurers' premiums. A policy was signed at 35 guineas in January 1758, but that was exceptional; the rate began to fall, and by the end of 1759 it was down to 10 guineas. For some reason it rose next year; at the beginning of 1761 it was 20 guineas, fell to 12 in the summer, but mounted to 30 on the declaration of war against Spain and the invasion scare of January 1762. The extremities of this fluctuation illustrate the temperamental anxiety of West Indians for their property and the panic which the news of a squadron at St. Domingue created. The low premiums of 1759 and 1761 are a testimony to England's mastery of the sea in the latter years of the Seven Years War.

Ships in the West India trade were insured much cheaper on the outward voyages; for instance, the premiums from London to Barbados and Jamaica never rose above 15 guineas in the war of 1744, while the homeward rate was 25. The probable reason of this difference is the greater likelihood of a convoy outwards. The ships had no reason to run for a market in the West Indies, because their cargoes were not exported for sale but were already the property of the planters. Therefore they almost always waited for a convoy.

These are the rates at which ships were insured which sailed without the protection of a man-of-war. For those which took convoy the premium was reduced by as much as 7, 10, or even 15 guineas. Sometimes, however, the underwriters refused to return anything for convoy. They pointed out that a ship might part company with her escort in a storm and be taken; no doubt this was one of the considerations which moved them to stipulate in 1746 that the return of premium should only be made if the ship sailed with convoy and arrived safe. For a few months at the beginning of 1747 they gave up this claim, but insisted on it more than ever after some of Commodore Legge's convoy had met with exactly the accident against which this condition was meant to safeguard them.[1] They were also very reluctant to allow for partial convoy clear of the islands. On the other hand, they consented readily to deductions for partial convoy through the Channel. This difference shows that the really dangerous part of the voyage to and from the West Indies was the Channel and the Soundings. Once clear of them, the outward trade ran a much smaller risk at the landfall of the West Indies; but a convoy clear of the islands on the way home left the ships just as much exposed to the greater danger in the Channel as no convoy at all.[2]

The convoy system was a necessary evil. The planters did not like it, for the arrival of so much produce together glutted the market.[3] It rendered the fluctuations of prices more violent than in times of peace. The London sugar markets generally suffered great oscillations when the trade fleets returned from the West Indies. The prices usually rose very high in the spring, before the convoys could begin to be expected. For a month or two the buyers lived from hand to mouth in the hope of holding out until the new sugars should arrive. When they did so, the prices came down with a run. The planters suffered by the depreciation of their goods in the London market without receiving any compensation from that of their plantation supplies, because they ordered out manufactures from Europe on their own account and bought most of their victuals from the North Americans who did not come in convoys. They thus lost at one end without gaining at the other. The convoy system was also hard on the factors, and obliged them to find a very large capital at once for the duties which had to be paid before the sugars could be landed. According to Kinnoull, a good judge and a clever observer, the money market was disturbed by the

[1] Lascelles and Maxwell to Edward Pare, Sept. 17, 1746, W. & G. iii; to John Fairchild, March 25, 1747, to Lucas and Scott, Jan. 25, 1747/8, ibid.
[2] For a further discussion of convoys from the naval point of view, see pp. 303–11.
[3] Letter of James Knight, Aug. 15, 1745, Add. MSS. 22677, f. 48. There are many confirmations in the correspondence of Messrs. Lascelles and Maxwell.

annual withdrawal from circulation of the great sums necessary for this purpose.[1]

I cannot estimate the cost to the planters of these consequential injuries, but must be content with calculating that of the increased insurance itself. If the premium from London to Barbados rose from $2\frac{1}{2}$ guineas per cent. to 15, and that of the homeward voyage from $3\frac{3}{4}$ to 25 (the figures in the war of 1744), the whole addition to the sugar-planter's expenses was $12\frac{1}{2}$ guineas out and $21\frac{3}{4}$ home; or, if convoy was always taken, $7\frac{1}{2}$ guineas out and $11\frac{3}{4}$ home. These two figures cannot simply be added together, because the value of the goods brought out from England was only a fraction of that of the crop which returned.

The insurance also rose, of course, upon the vessels which carried slaves and provisions to the islands. I have hardly any statistics for the African trade and too many for the North American; it is hard to fix an average from the bewildering multitude of premiums at different towns, for different voyages, in different conjunctures to which the North American insurers were more sensitive than anybody. So far as I can tell, the average insurance for a voyage between North America and the English sugar colonies seems to have been about 4 per cent. in time of peace; it was usually a little less for the Barbados trade and a little more for that of Jamaica. The rates were vastly higher in war. Insurances were made at Salem for voyages to Barbados at 18 to 23 per cent. in 1747 and 1748, and to Jamaica at 22 to 25 per cent. At the beginning of the next war the premiums rose to about 20 per cent.—rather more for the Leeward Islands, where the French privateers were most dangerous. They declined after the beginning of 1758; policies were signed for ships bound to Barbados and Jamaica at 10 and 12 per cent. The success of the Martinique privateers raised them in 1760 to 14 or 16 per cent. and the Spanish war affected those

---

[1] Kinnoull to Newcastle, Oct. 17, 1759, Add. MSS. 32897, f. 181; Lascelles and Maxwell to James Bruce, Jan. 27, 1747/8, W. & G. iii. There were also some smaller inconveniences which barely deserve a mention. When a large convoy came home there was a run on the lighters which carried the sugars to the wharf; a captain who had got a lighter was in a hurry to disembark his cargo and sent the cask on shore in bad condition so that it sometimes burst. The crews of the merchant ships in the convoy were often pressed as soon as they arrived in the river, and the factors could only get the goods into the warehouses by hiring 'lumpers' who pilfered whatever they could (Lascelles and Maxwell to John Frere, Feb. 22, 1744/5, W. & G. ii; to Gedney Clarke, Feb. 1, 1762, vol. ix).

of the Jamaica trade still further. The premiums for the homeward voyages were usually 4 or 5 per cent. below these rates. The trade of North America to the islands differed from that of England, in that the outward voyage was much more dangerous than the return. The traders could hardly ever get convoy to the islands, but could very often get themselves escorted clear of them on the way home; enemy privateers were seldom met with on the coasts of North America.[1]

Since this trade was commonly carried on at the risk of the North American merchants, it is to be questioned how much of the extraordinary premiums they made the planters pay in the prices of their goods. At any rate, it need not be reckoned here, because it entered into the cost of necessaries. The only part of the additional insurance which can be taken into consideration here is that of the trade between the West Indies and England, which may perhaps be reckoned at 21 per cent.[2]

Nobody was compelled to insure; some planters preferred to be their own insurers, and to divide their risk by shipping a small consignment on as many vessels as possible.[3] That makes little difference to the calculation: if the risk was rightly represented by the premium, the uninsured planter must lose as much in the long run as he would have done if he had paid it. Some instructed their factors to have no insurance made if their goods were shipped with convoy. This was inconvenient and dangerous. It was sometimes uncertain, until she was actually gone, whether a ship would sail with convoy. She might be separated from the escort in a storm and taken by the enemy.[4] Others increased the crews and armament of their ships and trusted

---

[1] John Moffatt, Portsmouth, N.H., to John Reynell, Sept. 14, 1758, Coates-Reynell Papers, H.S.P. The best collections of insurance policies, or lists of premiums, are to be found in the insurance note-book of Obadiah Brown, R.I.H.S., and the Timothy Orne MSS., vols. i to iv, Essex Institute; there are a few more notices for Salem in the Derby family MSS., vol. i, ibid., and many other details scattered among the merchants' letters in the collections of other Historical Societies of the United States. Lascelles and Maxwell also made some insurances for these voyages, but the London premiums were considerably higher than those of the colonies, and less responsive to conjunctures.

[2] I have assumed that three-quarters of the planters took convoy out and home; that the cargoes brought out from England were only a third as valuable as the consignments of sugar; and that the valuation of sugars on which insurance was made rose in the islands about a quarter. This appears to give the figure of 20·3/8 guineas per cent. for the increase. That is to say, the premiums rose not by 21 per cent. of themselves but by 21 per cent. of the sum insured.

[3] Lascelles and Maxwell to Benjamin Charnocke, Sept. 10, 1744, W. & G. ii.

[4] Lascelles and Maxwell to Lucas and Scott, Jan. 25, 1747/8, W. & G. iii.

to their own defences. This only answered when they were to run without convoy, for the underwriters made no allowance for it. Besides, it increased the shipowner's expense; but it entitled him to charge more for the freight.[1]

The common rate of freight from Barbados to London was 3s. 6d. a hundredweight of sugar. It rose a shilling at the beginning of the Spanish war; the shipowners were not satisfied with that, but they had to put up with it. The rate seems to have been 7s. 6d. or 8 shillings at the height of the war with France. The absentee planters in London agreed with the shipowners in February 1746 that 9 shillings should be charged that year, but the colonists repudiated the bargain. They could well afford to do so, because there was plenty of shipping at the island to take home the crop; the captains had to sign their bills of lading at 7s. 6d.[2] The rates do not appear to have been very different in the Seven Years War: freight from St. Kitts to London was at 8 shillings in May 1757, from Antigua to London at 7 shillings in May 1758. At some time in the Seven Years War the freight from Jamaica was 10 shillings, but in 1758 it was only 6.

The rate between North America and the islands did not rise quite so much: 5 shillings a hundredweight seems to have been a fair freight from Philadelphia to the Leeward Islands in peace; in war it seems to have varied between 7s. 6d. and 9 shillings.

Although particular bargains like that of 1746 might fail, the rate of freight was governed more or less by the shipowners' costs. There was nothing mechanical in this determination, for there was quite as much English shipping at the islands in war as in peace, and hardly more goods to carry home.[3] Since the size of each island's crop varied considerably from year to year, there might be too many or too few ships to take it to market and their competition would lower or raise the rate, regardless of war and peace. Thus sugar was carried home from Antigua for only 5 shillings a hundredweight in 1747, because that year's crop was less than half the average, and those of all the islands

---

[1] Lascelles and Maxwell to Richard Gosling, Sept. 12, 1744, W. & G. ii; to A. Lynch, Jan. 7, 1744/5, ibid.; to Gedney Clarke, Sept. 4, 1756, vol. viii; to Samuel Carter, July 9, 1760, vol. ix.

[2] Lascelles and Maxwell to Thomas Applewhaite, March 1, 1745/6, W. & G. iii; to Foster March, Feb. 13, 1746/7, ibid.

[3] Prize goods were sent to England, but usually in prize ships.

were low. The shipowners appear to have relied on the equity of the planters to fix a reasonable rate; and though they often complained that the advance in freight did not keep up with the increase of their costs, they acknowledged at other times that the planters had treated them better than they were obliged to do.[1] They had always a remedy in reserve, for if they were disgusted by too many losses they might employ their vessels in another trade next year, or get them into the service of the Government.[2]

That threat, however, was not so easily executed, because most of the regular ships in the trade were partly owned in the island. The arrangement was useful to both parties in time of peace; the planter hoped to be sure of a passage for his goods on a vessel in which he was interested, and in the same way the shipowner counted on finding enough goods to make him a fair profit. Perhaps it was partly because they were also interested in the profits of shipping, that the planters sometimes consented to raise the rates of freight higher than they need. This connexion of interests must, however, have made it difficult to divert the ships to other uses, and the interest of the captains must have added to the embarrassment. The captains were very important people in this trade, for it was their influence as much as anything else which procured the homeward freights; indeed, it was often the captain rather than the ship, or even the shipowner, that determined the planters to load their goods on a particular vessel. This experience and prestige would be wasted if the ship were taken out of the trade; moreover, many captains were also part-owners, and seem to have had a veto on anything they did not like.[3] For these

[1] H. Lascelles and son to Thomas Applewhaite, March 17, 1739/40, Sept. 13, 1740, Aug. 29, 1741, W. & G. i; to Richard Morecroft, Feb. 20, 1740/1, ibid.; Lascelles and Maxwell to Applewhaite, Aug. 6, 1748, vol. iii.

[2] There were not enough ships in the West Indies to take off the crops of 1740, because so many owners had been tempted to take Government contracts (H. Lascelles and son to Francis March, Jamaica, Sept. 13, 1740, W. & G. i). At the same time it was reported in Philadelphia that the freight to the West Indies was very dear, because so many vessels were taken up for transports; shipowners refused cargoes of lumber which could only afford to pay a low rate, and reserved their vessels for cask goods (John Reynell to Samuel Dicker, Oct. 29, 1740, Reynell Letter-book, H.S.P.).

[3] Lascelles and Maxwell to Samuel Husbands, Feb. 5, 1757, W. & G. viii. In 1750 they talk of building a ship for Captain Husbands, as if it were his goodwill rather than theirs or the ship's that was important (to John Fairchild, Dec. 29, 1750, vol. v; to Samuel Husbands, Jan. 10, 1750/1, ibid.).

reasons many ships continued in the trade through good years and bad, and took whatever rates of freight the planters could be brought to give. If they had not done so, there were always some North Americans ready to take a cargo from the islands to England. The London shipowners particularly disliked their competition, and dwelt on the folly of trusting sugars to cheap and bad vessels.[1]

The war increased the cost of shipowning. Wages went up from 30 and 35 shillings a month to 70 and 80. This was not all the sailors' doing, for the press-gang made them really scarce. Sometimes they were not to be had at all; the delay of waiting for them added to the expense and made the vessel late for her market. The wage-bill was also increased by the necessity of waiting for convoy. Ships' stores and repairs were dearer, and the price of the ships themselves was kept up until 1759 by the demand for privateering; on the other hand the scarcity was somewhat eased by the sale of prize ships. In spite of all these discouragements, Messrs. Lascelles and Maxwell believed in 1744 that war was the best time to make a profit out of shipping; though they sometimes complained of difficulties in the Seven Years War, they afterwards looked back to it with regret.[2]

Many planters seem to have felt that these high rates of freight and insurance made all remittances of produce unprofitable. They did more than air this opinion in pamphlets;[3] some of them ceased to consign their sugars to London on their own account, and sold them in the islands, remitting bills to England for such expenses as they might have there. This often answered their purpose very well, but involved the buyer in a loss.[4] Besides, there were limits to it. Somebody had to send the produce to England, and if the planters would not do it on

---

[1] Lascelles and Maxwell to Thomas Applewhaite, March 1, 1745/6, W. & G. ii. They appear to have meant what they said (Henry Lascelles to John Frere, W. & G. A, p. 5).

[2] Henry Lascelles to Edward Lascelles, Nov. 6, 1740, W. & G. i; to Richard Morecroft, Jan. 30, 1740/1, ibid.; Lascelles and Maxwell to Nicholas Wilcox, Sept. 11, 1744, vol. ii; to John Newton, Jan. 10, 1750/1, vol. v; to Harriet Lynch, April 27, 1756, vol. vii; to Gedney Clarke, June 2, 1756, ibid.; to Samuel Husbands, June 6, 1768, vol. x.

[3] *Considerations relating to a New Duty upon Sugar* (2nd ed., with supplement, 1746), pp. 33, 41.

[4] Lascelles and Maxwell to John Harvie, Nov. 6, 1745, W. & G. ii; to John Brathwaite, March 25, 1747, vol. iii; to Nicholas Wilcox, Nov. 20, 1747, ibid.; to Philip Gibbes, Oct. 9, 1758, vol. viii.

their own accounts, they must accept some questionable bills from the merchants, whose credit was probably less established than their own.

§ vi. *War Taxes*

There remains to be considered one other charge upon the sugar-planter. He was more heavily taxed in war than in peace, both by Parliament and by his own legislature. With the worst will in the world, the islands could not avoid raising money for their defences; they sometimes had to pay for the years of neglect by a heavy and sudden increase in taxation. Thus the poll-tax of Montserrat rose from 7 shillings in 1743 to 32 in 1747; Mathew called this last tax the highest that any island had raised, and he was probably right.[1] It appears, however, from the figures that taxes by no means always rose in war time; some of the highest were laid in times of peace, or in the Spanish war which affected the Leeward Islands very little. There was nearly always some delay in passing the accounts, so that it is hard to tell whether the money was paid for present expenses or old debts. On the other hand, the levies of negro labour for the fortifications cost the slave-owners a great deal,

[1] I give the figures of all the islands for the sake of comparison:

	Antigua	Barbados	Montserrat	Nevis	St. Kitts	Jamaica
1739			6s. 9d. negro tax	4s. 6d. negro tax		
1740			..	9s. 6d.		
1741			4s. 6d.	7s.		
1742			5s. 6d.	3s. 7½d.		
1743			7s.	2s. 6d.		
1744			11s.	3s.		
1745			22s. 6d.	..		
1746			..	3s. 6d.		
1747			32s.	4s. 6d.		
1748			..	3s.		
1754		1s. 3d. negro tax		8s.	15s. negro tax	
1755		1s. 3d.		4s. 6d.	6s.	
1756	Sugar 9d. per cwt.	1s. 3d.			5s.	1s. negro tax
1757	8d.	7½d.			10s.	2s.
1758	1s.	1s. 10½d.			8s.	1s.
1759	6d.	2s. 6d.			7s.	1s.
1760	..	1s. 3d.			2s.	
1761	6d.	5s.				
1762	1d.					

for they were usually exacted without payment; the amount cannot be estimated.

The Assemblies were elected by the resident planters, and were naturally ready to throw as much of the burden as they could upon the absentees. St. Kitts and Antigua discriminated against them by taxing them at more than the ordinary rates. There was some excuse for this policy. If the tax had any effect upon the absentees, it would make them return to their plantations, where they would add to the military strength of the island and reinforce the discipline of the negroes.[1] It seemed a little hard that some planters should enjoy themselves in London or Bath upon the profits of estates which they left others to defend. There might, however, be some doubt whether a colonial legislature could decently or even lawfully punish His Majesty's subjects for living in whatever part of his dominions they thought fit; and since every planter aspired to be an absentee as soon as he could afford it, the Assemblies might be said to be discouraging honest industry.[2] Be that as it might, the absentees were a powerful body and could look after themselves. They had the ear of the Government; the Board of Trade allowed some of the taxing Acts to stand, but told Governor Mathew to reject such a clause for the future. The Assembly of Antigua held out for a time and refused to pass a money bill without it, but came to heel in 1746.[3]

Though their own legislatures laid upon them no insupportable burdens, the planters had to reckon with Parliament. The cost of the war was paid largely by loans, which needed to be secured by funds of additional taxation. The Treasury natur-

---

[1] There were presumably some absentees who thought it their interest or their duty to return to the islands in war-time; John White, an absentee Councillor of St. Kitts, told the Board of Trade in 1755 that he should not go back unless he was obliged to do so by a war with France (White to Pownall, June 21, 1755, C.O. 152/28, BB 52).

[2] Fane to the Board of Trade, Nov. 26, 1744, C.O. 152/24, Y 73; Antigua Council Minutes, July 23, 1742, C.O. 9/14; compare this with the argument of the Governor and Intendant of St. Domingue, that the luxury of absentees advertised the colony and drew new settlers to it (Vaudreuil and Laporte-Lalanne to Machault, June 10, 1755, A.N. Colonies C⁹ A 96).

[3] Mathew to the Board of Trade, April 15, 1743, C.O. 152/24, Y 61; Fane to the Board of Trade, Nov. 26, 1744, Y 73; Order in Council of March 7, 1744/5, C.O. 152/25, Y 133; Douglas to the Board of Trade, March 19, 1744/5, ibid., Y 77; Mathew to the Board of Trade, July 6, 1745, ibid., Y 139. A tax of this kind was proposed by the Assembly of Barbados but rejected by the Council (Henry Lascelles to Thomas Applewhaite, April 20, 1741, W. & G. i).

ally cast its eye upon sugar and its by-products. The West
India interest was always on the alert against a new duty. It
was talked of in the session of 1742–3, but Sandys, the Chancellor of the Exchequer, contented himself with taxing molasses.
The West India pamphleteers said that this reduced the price
of molasses from 16 shillings to 9s. 6d. the hundredweight, which
was equivalent to a duty of 2s. 7d. on every hundredweight of
sugar. The distiller could not raise the price upon the consumer, because the smuggler of French brandy would undersell
him, and the refiner who received less for his molasses had to
pay the planter less for his sugar.[1] The price of sugar did not
fall much in 1743 on account of this duty, because a great deal
was re-exported to the Continent that year; but the distilling
of molasses seems to have been affected, for the quantity excised
as low wines fell.[2] According to a later writer, the additional
duty did not even increase the revenue.[3] It continued nevertheless to be paid; the Jamaica Assembly complained later that while
it might have been bearable in war-time, it weighed very heavily
on the low prices of peace. That was the worst of duties raised
to fund loans; they had to be borne until the loans were repaid.[4]

There was a much more serious controversy in 1744 over
Henry Pelham's proposal to lay a new duty on sugar, and again
in 1759 over Legge's budget. The great question was, who
would pay the tax—the planter or the consumer? The Government and its supporters seem to have thought in 1744 that the
consumer would do so; they argued that the price had been
rising for some time without affecting the consumption, and
could safely go a little farther.[5] The planters and their advo-

---

[1] *Considerations relating to a New Duty on Sugar* (2nd ed.), pp. 25–6.

[2] The figures are:

1742	.	.	.	1,175,924 gallons
1743	.	.	.	980,494 ,,
1744	.	.	.	410,697 ,,
1745	.	.	.	543,415 ,,

The table (C.O. 390/3, f. 21) ends in 1745. The quantity had been over a million
gallons in every year but one since 1725.

[3] *Considerations relating to the laying any Additional Duty on Sugar from the British
Plantations* (London, 1747), p. 22.

[4] Address of the Council and Assembly to the King, April 14, 1749, C.O. 137/58.
Rum was exempted from a new duty on spirituous liquors in 1751 (Lascelles and
Maxwell to Edmund Duany, July 9, 1751, W. & G. v), but not from that of 1760
(Memorial of the Agents to Newcastle, Feb. 28, 1760, Add. MSS. 32902, f. 460).

[5] *Parl. Hist.* xiii. 640; Lascelles and Maxwell to Thomas Applewhaite, Jan. 17,
1743/4, W. & G. ii; to William Gibbons, Jan. 17, ibid.

cates earnestly denied it, though it is worth noticing that when the sugar duty was talked of, some of the very merchants who refused to admit that it could possibly raise the price, warehoused their sugars in the hope that it would.[1]

The planters' arguments were a little obscure. Duties, they said, had nothing to do with prices, which depended only on supply and demand. The additional duty on molasses had not raised the price but lowered it (they added, in the later controversies on this subject, that the duty of 1748 upon sugar had not prevented the fall of prices after the peace in that year).[2] They made out that the English market was always slightly overstocked with sugars because the colonies produced more than it could consume. They admitted that some sugar was re-exported, in fact they sometimes exaggerated the amount, in order to appeal to the zealots of the balance of trade; but they argued that the re-exportation only took place when there was an exceptional plenty in England and the prices were very low there, because the French could undersell the English at all other times.[3] This was quite wrong: sugar was rather re-exported when the price abroad was particularly high because the crops of the foreign colonies had failed or been detained by war. Since the Act of 1739 the planters had a weapon which they could use against the English consumer when they were not satisfied with the price he offered—they could send their sugars directly to the south of Europe. Although they had complained of the limitations which prevented them from taking advantage of this permission, they now said that the additional duty on sugar imported into England would compel them to resort to it.[4] Here they made a tactical mistake, for it was impossible to argue against everybody at the same time; some of their adversaries replied that they were delighted to hear this, for they welcomed anything that would increase our exports and the favourable balance of trade.[5] The planters did not really mean to put this threat in force; indeed they could not do so for ever, for, as Beckford said in 1748, the direct exportation to Europe was only profitable in war-time when our

---

[1] Lascelles and Maxwell to Florentius Vassall, Feb. 4, 1743/4, W. & G. ii.
[2] *Reasons against laying any new Tax upon Sugar*, in St. Kitts Council Minutes, June 25, 1759, C.O. 241/7.
[3] *Considerations relating to a new duty upon Sugar* (2nd ed.), pp. 8–10.
[4] Letter of James Knight, 1744 (undated), Add. MSS. 22677, f. 64.
[5] Watkins to Newcastle, Feb. 21, 1759, Add. MSS. 32888, f. 214.

control of the sea hindered the carriage of French sugars to market.[1]

The planters did not think it made much difference in the end whether they or the consumer bore the burden of this tax. If the consumer paid it, the high price would reduce his consumption, and production must begin to diminish soon afterwards. The small cultivators would be driven out of the business, and emigrate to the foreign islands. Many people had already gone to Essequibo and St. Croix, where they could continue to make sugar with advantage, rather than stay in the Empire and turn their hands to other crops;[2] for indeed the capital, labour, and experience of a sugar-planter could not be diverted to cotton, coffee, or ginger without disastrous loss. Thus the tax would turn our own planters into foreign competitors. The defence of the islands would be weakened by this emigration, and they would become a prey to the negroes or the enemy. Only the great capitalists would remain, and even they would be forced to stint their crops. The price of sugar would be kept down abroad while it rose at home, and the English refiners would suffer by the smuggling of Dutch refined sugars into the eastern counties.[3] Lastly, the planters reminded the Government that it had already killed the cultivation of indigo by a tax; they asked whether it wished to treat sugar in the same way. They repeated once more their invariable argument that it was lower duties that enabled the French producers to undersell them.[4]

This was not enough to convince. Money had to be found for the war, and if the sugar-planters did not pay it, somebody else must. Much was made of the antagonism between the landed and the planting interests. Light-headed Dodington

[1] *Parl. Hist.* xiv. 193.

[2] *Considerations relating to the laying any Additional Duty on Sugar from the British Plantations* (London, 1747), p. 16. The argument assumes that it was the poor who emigrated; that may have been true in the seventeenth century, but I do not believe it still was. It appears to have been rich capitalists who founded new plantations in Essequibo; indeed it is unlikely that anybody else would have been welcome there. We hear of servants, slaves, and tools imported there from Barbados, and new comers who taught the inhabitants how to make sugar—always a rich man's industry (*Storm van 's Gravesande*, ed. Sir C. Harris, Hakluyt Society, 1911, i. 211–13). In fact some of these planters continued to live in Barbados, like Gedney Clarke, who was Collector of Customs there.

[3] *Parl. Hist.* xiv. 192–5 (Beckford).

[4] *Considerations relating to a New Duty upon Sugar*, pp. 13–16; *Considerations relating to the laying any Additional Duty on Sugar from the British Plantations*, p. 8.

promised to vote against the duty in 1744 because it would ruin the planters, but admitted that they were the only people left to ruin since every other interest was undone by taxes already. Vernon acknowledged the same thing in other words.

'He is perhaps the only man in the opposition that declared to the committee that attended him, he would vote for the Sugar Bill, not but he was convinced the duty would fall upon the planter, and for that reason, because, he said, they would otherwise be for raising a new tax upon the people here, which would affect himself, and concluded that his shirt was near him but his skin was nearer.'[1]

The land-tax had already been raised on account of the war; why should not the sugar-planters pay something too?

The West India pamphleteers had to meet this argument. They pointed out truly that a land-tax of four shillings in the pound did not effectively amount to more than three because the assessments for it were too low; they added that the English landowner was only taxed upon his rental while they had to pay duty on their gross income. When the planters were asked why they did not contribute to the war, they answered that they did. Not only were their freights, costs, and premiums of insurance increased, but they raised additional taxes for their defence besides paying, in all the islands but Jamaica, the $4\frac{1}{2}$ per cent. duty which was supposed to be granted for the expenses of their own Government but was applied chiefly to other objects.[2]

Nevertheless, the sugar-planters were beginning to incur envy and dislike. The House of Commons was reported to be downright vindictive against them in 1759, and there was a strong feeling of hostility to them in certain quarters of the City.[3] The rising price of their produce and the fortunes which their absentees flaunted, had created a bad impression. They could not remove it by arguing that the prices were affected by transient influences which brought them no profit, or that the absentees were few and unrepresentative, and lived beyond

[1] Lascelles and Maxwell to James Bruce, Jan. 17, 1743/4, W. & G. ii; to George Hannay, Feb. 12, ibid.

[2] Antigua Assembly Minutes, Sept. 22, 1743, petition of the legislature, C.O. 9/15; *Considerations relating to the laying any Additional Duty upon Sugar from the British Plantations*, p. 13; *Considerations relating to a New Duty upon Sugar*, pp. 20–4.

[3] Henry Wilmot to the St. Kitts Committee of Correspondence, March 24, 1759, in St. Kitts Council Minutes, June 25, 1759, C.O. 241/7; Watkins to Newcastle, Dec. 19, 1758, Add. MSS. 32886, f. 401; Feb. 21 and 26, 1759, vol. 32888, ff. 214, 256.

their means.[1] (Beckford went farther and argued that nobody could be expected to spend his life in the disagreeable climate of the West Indies without the inducement of a handsome fortune.)[2] The landed gentry had a political grievance against them, too, for they had begun to usurp the Parliamentary representation of too many boroughs.[3] Beckford tried to defend his fellow planters in the House of Commons, but was interrupted by horse-laughs every time he uttered the word 'sugar'. Pitt tried to stem this tide of malice.

'He said the produce of the Sugar Colonies ought not to be put upon the foot of foreign luxury, that their produce was the labour of our own people, that they are supplied with everything from hence, that they sent home all their produce and are the support of our marine, that he did not know but the landed gentlemen seemed to consider themselves in a separate interest from the colonies, that he should ever consider the colonies as the landed interest of this Kingdom and it was a barbarism to consider them otherwise.'

These were fine sentiments, but they did not go down.[4]

The political history of the sugar taxes during these wars is worth following in some detail. The West India interest first tried to dissuade Pelham from laying one in 1743, and only had recourse to pamphleteering and canvassing against the Government when his mind appeared to be made up. It was a difficult thing to resist a tax proposed by the Chancellor of the Exchequer; the more so because the House had lately resolved to receive no petitions against money bills. A Barbadian Member of Parliament named Drax conceived the idea of effecting the same purpose by remonstrating against the existing duties as already too high; the ranting Alderman Heathcote, who would do anything to spite any Ministry, concurred with him, but the Speaker condemned this quibble.[5] Nevertheless, the planters had everything on their side. The Opposition voted, of course, against anything the Government proposed; Pitt, already regarded as the most dangerous speaker in the House, 'desired and received a brief' against the Bill. Sandys, whom Pelham had lately superseded as Chancellor of the Exchequer,

---

[1] Antigua Assembly Minutes, Sept. 22, 1743, C.O. 9/15; *Considerations relating to a New Duty upon Sugar*, pp. 11, 36; *Reasons against laying any new Tax upon Sugar*, C.O. 241/7. [2] *Parl. Hist.* xiv. 189.
[3] Watkins to Newcastle, Feb. 21, 1759, Add. MSS. 32888, f. 214.
[4] St. Kitts Council Minutes, June 25, 1759, C.O. 241/7.
[5] Lascelles and Maxwell to Thomas Applewhaite, Feb. 11, 1743/4, W. & G. ii.

would not do anything to help his supplanter; Carteret was struggling with Pelham for the control of the Cabinet and was suspected of instructing his friends underhand to vote against the tax. The Prince of Wales was said to have done so too.[1]

The planters struck a most fortunate bargain with the Irish and Scotch members who represented the linen interests. The object of the latter was to lay an additional tax on foreign linens, or to abolish the drawback of the duty on foreign linens exported to the colonies. The planters, as consumers in the colonies, had opposed this successfully in 1739, but now joined with the Scotch and Irish members in recommending this way of raising revenue as an alternative to the sugar tax.[2] Pelham got his duty through the committee but was defeated by twelve votes on the report stage of the Bill. He might perhaps have forced his measure upon the House, but he preferred to yield. He did not, however, allow the linen-manufacturers to tax the colonial consumer, but found the necessary revenue in another way. The linen interest had now served the planters' turn; some West India merchants thought it imprudent to keep up the alliance, for its success could only save the islands from the sugar duty at a heavy cost to their pocket. The Planters' Club in London thought otherwise; the sugar tax was only put off, and would sooner or later be revived unless an alternative source of revenue was kept in reserve. In fact the sugar and linen interests were still supporting each other in 1755; the legislature of Antigua then instructed its agent to resist the Hamburg linen-importers' proposal to abolish the bounties on Scotch and Irish linen.[3]

The planters were right in thinking that the sugar tax was only postponed. They were saved from it in 1745 by an additional duty on wines and in 1746 by one on glass and malt spirits. Pelham continued to think that sugar would bear another duty, and made up his mind in 1747 to impose one in

[1] Lascelles and Maxwell to Thomas Applewhaite, Jan. 17, 1743/4, W. & G. ii; to James Bruce, Jan. 17, to John Frere, Feb. 14, 1743/4, ibid.; Parliamentary diary of the Hon. Philip Yorke, Feb. 13 and 20, 1743/4, Parl. Hist. xiii. 640, 652-5.

[2] Samuel Martin to the Montserrat Committee of Correspondence, Feb. 24, 1743/4, Montserrat Assembly Minutes, May 26, 1744, C.O. 177/4; Lascelles and Maxwell to John Fairchild, Jan. 17, 1743/4, W. & G. ii; to George Hannay, Feb. 12 and March 12; to James Bruce, March 12; to Conrade Adams, April 20, 1744; to John Fairchild, March 2, 1744/5, ibid.

[3] Ibid.; Nathaniel Newnham to Stone, Feb. 19, 1744/5, Add. MSS. 32704, f. 77; Antigua Council Minutes, Sept. 23, 1755, and April 20, 1756, C.O. 9/21.

the form of a subsidy on dry goods imported. The planters found that the country party had deserted them; they had no choice but to submit.[1]

The sugar duty of 1759 nearly caused a Cabinet crisis. It was Legge's tax, and Newcastle was for it, though he had fulsomely assured Pitt that he looked upon the Sugar Colonies as a most valuable part of the possessions of the Crown.[2] His friends and advisers in the City strongly urged to him to support it, representing that nothing would be so popular with the landed interest. Pitt disliked it, but he would consent even less to any of Legge's other schemes. He disclaimed responsibility for it, and told the West India Agents that taxes were not in his department and he should consider them as a private Member of Parliament from his place in the House. This was a curious attitude for a Secretary of State, even in a coalition Ministry and in those days. Legge compromised on an additional 5 per cent. on certain dry goods, of which sugar was the most important. It amounted to 1s. 6d. on each hundredweight.[3] In the event Pitt dared not openly resist, though he defended Beckford from the mockers. He could not deny that the Government must have money. He sulked, and contrived to quarrel with Legge over the manner while he assented ungraciously to the substance of the measure. In fact this dispute dissolved for ever the partnership of Pitt and Legge, which they had so much aired a few years earlier.[4] The planters were powerless, for the House was so hostile to them that it would have voted any tax on sugar which Legge could have asked. The duty certainly cannot be said to have raised the price of sugar, which fell at

[1] Lascelles and Maxwell to Applewhaite, Bruce and Lake, Dec. 20, 1747, W. & G. iii; to Joseph Jordan, Dec. 19, ibid.; *Parl. Hist.* xiv. 155–95 (Henry Pelham and Beckford).

[2] Newcastle to Pitt, March 27, 1755, G.D. 8/51. There was a doubt whether Newcastle intended to alter the drawbacks on refined sugar; Pitt was up in arms about it, and Newcastle swore, falsely as it would appear, that he had never meant it.

[3] Wilmot to St. Kitts Committee of Correspondence, March 24, 1759, St. Kitts Council Minutes, June 25, 1759, C.O. 241/7; Legge to Newcastle, Jan. 25, Add. MSS. 32887, f. 333; Newcastle's memoranda of Feb. 19 and 28, March 8, 1759, vol. 32888, ff. 173, 275, 408; Hardwicke to Newcastle, March 8, f. 287.

[4] West's House of Commons report, March 9, 1759, Add. MSS. 32888, f. 428. (West mentions one remarkable fact : the politician Samuel Martin, though a West Indian, supported Legge, saying he believed the tax would fall on the planters but they could well afford it.) Watkins to Newcastle, March 22, 1759, vol. 32889, f. 197; Newcastle's notes of a conversation with Viry, March 24, f. 221.

the end of the year and never rose again to such a height. This tax, like the others, was permanent, and as it was levied at the artificial valuation of the Book of Rates it weighed heavier in peace than on the higher prices of war. On the other hand the price of sugar never came down to the level of the thirties, and it might be argued that it was the tax, among other things, that prevented it from doing so.

§ vii. *The Planter's Profit and Loss in War-time*

We are now able to calculate very roughly the cost of the war to the planters. The insurance rose by about 21 per cent. of the value of the homeward cargoes. Exactly how the sugars were valued for insurance, does not clearly appear, but perhaps the safest figure to take is the price of sugars in the islands; it probably represents in the long run the equivalent of the net proceeds in London. If we take Barbados as our example, let us say 21 per cent. of 30 shillings currency, which is 6s. 3d. currency. Freight rose by 4s. 6d. sterling upon an average, and English duties by 3 shillings, of which only 1s. 6d. was imposed in the war of 1744, and that at the very end. It may be uncertain who lost most by the duties in the last resort, but the importer certainly had to pay them before the sugars could be sold, so they may justly be included in this calculation. The cost of necessaries may be held to have increased 35 per cent., but it is difficult to know how to assess this article in terms of shillings per hundredweight. The most reliable West India pamphleteer reckons it at 8s. 11d. sterling in the war of 1744, but even his figures and calculations are rather doubtful.[1] It is impossible to define plantation necessaries, or to guess the value of the imports from Africa and North America to the islands— even the statistics of the imports from England rest upon purely conventional values. We do not know how much of the cost of these articles was met by the rum and molasses; estimates varied from a third to very nearly the whole. The figure of 8s. 11d. sterling looks somewhat high, from what little is known of these factors, so it would perhaps be safe to allow something for West India exaggeration and guess 8s. 11d. currency. This is an arbitrary figure, but it needs some effrontery to publish a calculation of this sort at all. The result for the War of 1744 is 15s. 2d. currency and 6 shillings sterling; translate the whole

[1] *Considerations relating to a New Duty on Sugar* (2nd ed.), p. 42.

into sterling at 35 per cent. and the amount is nearly 15s. 9d. sterling. If I am right in thinking that the prices rose from about a guinea to 38 shillings, it will appear that the planter neither gained nor lost very much by the war.[1]

The price did not rise by nearly so much in the Seven Years War; but then it had not fallen back during the peace to the level of 1739. There were never more complaints from the consumer.

The other tests which can be applied produce very much the same results. The price of sugar in the islands did not vary much from war to peace. The highest prices of all are peace prices, but so are the lowest; the average seems to have been somewhere near 30 shillings in Barbados and 35 shillings in Antigua from 1748 to 1763, the period for which the statistics are fullest. This stability is a strong testimony to the efficiency of the navy if it is compared with the great fall of prices which took place at the French islands as soon as a war began.

It is almost impossible to make any sense of the rates of exchange: they did not correspond with the size of the crops or the price in London: war and peace seem to have made no ascertainable difference to them.[2] The Government spent more

---

[1] This calculation differs a little from that of the *Considerations*. The author does not include the duty, which had not yet been laid; but he underestimates the increase of the price of sugar, because he takes as his starting-point the price of 1739, which was somewhat higher than the average for the decade before the war.

[2] The following table will make clear the difficulties of the subject:

| | Antigua | | Barbados | | London Sugar Price |
	Exchange Premium	Crop	Exchange Premium	Crop	s.　d.
1739	High	Large	Low	Rather small	25　8
1741			Very low	Large	30　5
1744			High	Very small	30　7
1746	Moderate	Moderate	High	Rather small	39　5
1747	Moderate	Very small			42　5
1750	High	Moderate			27　9
1751	High	Moderate	High	Rather small	30　6
1752	Very high	Rather small			38　7
1753	Low to moderate	Very large			33　0
1754	Moderate to high	Very small	High	Moderate	35　8
1757			Moderate to high	Moderate	37　1
1758	Very low	Very large	Moderate to high	Moderate	42　5
1760			Moderate	Moderate	..
1761	Moderate	Large	Moderate	Rather large	..
1762			Low to moderate	Rather large	..
1763			Moderate to high	Rather large	..

in the West Indies and drew more bills in war-time; the Dutch of St. Eustatius bought prize goods and paid for them with bills. Undoubtedly the discount tended to diminish for these reasons, but even stronger forces seem to have been driving it up.[1]

The islands often complained of scarcity of money, but the legislatures made no attempt in this period to keep it in circulation by arbitrarily raising its value, until the end of the Seven Years War. Then Jamaica passed a law to increase the nominal value of Spanish dollars, and Barbados later considered following the example. The absentees and merchants in England were up in arms. Alderman Beckford, though an ostentatious lover of his native island, appeared before the Board of Trade to complain of the injury to credit, by which he meant creditors. This is not surprising, for the Beckford family had made its huge fortunes by a judicious combination of money-lending with planting. Daniel Lascelles, who had lent very large sums to the planters of Barbados, was equally indignant when he heard of the law which had been proposed there. The Board of Trade recommended the repeal of the Jamaica Act.[2]

Probably the conditions of exchange and currency were more affected by the demand for money in Europe than was usually recognized. An anonymous writer suggested this soon after the Peace of Paris. He accounted for the scarcity of cash in the colonies in this way among others: 'For that the want of money

A 'high' rate of exchange in this table means a high premium of exchange—45 per cent. for Barbados or 80 per cent. for Antigua; 'low' means 30 per cent. for Barbados and 50 per cent. for Antigua. I have not thought it right to make any reference to the imports into the colonies, because they were constantly rising and it would be difficult to classify them as high or low, also because the imports from England, the only ones for which we have any figures, were seldom paid for by bills: they were ordered by the planters and set against their credit balances in the hands of the factors. The prices of sugars—presumably Barbados and Leeward Island sugars—are taken from the sales of the King's sugars in London. They are not very good averages to take, but are better than none. They appear to be a little below such other market rates as I can discover; that was to be expected, since the worst sugars were usually given in payment of the $4\frac{1}{2}$ per cent. tax.

[1] Thus though the Government bills for subsisting Cathcart's forces affected the Jamaica rate of exchange, and although a ring of moneyed men tried to keep it at 110, it soon recovered to the normal rate of 125 and even rose to 135 and 140. The contractors for the remittance attributed this to the cash they had sent to Jamaica in order to break the ring (*Calendar of Treasury Books, 1742–5*, p. 7), but others ascribed it to the brisk trade with the Spanish Main. (Colebrooke to Pelham, Sept. 1, 1741, Bodleian Library, North MSS. a 6, f. 126.)

[2] *Journal of the Commissioners for Trade and Plantations, 1759–63*, pp. 85, 87, 90–1. Lascelles and Maxwell to T. Stevenson and sons, April 28 and Oct. 2, 1762, W. & G. ix.

in Europe in the last years of the war, drew specie from all parts of the globe, where it was to be found, and therefore must have drawn from our colonies.'[1] It was not that the planters invested in English funds—there are very few records of it—but the shortage of money in Europe caused the creditors to make special efforts to draw home their debts. This would increase the demand for bills in the colonies and might even make it profitable to send gold to England.

Perhaps this will become clearer from an examination of the effect of war upon the planter's credit. It exposed his estate to some danger of invasion and therefore lessened its value. Old creditors became anxious about the security of their debts, and new correspondents refused to agree to advances. Messrs. Lascelles and Maxwell, for example, made many efforts to contract their credits on account of the war.[2] It is true that they used the peace as an argument to the same purpose, alleging the low price of sugars as a reason for securing themselves against the bankruptcy of the planters; the logic of creditors, like that of debtors, is versatile and can turn opposite premisses to the same conclusion. However, the sincerity of their arguments to their old debtors is proved by their reluctance to enter into engagements with new ones.[3]

Security was not the only consideration. The planter's chief creditor was usually his factor, with whom he first ran into debt by casual overdrafts and often ended by giving a bond or a mortgage for a loan. The high freights, insurances, and taxes of war-time obliged the factor to employ in his trade a larger capital than he would have wanted in peace; the sugars could not be sold till these had been paid, and the buyers were unusually slow in settling their accounts.[4] Meanwhile half the planters had drawn bills on the strength of their sugars, and these had to be honoured.[5] Besides, it might be a factor's duty to his correspondents to warehouse their sugars and wait for a better market. How could he do this if he was distressed for

[1] Add. MSS. 38373, f. 130.
[2] Lascelles and Maxwell to John Fairchild, Feb. 13, 1743/4, W. & G. ii; to Nicholas Rice, Sept. 6, 1744; George Maxwell to Henry Slingsby, May 4, 1745; to John Brathwaite, Nov. 1745, ibid.
[3] Lascelles and Maxwell to Nicholas Newton, Aug. 6, 1748, W. & G. iii; to Edward Pare, Dec. 9, 1746, ibid.
[4] George Maxwell to James Bruce, Feb. 5, 1747/8, and June 16, 1748, W. & G. iii.
[5] Lascelles and Maxwell to Jacob Allin, Nov. 27, 1745, W. & G. ii.

money? When they were very hard put to it in the rebellion of
1745, Lascelles and Maxwell had to sell off their correspondents'
sugars at any rate in order to save their own credit; they began
with the property of those who had drawn large bills on them,
but were forced to go farther and sell all the sugars consigned
to them.   In such an emergency, how could they be blamed?[1]

The factor had the less to spare for loans when the ordinary
demands of his profession increased in this way. Moreover he
was himself forced to borrow in emergencies: in some degree he
seems to have been a mere channel through which the credit
of the London banker reached the planter.[2] Money was always
harder to borrow in war-time; the reason which Lascelles and
Maxwell usually gave was the universal desire to speculate in
the public funds. They asked their debtors how anybody could
expect money at 5 per cent. on a West India security when the
possessors could make 10 or 20 per cent. in six months by buying
and selling Government stocks? At the beginning of the Seven
Years War all the money was mobilized for speculation on the
war, and towards the end it was all called out again for speculation on the peace.[3] Accordingly it was at the crises of English
credit that the factors cried loudest for repayments—the rebellion of 1745, the great fall of the stocks in the winter of 1747–8,
another financial crisis in 1753, and the chronic shortage of
money at the end of the Seven Years War. It mattered very
little whether the colonial legislatures tinkered with the currency, or the drawers of bills combined to raise the rate of
exchange: the credit of the Sugar Colonies, and perhaps their
plenty or scarcity of money too, depended most of all on the
financial weather in London.

---

[1] Lascelles and Maxwell to Joseph Jordan, Jan. 8, 1745/6, W. & G. ii; to
William Gibbons, Jan. 15, ibid.

[2] Lascelles and Maxwell to Benjamin Charnocke, Nov. 3, 1746, W. & G. iii;
to Samuel Husbands, Nov. 20, 1747, ibid.; to Jeremiah Browne, May 20, 1751,
vol. v.

[3] George Maxwell to J. and A. Harvie, Aug. 21 and Nov. 8, 1755, W. & G. vii;
to Richard Husbands, Feb. 5, 1757, vol. viii; to T. Stevenson and sons, April 29,
1760, vol. ix.

XI

ENGLAND AND SPAIN IN THE WEST INDIES, 1748–61

THE period of colonial warfare which is discussed in this book began with a single combat against Spain which was complicated in 1744 by a war against France; it ended with a single combat against France, to which was added in 1762 a war against Spain. The first Spanish war of 1739 was described in the earlier chapters of this book; the description was followed by an account of the strategy and economic effect of the French wars. It is time now to say something of the second Spanish war of 1762. The West India colonies were, for the most part, more immediately concerned with the French wars and more profoundly affected by them; but the picture of England's imperial policy would not be complete without an account of her intricate dealings with France and Spain, which led up to the Family Compact and the War of 1762. For this purpose, it is necessary to turn back to the story of Anglo-Spanish relations, and to take it up at the Peace of Aix-la-Chapelle, which put an end to the War of 1739.[1]

§ i. *The Treaties of 1748 and 1750*

The South Sea Company assumed that the Government would get the Assiento renewed for it at the peace; but that was by no means certain. The attitude of the Court of Spain on this subject was constant and definite. It had no intention of suffering any revival of the Assiento trade, if that could possibly be avoided; indeed it does not seem to have wanted to grant a single monopoly to the subjects of any nation.[2] Instead, it allowed the enthusiastic dotard Macanaz, who represented it at the conferences of Breda in 1746–7, to propose the establishment of a free port for slaves, to which the subjects of all nations might trade. This scheme, as he pointed out, would work to the advantage of England, as she was the strongest slave-trading power on the African coast.[3] The Court of France, which took upon itself the direction and representation of Spanish foreign

[1] For the earlier history of these relations, see Chapters I to III.

[2] See the denunciations of the Assiento by Ulloa (*Restablecimiento de las Fabricas y Comercio Español* (Madrid, 1740), ii. 17, 100). His chief objection to it is the excuse and opportunity it affords for smuggling.

[3] Macanaz's scheme transmitted by Sandwich, April 21, 1747, S.P. 84/425, f. 79.

policy in the conferences with England, was not anxious to snatch the Assiento for its own subjects. It had consented to go without it by the Treaty of Fontainebleau (1743), but some of its advisers hoped that England could be induced to accept a compensation for both Assiento and Annual Ship, which gave her an advantage by furnishing too many occasions for smuggling.[1]

The South Sea Company on the other hand seems to have hoped at least to enjoy the Assiento for the years which were unexpired at the outbreak of the war in 1739. Indeed it went farther, and revived the arguments for a longer period; it claimed that the thirty years must be interpreted as thirty trading years, and added that the debts which the Crown of Spain owed it could not conveniently be paid except by such an extension.[2] If the Assiento were renewed for no more than the four years which were due according to the Spanish interpretation, it would hardly be worth the Company's while to resettle the factories and start the whole machine again. Be that as it might, the Directors thus set the English Ministry, in so far as it accepted their claims, a much more complicated problem than the mere renewal of the contract. The period must be defined, and the question of indebtedness between the Company and the Crown of Spain must be brought into consideration.[3]

It is not very easy, even on a small point like this, to follow the distracted and tortuous motions of the English Ministers. In 1747 Newcastle was pressing very hard to detach Spain from France, and was willing to sacrifice to that political advantage a purely commercial point like the Assiento. His colleagues were a little less ready for this, though some of them, like Bedford, were willing then and later to buy a separate peace with Spain by concessions of an even more striking nature.[4] Newcastle had his way. He told Sandwich, the English plenipotentiary, that though he was to try to have the Assiento ques-

---

[1] Instructions to St. Séverin, Feb. 29, 1748, *Recueil des Instructions aux Ambassadeurs de France, Hollande*, iii. 128; A.E. Mém. et Doc. Espagne, 80, f. 111; Angleterre, 41, ff. 188, 200.   [2] *V. supra*, pp. 53–4.

[3] Court of Directors, South Sea Company, to Keene, March 16, 1748/9, Add. MSS. 32816, ff. 258–9; Bedford to Keene, Aug. 17, 1749, S.P. 94/136, with enclosed paper of Burrell and Bristow.

[4] I refer to the scheme for giving back Gibraltar; some account of it will be found in Sir Richard Lodge's *Studies in Eighteenth Century Diplomacy*, pp. 238–52, 295, 314–16.

tion left to be decided after the peace by commissioners, he might at last yield, give up the Assiento altogether (but not the private debts of the Crown of Spain to the Company), and accept Macanaz's scheme of a free port.[1] After the conferences of Breda had come to nothing (for European, not for American reasons), the attitude even of Newcastle seems to have hardened. In fact he had ceased to wish for a separate peace with Spain, because it would not end the war of France against England or of Spain against Austria.[2] Bedford too was perhaps less anxious for it, since he had been forced to see that it would not enable England to preserve his favourite conquest of Louisbourg. Sandwich was therefore instructed in 1748 to get the Assiento Treaty renewed.[3]

So he did; but that was only the beginning of the difficulty. First, what was to be the period of the renewal? By the preliminary treaty the contract was continued for the number of years during which the Company had not enjoyed it—the phrase was *non-jouissance*. This left the question between the King of Spain's and the Company's interpretations perfectly open; but the Court of Spain, if it had to yield to any renewal at all, had certainly intended to have that question closed, and in its own way. It was not Sotomayor, the Spaniard, but St. Séverin, the Frenchman, who had negotiated the preliminaries with Sandwich, and had accepted from him the fatal phrase *non-jouissance*. He turned this blunder—if indeed it was a blunder—very ingeniously to account by taking Sotomayor's part against Sandwich, and averting, at least for the period of the conferences, that detachment of Spain which England had worked hard to obtain. Sandwich and Sotomayor concerted a declaration that England and Spain would discuss an equivalent for the unexpired years of the Assiento; but as long as Spain depended on the support of France, for reducing those years from ten or fifteen to four, Sotomayor could do nothing very dangerous behind St. Séverin's back.[4]

[1] Newcastle to Sandwich, April 11, 1747, Add. MSS. 32808, f. 61.
[2] Tabuerniga to Carvajal, with Newcastle's emendations, March 1748, Add. MSS. 32811, f. 411. See the discussion of these questions in *An Apology for a late Resignation, The Resignation Discuss'd*, and *National Prejudice Opposed to the National Interest*, three pamphlets of 1748; also Lodge, op. cit., chapters vi and vii.
[3] Newcastle to Sandwich (very private), March 29, 1748, S.P. 84/431.
[4] For the history of this negotiation, see S.P. 84/431 to 435 and Add. MSS. 32811 to 32814, *passim*; also Lodge, op. cit., pp. 337–410.

It would be tedious to describe the delays, obstinacies, and recriminations through which this question passed to Newcastle's final surrender—especially as there was more noise than real importance in them. It was not really the Assiento so much as Newcastle's refusal to proceed without the co-operation of Austria, that caused the delays at Aix-la-Chapelle and the estrangement between him and Sandwich; though some part of both was ascribed to the smaller and less important question. Sandwich was always for yielding to Spain on this point. He argued that as he had been authorized to give up the Assiento altogether in the last resort at Breda, he might surely be permitted now to accept the renewal for four years. It was no less important and possible now than it had been then to detach Spain from France, and a direct concession to her on this small point would put her under an obligation to us instead of France.[1] Even our allies the Dutch, who were also our rivals in trade, showed no desire to support our demand for an extended Assiento. Their chief plenipotentiary plainly told Sandwich and Newcastle that we were in the wrong. Newcastle yielded at last; the four years were accepted.

According to the declaration of Sandwich and Sotomayor, the South Sea Company was not to be put in possession of its rights until the two Crowns had made some attempt at negotiating an equivalent for them. The question which the English Ministry had to face was, what were those rights, and who was to receive the equivalent?

The claims of the Company were of three kinds. First, the privileges of the Assiento and the Annual Ship. Second, the debts due from the King of Spain, which could be described as public or national in their nature, that is, caused by the diplomatic relations of England and Spain; the most important of this class were the Reprisalia, or seizures of the Company's property during hostilities between the two countries. Lastly there were the private debts of the King of Spain, for money actually advanced him by the Company acting as his banker or partner in the South Sea trade—such as the sum lent him at the beginning of the contract, or his quarter part of the capital stock which the Company advanced on his behalf.

The value of the first class in equity was very doubtful. The

---

[1] Sandwich to Newcastle, May 31, 1748, Add. MSS. 32812, f. 220; Sandwich to Anson, June 26 and Aug. 7, 1748; Add. MSS. 15957, ff. 69, 78.

Company's adversaries renewed their argument that the Assiento and Annual Ship damaged the trade of the nation as a whole; and the Company itself had always underrated them for purposes of its own. On its own showing it ought to be glad to get rid of those onerous privileges for nothing; the only excuse for demanding a recompense was the inconvenience and loss of revenue which they caused to the King of Spain so long as they subsisted.[1] Of course the Company did not draw these deductions, but asked cheerfully for the revival of its privileges as if for something valuable, in order to raise the price at which it would abandon them. It even exploited the unprofitableness of the Assiento proper. When it asked for a prolongation of the contract in order to repay itself out of the negro duties the debts due from the King of Spain, it was careful to point out that the Assiento itself brought in nothing but loss and that its continuation must therefore be accompanied by that of the Annual Ship.

The second class, the 'public' debts, had been the subject of much negotiation and complaint before the war broke out; in fact, as the reader will remember, it furnished the occasion of the outbreak.[2] The Company had demanded huge sums on account of the Reprisalia, ignoring (according to the Spaniards) the fact that a part of these sums had been paid, or the seized effects restored, to its own agents. It had added, with very little justification, such secondary charges as the maintenance of its factories during the suspensions of their activity which arose from the same cause. It now made a further claim for the effects seized in the 'third Reprisalia' of 1739. The directors piled item upon item in this account, and Newcastle was quite right to regard it as 'swollen'. Moreover, demands of this nature were incidental to the wars which had broken out between England and Spain. The English Government considered that it might lawfully give them up as an affair which properly belonged to the relations of the two Crowns, or that it might even regard them as annulled by the outbreak of war which put an end to all engagements between the two countries.[3]

The private debts of the King of Spain to the Company were a different matter. Although the Assiento Treaty was a public engagement between the two Crowns, some of the transactions

---

[1] 'The British Trade to the Spanish West Indies considered', Add. MSS. 32819, ff. 188–99.   [2] V. supra, pp. 52–5.
[3] Newcastle to Keene, Feb. 12, 1749/50, Add. MSS. 32820, ff. 193–8.

which were founded upon it were exactly like any other business transactions between partners in trade or between banker and client. The Company had paid orders drawn upon it by the King of Spain, sometimes more than it was in cash for his account, and had advanced money for him, with his consent, in its own operations. These demands would have been incontestably valid if only the amounts had not been in question. But the Company, whose financial character was universally regarded as shady after the Bubble, had never produced its accounts in such a form as to convince the King of Spain that he was credited with all the real profits, or that the capital of which he was debited with a quarter was really used in trade. The Spanish Ministers hinted that if the accounts were sifted on both sides the balance would prove to be due not to the Company but to the Crown of Spain. The English Ministers believed, however, that the Company had a large and valid demand against Spain on this account,[1] and that the King could not in any negotiation sign away the private rights and properties of his subjects without their consent. Lord Chancellor Hardwicke was particularly strong on this point: the Crown could not give up the Company's rights for nothing, though it could give them up for a compensation of a hundred thousand pounds—a view which the Duke of Newcastle found rather strange.[2]

It was not often that Hardwicke and Newcastle disagreed for long; but there was an important question at issue here. If the Company's real claims could be ascertained, and Spain induced to admit them as valid, what form was the compensation to take? To whom was it to be paid—to the Company or to the nation? At first sight it would naturally be due to the Company; but that was not so clear to Newcastle.

He did not view the subject in a purely commercial light; still less did he regard it as one which concerned the Company alone. He said many times, in the negotiations which led up

---

[1] Deputy-Governor Bristow was reported to have said, disclaiming all affectation, that he believed the Company would be awarded half a million if the cause were taken into Chancery; this was certainly a great reduction from the original demand of £1,367,567 (Wall to Ensenada, Sept. 25, 1750, Add. MSS. 32823, f. 305).

[2] Wall to Ensenada, ibid.; to Carvajal, Sept. 25, f. 309; Newcastle to Hardwicke, Sept. 8/19, 1750, Add. MSS. 32722, ff. 369–70; Hardwicke to Newcastle, Sept. 15, 1750, f. 422.

to the Treaty of 1750, that the value of a satisfactory commercial agreement with Spain was chiefly political. He had already been so inept as to imagine, in the middle of the crisis of 1738, that he could tempt La Quadra to adjust the commercial and maritime disputes by hinting at the advantages of a political alliance.[1] He had been willing in 1747 (though less so the next year) to sacrifice the Assiento in order to detach Spain from France. He now wanted to complete the process of detachment, which had begun at Aix-la-Chapelle on account of some concessions into which St. Séverin forced Sotomayor. He wanted, in fact, to drive a wedge between France and her ally Spain, as the French Court was beginning to drive one between him and his ally Austria.[2]

He had help in the Court of Spain itself. Although the Ministers Carvajal and Ensenada had differentiated themselves by 1754 as the Anglophile and the Francophile, they were still in 1748 or even 1750 comparatively indistinguishable in their foreign policies. Both were 'national' Ministers of a national King (for Ferdinand VI, unlike Philip V, had been born a Spaniard), and their policy was: Spain for the Spaniards, and independence in foreign affairs. This independence could only be achieved by a slight relaxation of the tie which bound Spain to France. Ensenada never meant to go farther. He believed that a renewal of the conflict between England and France was inevitable, and wished to make Spain the arbiter between them —an arbiter to be handsomely paid by such bribes as the restitution of Gibraltar. In the meantime he was for contracting a neutrality of limited duration.[3] Carvajal was more inclined to England; but even he told Keene, in a parable, that while he desired the friendship of England he had no intention of burning his boats with France. Keene credited him with the maxim 'To live well with England, tho' at as cheap a rate as he can'.[4]

Newcastle seldom thought anything impossible that he strongly desired. He did not mean to let Spain remain

[1] Newcastle to Keene, Jan. 26, 1738/9, S.P. 94/134; Keene to Newcastle, Feb. 23, 1739, S.P. 94/133.

[2] Newcastle to Keene, Oct. 26, 1749, Add. MSS. 32819, ff. 37–8; Feb. 12, 1749/50, vol. 32820, f. 193; Dec. 20, 1750, vol. 32825, f. 295; Wall to Carvajal, Feb. 5, 1750, vol. 32820, ff. 132–4.

[3] Ensenada, memorandum of 1746, in A. Rodríguez Villa, *Don Cenon de Somodevilla* (Madrid, 1878), pp. 37–41; memorandum of 1751, ibid., pp. 119–21.

[4] Keene to Newcastle, March 22, 1750, Add. MSS. 32820, ff. 309–13; Aug. 13, 1750, *Private Correspondence of Sir Benjamin Keene* (ed. Lodge), p. 244.

merely neutral, but was determined to attract her, if not to an English alliance, to something not far short of it. He wanted to reconvert her to 'the old, Spanish, venerable principle, *Pace con Inguilterra, Guerra avec toute la Terra*'.[1] Indeed he did not see how Spain could, in the circumstances of the time, cease to be pro-French without becoming pro-English. Here he proved to be wrong; but the first steps to neutrality and to an English alliance were the same. They both led away from France, and thus Newcastle was helped more than he was hindered by the 'national' dispositions of the Spanish Ministers.

He wanted a commercial agreement which should symbolize the independence of Spain by the very fact that it had been negotiated without French help or intervention. It should create good relations between the English trading interest and the Spanish Government, whose mutual grievances had been such a source of war in the past. Lastly it should irritate France against the diplomatic infidelity of Spain and against the preference shown to the rival English manufactures. For these reasons Newcastle and Keene refused to be content with tacit or underhand exemptions and privileges. It was not only the privilege itself but its publicity that they desired, for the ostentation of Anglo-Spanish cordiality in the face of the world and the mortification of French diplomats.

Newcastle was therefore indifferent to the interests of the Company, so long as he was not terrified by the prospect of Parliamentary noise. At first he saw little reason to be afraid of that. The Company no longer had all the influence that so large a financial corporation might expect to have. Newcastle had been ready to sacrifice its Assiento for political considerations in 1747, and would have no objection to doing so again, but for the legal difficulties that oppressed his friend Hardwicke. Still less would he object to sacrificing it for another commercial advantage of a different kind.

What commercial advantages could we want from Spain? A direct participation in the trade of Spanish America was not to be hoped for. The trade of Spain in Europe was by no means to be neglected, especially as a great deal of it was indirectly a trade with the Spanish colonies, and according to some writers—chiefly, it is true, interested parties—the only proper or advan-

---

[1] Newcastle to Keene, Aug. 22, 1750, Add. MSS. 32823, f. 112. The Spanish is Newcastle's.

tageous kind of trade with them. Since the Treaty of 1667, however, we had had little to ask for our traders to Spain, who had been placed on a very favourable footing. The privileges of that treaty had been renewed and confirmed by another, negotiated in 1715 by the notorious George Bubb Dodington. Persuaded by money or despair, the Spanish Court had then been ready to grant almost anything England could ask: it promised that the English traders should never be obliged to pay higher duties than those they had paid upon the same goods in the reign of Carlos II, or those paid now by the King of Spain's own subjects or any other foreigners.

Dodington's treaty had protected the English trade until the outbreak of the war in 1739. The Spanish Government then took advantage of the absence of the English merchants, who had always joined with the French and the Dutch in defending the privileges of foreign traders at Cadiz. It raised the duties on several classes of goods and the valuations on yet more. In some cases the increase amounted to 6 or 7 per cent. (England, by the way, had likewise raised the import duties on Spanish goods during the war, although none were supposed to be imported.) Raising the valuations was probably fair enough: the money price of many kinds of goods must have altered considerably since the reign of Carlos II, but they still paid duties at the old rate. The English traders, however, would have had a clear case for exemption from these increases upon their return to Spain, if only Dodington's treaty had been renewed at Aix-la-Chapelle. By some unexplained oversight it was not. Newcastle had in the end to admit that he had forgotten to give any instructions about it, and Sandwich had been hurried into the preliminary treaty by St. Séverin, so that it slipped his memory too. At first sight the omission did not seem very important, and it might be rectified in the definitive treaty; but when it came to that point, Sotomayor would not allow a clause to be put in for confirming the Treaty of 1715 without fresh orders from his Court. Sandwich was once more in a hurry to sign, and decided not to wait a month for Madrid to declare itself on this petty point.[1]

Sandwich and Newcastle ought to have foreseen the trouble which arose from their neglect, for a point once missed in the game of diplomacy with Spain was lost beyond recovery.

[1] Sandwich and Robinson to Newcastle, Sept. 25, 1748, S.P. 84/435.

Perhaps, however, they could hardly have known how great this particular difficulty was to be.

The Spanish Government was beginning to look upon commercial affairs in a new light. This change is partly to be accounted for by the publication of two books. Don Geronimo Uztaritz and Don Bernardo Ulloa were perhaps the two most popular economists of the eighteenth century in Spain. They were mercantilists of a common enough type: they lamented the passive trade of their country, and preached the importance and practicability of promoting manufactures, especially those of textiles. A great deal of their doctrine was aimed at the heavy taxation which they believed to have destroyed Spanish industry since the sixteenth century. They had some other tenets which had a more immediate bearing upon foreign policy. It was industry, rather than agriculture, that they wished to develop. Ulloa indeed said that Malaga was a more useful port than Cadiz because its trade was active; but he was not content that Spain should remain an exporter of wines and fruits only. This preoccupation with industry destroyed the foundation of a commercial accord between England and Spain. English writers used to argue that Spain ought to prefer our manufactures to those of France because we were better customers for her agricultural produce.[1] That was a true argument, but it did not avail against the industrial protectionism of Uztaritz and Ulloa.

Ulloa recommended something like a Navigation Act; England had one, and discriminated between native and Spanish shipping in spite of the commercial treaties. Ensenada took very seriously this claim of reciprocity, though Carvajal seems to have treated it as a mere debating-point.[2] In the protection of Spanish manufactures Carvajal was much more interested; he must have been particularly struck by Uztaritz's and Ulloa's denunciation of the Government's fiscal policy. It was indeed the opposite of everything a good mercantilist could have desired: low duties on imported manufactures and exported raw materials; high duties on imported raw materials, such as silk, and on some exported manufactures. The internal customs duties prevented the manufacturers of the rest of Spain from

---

[1] Josiah Tucker, *A Brief Essay on the Advantages and Disadvantages which respectively attend France and Great Britain, with regard to Trade* (in Lord Overstone's *Select Collection*, 1859, p. 338). [2] A. Rodríguez Villa, op. cit., pp. 100, 266.

sending their goods to the colonies through the Kingdom of Seville.[1] The revenue-farmers had attracted foreign trade by granting unauthorized rebates of import dues, which had become established by custom or even by treaty. The only way to free Spain from the domination of the foreign manufacturer was to raise the duties upon him wherever he was not protected by a commercial treaty; such treaties as existed must be interpreted as restrictively as possible, and the principle of reciprocity insisted upon.[2]

Newcastle was unprepared for the obstinacy with which Carvajal and Ensenada held to these opinions. He hoped to pass off the difficulty by overlooking it. He affected to believe that Dodington's treaty was virtually revived at Aix-la-Chapelle, or that its renewal was unnecessary because it conferred no more rights than other treaties which were unquestionably in force. This was not quite unreasonable, considering the relation which the treaties of 1667 and 1715 were supposed to bear to each other. Besides, as Newcastle truly but vainly pointed out, the commerce with Spain in Europe had given rise to none of the difficulties which had caused the war or obstructed the peace; so that there seemed to be no excuse for deliberate innovations in this field. Keene, returning to his old post at Madrid, was told to make no fuss over the omitted treaty, and to encourage the Spaniards to believe, by appearing himself to assume, that it was to all intents and purposes in force. He did so; but he could not support his arguments against the new duties and valuations without recourse to the treaty. In one way or another it came out that the Spanish Government did not mean to consider it as renewed. Ensenada affected not to have noticed the point until Keene brought it to his attention; Carvajal acknowledged that he had always meant to drop the treaty, and had expressly told Sotomayor not to revive it.[3]

---

[1] According to Uztaritz the Kingdom of Seville was the only one which still had the right to levy duties upon such Spanish manufactures; unfortunately it was the most important one because Cadiz lay within it (*The Theory and Practice of Commerce and Maritime Affairs*, translated by J. Kippax, (London, 1751), i. 250 *bis*).

[2] Uztaritz, op. cit.; Ulloa, *Restablecimiento de las Fabricas y Comercio Español* (Madrid, 1740). The argument is so scattered and repetitive that it is impossible to give particular references. Similar opinions were expressed in the *Nuevo Sistema de Gobierno Económico para la America*, attributed to the Minister of Finances, Joseph del Campillo y Cosio. But as Campillo died untimely in 1743 and the book was not published until 1789, his ideas cannot be said to have had much influence.

[3] Keene to Newcastle, Oct. 8, 1750, S.P. 94/138. There were also Frenchmen

Ensenada made a polite attempt to swap a confirmation of it for an accidentally omitted guarantee of Don Philip's possessions in Italy, but the English Government treated that as mere mischief-making between England and her allies.[1]

This was a tiresome check indeed, and no way of getting over it appeared, for Carvajal declared that the renewal of Doding-ton's treaty would be a new privilege from which he could not exclude the subjects of states which had most-favoured-nation clauses in their treaties with Spain.[2] Keene plied him with arguments in vain; the English Government made a merit in vain of its complaisance in curtailing and then abandoning Anson's project of an exploring voyage to the Falkland Islands and the South Seas. No way through the difficulty appeared until an opening came from General Wall.[3]

Don Ricardo Wall, a Spaniard of Irish origin, first came over in 1748 to try to arrange a peace between England and Spain without the intervention of France. He did not succeed in his mission, but he had recommended himself to Newcastle, and remained as the official representative of his Court. When the difficulty arose over the years of *non-jouissance*, he pressed the English Government to yield to Spain on that subject, in order to oblige her and to detach her from France. Newcastle declined to yield outright, but suggested that the two nations might treat of a compensation which should include not only something for the South Sea Company, but some advantage for the nation at large, to make up for the British manufactures which would have been exported in the Annual Ships.[4] Perhaps it was this

who saw beforehand the importance of dropping the Treaty of 1715 (A.E. Mém. et Doc. Espagne, 82, ff. 116 et seqq.).

[1] The early stages of this negotiation are to be found in S.P. 94/135 and 136, *passim*, and in Newcastle's letters to Keene, Dec. 8, 1748, Add. MSS. 32815, f. 289; March 9, 1748/9, vol. 32816, f. 216; Oct. 26, 1749, vol. 32819, ff. 37–8.

[2] Keene to Bedford, June 26, 1749, S.P. 94/135. The possibility of exclusive privileges had also occurred to the French negotiators who had been trying to extort a commercial treaty from Spain. As the peace approached, they asked themselves whether it was worth while to obtain privileges which would probably have to be communicated to England by the most-favoured-nation clause; they had decided that it was better to wait until England should be at liberty to join in demanding favours. They were therefore outwitted by Keene, who achieved the unexpected result of privileges from which France herself was excluded (A.E. Mém. et Doc. Espagne, 80, f. 111; 82, f. 62).

[3] Tabuerniga to Newcastle, May 21 and June 25, 1749, Add. MSS. 32817, ff. 27, 172; Keene to Bedford, May 21, 1749, S.P. 94/135; Bedford to Keene, April 24, ibid.

[4] Newcastle to Sandwich, May 6 and 27, 1748, S.P. 84/431.

seed which brought forth Wall's proposal in 1749. Since Carvajal objected to granting the English any new privileges which
would have to be communicated to other nations, and the two
Governments had not yet begun seriously to discuss the equivalent for the four years' Assiento, Wall proposed to combine the
two negotiations. England should 'purchase' the renewal of
Dodington's treaty by giving up the claims of the South Sea
Company. Carvajal would then be able to justify the exclusiveness of the privileges to be granted, by the receipt of a valuable
consideration which no other nation had paid for them. It
would also be an excellent way to get rid of the stale demands
of the South Sea Company, which there was no prospect of
settling if Keene and Carvajal had to descend into a minute
examination of so many swollen and unverifiable items.[1]

The two Governments took a year to come to terms. Some
of the English Ministers were impressed by the legal difficulty
of yielding all the Company's demands without its consent.
Others were just as intimidated by the political dangers. What
would the country say to a complete abandonment of the South
Sea Company? Some compensation must be had, either directly
or indirectly. The Cabinet in fact would rather have a sum of
money paid by Spain than anything else. This met with great
difficulty from Carvajal. He had been asked, he said, for special
favours.[2] He could only justify them to the rest of the world if
they were paid for; but when the payment came to be adjusted
the English Government proposed that Spain should make it.
Keene might point out that the suggested sum was very much
smaller than the balance due to the South Sea Company, and
that therefore Spain would be receiving something in return for

[1] Keene to Bedford, Sept. 28, 1749; Bedford to Keene, Oct. 26, 1749 (two
letters), S.P. 94/136; Newcastle to Keene, Oct. 26, 1749, Add. MSS. 32819,
ff. 37–8; Wall to Carvajal, Feb. 5, 1750, vol. 32820, ff. 132–4.

[2] There was a difference between Newcastle's and Bedford's attitude to this
affair. While Newcastle had no great objection to giving up the Company if he
could obtain some exclusive commercial privilege of another kind, Bedford took
more seriously his duty to defend the Company's interests, and was less intent upon
the political consequences of an exclusive concession. As he was prepared to yield
less, he must ask less too; so he reasoned that we only wanted the continued enjoyment of Dodington's treaty, and did not insist upon keeping other nations out of
the same benefit. Perhaps he did not quite understand that the renewal of the
treaty, after the new taxes had been imposed during the war, would amount to an
exclusive favour, whether the exclusiveness was expressed or no (Wall to Carvajal,
Feb. 5, 1750, quoted above; Bedford to Keene, Feb. 12, 1749/50 (two letters),
S.P. 94/137).

the renewal of Dodington's treaty. Carvajal denied his premisses and also dismissed them as irrelevant. Surely the rest of the
world would think it too much that Spain should pay England
to receive privileges at her hands?[1]

For some time, therefore, the first alternative seemed unattainable; Keene never quite dropped it, but the Ministers in
England thought he was wasting his time. Their second choice
was to revalidate the Treaty of 1715 without saying anything
at all about the South Sea Company. It would amount to
giving the Company up, but it would avoid the political danger
of openly doing so and the legal impropriety of abandoning the
claim to the private debts of the King of Spain. This also was
too little for Carvajal. His object, in making any bargain on
this affair, was to guard against any demands the Company
might put forward in future. It was all very well for the present
English Ministers to say they would give it no help. They could
not bind future Ministers; in fact, they could not bind themselves. If Sir Robert Walpole could have had his way, the
Company's affairs would never have been allowed to aggravate
the difficulties of 1739; but Sir Robert could control neither the
Court of Directors nor the Parliamentary Opposition. What
was to prevent some future Opposition from forcing a future
Government, or this Government for that matter, into another
crisis over the Company's demands?[2] Carvajal therefore refused
to accept the plan of passing the Company *sub silentio*, unless
King George would secretly declare that he would not support
any demands it might make. This was as bad as giving up the
Company outright, or worse. Nobody in the English Cabinet
would hear of it, except Newcastle, who had always been more
anxious than Bedford to close with Spain on any terms and was
now working himself into a frenzy because nothing had been
done.[3]

There seemed to be nothing for it but the third alternative,
which was to give up openly all but the Company's private

[1] Keene to Bedford, Jan. 9 (secret) and March 22 (secret), 1750, S.P. 94/137;
Wall to Carvajal, Sept. 25, 1750, Add. MSS. 32823, f. 309.

[2] Wall to Carvajal, Feb. 5, 1750, Add. MSS. 32820, ff. 132–4; to Ensenada,
Sept. 25, 1750, vol. 32823, f. 305.

[3] Newcastle to Bedford, Aug. 19, 1750, S.P. 94/138; Bedford to Keene, Aug. 30,
1750, ibid. (printed in *Bedford Correspondence*, ii. 51–7); Henry Pelham to Newcastle,
Aug. 31, 1750, Add. MSS. 32722, f. 280; Hardwicke to Newcastle, Aug. 31, 1750,
f. 283. Wall taxed Newcastle with having been the first to invent the secret article
(Wall to Carvajal, Oct. 9, 1750, Add. MSS. 32824, f. 78).

claims on the King of Spain. This was originally meant to be conditional on Spain's granting new and exclusive privileges which we had never enjoyed before; but Newcastle could wait no longer for a settlement (since he dared not face Parliament for a third session with nothing to show).[1] He therefore forgot or omitted this qualification, and pressed Keene to offer an almost unconditional surrender.[2] Fortunately Keene kept his head and his courage. While the Secretary of State was preparing at Hanover to yield almost anything rather than delay the settlement, the Minister Plenipotentiary was edging Carvajal back to the first alternative. Spain offered a small compensation to the Company, in return for which all its demands, even the private debts, were given up. Nothing was said of exclusive privileges in the treaty, but all the important benefits of 1715 were secured. The dispute over the valuations for duty was settled in our favour, and Keene slipped in a phrase which might be represented as a renunciation by Spain of all claim to Gibraltar.[3]

Even at the last moment the settlement came near to being embroiled. In an earlier interview with the Cabinet Wall had made the most of the exclusive advantages he was empowered to offer, and Hardwicke, like a good bargainer, had tried to belittle them by suggesting that whatever Carvajal might now think, he would find it legally impossible to refuse the same advantages to other nations. This idea had penetrated into Carvajal's head in a curious form: he offered to get over the difficulty by granting the exclusive privileges for a limited term of years only. How that would have removed any legal difficulty, is not clear; but the proposal caused the greatest consternation in England, where it appeared, and rightly as it would seem, that what Carvajal was proposing to limit was not the exclusiveness of the advantages, but the advantages themselves. These would have been perpetual, but for the unlucky omission of Dodington's treaty, and a renewal for six years only would

[1] The Opposition had already made a few complaints of the omission of Dodington's treaty, and of the delay in carrying out the terms of the Sandwich-Sotomayor declaration (*Parl. Hist.* xiv. 384 (Thomas), 581 and 670 (Egmont)).

[2] Newcastle to Keene, June 15, 1750, S.P. 94/137.

[3] Keene to Newcastle, Oct. 8, 1750, S.P. 94/138. The concession of the valuations was not so easily extorted in practice: a paper of 1762 or 1763 complained that the valuations and therefore the duties were still higher than they ought to be (Add. MSS. 36807, f. 250).

therefore have been a very poor concession to buy with the South Sea Company's money. When the six years were up, what should we have to pay for a further lease of them? No doubt Gibraltar would have been asked: this limitation of years was first suggested to Carvajal by Ensenada, who had determined to sell Spain's friendship and goodwill to England and France for concessions of that kind, and had his eye on Gibraltar particularly. Although there were men in the English Ministry who had warmly advocated giving up Gibraltar for other solid advantages, they would not endanger the ultimate abandonment of it to repair a stupid mistake of Newcastle and Sandwich; and the limitation was rejected as inadmissible. Keene induced Carvajal to conclude without it.[1]

Keene's treaty may be represented as a proof that the English Government was really more concerned for European than for American trade, or as a final victory of the Cadiz traders over the South Sea Company. I think it would be a mistake to draw such conclusions: the interest of the Government in the matter was predominantly political; not only Newcastle, but his agent Keene and, in a less degree, his colleague Bedford made this clear.

Something had still to be done to content the South Sea Company; but Henry Pelham found a happy opportunity in the conversion of the public funds. The Company claimed that its stock was not on the same footing as other Government securities, and that the interest could not be reduced. Pelham did not really accept this view, but thought a compromise on this head would be a way of compensating the Company for having to sit down with the £100,000 obtained from Spain.[2] The Treaty of 1750 put a formal end to the South Sea Company's trading career, which had never been so important or so profitable as the founders had hoped. All that remained of the Company was a bad reputation, a large capital lent to the Government or otherwise incorporated in the public funds, and a staff of clerks which later had the honour of having its peculiar manners preserved to immortality by Charles Lamb.

The English traders continued to supply slaves to the Spanish

---

[1] Keene to Newcastle, July 30, Aug. 10 and 13, Sept. 21, 1750, S.P. 94/138; Keene to Castres, Aug. 23, 1750, *Keene Correspondence*, p. 246; Newcastle to Keene, Aug. 22, 1750, Add. MSS. 32823, f. 111; Newcastle to Henry Pelham, Aug. 23, 1750, vol. 32722, f. 228; Hardwicke to Newcastle, Aug. 31, 1750, f. 283.

[2] Henry Pelham to Newcastle, June 1, 1750, Add. MSS. 32721, f. 13; Oct. 19, 1750, vol. 32723, f. 176.

colonies, by virtue of special licences granted to Spaniards who entered into contract or partnership with merchants of Jamaica.[1] The Havana Company offered to make a very large contract, but insisted that its business must be carried on in Spanish ships. This proviso was contrary to the Navigation Acts, so that Governor Knowles had to reject the scheme, though he and the merchants of Jamaica would dearly have liked such an alteration in the Acts as would have enabled them to trade on these terms.[2]

§ ii. *The 'Guarda-Costas' again*

While all this attention was paid to the comparatively unimportant affairs of the South Sea Company, what had become of the grand controversy over the right of search? It had been almost forgotten, in spite of the addresses of Parliament and George II's promise at the outbreak of the war. When Walpole was removed it had served its turn, and many of the loudest shouters for the freedom of navigation came to recognize that the question could not and need not be formally settled at all, or that their demands had been entirely unreasonable. Not all of them had the courage to admit it, as Pitt did in the House of Commons. Perhaps even he would hardly have made such a confession had he not been obliged to it by the necessities of his dreary apprenticeship in the Pelham political machine, where, 'eyeless in Gaza at the mill with slaves', he unsaid a great deal of what he had said before and was to say again.

Carteret in power had made one or two attempts to come to terms with Spain on this matter. He seems to have demanded little, and to have made even less impression on Villarias (formerly La Quadra), who continued to insist that English ships found a long way out of their course in the American seas must be subjected to search. It was not want of agreement on this point, but difficulties in the settlement of Don Philip in Italy, that put an end to any arrangement between England and Spain in Carteret's time.[3] Several years after his fall, when the Governments of Europe began to make closer approaches to

---

[1] For details of such a contract at Cartagena, which had been enjoyed at one time by Edward Manning, see the cases of the *Isabella*, Joseph de Micolta master, H.C.A. 42/76, and *N.S. del Carmen y las Animas*, Joseph Rapalino, H.C.A. 42/83.

[2] This question raised great difficulty after the Peace of Paris.

[3] Villarias to St. Gil, Oct. 22, 1742, Add. MSS. 32802, f. 347; Bussy to Amelot,

peace, it was still Don Philip, not the liberty of navigation, that caused all the difficulty and controversy. The English project of peace in April 1747 perfunctorily demanded that the question should be settled according to the Treaties of 1670 and 1713. Perhaps Newcastle had forgotten, or else he had never understood, that those treaties did not conclude the point.[1] Marchmont, who had taken a great part in the agitation against the right of search, might remind Chesterfield, who had done the same, that such an arrangement would hardly comply with the resolutions of 1739. Chesterfield was now Secretary of State, and could not afford such scruples. He merely advised Sandwich to 'hook in the words *No search*', if he could. It is true that he rejected Macanaz's proposal to leave these questions to commissaries once more, but he was not exacting on the substance of the dispute: he only demanded that the claims on both sides should be cancelled.[2]

Newcastle repeated to Sandwich the next year that our rights must be established on the foundation of the treaty of 1670; but the matter hardly seems to have been mentioned at Aix-la-Chapelle. In fact the Dutch took more interest in it than the English.[3] Ensenada hoped that England would be induced to put off discussing the matter until after the peace was made, but he feared she would not consent.[4] He reckoned without the inattention of the volatile Newcastle, who was immersed in politics of a grander and more exciting kind. Perhaps everybody concerned accepted the view laid down in St. Séverin's instructions: that no form of words could exactly reconcile the rights of England and Spain, that both sides had been right in principle and wrong in practice, and that a real settlement of the controversy was more likely to be achieved by the good relations of the two Crowns than by any promise that could be written on paper.[5]

Aug. 12, 1742, A.E. Angleterre, 415, f. 180; Tabuerniga to Harrington, Dec. 28, 1744, and Feb. 22, 1744/5, S.P. 100/59.

[1] Add. MSS. 32808, ff. 45–51.

[2] Marchmont's diary, Sept. 16, 1747, *Marchmont Papers*, i. 213; Chesterfield to Sandwich, April 7 and 17, 1747, *Letters of Chesterfield*, Dobrée's edition nos. 1161, 1177.

[3] Newcastle to Sandwich, March 29, 1748, S.P. 84/431; Paper enclosed by Newcastle to Sandwich, July 11, 1748, ibid.; Sandwich to Newcastle, April 28, S.P. 84/433.

[4] Memorial of 1746, quoted above.

[5] *Recueil des Instructions, Hollande*, iii. 125–6. The same view is expressed in the

No mention, therefore, was made of these disputes in the treaty of peace. The Opposition made the most of this singular omission. The arguments of 1739 did duty again: the Government had recognized the claim of Spain by not insisting upon our own; besides, it had broken the King's promise.[1] The Government speakers might dispute the propriety of determining a technical and commercial question in a treaty of peace, and justify reserving it to a later discussion; the Opposition retorted that this was a singularly negligent way of treating the controversy which had been the cause of the war. Besides, months and sessions went by, and no such subsequent discussion was begun. Henry Pelham excused the Government for disregarding the resolution of both Houses, which demanded the abolition of the right of search. Such resolutions, he said, cannot affect the course of wars, therefore should not control the terms of peace; the war had not been very successful, so the peace could not be very advantageous. This was a difficult row to hoe for the man who had been conducting the war as Prime Minister for the last four years. He could only escape from it into a worse; for if he pleaded that circumstances had altered the case, and that the war, having become a continental war, had changed its objectives, he brought down upon himself the gallant Admiral Vernon and all the loud declaimers against continental politics.[2]

Pelham and Pitt argued better and more truly when they said that the war had been occasioned by a conflict of two rights, neither of which could be abandoned entirely, and that nothing could reconcile them but mutual forbearance, and restraint of the worst excesses of both smugglers and *Guarda-Costas*.[3] Even if Spain had complied with the resolution of the two Houses, that would not have settled the controversy without some further explanation. As Pelham pointed out, every case would still have been open to dispute as to the facts—whether the ship had really been on a voyage from one English dominion to another when she was seized by the *Guarda-Costas*. Pelham may have hoped, besides, that the treaty of 1750 would eliminate the causes of jealousy and complaint in the West Indies, by

instructions to Vaulgrenant, April 11, 1749 (*Recueil, Espagne*, iii. 294–5), and in A.E. Mém. et Doc. Angleterre, vol. 9, f. 104.

[1] *Parl. Hist.* xiv. 342 (Lee), 595 (Hynde Cotton).
[2] *Parl. Hist.* xiv. 341 (Lee), 587, 597 (Pelham), 601 (Vernon).
[3] *Parl. Hist.* xiv. 686 (Pelham), 800–1 (Pitt).

making the trade through Cadiz more profitable to the English merchants.[1]

A good disposition existed on both sides after the Peace of Aix-la-Chapelle. There were still some grievances, and tempers were heated once or twice. Ensenada complained with justice that the commanders of English warships continued to convoy the smugglers, and even to trade on their own account, as they had done in the war.[2] The English Government did nothing, and perhaps could have done nothing effective, to stop the smuggling trade. The honest Bedford appears to have seen that an Act of Parliament ought to be passed for the purpose; but he asserted that he knew of no illicit trade which he could prevent without one.[3]

The English traders, on the other hand, still had to contend with a number of petty malpractices and obstructions. Neither Government showed very much desire to discuss these incidents in general terms of right.[4] Keene carefully avoided demanding a free navigation while he was negotiating his treaty. Afterwards he promised to work at a project of arrangement which should establish the rights of both parties on a firm foundation; but he was now too old, too tired, and too ill to grasp the nettle gratuitously. Especially after the question of depredations took a new and ominous turn, he seems to have resigned his ambitions of any far-reaching scheme, and was content to live from hand to mouth for the rest of his days.[5] The enterprising genius of Ensenada had turned for a moment in the same direction of a new and radical settlement: he once told Keene that the best thing the Spanish Government could do was to burn all the

[1] Bedford to Keene, May 11, 1749, S.P. 94/135.

[2] Keene to Bedford, Oct. 6, 1749, S.P. 94/136. Knowles continued to grant convoys to the Spanish colonies for some little time after the war. He complained that the English newspapers aroused the vigilance of the Spanish Government by foolishly parading the quantity of Spanish treasure which reached England from Jamaica (Knowles to Secretaries of the Admiralty, Dec. 20, 1748, Adm. 1/234). Commodore Townshend received in 1751 a severe rebuke from the Viceroy of Santa Fé for allowing the ships under his command to convoy the trade and to engage in it themselves (Villar to Townshend, May 29, 1751, ibid.). See also a letter of Dec. 8, 1753, on the prevalence of English trade at Havana, quoted by Duro, *Armada Española*, vi. 392.

[3] Bedford to Keene, Feb. 11–17, 1751, *Bedford Correspondence*, ii. 70.

[4] Keene to Bedford, Oct. 6, 1749, S.P. 94/136; Dec. 1750 (separate), S.P. 94/138.

[5] Keene to Castres, April 16, 1751, *Keene Correspondence*, p. 295; to Newcastle, Nov. 6, 1751, p. 314; to Castres, Aug. 2, 1753, p. 342.

laws of the Indies. Here Carvajal was on the conservative side: he could not foresee the consequences of a total reform, and thought justice and chastisement in particular cases were all that was needed. Ensenada never got farther than projecting a revision of the instructions to Spanish Governors.[1]

Most of the correspondence of this period deals with minor nuisances and their redress. Some of them in fact arose, not out of depredations but out of prizes of war which had been improperly made after the time fixed for cessation of hostilities. Keene had once more to batter his way through the same difficulties that had always hindered the perfect restitution of effects seized and condemned in the Spanish colonies. The *Guarda-Costas* still plundered their prey before the formality of condemnation. They still sold the ships and cargoes, whether collusively or in good faith, at a price very much below what was claimed as the real value. They still distributed the proceeds at once without waiting for the result of an appeal or giving security to restore them in case the sentence should be reversed; if the claimants arrived with a decree of restitution from Madrid, there was little or nothing to be had.[2] The Governors still granted commissions to *Guarda-Costas* of insufficient fortune and reputation, and still received a share of the forfeitures, which tempted them to condemn whatever they could.[3]

Keene overcame these difficulties one by one. By threats of his Court's severe displeasure, or even of war, he procured in July 1752 an order for paying the value of some cargoes out of the King's revenues, so far as the captors could not be made to pay their shares.[4] This was not an entirely effective reform, for

[1] Keene to Bedford, Dec. 1750, S.P. 94/138; Feb. 8, 1751, S.P. 94/139; to Holdernesse, March 21, 1752, S.P. 94/141.

[2] The French had found the same difficulty in getting their effects restored even with a royal order for the purpose. Larnage said of Horcasitas, Governor of Havana, that he probably would not restore a certain ship but would force the claimants to compound with him for 25 per cent., 'according to the laudable practice of the Spanish Governors, and particularly of that one' (Larnage to Maurepas, April 28, 1745, A.N. Colonies C⁹ A 66). The French Government proposed to take vigorous measures against the *Guarda-Costas* after the war—much stronger than anything the English Government allowed (Minute of Nov. 1, 1749, A.N. Marine B⁴ 62, f. 217). The authorities at St. Domingue still complained of the *Guarda-Costas* in 1755 (Vaudreuil and Laporte-Lalanne to Machault, Jan. 10, 1755, A.N. Colonies C⁹ A 96).

[3] Bedford to Keene, Jan. 10 and Feb. 11, 1750/1, with enclosures, S.P. 94/139; Keene to Carvajal, June 18 and 30, 1752, with enclosures, S.P. 94/142. See also Carvajal to Keene, Dec. 21, 1753, S.P. 94/144.

[4] His success in this object was long obstructed by the case of the *Anna Maria y*

the Governors of colonies sometimes made difficulties, by pretending they had not received the originals of the royal orders and refusing to accept authenticated copies; sometimes again they would allege, truly or falsely, that the provincial treasuries were empty. Keene persuaded Carvajal to go farther, and promise that no prizes should be distributed to the *Guarda-Costas* in future before the King's pleasure should have been signified from Madrid.[1] The question of the valuation was never settled to Keene's satisfaction. The English claimants wanted their property restored at the value expressed in the invoices or insurance policies. The Spanish Government continued in general to pay no more than the net sales in the colonies, though there were some fortunate claimants who received nearly all they asked.[2] As for the personnel of the *Guarda-Costas*, Carvajal could not promise to employ none but the King's ships in that work; the Royal Navy had neither men nor money for the purpose, and he doubted whether the English traders would be any safer than they were already, for the *Guarda-Costas* were supposed to give security for good behaviour. However, he accepted the suggestion that only the Governors of important provinces, in whom confidence could be placed, should be allowed to commission *Guarda-Costas*.[3] Wall was to have proposed other reforms on this head, and Keene credited Arriaga, the successor of Ensenada as Secretary for the Navy, with the intention to suppress the *Guarda-Costas* altogether and have the work done by the King's ships.[4]

These matters could be debated and settled without touching any question of right or principle. There were others that could

---

S. Felix, in which the English Government used the same arguments to Wall that Carvajal had brought forward about the English vessels. Admiral Knowles had taken her after the time prefixed for the conclusion of hostilities, and had improperly distributed the proceeds after condemnation. The English Ministers would not order anything to be restored until an appeal had been properly lodged and heard; then they offered to apply to Parliament for the payment of the value out of the Treasury, but this application was delayed for a long time by Pelham's indecision whether Knowles should be prosecuted for his share. The money does not seem to have been finally asked and granted before 1756 (Legge to Newcastle, Feb. 2, 1755, Add. MSS. 32852, f. 335; Fox to Keene, Jan. 20, 1756, S.P. 94/151).

[1] Keene to Holdernesse, March 13, 1752, S.P. 94/141; June 30, July 4, 1752, S.P. 94/142; Carvajal to Keene, Aug. 16, 1752, ibid.

[2] Newcastle to Keene, July 12, 1753, S.P. 94/144; Holdernesse to Keene, Sept. 20, S.P. 94/145; Carvajal to Keene, Dec. 2, 1753, S.P. 94/144.

[3] Ibid.

[4] Keene to Robinson, 'most, most secret', Sept. 21, 1754, S.P. 94/147.

not; and in spite of all Keene's and Carvajal's little alleviations, the cry against depredations began to rise again in 1751. The Ministers in England insisted that something must be done— that new and very different instructions must be delivered to the *Guarda-Costas*.[1] In spite of Ensenada's reforming zeal their commissions were not changed; the anger of the English press continued to increase, and with it the alarm of the English Ministers. Newcastle and Holdernesse warned Keene again and again that the friendship of the two countries could not endure the strain for long; in July 1752 Newcastle prophesied that letters of reprisals would soon be asked for and could hardly be refused.[2]

A violent incident soon afterwards brought matters near a crisis. Admiral Knowles, the new Governor of Jamaica, was constitutionally inclined to strong measures and hard words, and had inherited from his friend Trelawny an idea that the *Guarda-Costas* could be intimidated by a little force. He caught some of them on private business at Jamaica, and had them tried and condemned to death for piracy.[3] Fortunately, he had at least the good sense not to execute them without orders from home; but he aggravated his imprudence by a most offensive letter to a Spanish Governor.[4] The Secretary of State reproached him for his silly fulmination, and at least one of the 'pirates' was promptly pardoned; but the Court of Spain was very upset by the insult—the more so, as one of the *Guarda-Costas* had carried with him, at the time of his arrest, a commission from the King of Spain which should have secured him from such treatment.[5]

This little thunderstorm cleared the air, and for some years afterwards the complaints of Spanish depredations almost ceased.[6] The two nations had not even approached a settlement of the great controversy. Spain still thought herself

---

[1] Holdernesse to Keene, May 28, 1752, S.P. 94/141; Sept. 20, 1753, S.P. 94/145; Newcastle to Keene, July 26, 1752, S.P. 94/142; Newcastle to Wall, April 2, 1752, Add. MSS. 32825, f. 38.

[2] Newcastle to Keene, July 26, 1752; Holdernesse to Keene, Sept. 20, 1753, quoted above.

[3] Trelawny to Knowles, March 6, 1750/1, C.O. 137/57; Knowles to Holdernesse, Nov. 18, 1752, C.O. 137/59.

[4] Knowles to Caxigal de la Vega, Nov. 13, 1752, C.O. 137/59.

[5] Holdernesse to Knowles, May 26, 1753, C.O. 137/60; Holdernesse to Keene, May 26, 1753, S.P. 94/143; Report of the Fiscal of the Council of the Indies, enclosed by Duras to St. Contest, Jan. 15, 1754, A.E. Espagne, 515.

[6] Knowles to Holdernesse, Jan. 12, 1754, C.O. 137/59.

entitled to confiscate foreign ships found with 'contraband' goods such as silver or logwood on board. The English Ministry no longer insisted on a general renunciation of the right of search; even Newcastle admitted that 'No Search' may have been a cant word. But he and his colleagues still regarded any kind of examination of English ships on the high seas as an unjustifiable molestation, and particularly objected to the treatment of logwood and silver as contraband.[1]

Such articles as silver raised no special difficulties. Logwood was a very different question; indeed, Keene said 'we justify from what these people think the greatest offence'.[2] At this point, even when the outcry against the depredations themselves had died away, the controversy took a new and far more dangerous form, and became a territorial question. Nothing was heard of the right of search for some years after 1754, but the dispute over logwood and the Moskito Shore more than filled its place.

§ iii. *The Logwood Settlements after the Peace of Aix-la-Chapelle*[3]

The Treaty of Aix-la-Chapelle provided that conquests should be mutually restored. There could be no doubt that this clause applied to Rattan, which was accordingly evacuated; but the English Government declined to withdraw the settlers from Belize and Black River. It even took a new step forward, and appointed a superintendent on the Moskito Shore.[4] Presumably, if it thought about the matter at all, it argued that the Shore and the Bay were not new conquests but old possessions, or at least establishments, dating from before the treaty of 1670. Even this does not explain why it paid this attention to the Moskito Shore and not to the more important settlement on the Bay of Honduras; perhaps that was due to the influence of Trelawny and the arguments of Hodgson, who came home to advise the Government and to obtain the superintendency. The annual produce of the Moskito Shore was so small that, according to statistics afterwards supplied by Knowles, it fell short of the expenses of the Government and fortifications; but Hodgson gave other figures, which put a different face on this

---

[1] Newcastle to Keene, Jan. 15, 1753, Add. MSS. 32842, f. 152.
[2] Keene to Castres, July 12, 1753, *Keene Correspondence*, p. 338.
[3] For the earlier history of this subject *v. supra*, pp. 97–104.
[4] Bedford to Hodgson, Oct. 5, 1749, C.O. 137/57.

question.[1] There had been a considerable trade at Black River in 1745 and 1746; but it had fallen off since then, and though Hodgson was always expecting it to revive, for one reason or another it never did so.

The usefulness of the establishment was not thought, however, to depend only on its own commerce or agriculture: it had already been invaluable as a last resort for the logwood-cutters in times of Spanish invasion, and was to prove so again.[2] It could be made to serve still more ambitious purposes. Trelawny had not given up his dream of disrupting the Spanish Empire; in fact he still thought it would come about one day. He was still preparing the way for annexing the isthmus of Darien and the passages to the South Seas, and still believed it could best be done by means of the Indians and Creoles. He therefore wanted to keep up an establishment which would give England a foothold in Central America, and enable her to extend her diplomacy from one tribe of Indians to another.

Trelawny wanted the Moskito Shore to retain the character of a trading-station and outpost of Indian diplomacy, not to degenerate into a plantation colony. Here no doubt he thought as Governor of Jamaica. He earnestly pressed Bedford to forbid slavery on the Shore, or to restrict it as far as possible. He drew many specious reasons from the unsuitability of such a colony for the purposes he had in view; he also argued that as the English settlements were not islands, like the older sugar colonies, the slaves would be constantly running away to the Spaniards. Here history proved him right. The slaves of the Moskito Shore had run away in a body some time before he wrote, and been subdued with difficulty by the Indians. For many years afterwards the settlers often complained against the neighbouring Spaniards for enticing their slaves, and refusing to restore them on the grounds of their conversion to Catholicism, which would be endangered by their return to heretic masters. Trelawny's real object, however, probably was to protect Jamaica from being weakened by emigration and injured by the competition of new sugar-plantations. So far as the existing settlers were concerned, he need perhaps have given himself little trouble:

[1] Knowles to Holdernesse, Jan. 10, 1753, C.O. 137/60; the younger Hodgson's *First Account of the Mosquito Shore*, C.O. 123/1.

[2] Hodgson to Under-Secretary Aldworth, April 10, 1751, C.O. 137/59; Pitts to Knowles, Aug. 1, 1754, C.O. 137/60.

very few of them had much capital, or the inclination to desert their occasional seafaring and turtling to become tillers of the soil. But new sugar colonies were generally made, in that age, by a migration of planters from the old, and Trelawny feared that the reported excellence of the land would persuade those of Jamaica to remove themselves and their slaves to Black River.[1]

It was necessary to Trelawny's schemes that the Indians should be kept quiet. They had once undertaken to observe the King of England's times and occasions for war and peace rather than their own; this promise must be strictly exacted. It was indeed one of the chief articles of Hodgson's instructions. He was not to hinder the Moskitomen from defending themselves against an attack, but he was to restrain them from active hostilities against the Spanish settlements.[2] Trelawny intended to point out to the Spanish Governors, as often as possible, that Hodgson's presence on the Moskito Shore was not a step in encroachment, but a safeguard and advantage to the Spaniards; but for his presence, the unregulated English settlers would incite the Moskitomen to worse and more frequent outrages.[3] This argument, as Trelawny's successor thought, would have been a stronger one if Hodgson himself had shown any more discretion than the other Englishmen on the Shore. However that might be, before he arrived at his post the Moskitomen had executed a great expedition against the Spaniards and their allies, and had carried off a number of Indian prisoners. Heredia, the Captain-general of Nicaragua, demanded the return of the prisoners and the withdrawal of all the arms which the English had furnished to their allies. He claimed the Moskitomen themselves as Spanish subjects, and denounced the English for inciting them to rebellion against their lawful lord. Soon afterwards he asked for the evacuation of Belize and Black River as provided for by the Treaty of 1748.[4] Of course Trelawny could not grant this.

---

[1] Trelawny to Board of Trade, Oct. 7, 1748, C.O. 137/25; Trelawny to Bedford, April 8, 1749, C.O. 137/58; April 14, 1750, and private letter of the same date, C.O. 137/59.

[2] Trelawny, instructions to Hodgson, April 14, 1750, C.O. 137/57; May 20, 1752, C.O. 137/59.

[3] Trelawny to Heredia, Oct. 16, 1750, C.O. 137/59; Trelawny to Bedford, July 17, 1751, ibid.

[4] Hodgson to Aldworth, April 10, 1751, C.O. 137/59; July 11, 1751, C.O.

Heredia soon sent an envoy to make a treaty with the Moskito Indians, who received his proposals with tolerable respect.[1] He hoped also to detach them, if not perhaps the Englishmen too, by the insinuations of Spanish missionaries. He asked Hodgson's leave to send one among the Indians. Hodgson professed that he was no bigot in religion but could not answer for the safety of a Spanish priest. While he was away, however, there soon arrived a clerical emissary from the President of Guatemala. This was Father Solis, who had appeared among the English about 1745 in order to arrange an illicit trade at Black River. (Trelawny had reported at that time that most of the smuggling was in the hands of the clergy.) He now turned up again, with a curious story of disagreement among the Spanish Governors about the way to treat the English. Heredia, he told them, was for destroying their settlements, but the new Governor of Leon preferred to try gentler methods first. If they would allow him to reside among them and convert the Indians, he would arrange a trade with Guatemala for certain small articles, and the Governor would obstruct any violent measures against them.[2]

At this time the Spanish Governors seem to have had two policies in this affair. On the one hand they prepared an expedition to evict the English; on the other, they tried the method of peaceful penetration. In some degree this alternation of methods resulted from the conflict of different authorities; but the same Governors pursued both the one and the other.

The settlers also appear to have been in two minds. They had long been pressing Trelawny to withdraw the detachment of twenty soldiers which had been at the Shore since 1747, or else to strengthen it so that it could afford them real protection. This little force was not enough to defend them and could only get them into trouble with the Spaniards if its presence was proved.[3] Trelawny and Hodgson assented to this reasoning and withdrew the men. Trelawny afterwards tried to make a

137/57; Heredia to Trelawny, June 23, 1750, and April 30, 1751, C.O. 137/59; Heredia to Hodgson, June 22, 1750, ibid.
[1] Ruiz to Heredia, March 7, 1751, ibid.
[2] Heredia to Hodgson, June 22, 1750; Hodgson to Heredia, Dec. 3, 1750, ibid.; Pitts to Trelawny, April 8, 1751, ibid.; Inhabitants of Moskito Shore to Trelawny, April 7, 1751, C.O. 137/57.
[3] Pitts to Trelawny, July 17, 1749, C.O. 137/59; Trelawny to Bedford, Dec. 7, 1750, and July 17, 1751; Hodgson to Aldworth, April 10, 1751, ibid.

merit of this, by declaring that he had only done it on Heredia's promise to leave the settlements as they were, pending a reference of the whole question to the Courts of London and Madrid.[1] Pitts and the other Englishmen on the shore then asked that the cannon should follow the soldiers. Perhaps they had made up their minds to try what terms they could get from the Spanish authorities by representing themselves as defence-less stragglers without any connexion with the English Government. Some of them, especially Pitts, had an old-standing grievance, for they had established themselves at Rattan on the faith of official encouragement, and had had to withdraw at the end of the war; now they were afraid they should be abandoned again in the same way.[2] At any rate they did not send Solis away, and within a few months Hodgson had to complain that he had baptized the Moskito 'King' and formed a party for himself among the Indians and English. However, 'General Handyside', a Moskito notable, obliged the King to retract his conversion, and the sounder part of the Indians were for murdering Solis on the spot if Hodgson would let them. Of course he could not suffer it, but suggested as a counter-attack that an Anglican clergyman should be sent to the Shore. Trelawny had already applied for one in vain to the Society for the Propagation of the Gospel, and the English settlers said that the Government deserved to lose the possession of the Shore for want of such precautions.[3] I cannot say whether this new proposal resulted in the dispatch of anybody; but if the battle of the missionaries ever began, it was soon ended by the suppression of Solis. He seems to have been sent to Jamaica to answer the charge of stirring up rebellion among His Majesty's subjects. Once there, he was conveniently arrested for an old debt of his smuggling days, and died in prison. Hodgson was instructed to allow no more priests among the Indians.[4]

[1] Trelawny to Heredia, May 15, 1752, C.O. 137/59; Vasquez Prego to Trelawny, Nov. 25, 1752, C.O. 137/57.

[2] Hodgson to Aldworth, July 11, 1751, C.O. 137/57; Hodgson to Knowles, Dec. 19, 1752, C.O. 137/60.

[3] Hodgson to Aldworth, July 12, 1751, C.O. 137/57. There had been one, who went by the name of 'the Irreverend Mr. Holmes'.

[4] Trelawny to Holdernesse, Nov. 25, 1751, C.O. 137/59; Trelawny, instructions to Hodgson, May 20, 1752, ibid.; Trelawny to Heredia, May 15, 1752, ibid.; Hodgson to Knowles, Jan. 19, 1753, C.O. 137/60; Report of the Fiscal of the Council of the Indies, enclosed by Duras to St. Contest, Jan. 15, 1754, A.E. Espagne, 515.

Meanwhile the Spanish preparation for warlike enterprises had been pushing slowly on. Heredia complained that the equipment of the galleys was perpetually obstructed by the idleness and 'juridical diligence' of the President of Guatemala, whose love of forms and zeal for economy may have been stimulated by dissent from the violent policy. Heredia had received orders of September 1750 from Ensenada, to destroy and dispeople the English settlements. Pitts discovered this by intercepting a Spanish messenger, and spread an alarm; but Trelawny thought there was no immediate danger.[1] Next year, however, he sent back to the Shore not only the detachment he had lately withdrawn but a whole company of soldiers. His relations with the Spanish Governors had not improved. A few years earlier he had refrained from demanding a vessel taken between the Moskito Shore and Jamaica as having been interrupted in a voyage from one British dominion to another. He now claimed the Shore as absolutely for England as they for Spain; but he tried to gain time by entreating that no violence should be done until the Governments in Europe could settle the matter. This request could hardly meet with much favour, accompanied as it was by a reinforcement of the English defences; and the President of Guatemala hinted that he should be obliged to use force to dislodge the settlers.[2]

At this moment a new Governor arrived in Jamaica. If the plausible Trelawny had allowed matters to come so far towards a crisis, it was not likely that Admiral Knowles would keep the peace long. Knowles, however, did not think very much of the Moskito Shore. It did not even earn the expenses of its Government by its exports. Hodgson's residence and the fort were wrongly placed at Black River, some hundred miles from the strongest Moskito head-quarters near Cape Gracias à Dios. Black River, with its ninety miles of navigable stream connected with a hundred miles of Indian road, might be the best place for a trade with the Spaniards, for which reason Hodgson had chosen it; but it was too far to receive help in an emergency from the Moskitomen. Besides, they were beginning to be disaffected: they had received the Spanish overtures without

[1] Heredia to Yscar, Jan. 12, 1751, C.O. 137/59; to Ensenada, April 26, 1751; to the Viceroy of Mexico, April 30, 1751, ibid.; Trelawny to Bedford, July 17, 1751, ibid.

[2] Trelawny to Heredia, May 15, 1752, ibid.; Vasquez Prego to Trelawny, Nov. 25, 1752, C.O. 137/57.

disfavour in 1751, and three years later General Handyside actually abandoned Hodgson in his greatest necessity. Perhaps this was attributable to Hodgson's embezzlement of the Government's Indian presents. Knowles said so; and although Knowles threw his accusations about as he needed them, there is more significance in the repetition of the charge by Governor Haldane.[1]

Hodgson indeed made a very good thing of his superintendency. He spent large sums of public money on heaven knew what; he wished also to engage the Government in a great commercial venture by buying negroes on its account, to hire them out afterwards to new settlers. This perhaps accounts for his antipathy to Pitts, the chief trading and negro-owning magnate upon the Shore.[2] Knowles thought the whole establishment on the Moskito Shore a job; so it was, and what was worse, it was not Knowles's job.

Hodgson now demanded that the ships of war should make an offensive campaign against the small Spanish *Guarda-Costas* who molested the Shore; but Knowles snubbed him. When the Moskito Indians made an expedition against the Spaniards at Carpenter's River, Knowles ordered Hodgson to send any white settlers who had engaged in it to Jamaica to be tried, and to recover and return the booty. On the other hand the temptation of affronting a Spanish Governor by a display of stern inflexibility was too much for him; he told the President of Guatemala that if the English settlements were molested he would repel force by force. This declaration received the approval of the Government in England.[3]

The Spanish blow fell in 1754, not on the Moskito Shore but on the logwood-cutters in the Bay of Honduras. Though that was the more important of the two settlements, there is little mention of its history in the English archives—presumably because there was no superintendent to send home reports, and the Baymen, who made their living by disregarding the Acts of Trade, did not wish to say too much about themselves.

---

[1] Hodgson to Aldworth, July 11, 1751, C.O. 137/59; Knowles to Holdernesse, Jan. 10 and March 26, 1753, C.O. 137/60; Hodgson to Reid, Aug. 3, 1754, ibid.; Haldane to Board of Trade, July 10, 1759, C.O. 137/30, Z 60.

[2] Hodgson to Aldworth, April 10, 1751, C.O. 137/59.

[3] Hodgson to a friend, end of 1752, C.O. 137/57; Hodgson to Knowles, Dec. 19, 1752, C.O. 137/60; Knowles to Hodgson, Jan. 24, 1753, ibid.; to Vasquez Prego, March 20, 1753, ibid.

Diplomacy, however, had been handling the logwood question very gingerly and reluctantly. Keene, in particular, wished to have as little to do with it as possible. As he had avoided discussing the right of search while he negotiated the Treaty of 1750, he now kept logwood in the background while he adjusted the disputes over new depredations.[1] Both he and Ensenada once thought of working out a definite compromise; it is to be wished they had done it, for they might thereby have saved their countries a war.

Ensenada's scheme appears to have consisted in a licensed monopoly of the trade, jointly in English and Spanish hands; but he soon came to prefer an exclusively Spanish monopoly, and proposed to set up a company at Santander for the purpose. He believed that the Spanish merchants, having all the supplies in their hands, could raise the price upon the dyers of Europe. The English thought so too, and it was exactly what they wanted to avoid. Hardwicke believed that even an Anglo-Spanish monopoly would be objectionable. There were other people in England who thought a monopoly harmless, provided it were an English one. That was the point of the often expressed desire to oblige the logwood-cutters to conform to the Acts of Navigation, and of the younger Hodgson's suggestion that the cutting needed some regulation in order to prevent over-production and the steady fall of prices. At any rate no Englishman of any school of thought wished to be at the mercy of Spain for the supply of logwood, or to pay whatever prices the Spaniards chose to ask.[2] This was the great reason for the obstinate refusal of the English Government to accept any such settlement of the question. It was quite useless for the Spanish Ministers to protest that they did not wish to deprive us of logwood and that they would arrange for its sale on reasonable terms. They could not prevail against an ineradicable suspicion, and perhaps a very justifiable one, since the whole tendency of commercial policy in the Spanish Empire was towards high prices and small supplies.[3]

---

[1] Keene to Newcastle, April 19, 1751, Add. MSS. 32827, f. 197; Keene to Holdernesse, July 4, 1752, S.P. 94/142; June 30, 1753, 94/143.

[2] See a letter to the *Craftsman*, no. 605. I shall not try to enter into the justice of this reasoning. It was then a commonplace of economics that a nation which had a monopoly of an article would ask and could get any price it chose.

[3] Keene to Newcastle, Aug. 27, 1751, Add. MSS. 32829, f. 163; Newcastle to Keene, Sept. 5, 1751, vol. 32830, f. 6; Keene to Newcastle, March 21, 1752,

Poor Keene was forced to bring forward the English claim to cut logwood, though he did not believe in it, and understood that it raised difficulties far greater than those which were involved in the right of search. He did his best to dissuade his Government from patronizing the logwood-cutters; and as for the Moskito Shore, he said with perfect truth that he had never heard of our right to it. He could not convince Holdernesse. Newcastle never got farther than understanding that the logwood question was a very important one, which must be settled; he could not see what difficulty there could be in making out the English title.[1] If only he and Hardwicke had entertained at this period the doubts they felt in 1760, there might have been a different story to tell; but it was not to be expected that Newcastle should question the foundation of a right before he could see a grave political danger in asserting it.[2] Be that as it might, the controversy about logwood could not remain dormant. Keene could not reclaim the ships confiscated for carrying 'contraband' logwood without starting this question; and even if England had made no complaint of the state of affairs, Spain was determined to put an end to it. Carvajal raised the question several times. He always denied that England had any right, and apparently hoped to get the settlements evacuated peacefully by convincing the English Government.[3]

While Carvajal argued, Ensenada acted. He had long inclined somewhat more to France than his rival. As the Secretary for the Indies he had the power not only to magnify the complaints of English encroachments but also to give what turn he pleased to the orders which the colonial Governors received. Exactly what he did in this affair of the logwood, and why he did it, are not very clear from the English archives. He afterwards maintained that he had given no special orders to promote

vol. 32834, f. 204; Hardwicke to Newcastle, Sept. 10, 1751, Coxe's *Pelham Administration*, ii. 410; Keene to Holdernesse, March 21, 1752, S.P. 94/141; Ensenada's justification, quoted by Rodriguez Villa, op. cit., pp. 263-4.

[1] Keene to Holdernesse, June 30, 1753, S.P. 94/143; Newcastle to Keene, June 20, 1751, Add. MSS. 32828, f. 110; July 26, 1752, vol. 32839, f. 27; July 12, 1753, S.P. 94/144.

[2] Newcastle to Hardwicke, Sept. 13, 1760, Add. MSS. 32911, f. 270; Hardwicke to Newcastle, Sept. 14, f. 286; but see also Newcastle's letter to Joseph Yorke, May 27, 1760, vol. 32906, f. 348.

[3] Keene to Holdernesse, Jan. 17, 1752, S.P. 94/141; Carvajal to Keene, Dec. 2, 1753, S.P. 94/144; Duras to St. Contest, Jan. 15, 1754, A.E. Espagne, 515.

aggression against the English, and had King Ferdinand's full assent to what he did.[1] This can hardly be true, for the King (who was a spectator and not an accomplice of his fall) was apparently horrified at the consequences of those orders.[2]

The English version of the affair was as follows. The Spanish Court was in two minds whether to apply first to England for the withdrawal of the settlements, or to send orders for hostilities at once. The committee, to whom the question was referred, decided to try the amicable negotiation first; but Ensenada, apparently without the King's full knowledge or consent, ordered, in the royal name, that the English settlements should be attacked immediately.[3] Keene had already sent home in 1753 an elaborate plan drawn up by one Flores da Silva for penetrating in various disguises near the English settlements and cutting off the inhabitants in their cups one Sunday or holiday. This plan, according to Keene, had been sanctioned by Ensenada; but it is no evidence against him.[4] This expedition against Belize, duly authorized or not, was not the only charge against Ensenada; and all the charges put together were rather the pretext than the cause of his fall. His real crime was his French sympathies, and the danger that he would be too powerful after the death of Carvajal who had balanced him. His disgrace was arranged with Newcastle before Wall left London to succeed Carvajal;[5] and the horror which was felt in England upon the discovery of his black designs was no more than an excellent piece of acting, for the discovery must have been made a long time before it was announced.

The consequences of Ensenada's orders were more than theatrical in the Bay of Honduras. A land and sea force was mustered from Havana and Guatemala. A body of soldiers penetrated unexpectedly, by a newly cut path, to the houses of some settlers at Labouring Creek, and overpowered them. After this the Baymen took to flight, leaving their huts and their cut logwood to the Spaniards. They retreated to Black River, where Hodgson himself was preparing to meet an attack. He

---

[1] Rodriguez Villa, op. cit., pp. 263–6.
[2] Keene to Robinson, July 31, 1754 (most secret, nos. 1 and 2), S.P. 94/147.
[3] Ibid.; Robinson to Albemarle, Aug. 15, 1754, Add. MSS. 32850, f. 90.
[4] Keene to Holdernesse (very secret), June 30, 1753, with annexed memorandum, S.P. 94/143.
[5] Newcastle to Albemarle, Aug. 1, 1754, Add. MSS. 32850, f. 6. Carvajal had died in the spring of 1754.

was seriously embarrassed by their presence, for when they were all assembled together it was almost impossible to victual them. They furnished him, however, with five hundred armed men, who compensated him for the disappointments he had just received: Knowles had sent him a very ill-timed order to send back the regular soldiers to Jamaica, and General Handyside, with many of the Moskito Indians, had deserted him. No further attack came. The Spaniards retired without even burning the piles of logwood properly, and within a few months the Baymen were back in their settlements without the least molestation. Knowles sent them an engineer to rebuild their forts, and a few soldiers, disguised as Baymen in frocks and trousers, to protect them.[1]

There is little that is of interest in the history of the Shore or the Bay for the next few years; but Ensenada's indiscretion had unhappy consequences in diplomacy. Before anybody in Europe knew what had happened in the West Indies, the English and Spanish Governments found themselves entangled in a misunderstanding. Wall sent counter-orders to the Spanish Governors, to suspend their measures against the English settlements while the two Crowns came to an amicable agreement on the rights and wrongs of the matter.[2] The English Ministers expected more—indeed, they construed this very action of Wall as a promise of more. It was not enough, they said, to leave off hostilities: if the settlers had been dispossessed, they must be restored to their establishments.[3]

This was more than Wall could admit. He had been willing enough to use the crisis in order to get rid of Ensenada; and perhaps, as an Anglophile, he sincerely deplored so violent and provocative a method of handling a delicate matter, which might have involved Spain in a war with England for interests whose importance did not warrant it. But he no more recognized the justice of England's pretensions than Carvajal or Ensenada himself. Keene therefore had great difficulty in get-

---

[1] Pitts to Knowles, Aug. 1, 1754, C.O. 137/60; Hodgson to Reid, Aug. 3, 1754; Settlers of the Shore to Knowles, Sept. 5, 1754; Knowles to Robinson, Dec. 11 1754, Jan. 13, Feb. 25, July 12, 1755; Hodgson to Knowles, March 16, 1755; Hodgson to his son, May 14, 1755, ibid.

[2] Keene to Robinson, July 31, 1754 (most secret, no. 2), S.P. 94/147; Wall to Keene, Sept. 15, 1754, ibid.; Arriaga, orders to Governors, Jan. 5, 1755, S.P. 94/148; Wall to Newcastle, Sept. 25, 1754, Add. MSS. 32850, f. 387.

[3] Keene to Robinson, Jan. 12, 1755 (secret and confidential), S.P. 94/148; Robinson to Keene (no. 1), Jan. 27, 1755, ibid.

ting from him satisfactory orders to the Governors. He would give back the captured ships, but to restore the settlers would be to acknowledge the validity of the English claim or at least to increase its force. Besides, who and where were these 'illustrious exiles'? If the English Ministry would undertake to collect and present them in order to their re-establishment, the next thing that would follow was a settled English government in the Bay, and this furtive intrusion would thus be regularized as an English Colony. Keene urged that we were not asking for anything new: a mere re-establishment of the *status quo ante* would commit Spain to nothing. Wall did not accept his argument, and still thought that a negotiation on such terms would be useless because England's demand would be conceded before it was discussed. However, he went so far as to instruct the President of Guatemala to restore everything to the condition in which it was before the hostilities. The English Ministry was not satisfied with these orders, and detained them nearly six months in the hope of extorting better.[1] None were needed in the end, for the Baymen had restored themselves. The whole affair became less pressing and was almost forgotten for a time while a new war between England and France drew near.

Nothing had been settled. The negotiation, if it can be called so, advanced little farther. Wall continued to insist, in one way or another, that the affair could not be discussed on equal terms unless England would withdraw the establishments in dispute. He had promised Keene that he would not force concessions from England by taking advantage of her embroilment with France. He kept his promise so well that Ensenada, emerging from disgrace in the next reign, might well have boasted that Spain would not have been paid so little for her neutrality if he had remained Minister.[2] Yet Wall did not wish to leave the matter for ever in suspense. His anger and impatience rose as the English logwood-cutters repaired and fortified their habitations with the connivance of the Governor of Jamaica, and the English Ministers continued to deny him the negotiation which he looked upon as the price for revoking Ensenada's orders.[3]

[1] Ibid.; Wall to Newcastle, March 5, 1755, Add. MSS. 32853, f. 115; Robinson to Newcastle, July 5, vol. 32856, f. 482.

[2] Keene to Fox, Sept. 8, 1756 (secret and separate), S.P. 94/153; Rodriguez Villa, op. cit., p. 266.

[3] Keene to Robinson, Sept. 22, 1755, S.P. 94/150; to Fox, Sept. 8, 1756, quoted above.

He suspected them of playing for time; and indeed that was just what they did. Trelawny had played for time when he pretended that Heredia ough: to leave the settlers alone until the two Courts had come to an agreement; the English Ministers, finding that matters had righted themselves in the West Indies without intervention, seem now to have made up their minds to avoid further discussion so far as they decently could. They took what Wall gave in 1755, and eluded their part of the bargain; indeed, they often quoted Wall's letter to Keene as a kind of charter to preserve the *status quo* until further order should be taken. They even made a show of distracting Wall's attention to a settlement of French buccaneers on the isthmus of Darien, which was thought to have some official countenance from the Governor of St. Domingue. 'If we can get these thorns out of our sides', Keene wrote, 'it will not be hard to stick them into those of the French, who cover their own encroachments upon Spain by bawling against us.'[1] The English Ministers were hardly to be blamed for neglecting a minor negotiation during the war, or for avoiding explanations on a point they did not wish to yield, with a great power which might set a price on its neutrality.

Wall and Keene faintly tried to quiet the controversy in 1755

[1] Keene to Newcastle, Sept. 25, 1754, Add. MSS. 32850, f. 378; Duras to St. Contest, June 17 and July 27, 1754, A.E. Espagne 515. This settlement was not a new one. There were always a few good-for-nothing Frenchmen, who had made the regular colonies too hot to hold them. They were scattered hugger-mugger up and down the Darien coast; they had been there since the days of the buccaneers, and no doubt they led the same kind of life as the English on the Moskito Shore. They seem to have received reinforcements and encouragement from St. Domingue about 1750. Conflans, then Governor, entertained some Indian chiefs and even sent some kind of trading expedition to them. A few years later a certain Father Louis, who was wanted by the police for malversations, led a party of young gentlemen from the south side of St. Domingue to make a new French colony at Darien. The old settlers had some connexions with the Spaniards (who nevertheless suspected them), but the new seem to have aspired to establish a regular plantation with a Governor and legislature. The Spanish Government was alarmed, but without reason, for neither Machault nor the local authorities at St. Domingue wanted to support Father Louis. The Darien Indians massacred sixty French families in 1757, and renewed their friendship with Jamaica. Lieutenant-Governor Moore gave them some arms against the possible arrival of a French reinforcement (Maurepas to Conflans, July 21, 1747, A.N. Colonies B 85; Vaudreuil to Machault, Jan. 13, 1755, C⁹ A 99; Machault to Vaudreuil, Oct. 31, 1756, B 103; Mémoire in A.E. Mém. et Doc. France, 2008, ff. 82, 88; Townshend to Clevland, Dec. 2, 1750, and Jan. 19, 1750/1, Adm. 1/234; intercepted letter of Dulac to Dutruch, April 4, 1755, C.O. 28/42; settlers to Marcillan, April 1, 1755, C.O. 137/60; Dulac to Marcillan, ibid.; Moore to Holdernesse, Aug. 31, 1757, C.O. 137/60).

by reviving something like Ensenada's scheme for furnishing logwood to the English dyers through Spanish channels. This project, for which Newcastle had called loudly, would have involved breaking the Navigation Acts by allowing the logwood to be imported into Jamaica in Spanish ships. Just before his resignation in 1756 Fox announced that the English Government would prepare a convention of its own for this purpose.[1] At this point Abreu, the Spanish Minister in London, once more demanded the complete evacuation of the Bay and the Moskito Shore, and requested, not for the last time, an answer in writing. Fox thought he ought to have distinguished between the two settlements. The King would give immediate orders about the Moskito Shore, but the old-established logwood settlements were another affair.[2] Pitt adopted this distinction in 1757. He would make the settlers withdraw from all encroachments made on Spanish jurisdiction since the peace of 1748—so, at least, he said, but I can find no hint of orders for the purpose. Wall, in a passion, had this answer returned to Pitt as inadmissible, and refused to listen to his excuse that Abreu had misled him into thinking this was all that was immediately wanted.

The whole affair stuck there for three years. Pitt would take no further step till Wall had explained why the answer was inadmissible; Wall would explain nothing, but threatened to leave it to time and circumstances to do him justice.[3] When the Conde de Fuentes went Ambassador to England in 1760, with high hopes of clearing up all outstanding controversies, that of the logwood settlements was disagreeably renewed.

Wall still required an unconditional withdrawal of the settlers. Pitt professed a great desire to come to an amicable agreement, but could not do so if Spain precluded discussion by demanding everything—an accusation which Wall retorted, with about as much justice, on Pitt's own head. Pitt acknowledged that some of the settlements might be unjustifiable encroachments, but could not consent in any circumstances to give up the right of

---

[1] Keene to Robinson, Dec. 10, 1755, Add. MSS. 32861, f. 269; to Fox (secret and separate), Sept. 8, 1756, S.P. 94/153; Fox to Keene, Oct. 5, 1756, ibid.

[2] Abreu to Fox, Sept. 25, 1756, G.D. 8/92; Fox to Keene, Oct. 5, 1756.

[3] Pitt to Abreu, Sept. 9, 1757, S.P. 94/156; Pitt to Keene (secret), Nov. 29, 1757; de Cosné to Pitt, Dec. 26, 1757, ibid.; April 24, 1758, S.P. 94/157; Pitt to Bristol, Aug. 1, 1758, S.P. 94/158, printed in Thackeray's *History of William Pitt* (London, 1827), i. 380–5.

cutting logwood. Wall took advantage of Pitt's admission and complained that England, having acknowledged the invalidity of all the settlements, still refused to evacuate any of them until she had extorted the conditions she wanted for the logwood-cutters. Each party, in fact, would negotiate, provided the negotiation should proceed on a basis which would imply an acceptance of its own position. Each party insisted on a *status quo* so favourable to itself that it would suffer nothing if the discussion never came to an end. Wall accused Pitt of trying to keep, in the continued occupation of the settlements, a pledge that England would never have to accept a final agreement which did not satisfy her. His accusation was perfectly just, but he might as fairly have taxed himself with exactly the same thing; for if the settlers were removed, Spain would be under no necessity to agree to anything except on her own terms. It is ill work criticizing in detail the interested logic of diplomacy. Each party wished to negotiate, but to accept no conditions but his own—not an uncommon fault in Ministers for Foreign Affairs.[1]

A sort of negotiation was continued. It seems to have been Charles III of Spain, rather than Wall, who prevented an agreement. Wall tried to persuade him to treat without the preliminary evacuation; but Charles III was determined to expel the logwood-cutters altogether, and to furnish the English with ready-cut logwood at some European or American port.[2] Wall therefore had to insist once more on the total evacuation of all the encroachments. He brushed aside the distinction between the logwood settlements and the Moskito Shore with the very reasonable argument, founded on experience, that it was useless to expel or withdraw the English from one establishment on the coast if they were to have the liberty of repairing to another. However, he made a great concession, which was the basis of the agreement finally reached in the Peace of Paris. He would only ask Pitt to withdraw the soldiers and artillery and to demolish the forts; the cutters might continue their business until a final convention should be made for supplying England with logwood. Perhaps Wall only meant to place Pitt

---

[1] Pitt to Bristol, Sept. 26, 1760, S.P. 94/162 (Thackeray, i. 487–92); Bristol to Pitt, Jan. 14 and 28, 1761, S.P. 94/163; Wall to Bristol, Jan. 24, 1761, ibid.; Pitt to Bristol, July 3, 1761 (Thackeray, i. 560).

[2] Ossun to Choiseul, July 16, 1761, A.E. Espagne, 533.

in the wrong by this, for he was already far advanced in the adjustment of the Family Compact with France. The destruction of the military defences was something more than a concession of mere form, and would at least help Spain to enforce her own terms in the last resort by removing the settlers altogether. Pitt did not accept unconditionally; before he ordered any sort of evacuation he must know the details of Wall's scheme for supplying the logwood. Here the struggle for advantage began again. Pitt would only treat if he knew beforehand that he would approve the terms which Spain would propose. Wall would only do so if he should be placed in a position to propose any terms he chose and have them accepted.[1] Here the matter rested when the sands of patience ran out in both countries; for Wall's last offer to be content with the military evacuation of Black River alone can hardly be regarded as a serious one, since it was made after the Family Compact was signed.[2]

Thus the attempt to clear up the outstanding disputes between the two countries ended in failure. The contest of pride and obstinacy over the logwood settlements destroyed the hopes which Newcastle had founded upon the Treaty of 1750. That contest might have ended less violently had Europe been at peace; but it was unhappily prolonged into the Seven Years War and became one of the most important incidents in the struggle of England and France for the alliance or at least the neutrality of Spain.

[1] Pitt to Bristol, April 24, 1761, S.P. 94/163; Bristol to Pitt, May 20, 1761, ibid.; Aug. 6 and 31, 1761, S.P. 94/164 (the latter printed in Thackeray, i. 579–88); Wall to Bristol, Aug. 28, 1761, S.P. 94/164.
[2] Bristol to Pitt, Sept. 28, 1761, S.P. 94/164.

XII

ENGLAND, FRANCE, AND SPAIN, 1756–62

§ i. *The Bidding for the Spanish Alliance*

THE English and French Governments never ceased in these years to struggle for the control of Spanish policy. For a short time after 1748 the effort was relaxed a little: each party could see that too much zeal would do more harm than good with Ferdinand VI and his ministers. But when the impermanence of the settlement of Aix-la-Chapelle became more and more apparent, the rivalry of the two countries for the favour of Spain became keener than ever.

In the ten years after the Treaty of Aix-la-Chapelle, the relations of England and Spain were more friendly than at any other time in the century. The Spanish Court was no longer grateful for the French intervention of 1744, and only remembered the rather high-handed way in which France had treated the interests of Spain at the Peace Congress. Sir Benjamin Keene successfully removed some of the outstanding causes of ill will, and avoided the consideration of those he could not remove. The French Ambassadors, Vaulgrenant and Duras, tried harder and harder to resist him as they watched his successes grow, and as their own Government saw less and less chance of keeping the peace with England in America. Keene held his own as long as Carvajal lived. Duras tried in 1753 to persuade Carvajal to make a close alliance between France and Spain, but he was put off with vague phrases, to the effect that Ferdinand VI would come to the rescue of France if he saw her oppressed or in great difficulties.[1] Duras believed that he made more impression on Carvajal in the last months of his life, and was almost sorry for his death though he had passed for an enemy of France; but Duras was not a very sensible man, and founded his belief on the report of stormy interviews between Keene and Carvajal which do not seem to have taken place.[2]

The death of Carvajal in 1754 was to have opened to his rival Ensenada a position of unquestioned authority, in which

[1] Keene to Holdernesse (most secret), Dec. 22, 1753, S.P. 94/144.
[2] Duras to St. Contest, Feb. 23, March 9 and 26, April 9, 1754, A.E. Espagne, 515.

he would have been able to provoke a war with England whenever he pleased; for though Wall was to have the department
of Foreign Affairs, Ensenada would be able to regulate the
volume of complaint against England, having the supervision
of the Indies and internal trade from which it must arise.[1] The
fall of Ensenada and the appointment of Wall to the Ministry
of Foreign Affairs were part of a preliminary struggle for
influence at the Court of Spain, between two nations which
were aware of the necessity for renewing their great contest in
America. Newcastle still hoped for a defensive alliance with
Spain, who had done enough to annoy France but not enough
to get clear of her. This consummation of his policy could only
be achieved through the fall of Ensenada.[2] Newcastle believed,
or professed to believe, that some collusive design accounted
for the coincidence of Ensenada's expedition against Honduras
with the French aggressions in North America.[3]

After his disgrace, Wall and Alva controlled the policy of
the Court, and Keene appeared stronger than ever. Wall had
passed through France on his way from London to Madrid, and
had a curious interview with St. Contest, the French Foreign
Minister. He owned it was to be desired, in the interests of
France and Spain, that a prospective aggressor should know
they stood together; but he did not admit Duras's and St.
Contest's minor premiss, that the relations of England and
Spain were critical, and that Spain would therefore need the
help of France. St. Contest had regretfully to conclude that
Wall would follow the system of Carvajal; in fact he did more
when he came to power, and set himself to finish for ever the
misunderstandings that subsisted between England and Spain.[4]

Ensenada was gone, but the defensive alliance between England and Spain was very little nearer. However, the triumph
of English diplomacy was celebrated ostentatiously by Keene's
long-coveted knighthood and by a self-satisfied announcement
in the King's speech of November 1754. Although the Opposition, through the mouth of Potter, congratulated the Government on its success, Beckford pointed out that the reality hardly
squared with the boasted professions of Spanish friendship.

[1] Duras to St. Contest, June 17, 1754, ibid.
[2] Newcastle to Keene, Jan. 24, 1754, Add. MSS. 32848, f. 146.
[3] Newcastle to Albemarle, Aug. 15, 1754, Add. MSS. 32850, f. 90.
[4] St. Contest to Duras, May 7, 1754, A.E. Espagne, 515.

Newcastle himself felt this discrepancy. He told Wall that people would contrast our behaviour to France and Spain: we armed against the one while we complimented the other, though both alike withheld from us our due. Wall replied that he did not know what to do between the French and English: they criticized him for yielding too much, while we were not satisfied with what he yielded.[1]

For many years his attitude continued to be that of the friend who wished to serve us if only we would enable him to do so by going half-way to meet him. He pointed out the difficulty of his position: a foreigner, Irish by birth, lately Ambassador in London and notoriously an intimate friend of English statesmen, he was exposed to the reproach of sacrificing Spain to England. He must therefore be at least as careful as another man to defend the essential interests of his country.[2] No doubt this was a profitable way of extorting concessions: a diplomat is not worth his hire if he cannot make his friends pay dearer than his enemies by such means. It does appear, however, that Wall was for a long time a real well-wisher to England, and that he would have liked to make it the glory of his Ministry that he had established a solid friendship with her. This explains very well the warmth with which he resented the outrages of the English privateers and Pitt's refusal to come to terms about Honduras. He was concerned to find that we ourselves made his policy impossible on his own terms. He would have liked to resign; and if he entered at last in cold blood upon measures against England, he only did so under the guidance of his master, when he had already given Pitt more than enough time for concessions and agreement. He kept up his air of pained benevolence to the last, even after the Family Compact was signed.[3] This excellent acting casts a little doubt on his earlier sincerity, but not enough to call it seriously in question.

Instead of pursuing in detail the ups and downs of English and French influence at the Court of Spain, it is more profitable

[1] King's Speech of Nov. 14, 1754, in *Parl. Hist.* xv. 330; see the debate which follows, especially Beckford's speech, p. 350. Newcastle to Keene, Jan. 27, 1755, Add. MSS. 32852, f. 275; to Wall, Jan. 26, f. 272; Wall to Newcastle, March 5, 1755, vol. 32853, f. 115.

[2] Keene to Fox (private), Sept. 8, 1756, S.P. 94/153; Keene to Holdernesse (secret and confidential), July 21, 1757, S.P. 94/155; Holdernesse to Newcastle, Sept. 8, 1757, Add. MSS. 32873, f. 464; Keene to Pitt (most secret and confidential), Sept. 26, 1757, S.P. 94/156.

[3] Bristol to Pitt (most secret), Aug. 31, 1759, S.P. 94/164.

to examine in general the arguments and offers which each nation put forward in order to gain its cause. France possessed one card which England could not play—the dynastic appeal. The French and Spanish diplomatic correspondence of this century is full of 'Bourbonism'—grandiose schemes of domination in southern or western Europe, and desperate calls for help in wars and crises, all backed by references to the ties of blood and the honour of the family. Many of these expressions were hollow and interested, but they probably counted for something, especially with Charles III, who had extended the Bourbon estate to Naples. Appeals of this kind were often made to Ferdinand VI at the beginning of the Seven Years War, coupled with a reminder of Carvajal's vague promise of 1753. His answers, however, were for the most part vague or tepid, and if he took one or two resolutions of preparing to help his cousin, they were traversed by accident or stronger influences. Duras carried his entreaties too far in the summer of 1755: he denounced the King of Spain's Ministers to his face. Ferdinand VI was really angry, and Duras had to go. Keene had the field to himself for some time after that, but his opportunity was spoilt by the depredations of our privateers, which were Wall's chief grievance in 1757.[1]

Though England had no dynastic argument of her own, she had some influence at Court. Ferdinand's Queen Barbara was a Portuguese princess, related to the Austrian Hapsburgs. Neither the Court nor the Minister of Portugal was so warmly in our interest as we were used to expect, and the Austrian connexion became a hindrance rather than a help to our designs after the reversal of the alliances in 1756. Nevertheless his Queen generally inclined Ferdinand VI to our side, and her death in 1758 gave us another year's valuable time by reducing her husband to a pitiable incapacity which paralysed Spanish policy.

The game became more complicated with the accession of Charles III, the King of Naples, to the Spanish throne in 1759. Italian ambitions were called into play. He wanted to bequeath Naples and Sicily to his son, instead of giving it up to his brother Don Philip, which the treaty-makers of 1748 appear to

---

[1] A. Soulange-Bodin, *La Diplomatie de Louis XV et le Pacte de Famille*, pp. 35–57; Keene to Robinson (secret), April 7, 1755, S.P. 94/148; Keene to Holdernesse (most secret), July 24 and 29, Aug. 27, 1755, S.P. 94/150.

have expected him to do on his accession to the Crown of Spain. George II was more free to oblige him in this respect than Louis XV, whose favourite daughter was married to Don Philip. The affair was entangled, however, by the Treaty of Aix-la-Chapelle, which provided that Don Philip should give up some of his Italian patrimony when his brother left Naples. Sardinia, who was looked upon as our ally, stood to gain by this, so the problem was quite as difficult for England as for France. Austria too was concerned, and since Maria Theresa was no longer any friend of ours, we wanted Charles III to join with Sardinia against her and sweep the board in Italy, by which method Charles III, Don Philip, and Sardinia might all have been contented without treading on each other's toes. The English Ministers, and Newcastle in particular, expected great thanks for this interesting scheme, and for their consent to the devolution of Naples upon Charles III's younger son. Newcastle relied upon this to divert Charles III's attention from his American complaints to Italy, and to stop his mouth by rendering him dependent upon us for help against Austria. Unfortunately Charles III refused to be grateful for our acquiescence in his disposition of his own property, and France removed the cause of conflict with Austria by squaring the Italian circle in such a way that everybody was satisfied. The effect of this contrivance was spoilt, however, by a ladies' quarrel over a marriage. The Archduke Joseph was intended for a daughter of Charles III, but Don Philip's wife used her influence with her father Louis XV to get the young man for her own child. The influential prejudice of Queen Maria Amalia for a neutrality between England and France was attributed, perhaps unjustly, to her resentment of this manœuvre. Her death at the end of 1760 was followed very quickly by the first steps towards the Family Compact, but whether she could have prevented it, may well be doubted.[1]

The solid interests of Spain in Europe and America required more immediate sacrifices from the belligerent powers. England

---

[1] See the accounts of Soulange-Bodin, op. cit., pp. 70–91; F. Rousseau, *Le Règne de Charles III d'Espagne*, pp. 3–7. Newcastle still believed in the summer of 1760 that Charles III was too much interested in Italy, and too dependent on us for help there, to quarrel with us for America (Newcastle to Yorke, May 29, 1760, Add. MSS. 32906, f. 350; to Kinnoull, June 6, vol. 32907, f. 21). Fuentes gave him little encouragement: 'And tho' I hung pretty much upon that string, to avoid the other, Mor Fuentes did not seem to enter into it' (Add. MSS. 32908, f. 36).

had kept for herself, at the Treaty of Utrecht, two morsels of the Spanish dominion in Europe. The recovery of Minorca and Gibraltar was one of the constant aims of Spanish policy. In ordinary circumstances no English Government would have consented to give them back, but the Seven Years War began with such disasters that the Ministers had to think seriously of yielding something. Minorca itself was taken by the French, who therefore had it to offer if the Spanish Court would take their part in the war. The French Ambassador suggested this once or twice. Wall had enough influence to get the offer repelled.[1] He had determined upon neutrality, and was not to be moved from it but by the conduct of England herself. When the Family Compact was made at last in 1761, the Spanish Ambassador in Paris tried to persuade Choiseul to put Spain provisionally in possession of Minorca. France was now disinclined for any bargain upon that island, because she had lost so much in the war that she must keep it to buy back some of her own colonies from England.[2]

The English Ministers were afraid in the first years of the war that Spain would be tempted by this offer of Minorca. They therefore brought themselves to counteract it by a sacrifice of their own. Fox was suspected of hinting to Abreu in July 1756 that we should give Spain Gibraltar if she would help us to recover Minorca. Newcastle did not like this, and Fox denied that he had ever spoken of it.[3] A year later, however, the situation of England was so little better that even Pitt proposed, and Newcastle agreed, to instruct Keene to put forward this suggestion again. Perhaps we should only have suffered in our pride if our terms had been accepted: Spain was not only to get back Minorca for us, but she must also give us Oran, Ceuta, or some port on the African shore instead of Gibraltar. Pitt offered at the same time to evacuate the new logwood settlements made since the Treaty of Aix-la-Chapelle. His language was almost that of despair: after lamenting the French victories in Lower

---

[1] Keene to Fox, May 31, 1756, S.P. 94/152; *Recueil des Instructions des Ambassadeurs, Espagne*, iii. 323.

[2] A. Bourguet, *Le Duc de Choiseul et l'alliance espagnole*, p. 210. A little later, however, Choiseul seems to have been converted to the necessity of promising Minorca to Spain (M. Danvila y Collado, *Reinado de Carlos III*, ii. 128, 137). Since France and Spain were no more successful than France alone, Minorca had to be restored to England in 1763, and Spain had to wait twenty years longer for it.

[3] Newcastle to Hardwicke, July 12, 1756, Add. MSS. 32866, f. 143.

Saxony and the danger to Cumberland's army of observation, he concluded in these words: 'The day is come, when the very inadequate benefits of the Treaty of Utrecht, that indelible reproach of the last generation, are become the necessary, but almost unattainable wish of the present; when the Empire is no more, the ports of the Netherlands betrayed, the Dutch barrier an empty sound, Minorca, and with it the Mediterranean, lost, and America itself very precarious.'[1]

Hardwicke doubted the wisdom of all this. He did not think giving up Gibraltar would be any more popular than making peace without Minorca, and he believed that if Spain procured these terms for us by interceding with France, it was to France, not to us, that she would really be obliged for the recovery of Gibraltar.[2] Perhaps it was not settled at first among the English Ministers, as it came to be later, that Spain was to procure Minorca for us not by a peaceful intercession with France, but by taking our part in the war. That would have been an end in itself, in view of the advantages which English trade in Spain would have had over the French during such a war.

The outrages of our privateers and the delay in the logwood negotiation prejudiced Wall against us so much that he could not think of accepting the proposal. His colleagues were averse to entering the war on our side; some, like Eslava, would rather have taken part against us, and Wall's own credit was ruined by the English Government's neglect. He would not promise even to represent Keene's offer to his master; Keene thought he observed 'something of a regret, either that this proposition should come too late, or in circumstances when he would not or dared not, make use of it'. 'Are these times and circumstances', he asked Keene a few days later, 'to talk on such points as the liberties of Europe and a close union with Spain, when you have given *us* so much room to be dissatisfied with you?'[3]

---

[1] Pitt to Keene (most secret and confidential), Aug. 23, 1757, S.P. 94/155; Newcastle to Hardwicke, Aug. 9, 1757, Add. MSS. 32872, f. 492; Newcastle's memorandum of Aug. 16, vol. 32997, f. 245. Pitt appears, but not certainly, to have thought of this first.

[2] Hardwicke to Newcastle, Aug. 11, 1757, Add. MSS. 32873, f. 25.

[3] Keene to Pitt (most secret and confidential), Sept. 26, 1757, S.P. 94/156, printed in *Chatham Correspondence*, i. 263-77. The idea of giving up Gibraltar was strongly denounced, and even the value of Spanish neutrality was questioned, by Postlethwayt (*Britain's Commercial Interest Explained and Improved* (London, 1757), ii. 490).

§ ii. *The Spanish Grievances—the Prizes and the Fishery*

What were the injuries which so estranged Wall from his friends in England, and drove him at last into war? First of all, the violations of Spanish neutrality by English warships and privateers. It would be impossible to discuss these in a satisfactory manner, without entering into the vast subject of neutral rights.[1] The English Ministry knew very well the bad consequence of offending Spain during the war with France, and tried hard to avoid it; indeed, it treated Spain with more favour or justice than it allowed to any other neutrals. But the proper pride of the Admiralty, the difficulty of controlling the privateers, the reluctance of the Government to interfere with the Prize Courts, and a kind of *raison d'état* which has always been the curse of belligerent nations—all these things prevented the best-intentioned Ministers from satisfying the claims of any neutral power. The molestation of Spanish merchant vessels, and seizures within Spanish territorial waters, continued to incense Wall to such a pitch of fury that even his old friend Keene could do nothing with him. Poor Keene can truly be said to have died of these disputes. His successor Lord Bristol was able to calm Wall, but the mischief was done. Neither Wall nor Charles III could forget the tactless inflexibility with which the navy and the courts of England asserted their very questionable doctrines of international law—the most odious possible reminder of the rights of the strong.

The second of the grievances for which Spain went to war with England arose out of the first. But for the seizures of Spanish ships in the French North America trade, the question of the Newfoundland fishery need not have arisen at this time. It was first mentioned in one of Abreu's complaints about prize cases. Some of the ships which were brought up before the English courts seem to have had Spanish passports for going to fish in Newfoundland. This errand was presumably no more than a pretext for carrying provisions to the French colonies; but the validity of the excuse was unavoidably called in question. Abreu quoted the treaties from which Spain claimed the right to take part in this fishery, and Pitt very soon joined issue by denying the whole Spanish case.[2]

---

[1] I hope to do so in a book to be published shortly.

[2] Abreu to Pitt, June 16, 1758, S.P. 94/157; Pitt to Bristol, Aug. 1 and 15

There was little to be said for the Spanish claim to the fishery, so far as it was founded upon the right of first discovery; but the English argument for excluding the Spaniards altogether was supported by some rather dubious sophistries. Obviously the rights had been far from clear when the Treaty of Utrecht was signed, for it begged the question by preserving to the Spaniards any privileges to which they could make good a title. Neither Government had ever meant to yield anything by this formula; England tried to entrap Spain by granting licences for Spanish voyages to Newfoundland, but it does not appear that their acceptance really prejudiced the Spanish case. The dispute had slept at any rate since the Treaty of 1721, which avoided a determination in the same way as that of Utrecht.[1] It now became a burning question, because the Ministers of England, France, and Spain were all intent upon improving their navies, and thought of the fishery as the best possible training for sailors. Pitt and Choiseul attended to this point so earnestly that their peace negotiation came to grief on it in 1761. Spain, who had so long disused the fishery, could hardly pretend that it was of the same importance to her; but the middle of the eighteenth century was a time of colonial and maritime revival, in which the fishery may have been meant to play a part.[2]

Neither Pitt nor any other English Minister seems to have thought seriously of yielding this point to Spain. England had already got the sole possession of Newfoundland by the Treaty of Utrecht; the French still enjoyed the fishery on the banks, besides that of the St. Lawrence which naturally belonged to the sovereignty of Canada. After the conquest of Montreal,

S.P. 94/158; Pitt to Abreu, Aug. 11, ibid.; see Fuentes's later memorial, Sept. 9, 1760, S.P. 94/162.

[1] See the article of Miss Vera Lee Brown on this subject, in the *Annual Report* of the Canadian Historical Association for 1925.

[2] Historians generally make the most of Charles III's interest in this question and in the revival of the Spanish navy. That seems to have begun under Ensenada and continued by Arriaga, though Charles III still found much to do when he came to the throne. Ensenada had been aware of the Spanish claims to the fishery in 1746, though he did not expect to have them recognized at once. Macanaz had tried to get them established by his peace project of 1747 (S.P. 84/425, f. 80). The Spanish Government first took up the Newfoundland question, and demanded an answer in writing, before the accession of Charles III. The mercantilist writers Uztaritz and Ulloa had complained of the loss of this fishery, though in a rather academic way (Uztaritz, op. cit. ii. 135–45; Ulloa, op. cit. ii. 42–9). Their aspirations were noticed and condemned in 1757 by Malachy Postlethwayt in *Britain's Commercial Interest Explained and Improved* (ii. 282), so the Newfoundland question was a familiar one before Abreu reopened it.

Pitt seems to have aimed at a monopoly of both these fisheries, by excluding even the French from them. The other members of the Cabinet were less ambitious to deprive France of the fishery, but even Newcastle hardly wanted to allow it to Spain, and if he would have done it, he dared not. Hardwicke thought the Spanish pretensions very thin, and Pitt never varied his absolute denial of any concession or even discussion of the point. It was 'sacred'; it was even more than the friendship of Spain was worth.[1]

It was hardly one of Spain's essential interests to insist on this privilege, even if it was one of England's to deny it (which is somewhat doubtful). If the prizes and the Newfoundland fishery had been their only grievances, Charles III and Wall would hardly have had any solid reason for departing from their neutrality. The controversy over the logwood settlements was a far more important affair;[2] but the worst thing of all was the spirit in which the English Government treated all these questions. Two things became more and more evident after the tide had begun to turn in our favour against France. Pitt meant to sweep the board in North America and perhaps in the West Indies too. By conquering one French colony after another, he must necessarily make England the strongest power in that part of the world, and bring her face to face with Spain. Moreover, he clearly wished to avoid dealing with the Spanish claims in Newfoundland and Central America until he had finished the war with France. Spain would then have to confront him alone, and to settle her accounts with him on any terms he thought proper to impose.

§ iii. *The Balance of Power and the Family Compact*

The successive conquests of Louisbourg, Guadeloupe, and Quebec gave Spain increasing cause for anxiety. Wall expressed some private satisfaction as a friend of England, but this may have been a mere compliment.[3] Charles III was without Wall's partiality to us, and was seriously impressed by the appeals of

---

[1] Newcastle to Hardwicke, July 15, 1760, Add. MSS. 32908, f. 308; to Mansfield, July 18, f. 353; to Hardwicke, Sept. 13, vol. 32911, f. 270; Hardwicke to Newcastle, Sept. 14, f. 286; Pitt to Bristol, Sept. 26, 1760, S.P. 94/162, and July 28, 1761, S.P. 94/163 (these two dispatches are largely printed in Thackeray's *History of William Pitt*, i. 487-90, 570-3). See also Bristol's account of his arguments with Wall, in his dispatch of Nov. 6, 1760 (most secret), S.P. 94/162, and Wall's paper of Jan. 24, 1761, S.P. 94/163.   [2] *V. supra*, pp. 550-5.

[3] Bristol to Pitt, Nov. 12, 1759, S.P. 94/160.

the French Court to the common interests of France and Spain
in America. Ossun, the French Ambassador accredited to him
both at Naples and Madrid, declared that the French colonies in
North America were the bulwark of the Spanish Indies against
the aggressions of England. Cape Breton, Canada, and Louisiana
lay successively between the English and the mines of Mexico;
but those defences were falling one by one. Charles III's blood
froze at the news of Quebec; Montreal was to surrender next
year, and the English army would be free to proceed against
New Orleans. In the same way the loss of Guadeloupe was
likely to be followed by that of Martinique and perhaps St.
Domingue too; what sort of neighbours would the English be
to the Spaniards on Hispaniola?[1]

The English Ministers did their best to repel these suspicions.
While the controversy with France was still maturing, they
tried to retort the charge of encroachment by pointing out that
the French memorials made claims to North America which
Spain would be sorry to see us admit.[2] Pitt assured the Neapoli-
tan Ambassador Sanseverino in 1759 that we did not mean to
attack French Hispaniola, but should only conquer the Windward Islands.[3] Even this limitation did not quite satisfy Spain,
who still held some sort of a claim to the Neutral Islands, upon
the principle that whatever she had not formally conceded in
America to a foreign nation was still hers by right. During the
peace negotiation of 1761, Wall warned Choiseul not to sign
away those islands to England without regard to this interest;
but it was a small matter, and Spain only put it forward in
order to acquire a title to some compensation in another field.[4]
In North America, Pitt made a merit of abstaining from any
conquest which might give umbrage to Spain; perhaps this was
the reason why Amherst never made any attack on Louisiana.[5]
The Spanish Government particularly desired that the English
should have no settlement near the Gulf of Mexico, for that
would bring them to the treasure route by a side-door.

---

[1] Rousseau, op. cit., p. 39; Duras had tried the effect of these arguments before
the war began (Keene to Robinson, April 7, 1755 (secret), S.P. 94/148).

[2] Robinson to Keene (secret), March 11, 1755, ibid.

[3] Pitt to Bristol, June 5, 1759, S.P. 94/159.

[4] Bristol to Pitt, July 13, 1761, S.P. 94/163. Wall discussed the matter with
Bristol as well (Bristol to Pitt, Aug. 10, 1761, S.P. 94/164).

[5] Pitt to Abreu, Dec. 13, 1759, S.P. 94/160; Hardwicke to Newcastle, Oct. 19,
1760, Add. MSS. 32913, f. 210.

Besides these considerations, Choiseul and Ossun brought forward once more the doctrine of the American balance of power. This was the natural retort to the English cant upon the liberties of Europe. It took several forms. Sometimes Ossun or Sanseverino would imply that there ought to be a local balance of power in every region of the world, which it was the interest of neutrals to keep even. Something of the sort had been established in America by the Treaty of Utrecht, and it was now upset by the English conquests. When Sanseverino repeated this language in London, Pitt asked him how Charles III would like it if we were to talk about the balance of power in Italy? This shaft fell wide of the mark, because Charles III did not accept Pitt's encouragement to upset that particular equilibrium for his own advantage. Pitt further denied that the Treaty of Utrecht had meant to establish an American balance of power, and if it had done so, France as the first encroacher and aggressor was more responsible than we were for its alteration. He thought it neither very friendly nor very neutral of Charles III to say that he could not see with indifference our conquests in America. We only took, and meant to keep, what was necessary to our security and to the prevention of future wars. (This was almost an admission that we meant to upset the balance, which can hardly be said to exist when one party is permanently secure from attacks by the other.)[1] Sir James Gray, at Naples, replied to the same arguments in another way: he denied the existence of such regional balances of power, and maintained that there was only one in all the world, which France, through her preponderance in Europe, was more likely to upset than we were.[2] The French diplomats overcame this objection by arguing that the military balance on land was no longer important; it was commerce, wealth, and sea power that carried the day, therefore the colonial and maritime balance was the most essential of all.[3]

Choiseul meant to establish on these grounds a case for

---

[1] Newcastle to Hardwicke, Oct. 22, 1759, Add. MSS. 32897, f. 287; Abreu to Pitt, Dec. 5, 1759, S.P. 94/160; Pitt to Abreu, Dec. 13, ibid.

[2] Gray to Pitt (extract), Sept. 27, 1759, Add. MSS. 32896, f. 132.

[3] Choiseul to Ossun, Sept. 7, 1759 (*Recueil des Instructions des Ambassadeurs, Espagne*, iii. 349). See also the letter of Choiseul to Ossun quoted in Bourguet, op. cit., p. 159. Duras had already held this language in 1755 (paper enclosed by Keene to Robinson, April 7, 1755, S.P. 94/148). See also *Le Politique danois*, pp. 141-3, 281-4.

Spanish mediation. At the beginning of the war, France had been no more anxious for such a thing than England, but after so many disasters she had changed her opinion. Bernis wanted a Spanish mediation in 1758, but the eclipse of Ferdinand VI's understanding made it impossible.[1] Choiseul returned to the plan next year with more hope of success. He was for dividing the separate peace with England, under the mediation of Spain, from the general congress, because he hoped to extort better terms by isolating England in a three-cornered discussion with France and Spain on those questions in which alone Spain had an interest opposite to that of England. The English Ministers seem to have guessed something of the sort.[2] Newcastle was not for rejecting a Spanish offer altogether, because he thought Pitt would prefer Charles III's mediation to any other, and therefore regarded it as the only way to reconcile Pitt to a peace. George II did not like it at all, and as it turned out, Newcastle must have been mistaken about the attitude of Pitt, who went to considerable shifts to avoid the intervention of Spain; he was afraid of a private peace between England and France, because once our own war was over and we had nothing more to gain, the Ministry could not easily get Parliament to continue supporting Frederick II, whom he was determined not to desert. Newcastle admitted this, but seems to have thought there could be no harm in a separate negotiation so long as it did not lead to a separate peace. That was both silly and dangerous, and Pitt was no doubt in the right to avoid the interposition of Charles III altogether.[3] He put it aside, professing his readiness to accept good offices, and at the same time he tried to render it unnecessary by proposing, in concert with Prussia, a general peace congress at which everything should be treated.

Choiseul really wanted a peace; even the Spanish mediation was designed as a means to it, not as an excuse for embroiling Spain in the war. He would still have preferred to settle his affairs with England through the mediation of Spain, but he

---

[1] *Mémoires et Lettres du Cardinal de Bernis* (ed. Masson, 1878), ii. 44, 98, 191, 259.

[2] Hardwicke to Newcastle, Jan. 3, 1760, Add. MSS. 32901, f. 48.

[3] Newcastle's memoranda of Aug. 27, 1759, Add. MSS. 32894, f. 477; Hardwicke to Newcastle, Aug. 30, Sept. 2 and 12, vol. 32895, ff. 32, 117, 363; Newcastle to Hardwicke, Aug. 31, f. 80; Newcastle's memoranda of Oct. 8 and 11, vol. 32896, f. 349 and 32897, f. 11; Newcastle to Hardwicke, Oct. 15 and 31, vol. 32897, ff. 88, 513; Hardwicke to Newcastle, Oct. 24, f. 351; Dec. 5, vol. 32899, f. 301; Newcastle to Hardwicke, Jan. 2, 1760, vol. 32901, f. 42.

could not afford to reject the congress. Meanwhile Charles III had met Wall, and seen for himself the unreadiness of the Spanish army and navy. Wall had not been consulted on the mediation; he had always disliked it as a step which might lead Spain into the war, and he was supported in this by Queen Maria Amalia and perhaps by Charles III's own conviction of the necessity of waiting his time. Spain therefore accepted Pitt's snub, and offered good offices instead of mediation. Choiseul still tried hard to keep her to the original plan, and Charles III finally allowed him to say that England had refused mediation. The first months of 1760 were taken up with a futile controversy over the truth of this, and perhaps Charles III was as much angry with Choiseul as with Pitt for so unpleasant an advertisement of his failure.[1]

While Charles III strengthened his resources and increased his navy, the controversy between England and Spain took a more dangerous turn. The Conde de Fuentes, who had been his named Ambassador to England long ago, was at last sent to post with orders to press for satisfaction of the various injuries which Spain had suffered from the English. The discussion of those grievances, especially that of the logwood affair, had been hung up too long already, and if Spain was to take any advantage of England's war with France, her opportunity was beginning to run out. This mission of Fuentes seems to have been England's last chance of making up her differences with Spain. Presumably Charles III and Wall had determined to know where they stood, in order to decide whether Spain's own interests required her to take part in the war while France was still able to wage it. It was not only the balance of power that was the question, but the prizes, the fishery, and the logwood settlements.

Fuentes presented a batch of memorials and demanded an answer in writing. Pitt gave one in September about the prizes, but avoided saying anything definite on the other two questions, since no answer which we could bring ourselves to give was likely to satisfy Spain. Even Newcastle disputed the points of Newfoundland and the logwood; but after a closer attention

[1] See Yorke's letters to Holdernesse at the beginning of 1760, S.P. 84/487, also Newcastle to Yorke, Feb. 26, 1760, Add. MSS. 32902, f. 408; see also Bourguet, op. cit., pp. 41–88; Rousseau, op. cit., pp. 33–51; Soulange-Bodin, op. cit., pp. 111–37.

to Fuentes's arguments, he began to think we were in the wrong about the latter. Kinnoull and Hardwicke, the two best informed and most judicious of his friends, agreed with him. Bute was as firm as Pitt about the fishery, but hoped we might accommodate the affair of the logwood.[1] Even Pitt himself seems to have thought we might have to yield this point, for he prepared to throw the blame of doing so upon Newcastle.

'He told me, in a very extraordinary manner, and persisted in it to the last, that, when the affair came to be decided, which he thought must be brought to an issue very soon, he (Mr. Pitt) would give no opinion. That it was the Duke of Newcastle, and My Lord Hardwicke, who must determine it.'

The reason he gave for this strange abnegation was that Newcastle had already compromised our case many years before by promising Wall that we would yield something; further:

'That he, (Mr. Pitt) was not in a situation in the administration to stand either breaking with Spain, or the giving up any right of this country—that he did not apprehend the consequences of a breach with Spain, so much as others might do; tho' he wish'd extremely to avoid it, in order to secure an alliance with that Crown, with regard to the affairs of Europe in general. He thinks, Spain will give up the point of the fishery on Newfoundland, and would propose some expedient with regard to the logwood. But whether that expedient should be accepted or not, he would not give any opinion. He said, the Duke of Newcastle is the person, who has the confidence of the King, the Duke of Newcastle has the support of the Parliament, and a power, which may enable him to stand the one or the other. That his situation was very different.'[2]

This may have been a momentary outburst of ill humour, or a clever threat calculated to paralyse Newcastle, or Pitt may

---

[1] Newcastle's memorandum of his interview with Fuentes, July 3, 1760, Add. MSS. 32908, f. 36; Kinnoull to Newcastle, July 10, 1760, f. 171; Memorandum of conversation with Viry, July 25, vol. 32909, f. 46; Newcastle to Hardwicke, Sept. 13, vol. 32911, f. 270; Hardwicke to Newcastle, Sept. 14, f. 286.

[2] Newcastle's memorandum of July 4, 1760, Add. MSS. 32908, ff. 80–1. I hardly know what credit to give to this sort of report. No doubt Newcastle thought he understood Pitt right, but he was himself so anxious to escape responsibility for anything unpopular, that he may have erred in thinking that others were trying to get rid of it by thrusting it on him; that is, he may have judged Pitt too much by himself. Nevertheless Hardwicke, whose judgement I would take against that of any of his contemporaries, seems to have shared Newcastle's opinion of Pitt, and I am inclined to believe, from this and many other instances, that Pitt was an exceedingly artful demagogue, who took the credit for anything popular and often —but not always—shirked the responsibility for things that would not go down.

afterwards have changed his mind. He seems to have determined to avoid giving Fuentes a definite answer. He received a most unfortunate encouragement in this fatal course from the indolence of Hardwicke, without whom Newcastle dared not face him. Hardwicke did not want to come to town, and acquiesced the more readily in Pitt's policy of delay. He argued it neither proper nor necessary to return answers at once to Fuentes's memorials.

'They can never be such, as will please the Court of Spain, neither do I think that the people of England, in their present temper, will bear it. Therefore I think it will be right to gain time, as much as possible, especially till you see the winding up of this campaign, both in Germany and America: for according to those events, it may be right to speak more or less strongly to Spain.'[1]

This may have been true. It certainly was so, if the Ministers were determined to be afraid of their own supporters (which was quite unnecessary before the death of George II) or to vindicate at all costs what Pitt thought, but Newcastle and Hardwicke did not think, the just and essential interests of their country. At any rate it coincided with Pitt's own reasoning. He contented himself with declaring, in a long dispatch to Bristol, that he was ready to negotiate the logwood question, but not on the basis of Fuentes's memorial. As for the fishery, Spain must 'cease to expect, as a consideration of an union, which it is at least as much to her interest as to ours to maintain inviolate, a sacrifice which can never be made'.[2]

It was here that the negotiation took the wrong turning from which it never came back. Wall and Fuentes had long suspected that Pitt was only trifling with them until he should have his

---

[1] Hardwicke to Newcastle, Sept. 14, 1760, Add. MSS. 32911, f. 286.

[2] Pitt to Bristol, Sept. 26, 1760, S.P. 94/162. Pitt did not make clear his reasons for saying that Spain gained at least as much as England from their mutual friendship. He may have been thinking of the argument that England was a much better customer for Spanish produce than France, though the balance of the trade between the two countries was supposed to turn in favour of England. English pamphleteers often used this argument in order to prove that Spain must lose more by a war than England. (For example, *The Advantages and Disadvantages which will attend the Prohibition of the Merchandizes of Spain, impartially examined* (London, 1740), p. 29.) Postlethwayt complained in 1757 that the Spaniards took more French than English textiles, although England was a better customer for Spanish goods (*Great Britain's True System*, p. lxxxiv). So far as the trade statistics prove anything, the exports from England easily overbalanced the imports in every year of peace between 1730 and 1770 (see Sir C. Whitworth's figures, *State of the Trade of Great Britain*, ii. 31-2).

hands free of the French war; now they were sure of it. Ossun
held the same language to Charles III.[1] Wall pressed Bristol
for an answer in writing, ostensibly because he needed it to
defend himself against this suggestion of Ossun; but Bristol
would not even give him a copy of Pitt's dispatch. Pitt continued to withhold a written answer, on the pretext that a paper
war of memorials would only irritate the Court of Spain; he
was willing instead to 'negotiate' the points in dispute by word
of mouth.[2] At the same time Wall ordered Fuentes to try once
more to obtain something in writing about the logwood settlements.

'If they should confess, as they do verbally, that they ought not to
keep those settlements, and that they will evacuate them upon such
a condition, we always obtain, by their confession, a new pledge of
our justice. Do you therefore continue to press strongly for an
answer in writing, which at all events must be of use to us, in order
that the King's measures may have a solid support.'[3]

The last sentence has an ominous look; but no danger could
draw any concession from Pitt. There was a race between the
exhaustion of France and the rising anger of the Court of Spain,
and the English Government had some reason for hoping that
France would submit before Spain was ready.

That was just what Charles III and Wall feared. Wall asked
Bristol again and again whether he thought Spain could be so
foolish as to pick a quarrel with England at the height of her
power and triumph. In truth, however, this was his last good
chance, and he knew it. Choiseul had never concealed that if
Spain allowed France to be defeated in this war, he should not
be able, if he wanted, to support Charles III in his quarrels
with England.[4] Spain must soon make up her mind once for
all whether she was likely to procure satisfaction from England
without fighting, and whether France could hold out against
England long enough for her to enter the war. Grimaldi and
Fuentes, at Paris and London, were already convinced at the
beginning of 1761 that it would be a disaster for Spain if
England and France were to make peace before she had per-

<hr/>

[1] Bristol to Pitt, Nov. 6 (most secret), Dec. 1, 1760, S.P. 94/162.

[2] Pitt to Bristol, Sept. 26 and Dec. 23, 1760, ibid.; Bristol to Pitt, Nov. 6 (two
letters) and Dec. 22, ibid.

[3] Wall to Fuentes, Dec. 22, 1760, intercepted, Add. MSS. 38197, f. 102.

[4] Bristol to Pitt (most secret), Nov. 6, 1760; Choiseul to Ossun, Sept. 7, 1759,
Recueil des Instructions des Ambassadeurs, Espagne, iii. 350.

suaded the former to yield or the latter to support her.[1] Wall
must have come round to this opinion at the same time. At the
beginning of January he heard from London, through Bristol
and Fuentes, that Pitt had once more refused a written answer
about Honduras; at the same time he procured a document
which informed him clearly enough what the answer would
have been, if it had been given. This was Pitt's dispatch to
Bristol of September 26, which Pitt had consented to let him
see. Wall was so displeased with it that he would not even
show it to his master, or so he told Bristol.[2] However, he now
knew where he stood: he was 'at length fully convinced of what
he might expect from Great Britain'. He could look for no
concession on the fishery, and England would insist on negotiating the logwood question before she evacuated the settlements,
whereas Spain had demanded that the evacuation should take
place first.

Wall saw the dispatch not long before the 14th of January;
on the 19th Ossun told Choiseul that if he could make a good
peace with England he ought to do so, but there was no need
to accept a bad one in a hurry, because Spain would soon be
ready to come to his help.[3] Soon afterwards Grimaldi, the new
Spanish Ambassador at Versailles, made overtures for a closer
union of the two Bourbon powers. Whether he made his first
proposal by order, is an unimportant question; he soon enough
got his conduct approved. It was the fear of a peace between
France and England that inspired Grimaldi with such a precipitate zeal for the Family Compact. Convinced that Spain
could only get her grievances redressed by war, he saw that it
was her advantage to throw her weight into the scale of France
now, rather than fight single-handed a few months later.[4] As
he told Fuentes on March 5: 'It appears to me of the utmost
importance for us, to assure ourselves of France, and engage her
before she makes her peace; for afterwards, I don't know what

[1] Fuentes to Wall, Jan. 30, 1761, G.D. 8/93; Grimaldi to Fuentes, Feb. 26
and March 5, 1761, *Chatham Correspondence*, ii. 92, 95; Fuentes to Grimaldi,
March 10, p. 96.
[2] Bristol to Pitt, Jan. 14 and 19, 1761, S.P. 94/163; Fuentes to Wall, Jan. 23,
1761, Add. MSS. 32918, f. 27.   [3] Bourguet, op. cit., p. 176.
[4] In this he seems to have differed from Wall, who repeatedly told Ossun he
hoped a war could be avoided. Wall may even have welcomed the French intervention in the Anglo-Spanish dispute because it would enable Spain to yield with
dignity what she could not give up to England alone (Ossun to Choiseul, June 29,
1761, A.E. Espagne, 532; July 16, vol. 533).

inclination she may have to go to war again for our sake.'[1] At the same time he had to conceal from Choiseul the obvious self-interest of the scheme, and to represent it as the overflowing of Charles III's compassion for his cousin.[2] For this affectation of generosity Choiseul made Spain pay heavily at the Peace of Paris.

Choiseul now had two strings to his bow. He can hardly be said to have made up his mind whether he would rely more on making a peace with England or continuing the war with the help of Spain. Much would depend on the terms which could be obtained from the enemy and the ally. Choiseul was ready to make Spain pay for helping him. He can hardly be blamed for that, since she had often refused help when France needed it, and only offered it now in her own interest, when France was bled white by the war.

He seems to have given up the idea of a new Treaty of Commerce,[3] convinced that France already enjoyed by prescription such rights as could hardly be improved by a new tariff.[4] He did, however, ask Charles III to prevent neutrals from importing English manufactures during the prospective war with England. The ostensible purpose was to aggravate England's financial exhaustion by cutting off her export markets; but presumably there was the ulterior motive of enabling French counterfeits to establish themselves securely in the market under this protection.[5] That was exactly one of the things England most feared from a war with Spain.[6] Further, the Family

[1] Grimaldi to Fuentes, March 5, 1761, Add. MSS. 32919, f. 446.
[2] Fuentes to Grimaldi, March 10, 1761, vol. 32920, f. 40.
[3] He had suggested it at first—see his letter to Ossun of Jan. 27, 1761, quoted by Bourguet, op. cit., p. 180.
[4] See the *mémoire* sent to Ossun with Choiseul's approval on May 5 (A.E. Espagne, 532). Ossun disagreed with Choiseul; he thought it was to Spain's advantage to resign any attempt at manufactures, for which her working population was too small, and to live by exporting raw materials to the industrious French, from whom she should receive them back as finished products (Ossun to Choiseul, with *mémoire* annexed, June 29, 1761, ibid.). Even the English had never asked more than this: Ensenada and the Spanish mercantilists would not have thanked Ossun for the suggestion.
[5] Choiseul to Ossun, July 7, 1761, A.E. Espagne, 533. Such a clause was finally included in the Family Compact and was very strictly executed. The shop-keepers of Madrid ran out of English cloth and would have been glad to supply themselves with French substitutes, but the local regulations of Nîmes about sizes and standards obstructed the contract, and the help of the French Ministry had to be invoked (Ossun to Choiseul, May 27, 1762, A.E. Espagne, 536).
[6] Bristol to Egremont (separate and secret), Dec. 6, 1761, S.P. 94/164.

Compact finally included a vaguely worded clause by which each nation communicated to the subjects of the other the same rights that were enjoyed by its own natives, and no other country might claim the privilege so imparted, even by virtue of a most-favoured-nation clause. If this article had been at all precise, France would at last have gained the position of unique and exclusive commercial privilege for which she had so long striven at Madrid; but in fact it seems to have had very little importance.

Although France did not ask for many tangible advantages from the Spanish alliance—for indeed the alliance itself appeared to be advantage enough—Grimaldi and Choiseul had nevertheless a violent tug-of-war over the terms. It was Grimaldi's object to prevent France from making peace with England without procuring redress of the Spanish grievances into the bargain. For this purpose he suggested that each power should communicate to the other all its negotiations, and that neither should make peace without the consent of the other. Choiseul thought this unreasonable, especially as Grimaldi proposed to avoid if possible the entry of Spain into the war. This was asking France to pay the reckoning while Spain called the tune.[1] Choiseul (as he later said in his justification) regarded the question between peace with England and the Spanish alliance as an open one—or rather, he would prefer a peace with England if it could be had on reasonable terms; the Spanish alliance was only to guarantee him against bad ones.[2] His negotiation with Pitt, through the missions of Bussy and Stanley, had already begun in the middle of his more secret one with Spain, and if it succeeded, he did not mean to spoil it by drag-

---

[1] Choiseul to Ossun, May 26, 1761, A.E. Espagne, 532. There were other causes of disagreement. Spain wanted to limit so far as possible the contingencies against which she was to guarantee France—that is to say, she did not want to follow France into an offensive German war. Besides, she only offered at first to guarantee France the territories she should possess at the peace with England, while France was to guarantee all that Spain possessed now. That is to say, France was to undertake that Spain should lose nothing at all, while Spain would not undertake that France should lose nothing more (Choiseul to Ossun, May 26 and June 2; Ossun to Choiseul, June 22). This inequality was removed in the Family Compact, by which each power only guaranteed to the other what it should hold at the next peace.

[2] See Choiseul's *mémoire* printed by Soulange-Bodin, op. cit., pp. 242–3; Choiseul's instructions to Bussy, May 23, 1761, A.E. Angleterre, 443. He continued to say so as late as July 7, when he was on the point of deciding to unite himself with Spain (Choiseul to Ossun, July 7, A.E. Espagne, 533).

ging in Spanish affairs. He therefore told Bussy to keep Fuentes quiet in London so long as there was any hope of a peace, and only to play upon his animosity if there was none.[1] At the same time, while offering to sign the Family Compact as soon as Spain pleased, he only promised to make the satisfaction of Spain's demands on England an indispensable condition of his own peace if he had not succeeded in making it within eleven months; in that case, Spain was then to declare war on England.[2] The only point on which Spain was to be consulted in all events was the partition of the Neutral Islands between England and France. This was reasonable, because Spain asserted some claim to them; but it might serve, if the negotiations for peace went badly, as a hook to draw Spain into the general discussion of the terms.[3]

It was therefore clear that if Pitt and Choiseul came to an agreement at once, Spain would be left out. The issue of Choiseul's double game turned on the intrigues within the English Ministry. As early as January 1761, Fuentes reported that England would never yield anything so long as Pitt controlled her policy, but a little pressure might hearten the peace party and bring about his fall. The Russian Ambassador in London gave Choiseul the same advice in April, and advised him not to show too much facility. Finally Choiseul himself claimed, after the event, to have discerned at a very early stage of the peace negotiation that it turned on the struggle of Pitt and Bute for ascendancy.[4]

The affair was not quite so simple as Choiseul believed. Bute wanted Pitt's power and popularity, but he was not sure whether it was yet safe to dispense with him, and he did not know how to beat him except with his own weapons.[5] It is a

---

[1] Instructions to Bussy, May 23, 1761, A.E. Angleterre, 443. Unfortunately Bussy despaired at once of the peace and began to work up Fuentes too soon.

[2] Choiseul to Ossun, June 2, 1761, A.E. Espagne, 532.

[3] In fact it did so (Choiseul to Bussy, June 19 and July 4, A.E. Angleterre, 443; see also Bussy's instructions, ibid., and Choiseul to Ossun, May 26).

[4] Fuentes to Wall, Jan. 23, 1761, Add. MSS. 32918, f. 27; Galitzin to Choiseul, April 26, 1761, A.E. Angleterre, 443; Choiseul's mémoire of 1765, printed by Soulange-Bodin, op. cit., pp. 242-3.

[5] Fox afterwards attributed this to Gilbert Elliot's attempt to bring Bute and Pitt together, which 'raised, or at least fomented and increas'd in Ld Bute that vain imagination of gaining equal popularity with Pitt; in order to which, his Lordship was, in such points as he thought would at all effect that, of Pitt's side in the Council, and carrying the cyphers of the Cabinet with him outvoted the sound part' (Memoir, in Life and Letters of Lady Sarah Lennox, i. 51).

mistake to treat Bute as the head of the peace party during this summer of 1761. He pursued peace, it is true, but dared not make an unpopular one; for a long time, therefore, he was half an accomplice of Pitt, and the task of insisting on peace at any reasonable price fell upon Newcastle and Hardwicke, and most of all upon Bedford. In fact it was Bute as much as Pitt who suggested on June 26 the fatal decision to refuse France any fishery in America—even that of Newfoundland which she had always enjoyed. Pitt and Temple were for claiming the monopoly of the fishery. Newcastle and Bedford disliked that, but Bute persuaded the majority of the Cabinet to try once more whether France would yield it, without meaning to insist if she held firm. Though Pitt condemned this trial of Choiseul's resistance as 'puerile and illusory', he did not reject help in any form, and altered his dispatch so as to declare that we would not allow France any share of the fishery without some great and important compensation—by which he meant the almost equally unacceptable condition of demolishing Dunkirk.[1]

By all accounts this was the turning-point of the negotiation. There were indeed other matters in dispute, even in the fishery itself. Choiseul wanted not only the Newfoundland fishery but that of the St. Lawrence as well, and a settlement to which the French fishermen could resort; without this, he said, the right of fishing was illusory. Bute's unfortunate suggestion only covered the first of these points; at that stage of the negotiation the Cabinet was almost unanimous in refusing the other two, which were equally indispensable in Choiseul's eyes. It would therefore be wrong to blame any one party in the Ministry for the failure to bridge the gulf between Pitt's concessions and Choiseul's demands. It is nevertheless true that if Bute and his fellow waverers had agreed in June to what they allowed in September, the peace might have been made between England and France, and the Family Compact might never have come into being.

There is plenty of evidence that the refusal of the fishery convinced Choiseul that he must ally himself with Spain and continue the war. A day or two after he heard of it, he first told Stanley, who was negotiating with him in Paris, that he

---

[1] Newcastle to Devonshire, June 28, 1761, Add. MSS. 32924, ff. 312–20; Pitt to Stanley, June 26, printed in Thackeray's *History of William Pitt*, i. 546.

had been offered a Spanish alliance.[1] At the same time he
ordered Bussy to introduce Spain into the negotiation by
declaring that France could only discuss the Neutral Islands
with the consent of Spain; he warned Bussy that this was only
the first move, and that the next messenger would bring him
further instructions.[2] It is true that he still tried to convince
Charles III that he would prefer a peace with England on good
conditions to a prolongation of the war; but he may have meant
to sharpen Charles III's desire for the Family Compact by an
affectation of reserve.[3]

He took an irrevocable step on July 15. He had made up his
mind not to yield the fishery, and if Pitt persisted in withholding
it, he should only spin out the negotiation in order to gain time.
He sent Bussy a memorial, which set forth the grievances of
Spain and argued that the peace between England and France
would only be solid if Spain was satisfied as well, because, if
Spain went to war with England, France would be obliged to
take her part.[4] In this and other ways he not only revealed that
he was about to enter into some engagement with Spain for
that purpose, but gave Pitt the impression that he had already
done so. Perhaps Choiseul had still half a hope of peace, for
he would have wished Bussy to keep this memorial up his sleeve
until Pitt should have answered the French ultimatum, which
was sent at the same time and demanded the fishery once more.
He wanted to give Pitt a last chance, and to avoid prejudicing
the French case by the addition of the Spanish; for which
reason he had refused to sign the offensive alliance with Spain
until he should be convinced by Pitt's next answer that there
was no hope of a good peace.[5] Louis XV, however, decided
that Bussy must leave it to Fuentes to judge whether to present
the French and Spanish demands at once. In spite of Bussy's
persuasions, Fuentes insisted upon his doing so. Bussy finally
agreed to be guided by the temper in which he found Pitt; but
Pitt was so violent when he began to discuss the Spanish

---

[1] Stanley to Pitt, postscript of July 5, Thackeray, op. cit. ii. 541.
[2] Choiseul to Bussy, July 4, A.E. Angleterre, 443.
[3] Choiseul to Ossun, July 7, A.E. Espagne, 533.
[4] Choiseul to Bussy, July 15. The memorial is translated in Thackeray, ii.
552–3. It was originally a part of the French ultimatum, but Stanley remonstrated with Choiseul and persuaded him to cut it out and to leave Bussy to discuss
the Spanish affair with Pitt by word of mouth. Finally Choiseul compromised on
a separate memorial (Stanley to Pitt, Aug. 6, Thackeray, ii. 585–6).
[5] Choiseul to Ossun, July 7; Ossun to Choiseul, July 27, A.E. Espagne, 533.

grievances by word of mouth, that he decided to give him the written memorial, and the mischief was done.[1]

For all the excuses of Wall, this looked uncommonly like a threat, or 'reversionary declaration of war from Spain'. It was not quite without precedent, for Spain had communicated to France, a year earlier, a copy of Fuentes's memorial to Pitt on the Newfoundland fishery. That had annoyed the English Ministers, though there was this to be said for it, that as the fishery was sure to be an object of negotiation between England and France, Spain might well remind both parties that they did not possess between them the sole claim to it.[2] The same pretext might be given for Choiseul's reference to Spain's claim to the Neutral Islands—on which she had just made a similar communication to France.[3] This fresh memorial, however, was far more objectionable, for it clearly indicated that France and Spain meant to make common cause against England in their colonial affairs, unless she satisfied both of them at once. This came out later in some expressions of Wall, who blamed Pitt for rejecting the very handsome conditions offered by Choiseul, and judged from that how unlikely he was to yield to the reasonable demands of Spain.[4]

Pitt did not hesitate to denounce this interference of our enemy with the affairs of our ally; he returned the memorial to Bussy as inadmissible, and the conclusion of the Family Compact was brought about at once by this indignity. Bussy was forbidden to sign any peace between France and England without satisfaction for the demands of Spain as well.[5]

[1] Bussy to Choiseul, July 21 and 26. See also Stanley's letter to Pitt of Aug. 6. Bussy seems to have apologized to Newcastle for this paper (see Newcastle's memorandum of July 29, Add. MSS. 32926, f. 50) and perhaps he really thought it a mistake to present it.

[2] Fuentes to Pitt, Sept. 9, 1760, S.P. 94/162; Pitt's reply of Sept. 16, ibid.

[3] Bristol to Pitt, July 13, 1761, S.P. 94/163. Choiseul does not seem to have taken the Spanish claim seriously; he finally persuaded Charles III to give it up to France.

[4] Bristol to Egremont, Nov. 2, 1761, S.P. 94/164. Pitt had given Wall an opportunity to disavow Bussy's step, but Wall expressly took the responsibility for it (Pitt to Bristol, July 28, S.P. 94/163; Bristol to Pitt, Aug. 6 and 31, S.P. 94/164, with Wall's paper of Aug. 28).

[5] Choiseul to Ossun, July 30, A.E. Espagne, 533; Choiseul to Bussy, Aug. 10, A.E. Angleterre, 444. Bute was no less angry than Pitt with Bussy's intervention in the Spanish dispute; indeed the violence of his expressions on this subject alarmed Frederick II, who was afraid it would needlessly embroil England with Spain (*Politische Correspondenz*, vol. xx, no. 13130).

§ iv. *The Resignation of Pitt*

Since the war between England and Spain was virtually decreed by the beginning of August 1761, there is not very much interest in the later stages of the peace negotiation. Choiseul and Pitt only tried to put each other in the wrong. Bute was converted from war to peace in the middle of August.[1] Consequently the English Ministry yielded first the Newfoundland fishery, then that of the St. Lawrence, and finally a very small settlement for the French fishermen. The dispute centred more and more on the exigencies of Austria and Prussia, whom Choiseul and Pitt were less and less willing to sacrifice as they saw less hope of satisfaction on their own national points. Choiseul retracted in July a very important concession which he had, perhaps inadvertently, made at Maria Theresa's expense in June.[2] Stanley seems to have understood that the fishery

[1] Bute's fluctuations in July and August are hard to follow. Bedford wrote him a long letter on July 9, to persuade him that we ought to allow France the Newfoundland fishery. Bute replied that he agreed to that, but Choiseul wanted an establishment on land for his fishermen as well—which would be objectionable because it would grow into another Louisbourg. He claimed to be as ready for peace as Bedford himself, but 'let that peace prove in some measure answerable to the conquests we have made. Can ministers answer for it to the public, if they advise the King to sit down with a barren country' (this is Canada) 'not equal in value to the Duchies of Lorrain and Barr, and yet an acquisition invidious from its vast extent, while the French have restored to them the very essence of the whole? Why not rather, out of all our rich conquests, reserve to posterity something that will bring in a clear and certain additional revenue, to enable them to pay the interest of the enormous debt we have by this most expensive war laid upon them?' (Bute to Bedford, July 12, *Bedford Correspondence*, iii. 32). On the same day he seems to have promised Devonshire to agree to a sort of compromise suggested by Sir William Baker (Devonshire to Newcastle, July 12, Add. MSS. 32925, f. 28). On the 21st, his under-secretary reported that Bute was 'very much disgusted' by the last French terms, and had been 'endeavouring, for the last three or four days, to spirit up the Dukes of Newcastle, Devonshire, and Bedford to something vigorous' (Jenkinson to George Grenville, July 21, *Grenville Papers*, i. 376). When the Cabinet replied sternly to those terms and resolved to reject Bussy's memorials about Spain and Austria, the same under-secretary gave Bute the credit of it (Jenkinson to Grenville, July 28, ibid., p. 380). Not until August 18 did he give up his objection to the *abri* for the French settlement, and join the peace party (Devonshire to Bedford, Aug. 18, *Bedford Correspondence*, iii. 41; Devonshire to Newcastle, Aug. 21, Add. MSS. 32927, f. 154).

[2] This was the evacuation of Wesel and Cleves. Choiseul seems to have yielded it in his proposals to Stanley of June 17 (Thackeray, op. cit. i. 541) but he expressly refused it in those of July 15 (ii. 550). Stanley accounted for this inconsistency by carelessness or ignorance, but that is hardly plausible, for Choiseul had been Ambassador in Vienna and knew as well as anybody the engagements between France and Austria. Pitt regarded this 'tergiversation' as one of the decisive proofs of Choiseul's insincerity.

was the real centre of the negotiation, but prophesied that when Choiseul despaired of obtaining it, he would express a more ostentatious attachment to Austria and Spain.[1] The English Cabinet never offered it, until the Family Compact was made and it had to be refused; so Choiseul gave more prominence to the interests of his allies in order to have a nobler excuse for breaking off. Pitt at the same time accepted Frederick II's demands, and embodied them in his own, without the reservations which he might have made at the beginning of the campaign; but here he was somewhat more consistent than Choiseul, as he had never promised anything to Frederick's disadvantage.[2]

If the last stages of the negotiation were illusory, the dissimulation of Wall is not much more important. Fuentes at least seems to have tried to keep a door open, especially after the fall of Pitt, which gave Wall a slight return of hope.[3] Perhaps if that event could have been known in Paris before Stanley came away, it might have made a difference, for Choiseul seems to have thought Pitt the great obstacle to a peace.[4] The one place, however, where a real decision remained to be taken was the English Ministry, which was only half enlightened as to the intentions of France and Spain.[5]

In this dispute, as in the earlier one over the terms of peace with France, there were not two parties but three. Pitt had made up his mind to a war with Spain, Newcastle wanted to avoid it if he could; but between them, several members of the Cabinet wavered or regarded the question as open, and hoped to hit upon a compromise. Pitt was prepared with schemes of

---

[1] Stanley to Pitt, Aug. 1 and 6, Sept. 4, 1761 (Thackeray, ii. 565, 584–5, 612). Stanley had the wit to notice, in particular, that Choiseul did not introduce the Spanish question before Pitt's refusal of the fishery.

[2] Pitt raised his demands on Frederick's behalf in his ultimatum of Aug. 16 (Thackeray, ii. 596).

[3] Wall to Fuentes, Oct. 26, 1761, Add. MSS. 32930, f. 48. Fuentes himself seems to have hoped that England, France, and Spain might yet come to terms if France would repeat her last offer (Fuentes to Grimaldi, Nov. 10, f. 394; to Wall, Dec. 18, vol. 32932, f. 230).

[4] Newcastle's memorandum of Dec. 4, 1761, Add. MSS. 32931, f. 408.

[5] Its deliberations have been analysed again and again; for example, by Sir J. S. Corbett, *England in the Seven Years' War*, ii, chap. 6; R. Waddington, *La Guerre de Sept Ans*, iv, chaps. 10 and 11; A. von Ruville, *William Pitt, Graf von Chatham*, ii, chaps. 15 and 16; Basil Williams, *Life of William Pitt*, chaps. 17 and 18; L. B. Namier, *England in the Age of the American Revolution*, i. 339–43; D. A. Winstanley, *Personal and Party Government*, chap. 2; H. W. V. Temperley, in the *Cambridge History of the British Empire*, i, chap. xvii.

conquest, and converted Mansfield to them for a moment;[1] but Mansfield seems to have veered round again in the meeting of October 2, when Anson and Ligonier, the heads of the fighting services, spoke against the war as impracticable.[2] Pitt's plans for carrying on a Spanish war are not known; he afterwards claimed the credit of projecting the expedition to Havana, and he may have cast his eye upon Panama.[3] He certainly meant to seize the Mexican *flota*, which was daily expected at Cadiz. This was the old method of putting a kind of preventive pressure on Spain. Newcastle and Hardwicke must have remembered Vernon's failure to catch the *azogues* in 1739. One of the peace party mentioned it in the meeting of September 18, and added that the length of the present war with France was a lesson against relying on a brisk decision at the beginning.[4] Besides, the financial and economic effects of such a war must be considered. Newcastle was justly nervous about them, as he was raising the next year's supplies, and met with disquieting reservations in the City upon the contingency of a Spanish war.[5] Not only Pitt but Bute had argued in August that a Spanish war would pay for itself in prizes[6]—a venerable fallacy which had misled English statesmen from the days of Elizabeth. On the other hand, our flourishing trade with Spain, which would be cut off by a war, was one of the things which had enabled us to maintain the struggle with France. Besides, somebody suggested that if once we broke off relations with Spain, we should find it difficult to get our favourable treaties of commerce renewed at the peace; this foresight was justified next year by the almost invincible obstinacy of Grimaldi on the subject.

[1] Newcastle to Hardwicke, Sept. 21, 1761, Add. MSS. 32928, f. 304.

[2] Add. MSS. 32929, f. 20.

[3] The evidence of this is only a 'supposed conversation between Mr. Pitt and a General Officer, related from memory' and quoted by Almon in his *Anecdotes of the Life of the Earl of Chatham*, 1797, i. 366.

[4] Add. MSS. 32928, ff. 230-1.

[5] He noticed on Oct. 8 that one of the chief underwriters of the loan 'hopes he may bring £1,000,000; but in the case of a Spanish war, he does not believe he can get any subscribers at all, at least he can't subscribe himself' (Add. MSS. 32929, f. 111). Bussy had always advised Choiseul that English credit could support many more years of French war but would break down if one with Spain were added (Bussy to Choiseul, June 11 and 19, 1761, A.E. Angleterre, 443).

[6] Newcastle to Hardwicke, Aug. 7, 1761, Add. MSS. 32926, f. 282. Barrington pointed out later that if the prizes were insured in England, as many of them were, the captures would increase the immediate financial difficulty, because the insurance must be paid at once while the prize-money took much longer to distribute (Barrington to Newcastle, Jan. 3, 1762, Add. MSS. 32933, f. 50).

More attention was given in the Council to the moral justification of a breach. The question was: how far and in what way were France and Spain known to be committed to each other? Historians have spilt a great deal of ink on this subject. The only certain thing is that besides Bussy's ominous memorial of July, the Ministers were in possession of three documents. Grimaldi wrote to Fuentes that the Spanish Court must gain time until the *flota* reached Cadiz; that two conventions had been signed between France and Spain on August 15, but had not yet been ratified, and that France was bound by them not to make peace without settling the affairs of Spain. This letter was intercepted on September 8.[1] Wall gave Bristol on August 28 a paper which was a masterpiece of ambiguity. On the one hand he avowed Bussy's memorial about the Spanish disputes, but on the other he represented it as inoffensive to England. He defended the right of France and Spain to interfere in each other's disputes with England, and asserted that 'There is the greatest harmony between the two Courts; and who, in this age, can be surprised there should be that harmony between the Kings of Spain and France?' He owned that Louis XV had promised to defend Spain against England in case there was a rupture after the peace between England and France; and he asked whether Spain was to despise so generous an overture? But he hinted that if England had tried, or should still try, to make up her differences with France and Spain separately, she would meet with the utmost goodwill.[2] Finally, Stanley wrote on September 2 that he had seen the draft of a secret article between France and Spain, by which the former undertook to support the interests of the latter at the peace negotiations. That, however, was no more than appeared from Bussy's behaviour in July, and Choiseul told Stanley that he hoped to be able to disengage himself from Spain if we would agree to his final terms.[3]

This was all the evidence that the rest of the Cabinet had, and I am not inclined to believe that Pitt and Temple had any other.[4] Their colleagues did not think it enough, and refused

---

[1] Add. MSS. 32927, f. 299.   [2] S.P. 94/164.
[3] A copy is in Add. MSS. 32927, f. 336.
[4] Bute later said in the House of Lords 'that when Lord Temple advised the war, they knew nothing of this treaty between France and Spain, nor that there was such a thing, but by mere rumour'. Temple's contradiction need not prove much, for he may have been thinking of Grimaldi's letter (Ilchester, *Henry Fox*,

to commit the irregularity of declaring war on the strength of it. That decision, however, can by no means be regarded as a vote for peace with Spain, and there was a serious political struggle underneath the rather pedantic dispute over the evidence.

Pitt himself rested the case for war on wider arguments than the proofs of the Family Compact. He had never been a friend of Spain: from his first days in Parliament to his last, he was too easily fired by patriotic rant against the whole House of Bourbon. He kept this feeling in check as late as 1759, in order to avoid provoking what he called 'a half-enlightened, irritable, but too necessary Court'. The necessity, however, was passing away. Pitt understood what Newcastle never believed, that we were now a match for Spain as well as France; and soon after Bussy's intervention in the Spanish dispute, he began to think of seizing the *flota*.[1] He relied less and less on proofs of a written agreement between the Bourbon powers, or of Spain's resolution to declare war, and more on the inconvenience of suffering Spanish neutrality at all. 'Spain', he said at his last Cabinet meeting, 'is now carrying on the worst species of war she can for France—covers her trade, lends her money, and abets her in negociation. This puts you actually in war with the whole House of Bourbon.' He held this language later to Hardwicke, and again in the House of Commons.[2] In fact, Pitt seems to have been resolved on a war with Spain, whatever reasons he might choose to give for it. Perhaps he repented of his compliance with the concessions to France, and determined to find an excuse for resigning rather than stay in the Ministry to be responsible for measures which he did not approve. He almost said as much in the meeting of September 21, and the impression is confirmed by his needlessly dictatorial behaviour in October.[3]

First Lord Holland, ii. 162). Pitt said in the meeting of October 2 that 'the papers he had in his bag fix'd an eternal stain on the Crown of England, if proper measures were not taken upon it'; but Newcastle understood him to mean Bristol's dispatch and Wall's paper of Aug. 28 (Add. MSS. 32929, f. 22). Newcastle might not understand right; but if Pitt had more than that in the bag, why not show it? In Dutens's *Mémoires d'un voyageur qui se repose* (London, 1806), i. 152, there is a very vague story about a secret dispatch of Squillace, Spanish Minister of Finance, which Dutens got hold of at Turin and sent to Pitt. This dispatch, if it existed, was not mentioned at any of the Cabinet meetings.

[1] Newcastle's letter of Aug. 7, quoted above.

[2] Minute of Oct. 2, 1761, Add. MSS. 32929, f. 22; Hardwicke to Newcastle, Oct. 13, f. 228; West's report of the House of Commons, Dec. 11, vol. 32932, f. 141.

[3] Newcastle heard on Sept. 13 that Pitt thought of resigning; that was before

His enemies put a more sinister interpretation upon his resignation. They thought he had begun to see that the war could not be carried on in his way, nor the peace made on the terms he had taught the country to expect; he therefore determined 'by going out upon a spirited pretence, to turn the attention and dissatisfaction on those, who, at a ruinous expense, are to carry on his wild measures'.[1] Without wishing to pay Pitt too high a compliment, I do not think we can hope for much light on his motives from two cynical, calculating self-seekers like Fox and Dodington. At the same time it can hardly be denied that Pitt did contrive to have the best of both worlds: his reputation suffered far less from the events of 1762 than those of Bute, Newcastle, and Fox himself. Newcastle, unlike Bute, never exactly accused Pitt of resigning on purpose to avoid responsibility for the peace; but he and Hardwicke had seen long ago that Pitt would find it very hard to save his face when he came to treat with France.

'Your Grace says that you begin to be of my opinion about Mr. P.'s disposition as to peace. I never said that he might not wish it; but I have said, & do think that he hardly knows how to set about it. He sees that, in order to obtain peace, so much of our acquisitions must be given up, and the populace, who have been blown up to such an extravagant degree, and of whom he is unwilling to quit his hold, will be so much disappointed, that he is ready to start at the approaches to it.'[2]

These considerations might account for Pitt's difficulty in the negotiation with France; but why should he force himself out of office just when peace was indefinitely postponed? Perhaps it is best to accept the reason which Pitt himself gave; it was a just and constitutional one. The next step in the Spanish affair, whatever it might be, must involve orders to Lord Bristol. They must be signed by Pitt, for Spain was in his department, and he must therefore be responsible for them.[3] If he did not

the Spanish business came before the Cabinet (Newcastle to Bedford, Sept. 13, vol. 32928, f. 131).

[1] Melcombe to Bute, Oct. 8, 1761, printed in Adolphus's *History of England from the Accession of George III*, i. 549. See Fox's memoir in *Life and Letters of Lady Sarah Lennox*, i. 46, 57.

[2] Hardwicke to Newcastle, April 10, 1760, Add. MSS. 32904, f. 303.

[3] Apparently he suggested on Sept. 21 that Bute, the other Secretary of State, should send Bristol the orders he could not bring himself to sign (Newcastle's memorandum of Sept. 21, 1761, vol. 32928, f. 299). The same reason which induced him to resign was an excellent one for accepting his resignation; as Bute

choose to accept this responsibility, he was quite right to resign. Finally, one thing more must be remembered. Pitt went out of his mind a few years later, and the undue violence of his decision in October 1761 may perhaps be accounted for by the approaches of insanity.

The motives of Pitt's adversaries were various. The extreme pacifist Bedford regarded Pitt as a danger to his country and might fairly be glad to see him go. Newcastle's attitude, though vague and scared, was equally logical. He had always lamented the difficulties which Pitt had cast in the way of the peace negotiation; had always been for lowering our terms to France, and continued after Pitt's fall to resist the measures which led to a breach with Spain. Newcastle cannot in any sense be said to have betrayed Pitt on this occasion. He might be mistaken as to the chance of avoiding a war with Spain; indeed he had nothing to propose but leaving well alone and forbearing to press Wall for explanations where only disagreeable ones were to be expected. He admitted that the Family Compact might contain some articles which would be offensive to us and, if known, would make it harder to settle our differences with Spain. That, in his opinion, was a reason against demanding to know what they were. If we could, after all, come to an agreement with Spain, we need never know them, and we might detach her from France without war.[1] This argument had two weaknesses. Newcastle could not or durst not propose any plan of settlement which should at the same time maintain our honour and satisfy Spain. Moreover, the facts were against him: Spain was actually bound to declare war on us before May 1, 1762. That, however, was more than Newcastle or anybody else knew. Besides, Choiseul was already treating with England before May 1, so that Newcastle had some justification for thinking that if we had kept quiet, swallowed our pride, and asked no questions for a few months, we need never have gone to war at all.[2]

said, there was no doing business with a man who would not execute the resolutions of the Council when he did not concur in them (Newcastle to Hardwicke, Sept. 21, f. 305).

[1] Newcastle to Hardwicke, Oct. 20 and 21, Add. MSS. 32929, ff. 406, 421; his observations on Egremont's dispatch, Oct. 26, vol. 32930, f. 57.

[2] Hardwicke did not agree. He did not repent of resisting Pitt's desire for an immediate war in October, but he believed later that the real point was not the Family Compact but the logwood settlements. Nothing would have satisfied Spain but their evacuation, especially after she had fortified herself by a close connexion with France; but no English Minister would have dared to give orders for the

Mansfield and Hardwicke were judges. Perhaps they were really affected by the considerations of evidence and diplomatic propriety which the Council discussed before Pitt's resignation; but what was Bute's game? He had supported Pitt in standing out for high terms against France, and now he neither wished nor expected to renew the negotiation at once. He disliked the war, but he dared not put his name to a bad peace. A few days after Pitt's resignation, Bute wrote that 'the change of a minister cannot, at present, make any remarkable change in measures'.[1] He was thinking of the French negotiation, but what he said was equally true of the Spanish.

At the meeting of September 18, the Council resolved against recalling Bristol at once and declaring war; but at a private meeting next day, four of Pitt's opponents 'were unanimously of opinion, that before any hostilities should be committed, a notification should be given to the Court of Spain tantamount to a declaration of War, and Lord Bristol recall'd'. The difference then was one of punctilio, especially as this was so near to what Pitt and Temple had proposed to the King the day before.[2] Pitt's adversaries only proposed to allow a somewhat fuller trial of Wall's intentions. Bristol was to refuse peremptorily to discuss the prizes and Newfoundland; but he might offer to evacuate the logwood settlements, if Charles III would promise that the logwood-cutting should go on until further arrangements were made. This was almost exactly what Pitt had already offered, and Charles III was resolved not to grant. Bristol was to ask whether Charles III was under any engagements to take part with France; and if the answer was unsatisfactory, he was to treat it as a declaration of war and come away. This course offered very little prospect of avoiding war; Newcastle objected to it, but the others answered that the conduct of Spain was very offensive, and that if she would not take hold of this very slight 'handle to get off', then 'we should give Mr. Pitt such a handle against us, as might have very bad consequences, if we did not take such a refusal, as a declaration of war on their part'.[3] Newcastle acquiesced, but Hardwicke got the resolution

purpose without the assurances which Wall had refused to Pitt (Hardwicke to Newcastle, Dec. 25, 1761, Add. MSS. 32932, f. 349).

[1] Bute to Melcombe, Oct. 8, 1761, Adolphus, op. cit., p. 549.

[2] The original Minute of Sept. 19 is in Add. MSS. 32928, f. 248; the amended version on f. 233; Pitt's and Temple's paper on f. 225.

[3] Newcastle to Hardwicke, Sept. 20, 1761, Add. MSS. 32928, f. 261.

toned down.[1] It was not executed for some weeks, because the situation was altered by more reassuring letters from Stanley and Bristol, and then the resignation of Pitt caused a new delay.

This delay could not be prolonged for ever: on the one side Wall was clamouring for a written answer to his last paper about the logwood, and on the other Bute and his new colleague Egremont soon determined to 'out-war Mr. Pitt'. Newcastle did his best to dissuade them from asking for an explanation of Spain's intentions, but he might have spared himself the trouble. At first the news from Lord Bristol was so comfortable that Egremont was induced to express his demand in the softest and least peremptory terms. Unfortunately this mild dispatch crossed a most alarming one from Bristol. Too true, perhaps, to the policy of Pitt, he had hammered at Wall in order to find out the terms of the Family Compact. Wall completely changed his tone, burst out into violent denunciations, and accused us of aiming at the conquest of all the French and Spanish colonies in the West Indies. 'He would himself be the man to advise the King of Spain, since his dominions were to be overwhelmed, at least to have them seized with arms in his subjects' hands, and not to continue the passive victim he had hitherto appeared to be in the eyes of the world.' Worse still, he put Bristol off without any information. He only admitted that there had been some renewal of the Family Compacts between France and Spain. Bristol did not know how to account for this sudden change, except by the safe arrival of the *flota*, which made it unnecessary to wear the mask any longer.[2]

Even Newcastle doubted the necessity of war no more. Bristol received the peremptory orders which the peace party had avoided in September, and left the Court of Spain after Wall's equally peremptory refusal to reveal the treaty with France.

The behaviour of Bute and his party needs some explanation. Bute had already begun to think of the Spanish and the German wars as alternatives, but it can hardly be believed that he resisted Pitt's Spanish war in order to force him out, then took it up in order to render the German war impossible and force out Newcastle.[3] That was the effect of his policy in the

---

[1] Newcastle to Hardwicke, Sept. 20, 1761, Add. MSS. 32928, f. 264.
[2] Bristol to Egremont, Nov. 2, 1761, S.P. 94/164.
[3] He said on Sept. 26 that 'If we have a war with Spain, we must give up the

end. He first got rid of the war Minister and carried on the war, then got rid of the peace Minister and proceeded to make the peace. Since Bute probably meant from the beginning to drive out Pitt and Newcastle sooner or later, there is a temptation to suspect him of a very subtle design; but that mediocre Scotch amateur was incapable of anything so clever, and it is far more likely that he blundered into the position he desired.

As soon as Pitt's retirement became possible, Bute probably began to ask himself what was the point on which it would be most to his advantage that it should take place. Newcastle did the same;[1] but neither of them was glad of the resignation when it came. Bute wrote to Dodington, whom he can hardly have hoped to deceive, 'Whatever private uneasiness I might have in the late administration, I am very far from thinking it favourable in the present minute to the King's affairs.' He gave a convincing reason for his embarrassment. For the moment, he was afraid of having to carry on Pitt's war without Pitt's help; afraid of being answerable 'for the miscarriage of another's system, that he himself could not have prevented'.[2] That is to say, he probably shared at that time the opinion that Pitt had forced his resignation because he knew he could not perform the impossible.

Why did Bute rush into the Spanish war? Once more, because he was afraid—not of the consequences but of Pitt's popularity. Egremont thought his safety was concerned in sending a strong dispatch to Spain; and Newcastle justly said of the whole set of them that 'They breath war as much as Mr. Pitt did: But from this principle, for fear of Mr. Pitt's popularity, which *they* would endeavour to gain but will never obtain it'.[3] Henry Fox and the Spanish Ambassador took the

German war; it is impossible to carry on both; and then Mr. Pitt will quit for that' (Newcastle to Hardwicke, Sept. 26, Add. MSS. 32928, f. 363).

[1] Newcastle calculated that if Pitt was to resign, he had better do so over his refusal to continue the negotiation with France, because he was more obviously in the wrong there, and Newcastle would have more advantage over him (Newcastle to Hardwicke, Sept. 23, vol. 32928, f. 303). The King was more candid: in the register of Bute's correspondence (Add. MSS. 36796, f. 256) there is a reference to an undated letter of George III to Bute: 'Desires to get rid of Mr. Pitt but must select a favourable opportunity for so doing.'

[2] Bute to Melcombe, Oct. 8, 1761, Adolphus, op. cit., pp. 548–9; Newcastle to Hardwicke, Sept. 20, 1761, Add. MSS. 32928, f. 260.

[3] Newcastle to Hardwicke, Oct. 23, vol. 32929, f. 472, and Hardwicke's reply, f. 470.

same view.[1] Bute's anxiety was quite natural. He did not yet know whether Pitt meant to make trouble; he and Egremont were new to politics, desperately anxious to make good reputations, and without the *sangfroid* of experience—they were still talking to Nivernois of scaffolds and impeachments a year later. Bute, moreover, held in his hands the most precious treasure of all, and was determined not to spill it—the popularity and credit of the young King, which it was his life's purpose to establish.

§ v. *The Spanish War and the Conquest of Havana*

The Spanish war of 1762 revived the hopes and projects which had obsessed the English public twenty-three years ago.[2] Privateering received a new lease of life.[3] The Government once more prepared to conquer Havana; but the execution of the design left nothing to be desired this time. The English fighting-machine was in full working order, and the experience of the earlier failure seems to have taught the Admiralty what to avoid. There was none of the delay, cross-purposes, and uncertainty which did so much harm to Cathcart's expedition in 1740. The choice of objective was not left to the commanders: even the route and rendezvous were worked out beforehand.[4] The Government thought this enterprise so important that it commanded Rodney to give up the siege of Martinique in case he should not have succeeded already, in order to hold his forces in readiness for the grand expedition under Pocock and Albemarle.[5]

Nevertheless the whole plan came near to being ruined. It might be thought that this time, at least, there would be no fear of a French intervention, for France was already an enemy, and a beaten one; yet there was a French force in the West Indies, and it had an unexpected chance of destroying the English expedition. The Comte de Blénac had been sent out to relieve Martinique. He was to have sailed in November 1761,

[1] Fuentes to Grimaldi, Nov. 10, 1761, vol. 32930, f. 394; Fox's memoir in *Life and Letters of Lady Sarah Lennox*, i. 56.

[2] *V. supra*, pp. 65–97.

[3] The number of new commissions taken out, which had diminished greatly since the Privateers' Bill of 1759, suddenly rose again upon the expectation of Spanish treasure. However, part of this number is accounted for by the privateers already in existence; for a commission against France did not warrant captures upon the Spaniards, and a new one had to be taken out against France and Spain.

[4] Secret instructions to Pocock, Feb. 18, 1762, Adm. 2/1332, pp. 25–33.

[5] Orders to Rodney, Feb. 5, 1762, Adm. 2/1332, p. 17.

but was held up in Brest till January by the winds and the English blockade which prevented his storeships from reaching him in time.[1] When he arrived at Martinique he found it lost, so he sailed away to St. Domingue. There he was to co-operate with the colonists and the Spaniards in the conquest of Jamaica.

The authorities at Jamaica had already discovered from intercepted letters that the French were preparing to invade the island. Commodore Forrest wanted to take out his whole force and intercept the enemy's fleet before it arrived at St. Domingue. He was in good time, for Blénac had hardly started from Brest; and he judged rightly that the Brest and Rochefort squadrons would not be able to get out of port together, but would have to come to the West Indies separately. (In fact only one detachment ever reached the West Indies, because d'Aubigny could not break out of Rochefort at all; but if the whole of Choiseul's scheme had been executed, two squadrons, neither of them larger than Forrest's own, would have arrived at St. Domingue one after the other.) Forrest's plan was therefore to lie off Cap François, where they were most likely to arrive, and cut them off one by one. It was the best thing he could have done; but unhappily he thought himself obliged to defer to the Governor and Council of Jamaica, who believed that the safety of the island could only be assured by mooring the capital ships in Kingston Harbour and sending out the frigates for news. So Forrest lost the chance of catching Blénac and destroying almost the last sizable French squadron at sea. Twice more he wanted to go out—when he heard of Blénac's arrival at St. Domingue, and when Rodney sent word from the Leeward Islands that he was coming down with reinforcements which Forrest was to meet at Cape Tiburon. Both times the block-headed cowardice of the Governor and Council baulked him.[2]

Meanwhile Rodney, with his large fleet to windward, was so alarmed for the safety of Jamaica that he sent down a great part of his force under Sir James Douglas to protect it. Now

[1] Choiseul to Blénac, Oct. 19, 24, 26, and 31, Nov. 7, Dec. 12, 1762, A.N. Marine B² 368, ff. 137, 140, 144, 150, 159, 203.

[2] Forrest to Anson, Jan. 28, 1762, Adm. 1/1788; to Clevland, Jan. 28, Feb. 25, and April 14, ibid.; Jamaica Council Minutes, Jan. 24 and March 16, 1762, C.O. 140/42; Admiralty Minutes, May 1, 1762, Adm. 3/70. The mystery is, why Forrest was so stupid as to think himself bound to obey the Governor and Council. Perhaps it was because he had only just succeeded to the command by Holmes's death, and had no time to make himself familiar with his instructions.

Pocock was to have picked up most of Rodney's ships in the Windward Islands and gone down towards Cuba in force; but when he reached Martinique he found nothing there, for the ineffable Rodney had sent away the few ships of the line he had left to cruise for prizes on the Spanish main.[1] Therefore, if the French and Spaniards had joined, they would have been superior to Pocock until he met with the Jamaica squadron commanded by Douglas.

Blénac in fact was in the same position as d'Antin in 1740: with the help of the Spaniards at Havana, he ought to have cut off the force from England before it could unite with the force on the spot. But the parallel between Blénac and d'Antin fortunately went farther. Both were irresolute, and neither could get the Spaniards to join him.[2] This time the Spaniards at Havana may not have been in fault, for none of the five *avisos* sent out to warn them had ever arrived.[3]

Perhaps Blénac ought to have taken the initiative, but he was kept in harbour by trifling accidents and duties, and finally by the report that St. Domingue itself was to be invaded. In short, he was so weak and useless that Douglas at Jamaica was able to divide his squadron again and blockade him in Cap François; so the concentration of the English force, which could easily have been upset, took place without danger.

Blénac still had a chance to do some good. In the middle of June he received from Havana pressing entreaties for help; but his troops were beginning to fall sick, the colonists of St. Domingue were still afraid of an English invasion, and it was difficult to see how his squadron would ever be able to reach Havana while Pocock was lying before it. The next thing proposed was an attack on Jamaica. That island was left very bare of ships and soldiers, but Blénac's forces were reduced so low by accident and sickness that the French commanders could not promise themselves a decisive victory, and therefore preferred to attempt nothing. They then thought of sending some troops to Santiago de Cuba, and as much farther towards

[1] Pocock to Clevland, May 26, 1762, Adm. 1/237; Rodney to Clevland, March 24 and 26, May 27 and 31, 1762, Adm. 1/307.

[2] Private instructions to Blénac, Oct. 12, 1761, A.N. Marine B² 368; project of a letter to be sent to Blénac, Feb. 10, B⁴ 104; Blénac to Choiseul, March 28 and May 18, ibid.; Minutes of a Council of War, ibid.

[3] Choiseul to Ossun, July 13, 1762, A.E. Espagne, 536; Ossun to Choiseul, July 26, ibid.; Prado to Bory, April 6, A.N. Colonies C⁹ A 111.

Havana as the squadron would safely carry them. Governor de Bory seems to have thought that something ought to be done, but the other commanders made all the difficulties they could out of the vagueness of the Spanish requests and the uncertainty of the situation. Finally the Intendant finished the controversy by announcing that he could not find enough victuals to enable the troops or the squadron to make an expedition which would probably require a long journey and much waiting.[1]

The English forces were thus suffered to reduce Havana undisturbed, without paying for their serious mistakes of strategy. A third of the Spanish navy was destroyed, a great sum of prize-money was distributed, some English merchants rushed slaves into the market and found great difficulty in recovering payment for them;[2] and the Earl of Albemarle, not content with the vast share of plunder which had fallen to him and his family, got himself into a series of lawsuits by exacting illegal duties from the English importers who flocked to the market.[3] The conquest made a great public impression and affected the negotiations for peace.

Walpole's Ministry had meant to combine the conquest of Havana with a 'side-show' at Manila. That had to be given up then, but the intention was fulfilled in 1762. There was a difference in the execution: the earlier expedition was to have gone round Cape Horn, but Draper started from the East Indies. Greater secrecy could be observed, and Draper was not, like Anson, dogged by a Spanish Admiral. The conquest of Manila was not known when the peace was made, therefore it could not enter into the terms. It may only have been meant to procure a compensation from Spain in some other part of the world; but the Government certainly would have liked to

[1] Bory to Choiseul, June 13 and 15, July 17, Aug. 22, and Sept. 2, 1762, A.N. Colonies C⁹ A 111; Bory's speech to a Council of War, Aug. 16, ibid.; Blénac's justification, A.N. Marine B⁴ 104, ff. 185 et seqq.

[2] Lascelles and Maxwell to Gedney Clarke, Jan. 31, March 5, and May 20, 1763, W. & G. ix; Lascelles and Daling to William Harvie, March 13, 1766, W. & G. x.

[3] See the opinion of the Law Officers, Norton and de Grey, to the Treasury, May 14, 1764, Add. MSS. 36223, f. 424. They held that, according to the capitulation, Albemarle might impose Spanish duties on conquered Spanish subjects, but not on His Majesty's native-born subjects who imported goods into the conquered territory. This seems to differ from the practice of Governor Dalrymple in Guadeloupe (v. supra, p. 192).

keep Mindanao, nor does Sir Julian Corbett appear to be right in saying that it never thought of keeping Manila too.[1]

The Spanish war enabled Choiseul to revive his plans for invading England or Ireland, or both. He wanted to make a feint against Ireland in the summer and to conquer Portsmouth and the Isle of Wight in the autumn; but the King of Spain could not spare troops for the first, and it is doubtful if Choiseul could ever have undertaken the second, even though it did not demand a large naval force.[2]

The one new thing in the war of 1762 was the attack on Portugal. It seems to have been Wall who first suggested that Portugal should be given the option of closing her ports to English shipping or submitting to an invasion.[3] It was a good plan. If Portugal complied, the Bourbon powers had the beginnings of a 'continental system' in southern Europe, and in particular they deprived England of the Brazil trade, which was to her almost what the Cadiz trade was to France.[4] Her exports must fall, and her financial stability might be threatened by cutting off the imports of gold which she drew chiefly from this source. The English navy and privateers had used the port of Lisbon and found it in some ways more convenient than Gibraltar. If Portugal resisted this attempt to detach her from her English alliance, Charles III had no doubt of his ability to conquer her. Once in his power, she would serve a hostage for all sorts of concessions. England would be forced to buy her

[1] The instructions to Steevens recite that the East India Company thought Mindanao a good thing to keep at the peace, but both Manila and Mindanao were to be handed over to the Company if taken, and both were to be disposed of by the King at the peace (Adm. 2/1332, p. 13). It is true that we only mentioned Manila in the negotiation in order to frighten Spain into agreeing to our terms quickly; but we could not tell then whether we had taken it.

[2] Choiseul to Ossun, April 5, May 4 and 29, 1762, A.E. Espagne, 536; Ossun to Choiseul, Aug. 2, vol. 537.

[3] Choiseul congratulated Wall on the idea, which he described as 'luminous' (Choiseul to Ossun, July 2, 1761, A.E. Espagne, 533).

[4] Choiseul also intended an expedition against Brazil itself, which might have the same effect upon the trade and revenues of England that an attack on the Spanish West Indies had upon France—to dry up the sources of our wealth. At the beginning of 1762 he seems to have meant to send a small force against the northern provinces of Brazil ('Plan de campagne par mer pour l'année 1762', in A.N. Marine B⁴ 104). In the autumn he projected a much larger and more important conquest. Beaussier's squadron was to attack both Bahia and Rio de Janeiro. The instructions were dated as late as Oct. 19 and 20, 1762—a fortnight before the preliminaries of peace were signed. They breathe an extraordinary spirit of desperate resolution. Beaussier's expedition was to be a kind of 'death ride' of the remnants of the French navy (A.N. Marine B⁴ 105, ff. 38 et seqq.).

back by restoring her conquests to France, and, if the war went well enough, by giving up Gibraltar to Spain.[1] In fact the Portuguese war was to Spain what the German war was to France—a means of distracting England's energy from her other enterprises, of holding her to ransom and cancelling the effect of her conquests in America.

This plan rested on some miscalculations. In the first place, England did not allow her attention to be diverted from Havana. Newcastle, it seems, would rather have sent the fleet to Lisbon, but nobody listened to him.[2] The Portuguese war did in fact have a very important effect on the attitude of the English Government to the German war; but it seems to have been rather an excuse than a reason for abandoning the Continent. Besides, after all, Prince Ferdinand's army continued to fight in Germany with a good deal of success in 1762. Furthermore, there was some doubt whether England would have been ready to sacrifice much at the peace for Portugal's sake. Nivernois found in September that many Englishmen, rather than sacrifice Cuba for Portugal, would leave the latter, for the time, in the possession of Spain, while the English forces went on from one conquest to another in Spanish America; then they could repurchase Portugal by giving up these further acquisitions and keep Cuba as pure gain.[3] It is to the credit of Bute that he did not reason upon such principles; but the Spanish army had to evacuate Portugal without any compensation.

Charles III overrated his own strength and prospects. The Family Compact was to improve the terms for France and procure satisfaction to Spain, because Lisbon was sure to fall and Havana was impregnable. In fact Havana was conquered and Lisbon was never in serious danger from the inept Spanish commander. This reversal of all expectations is the reason why Spain suddenly capitulated on every point in dispute at the end of October 1762, and why the Bourbon alliance was so disastrous to her and so little advantageous to France.

---

[1] Ossun to Choiseul, April 19 and 26, 1762, A.E. Espagne, 536.
[2] Newcastle's memorandum of Feb. 11, Add. MSS. 32934, f. 275.
[3] Viry to Solar, July 12, 1762, A.E. Espagne, 536; Nivernois to Comte de Choiseul, Sept. 15, A.E. Angleterre, 447; Choiseul to Ossun (private), Oct. 9, A.E. Espagne, 537.

§ vi. *The Peace of Paris*

Choiseul renewed the negotiation of peace surprisingly soon after his failure to come to terms with Pitt, and prepared to put an end to the new war into which he had dragged Spain, almost as soon as it was begun. He felt that he was incurring some just criticism by this haste, and defended himself by saying that Charles III had always meant the Spanish intervention to be the instrument of a better peace for France; if that peace should offer itself quickly, Spain had no reason to complain.[1] Historians have generally attributed the change to the fall of Pitt. No doubt that had something to do with it, for hints and invitations began to be exchanged soon afterwards, before any event had altered the situation of France for the worse. But above all it was the diplomatic changes in eastern Europe that rendered the peace so much easier to make in 1762. On the one hand Bute, having quarrelled with Frederick II, was more eager for a separate peace with France and less inclined to insist on safeguards for the interests of Prussia; on the other, Choiseul's ally Maria Theresa was thoroughly frightened by the defection of Russia, and ready for peace at last—so ready that Choiseul was afraid she would make it without him.

Choiseul's sincerity to Spain is doubtful. He began the conversations in secret, and only revealed them to her when he was sure that England would offer enough; even then he contrived, with Egremont's collusion, to conceal from her the fact that he had already been treating for over two months.[2] He insisted, however, from the first, that Spain alone of all his allies must be consulted sooner or later, and he afterwards declared with ostentation that France could make no peace without her.[3] The English Ministry was in two minds whether to accept the solidarity of France and Spain, or to try to treat with them separately. Newcastle was impressed by Choiseul's declaration that France could do nothing without Spain, but Bute and Egremont would not at first recognize the Bourbon Family Compact by consenting to approach one power through the

---

[1] Choiseul to Ossun, May 17 and June 13, 1762, A.E. Espagne, 536; Aug. 17 and 27, vol. 537.

[2] Choiseul's *mémoire* to Grimaldi, inclosed in his letter to Ossun, April 17, 1762, A.E. Espagne, 536; Choiseul to Ossun, May 12, ibid.; Solar to Viry, May 12, Add. MSS. 32938, f. 175.

[3] Solar to Viry (most secret), Feb. 1, 1762, vol. 32934, f. 125; Choiseul to Solar, April 15, vol. 32937, f. 112; May 10, vol. 32938, f. 133.

other; they changed their minds several times and agreed at last to a half-measure which only maintained the technical distinction of the two negotiations.[1] This was in March; by July it was England who insisted on making peace with her two enemies together. The change is to be accounted for by the discussions over the Louisiana boundary.

The more Choiseul was sure of satisfactory conditions in his peace with England, the harder he pressed Charles III to conclude even at the cost of some sacrifices. First the reason was his increasing consternation at the effects of Peter III's accession in Russia; then, though Peter III was deposed, the French army in Germany was in a desperate situation. A little later, he urged Spain to sign the peace before Havana should fall, and last of all, when that news arrived, he declared that France and Spain together were no match for the English navy. No doubt the reasons he gave reflected a succession of very real alarms, but it is impossible not to see in his dispatches to Ossun a great deal of exaggeration and special pleading, and to suspect that he made up his mind to peace, let the arguments for it be what they might.[2]

There is no need to discuss here the terms between England and France, except where they affected Spain. On one very important matter they did so, and perhaps it was the turning-point of the whole negotiation. This was the Mississippi boundary. Choiseul had agreed to buy back Martinique by yielding to England all the French territory in North America east of the Mississippi.[3] As a compromise between England and France, it was a statesmanlike piece of work. But it was a matter which did not concern England and France alone. Such an extension of English territory would isolate Florida and bring the English to the shores of the Gulf of Mexico. Here the North

[1] Newcastle's memorandum of March 10, 1762, Add. MSS. 32999, f. 423; of April 1, vol. 33000, f. 3; Newcastle to Hardwicke, March 11, vol. 32935, f. 312; Egremont's draft letter to Viry, March 21, vol. 32936, f. 1; Newcastle to Hardwicke, March 31, f. 234; Egremont to Choiseul, April 8, f. 418.

[2] The most important documents in this series of lamentations are Choiseul's letters to Ossun of April 17, May 12, 16, and 17, June 13, July 13 and 19, all in A.E. Espagne, 536; those of Aug. 17, Oct. 3 and 20, vol. 537. Choiseul really did not believe that Havana would fall, and was extremely disconcerted when he heard the news; see his letter to Nivernois, Oct. 3, in Nivernois's *Œuvres posthumes*, vol. ii, pt. iii, pp. 62–3.

[3] For the details of this compromise, and of the terms of the Peace of Paris so far as they affected England and France in the West Indies, see Chapter V, pp. 225–6.

American question became a West Indian one, and the French question a Spanish one. While Spain had been neutral, the war-makers had not dared to order an expedition against Louisiana for fear of offending her; she was now an enemy, and the peace-makers had no reason for sparing her feelings.

As soon as Charles III found out what was in the wind, he began to make objections. He did not want the English to have a new advanced post for smuggling and for intercepting the Mexican *flota*. Wall explained to Ossun that so long as the English had no lawful excuse for sailing in the Gulf, they could properly be seized there as interlopers (an argument which shows how little Spain had departed from her old doctrine of 'suspected latitudes'). If England had a colony on its shores, the *Guarda-Costas* could not exercise their profession with the same safety or excuse.[1] Ossun replied that the English were often found in the Gulf of Mexico already, and that if any posses-sion could enable them to intercept the *flota* it was the Bahama Islands, which belonged to them and had never been used for the purpose. Charles III would still have preferred a boundary which would have kept them away from the Gulf, and proposed that all the land between Florida and New Orleans should be neutral Indian territory.[2]

The English Government was not blind to this side of the question. It might pretend that the Mississippi valley would be of no manner of use, and that its only object was the estab-lishment of an ideal frontier;[3] but its words were belied by the vehemence with which it insisted at first upon New Orleans, the capital of Louisiana, which happened to lie on the eastern bank of the river. Choiseul affected to believe that England only claimed New Orleans by a geographical oversight. He proposed another boundary farther east, which ran from the Mississippi down the Iberville river through two lakes into the Gulf. It can hardly have been a geographical oversight which prompted the violent resistance of Granville, Egremont, and George Grenville to this change.[4] Bute overcame them, and the Iberville boundary was accepted; but the whole English

---

[1] Ossun to Choiseul, July 12, A.E. Espagne, 536; Aug. 2, vol. 537.

[2] Ossun to Choiseul, Aug. 2 and Sept. 27, vol. 537.

[3] Observations accompanying the English project of July 10, A.E. Angleterre, 446.

[4] Cabinet meeting of June 21, Add. MSS. 34713, f. 106. We still insisted on New Orleans in our project of July 10 and only gave it up on July 31 (Egremont to Choiseul, July 31, A.E. Angleterre, 446; Viry to Solar, Aug. 1, ibid.).

Government continued to demand not only the Mississippi boundary, with this small alteration, but the right to navigate the river as well. If the Iberville and the Lakes proved to furnish a satisfactory channel for large ships between the Gulf and the river, we would be content with that at a pinch; but if there was any doubt on that point, we were to enjoy the right of sailing down the Mississippi to the very mouth, even though both the banks at New Orleans were under French sovereignty.[1] When the news of Havana came and the enemy's negotiators were at our mercy, we exacted the entire navigation of the Mississippi without even this condition.

This question embarrassed Choiseul more than any other, and he entangled himself in lies over it. Grimaldi made a fuss as soon as he heard of it in June. Choiseul contented him by altering the article, and assuring him that it could give Spain no cause for alarm because there was no good harbour in that part of the world except New Orleans, which he did not mean to let England have.[2] At the same time he told Ossun that he would not let the peace come to grief for this. He promised England that she should have both the boundary and the navigation of the Mississippi down to the Iberville—and thence presumably through the lakes into the sea. This concession was made in a secret article which could not be shown at present.[3] On the very same day Choiseul told Grimaldi that the English were to have no access to the sea.[4] He seems to have distinguished the navigation of the river from that of the Gulf of Mexico into which the river ran. France could lawfully allow England to share in the former, but could not transfer any right to the latter without the consent of Spain. In fact Choiseul does not appear to have seen his way through this difficulty even as late as the beginning of September, when the English and French plenipotentiaries were exchanged.[5]

It seems to me that the duplicity of Choiseul on this point

[1] Cabinet meeting of July 26, Add. MSS. 34713, f. 110; Egremont to Viry, July 31, A.E. Angleterre, 446; Instructions to Bedford, Sept. 4, S.P. 78/253; Egremont to Bedford, Sept. 7; Bedford to Egremont, Sept. 12, ibid.

[2] Choiseul to Ossun, June 29, A.E. Espagne, 536.

[3] Choiseul to Ossun (private), June 30, ibid.; Comte de Choiseul to Solar, July 21; to Viry, July 21, with the secret articles, A.E. Angleterre, 446.

[4] Choiseul to Ossun, July 21, A.E. Espagne, 536.

[5] *Mémoire instructif* for Nivernois, A.E. Angleterre, 447, f. 30. It is plain from this document that Choiseul meant to try once more whether he could somehow escape from the concession which he had made to England in the secret article.

may have something to do with the mysterious Cabinet crisis of July, when even the ultra-pacifist Bedford[1] refused to make peace with France unless Spain acceded at the same time. The ostensible reason for this refusal was that if the war against Spain was continued after the peace with France, English and French troops would have to face each other as auxiliaries in Portugal. That would certainly be an awkward situation, and at the time it seemed to be a likely one, for Grimaldi had presented on behalf of Spain a set of articles which were inacceptable in almost every detail.[2] But the Ministry had been willing enough in March to divide the Bourbon powers; why should it object to doing so in July, unless it was afraid that Choiseul had made a proposal which might at worst involve England and Spain in endless disputes over which he would stand as arbiter, and was at best only valid if he would guarantee Spain's acquiescence in it? Choiseul must be made to buy the concessions we made him, by obliging Spain to consent to those which he made us; otherwise we might have to pay for them twice over, first to France and then to Spain.

In fact, though Choiseul obtained from Charles III a promise to set about peace-making in earnest, the danger to the Mississippi navigation was not over. The French plenipotentiary Nivernois was convinced, as soon as he arrived in England, that it was the most difficult point of all. Bute lived in fear that this article, which he had invented and looked upon as his 'shield against Parliament', might be open to new discussion and retraction; if he allowed it, the patriotic Opposition in his own Cabinet would denounce him as the betrayer of his country.[3]

Bedford went to Paris as plenipotentiary at the same time that Nivernois came to London;[4] when he arrived he found

---

[1] It is worth noticing that Bedford was much more exacting in the Spanish than in the French affair : at one point he raised objections to a concession which even Egremont did not object to making (Bedford's minute of July 19, *Bedford Correspondence*, iii. 89).

[2] Bute to Egremont, July 26, Add. MSS. 36797, f. 7; Egremont to Comte de Choiseul, July 31, A.E. Angleterre, 446; Viry to Solar, Aug. 1, ibid.; Fox's memoir in *Life and Letters of Lady Sarah Lennox*, i. 69; Egremont to Bedford, Sept. 7, 1762, S. P. 78/253.

[3] Nivernois to Comte de Choiseul, Sept. 15 and 16, A.E. Angleterre, 447 (the latter is printed in Nivernois's *Œuvres posthumes* (1807), vol. ii, pt. iii, p. 9); Egremont to Bedford, Sept. 16, S.P. 78/253; Bute to Bedford, Sept. 28, Add. MSS. 36797, f. 12.

[4] At the beginning of September 1762.

that the news of Choiseul's secret arrangement had not yet been broken to Grimaldi. This was bad enough; but Bedford would have been much angrier if he had known that Choiseul then proceeded to console Charles III by explaining that he had only granted England the right to sail *down* the river. That could not have hurt Spain, for the Mississippi valley produced no contraband goods, nor would it be easy to introduce them from Europe into its upper waters. It was only the ships that sailed *up* the river that could bring any merchandise fit for smuggling into Mexico.[1] Charles III naturally wanted to have this stipulated in so many words, and once more suggested a proviso that England should have no port in the Gulf of Mexico.[2] It is doubtful if Choiseul would have put this forward, as he was already pledged to England; besides, in the last resort he did not care what Charles III thought of the matter. Louisiana, he said, was the property of France, and he would not let Spain dictate to him how he should dispose of it—a curious argument from the man who had persuaded Charles III into the Family Compact by telling him that the French possessions in North America were the bulwark of the Spanish West Indies.[3] But however Choiseul may have meant to equivocate, the time for double dealing had gone by when the conquest of Havana was known, and Grimaldi was made to yield the point without any reservation. Choiseul made amends at the last. He felt himself obliged to give Spain some consolation for her losses at the treaty, and he chose Louisiana as the sacrifice. He may have had many good reasons for his choice. He did not think much of the colony, and when so much was lost in North America it was hardly worth keeping by itself. So far as Spain found this present worth accepting at all, it was because it would enable her to keep a closer watch on the approaches of England to her treasure-colonies.

The immediate terms between England and Spain had still to be settled. The three old disputes of the prizes, the fishery,

---

[1] Bedford to Egremont, Sept. 13 and 19, S.P. 78/253 (the latter is partly printed in *Bedford Correspondence*, iii. 101–13); Choiseul to Ossun, Sept. 20, A.E. Espagne, 537. It appears that Bedford proposed a clause for safeguarding Spain against smuggling in the Gulf of Mexico, but it was unacceptable because it applied equally to English and French subjects trading to the Mississippi (Comte de Choiseul to Nivernois, Sept. 19, 1762, A.E. Angleterre, 447).

[2] Ossun to Choiseul, Sept. 29, A.E. Espagne, 539.

[3] Choiseul to Ossun, Sept. 20, ibid.; Comte de Choiseul to Nivernois, Sept. 20, A.E. Angleterre, 447.

and the logwood gave the least trouble of all. The prizes had to be left to the English courts. There was no practicable alternative. Spain might stipulate that the treaties and the law of nations should be applied, but that meant as much or as little as the Court of Prize Appeals chose to allow. Charles III did not insist on the express recognition of the Spanish fishery: he was content to perpetuate the ambiguity of that affair by a simple confirmation of the Treaty of Utrecht. England would have accepted this, if the conquest of Havana had not given her the power to impose her own conditions. Grimaldi was obliged at last to renounce the fishery altogether.[1]

The affair of the logwood settlements promised to be more difficult. Charles III meant at first to exclude the English altogether from the mainland of Central America, in order to prevent them from stirring up the Moskito Indians to rebellion. For this reason he demanded their unconditional removal. He was ready to make an agreement to supply a quantity of cut logwood in some Spanish port; but he did not want to make even this concession a condition of the evacuation.[2] The English Ministers did not intend to sacrifice the right to cut logwood; they recurred therefore to a suggestion which Wall had dropped in 1761. The settlements should be disavowed, but the King of Spain should promise not to disturb the logwood-cutters, pending a further agreement.[3] This provisional toleration would probably have lasted for ever, or at least until England gained her point by negotiation. Charles III held out at first, but yielded in September. Before the terms could be adjusted the news from Havana encouraged England to press for something more. Egremont would have liked to demand the sovereignty of part of Yucatan as a compensation for restoring Havana. This plan would have given a concrete fulfilment to the long-standing ambition for an English foothold in Central America, and it is most unlikely that Spain would have yielded it. Bute obliged Egremont to propose more harmless alternatives, but

[1] Ossun to Choiseul, June 12 and July 12, A.E. Espagne, 536; Grimaldi's proposals of July 20, ibid.; Viry to Solar, May 22, with annexed note, A.E. Angleterre, 446; separate instructions to Bedford, Sept. 4, S.P. 78/253; Bedford to Egremont, Sept. 19, ibid.; English project of Oct. 26, articles 15 and 17, ibid.

[2] Ossun to Choiseul, April 26, May 31, and June 12, A.E. Espagne, 536. Choiseul approved of Charles III's attitude at first (Choiseul to Ossun, June 29, ibid.).

[3] Egremont to Comte de Choiseul, July 10, with English proposals, ibid.; separate instructions to Bedford, Sept. 4, S.P. 78/253.

he could not resist the temptation to screw up the terms of the logwood clause a little higher.[1] Instead of evacuating the settlements, England would only destroy the forts; the King of Spain must promise to tolerate the logwood-cutters indefinitely without any hint of a further agreement to be made, and he must even guarantee the huts and property of the cutters. Grimaldi had to yield all this, and the settlements in Honduras received a precarious and indefinite recognition—precarious because they could have no military protection against Spain, and indefinite because neither their boundaries nor their rights were ascertained. In no other part of the world was the Peace of Paris less conclusive: the Governments and colonists of both countries bickered continually about their rights for the next twenty years.[2]

The English Ministry was surprised to find that the three old disputes were not all. The war had automatically put an end to all treaties of commerce between the two nations, and Spain meant to take the opportunity of revising her commercial system. No nation's privileges cost the Spanish treasury more than those of England, or did more to prevent the growth of native industry in Spain. The doctrines of Uztaritz and Ulloa were beginning to have their effect, and the Marqués de Squillace, who controlled the Spanish treasury, was determined to make at least three reforms. English shipping was to be subjected to closer search for smuggled goods; the exemption of the *Pié del Fardo*, which amounted to 40 per cent. of the duties, was to be abolished; and reciprocity was to be claimed for Spanish shipping. English ships were allowed to import goods from any European countries into Spain, so it seemed quite fair that Spaniards should have the same privilege in England; but this last demand was quite impracticable, for it required the repeal of the English Act of Navigation.[3]

In order to procure these alterations, Grimaldi was instructed to renew the old treaties for six months or a year at most, and

---

[1] Nivernois to Comte de Choiseul, Oct. 12, A.E. Angleterre, 447; Bedford's note of Aug. 23, *Bedford Correspondence*, iii. 96; English project of Oct. 26, article 16, S.P. 78/253.

[2] See the account of these disputes in Miss Vera Lee Brown's article in the *Hispanic American Historical Review*, v, no. 3, pp. 351–68; also the *Archives of British Honduras*, ed. Sir John Burdon, vols. i–iii (London, 1931–5). The logwood settlement was not recognized as a British colony until 1862 (iii. 247). The British claim to some authority on the Moskito Shore was not finally renounced before the Bulwer-Clayton Treaty of 1850.

[3] Ossun to Choiseul, April 26 and June 12, A.E. Espagne, 536.

to stipulate that a new one should be made within that time. The English Ministry would not hear of this, and insisted on the unconditional renewal; a fresh treaty might indeed be negotiated, but that was not to be a condition of the peace.[1] Choiseul had to deal with the old dilemma. If English merchants were badly treated, French merchants gained relatively; but the rights of France were badly defined, and she could not wish the curtailment of English privileges to develop into a general attack on all foreign trade in the interest of Spanish industry. Besides, since France was to be treated as the most favoured nation, anything which England gained would accrue to her, and it might be worth her while to let England fight her battles. Choiseul seems to have been sure of only one thing: he hoped Spain would avoid renewing Keene's Treaty of 1750—it was a symbol of England's influence and gave her merchants exclusive privileges.[2] Some of the English Ministers returned this attention. They suspected that France had obtained some special rights in the Family Compact, and wanted to defeat it by stipulating that all treaties of commerce should be renewed, notwithstanding any engagements which Spain had undertaken to the contrary. Bedford was able in the end to get this put into the preliminaries; for Choiseul, after proposing in vain a very ambiguous compromise, had to force Grimaldi to accept Bedford's terms on this point as well as the others, when the news from Havana gave England the power to dictate.[3]

The conquest of Havana very nearly upset the negotiation. Everybody in England counted on success, and even the prospect of it cruelly embarrassed the peace party. That was the reason why Bute hoped the peace would be made before the news came. Pitt would have delayed the negotiation until it should come, in order to have an excuse for raising his terms.[4] Bute was too anxious for peace to do such a thing. He knew that nobody in England would consent to give Havana back for nothing. For himself, he would have been content with obliging Spain to show greater facility on the points already

[1] Bedford to Egremont, Sept. 19, with enclosures D, G, and I, S.P. 78/253.
[2] Choiseul to Ossun, May 24 and 29, A.E. Espagne, 536.
[3] Bedford's note of a conversation with Mansfield, Sept. 4, *Bedford Correspondence*, iii. 98; Bedford to Egremont, Sept. 19, S.P. 78/253; article 24 of the preliminaries.
[4] He was suspected of delaying the negotiation in May 1761 until we should have conquered Belle Isle.

in dispute, but his colleagues were sure to insist on some new acquisition of territory. Egremont had always warned Choiseul to expect such a demand, but Bute seriously doubted whether Spain could ever be induced to satisfy it, and was afraid that if the case should arise the peace would be wrecked.[1]

At the end of September the news was expected hourly. The mulish George Grenville, who had held out against every concession to everybody throughout the summer, announced that he should ask for a compensation for Havana before it was known to be taken, and thus started Bute's second Cabinet crisis.[2] Bute was in even greater difficulties a few hours later, when the victory was known. Egremont had lately worked hand in hand with Grenville, and affected a certain patriotic intransigence which was meant to commend him to the Opposition. He now began to flatter himself that he could throw Bute over and stand at the head of a national party.[3] He and Grenville had already insisted that Bedford should submit his terms to the Cabinet before he signed them, in order to keep a check on his immoderate inclination to peace.[4] They now joined with Granville, Mansfield, and the Chancellor to ask an impossibly high price for restoring Havana to Spain: we must have Porto Rico and Florida, besides forcing Spain to yield on all the points already in dispute. Worse still, Grenville now demanded that the preliminary treaty should be laid before Parliament before it was signed. He can only have meant to lead the resistance to concession as Secretary of State.[5]

[1] Egremont to Viry, May 1, 1762, A.E. Angleterre, 446; Viry to Solar, July 12, A.E. Espagne, 536; Bedford's note of a conversation with Bute, Aug. 23, *Bedford Correspondence*, iii. 96. Bedford was instructed to exact a good compensation for Havana if it was taken before the peace was signed. For this reason he tried to get the peace signed first, or at any rate he used this threat as a lever to accelerate the consent of Spain (Comte de Choiseul to Nivernois, Sept. 14, 1762, A.E. Angleterre, 447).

[2] Fox to Cumberland, Sept. 29, printed in Albemarle's *Rockingham*, i. 128–32.

[3] Nivernois to the Comte de Choiseul, Sept. 25, Oct. 4 and 7, 1762, A.E. Angleterre, 447. Nivernois believed it was the peace, rather than Bute, that stood in danger after the fall of Havana; Bute could at least meet Parliament with a success in hand, and Nivernois thought this made him less anxious to conclude peace before the session began.

[4] Egremont to Bedford, Sept. 7 and 19, S.P. 78/253; Bute to Bedford, Sept. 28, Add. MSS. 36797, f. 11; Rigby to Bedford, Sept. 29, *Bedford Correspondence*, iii. 125. Choiseul saw this point quite as clearly as Egremont, and therefore wanted the English Ministry to leave Bedford's hands free.

[5] Bute to Bedford, Oct. 14, *Bedford Correspondence*, iii. 137; Grenville's memorandum in *Grenville Papers*, i. 483.

Parliamentary discussion of the peace before it was signed was just what Bute had always meant to avoid, because he was sure that the only way of getting Parliament to agree to it was to present it ready-made. His reasons for believing this are not very clear. No doubt there was a danger that the Opposition, perhaps secretly abetted by Grenville, would carry through the House of Commons some violent and extravagant resolution as to the terms, which could hardly be resisted and would tie the negotiators' hands. Moreover, Bute, whose somewhat rigid mind could only defend a carefully prepared position, seems to have wanted to know where he stood before Parliament met in order that he might take the lead, whether for war or for peace, in the King's speech from the throne. It is barely possible that Bute's anxiety to make peace before the Session began was affected for the purpose of hurrying Choiseul into signing quickly. If this was so, it becomes easier to see why he made difficulties, or allowed them to be made, when Nivernois asked him to have the opening of Parliament postponed. The Comte de Choiseul appears to have taken this view when he said: 'The English profit not only by their superiority and their advantages, but also by their own divisions, their internal difficulties and their constitution, to impose hard conditions upon us.'[1]

Bute had deprived himself of his natural allies against Grenville, when he had acquiesced in the resignation of Newcastle in May. Newcastle had stood for peace at any price, and he might have been expected to come to Bute's help now; in fact Bute had made advances to him for that purpose, and Bedford strongly desired his return to the Ministry. But Newcastle had changed for the worse since he left office. He had an avowed and legitimate grievance against Bute's German policy, and his personal dislike of Bute was natural enough; but that was not all. Newcastle had been in politics for forty years, and he had an itch for it. He could not sit still, and rather than do nothing he had drifted into the situation of leader of the Opposition— an unconstitutional one by his own doctrine. He had even begun to object to the peace. His reasons might be superficially valid, for it was true that since his retirement Bute had made

---

[1] 'Memoire pour servir d'instructions au Sr Duc de Nivernois', A.E. Angleterre, 447; Nivernois to Comte de Choiseul, Sept. 15 and 24, ibid. (Nivernois, Œuvres posthumes, vol. ii, pt. iii, pp. 40–1); Comte de Choiseul to Nivernois, Oct. 31, ibid.; Egremont to Bedford, Sept. 16 and Oct. 30, S.P. 78/253; Bute to Bedford, Oct. 24, Bedford Correspondence, iii. 138.

some new concessions; but if Newcastle had still been Prime Minister he would have been the loudest for making them.[1]

Bute could not turn to Pitt; if anybody could have got his support in this controversy it would have been Egremont and George Grenville. Bedford had some influence, but he was in Paris. There was nobody but Fox who could save Bute. Historians have denounced this alliance without reason. No doubt Fox was glad to come back to the Cabinet, and wanted a peerage; but it is evident, unless he lied in his memoirs and his letters, that he sincerely agreed with Bute and Bedford about the peace.[2] Also he believed that the only alternative to Bute was Pitt, whom he had hated so long that he sincerely thought him a danger to his country. Unless somebody stepped in to save Bute, a great popular party, headed by Pitt, Egremont, and George Grenville, might obtain such a monopoly of power as to enslave the King for life.[3] Fox's greatest strength as a politician was his connexion with the Duke of Cumberland, who was now at the bottom of Newcastle's opposition. If the admission of Fox to the Ministry could buy off Cumberland, Newcastle might be reduced to silence.[4] Fox proposed to Cumberland the office of mediator between all the parties which really wanted a peace; but Cumberland was too far gone in faction to listen, and the only result of Fox's adhesion to Bute was to break his old friendship with his patron.

Even without Cumberland, Fox had his value. All Bute needed was somebody who could stand up to Pitt in the House of Commons, for Pitt was the only sincere opponent of the peace, and therefore the only one likely to make an impression. Fox was the man for this uncomfortable but not dangerous position. George Grenville had to be degraded from the leadership

[1] This accounts for the persecution of his friends, and especially the dismission of Devonshire. The King wanted Devonshire to share the responsibility of a peace which he had always approved in his heart. Devonshire might naturally dislike the task of protecting Bute against the criticism of his own party, but George III had quite as much right to dismiss a servant whom he suspected of factious treason to his conscience (Bute to Granby, Nov. 5, Add. MSS. 36797, f. 20). For the whole of Newcastle's conduct in the summer and autumn of 1762, see Professor Namier's brilliantly entertaining account in *England in the Age of the American Revolution*, i. 380–468.
[2] See his memoir in *Life and Letters of Lady Sarah Lennox*.
[3] Fox to Cumberland, Sept. 29, in Albemarle's *Rockingham*, i. 131; see Nivernois's account of Bute's situation in his letter to the Comte de Choiseul, Oct. 9, A.E. Angleterre, 447.
[4] Nivernois to the Comte de Choiseul, Oct. 13, A.E. Angleterre, 447.

of the House of Commons, but still imprisoned in the Cabinet, for if he was a free man, he would carry a considerable strength to the Opposition, and his tongue would be loosened to reveal many details of the negotiation which Bute did not wish to make public. The admission of Fox was therefore accompanied by an exchange of offices between Grenville and Halifax.[1] Bute was in smooth water again, as Fox had prophesied.

The reunited Ministry offered to restore Havana on condition that Spain gave way on all the other questions and surrendered Florida or Porto Rico.[2] The crisis was now transferred to France, where Choiseul had to procure the acquiescence of Spain in these hard terms. The war could not go on, for what was left of the Spanish navy must be sent out to protect the West Indies, and the invasion of England was out of the question. France must not make a separate peace: she could only force or bribe Spain to make sacrifices. Yet that was exactly what Choiseul did not wish to have the air of doing, for so disastrous a beginning could not recommend the Family Compact to patriotic Spaniards, and the parallel with the treaty of 1748, which France made to some degree at Spain's expense, was becoming unpleasantly close.[3] The greatest danger was that Spain would refuse to admit the disaster. Choiseul was very alarmed by the heroic posture in which Charles III and Wall received the news: they would fight on till all the West Indies were lost, rather than yield an inch of land to England in negotiation. Choiseul deprecated these violent resolutions: he really believed that Mexico might be conquered next year, and foresaw that French trade would lose twenty million livres by the loss of the market to the English.

After a few days' reflection Charles III gave way to necessity,

---

[1] The question arises, why had Grenville to be degraded from the Secretaryship of State as well as the lead in the House of Commons? I think the reason may be, that as Secretary for the Northern Department he could still have obstructed the peace by insisting on such safeguards for Frederick II's interests as France might not be willing to grant (see Nivernois's letter to the Comte de Choiseul, Sept. 20, A.E. Angleterre, 447). Perhaps, however, the explanation was simpler: when a Secretary of State was in the House, it would be almost irregular for the Paymaster-General to take the lead.

[2] Bute was so anxious to save time in the negotiation, that he had the French Ministry informed privately of these terms, through Viry and Nivernois, a fortnight before Bedford received his official instructions upon the subject (Nivernois to the Comte de Choiseul, Oct. 11, 1762, A.E. Angleterre, 447, f. 279; Œuvres posthumes, vol. ii, pt. iii, pp. 73–8).

[3] Choiseul to Ossun, Oct. 3 and 9, A.E. Espagne, 537.

and authorized Louis XV to sign the English terms if it could not be avoided.[1] Choiseul not only used this permission, but took advantage of it to extract a few paltry concessions for France at the last minute: Bedford had to bribe him to smooth the Spanish affairs by giving up, for example, the inspection of the French fishing settlement in the St. Lawrence.[2] Florida came into the possession of England; Bute's honour was satisfied and his skin was safe.

He cared for little else; Fox thought him calm, but he and Bedford had talked of nothing but scaffolds and impeachments until Choiseul was tired to death.[3] This way of talking might be partly cant and partly even bluff; but there seems to be no doubt that their personal reputation, even their personal safety, was the ruling consideration in the minds of the English peacemakers. Bute at least was reduced to a pitiable state of nerves and glad to get out of the war on any terms which his countrymen would not condemn. He and his colleagues were, after all, pure politicians, to whom popularity and prestige were the realities; this is equally true of those who held out and of those who yielded. Newcastle would have acted in no other spirit, and Egremont with his care for his reputation was no more a realist than Bute with his fears for his safety. Although it was a mercantilist age, Pitt was the only man in the first rank of politics who dealt in terms of economic or strategic value, and considered colonial acquisitions as something more than so many debating-points for or against the Ministry. That is why, in spite of its exaggerations and inconsistencies, Pitt's is the only opposition to the Peace of Paris that can be justified or pardoned, and why Pitt remains, for all his insincerity and demagogy, the one living figure among a generation of shadows.

When the Preliminaries of Peace came to be debated in the House of Commons, Bute's fears and the noisy confidence of the Opposition were made to look equally ridiculous. Fox prophesied in his memoir (perhaps after the event) that Bute would get a majority, with the help of the Tories and the Scotch, after a few angry debates. 'So many of the leaders on

[1] Choiseul to Ossun (private), Oct. 9; Ossun to Choiseul, Oct. 10 and 22; Choiseul to Ossun, Oct. 20 and Nov. 3, ibid.

[2] Bedford to Egremont, Nov. 3, S.P. 78/254.

[3] Nivernois to Comte de Choiseul, Sept. 15 and 16, A.E. Angleterre, 447 (the latter is printed in Nivernois's *Œuvres posthumes*, vol. ii, pt. iii, p. 18); Choiseul to Ossun, Sept. 20, A.E. Espagne, 537.

the other side are in their hearts for peace, have declared so, and the comparison between this and that which even Mr. Pitt offer'd his consent to last year is so obvious, that they will be embarrass'd to let out all their fury against it. I mean all but Mr. Pitt, who like his mob is never embarrass'd by any degree of shame.'[1] It came to pass as he said. After a long and bad speech by Pitt in the Commons,[2] and a half-hearted one by Hardwicke in the Lords, the Opposition collapsed and the terms were approved by large majorities. There is no need to have recourse to the myth of proscription or bribery in order to explain the acquiescence of Parliament in a settlement which secured the original objects of the war and satisfied the reasonable ambitions of all Englishmen but those who lived by war or war-mongering.

The Peace of Paris was by no means the end of the long conflict of England, France, and Spain; but it concluded a stage in that conflict which differed from those which went before it. This is the period of the single-handed but successful English aggression. We fought without receiving, and almost without expecting, the help of the Dutch, or of any other sea-power. The French pamphleteers might well alter, in the middle of the Seven Years War, the terminology of their cant effusions, so as to denounce 'the Maritime Power' instead of 'the Maritime Powers'.[3] It is true that we were helped on land by Maria Theresa and then by Frederick the Great; but in each case the continental fighting was no part of our original plan, and we began the struggle in the expectation of a purely naval war against France and Spain. Even when the war became general, our allies did not so much join in an attack as repel a counter-

---

[1] *Life and Letters of Lady Sarah Lennox*, i. 77.

[2] If the speech given under his name in the Parliamentary History represents him truly, Pitt said some things he had no right to say. It was all very well to denounce the Government for making peace without crushing France and reducing her to a second-class power. That was Pitt's considered opinion, though we may agree with Bedford that he demanded the impossible. But it was factious to run down North America and to exalt the value of Martinique and Guadeloupe by comparison, because Pitt was the man who had always insisted that the security of North America was the first object of the war, and the conquest of the West Indies a thing of second-rate importance (*Parl. Hist.* xv. 1263-7). In this respect alone Bute had the advantage of Pitt, for he had obtained much better terms than Pitt had been willing to accept—as a result, it is true, of the success of Pitt's conquest of Martinique.

[3] This change is made, for example, from the first to the second editions of *Le Politique Danois*.

attack upon a flank which in the opinion of many representative Englishmen was not really exposed.

Not only had we no allies at sea, but we were equal there to the united force of our two nearest rivals. This conclusion which was hinted in 1747 was apparently proved in 1762, when the Bourbon Family Compact broke down. The proof was not quite so decisive as could be wished, because history might have been written differently if Spain had entered the Seven Years War when it began, instead of waiting till the French navy was destroyed; but Spain was probably still weaker in 1756 than in 1762, so the final result, if the war had lasted long enough, is not likely to have been very different.

The failure of the Family Compact was a great disappointment to Choiseul. As he explained to Ossun in 1764, Spain was so useless an ally that

'the first care of France, if another war should arise between her and England, must be to prevent Spain from having anything to do with it, in spite of the stipulations of the Family Compact; on the other hand, if Spain should start the war first, we should be obliged by sentiment and policy to take her part, without which I think she would lose America in two years.'

Spain, in fact, was a liability in war. Choiseul regarded this as a reason why she should consent to be an asset in peace by granting favours to French commerce.[1]

This was not always Choiseul's language. While he was pressing Charles III to make peace, he held out hopes of renewing the struggle. He spoke of peace as a rest, or a truce, necessary for the reform and repair of the French and Spanish fighting machines. Pitt called the peace a ten years' armed truce; Choiseul only expected it to endure for five.[2]

Historians have often remarked that England gained too little or too much at the Peace of Paris. In this they only echo Pitt, who was justified by events within his own lifetime. As a criticism of the details of the peace, this seems to be a little severe. It is not the loss of territory, but the loss of the war itself that creates the desire for revenge; and in spite of Choiseul's cant about a 'solid' peace, it is hard to believe that further concessions would have diverted him or his successors from preparing for another war. Yet in a more general way, Pitt was

---

[1] Choiseul to Ossun, Dec. 16, 1764, *Recueil des Instructions des Ambassadeurs, Espagne*, iii. 354.   [2] Choiseul to Ossun, Oct. 9, A.E. Espagne, 537.

right. France and Spain were neither appeased nor crushed. Perhaps they could not be appeased; that was what Pitt seems to have thought, for all his arguments pointed to the conclusion that the Bourbon powers must be crushed. France and Spain were not yet second-rate powers, and they had not to wait very long for a chance to turn the tables on England.

APPENDIX I

PRINCIPAL EVENTS IN THE WEST INDIES, 1739–63

I. *War of 1739–48*

1739 Jan.   Convention of El Pardo.
     June.   Declaration of reprisals against Spain.
     Oct.   Vice-Admiral Vernon arrives at Jamaica.
             Declaration of war against Spain.
     Nov.   Vernon reduces Portobello.
1740 Mar.   Vernon reduces Chagre.
     Aug.   D'Antin and Laroche-Alart sail for the West Indies.
     Oct.   Ogle and Cathcart sail for the West Indies.
     Dec.   They arrive at Jamaica.
1741 Mar.–Apr.   Vernon attempts Cartagena.
     July–Oct.   He attempts to conquer the east end of Cuba.
1742 Mar.   He attempts an overland expedition against Panama.
     Oct.   Vernon sails for England.
1743 Feb.–Apr.   Knowles attempts La Guayra and Porto Cabello.
1744 Mar.   Declaration of war against France.
1745 Mar.   Caylus arrives at Martinique.
     Sept.   Townsend arrives at Barbados.
     Nov.   Engagement between Mitchell and Macnémara off St. Domingue.
1746 Aug.   Engagement between Mitchell and Conflans off St. Domingue.
1747 Mar.   Engagement between Dent and Dubois de la Motte off St. Domingue.
     June.   Fox intercepts Dubois de la Motte's homeward convoy.
     Oct.   Hawke intercepts L'Étandùere and the outward convoy.
1748 Mar.   Knowles takes St. Louis and attempts Santiago de Cuba.
             Preliminaries of peace signed between England and France.
     Oct.   Knowles fights Reggio between Vera Cruz and Havana.
             Peace of Aix-la-Chapelle.

II. *Seven Years War*

1756 May.   Declaration of war against France.
             Périer de Salvert at St. Domingue; alarm at Jamaica.
1757 Feb.   Beauffremont at St. Domingue; more alarms at Jamaica.
     Oct.   Engagement between Forrest and Kersaint off St. Domingue.
     Nov.–Mar. 1758.   Osborn prevents La Clue from going out to the West Indies.
1759 Jan.   Moore and Hopson attack Martinique without success.
     Feb.–Apr.   They reduce Guadeloupe.
     Mar.   Bompar arrives at Martinique but fails to relieve Guadeloupe.
1761 May.   Peace missions of Bussy and Stanley.
     June.   Capture of Dominica.
     Aug.   Family Compact signed between France and Spain.
     Sept.   Withdrawal of Bussy and Stanley.

1761 Oct.	Resignation of Pitt.
1762 Jan.	Declaration of war against Spain.
	Rodney conquers Martinique.
Feb.–Mar.	He reduces the Neutral Islands.
Mar.	Blénac arrives at St. Domingue; alarm at Jamaica.
Apr.	Pocock and Albemarle arrive in the West Indies.
June.	They reach Havana.
Aug.	They take it.
Sept.	Peace missions of Bedford and Nivernois.
	The news of Havana arrives.
Nov.	Preliminaries of peace signed at Paris.

APPENDIX II

ENGLAND

Secretaries of State

Northern Department

1739	William Stanhope, Lord Harrington.
1742	John, Lord Carteret.
1744	William Stanhope, Earl of Harrington.
1746	Philip Dormer Stanhope, Earl of Chesterfield.
1748	Thomas Pelham-Holles, Duke of Newcastle.
1754	Robert D'Arcy, Earl of Holdernesse.
1761	John Stuart, Earl of Bute.
1762 (June).	George Grenville.
(Oct.).	George Montagu Dunk, Earl of Halifax.

Southern Department

1739	Thomas Pelham-Holles, Duke of Newcastle.
1748	John Russell, Duke of Bedford.
1751	Robert D'Arcy, Earl of Holdernesse.
1754	Sir Thomas Robinson.
1755	Henry Fox.
1756	William Pitt.
1757 (Apr.).	Robert D'Arcy, Earl of Holdernesse.
(July).	William Pitt.
1761	Charles Wyndham, Earl of Egremont.

Governors of Jamaica

1739	Edward Trelawny.
1752	Rear-Adm. Charles Knowles.
1756	Henry Moore, *Lieut.-Governor.*
1759 (Apr.).	Brig.-Gen. George Haldane.
(Aug.).	Henry Moore, *Lieut.-Governor.*
1762	William Henry Lyttelton.

Governors of Barbados

1739	James Dottin, *President.*[1]
(Dec.).	Hon. Robert Byng.
1740 (Oct.).	James Dottin, *President.*
1742	Sir Thomas Robinson, Bt.
1747	Hon. Henry Grenville.
1754	Ralph Weekes, *President.*
1756	Charles Pinfold, LL.D.

Governors of the Leeward Islands

1739	William Mathew.
1752	George Thomas.

Ambassadors, &c., at Versailles

1739	James, Earl Waldegrave.
1740 (Oct.).	Rev. Anthony Thompson, *Chargé d'Affaires.*
1749 (Feb.).	Hon. Joseph Yorke, *Chargé d'Affaires.*
(July).	William Anne Keppel, Earl of Albemarle.
1761	Hans Stanley (special mission).
1762	John Russell, Duke of Bedford.

Ambassadors, &c., at Madrid

1739	Benjamin Keene.
1749	Benjamin Keene.
1757	Ruvigny de Cosné, *Chargé d'Affaires.*
1758	George Hervey, Earl of Bristol.

Ambassadors, &c., at The Hague

1739	Rt. Hon. Horatio Walpole.
(Oct.).	Robert Trevor.
1745 (Feb.).	Philip Dormer Stanhope, Earl of Chesterfield, and Robert Trevor.
(May).	Robert Trevor.
1746	John Montagu, Earl of Sandwich.
1749	Robert D'Arcy, Earl of Holdernesse.
1751	Hon. Joseph Yorke.
1758 (Feb.).	Daniel Delaval, *Chargé d'Affaires.*
(June).	Hon. Joseph Yorke.

First Lords of the Admiralty

1739	Sir Charles Wager.
1742	Daniel Finch, Earl of Winchelsea.
1744	John Russell, Duke of Bedford.
1748	John Montagu, Earl of Sandwich.

[1] Senior Councillor acting as Commander-in-Chief.

First Lords of the Admiralty (cont.)

1751   George, Lord Anson.
1756   Richard Grenville-Temple, Earl Temple.
1757 (Apr.).   Daniel Finch, Earl of Winchelsea.
      (July).   George, Lord Anson.
1762 (June).   George Montagu Dunk, Earl of Halifax.
      (Oct.).   George Grenville.

Secretaries of the Admiralty

1739   Josiah Burchett.
1742   Thomas Corbett.
1745   Thomas Corbett and John Clevland.
1751   John Clevland.

Commanders-in-Chief, Jamaica Station

1739   Commodore Charles Brown.
      (Oct.).   Vice-Admiral Edward Vernon.
1742   Vice-Admiral Sir Chaloner Ogle.
1744   Vice-Admiral Thomas Davers.
1746   Cornelius Mitchell, *Acting Commodore.*
1747   Digby Dent, *Acting Commodore.*
1748   Rear-Admiral Charles Knowles.
1749   Commodore George Townshend.
1752   Commodore Thomas Cotes.
1755   Rear-Admiral George Townshend.
1757   Vice-Admiral Thomas Cotes.
1760   Rear-Admiral Charles Holmes.
1761 (Dec.).   Arthur Forrest, *Acting Commodore.*
1762 (Apr.).   Commodore Sir James Douglas.
      (July).   Rear-Admiral Hon. Augustus Keppel.

Commanders-in-Chief, Leeward Islands Station

1743 (winter).   Commodore Peter Warren.
1744 (summer).   Commodore Charles Knowles.
      (winter).   Commodore Peter Warren.
1745 (Mar.).   Commodore Charles Knowles.
      (May).   Commodore Hon. Fitzroy Henry Lee.
      (Sept.).   Vice-Admiral Isaac Townsend.
1746 (Mar.).   Commodore Hon. Fitzroy Henry Lee.
1747 (Apr.).   Commodore Hon. Edward Legge.
      (Nov.).   George Pocock, *Acting Commodore.*
1748   Rear-Admiral Henry Osborn.
1749   Commodore Francis Holburne.
1752   Commodore Thomas Pye.
1755   Commodore Thomas Frankland.
1757   Commodore John Moore.
1760   Commodore Sir James Douglas.
1761   Rear-Admiral George Brydges Rodney.

FRANCE

Ministers of Marine

1739	Jean-Frédéric Phélypeaux, Comte de Maurepas.
1749	Antoine-Louis Rouillé.
1754	Jean-Baptiste Machault.
1757	François-Marie Peirenc de Moras.
1758 (June).	Claude-Louis, Marquis de Massiac.
(Nov.).	Nicolas-René Berryer.
1761	Étienne-François, Duc de Choiseul.

Governors of St. Domingue

1739	Marquis de Larnage.
1746	De Chastenoye, *Acting Governor*.
1748	Comte de Conflans.
1751	Comte Dubois de la Motte.
1754	Marquis de Vaudreuil, *Acting Governor*.
1756	Bart.
1761	De Bory.

Intendants of St. Domingue

1739	Maillart.
1751	Laporte-Lalanne.
1758 (Dec.)	Lambert.
(Dec.)	Élias, *Acting Intendant*.
1760 (Mar.)	Peyrac, *Acting Intendant*.
(Dec.)	De Clugny.

Governors of the Windward Islands

1739	Marquis de Champigny.
1745	Marquis de Caylus.
1750 (Apr.)	Hurault de Ligny, *Acting Governor*.
(Oct.)	De Bompar.
1757	Marquis de Beauharnois.
1761	Le Vassor de la Touche.

Intendants of the Windward Islands

1739	La Croix.
1744	Ranché.
1749	Hurson.
1755	De Givry.
1759	Le Mercier de la Rivière.

Ministers of Foreign Affairs

1739	Denis Amelot de Chaillou.
1744	Louis-René de Voyer, Marquis d'Argenson.
1747	Louis-Philogène Brûlart, Marquis de Puysieulx.
1751	Barberie de St. Contest.

Ministers of Foreign Affairs (cont.)

1754	Antoine-Louis Rouillé.
1757	François-Joachim de Pierre de Bernis.
1758	Étienne-François, Duc de Choiseul.
1762	César-Gabriel, Comte de Choiseul.

Ambassadors, &c., in London

1739		Comte de Cambis.
1740	(Feb.)	De Vismes, *Chargé d'Affaires.*
	(Apr.)	De Bussy.
1749	(Jan.)	Durand.
	(July.)	Marquis de Mirepoix.
1761		De Bussy (special mission).
1762		Duc de Nivernois.

Ambassadors, &c., in Madrid

1738		Comte de Vaulgrenant.
1738	(Oct.)	Comte de La Marck.
1741		Vauréal, Bishop of Rennes.
1748		Comte de Vaulgrenant.
1752		Duc de Duras.
1755		Frischmann, *Chargé d'Affaires.*
1757		Marquis d'Aubeterre.
1759		Marquis d'Ossun.

INDEX